2ND
EDITION

DEBATING
TERRORISM AND
COUNTERTERRORISM

THE DEBATING POLITICS SERIES FROM CQ PRESS

- *Debating the Presidency: Conflicting Perspectives on the American Executive, Second Edition*
  Richard Ellis and Michael Nelson, Editors

- *Debating Reform: Conflicting Perspectives on How to Fix the American Political System, Second Edition*
  Richard Ellis and Michael Nelson, Editors

- *Debating Terrorism and Counterterrorism: Conflicting Perspectives on Causes, Contexts, and Responses*
  Stuart Gottlieb, Editor

2ND EDITION

DEBATING
TERRORISM AND
COUNTERTERRORISM

Conflicting Perspectives on Causes, Contexts, and Responses

STUART GOTTLIEB
Columbia University
EDITOR

Los Angeles | London | New Delhi
Singapore | Washington DC

Los Angeles | London | New Delhi
Singapore | Washington DC

FOR INFORMATION:

CQ Press

An Imprint of SAGE Publications, Inc.

2455 Teller Road

Thousand Oaks, California 91320

E-mail: order@sagepub.com

SAGE Publications Ltd.

1 Oliver's Yard

55 City Road

London EC1Y 1SP

United Kingdom

SAGE Publications India Pvt. Ltd.

B 1/I 1 Mohan Cooperative Industrial Area

Mathura Road, New Delhi 110 044

India

SAGE Publications Asia-Pacific Pte. Ltd.

3 Church Street

#10-04 Samsung Hub

Singapore 049483

Printed in the United States of America

A catalog record of this book is available from the Library of Congress.

978-1-4522-2672-9

This book is printed on acid-free paper.

Acquisitions Editor: Elise Frasier

Production Editor: Libby Larson

Copy Editor: Melinda Masson

Typesetter: C&M Digitals (P) Ltd.

Proofreader: Bonnie Moore

Cover Designer: Candice Harman

Marketing Manager: Jonathan Mason

Permissions Editor: Jennifer Baron

13 14 15 16 17 10 9 8 7 6 5 4 3 2 1

CONTENTS

FOREWORD

A s events since this volume was first published in 2010 have shown, the international terrorist threat has evolved, even in that brief three-year period. The demise of Osama bin Laden has, of course, been a watershed event and demonstrates that America's proficiency in tracking and eventually hunting down individual high-value terrorist targets has improved dramatically. U.S. special operations capability is currently at peak performance, and it is important that this asset be nurtured and maintained.

But we all know that intelligence and derring-do, though important and at times decisive, are factors that represent but part of the picture.

Indeed, dealing with terrorism and its underlying causes brings into play a broad range of instruments of statecraft in the fields of politics, economics, security, and development. Notwithstanding more than a decade of intense contemporary experience, the relative weight and relationships between these factors are still imperfectly understood. So it is important to update the discussion, which is exactly what this excellent second edition of *Debating Terrorism and Counterterrorism* has done under the editorial leadership of Stuart Gottlieb.

Can poverty be an underlying cause of terrorist recruitment and behavior? Where do religion and democracy fit in? Our recent experience certainly suggests that poverty can be an important element in recruiting foot soldiers of terrorism; but it is more ambiguous about the socioeconomic profile of terrorist leaders themselves, and the types of political systems from which they are most likely to emerge. And what about the perennial tension between the imperatives of human rights and civil liberties on the one hand and the need for order and security on the other? We now have a larger body of contemporary experience against which to measure each of these issues, which this volume accomplishes in cutting-edge fashion.

I should note that this edition contains a particularly welcome and more expansive discussion of what the international community and international organizations can do to help deal with terrorism. I arrived as Permanent Representative of the United States to the United Nations in New York barely a week after the 9/11 attacks. Within a matter of days thereafter our delegation was able to secure unanimous approval of UN Security Council Resolution

1373 (September 28, 2001), which became a basic reference document in the council's subsequent work in the fight against terrorism. Also, as a decision binding on the entirety of the UN's state members, Resolution 1373 became a benchmark for use by states in drafting their own domestic legislation, especially in the field of combating terrorism finance. Rather than being dismissive of the UN and international institutions, it is important to explore ways by which we can even further strengthen cooperation through them, instead of focusing exclusively on unilateral tools. Combating modern, global terrorism is a worldwide endeavor that can benefit immensely from cooperation with others, and it may be that we collectively have devoted insufficient imagination or attention to the opportunities for increased international collaboration.

There is no doubt that from the perspective of the United States we are safer today than we were before 9/11 from the kind of attacks that were perpetrated on that day. Our intelligence community is better coordinated and integrated. Our defenses are stronger, and we have successfully put the most significant international terrorist group, al-Qaeda, on the defensive.

But the threat from al-Qaeda and its expanding list of affiliates has not disappeared and remains a threat to the U.S. homeland and problematic for a number of countries in the Middle East, Africa, and South Asia. In other words, America's domestic security and interests abroad remain exposed to ongoing terror threats. Therefore, as this book so capably illustrates, now is not a time for complacency, and there remain many important, indeed fundamental, issues that require continued attention. The stable of outstanding authors render us service by virtue of their very thoughtful discussion of these issues and in so doing help us to think creatively about next steps regarding a problem that is likely to be an important policy concern for some time to come.

John Negroponte
Former Deputy Secretary of State
First Director of National Intelligence

CONTRIBUTORS

Max Abrahms

Max Abrahms is a postdoctoral fellow in the political science department at Johns Hopkins University. Previously, he has held fellowships at Dartmouth College, Stanford University, Tel Aviv University, Washington Institute for Near East Policy, and West Point Military Academy. His research focuses on the consequences of terrorism, its motives, and the implications for counterterrorism strategy. He has published on these topics in *Comparative Political Studies, International Security, International Studies Quarterly, Perspectives on Terrorism, Security Studies, Studies in Conflict and Terrorism, Terrorism and Political Violence*, and several edited volumes.

Matthew Bunn

Matthew Bunn is an associate professor at Harvard University's John F. Kennedy School of Government, and one of the principal investigators for Harvard's Project on Managing the Atom. His research interests include nuclear theft and terrorism; nuclear proliferation and measures to control it; the future of nuclear energy and its fuel cycle; and innovation in energy technologies. Before coming to Harvard, he served as an adviser to the White House Office of Science and Technology Policy, as a study director at the National Academy of Sciences/National Research Council, and as editor of *Arms Control Today*. He is the author or coauthor of more than twenty books or major technical reports (most recently *Transforming U.S. Energy Innovation*) and over a hundred articles in publications ranging from *Science* to the *Washington Post*.

David Cole

David Cole is a law professor at Georgetown University Law Center, the legal affairs correspondent for *The Nation*, and a frequent contributor to the *New York Review of Books*. He is author of several books, including *Enemy Aliens: Double Standards and Constitutional Freedoms in the War on Terrorism* (2003) and *The Torture Memos: Rationalizing the Unthinkable* (2009).

Bruce Cronin

Bruce Cronin is a professor and the chair of political science at the City College of New York. He has published several books and numerous articles on international organization, the United Nations Security Council, international law, and human rights. Most recently, he coedited *The UN Security Council and the Politics of International Authority* (2008). He is currently writing a book titled *Civilians at Risk: Noncombatant Casualties and the Collateral Damage Exemption in International Humanitarian Law*.

Alan M. Dershowitz

Alan M. Dershowitz is the Felix Frankfurter Professor of Law at Harvard Law School. One of the world's best-known criminal and civil liberties lawyers, he has published more than one hundred articles in magazines, newspapers, and journals, including the *New York Times Magazine, Washington Post, Wall Street Journal, New Republic, The Nation, Commentary, Saturday Review, Harvard Law Review*, and *Yale Law Journal*. He is the author of nearly thirty works of fiction and nonfiction. He has been honored by the New York Criminal Bar Association for his "outstanding contribution as a scholar and dedicated defense of human rights."

Lindsay Fritz

Lindsay Fritz is an analyst at the Center for Civil-Military Relations at the Naval Postgraduate School in Monterey, California. She has studied at Tulane University, the Monterey Institute of International Studies, and the University of Hamburg.

F. Gregory Gause III

F. Gregory Gause III is a professor of political science at the University of Vermont and a nonresident senior fellow at the Brookings Doha Center. His most recent book is *The International Relations of the Persian Gulf* (2010).

Fawaz A. Gerges

Fawaz A. Gerges is the director of the Middle East Centre at the London School of Economics and Political Science and a professor of Middle Eastern politics and international relations. His interests include Islam and the political process, and mainstream Islamist movements and jihadist groups (such as the Muslim Brotherhood and al-Qaeda); Arab and Muslim politics in the twentieth century; and the international relations of the Middle East. He is author of several acclaimed books, including *The Arab Uprisings: A New Era of Politics* (forthcoming); *Obama and the Middle East: The End of America's*

Moment in the Middle East? (2012); *The Rise and Fall of Al-Qaeda* (2011); *The Far Enemy: Why Jihad Went Global* (2005); *America and Political Islam: Clash of Cultures or Clash of Interests?* (1999); and *The Superpowers and the Middle East: Regional and International Politics* (1994). His articles have appeared in the *New York Times, Washington Post, Los Angeles Times, Christian Science Monitor, International Herald Tribune, Baltimore Sun, Guardian, Independent, Foreign Affairs, Foreign Policy, Newsweek, Middle East Journal, Survival,* and many others. He has given scores of interviews for various media outlets throughout the world, including ABC, CNN, BBC, PBS, CBS, NBC, NPR, CBC, and Al Jazeera.

Rohan Gunaratna

Rohan Gunaratna is head of the International Centre for Political Violence and Terrorism Research and professor of security studies at the S. Rajaratnam School of International Studies at Nanyang Technological University in Singapore. He has more than twenty-five years of academic, policy, and operational experience in the fields of terrorism and counterterrorism. Author of twelve books, including *Inside Al Qaeda* (2003), he serves on the World Economic Forum's Global Agenda Council on Terrorism. Gunaratna has debriefed terror detainees in Asia, the Middle East (including Iraq), Europe, Australia, and North America, and testified as the U.S. government's expert in the José Padilla trial. He was invited to testify before the 9/11 Commission.

Ted Honderich

Ted Honderich is one of Great Britain's best-known and most prolific political philosophers. He has been the Grote Professor of the Philosophy of Mind and Logic at University College London and visiting professor at Yale University and the City University of New York, and he is now visiting professor at the University of Bath. Among many other books and dozens of articles, he is author of *How Free Are You? The Determinism Problem* (1993, 2002); *A Theory of Determinism: The Mind, Neuroscience and Life-Hopes* (1998); *The Oxford Companion to Philosophy* (2005); *Humanity, Terrorism, Terrorist War: Palestine, 9/11, Iraq, 7/7* (2006); and *Philosopher: A Kind of Life* (2001). His 2003 book *After the Terror* sparked controversy in Germany and elsewhere for its moral defense of Palestinian terrorism against Israel.

Walter Laqueur

Walter Laqueur is one of the world's foremost authorities on political violence and terrorism. Over a long and distinguished career, he has been director of the Institute of Contemporary History in London, founding editor of the *Journal of Contemporary History*, chairman of the International Research Council of the Washington-based Center for Strategic and International Studies, and founding editor of the *Washington Quarterly*. Author of countless articles, he has also written more than twenty books, including *Guerrilla* (1976), *Terrorism* (1977), *The Age of Terrorism* (1987), and, most recently, *Voices of Terror* (2004), *The Last Days of Europe* (2007), and *Best of Times, Worst of Times* (2009).

Susan B. Martin

Susan B. Martin is a lecturer in the Department of War Studies at King's College London, where she is also affiliated with the Centre for Science and Security Studies. Her research focuses on a neorealist explanation of the role of chemical, biological, and nuclear weapons in international politics. She is a coeditor of *Terrorism, War or Disease: Unraveling the Use of Biological Weapons* (2008). Her work has appeared in *International Security* and *Journal of Strategic Studies*, as well as various edited volumes.

Andrew C. McCarthy

Andrew C. McCarthy is the executive director of the Philadelphia Freedom Center, a senior fellow at National Review Institute, and a contributing editor to *National Review*. He formerly served as assistant U.S. attorney for the Southern District of New York, where he led the prosecution against the mastermind of the 1993 World Trade Center bombing, Sheikh Omar Abdel Rahman. McCarthy is the recipient of the U.S. Justice Department's highest honors: the Distinguished Service Award (1988) and the Attorney General's Exceptional Service Award (1996). His most recent book is *Spring Fever: The Illusion of Islamic Democracy* (2012).

Gordon H. McCormick

Gordon H. McCormick is a professor and the founding chairman of the Department of Defense Analysis at the Naval Postgraduate School in Monterey, California. He was formerly a senior social scientist with the RAND Corporation and has taught at the University of Pennsylvania, Johns Hopkins University, and the University of North Carolina at Chapel Hill. His interests lie in the areas of international politics, mathematics, and classical history and philosophy.

Tamar Meisels

Tamar Meisels is a professor of political theory at Tel Aviv University in Israel. Her primary research interests are liberal nationalism, territorial rights, and the philosophical perspectives on war and terrorism. She is the author of *Territorial Rights* (2005, 2009) and *The Trouble with Terror* (2008), as well as various articles on related topics. During 2009–2010, she served as the visiting Goldman Professor at Georgetown University's Government Department.

John Mueller

John Mueller is the Ralph D. Mershon Senior Research Scientist at the Mershon Center for International Security Studies and is an adjunct professor of political science at The Ohio State University. He is also a senior fellow at the Cato Institute. Mueller is currently working on terrorism, and particularly on the reactions (or overreactions) it often inspires. His books on the subject include *Overblown* (2006), *Atomic Obsession: Nuclear Alarmism from Hiroshima to Al-Qaeda* (2010), and (with Mark Stewart) *Terror, Security, and Money* (2011). His book on international and civil warfare, *The Remnants of War*, was awarded the Lepgold Prize for the best book on international relations in 2004.

Brigitte L. Nacos

Brigitte L. Nacos has taught for more than fifteen years at Columbia University, following a career as a newspaper correspondent. Her research and teaching interests are the links between the media, public opinion, and decision making, and domestic and international terrorism and counterterrorism. She has published many articles and book chapters as well as eight books, among them *Terrorism and the Media* (1994, 1996), *Mass-Mediated Terrorism* (2002), and *Terrorism and Counterterrorism* (2006, 2008, 2010, 2012), and is coauthor of *Selling Fear: Counterterrorism, the Media, and Public Opinion* (2011).

James A. Piazza

James A. Piazza is an associate professor of political science at The Pennsylvania State University. His research examines the socioeconomic root causes of terrorism, terrorism and human rights, state failure, and the impact of illicit narcotics trade on terrorist groups and activity. His work has appeared in a variety of journals, including the *Journal of Politics*, *International Studies Quarterly*, *Comparative Political Studies*, *Journal of Peace Research*, *Terrorism and Political Violence*, *Conflict Management and Peace Science*, and *Studies in Conflict and Terrorism*.

Michael H. Posner

Michael H. Posner is U.S. assistant secretary of state for democracy, human rights, and labor—the country's chief human rights official. Throughout his term, Posner has engaged in a wide range of human rights and democracy issues. He has been a vocal proponent of the Obama administration's integrated approach to human rights and the inexorable relationship between national security and economic, social, and political opportunities. He has played a leading role in implementing Secretary of State Hillary Clinton's vision for promoting sustainable democracies through partnerships with civil societies worldwide. He has also played a leading role in implementing Secretary Clinton's vision for Internet freedom, and frequently speaks on the role of the Internet in advancing human rights and helping people build sustainable democracies. Before entering government service, Posner was president of Human Rights First and served as its executive director from its founding in 1978 until 2006. A frequent commentator in newspapers across the country, he has testified dozens of times before Congress on a number of human rights issues and is a frequent speaker at conferences in the United States and abroad. From 1984 to 2009, he served as a lecturer at Columbia Law School, and he was Yale Law School's 2009 Bernstein Distinguished Human Rights Senior Fellow.

Michael Rubin

Michael Rubin is a resident scholar at the American Enterprise Institute and a senior lecturer at the Naval Postgraduate School. From 2004 to 2009, he edited the *Middle East Quarterly*, and from 2002 to 2004 he was an adviser for Iran and Iraq in the Office of the Secretary of Defense, during which time he was seconded to Baghdad. Rubin has also taught at Yale University, Johns Hopkins University, Hebrew University of Jerusalem, and three universities in Iraqi Kurdistan. He is author of two books about Iran and is completing a study of engagement with rogue regimes, *Dancing with the Devil: The Promise and Perils of Engagement*.

Zachary C. Shirkey

Zachary C. Shirkey is an associate professor of political science at Hunter College, City University of New York. His research focuses on the causes of war, deterrence and balancing, conflict resolution, and terrorism. He has published articles in journals including the *Journal of Peace Research* and the *Journal of Theoretical Politics*. He is the author of two books, the most recent of which, *Joining the Fray* (2012), explores the role that revealed information and commitment problems play in why and when states join ongoing civil wars.

Alexander Spencer

Alexander Spencer is assistant professor in global governance and public policy at the Ludwig-Maximilians University in Munich. His research centers on the potential of constructivist international relations theory for the field of terrorism research. His work has been published in journals including *Foreign Policy Analysis*, *Security Dialogue, Journal of International Relations and Development*, and *Critical*

Studies on Terrorism. He recently published a book titled *The Tabloid Terrorist: The Predictive Construction of New Terrorism in the Media* (2010), and an edited volume titled *Reconciliation after Terrorism* (2012).

Karin von Hippel

Karin von Hippel serves as the deputy assistant secretary for overseas operations in the U.S. State Department's Bureau of Conflict and Stabilization Operations. Prior to her current position, she was a senior adviser in the State Department's Office of the Coordinator for Counterterrorism. Before joining the State Department, she spent five years as codirector of the Post-Conflict Reconstruction Project at the Center for Strategic and International Studies. Von Hippel has advised the United Nations on peacekeeping, peace building, and its humanitarian system; the U.S. Agency for International Development on the development potential of Somali remittances; and the Organisation for Economic Co-operation and Development on the role of development cooperation in discovering the root causes of terrorism. Her numerous publications cover the full conflict spectrum, and include *Democracy by Force* (2000), which was short-listed for the Westminster Medal in Military History. She received her PhD in international relations from the London School of Economics, her master of studies from Oxford University, and her bachelor's degree from Yale University.

Jennifer L. Windsor

Jennifer L. Windsor is the associate dean for programs at the School of Foreign Service at Georgetown University. Previously, she served for ten years as the executive director of Freedom House. From 1991 to 2000, Windsor worked at the U.S. Agency for International Development, last serving as the deputy assistant administrator and director of the Center for Democracy and Governance. She is a graduate of Princeton's Woodrow Wilson School and received her undergraduate degree from Harvard University. She has written numerous articles on issues of democracy and human rights.

John Yoo

John Yoo is a professor of law at the University of California at Berkeley School of Law and a visiting scholar at the American Enterprise Institute. From 2001 to 2003, he served as a deputy assistant attorney general in the Office of Legal Counsel in the U.S. Department of Justice, where he participated in the development of counterterrorism policy in the wake of the 9/11 attacks. He has published more than seventy scholarly articles on foreign affairs, national security, and constitutional law in some of the nation's leading law journals. His work has also appeared on the editorial pages of the *Wall Street Journal, New York Times, Washington Post,* and *Los Angeles Times.* He is the author of *The Powers of War and Peace* (2005), *War by Other Means* (2006), *Crisis and Command* (2010), and, most recently, *Taming Globalization* (2012). He also coedited a book of essays on the tenth anniversary of the 9/11 attacks, *Confronting Terror* (2011).

PREFACE

I n many ways this book was an outgrowth of the crash of United Airlines Flight 175 into the south tower of New York City's World Trade Center at 9:03 a.m. on September 11, 2001. Seventeen minutes earlier, American Airlines Flight 11 had crashed into the World Trade Center's north tower. Even though the initial Flight 11 crash and subsequent collapse of the north tower would alone have been the deadliest terrorist attack in world history, the vast and skilled coordination shown by the al-Qaeda organization with its follow-on airliner attacks against the south tower and the Pentagon and the disrupted attack against the U.S. Capitol instantly, radically, and perhaps permanently transformed global perceptions of terrorism and counterterrorism.

Since the events of 9/11, and in the years since this volume was first published, a tremendous amount of global activity has, of course, surrounded terrorism in terms of both terrorist incidents and government responses. The United States remains at the forefront of recent counterterrorism efforts—Washington has spent many hundreds of billions of dollars since 2001 on new Pentagon priorities, homeland security initiatives, and increased counterterrorism-related activities around the world. And while the land wars in Iraq and Afghanistan have wound down (with mixed results), America's covert operations across multiple continents have only expanded. But the United States is certainly not alone. Terrorism, whether ethno-religious, territorial, or ideologically based, remains a top security and policy priority from western Europe to western China; from South America to South, Central, and Southeast Asia; and from northern and eastern Africa to the Middle East and Persian Gulf.

And yet, even though the world continues to live through what can fairly be described as an unprecedented era of terrorism, it is important to remember that terrorism as a form of political violence is as old as civilization itself. While much raised in its profile (and its purported lethality) by the 9/11 attacks, terrorism itself has not been transformed as a human social phenomenon. It will continue to be used by those around the world who choose violence as a means of redressing grievances and challenging established orders.

Along with the upsurge in global terrorism and counterterrorism activity since 9/11, there has been a tremendous amount of intellectual (and not-so-intellectual) discourse on the topic within and among academic, public policy, and think-tank communities, and across the spectrum of media. Whether measured by quantities of spilt ink or decibel levels, these debates can be enervating, difficult to navigate, hugely partisan, and simply overwhelming.

The purpose of this book is straightforward: to isolate, engage, and enrich debates on the most important contemporary terrorism and counterterrorism issues. To accomplish this goal, leading authorities from policy, academic, and think-tank communities were invited to write timely and original essays that juxtapose pro and con arguments on hotly contested topics of clear importance to understanding the past, present, and future of terrorism and counterterrorism. In a testament to this book's first edition, all of the authors have returned with fully updated essays for the second edition, with one significant change: a new debate chapter focusing on international organizations.

This book's contributors benefited, as will its readers, from the evolving hindsight of the last twelve-plus years. The intense flurry of counterterrorism-related activity that defined the first months and years after 9/11 has since become more settled, thereby giving the authors a unique opportunity to pause, reflect, and carefully analyze what the 9/11 attacks and the al-Qaeda organization have meant (or not meant) in the context of the broader history of terrorism and age-old questions related to terrorism. It has also allowed them to assess more recent events—such as the emergence of the so-called Arab Spring—in a deliberative fashion.

Both editions of this book have also benefited from the change in U.S. presidential administrations in 2009. The transition from Republican president George W. Bush, who had declared "war on terrorism," to Democrat Barack Obama, who has moved away from the hard-line rhetoric of his predecessor while maintaining nearly all of his hard-line counterterrorism policies, has helped to illuminate the consistencies in perceptions of the present threat and the ongoing challenges facing those who must address it.

The book's six chapters on terrorism and six on counterterrorism focus readers' attention on critical topics on which thoughtful people differ. Few subjects in the realms of policy, academia, and public discourse evoke as much passion and emotion as terrorism and the issues that surround it. This book does not pose straw man questions. Nor does it shy away from any controversial topics. Instead, it addresses these thorny problems head-on, firm in the belief that an open discussion aimed at bridging understanding of different perspectives is the best recipe for making proper sense of the challenges arising from terrorism and fashioning the most prudent and effective responses.

ORGANIZATION OF THE BOOK

Each of the twelve debate chapters—six in Part I, "Debating Terrorism," and six in Part II, "Debating Counterterrorism"—addresses a vital question related to the challenge of terrorism in a way meant to both evoke and illuminate. The comprehensive headnote at the beginning of each chapter introduces the nature of the controversy surrounding the topic and summarizes the two authors' forthcoming arguments. The following topics are debated in Part I, "Debating Terrorism":

- The nature of terrorist organizations, looking specifically at how al-Qaeda and other contemporary groups fit into the historical evolution of terrorism
- Whether poverty and socioeconomic underdevelopment serve as possible root causes of terrorism
- Whether and how terrorist violence can ever be justified
- The role played by religion—particularly radical Islam—in the modern wave of global terrorism
- Whether suicide terrorism is an effective strategy to advance political goals
- The likelihood that the nightmare of nuclear terrorism will become a reality

The following topics are debated in Part II, "Debating Counterterrorism":

- Whether diplomatic or military strategies should serve as the foundation of counterterrorism strategies
- Whether promoting democracy in the Arab and Muslim world can help combat terrorism
- What role, if any, international organizations can effectively play in fighting terrorism
- Whether an outright ban is the best way to address the practice of torture in counterterrorism intelligence operations
- Whether trade-offs with civil liberties are necessary to protect national security in an age of terrorism
- Whether the threat of terrorism is being overstated, and what that may mean for the future of terrorism and counterterrorism

Although the authors of the twenty-four essays in this volume may disagree on many things, we can all agree that terrorism will remain an important global challenge—both in terms of addressing its causes and in terms of reducing its effects—long after the 9/11 attacks fade from memory. The policy and intellectual activity of the last dozen years has opened an important door to increasing our collective understanding of terrorism—not just that of yesterday and today, but also that of tomorrow. By isolating the important questions and encouraging open and rigorous debate, this book hopes to seize the moment and contribute knowledge of and insights into one of the world's most enduring, complex, and high-stakes challenges.

ACKNOWLEDGMENTS

Both editions of this expansive and tremendously challenging project could not possibly have come together without the invaluable assistance of many special people. Brigitte L. Nacos at Columbia University and Zachary C. Shirkey at Hunter College selflessly assisted me with the initial conceptual development, as well as ideas for debate topics and prospective authors. I thank them for this, and for contributing excellent essays to both editions of the book. Erica Chenoweth at Wesleyan University provided helpful advice (and some important editing) early on, and served as a crucial sounding board as I wrestled with the many controversial issues and topics broached. Eric Lorber, Rachel Yemini, and Ahmed Salim provided crucial research assistance, editing, and creative ideas for the first edition, as did Heather Greenslate and Travis Evans for the second. Reviewers provided excellent guidance as we revised the essays for the second edition, and our thanks go to Barry Balleck, Georgia Southern University; John Fielding, Mount Wachusett Community College; Ryan Kennedy, University of Houston; Mary Manjikian, Regent University; Kelly Shaw, Drake University; Nahla Yassine-Hamdan, Central Michigan University; and Ayse Zarakol Jajich, Washington and Lee University. Special thanks to the Saltzman Institute of War and Peace Studies at Columbia for generously providing research support and access to its terrific personnel. I should also note that reviewers of the initial proposal for this volume provided excellent advice and criticism.

Finally, this book would not exist without the outstanding work of the professionals (in every sense of the word) at CQ Press. Special thanks go to acquisitions editors Charisse Kiino and Elise Frasier, as well as the editors involved with both the first and second editions: Allyson Rudolph, Sabra Bissette Ledent, Libby Larson, and Melinda Masson. All of you have made this ongoing project both enriching and far more enjoyable than it had any right to be.

is the "new terrorism" really new?

NO: The "new terrorism" of al-Qaeda is not so new.
Alexander Spencer, *Ludwig-Maximilians University, Munich*

YES: Al-Qaeda is an example of a "new terrorism."
Rohan Gunaratna, *Nanyang Technological University, Singapore*

Terrorism is an age-old phenomenon, extending as far back as human records take us. Although scholars and practitioners will likely never agree on a definition of *terrorism* (including many of the authors in this volume), at its core *terrorism* is the use of violence against noncombatants for political purposes.[1]

A primary challenge to developing a firm definition of terrorism, aside from the inherent subjectivity of the act itself, is that the term has evolved over time. In the 1790s, Robespierre employed the first modern usage of the word *terrorism* to describe his regime's coercive efforts to protect post-revolutionary France from counterrevolutionaries.[2] Yet since the mid-nineteenth century, the term has been used most often to describe organized substate violence against established political orders—monarchies, colonial powers, national governments—for purposes ranging from national liberation (e.g., the Jewish Stern Gang in pre-1948 Palestine), to territorial succession (e.g., the Basque separatist group ETA in Spain), to ideological revolution (e.g., the Revolutionary Armed Forces of Colombia). For many terrorism analysts, such groups and their motivations fall under the rubric of what is often called "traditional terrorism."

Beginning in the late 1960s with the hostage takings, skyjackings, and random out-of-area attacks by Palestine Liberation Organization (PLO)–affiliated groups, terrorism assumed a decidedly more international flavor. However, underlying grievances and motivations remained primarily local and territorial, and the violence utilized was often tempered by the need for groups to maintain organizational legitimacy and credibility as players in a possible future negotiated settlement. In this sense, the global terrorism sparked by the PLO had much in common with traditional terrorism.

Some terrorism experts believe that the 1990s witnessed the rise of a unique brand of terrorism—often referred to as "new terrorism."[3] This new incarnation is said to consist of groups with explicitly religious motivations, maximalist demands, and a commitment to inflicting mass casualties, potentially through the use of weapons of mass destruction. Such groups are further segregated from prior forms of terrorism by their purported ability to operate as independent global actors free from direct reliance on states.

Although the new terrorism was flagged as an emerging national security challenge years before the attacks on the United States on September 11, 2001, those attacks, and the al-Qaeda organization that perpetrated them, gave instant credibility to the notion of the coming-of-age of a new and more destructive form of terrorism. In response, the United States and other nations have recalibrated their assessments of the nature and threat of terrorism and altered their counterterrorism strategies accordingly.

But were these new assessments warranted and accurate? Do al-Qaeda and other groups often placed under the rubric of new terrorism—such as Aum Shinrikyo and the Christian Patriots—represent a truly novel form of terrorism?

Alexander Spencer believes the answer is no. He certainly agrees that al-Qaeda, the exemplar of the new terrorism, has been a highly effective terrorist organization. And he understands why, in the wake of the events of September 11, some experts sought to attribute newness to a very old phenomenon. But he takes strong exception to the notion that this form of terrorism is actually new. Indeed, Spencer argues that the very same characteristics that define the terrorism of today can be identified in the terrorism of generations past. To show this, he places three core aspects of the new terrorism—motives, tactics, and organization—into conceptual and historical frameworks, and concludes there is far less "new" than meets the eye. He warns that calling the current terrorist challenge "new" may permit acceptance of overly aggressive—and possibly unnecessary—"new" countermeasures.

Rohan Gunaratna contends that an identifiably new and more dangerous form of terrorism has in fact grown out of the post–Cold War globalized era. He specifically points to the post-1989 rise in internal ethnic and religious conflicts, the free flow of migrants and refugees, the proliferation of weapons and weapons technologies, and the revolution in digital communications as contextual contributors to the emergence and evolution of the new terrorism. Although some of the core characteristics of the new terrorism may be found in older forms, there are features—and combinations of features—that are unique to the new terrorism. Indeed, Gunaratna believes that what gives new terrorist groups such as al-Qaeda (his primary example) their strength and resilience are the creative ways in which they adopt and nurture the best of both old and new, and their ability to adapt to changing regional and global circumstances. That creativity and adaptability also makes such groups extremely difficult to combat, let alone defeat; innovative countermethods are essential, he says.

The emergence of al-Qaeda and similarly inspired groups has not altered the fundamental meaning of the word *terrorism*: as noted by both authors of this chapter, terrorism as a form of political violence may change over time and contexts, but it does not break radically from its past. Yet the degree to which today's terrorism differs from prior forms remains a vital question. The world is currently experiencing one of the most challenging periods in the history of terrorism. Understanding the nuances of contemporary terrorism is necessary both to counter current groups effectively and to recognize the early warning signs of emerging groups that may seek to emulate the highly effective terrorism template of today.

NO: The "new terrorism" of al-Qaeda is not so new. Alexander Spencer, *Ludwig-Maximilians University, Munich*

The Myth of "New Terrorism"

Terrorism is one of the most disputed terms in the social sciences.[4] The problem of defining *terrorism* is well known and has been examined extensively.[5] Apart from the challenge of distinguishing terrorism from guerrilla warfare, crime, or mad serial killers, the well-known phrase "one man's terrorist is another man's freedom fighter" is often used to highlight the problem of implying a moral judgment when classifying a particular act as "terrorism." If one identifies with the victim of the attack, then it is considered terrorism, but if one can identify with the perpetrator, it is not.

The field of terrorism research seems to have become bored with the subject; some scholars such as Walter Laqueur have concluded that "a comprehensive definition of terrorism . . . does not exist nor will it be found in the foreseeable future."[6] Others have struggled on in their quest for the all-encompassing definition. In one of the most rigorous attempts, Alex Schmid and Albert Jongman examine 109 different definitions of terrorism and issue a lengthy consensus definition incorporating the most common elements.[7]

In a more recent study, Leonard Weinberg, Ami Pedahzur, and Sivan Hirsch-Hoefler examine seventy-three definitions of terrorism from fifty-five articles in three leading academic journals on the topic, and come to the conclusion that "terrorism is a politically motivated tactic involving the threat or use of force or violence in which the pursuit of publicity plays a significant role."[8]

Regardless of whether or not one believes in the importance (or possibility) of a definition, it is generally accepted that terrorism has changed since the mid-1990s into an inherently new form with new characteristics. Many academics, government officials, and politicians have articulated the concept of "new terrorism," which they assert involves different actors, motivations, aims, tactics, and actions than the "old" concept of terrorism used previously.

This essay takes issue with the notion that this supposedly "new" terrorism is actually new. The aim is not to challenge the established characteristics of terrorism today, but to question the validity of the term *new terrorism* by showing that many of the trends underlying it can be identified in terrorism years ago.

The section that follows examines the concepts of old and new terrorism and illustrates what are commonly designated as their defining features. The next section questions the presumed nearly dichotomous relationship between old and new and—through an examination of terrorist motives, tactics, and organizational structures—argues that new terrorism is not new after all. The final section offers conclusions and indicates the possible consequences of using terminology such as "new terrorism."

THE OLD AND NEW TERRORISM

Terrorism as a form of political violence is by no means a new phenomenon. One of the earliest known groups was the Sicarii, a Zealot Jewish sect fighting against Roman rule in Palestine between AD 66 and 73. During the Middle Ages, a religious sect of Ismailis and Nizari called "Assassins" struggled against the empire of Saladin, and in the sixteenth century small "terrorist" groups in Albania and other regions resisted the armies of the Ottoman Empire. The term *terror* was first used around 1794 in association with a policy to protect the fragile government of the post-revolutionary French Republic from counterrevolutionaries. From about the mid-nineteenth century to World War I, revolutionaries and anarchists frequently used bombings and assassinations as weapons in their struggle against autocracy. After World War II, terrorism became a critical part of the anticolonial struggles. As Paul Wilkinson points out, this development has important significance as one of "the only clear instances in modern history where sub-state organizations using terror as their major weapon were able to achieve their long-term political goals, i.e., the withdrawal of the colonial power and establishment of a form of government favoured by the insurgents."[9]

Many scholars agree that the period prior to the early 1990s was marked by so-called traditional or "old terrorism," which can be roughly divided into different types such as left- and right-wing, ethno-nationalist, and separatist terrorism, as well as terrorism perpetrated by Palestinian groups after the late 1960s, which covers a number of these different types while adding an international element. Although in reality many of these "old terrorist" groups were a combination of these different types, it is argued that they all had some general common characteristics.

"Old Terrorism"

For one thing, traditional terrorist groups are classed as having predominantly secular motivations and rational political reasons for their acts of violence. For example, left-wing terrorist groups aimed to use violence to politicize the working-class masses and convince them to rise up against the capitalist system. And ethno-nationalist terrorists wanted independence for their ethnic group in the form of a separation of their territory from that of another country, the creation of their own sovereign nation-state, or the merger with another state. Whatever way, their specific demands were often rationally negotiable, such as when they demanded the release of certain jailed comrades, or payment in exchange for the release of hostages in a hijacking. Even when demands were difficult to meet, such as the reunification of a divided country, the creation of an ethno-national homeland, or the abolishment of the existing capitalist system, in many circumstances there appeared to be room for dialogue or negotiation.[10]

Related to this observation, it is believed that violence by "old terrorists" in general was "targeted and proportionate in scope and intensity to the practical political objectives being pursued."[11] Terrorists did not want to use excessive indiscriminate violence themselves because it would reduce their claim of legitimacy and alienate them from supporters, thereby reducing their access to new recruits and funding. Thus by keeping the level of casualties low, terrorists "preserved their eligibility for a place at the bargaining table and, ultimately, a role in successor governments."[12] "Old terrorism" was viewed as discriminate, with terrorist groups selecting their targets very carefully. They usually directed their precision attacks at well-defined, highly symbolic targets of the authority they opposed. These targets might include leading politicians; government officials; members of the aristocracy, military, or banking sectors; or other symbols such as government buildings. Groups tried to use their actions as a means of propaganda to increase their popular support. Terrorists sought maximum publicity for their acts, playing to an audience and spreading their ideological message. Brian Jenkins famously wrote that "terrorism is theatre" and that terrorist attacks were often choreographed for the media.[13] An attack was nearly always followed by a communiqué taking credit for the act, laying out demands, or explaining why it was carried out against that particular target. The targeted violence was generally perpetrated with conventional tactics such as handheld guns and machine guns, as well as bombs. Terrorists showed little interest in new tactics and nonconventional weapons such as weapons of mass destruction (WMDs). In general, they tried not to kill innocent bystanders because such casualties would alienate the population and go against their aim of inciting a popular uprising. At times, they even expressed sorrow for accidental deaths in the attack.[14]

Finally, the "old terrorism" has an obvious hierarchical organization with fairly well-defined command and control structures.[15] Although it is impossible to clearly demarcate the different layers, James Fraser argues that "old terrorism" is organized like a pyramid, with the leadership, who decide on the overall policy and plans, at the top. Underneath is a larger layer of active terrorists who carry out the attacks and are often specialized in certain activities such as bomb making, assassination, or surveillance. At the next level are the active supporters, who supply intelligence, weapons, supplies, communications, transportation, and safe houses. At the bottom are the passive supporters, who agree with the goals of the terrorist organization and spread their ideas and express their emotional support.[16]

"New Terrorism"

In contrast to "old terrorism," "new terrorism" is said to be characterized by a whole new range of attributes and to have begun around the early to mid-1990s. Many supporters of the "new terrorism" concept point to the prominence of religion as one of its main characteristics. Whereas old terrorism was primarily secular in its orientation and inspiration, terrorism linked to religious fanaticism is on the rise. According to Nadine Gurr and Benjamin Cole, in 1980 only two out of sixty-four identifiable international terrorist organizations could be classified as religious—a figure that rose sharply to twenty-five out of fifty-eight by 1995.[17] New terrorism is therefore often portrayed as terrorism that rejects all other ways and promotes an uncompromising view of the world in accordance with the belief of the religion. In contrast to old terrorism, new terrorism is said to lack a political agenda or precise political demands. Hoffman believes this religious motivation is the defining characteristic of the new terrorism, producing "radically different value systems, mechanisms of legitimization and justification, concepts of morality, and Manichean world view."[18]

Related to the religious motivation, many "new terrorism" supporters point to another of its main features: an increasing willingness to use excessive, indiscriminate violence. Laqueur, for example, argues that "the new terrorism is different in character, aiming not at clearly defined political demands but at the destruction of society and the elimination of large sections of the population."[19] These religion-based new terrorists see their struggle as good against evil, thereby dehumanizing their victims and considering all nonmembers of their group to be infidels or apostates. As a result, indiscriminate violence may be not only morally acceptable, but also a righteous and necessary advancement of their religious cause. Whereas "old terrorists" tended to strike only selected targets, "new terrorists" have become increasingly indiscriminate and try to produce as many casualties as possible.

Religious terrorists are often their own constituency, unconcerned about alienating their supporters with their acts of destruction, and holding themselves accountable only to God. Thus "new terrorists" do not always claim, and sometimes even deny, responsibility for their actions. They see the action itself as important and not the claim to it. They are not interested in any sort of negotiation. According to Matthew Morgan, "Today's terrorists don't want a seat at the table, they want to destroy the table and everyone sitting at it."[20] Moreover, "new terrorists" are deemed far more willing to engage in risky, complex, and seemingly irrational acts. Whereas most actions by "old terrorists" involved an escape plan, "new terrorists" are more willing to give their own lives while orchestrating a terrorist act; martyrdom is viewed as a way of reaching heaven.[21]

The threat of mass destruction is a fundamental part of the concept of "new terrorism." Many scholars believe that because "new terrorists" are motivated to use extreme violence, they are more likely to obtain and use biological, chemical, and radiological weapons, as well as nuclear WMDs. Hoffman warns that with the rise of the new terrorism "many of the constraints (both self-imposed and technical) which previously inhibited terrorist use of WMD are eroding."[22] And with the collapse of the Soviet Union, acquiring material that could be used for WMDs has become easier, and it no longer requires the cooperation of a state sponsor.

Another key characteristic of the new terrorism is precisely this inherent lack of state backers. Some academics believe that the explicit nonstate nature of new terrorism has enhanced terrorists' willingness to use extreme violence because it is virtually invulnerable to a direct backlash.[23] And the financing of new terrorism is based no longer on money received from state sponsors but on other illegal sources such as drug trafficking, video piracy, and credit card fraud, as well as legal business investments and donations from wealthy individuals and charities.

Finally, one of the most emphasized aspects of the new terrorism is its loose network and less hierarchical organizational structure, aided by the emergence of new communications technology. As Rohan Gunaratna points out, each group within this network becomes relatively autonomous, but all are still linked by advanced communications and their common purpose. They therefore become much more flexible and can adapt and react more easily to different situations. Although members do communicate with their leadership, groups can also operate self-sufficiently.[24] Steven Simon and Daniel Benjamin refer to this as a combination of "a 'hub and spoke' structure (where nodes communicate with the centre) with a 'wheel' structure (where nodes in the network communicate with each other without reference to the centre)."[25] This type of integrated structure is much more difficult to identify and penetrate than a traditional hierarchical structure. It is far more resilient because each cell can still operate even if the leadership of the organization is lost.

To summarize, proponents of the new terrorism believe its component parts consist of a fanatical religious motivation, excessive indiscriminate violence (with the possible use of WMDs), and an increasing independence from state sponsors, as well as a new ad hoc network structure aided by modern communications technology.

QUESTIONING "NEW TERRORISM"

A more detailed examination of the individual characteristics of the new terrorism raises questions about the validity of the concept and concerns about the common practice of dichotomizing the relationship between "old terrorism" and "new terrorism." This section examines three aspects of the supposedly "new terrorism"— motives, tactics, and organization—placing them in conceptual and historical perspectives. The results call into question the concept of new terrorism.[26]

Motives

Proponents of the "new terrorism" concept argue that the motivations of terrorists have changed, pointing to the growth of religious fundamentalism. Hoffman, for example, asserts that "the religious imperative for terrorism is the most important defining characteristic of terrorist activity today."[27] But does the rise in religiously motivated terrorist groups legitimize the existence of the term *new terrorism?* Historically, religious terrorism is by no means a new phenomenon. According to David Rapoport, religiously motivated terrorism aimed at killing nonbelievers has existed for thousands of years. From the first-century Zealots to the thirteenth-century Assassins, and even up to the nineteenth century and the emergence of political motives such as nationalism, anarchism, and Marxism, "religion provided the only acceptable justification for terror."[28]

Religious motivation is not so much a new characteristic as it is a cyclic return to earlier motivations for terrorism. Audrey Kurth Cronin, for example, suggests that "the forces of history seem to be driving international terrorism back to a much earlier time, with echoes of the behavior of 'sacred' terrorists such as the Zealots-Sicarii clearly apparent in the terrorist activities of organizations such as al-Qaeda and its associated groups."[29] In addition, many "old" terrorist organizations had close links with and were at least partly motivated by religion. The most prominent examples of this are the Irish Republican Army (IRA) with its predominantly Catholic membership, the Protestant Ulster Freedom Fighters or Ulster Volunteer Force, the primarily Muslim National Liberation Front (FLN) in Algeria, the Jewish terrorist group Irgun, and the National Organization of Cypriot Fighters (EOKA) in Cyprus, which was influenced by the Greek Orthodox Church.

It is also important to recognize that although the actions of modern Islamist terrorist groups may be religiously motivated, they still have specific political agendas. An examination of the demands and goals of al-Qaeda or other "new terrorists" associated with them reveals that many are based on clear political goals and targets—for example, the spread of political Islam, the withdrawal of foreign influence from the holy lands, the overthrow of the existing governments in Saudi Arabia and Egypt, the creation of a worldwide pan-Islamic caliphate, and the elimination of Israel. In reality, it is often extremely difficult if not impossible to distinguish between religious and political motivations. "Were the Jewish terrorists in British Palestine fighting for religion or against colonialism? Do the Tamil Tigers want their own homeland because they are Hindus in a Muslim nation or because they are Tamils in a Sinhalese country?"[30] The answer is both. As Chris Quillen points out, assigning religious motivations to individual terrorist attacks is subjective and open to interpretation. He cites the example of the 1995 Oklahoma City bombing, which one might interpret as an act motivated by Timothy McVeigh's devotion to the Christian Identity movement or as the reaction of a political terrorist to gun control measures and the bloody federal raids at Ruby Ridge and Waco.[31]

Tactics

In addition to the different motivations, "new terrorists" are said to use different tactics than "old terrorists," and they use new technologies—possibly weapons of mass destruction, suicide tactics, and, most important, excessive violence—to achieve their goals.

Use of Technology. The proliferation of technology and the accessibility of information useful to terrorists on the Internet are considered dangerous new trends that have contributed to the emergence and vitality of the new terrorism. However, the availability of information is arguably nothing new. Advice on bomb making and terrorist tactics has been available in newsletters and handbooks for well over a hundred years. An early example is the pamphlets published by the anarchist Johann Most at the end of the nineteenth century with "details on 'revolutionary chemistry' which included instructions on explosive devices, flammable liquid compounds, poison bullets and daggers, as well as on the best places to hide and use them."[32] Perhaps the most famous terrorist how-to guide is *The Anarchist Cookbook*, published in 1971.[33]

Weapons of Mass Destruction. To consider the use of WMDs as a characteristic of the new terrorism is also problematic. The example of the 1995 sarin gas attack on the Tokyo subway by Aum Shinrikyo is frequently cited to make the connection between the new terrorism and WMDs. However, terrorists have planned and attempted to use WMDs for many decades. In 1972 members of the right-wing group "Order of the Rising Sun" were arrested and found to be in the possession of 30–40 kilograms of epidemic typhus pathogens; they were seeking to poison the water supply of Chicago, St. Louis, and other midwestern cities in order to create a new master race. In 1984 members of the Bhagwan Shree Rajneesh's group contaminated salad bars with *Salmonella typhi*, thereby poisoning 750 people in Oregon. In the 1980s, European authorities discovered botulinum toxin and considerable quantities of organophosphorus compounds, used to make nerve gas, in Red Army Faction (RAF) safe houses in France and Germany. In addition, the Kurdistan Workers' Party (PKK) and the Tamil Tigers, both examples of "old terrorists," have used chemical weapons. In 1992 the PKK poisoned water tanks of the Turkish air force near Istanbul with lethal doses of cyanide, and in 1990 the Tamil Tigers attacked a Sri Lankan military camp with chlorine gas. The PKK and Tamil attacks are significant because they clearly disprove the idea that all "traditional terrorist groups would avoid using nuclear, chemical or biological weapons under any circumstances."[34]

The threat of nuclear terrorism has also been linked to the concept of new terrorism. So far, terrorists have not undertaken any attacks with nuclear weapons. The most devastating terrorist attacks have employed bombs, conventional explosives, and, most famously, box cutters. And yet, even though no nuclear bombs have been exploded, traditional terrorists made numerous attacks on nuclear power stations in the 1970s and 1980s. One of the first occurred in 1973 when a commando from a left-wing Argentinean group entered the construction site of the Atucha atomic power station north of Buenos Aires. During the years that followed, the separatist group Basque Fatherland and Liberty (ETA) conducted several attacks against the Lemoniz nuclear power station near Bilbao, Spain. Other attacks were directed against plants near San Sebastián, Pamplona, Tafalla, Berriz, and other sites in northern Spain. In 1982 the terrorist wing of the African National Congress (ANC) sabotaged two South African nuclear power plants. Both of their reactors were substantially damaged, but because they were not in operation at the time, there was no release of radiation.[35] Although it was not proven that any of these groups were seeking to cause a nuclear explosion or contamination, these incidents prove that even "old terrorists" were clearly willing to cross the nuclear line.

Suicide Tactics. The same can be said of suicide tactics, which are often included in the description of the fanatical nature of the new terrorism in general and Islamic fundamentalism in particular. However, suicide bombing has been used extensively by the separatist Tamil Tigers in Sri Lanka since 1983. For example, Robert Pape points out that the Tamil Tigers carried out 75 of 186 suicide terrorist attacks between 1980 and 2000.[36] Even before this, during the Middle Ages the Assassins' use of daggers at close range showed their "willingness to die in pursuit of their mission,"[37] and the anarchists of nineteenth-century Europe regularly died in the process of attacking their targets.

Use of Excessive Violence. Supporters of the "new terrorism" concept have argued that terrorists have become more lethal and willing to resort to unlimited violence to cause large numbers of casualties indiscriminately. In their view, the traditional terrorists were more restrained in their use of violence and the number of casualties they sought. On the one hand the indiscriminateness can be debated, as it may be argued that our understanding of what can be considered discriminate and indiscriminate is subjective. What we consider indiscriminate attacks on the Pentagon and the World Trade Center others may believe to be selective strikes on the military and financial center of the United States. New terrorists are still very selective in their targeting. They generally do not go about randomly killing everybody, but continue to carefully plan their attacks and consciously select their targets for maximum effect. Just because the selected target group is considered wider and now includes Western civilians does not make it indiscriminate. "Al-Qaeda is probably not interested in killing a native villager in the middle of the rainforest."[38]

On the other hand, one could argue that indiscriminate mass-casualty attacks have long been a characteristic of terrorism. Examples of the mass fatalities produced by the "old terrorists" are the simultaneous truck bombings of the U.S. and French barracks in Lebanon in 1983, which killed 367; the downing of Pan Am Flight 103 over Lockerbie, Scotland, which took the lives of 270; and the bombing of an Air India flight in 1985 by Sikh separatists with 329 fatalities. It is easy to forget that one of the most violent incidents of terrorism prior to September 11, 2001, was the 1979 attack on a movie theater in the Iranian city of Abadan that killed about five hundred people. And as Rapoport points out, evidence indicates that the Thugs of South Asia were by far the longest-lasting and most murderous terrorist organization in history, killing around half a million people over a period of roughly four hundred years.[39]

Even if the indiscriminate targeting of innocent people, such as the children in the attack on a school in Beslan, Russia, in 2004, is considered to be a characteristic of the new terrorism, one finds examples of "old terrorists" who did the same. For example, members of the Democratic Front for the Liberation of Palestine machine-gunned children in an Israeli school in 1974, killing twenty-seven and injuring seventy. And even if one disregards the numbers and argues that the gruesome violence of the "new" terrorism, such as the beheading of the *Wall Street Journal* reporter Daniel Pearl in 2002, is more excessive than before, the "old terrorists" could be just as ruthless. For example, Martin Miller describes how in 1884 "a Viennese banker and his eleven-year-old son were hacked to death with an axe in front of his other son" by anarchists.[40]

It is true that none of these examples can be likened to the casualties caused by the 9/11 attacks. However, the term *new terrorism* appeared long before 2001.

Marie Breen Smyth points out that "the scale of atrocity at the World Trade Center was unprecedented in the practice of modern terror; however, the emphasis on the scale of the attack has tended to negate the value of previous scholarship and experience of 'terrorism.'"[41] In fact, examination of the data on international terrorism incidences reveals that although the number of events has generally declined since the mid-1980s, the number of fatalities per incident has steadily increased over the same period. Considering that the new terrorism is supposed to have started in the 1990s, this increase in fatalities might not be directly linked to the phenomenon of the new terrorism. An equally plausible argument is that the increase in casualties is due at least in part to better technology. Explosives and timing and remote-control devices have substantially improved in recent decades, with a corresponding effect on the numbers of casualties. Furthermore, since the 1980s, governments have adapted to terrorist techniques such as kidnapping, hostage taking, hijacking, assassination, and sabotage by increasing security at airports, securing embassies, guarding likely kidnap targets, training specialist commando troops, and sharing intelligence with other states. In response, terrorists have adjusted their tactics by placing more emphasis on coordinated bombings and hit-and-run tactics. Although it has become increasingly difficult for terrorists to get close to their traditional targets, they continue to find other ways of capturing the public's attention. The use of more spectacular coordinated violent tactics is one way of gaining greater media coverage.

Scholars such as Ray Takeyh make a compelling case that public opinion plays as vital a role in the new terrorism as in the old terrorism. One example is the 1997 al-Gama'at al-Islamiyya attack on the Temple of Hatshepsut in Luxor, Egypt. The attack, which killed fifty-eight tourists and four Egyptians, was widely condemned not only by Western governments but also by many radical Islamists, who believed the attack damaged their cause. Takeyh points out that support for al-Gama'at al-Islamiyya fell dramatically in Egypt as a result of the attack. Although the group remained active, its attack alienated the people to whom it most wanted to appeal, and over time this development gravely hindered the group's efforts.[42]

The importance of public opinion is particularly true when one considers terrorists' political agendas. These political goals, such as the establishment of an Islamic state, will restrain terrorists. Public support will be required for the establishment of a new state, and therefore terrorists must be careful not to alienate their supporters and sympathizers by using excessive violence. This very concern was evident in a 2005 letter from al-Qaeda's second-in-command, Ayman al-Zawahiri, to the then-leader of al-Qaeda in Iraq, Abu Musab al-Zarqawi.[43]

Finally, the use of terrorist violence as "theater" has not faded with the emergence of the new terrorism. It is hard to think of a more symbolic and dramatically theatrical set of attacks than those of September 11. Targeting the World Trade Center (a symbol of Western capitalism), the Pentagon (the heart of the U.S. defense establishment), and the U.S. Capitol seems too much even for a Hollywood film. Terrorists still want a big audience, and the larger, more coordinated, and more dramatic the attack, the bigger the audience will be. Therefore, the rising level of fatalities can be viewed as an ongoing process, which does not necessarily represent a unique feature qualifying the concept of the new terrorism.

Organization

One of the main differences between the old terrorism and the new terrorism as postulated by proponents of the new terrorism is their form of organization. Whereas traditional terrorism was organized along hierarchical lines with a clear command structure, the new terrorism is a loose, stateless network that is more weakly organized and has no strong command structure. However, the network structure in the new terrorism is not a particularly new phenomenon in terrorism, and even Hoffman admits that the newness of the loose network structure associated with the new terrorism is debatable. For example, over a century ago the anarchist movement, responsible for a number of high-profile attacks against heads of state in Russia and across Europe, pursued a similar strategy of violence carried out by loosely networked, largely unconnected cells of like-minded radicals.[44]

Different forms of network structures also can be found in traditional terrorist organizations. For example, the Palestine Liberation Organization served as an umbrella group in which the dominant faction, Fatah, did not have a monopoly of power. For decades, the different factions within the PLO were fairly independent and had different policies and strategies. Hezbollah is as an umbrella organization of radical Shiite groups in which the relationship among members is unpredictable and does not follow strict lines of control. Network structures also existed in left-wing revolutionary groups such as the RAF in which second-, third-, and fourth-generation terrorists formed not really a hierarchical organization but rather a loose confederation with similar common goals.[45]

In the same way in which there are network structures in "old terrorist" groups, there are clear signs of hierarchical command structures in the "new terrorist" organizations such as al-Qaeda. They possess a clear leadership structure and operative subunits responsible for conducting attacks, as well as "specialized units directly below the top leadership level" that are responsible for certain tasks such as recruitment, finances, procurement, and public relations.[46] At the same time, today's terrorist organizations, including al-Qaeda, have many different types of members, including core members or professional terrorists, part-time terrorists, or amateurs, who also lead normal lives outside of the organization, as well as less closely associated supporters. These different types of members exist in both "old terrorism" and "new terrorism" to an equally fluctuating degree.

CONCLUSION

The emergence and effectiveness of terrorist organizations like al-Qaeda have sparked an understandable search for newness in a very old phenomenon. But as this essay has shown, there is actually far more consistency than difference between "old terrorism" and "new terrorism" in their key component parts, including motivations, tactics, and organization.

Some scholars may now ask, does it really matter what the kind of terrorism perpetrated by groups such as al-Qaeda is called? Some may argue that the predicate *new* is meaningless because it is a word devoid of any real significance. Others, this author included, would disagree and argue that words matter a great deal. Calling a problem "new" forces one to automatically buy into the belief that the appropriate solutions must also be new. Although it is certainly appropriate to adjust counterterrorism measures to address the terrorism challenges of the day, one should remain wary of accepting a whole new set of hastily formed, restrictive government countermeasures without their being debated, publicly discussed, and independently monitored. Such "new" measures may not be necessary.

Al-Qaeda is an example of a "new terrorism."
YES: Rohan Gunaratna, *Nanyang Technological University, Singapore*

Al-Qaeda and the "New Terrorism"

Since the onset of the contemporary wave of terrorism in 1968, the world has witnessed violence conducted by five categories of nonstate threat groups: left- and right-wing (ideological), ethno-political, politico-religious, state-sponsored, and single-issue.[47] Ideological, ethno-political, and state-sponsored terrorism were the most dominant forms of violence during the Cold War. But with the collapse of the Soviet Union in 1991, the ideology of communism lost its appeal and support, and left-wing groups diminished. With the end of the Cold War, the Soviet bloc of countries ended their support for socialist governments and left-wing groups, and the Western bloc of countries ended their support for right-wing governments and groups. Although the threat posed by ethno-political groups continued, a new form of terrorism emerged and grew steadfastly into the twenty-first century. Thus even though the end of the Cold War marked the decline of traditional or "old" terrorism, the post–Cold War era witnessed the emergence of a new and more dangerous form of terrorism.[48]

Skeptics of the existence of a "new terrorism" debated until al-Qaeda attacked America's most iconic targets on September 11, 2001. The continuity of attacks and plots since has made it clear that 9/11 was not an anomaly but a trend: the global threat of terrorism has only grown; it has not plateaued. Al-Qaeda and its operationally linked associates in the Muslim world as well as its ideologically affiliated cells in the West are the exemplars of this new terrorism. In addition to mobilizing thirty to forty groups in Asia, Africa, and the Middle East, al-Qaeda has successfully inspired segments of Muslims both in the territorial communities of the Middle East, Asia, and Africa and in the diaspora and migrant communities of the West. Despite being the world's most hunted class of terrorists, al-Qaeda, its associated groups, and its affiliated cells pose an unprecedented global threat. In the early twenty-first century, preventing and suppressing the new terrorism have become a high priority of most governments.[49]

THE CONTEXT

The rise in globalization in the 1990s transformed the thinking and behavior of politically motivated threat groups. As the conduct of terrorist groups that target civilians and of guerrilla groups that target combatants changed, both academics and practitioners began identifying their actions as the new terrorism. The post–Cold War globalized era can be characterized by four features that have significantly influenced threat groups:

1. *The ease of international travel, particularly migrant workers and refugees.* Most refugees came from internal conflict zones where they experienced human suffering and internal displacement. They were also the most vulnerable to indoctrination by virulent ideologies.

2. *Accessibility to weapons, dual-use technologies, and specialist trainers.* With the downsizing of Cold War armies worldwide, militaries privatized, and lethal technologies proliferated.

3. *A shift from international to internal disputes, especially ethnic and religious conflicts.* In contrast to ideological conflicts featuring left- and right-wing groups (Colombia, Philippines, Nepal, India), about 70–80 percent of contemporary conflicts worldwide are ethno-political and politico-religious.[50]

4. *The free flow of ideas, information, and technology through the proliferation of new platforms for communication, including the Internet.* Sustained propaganda disseminated through these platforms has been radicalizing both territorial and émigré Muslim communities. More than the territorial Muslims, the émigré Muslims—in North America, Europe, and Australia—are susceptible to radicalization.

A threat group's operational environment is the single most important parameter of influence. However, little if any research has been conducted to assess the impact of the environment on the origins, evolution, and trajectories of terrorist groups. Defining characteristics of the new terrorism proposed by scholars and practitioners include networked, not hierarchical; politico-religious, not secular; transnational, not territorial; autonomous, not state-sponsored; mass casualty, not restrained; destruction, not political goals; and amateurs, not professionals (see Table 1-1).[51]

Since the attacks of September 11, scholars' understanding of threat groups and their operational milieu, especially with regard to al-Qaeda, has grown. Against the defining features of new terrorism and old terrorism, it is time to test.

Table 1-1

New Terrorism versus Traditional Terrorism

Trait	New Terrorism	Traditional Terrorism
Motivation	Religious	Secular
Organization	Networked and ad hoc	Hierarchical and organized
Sponsorship	Autonomous	State
Violence	Extreme	Restrained
Aim	Destruction	Political goal
Personnel	Amateur	Professional
Range of operation	Transnational	Territorial

THE BACKGROUND

Terrorism is the threat or the act of politically motivated violence against non-combatants. Ideologically and operationally, terrorism is constantly evolving. Terror specialist Martha Crenshaw argues that "terrorism has changed over time, but the difference represents an evolution to the phenomenon and not a radical break between the past and the future of terrorism."[52] In every generation, the world has witnessed the emergence of groups with new intentions, capabilities, technologies, and tactics, and the range and types of threat they pose have differed. A confluence of factors—environmental, historical, intellectual, and other—create and shape new forms of terrorism.

When the contemporary wave of terrorism emerged in the Middle East in 1968, none of the identifiable international terrorist groups had a religious affiliation. However, after the Islamic revolution in Iran in 1979 and the anti-Soviet multinational mujahidin campaign in Afghanistan from 1979 to 1989, a new class of networked groups emerged. Like the groups over the previous decade, these threat groups had political aims, but they sought to use religion to justify their courses of action, which included violence.[53]

CHANGING LANDSCAPE OF THREAT

Since the end of the Cold War in 1991, the contours of the global threat have changed fundamentally. The threat of international conflict has receded, and the threat of internal conflict has advanced. With the exception of Iran and North Korea, no government currently poses a real threat to international security. At the global level, terrorism by nonstate actors has emerged as the tier-one national security threat. Despite sustained investment by the international community to reduce and manage the threat, terrorism remains the predominant challenge to the West. Ideological extremism and its vicious by-product, terrorism, have become more widespread. Existing and emerging classes of politico-religious groups, especially of the Islamist variety, dominate the global threat landscape.

Two principal operating environments are contributing to the current terrorist threat: the Global South and the Global North. Over 90 percent of threat groups—terrorist and insurgent—have emerged in the Global South. Asia, Africa, the Middle East, and Latin America, with their swathes of great poverty, illiteracy, injustice, and corruption, have witnessed the rise of economically and politically motivated violent groups. These threat groups or their representatives in migrant and diaspora communities have built state-of-the-art support networks in the Global North, where freedom of movement and protest, as well as human and minority rights, is protected by local constitutions.

Because of this political liberalism, North America, Europe, and Australia remain ideal arenas for the operation of terrorist support networks.

Conflict zones in the Global South (Palestine, Lebanon, Afghanistan, Chechnya, Kashmir, Algeria, Iraq) are the most conducive environments for the rise of extremist ideologies and terrorist recruitment and activity. Those affected then migrate to the Global North. Some bring ethnic and religious differences from their homelands and contribute to instability in the host nation. First- and second-generation migrant and diaspora youth searching for new identities, in the absence of finding one, become susceptible to terror recruitment through the use of virulent ideologies crafted and disseminated by groups like al-Qaeda. The core of the message has focused on U.S. intervention (Afghanistan), invasion (Iraq), and occupation (Saudi Arabia) in Muslim lands, as well as support for secular dictatorships (Egypt, Libya, Jordan, Pakistan, Uzbekistan) in the Muslim world.

Terrorist groups continually adapt to changing environments. What is unique today is the globalization of communication and social media, which has enabled terrorists to successfully penetrate ideologically the migrant and diaspora communities. As a result of this ideological penetration, terrorist groups enjoy support from both their territorial and their migrant and diaspora communities. Today's governments and societies therefore suffer not only from traditional group-centered terrorism but also from homegrown terrorism. These self-radicalized youth seek to link up with formally structured terrorist groups for training and guidance.

The single biggest threat emanates from al-Qaeda and its conglomerate of groups and cells that represent a new and increasingly dangerous form of terrorism. This global jihad movement, consisting of al-Qaeda, its associated groups in Asia, Africa, the Middle East, and the Caucasus, and the self-radicalized homegrown cells, is resilient, and the threat is enduring. In the coming years, through the Arab Spring uprisings and beyond, the movement will continue to challenge mainstream Islam and both Muslim and secular states. The narrative highlighting the suffering of Muslims (actual and perceived) finds resonance among territorial, migrant, and diaspora Muslims. Thus correcting and countering jihadi propaganda and reducing violence in conflict zones in Muslim countries will be paramount to lessening Muslim support for extremism and terrorism.

ORIGINS OF THE THREAT

The Islamist strain of the new terrorism emerged with the anti-Soviet jihad (mujahidin) in Afghanistan during the 1980s. In 1984 Abdullah Azzam, a Palestinian-Jordanian, founded Maktab al-Khidmat lil Mujahidin al-Arab

(MAK), known commonly as the Afghan Service Bureau, which provided the Arab mujahidin and their families with significant assistance. Osama bin Laden, member of a wealthy Saudi family, joined hands with Azzam and, as MAK's principal financier, was considered his deputy. At the height of the foreign Arab and Muslim influx into Pakistan-Afghanistan from 1984 to 1986, Azzam recruited several thousand Arab and Muslim youths, and bin Laden channeled several million dollars in financial and material resources into the Afghan jihad. MAK operated independently of Western and Pakistani governments that assisted in the fight against the Soviets, but it tapped into the vast Muslim Brotherhood network and the resources of the Saudi government.[54]

Toward the end of the anti-Soviet Afghan campaign, Azzam and bin Laden decided to form a vanguard group—al-Qaeda al-Sulbah—that could unite the whole Muslim world into a single entity. Azzam was the ideological father and the intellectual leader, but gradually bin Laden took over.[55] Although bin Laden's worldview was initially shaped by Azzam, formerly of the Muslim Brotherhood, around the time of the Soviet withdrawal in 1988 bin Laden's relationship with Azzam deteriorated, primarily over disputes about post-Soviet Afghan leadership and the next steps for the jihad movement. Along with the Egyptian members of al-Qaeda, bin Laden wished to support terrorist action against Egypt and other Muslim secular regimes. Having lived in Egypt, Azzam knew the price of such actions and opposed them vehemently. The issue was settled by Azzam's assassination in November 1989 by the Egyptian members of al-Qaeda in Peshawar, Pakistan.

After Azzam's death, the ideological vacuum was filled by Ayman al-Zawahiri, the leader of the Egyptian Islamic Jihad. A professional medical practitioner and qualified eye surgeon, al-Zawahiri became both bin Laden's doctor and his spiritual mentor. Bin Laden took over Azzam's MAK, and, using its trainers and camps, he built al-Qaeda. Al-Zawahiri became his deputy and the principal strategist of the jihad movement.

The group al-Qaeda takes its name from a concept—"al-qaedah al-sulbah" (the "solid base")—attributed to Sayyid Qutb, a mid-twentieth–century Egyptian Islamist scholar. The term al-Qaeda refers to the successful early Muslim generation, also known as Salafi, who received education and guidance from the Prophet Muhammad. They were companions of the Prophet, and their devotion and commitment to the Islamic struggle against Arab pagans were unmatched by later generations for whom the Salafi became a source of inspiration and a model for Muslims to emulate. In conceptualizing al-Qaeda, Azzam had drawn from the pages of Islamic history. He defined al-Qaeda's composition, aims, and purpose in the context of the struggle of the Islamist movement after the victory over the largest land army in the world—the Soviet military. Although the concept was transformed to meet the changing land-scapes, al-Qaeda was, in fact, never intended to be a terrorist organization.[56] Azzam stated in the founding charter of al-Qaeda in late 1987 early 1988 that he envisaged al-Qaeda as an organization that would channel the energies of the mujahidin into fighting on behalf of oppressed Muslims worldwide.[57] He viewed the organization as an Islamic "rapid reaction force," ready to spring to the defense of its fellow believers on short notice.[58]

Officially formed in August 1988, al-Qaeda became an organization with a global reach. Its real strength is not its membership, per se, but its overarch-ing, highly appealing ideology. In keeping with Azzam's original mandate, its principal aim is to inspire and incite Muslims worldwide to attack those who threaten Islam. Its principal strategy is to attack iconic targets in or belonging to the United States and its allies and friends in order to inspire and instigate a perpetual campaign.

Although al-Qaeda does not enjoy widespread support among Muslims worldwide, it opportunistically seeks to exploit the anger, suffering, and resent-ment of Muslims against the United States. America's lack of understanding of the Muslim world—for example, its unequivocal support for Israel, its assis-tance to secular Muslim rulers, its invasion of Iraq—has given Islamic terror-ism and extremism a new lease on life. In view of the current support for the global jihad movement in Asia, Africa, the Middle East, and elsewhere, the campaign has been a success. Al-Qaeda averaged one major attack every year before 9/11, but since 2001 the frequency of attacks by al-Qaeda and its associ-ated groups has grown exponentially.

AL-QAEDA, THE GLOBAL JIHAD MOVEMENT, AND THE NEW TERRORISM

A defining feature of the new terrorism is its network. Although al-Qaeda emerged as a centralized group, it has worked with other groups and individuals to form a network. Instead of building support for the group, it seeks to rein-vigorate its global capacity to strike.[59] Indeed, since the events of 9/11 al-Qaeda itself has been surpassed by the emergence of the global jihad movement, con-sisting of al-Qaeda and other groups that advocate global jihad. The movement has three overlapping components.

The first is the initial al-Qaeda group established by bin Laden and Azzam. Also known as al-Qaeda core, al-Qaeda central, or al-Qaeda classic, the post-9/11 and post–bin Laden al-Qaeda group is operationally weak but ideologi-cally potent, appealing to both associated groups waging local jihad in conflict zones and radicalized cells in migrant and diaspora communities in the West.

The second component is al-Qaeda's thirty to forty operationally associated groups in Asia, Africa, and the Middle East. Also known as the al-Qaeda network, these groups receive from al-Qaeda core training, weapons, financing, and ideology. The groups hold declared or undeclared membership in the World Islamic Front for Jihad against the Jews and the Crusaders, which was formed by fatwa, or religious decree, in February 1998. Members of the World Islamic Front include the Algerian Salafist Group for Call and Combat (GSPC), the Moroccan Islamic Combatant Group (GICM), Tawhid wal-Jihad (al-Qaeda of the Two Rivers), Lashkar-e-Taiba (LeT), al-Jamaah al-Islamiyah (JI), Abu Sayyaf Group (ASG), Yemen's Ansar al-Sharia, and Somalia's al-Shabaab.

The third component is al-Qaeda's ideologically affiliated cells and individuals, which are operationally unconnected to al-Qaeda but driven by an ideology of global jihad articulated by it. Examples include the cell responsible for bombing the trains in Madrid in March 2004, the disrupted British cell led by Omar Khayyám,[60] and the Fort Hood shooter in the United States in November 2009. Each was self-financed and independent of al-Qaeda's operational control. The Islamist milieu in North America, Europe, and Australasia has transformed support cells into execution cells.

Today, al-Qaeda's real power is the disparate groups and cells it has trained, financed, armed, and, most important, influenced ideologically. The al-Qaeda network (the al-Qaeda core plus its associated groups) and ideologically affiliated cells comprise the al-Qaeda movement. The threat is not monolithic. Members could be violent (for example, the extremist groups Laskar Jihad and Front Pembela Islam in Indonesia), or nonviolent (for example, Hizb ut-Tahrir and al-Muhajiroun in the United Kingdom). Some of these groups publicly criticized bin Laden and al-Qaeda, but they believe in global jihad. The groups in the Muslim territorial communities and cells in the Muslim diaspora represent a multidimensional threat against the United States and its allies. The global jihadists challenge both the "infidel" (non-Muslims) and "apostate" (Muslims who have forsaken their faith) regimes. The threat is both ideological and kinetic.

As a result of U.S.-led global counterterrorism policies in the dozen years since the 9/11 attack, al-Qaeda central has been severely weakened. Nevertheless, events such as the U.S.-led intervention in Afghanistan, the U.S. invasion and occupation of Iraq, and media reporting on Abu Ghraib, Guantánamo Bay, and drone attacks have strengthened support for like-minded or associated Islamist groups and cells.[61] Exploiting suffering, resentment, and anger of Muslims, the terrorist and extremist groups are now able to replenish their human losses and continue the fight. Indeed, al-Qaeda has morphed from a group of three to four thousand members in October 2001 to a movement of several tens of thousands of members, supporters, and sympathizers.

A MIXTURE OF OLD AND NEW TERRORISM

A closer look at al-Qaeda demonstrates that the group has features of traditional terrorism, as well as important features unique to the new terrorism. It has creatively adopted and nurtured the best of the old and the new in six ways.

First, although al-Qaeda is hierarchical, a classic feature of traditional terrorism, it is also part of a network of groups, a classic feature of the new terrorism. By organizing itself and its affiliated groups under the banner of the World Islamic Front for Jihad against the Jews and the Crusaders, al-Qaeda created a transnational network. In addition, although the central al-Qaeda members and members of affiliated groups in conflict zones are professionally trained, many operatives in diaspora communities are amateurs. In that sense, al-Qaeda is a hybrid, comprising both professionals, a characteristic of the old terrorism, and amateurs, a characteristic of the new terrorism.

Second, even though al-Qaeda operates globally through its network of groups and cells across regions and countries (classic new terrorism), most of the groups in this network are national or regional groups. These groups include Tehreek-e-Taliban, an alliance of Pakistani groups; the Islamic Movement of Uzbekistan and its splinter Islamic Jihad Union, groups seeking to create an Islamic state in Uzbekistan; the Eastern Turkistan Islamic Movement, a Uighur Chinese group seeking to create an Islamic state in western China; and the Libyan Islamic Fighting Group, a group seeking to establish an Islamic state in Libya. Although all of these groups believe in a global jihad, the model promoted by al-Qaeda, they are all fighting to establish Islamic states in their own countries, which is in line with traditional, particularly ideological, terrorism.

Third, al-Qaeda has used multiple sources of support, including state support. For example, it received the support of Sudan (1991–1996) and Afghanistan (1996–2001). However, unlike for the state-sponsored groups characteristic of traditional terrorism, no government has leverage over al-Qaeda. Indeed, al-Qaeda functions like a modern global business and investment firm, which also penetrates global charities. And it relies on its extraordinary global multimedia production arm, al-Sahab, to generate and sustain support. In its commercial outlook, al-Qaeda functions like a modern multinational corporation investing in a range of opportunities.

Fourth, al-Qaeda's ultimate aim is to establish a global Islamic state, or caliphate, which is clearly a "new terror" aspiration. This goal, however, is not a religious one but a political one, similar to that of traditional terrorism. Political leaders in the United States have often argued that al-Qaeda has no political goals. Some proponents of the new terrorism argument would go beyond that and claim that al-Qaeda seeks to destroy the world. However, al-Qaeda's goal is to create evermore Islamic states by carrying out an armed struggle—jihad or holy war—against those who, in its view, are trying to prevent the establishment of such states. Although some proponents of the new terrorism would argue that al-Qaeda is a religiously motivated organization, an examination of the group reveals that it is a political organization that is misusing religion to legitimize its actions. It is wrong and counterproductive to blame religion.

Fifth, al-Qaeda is a highly patient organization that is promoting a multigenerational campaign. Its meticulous and exhaustive preparation for attacks makes al-Qaeda truly unique, clearly differentiating it from traditional terrorism. Al-Qaeda is not event-driven but campaign-driven—it does not believe in an immediate reaction to an attack carried out against it. Indeed, al-Qaeda doctrine stipulates that it should always wield the initiative and calmly decide when and where to attack. For example, after the United States fired seventy cruise missiles into Afghanistan following the East African embassy bombings in 1998, al-Qaeda decided to strike America's homeland using U.S. airplanes, an operation that would take three years to plan, prepare, and execute.[62] Although al-Qaeda has appealed to Muslims across the world with its call that "it is the duty of every good Muslim to wage jihad," its primary tactical strength is an ability to meticulously study the gaps in security and patiently strike at targets that will have strategic implications. The challenge for intelligence services to prevent such attacks is extraordinary.

Sixth, parallel with building its conventional capabilities for "traditional"-style attacks, al-Qaeda has invested heavily in building a chemical, biological, radiological, and nuclear (CBRN) capability. A goal of mass destruction is a classic feature of the new terrorism, and al-Qaeda's structure includes a dedicated WMD committee under its military committee. As far back as 1993, bin Laden asked his personal pilot, Essam al-Ridi, to learn about crop dusting.[63] By the time the United States invaded Afghanistan in late 2001, al-Qaeda had established close links with Pakistani scientists, both nuclear weapons specialists and biochemists. The WMD committee, led by Abdul Aziz al-Masri, was dedicated to developing or acquiring a nuclear capability, but there were separate chemical and biological programs as well; the overall supervisor of the biological program was Ayman al-Zawahiri.

The centralized al-Qaeda CBRN programs fell into disarray after the U.S. intervention in Afghanistan, but since the 1990s other like-minded groups have developed similar programs for the production of chemical and biological agents. They included clandestine programs in northern Iraq, in the Pankisi Valley in Georgia, and in the southern Philippines. Because al-Qaeda had invested significantly in training members of its associated groups in its camps in Afghanistan in the use of chemical and biological agents, both the jihadist intention and the capability to use unconventional agents have proliferated.

In sum, al-Qaeda is an unpredictable adversary precisely because it draws from both traditional and new forms of terrorism. An examination of its ideology and ideological evolution provides further insight into the group.

THE POLITICO-IDEOLOGICAL DIMENSION OF THE NEW TERRORISM

Most Western scholars, whether for or against the new terrorism argument, do not discuss the ideological dimension. Traditional terrorist groups used violence as a means to a political end. Some scholars believe that the new terrorists aim at destruction as an end in itself. Although apocalyptic religious groups such as Aum Shinrikyo belong in this category, most of the politico-religious groups, including Islamist, are pragmatic. The politico-religious ideology of al-Qaeda offers an insight into the thinking of Islamist groups.

In terrorism, the more strategic and long-term threat is the belief system. At the heart of the sustained ideological campaign waged by al-Qaeda is the belief that the United States, the West, and Israel are leading a global conspiracy against Islam and Muslims. Al-Qaeda detests America's presence in the Arab Peninsula, especially in Saudi Arabia; U.S. support for Israel and neglect of the Palestinians; and U.S. assistance to pro-Western dictatorships around the Middle East. Al-Qaeda holds the U.S. government, the American people, and U.S. foreign policy responsible for bringing chaos to the Muslim world. The only way the Muslim nation could live under the shade of Islam, al-Qaeda ideologues argue, is to be united and work toward the establishment, by force if necessary, of an Islamic caliphate. It is with this in mind that bin Laden issued the 1998 fatwa. Since 9/11, the primary targets of the al-Qaeda movement have been U.S. allies—primarily Europe, Canada, and Australia—and friends—primarily Muslim countries that support the West.

Although its long-term wish is to create a global Islamic caliphate, al-Qaeda's immediate aim is to establish Islamic states wherever Muslims live. The methodology for achieving this goal is jihad.[64] Al-Qaeda's ideology is a composite of writings and speeches of past and present ideologues. Muhammad bin Abdul Wahhab, an eighteenth-century reformer, claimed that Islam became corrupted a generation or so after the death of the Prophet Muhammad. He denounced any theology or customs developed after that as un-Islamic and, in doing so, tried to reform more than a thousand years of religious scholarship. He and his supporters took over what is now Saudi Arabia, where Wahhabism remains the dominant school of religious thought. Sayyid Qutb, the Egyptian scholar, declared Western civilization an enemy of Islam and denounced leaders of

Muslim nations for not following Islam closely enough. He preached that jihad should be undertaken not just to defend Islam, but to purify Islam.

As an extension of these ideologies, the politically savvy al-Qaeda often couches its grievances in "Third Worldist" terms familiar to any contemporary antiglobalization activist and frames modern political concerns, including social justice, within a divine and religious narrative. Jihad in the form of an armed struggle in the name of God then becomes the means to attain freedom and rid the *ummah* (community of Muslims) of injustice. The jihad they wage is a "defensive jihad" in the face of perceived aggression by the enemies of Islam. In this sense, the presence of U.S. and other non-Muslim troops in Saudi Arabia after the 1991 Gulf War was a turning point in the life of bin Laden. He publicly criticized the Saudi royal family and alleged that their invitation of foreign troops to the Arab Peninsula constituted an affront to the sanctity of the birthplace of Islam and a betrayal of the global Islamic community.[65] After the Saudi government rendered him stateless, bin Laden advocated violence against it and the United States. Because it was difficult to strike inside Saudi Arabia, bin Laden increasingly focused his ire on the United States. After a period of exile in Sudan and Afghanistan, he sharpened his radical views. Jihad to al-Qaeda followers was deemed justifiable in order to defend the dignity and pride of the nation, a noble duty that had been neglected by Muslim leaders. Al-Qaeda's devotion to political ideology couched in religious terms is therefore not easily swayed by cheap promises and materialistic gains. So long as there is no sincere attempt to meet its demands, al-Qaeda will have sufficient support to continue the jihad.

Even though he did not possess Islamic religious credentials or authority, bin Laden issued the 1998 fatwa declaring jihad against the Jews and Crusaders. He claimed that the United States had made "a clear declaration of war on God, His messenger, and Muslims" through its policies in the Islamic world. This is another example of al-Qaeda's jihad ideology, which set the organization in motion.

With jihad comes the belief in martyrdom. Al-Qaeda operatives firmly believe that Allah guides and rewards those who sacrifice themselves for a noble cause. They are ever willing to sacrifice themselves without hesitation and often seek death as the best way to enter heaven.[66] When killed fighting for God, ideologues propagate that the "martyr" will enter paradise and receive an audience with God. In their ideological manuals, speeches, and one-on-one indoctrination, ideologues embellish the beauty of seventy-two virgins that would serve the "martyred Muslim hero" in paradise. As the "martyr" will be forgiven for his sins and vices, ideologues induce and exploit his fear of going to hell for wrongdoings on earth, compelling the gullible Muslim youth to kill and die. Furthermore, as the "martyr's" act will supposedly create the path for seventy relatives to enter paradise, some family members exposed to this ideology will clandestinely or openly support his mission to kill, maim, and injure.

The *baiah,* or pledge of allegiance, serves as an assurance that those affiliating themselves to the organization are committed to its ideology. By instituting it, the organization is freed from conceptual problems arising from differences in opinion. Through the *baiah* an acceptable level of uniformity is maintained that contributes to the organization's stability and ease of management and administration. *Baiah* unites all members to the notion that "true Islam or pure Islam" can only be established if the essence of Islamic society and its fundamentals are instituted. This requires the setting up of an Islamic state under *sharia,* or Islamic, law. Of course, to achieve this end, the present Muslim society needs an Islamic movement that will provide leadership and spiritual guidance.

Harnessing the forces of globalization, al-Qaeda has propagated the politico ideological belief that Muslims worldwide belong to a single global Muslim nation and has instilled the belief that whenever a group of Muslims suffer in any corner of the world, their brethren have a religious obligation to help. A convert to Islam, the American John Walker Lindh was motivated to travel to Afghanistan because as a "good Muslim" he felt a deep sense of obligation to help the "suffering Muslims to provide alms, train, and fight."[67] Despite international efforts to curb them, Muslim public sympathy, support, and participation in jihad are likely to continue and grow in coming years.

THE FUTURE OF AL-QAEDA'S NEW TERRORISM

Today, al-Qaeda is in a period of consolidation. It lost its leader, bin Laden, in a U.S. special operations raid in Abbottabad, Pakistan, in May 2011 but is now led by an even more capable leader, Ayman al-Zawahiri, who traveled extensively including to the United States. And it lost its territorial base, Afghanistan, but with the help of a new host, the Pakistani Taliban, al-Qaeda has reestablished itself and, together with some of its associated groups, continues to operate from the Pakistani-Afghan border.

And al-Qaeda's global message continues to appeal to cross sections of society—the old and the young, men and women, the educated and the illiterate, the rich and the poor. Al-Qaeda maintains a high capacity to reach out, resonate, and radicalize segments of the Muslim masses—a capacity that continues in the wake of the Arab Spring. Graphic scenes of battles, spectacular and bloody bombings, periodic pronouncements, and striking messages, including explicit threats, are brought to life by al-Qaeda and its propagandists. Radicalization of the periphery of Muslim communities—territorial, migrant, and diaspora—will continue to result in some tacitly supporting violence and others directly participating in violence, fully believing that the pinnacle of Islam is martyrdom.

Moving forward, the same environment driving al-Qaeda and "new terrorism" will continue to greatly influence insurgency and the popular uprisings in the Arab world that began in December 2010. Al-Qaeda, the Taliban, and their associated groups will continue spreading their influence in three directions: Afghanistan-Pakistan (Af-Pak), the broader Middle East, and beyond.

With the integration of terrorist tactics into insurgencies in Iraq and Afghanistan, the resilience and the staying power of "new terrorism" and "new insurgency" have been demonstrated in the Middle East and in Asia. The erosion of public and political will to remain in Iraq led to the withdrawal of all U.S. troops in early 2012, with al-Qaeda–inspired insurgent violence escalating ever since. And in Afghanistan, the U.S.-led coalition is planning to withdraw by 2014. In the eyes of the Islamists, both radical and violent, the United States suffered defeat both in Iraq and in Afghanistan; the same way the Soviet withdrawal from Afghanistan in 1989 was considered the defeat of a superpower, so too will America's withdrawals be judged by Islamists and their sympathizers and supporters.

The withdrawal of Western forces from Afghanistan will likely presage the swift return of the Taliban and al-Qaeda. Despite nearly twelve years of fighting, Nuristan and Kunar in Afghanistan and North Waziristan in Pakistan remain the epicenter of training, ideology, and finance for Muslim insurgents, terrorists, and extremists and continue to offer safe haven for threat groups from Afghanistan and Pakistan as well as from neighboring countries.

The Af-Pak region, particularly the Federally Administered Tribal Areas (FATA), has emerged as the world's most dangerous place. One of the world's poorest regions, FATA is 27,500 kilometers inhabited by 3.5 million Pashtuns and 1.5 million refugees from Afghanistan. A breeding ground for militancy, nearly all recent major attack operations were planned and prepared from this region, including the 2005 London transit bombings, the 2006 transatlantic aircraft plot, and the September 2009 plot against the New York City subway. It is from the Talibanized FATA and the adjacent North West Frontier Province (NWFP) that Ayman al-Zawahiri's al-Qaeda and its associated groups work together with more than two dozen groups globally.

Although the ten-plus–year campaign by U.S. special operations and Pakistani military and law enforcement caused al-Qaeda to suffer massive degradation—with its rank-and-file depleting from three thousand members to three hundred members—neither the death of its leader nor the general degradation of the core group has had an appreciable impact on the global threat landscape. The al-Qaeda organization remains a force multiplier and serves as "new terrorism's" quintessential ideological and operational vanguard. Al-Qaeda's return to Afghanistan will likely usher in an era of revival for both territorial and transnational threat groups, inspiring and instigating its associates globally to build their capabilities and conduct new acts of terrorism. Claiming that the West has been defeated both in Iraq and in Afghanistan, the groups will attract more youth to insurgent, terrorist, and extremist activity, creating a ripple effect that will ultimately impact global and U.S. security environments. The U.S. mainland will face threats from well structured groups such as al-Qaeda and its associated groups, most notably al-Qaeda in the Arabian Peninsula (AQAP). The United States and other Western states will also face threats from homegrown terrorism, as Muslim extremists expand upon the thousands of websites and other platforms they use to politicize, radicalize, and mobilize Muslim youth to hate and attack the West.

Internet and new communications technologies have also played a crucial role in mobilizing the pro-democracy movements in the Arab world, which are uniquely intertwined with the concept of "new terrorism." Unlike the new wave of terrorism and insurgency, whose aim is to destroy, the Arab Spring (Thawrāt al-Arabiyyah) has consisted of popular nonviolent and violent protests whose aim is to create new regimes. Like new terrorists, the participants of the popular protests are mostly amateurs. Although established opposition forces can join the group, the vanguard is ad hoc and networked as in the case of "new terrorism."

Islamists increasingly cooperate and collaborate with the pro-democracy movements, but with the intention of infiltration. Elements of the Libyan Islamic Fighting Group, Egyptian Islamic Jihad, Islamic Group of Egypt, and al-Nusra Front in Syria participated in the popular revolts. The Islamists will engage in politics to build their group and support base but retain the violent option. As such, the popular protest movements will evolve as violent or nonviolent depending on the situation. In all cases the movements are both territorial and transnational. Though the old participate, youth are the biggest component, and with youth spending more time on the Internet, their thinking and actions are increasingly influenced by social media. The traditional distinction that separated the real and cyber worlds is fading, and attitudes and actions are increasingly shaped by the convergence of both domains. This makes politically and socially marginalized Muslim youth susceptible to peaceful protest but also to radicalization and violence. New partnerships must be built with Muslim countries to counter the ideology of religious extremism; promoting moderation should be a part of any global strategy to counter "new terrorism," "new insurgency," "popular protests," and similar forces.

CONCLUSION: MORE CHANGE OR CONTINUITY?

Contemporary terrorist groups are in a phase of transition. Terrorism is constantly evolving. Is there more change than continuity? Considering the scale and frequency of attacks, the threat has increased. The earliest examples of attacks mounted by the new terrorists were the 1993 World Trade Center bombing in New York, the 1995 sarin gas attack in the Tokyo subway, the 1995 bombing of the federal building in Oklahoma, and the 1998 East Africa embassy bombings.[68] Fifteen years later, traditional terrorism still exists, and yet new terrorism is on the rise. Terrorist groups learn from one another; most are imitative, not innovative. Terrorism changes incrementally. There are neither typical traditional terrorist groups nor typical new terrorist groups. As such, the debate over the concepts of new and traditional terrorism will be ongoing.[69]

As described in this essay, al-Qaeda is certainly an illustration more of new terrorism than of old terrorism. But rather than label a terrorist group new or traditional, it is more useful to identify the characteristics that are new or traditional such as organizational structure, personnel, attitude toward violence, goals, and methods. As for al-Qaeda and its associated groups, research reveals that they are hybrids—picking among the most dangerous components of both old and new terrorism.

Moving forward, it is important to examine not only the Islamist strain of groups such as al-Qaeda or the Lebanese Hezbollah but the entire spectrum of threat groups. In addition to politico-religious groups such as Aum Shinrikyo, certain ethno-political and ideological groups have features of the new terrorism. For example, some ethno-nationalist groups such as the Kurdistan Workers' Party have established state-of-the-art transnational networks. Wherever there are opportunities for harnessing the forces of globalization, terrorist groups will network with like-minded groups, cells, and individuals and create transnational networks.

At its core, the new terrorism is more resilient than traditional terrorism. Even if al-Qaeda the group is dismantled, al-Qaeda the movement is likely to survive as a network. Unless there is a concerted operational and ideological campaign at the global level, both al-Qaeda and its network cannot be dismantled. Although a network, unlike a hierarchy, cannot be destroyed by decapitation,[70] over time governments can develop a greater understanding of the operational environment and knowledge of such threat groups, thereby enabling their security and intelligence services and law enforcement agencies to fight the new terrorism.

Notes

1. These attributes form the bases of definitions of terrorism for both the United Nations Security Council (though, notably, not codified by the UN as a whole) and the U.S. government. See UN Security Council Resolution 1566 (S/RES/1566), 2004; and U.S. Department of State, *Country Reports on Terrorism 2011* (Washington, D.C.: Office of the Coordinator for Counterterrorism, July 2012), chap. 7. For a detailed discussion of definitions of terrorism, see Bruce Hoffman, *Inside Terrorism*, rev. and exp. ed. (New York: Columbia University Press, 2006), 1–41.
2. Hoffman, *Inside Terrorism*, 3.
3. See, for example, Walter Laqueur, *The New Terrorism: Fanaticism and the Arms of Mass Destruction* (New York: Oxford University Press, 1999); and Steven Simon and Daniel Benjamin, "America and the New Terrorism," *Survival* 42 (Spring 2000): 59–75.
4. An earlier version of this chapter appeared in Alexander Spencer, *The Tabloid Terrorist: The Predicative Construction of New Terrorism in the Media* (Basingstoke, UK: Palgrave Macmillan, 2010).
5. Hoffman, *Inside Terrorism* (2006).
6. Walter Laqueur, *Terrorism* (London: Weidenfeld, 1977), 5.
7. Alex P. Schmid and Albert J. Jongman, *Political Terrorism: A New Guide to Actors, Authors, Concepts, Data Bases, Theories and Literature* (Amsterdam: North-Holland, 1988), 28.
8. Leonard Weinberg, Ami Pedahzur, and Sivan Hirsch-Hoefler, "The Challenges of Conceptualizing Terrorism," *Terrorism and Political Violence* 16, no. 4 (2004): 789.
9. Paul Wilkinson, "International Terrorism: New Risks to World Order," in *Dilemmas of World Politics*, ed. John Baylis and N. J. Rengger (Oxford: Clarendon Press, 1992), 230.
10. Kumar Ramakrishna and Andrew Tan, "The New Terrorism: Diagnosis and Prescriptions," in *The New Terrorism—Anatomy, Trends and Counter-Strategies*, ed. Kumar Ramakrishna and Andrew Tan (Singapore: Eastern Universities Press, 2002), 6.
11. Simon and Benjamin, "America and the New Terrorism," 65.
12. Ibid., 66.
13. Brian Jenkins, "International Terrorism: A New Mode of Conflict," in *International Terrorism: Fanaticism and the Arms of Mass Destruction*, ed. David Carlton and Carlo Schaerf (London: Croom Helm, 1975), 16.
14. Hans J. Horchem, "West Germany's Red Army Anarchists," in *The New Terrorism*, ed. William Gutteridge (London: Mansell Publishing, 1986), 199–217.
15. Ersun Kurtulus, "The 'New Terrorism' and its Critics," *Studies in Conflict and Terrorism* 34, no. 6 (2011): 489–491.
16. Described in Harry Henderson, *Global Terrorism—The Complete Reference Guide* (New York: Checkmark Books, 2001), 17.

17. Nadine Gurr and Benjamin Cole, *The New Face of Terrorism: Threats from Weapons of Mass Destruction* (London: I. B. Tauris, 2000), 28–29.
18. Bruce Hoffman, "'Holy Terror': The Implications of Terrorism Motivated by a Religious Imperative," *Studies in Conflict and Terrorism* 18, no. 4 (1995): 272.
19. Walter Laqueur, *The New Terrorism*: 81.
20. Matthew J. Morgan, "The Origin of the New Terrorism," *Parameters* 34, no. 1 (2004): 30–31.
21. Walter Enders and Todd Sandler, "Is Transnational Terrorism Becoming More Threatening? A Time-Series Investigation," *Journal of Conflict Resolution* 44, no. 3 (2000): 310.
22. Bruce Hoffman, *Inside Terrorism* (London: Indigo, 1998), 197.
23. David Tucker, "What's New about the New Terrorism and How Dangerous Is It?" *Terrorism and Political Violence* 15, no. 3 (2001).
24. Rohan Gunaratna, *Inside Al Qaeda: Global Network of Terror,* 3rd ed. (New York: Berkley Books, 2003).
25. Simon and Benjamin, "America and the New Terrorism," 70.
26. Other authors who support this line of argumentation include Thomas Copeland, "Is the New Terrorism Really New?" *Journal of Conflict Studies* 21 (Winter 2002/2003): 91–105; Tucker, "What's New about the New Terrorism," 1–14; and Isabelle Duyvesteyn, "How New Is the New Terrorism?" *Studies in Conflict and Terrorism* 27, no. 5 (2004): 439–454.
27. Hoffman, *Inside Terrorism* (1998), 87.
28. David C. Rapoport, "Fear and Trembling: Terrorism in Three Religious Traditions," *American Political Science Review* 78, no. 3 (1984): 659.
29. Audrey Kurth Cronin, "Behind the Curve: Globalization and International Terrorism," *International Security* 27 (Winter 2002/2003): 38.
30. Chris Quillen, "A Historical Analysis of Mass Casualty Bombers," *Studies in Conflict and Terrorism* 25, no. 5 (2002): 288.
31. Ibid., 287.
32. Martin Miller, "The Intellectual Origin of Modern Terrorism in Europe," in *Terrorism in Context,* ed. Martha Crenshaw (University Park: Penn State University Press, 1995), 45.
33. William Powell, *The Anarchist Cookbook* (New York: Lyle Stuart, 1971).
34. Gavin Cameron, "Weapons of Mass Destruction Terrorism Research: Past and Future," in *Research on Terrorism-Trends, Achievement and Failures,* ed. Andrew Silke (London: Frank Cass, 2004), 81.
35. Laqueur, *The New Terrorism,* 72.
36. Robert Pape, "The Strategic Logic of Suicide Terrorism," *American Political Science Review* 97, no. 3 (2003): 343.
37. John Gearson, "The Nature of Modern Terrorism," in *Superterrorism—Policy Responses,* ed. Lawrence Freedman (Oxford: Blackwell Publishing, 2002), 14.
38. Alexander Spencer, "Sic[k] of the 'New Terrorism' Debate? A Response to our Critics," *Critical Studies on Terrorism* 4, no. 3 (2011): 462.
39. Rapoport, "Fear and Trembling."
40. Miller, "The Intellectual Origin of Modern Terrorism," 45.
41. Marie Breen Smyth, "A Critical Research Agenda for the Study of Political Terror," *European Political Science* 6 (2007): 260.

42. Ray Takeyh, "Islamism: R.I.P.," *National Interest* 63 (Spring 2001): 97–102.

43. Director of National Intelligence, "Letter from al-Zawahiri to al-Zarkawi," July 9, 2005, www.fas.org/irp/news/2005/10/dni101105.html.

44. Bruce Hoffman, "Change and Continuity in Terrorism," *Studies in Conflict and Terrorism* 24, no. 5 (2001): 426.

45. Tucker, "What's New about the New Terrorism," 4.

46. Renate Mayntz, "Organizational Forms of Terrorism—Hierarchy, Network, or a Type sui generis?" MPIfG Discussion Paper 04/04, Max Planck Institute for the Study of Societies, Cologne, 2004, 11–12.

47. Hoffman, *Inside Terrorism* (2006), 63. The advent of modern international terrorism dates to July 22, 1968, when the Popular Front for the Liberation of Palestine (PFLP) hijacked an Israeli El Al commercial flight en route from Rome to Tel Aviv.

48. In the 1990s, a few preeminent specialists brought the threat of a new terrorism to the attention of the world. They include Ian O. Lesser, Bruce Hoffman, John Arquilla, David Ronfeldt, Michele Zanini, and Brian Michael Jenkins, *Countering the New Terrorism* (Santa Monica, Calif.: RAND, 1999); Walter Laqueur, *New Terrorism*; and Steven Simon and Daniel Benjamin, "America and the New Terrorism," 59–75.

49. Stephane Leman-Langlois and Jean-Paul Brodeur, "Terrorism Old and New: Counter Terrorism in Canada," *Police Practice and Research* 6 (May 2005): 121–140.

50. Interview with Dennis Pluchinsky, Office of Intelligence and Threat Analysis, Bureau of Diplomatic Security, U.S. State Department, Washington, D.C., 2001.

51. Scholars and practitioners continue to debate the distinguishing features between new and traditional terrorism. For example, Russell Howard argues that the new terrorists are better trained, while David Tucker argues that they are amateurs. Russell D. Howard, "Understanding Al Qaeda's Application of the New Terrorism— The Key to Victory in the Current Campaign," in *Terrorism and Counterterrorism: Understanding the New Security Environment*, ed. Russell D. Howard and Reid L. Sawyer (Guilford, Conn.: McGraw-Hill/Dushkin, 2004), 75–76; Tucker, "What's New about the New Terrorism," 1.

52. Martha Crenshaw, "Old and New Terrorism: Lessons Learned," paper presented at the Second IRRI Conference on International Terrorism, Jihadi Terrorism: Where Do We Stand? February 13, 2006.

53. Indeed, the first modern "religious" terrorist groups appeared in 1980, and, according to Bruce Hoffman, by 1992 eleven groups had strong religious affiliations, and by 1995 religious-based terrorist groups had grown to twenty-six out of fifty-six identifiable groups. Hoffman, *Inside Terrorism* (2006), 85–86.

54. "Al-Qaeda," *Jane's World Insurgency and Terrorism*, January 9, 2004, 1.

55. Gunaratna, *Inside Al Qaeda*, 2.

56. Ibid., 2–6.

57. The charter was published in April 1988 in *Al-Jihad*, the principal journal of the Arab mujahidin.

58. Azzam described his original concept as such: "Every principle needs a vanguard to carry it forward and, while focusing its way into society, puts up with heavy task and enormous sacrifices. There is no ideology, neither earthly nor heavenly, that does not require such a vanguard that gives everything it possesses in order to achieve victory for this ideology. It carries the flag all along the sheer, endless and difficult path until it reaches its destination in the reality of life, since Allah has

destined that it should make it and manifests itself. This vanguard constitutes Al-Qa'idah al-Sulbah for the expected society." See Abdullah Azzam, "Al-Qa'idah al-Sulbah," *Al-Jihad* 41 (April 1988): 46.

59. In addition to training its own group and support base, from 1989 to 2001 al-Qaeda trained more than twenty thousand members in its camps in Afghanistan.

60. "Briefing on Operation Crevice," SO 13, New Scotland Yard, December 2004.

61. For example, Faisal Shahzad, the individual behind the near–Times Square bombing in the United States in May 2010, stated the plot was in retaliation for U.S. drone strikes in Pakistan.

62. National Commission on Terrorist Attacks upon the United States, *The 9/11 Commission Report* (New York: Norton, 2004), provides information into the operation, including the different phases and timelines.

63. Interview with Essam al-Ridi, Texas, December 2003.

64. *Jihad* has different meanings. For al-Qaeda and its followers, *jihad* means holy war.

65. Robert Fisk, "Interview with Saudi Dissident Bin Laden," *Independent* (London), July 10, 1996.

66. Rohan Gunaratna, "Unleashed: Wiser Not to Execute the Bali Bombers," *ABC News* (Australia), December 17, 2007, www.abc.net.au/unleashed/stories/s2120383.htm.

67. Rohan Gunaratna, Debriefing of John Walker Lindh, Alexandria Prison, Alexandria, Va., 2002.

68. Simon and Benjamin, "America and the New Terrorism."

69. Duyvesteyn, "How New Is the New Terrorism?" 439–454.

70. Tucker, "What's New about the New Terrorism," 9.

does poverty serve as a root cause of terrorism?

NO: Poverty is a weak causal link.
James A. Piazza, *The Pennsylvania State University*

YES: Poverty is an important cause.
Karin von Hippel, *U.S. Department of State*

The notion that poverty is a root cause of terrorist violence is widely asserted, particularly in the Western world. The assertion is not surprising considering how well it fits with basic Western liberal economic theory, which presupposes that individuals are motivated primarily by material well-being. Those who have opportunities to sustain and better themselves will likely accept the system in which they live and behave peacefully. By contrast, those confronting socio-economic distress and deprivation are more likely to be drawn to radical and possibly violent movements, including terrorist movements.

This view has a long-standing pedigree. In 1994, for example, President Bill Clinton said that "the forces of terror and extremism . . . feed on disillusionment, on poverty, on despair." The way to end terrorism is, in his judgment, to "spread prosperity and security to all."[1]

After the attacks of September 11, 2001, the poverty-terrorism thesis was further bolstered. In December 2001, World Bank president James Wolfensohn remarked, "This war is viewed in terms of the face of bin Laden, the terrorism of al-Qaeda, the rubble of the World Trade Center and the Pentagon, but these are just symptoms. The disease is the discontent seething in Islam, and more generally, the world of the poor."[2] Secretary of State Colin Powell concurred, saying in 2002, "I fully believe that the root cause of terrorism does come from situations where there is poverty, where there is ignorance, where people see no hope in their lives."[3] In January 2010, President Barack Obama spoke of the near bombing of an airliner over Detroit on Christmas Day 2009 as a plot that originated from "Yemen, a country grappling with crushing poverty and deadly insurgencies."[4]

This thesis, however, has one glaring problem: it flies in the face of most evidence. Take the 9/11 hijackers. If one were to base an analysis of terrorism solely on the biographies of those nineteen individuals, one would conclude that the root cause of terrorism is not poverty and despair but privilege, education, and opportunity.[5] And in another telling example, the foot soldier in the near–Christmas Day bombing of which President Obama spoke, Umar Farouk Abdulmutallab, is son to one of the wealthiest families in Nigeria, and he himself lived in a multimillion-dollar apartment near Oxford Street in London. In fact, study after study, performed both before and after 9/11, confirms that most terrorists come from backgrounds more privileged than that of the average member of their national or regional population.[6] Furthermore, similar findings seem to hold at a more macro level: many of the poorest countries in the world experience no terrorism at all, while some of the wealthiest have been confronting terrorism for decades.

How can an assumption based on such deductive logic and enjoying such a renowned following be so wrong? The answer is that it may not be. Although both poverty and terrorism have been around for a long time, rigorous research into connections between the two is a relatively new phenomenon, and the jury is still out on definitive conclusions. Equally important, the criteria for judging the poverty-terrorism thesis may contain faulty assumptions—for example, perhaps poverty does not *directly* spawn terrorism but rather provides an important *context* in which radicalism and other support structures of terrorism may benefit. Most terrorists may not come from poverty, but their radical movements—be they religious, ideological, territorial-separatist, or other—gain influence when the communities they purport to represent suffer under dire socioeconomic conditions.

In this chapter, James Piazza and Karin von Hippel agree that terrorism is a highly complex phenomenon and that uncovering silver bullet causal explanations is unlikely. They differ, however, on the relationship between poverty and terrorism. Piazza maintains that the critics of the poverty-terrorism thesis have it right. Using the most current data available, he shows there to be little (if any) connection between poverty and terrorism at the global, national, and individual levels. These findings will not bring comfort to policymakers who, he says, have treated the poverty-terrorism thesis as gospel. But it will allow for a more honest—and ultimately more fruitful—investigation into the real roots of terrorism.

Von Hippel agrees that there is a paucity of reliable data supporting the poverty-terrorism thesis. But this does not mean the evidence against it is any more reliable. In fact, she argues that most research to date has been too narrowly focused and does not include many relevant countries and regions, rendering current findings inconclusive. In addition, most analyses fail to account for the ways in which terrorist elites take advantage of impoverished communities in order to expand their support base. This, she says, illustrates the specific ways in which poverty may play an important role in increasing both radicalism and terrorism—both certainly vital public policy concerns.

Addressing global poverty, irrespective of its relationship with terrorism, remains an essential humanitarian goal. But in order to devise better strategies for reducing both poverty and terrorism, policymakers need to have clear, fact-based assessments on the relationship between the two. The authors of this chapter take important steps in that direction.

Poverty is a weak causal link.
NO: James A. Piazza, *The Pennsylvania
          State University*

Poverty and Terrorism: A Hypothesis
in Search of Evidence

Poverty poses a serious threat to human life. It is responsible for an estimated one-third of all deaths each year worldwide. Roughly fifty thousand people die from poverty-related causes every day, and poverty has killed an estimated 270 million people since 1990, more than double the total casualties suffered by all sides during World Wars I and II.[7] Poverty also places a heavy toll on international security and political order. Poverty, unemployment, and income inequality have contributed to higher violent crime rates worldwide.[8] Unequal distribution of land and unequal access to material resources are key ingredients of civil wars, armed ethnic and sectarian conflicts, and riots.[9] Poverty and loss of livelihood help armed rebel movements and insurgencies with their recruitment efforts.[10] Economic distress as a result of poverty contributes to military coups, regime collapse, and the onset of nondemocratic rule.[11] Poverty also breeds social upheavals that produce refugees and illegal migrants, both of which have been linked to violence and armed conflict in the areas to which they migrate.[12]

But does poverty cause terrorism? In the wake of the September 11, 2001, terrorist attacks on the United States and subsequent attacks in Indonesia, Spain, Britain, Morocco, and Turkey, national politicians and United Nations officials were quick to identify poverty, global income inequality, unemployment, and low levels of education as key causes of terrorism. The reasoning behind their conclusion was straightforward: poor people who lack economic opportunities are resentful about their socioeconomic status and become alienated from mainstream society. This smoldering resentment is exacerbated by the large and growing gaps in living standards among rich and poor people, which result in intense feelings among the poor that they are being unfairly deprived of proper living standards and opportunities—a phenomenon that political scientist Ted Robert Gurr labeled "relative deprivation" and linked to increased likelihood of civil strife.[13] In this state of rage and hopelessness, the poor are more susceptible to the lures of political extremism. Ordinary law-abiding citizens who are placed under economic distress or who are confronted with opulence while they struggle to make ends meet become primed to the anti–status quo message that is part and parcel of many terrorist group ideologies, and therefore they are more likely to sympathize with terrorists. This sympathy can even lead them to aid, shelter, and provide information to terrorists, to refuse to cooperate with government agents fighting terrorism, and to be more likely to join terrorist groups themselves.

Thus poverty and inequality are deemed the natural fertilizers for terrorism. It stands to reason that the appropriate response to the threat of terrorism, as argued by a surprisingly wide range of public officials, is to increase aid to impoverished countries to foster economic development and to bridge gaps in wealth. More aid would remedy what President Bill Clinton called the "dark side of globalization," the fact that nearly half of the world's population survives on roughly $2 a day, despite the remarkable economic growth worldwide over the last fifteen years. Clinton's successor President George W. Bush outlined a new international security imperative affixed to the traditional moral imperative of foreign aid and poverty alleviation, famously stating before the 2002 Monterrey development summit (International Conference on Financing for Development), "We fight poverty because hope is an answer to terror."

The alleviation of poverty *should* be a top priority for developed countries, and wealthy countries should increase their international development and aid budgets. Doing so will undoubtedly produce humanitarian benefits and will likely yield real security dividends. However, humanitarian and development aid is not likely to reduce the threat of terrorism. Despite the very well-intentioned statements of policymakers eager to address the root causes of terrorism in the modern world, there is an absence of hard evidence that poverty, socioeconomic inequality, or low levels of economic development cause terrorism or elicit public sympathy for terrorist movements. Indeed, the experts who study terrorism agree on very few root causes of terrorism, but they have begun to produce a consensus that terrorism is not the direct by-product of economic factors.[14] As social scientists gain access to more comprehensive and precise data on human living standards, or what is known among development economists as "human development indicators," as well as to better statistics on terrorism and other types of political violence, the argument that poverty causes terrorism has begun to erode. Simply put, there is little empirical evidence to support the hypothesis that poverty, poor economic performance, or socioeconomic inequality is related to patterns of terrorism at any of the levels on which the causes of terrorism are traditionally investigated: the global level, the national level, and the individual level.

In this essay, I dissect and analyze the available empirical data to pinpoint vast evidentiary holes in the hypothesis that poverty directly causes terrorism.

I do so from three perspectives: global, state, and individual. I conclude, however, by discussing recent evidence on some specific socioeconomic factors that *are* important for explaining some patterns of terrorism.

TERRORISM AND GLOBAL POVERTY

The alleviation of global poverty has been a goal of the international community since the end of World War II. The urgent need to reduce poverty and to promote economic prosperity on the grounds that they both foment political extremism and increase the potential for violent conflict was a precept of the United Nations Charter drafted in San Francisco in 1945 and was a foundational concept upon which the U.S. Marshall Plan was built in 1947.

The threat of poverty to international order and the possibility that it could stoke terrorism was raised more recently in the negotiations that produced the 2000 United Nations Millennium Declaration. A by-product of this concern is a voluminous body of international statistics on poverty and on various types of political violence. Examination of these statistics reveals that global rates of terrorism, which increase and decrease in cyclical waves over time, are out of sync with changes in global poverty rates and measurements of global inequality, which do not show cyclical dynamics. As the percentage of the world's population living in poverty has steadily *declined* from about 66 percent in 1981 to about 47 percent in 2006,[15] the annual rate of transnational terrorist attacks has *fluctuated wildly,* exhibiting peaks of activity in the mid-1980s, around 1991, and between 2001 and 2005, and a steady decline in the mid- to late 1990s.[16] A similar pattern is found when one looks at casualties—persons injured or killed—in transnational terrorist attacks. By contrast, although global inequality, defined as differences in the gross domestic product (GDP) between the rich and poor countries of the world, has steadily increased since the 1970s,[17] the sharpest growth in the wealth gap, which occurred in the mid-1990s, was accompanied by the sharpest decrease in transnational terrorist attacks. It cannot be demonstrated that either economic good news—greater global prosperity—or economic bad news—a wide and growing gap in the global distribution of wealth—conforms to patterns of international terrorist activity.[18] This finding is a problem for the argument that poverty causes terrorism.

Another way to look at this argument is to examine the distribution of terrorism by regions of the world and by countries arranged by their level of economic development. Table 2-1 arranges terrorist activity by major world regions for the period 2000–2010. If economic privation were a cause of terrorism, it would be reasonable to expect that the poorer world regions would experience the highest proportion of world terrorism, would contribute the most transnational terrorist activity—defined as attacks perpetrated by a region's citizens against foreigners locally or abroad—and would host a greater number of terrorists than wealthier regions. However, such a straightforward pattern is not evident. The poorest world region—determined by comparing regional United Nations Development Programme (UNDP) Human Development Index scores that incorporate GDP per capita with literacy and life expectancy rates[19]—is sub-Saharan Africa. Yet, as a region it contributes modestly to the global distribution of terrorist activity. The lion's share of terrorist attacks, including transnational terrorist attacks, from 2000 to 2010 occurred in either the Middle East—a region categorized by "Medium" levels of human development—or South Asia, a poor region, producing a more complicated pattern. Moreover, in terms of hosting of active terrorist movements tracked by the U.S. Central Intelligence Agency, the Middle East and Western Europe and North America—a "High" human development region—contained more than three times the number of terror groups contained in Africa. Again, the pattern expected by the popular wisdom—that poor regions are more likely to be afflicted with terrorism—is not evident.

Analogous results are produced when one sorts terrorism globally by rich, middle-income, and poor countries irrespective of region, as illustrated in Table 2-2. "Low Human Development" countries, again classified using the UNDP's Human Development Index, on average experience fewer terrorist attacks, produce fewer transnational attacks, and see their territories used as a base of operations by fewer terrorist movements than the global average. The "Medium Human Development" countries, not the poorest states, were the biggest contributors to transnational terrorism and the sites of the largest concentration of terrorist activity in terms of attacks.[20] By contrast, the wealthiest countries—that is, those classified by the UNDP as "High Human Development" countries—had the highest average number of active terrorist groups operating within national boundaries, while poor countries had the lowest.

TERRORISM AND POOR STATES

A closer look at individual states is revealing. Do the poorest and least-developed states produce and experience the highest levels of terrorism? Are socially stratified countries more likely to produce resentment that manifests itself in terrorist activity per the relative deprivation model? Do economically stagnant countries experience more terrorism, and can afflicted countries therefore *grow* their way out of terrorism through economic development?

In 2005, the midpoint year for the 2000 to 2010 range examined here, the ten poorest countries in the world, measured using the Human Development Index,

Table 2-1

Regional Distribution of Terrorism, 2000–2010

	Sub-Saharan Africa	Middle East	East Asia and Pacific	Latin America	South Asia	Eastern Europe and CIS	Western Europe and North America
Global Share of Terrorist Attacks[a]	6.6%	32.1%	11.5%	4.3%	34.4%	5.7%	5.5%
Global Share of Terrorist Casualties[b]	20.1%	30.3%	11.5%	6.9%	22.9%	4.5%	3.8%
Contribution to Transnational Terrorist Attacks[c]	12.9%	38.3%	8.2%	9.1%	15.5%	4.8%	11.3%
Number of Active Groups[d]	79	320	92	133	143	75	380
Average Human Development Index	.465	.727	.743	.735	.558	.791	.926
Human Development Index Classification[e]	(Low)	(Medium)	(Medium)	(Medium)	(Medium)	(Medium)	(High)

Sources: Global Terrorism Database (GTD) (www.start.umd.edu); Terrorist Organization Profiles (TOPs) Database (www.start.umd.edu); International Terrorism: Attributes of Terrorist Events (ITERATE) Database (http://vinyardsoftware.com); United Nations Development Programme Human Development Index (http://hdr.undp.org/en/statistics/hdi).

Note: CIS = Commonwealth of Independent States (former Soviet Union).

[a] Share of global terrorist attacks occurring within region (derived from GTD).

[b] Share of global terrorism casualties: persons killed, injured, detained through a hijacking, or kidnapped through terrorist incidents within region (derived from GTD).

[c] Global share of transnational terrorist attacks perpetrated by citizens of region against foreign targets, either locally or abroad (derived from ITERATE). Data are for the period 2000–2006.

[d] Total groups listed having an active presence within countries in region (derived from TOPs).

[e] Average UNDP-reported Human Development Index measurement for region, accompanied by categorization of level of development: "High" (.800+), "Medium" (.799–.500), or "Low" (.499–.300).

Table 2-2

Distribution of Terrorism by Level of Human Development, 2000–2010

	Average terrorist attacks occurring in:[a]	Average transnational terrorist attacks perpetrated by nationals of:[b]	Average number of active terrorist groups operating out of:[c]
High Human Development countries (n = 51)	55.1	2.2	10.3
Medium Human Development countries (n = 01)	251.8	5.4	8.9
Low Human Development countries (n = 40)	106.7	3.2	2.7
All countries (n = 172)	159.7	4.0	8.4

Sources: Global Terrorism Database (GTD); Terrorist Organizations Profiles (TOPs) Database; International Terrorism Attributes of Terrorist Events (ITERATE) Database; United Nations Development Programme Human Development Index.

[a] Derived from GTD.

[b] Derived from ITERATE.

[c] Derived from TOPs.

were in order Sierra Leone (poorest), Burkina Faso, Guinea Bissau, Niger, Mali, the Central African Republic, Mozambique, Chad, Ethiopia, and the Democratic Republic of the Congo. Although many of these countries have indeed experienced civil war and serious political strife, terrorism has for the most part failed to appear in their lists of security challenges. Collectively, only 2 percent of all transnational terrorist attacks from 2000 to 2006 were committed by nationals of these least economically developed countries, and only one of them, Ethiopia, experienced significant terrorism within its borders (the perpetrators of most of these attacks were believed to be Muslim radicals of the al-Ittihad al-Islamiya movement based across the border in Somalia). Three of these countries—Guinea Bissau, Mozambique, and the Central African Republic— experienced and produced no terrorism whatsoever during the period, while Sierra Leone, Burkina Faso, and Chad each saw only one transnational attack launched from their territory, all of which resulted in no casualties.

By contrast, the countries that face the most serious challenges from terrorism seem to have no coherent socioeconomic profile. Table 2-3 lists in rank order the ten most terrorism-afflicted countries from 2000 to 2010, along with some of their macroeconomic indicators. One of them, Afghanistan, is without a doubt acutely underdeveloped as a result of more than thirty years of severe political turmoil and ongoing internal armed conflict. Both Pakistan and Iraq also face significant economic challenges, though they are classified by the UNDP as "Medium Human Development" countries and are far wealthier than most sub-Saharan African countries. Indeed, Pakistan's economic growth rate consistently outstripped global averages from its independence in 1947 until the present day with a short pause in the 1990s. Iraq, prior to the imposition of UN sanctions in 1991, had an industrial, health, and educational infrastructure that was widely admired throughout the Arab world. The Russian Federation, India, Colombia, the Philippines, Algeria, and Thailand are also all middle-income countries characterized by pockets of significant poverty alongside industrial development, functioning educational systems, relatively high literacy rates, and, with the exception of Russia, rising rates of life expectancy. One country/entity in Table 2-3, Israel and the Palestinian territories, sports a high level of development, placing it in the same cohort as the Western European countries though it experiences extremely high levels of terrorism. However, the Israeli case is unique given its forty-five-year occupation of the Palestinian territories—data that are aggregated in Table 2-3—the root cause of Israel's terrorism problem. Though, of course, poverty levels are higher in the Palestinian territories, this region's 2010 Human Development Index rating (.625) places it within the range of "Medium" developed countries and slightly below the median for the Arab states.

The countries listed in Table 2-3 are not noticeably unequal societies, as indicated by the Gini coefficients—a measurement used by development economists to determine income inequality in countries; the coefficient ranges between 100, indicating pure inequality of distribution, and 0, indicating pure equality. The countries mirror closely the rates of inequality found in the rest of the world with two exceptions. Both Afghanistan and Colombia have extremely high Gini scores, placing them in the top ten most economically stratified societies in the world. However, it is necessary to recognize complexities regarding both of these countries that muddy a straightforward relationship between inequality and terrorism. In the case of Afghanistan, it is difficult to determine whether economic inequality has been the source or the *product* of its acute security turmoil over the past several decades. The 1979 Soviet invasion prompted the emigration of six million Afghans, devastating the country's agricultural production, the mainstay of its employment and GDP, while exacerbating rural-urban gaps in development. Furthermore, Soviet counterinsurgency policy in the 1980s involved the destruction of irrigation infrastructure, roads, and communications in the rural areas of Afghanistan to weaken the armed resistance based there. This approach caused the standard of living to plummet in the hinterland relative to the cities, where the Soviet-backed Afghan regime was more firmly in control. The Soviet withdrawal in 1989 ushered in a decade-long civil war that chased away foreign

Table 2-3

Economic Development in the Most Terrorism-Challenged Countries, 2000–2010

	Terrorist attacks	Transnational terrorist attacks perpetrated by nationals	Number of active terrorist groups operating out of country	Human Development Index	Gini coefficient	GDP growth, 1990 to 2010
Iraq	6,077	100	77	.567	46.4	–1.5%
India	3,037	4	23	.592	32.5	6.2%
Pakistan	2,587	55	36	.500	31.9	2.7%
Afghanistan	2,426	38	16	.229	60.0	n.a.
Thailand	1,466	1	15	.768	42.6	3.4%
Philippines	1,187	18	16	.753	45.4	2.8%
Russia	1,157	14	24	.795	43.6	5.2%
Israel and the Palestinian Territories	999	2	59	.907	38.9	1.1%
Colombia	965	43	15	.772	57.6	2.5%
Algeria	959	16	10	.702	47.5	2.1%
Group average	2,806.0	29.1	29.1	.658	44.6	2.7%
World average	159.7	4.0	8.3	.685	41.4	2.6%

Sources: United Nations Development Programme, *Human Development Report* (Washington, D.C.: UNDP, various years); UNdata online database (http://data.un.org/Default.aspx); Global Terrorism Database (GTD).

aid and investment while giving rise to an opium industry that enriched local
warlords. After removal of the Taliban regime by the United States and coalition forces in 2001, Afghanistan received a sizeable infusion of humanitarian
and reconstruction aid from the international community. However, distribution of the aid monies remains uneven because of bureaucratic inefficiencies,
corrupt Afghan politicians and officials, and the fact that security remains
poor in the Taliban strongholds in the southern Pashtun regions bordering
Pakistan.

As for Colombia, Latin American countries are traditionally characterized
by high levels of socioeconomic inequality, and Colombia's Gini coefficient is
close to the regional median of 53.7 and is indeed lower than that of Bolivia,
Paraguay, and Brazil, three countries with insignificant levels of terrorism.
Table 2-3, then, provides little indication that domestic inequality produces
terrorism. This result is further validated by other evidence. On average, the twenty
most unequal countries in the world actually produce fewer transnational
attacks (3.1), sustain fewer terrorist attacks (72.8), and host fewer terrorist
groups (5.3) than the world average.[21]

But what about growth? If a paucity of economic opportunities creates pools
of disaffected and alienated people from which terrorists can garner support
and recruit, then economic growth is surely a panacea for terrorism. Terrorism
would then be a feature of countries with stagnating economies, whereas countries experiencing rapid economic growth would produce and sustain less terrorism. The countries listed in Table 2-3, as a whole, mirror worldwide GDP
growth rates, though it is striking that many of them have experienced rapid
GDP growth in the past decade and a half. One of them, India, a country with
one of the most vibrant and rapidly growing economies in the world and with
a burgeoning middle class, has endured some of the longest internal terrorism
campaigns in the world, including a dramatic spike since the 1980s in Islamist-
separatist terrorism related to the Kashmir crisis. Another, Thailand, has seen
a resurgence since 2001 of intense separatist terrorism in its Muslim-majority
Pattani region bordering Malaysia, even though it is one of the so-called East
Asian Tigers—a group of Southeast Asian countries noted for their spectacular
rates of economic growth and export-led rapid development in the 1980s and
the 1990s. Russia has also lately experienced rapid economic growth, largely
due to robust energy demand worldwide. In the shorter term, Afghanistan
grew by 12.4 percent in 2007 in the midst of an impressive spring offensive
launched against Afghan government and North Atlantic Treaty Organization
(NATO) troops by Taliban extremists.

Among the most terrorism-afflicted countries in Table 2-3, only Iraq and
Israel suffer from contraction or anemic economic growth. Iraq's posted

decline in GDP growth during the period is due to the severe political, economic, and social disruptions of the 2003 U.S. invasion, which led to the collapse of the Iraqi state. Since 2005, Iraq's GDP per capita has actually grown by an average of 1.3 percent per year; however, ongoing political disputes about control of oil revenues among the Iraqi provinces have forestalled crucial capital investment and robust growth. Israel's slow economic growth rate actually places it on par with many other Organisation for Economic Co-operation and Development (OECD) countries during the same time period. However, included within the data are growth rates within the Palestinian territories. The occupied territories experienced negative economic growth in much of the 2000 to 2010 period, mostly because of limitations imposed by the forty-year Israeli occupation, and are plagued by a notoriously corrupt domestic administration, the Palestinian Authority, and unemployment rates that reach 20 percent in Gaza. However, the Palestinian territories receive significant foreign assistance, benefit from preferential trade agreements from the European Union, and are marked by literacy rates higher than those found in other Arab countries. This again explains why they remain within the "Medium Human Development" cohort.

As was true for level of economic development, a broad survey of countries' economic growth rates fails to reveal a pattern consistent with the argument that economic stagnation generates terrorism. Indeed, some of the data provide evidence to the contrary. Looking beyond the countries listed in Table 2-3, of the nineteen countries that experienced negative growth during the period 1990–2010, nine experienced no terrorism at all while most of the others experienced significantly lower-than-average levels of terrorist activity. Only two of the negative growth countries, Iraq and Italy, experienced higher-than-average rates of terrorism. Yet the cohort of fastest-growing countries includes a sampling of countries with significant terrorism challenges, such as India, Angola, Georgia, Jordan, Indonesia, and Sri Lanka.

Finally, patterns of terrorist activity *within* states also fail to yield a discernible relationship between poor economic development and terrorism. The case of India is particularly useful here. At first glance, terrorist activity in India seems to vindicate the hypothesis that poverty and social class stratification incubate terrorist activity. Indeed, India has many poor people, and it has struggled for more than forty years against an internal Maoist terrorist insurgency—the Naxalites, recently renamed the People's War Group—that bases itself in impoverished rural communities and conducts terrorist attacks allegedly on behalf of peasants and low-caste Hindus exploited by rural landlords.[22] However, an examination of the distribution of terrorist incidents across the states of India demonstrates that terrorism plagues *both* poor and wealthy areas and that the pattern of terrorist activity is inconsistent with regional economic development rates.

The lion's share of Indian terrorism, over 60 percent, occurs in the state of Jammu and Kashmir, a region whose status has been disputed by India and Pakistan since 1947. Today, Jammu and Kashmir is the seventh least economically developed state of India. However, before intensification of its separatist insurgency in 1989 it was a middle-income state with a thriving tourist industry. Terrorism in Jammu and Kashmir also has a transnational dimension that has little to do with the economic status of the residents of Jammu and Kashmir in that Kashmiri militants are alleged by Indian intelligence to be armed and trained by Pakistan (Pakistani officials counter that India is arming Baluchi separatists in Pakistan). Impoverished Indian states such as Assam and Chhattisgarh share the dubious distinction of being high-terrorist activity states along with middle-income Andhra Pradesh and wealthy Maharashtra and the Delhi municipality. The poorest Indian state, Madhya Pradesh, suffered *only one* terrorist attack between 1998 and 2006. The caste-based Naxalite terrorist movement accounts for most contemporary terrorist activity in the poor and middle-income states of Chhattisgarh, Jharkhand, and Andhra Pradesh. Terrorism in underdeveloped Assam is separatist-inspired and draws energy from ethnic conflict between the native Assamese population and recent immigrants from Bangladesh, whereas terrorism in rich Maharashtra and poor Uttar Pradesh is tied to religious-sectarian tensions between Hindus and Muslims in those states. This is all to say that empirical patterns of domestic terrorism in India mirror those found on the global level: poor places do not produce or experience more terrorism than rich places.

All of these outwardly contradictory empirical findings make sense once one considers the theoretical disadvantages poor societies foist upon terrorists as opposed to the advantages that affluent societies offer terrorists. Like all organizations, terrorist groups need a stable, predictable environment in which to operate. Political scientist Ken Menkhaus provides important insight in explaining that severely underdeveloped states such as Somalia, one of the poorest countries in the world, are actually suboptimal operational venues for terrorist groups because these states offer poor infrastructure, provide a paucity of desirable targets such as foreign firms or tourists, and expose terrorist cadres themselves to harassment, extortion, or co-optation by corrupt authorities.[23] In theory, more developed countries are more attractive to terrorist groups because these countries have better transportation and communication infrastructures and are more likely to be political democracies that afford their residents rights of assembly and privacy and place constraints on police power. These features facilitate the free movement of terrorists, terrorist recruitment, and organization and training activities, and they hamper police counterterrorism efforts. More developed countries also contain an abundance of lucrative targets for terrorist groups and are more likely to have free media that will cover terrorist attacks when they occur, giving groups an outlet for their propaganda. In this sense, it is not the poverty of underdeveloped countries that incubates terrorism but the opportunities afforded to terrorist entrepreneurs by wealthier countries.

TERRORISM AND POOR PEOPLE

The release of the identities and biographies of the nineteen September 11 hijackers revealed a puzzling profile: all were well-educated young men with middle- and upper-middle-class family backgrounds who had traveled, some extensively, in the West and had attended Western educational institutions. The lead terrorist, Muhammad Atta, an Egyptian national who had lived for a time in Hamburg, was a trained engineer. None of them seem to fit the profile of the poorly educated, economically deprived, and socially marginal individual that makes up the popular stereotype of a terrorist. The suspected perpetrators of subsequent al-Qaeda attacks in Madrid, London, Casablanca, Istanbul, and Bali also do not fit the popular profile. Notorious al-Qaeda leaders such as the late Osama bin Laden, Ayman al-Zawahiri, 9/11 mastermind Khalid Sheikh Muhammad, and the late Abu Musab al-Zarqawi tend to be significantly better educated than their co-nationals—bin Laden earned a degree in civil engineering, al-Zawahiri is a trained physician with surgery credentials, Khalid Sheikh Muhammad is a U.S.-educated mechanical engineer, and al-Zarqawi for a time worked as a journalist—and to have been born to economically comfortable families.

However, unlike tracking patterns of global, national, or subnational terrorist incidents, surveying socioeconomic profiles of individuals who join terrorist groups or participate in terrorist attacks is fraught with statistical difficulty. Because it is challenging for researchers to obtain a reliable and representative sample of individual terrorists, most surveys have been limited to specific groups or populations. Nevertheless, the existing studies of the socioeconomic backgrounds of terrorists and their supporters fail to provide evidence that poor people are more likely to become or to sympathize with terrorists. In fact, the opposite seems likelier. Statistical studies have shown that the individuals more likely to engage in terrorism are also more likely to come from materially better-off backgrounds, to have obtained higher levels of education, and to enjoy higher standards of living. And this finding seems to be consistent across groups, nationalities, and time periods.[24] The common experience for most terrorists has been recruitment while at university, rather than in the street, an urban shanty, or a poverty-stricken rural tract. The individuals who sympathize with terrorists—a critical population because many terrorist groups rely heavily on networks of noncombatant supporters who provide safe houses, material support, and information and who refuse to cooperate with police—are also not more likely to be poor, unemployed, or uneducated. Surveys of ordinary Palestinians and Lebanese Muslims show no correlation between income, employment status, and educational background and support for suicide bombings and the September 11 attacks.[25] As a consequence, constructing a discrete demographic profile that can be used to neutralize terrorism has been fruitless.

And, again, there are theoretical reasons that individuals with a higher socioeconomic status might be more likely to become terrorists than their downtrodden brethren. As counterintuitive as this observation may seem, terrorism expert Edgar O'Ballance explains that an effective terrorist operative must be able to carry out often complex logistical and technical tasks, must have sufficient intellectual sophistication to evade security personnel, must have the educational and social backgrounds—or have acquired the requisite social comfort—to appear inconspicuous when traveling abroad, and often must be able to communicate in one or more of the international business languages, particularly English.[26] In addition to being committed, terrorists need to be reliable, adaptable, and polished, not unlike an employee of a multinational business enterprise, in order to launch their attacks successfully. Officials of the Palestinian terrorist group Hamas admit that because they are inundated with volunteers for suicide missions, they have implemented tough selection criteria for prospective martyrs that include educational achievement, intellectual ability, and social and professional aptitude.

DOES TERRORISM HAVE ANY SOCIOECONOMIC DIMENSION?

These assemblies of empirical information do not provide much comfort to those who wish to reduce terrorism by attacking poverty and remedying economic inequality. The idea that poverty and inequality promote terrorism is, in many ways, a very attractive one because it gives policymakers a cogent tool to use in the fight against terrorism—promotion of economic development—and it fortifies humanitarians' pleas for more attention to alleviating poverty. But there simply is no evidence of a direct relationship between poverty and terrorism.

Does this, therefore, close the book on the argument that terrorism has socioeconomic roots of any kind? Findings from recent cross-national research actually suggest the answer to this question is no, but for reasons that differ significantly from the traditional poverty-terrorism thesis. In two new empirical studies, I examined the economic status of ethnic and social minority groups within countries to see if it explained patterns of (mostly domestic) terrorist activity. [27] Both found minority economic discrimination to be a crucial factor explaining terrorism. Countries containing minority communities that suffer from economic discrimination, formal or informal government neglect in services and social spending, lack of opportunities, or socioeconomic exclusion from the wider society are statistically much more likely to experience domestic terrorist activity. Conversely, there is some evidence that improving the economic status of such minority groups, or eliminating the economic discrimination they face, reduces domestic terrorism. These findings reinforce earlier qualitative case studies of terrorist movements in Northern Ireland, the Basque region in Spain, and the Tupamaro and EOKA movements in Uruguay and Greece that link economic grievances of ethnic minority and sectarian groups to support for terrorism, as well as work by Christopher Hewitt crediting British government affirmative action programs in employment and housing for Catholics in Northern Ireland for dampening support for Provisional Irish Republican Army (PIRA) terrorism in the later 1980s.[28]

Moreover, when comparing the impact of minority political discrimination, economic discrimination, and minority cultural-linguistic and religious restrictions within countries, I find that it is economic discrimination, rather than practices designed to prevent minority groups from exercising political power, speaking traditional languages, or engaging in traditional modes of worship, that propels terrorism. This would suggest that actions by the Turkish government since 2000 to recognize the existence of the Kurds, to respect their political rights and allow the formation of ethnic Kurdish political parties, and to lift bans on the public use of the Kurdish language is not likely to significantly reduce the resurgence of Kurdistan Workers' Party (PKK) terrorism in the last several years absent addressing the economic discrimination Kurds still face in Turkey.

So, these two new empirical investigations do find a socioeconomic factor—minority group experience of economic discrimination—that contributes to terrorism. How, then, can we square this with the evidence above, and the evidence produced in the aforementioned empirical studies, showing that poverty, regional poverty, poor countries, and poor people, per se, do not drive terrorism? I believe that the key lies in a realization about the nature of terrorist activity and how it is different from other forms of political violence—such as rebellions, riots, or violent protests—and in a recognition of the mismatch between the measurement tools traditionally used to assess socioeconomic status and terrorist activity. Terrorism is recognized to be a low-intensity and clandestine activity engaged in by small bands of people who often populate the political and social margins of society. As Martha Crenshaw notes, historically terrorists have been political ideologues who lack mass political appeal and support and who frequently seek to defend or advance the interests of alienated and aggrieved segments of society.[29] Terrorism is not a mass behavior that can be assessed by looking at the typical person within society. Yet the tools used to assess poverty and economic development do just that: measure the status of the whole society and of the modal individual within society. This leads to a mismatch that may obscure the true relationship between economic factors and terrorism. It is therefore understandable that metrics that target the internal communities within countries with the highest level of socioeconomic grievance are found to be linked to terrorist attacks.

This paints a more complex picture of the poverty-terrorism relationship. Poverty itself, as it is traditionally measured and discussed by counterterrorism officials as a root cause, is not a proven driver of terrorism. However, socioeconomic status of marginalized (though not necessarily impoverished) people within society might be, and therefore affords counterterrorism officials a possible new policy angle for addressing the threat of terrorism.

YES: Poverty is an important cause.
Karin von Hippel, *U.S. Department of State*[30]

The Role of Poverty in Radicalization and Terrorism

O f all the debates on terrorism that have taken place in the twelve years since the attacks of September 11, 2001, the impact of poverty on terrorism has been the most emotional, anecdotal, and difficult to quantify. Several prominent economists and researchers have mined the data to demonstrate that—contrary to conventional wisdom—terrorists are not poor and uneducated. If anything, they tend to come from the ranks of the middle and upper classes—the "haves" rather than the "have-nots."[31] Alan Krueger concluded, "The bottom line . . . is that poor economic conditions do not seem to motivate people to participate in terrorist activities."[32]

Even when confronted by this research, world leaders tend to disregard it: they continue to blame poverty and its corollaries (alienation, humiliation, marginalization, and globalization) for "growing" terrorists, relying more on intuition rather than any rigorous research. At the March 2002 world development summit in Monterrey, Mexico, leaders such as President George W. Bush and former UN secretary-general Kofi Annan declared that the fight against poverty was intrinsically linked to the fight against terrorism.[33] In his farewell address to the United Nations on September 23, 2008, President Bush remarked, "The extremists find their most fertile recruiting grounds in societies trapped in chaos and despair, places where people see no prospect of a better life. In the shadows of hopelessness, radicalism thrives. . . . Overcoming hopelessness requires addressing its causes: poverty, disease, and ignorance." In 2010 U.S. Secretary of State Hillary Clinton said, "We cannot stop terrorism or defeat the ideologies of violent extremism when hundreds of millions of young people see a future with no jobs, no hope, and no way ever to catch up to the developed world."[34] These leaders' proclamations have, in turn, put enormous pressure on bilateral and multilateral development agencies to formulate policies and programs to counter radicalization, based on an insufficient empirical database.

Should we spend more time educating leaders and policymakers so that we can officially close the case on this debate and move on to the arguably more important, hard-edged counterterrorist challenges, such as policing and intelligence sharing? Or is there a chance that the emotion-driven, data-poor poverty defenders may at least be partially correct, while the coldhearted, data-rich number crunchers may be overlooking critical aspects in the debate?

This essay indeed posits that the focus of the research conducted thus far has been too narrow and not current enough to rule out poverty as a critical contributing factor in terrorism. In particular, such research has not taken into account the socioeconomic dynamics of the communities in which terrorists operate (that is, the enabling environment, discussed below); it has not fully explored the drivers for the ordinary foot soldiers; nor has it taken into account recent manifestations of the terrorist threat, such as the strengthening of more recent al-Qaeda affiliates in impoverished areas of Africa and the Arabian Peninsula. This is to argue not that poverty is *the* primary cause of terrorism but rather that socioeconomic conditions are relevant to understanding the rise of radicalism and the development of and support for terrorism in a growing number of situations. An improved understanding of the connections between economic vulnerability, on the one hand, and radicalism and terrorism, on the other, should help governments and multilateral agencies determine more appropriate and effective policies.

COMMUNITY DYNAMICS: THE ENABLING ENVIRONMENT

Today, it is well recognized that the more successful terrorist (and insurgent) groups thrive by building, expanding, and/or silencing their constituencies. For the al-Qaeda network and affiliated movements, this "enabling environment"[35] includes potential sympathizers not only in the Arab and Muslim world but also in Europe, North America, Australia, and other Western societies. These adherents may not themselves use violence, but they either endorse the arguments and platforms of the terrorists or are intimidated into silence.

The members of this wider community need to be won over so that they *oppose* terrorism in their neighborhoods, cities, and states, and, critically, in the virtual world of the Internet, where many of the battles are taking place. Appealing to the enabling environment may be the only way in the long term to isolate terrorists and end terrorism. Severing the connection between terrorists and their constituents would allow the former to become much more vulnerable to informants and standard policing surveillance. Experiences in Afghanistan, Greece, Iraq, Northern Ireland, Somalia, Pakistan, and, at times, Yemen demonstrate that this strategy can work and that it can be internally or externally driven. Conversely, in cases in which the government has limited capacity to impact positively or even reach its more at-risk communities—as seen recently in Yemen, Mali, and northern Nigeria—we witness an expanded support base for radical ideologies and movements.

It is in the enabling environment that poverty can be a factor. By providing the poor with social services, a number of nationally focused Islamist groups and political parties,[36] and the al-Qaeda movement and its formal and informal affiliates more generally, have been able to significantly broaden their appeal. It is not clear whether this support has increased the numbers of people who have become fully radicalized, but evidence does exist that terrorist groups have expanded their influence in their constituencies because of the assistance.

The connection between religion, charity, and group solidarity is, of course, nothing new. In the late 1880s, the anticolonial Libyan insurgent hero and holy warrior Omar al-Mukhtar ("Lion of the Desert") belonged to a conservative Islamic order, influenced by the Wahhabi movement. He was able to gain converts through the provision of social services such as schools and wells. Likewise, Christian missionaries in Africa during the colonial period competed for souls by providing health care and education.

The provision of economic and social welfare services has been central to the growth of the Muslim Brotherhood movement in Egypt and elsewhere in the Muslim world and of more nationally focused Islamist groups such as Hezbollah in Lebanon and Hamas in the Palestinian territories. From 2010 Islamist groups in Yemen redirected their recruiting message to focus on weak state capacity and the government's inability to meet local needs in the southern parts of the country, and the ranks of their supporters grew.[37]

Though there are many ways for substate organizations to provide poor communities with economic and social services, religious charities are the most effective—and potentially the most problematic. Many Islamic charities and their affiliated parent organizations are perceived as not being corrupt, and these charities often are the first to arrive on the scene in a disaster or a war zone. For example, in the aftermath of the 2005 Pakistani earthquake, the charity group Jamaat ud-Dawa (JuD) was an early provider of relief.[38] JuD is accused of being affiliated with Lashkar-e-Taiba (LeT), a radical Islamist group fighting in Kashmir and an affiliate of al-Qaeda. LeT was blamed for several high-profile terrorist attacks, including the November 2008 attacks in Mumbai, India.

After the Israeli bombings in Lebanon in July and August 2006, the international press featured Hezbollah-sponsored charities bulldozing bombed-out areas and providing cash to families that had lost their homes, whereas international agencies and the Lebanese government were much slower off the mark. According to focus groups in Lebanon, Hezbollah's increasing popularity among the Shia population can be attributed to the view, as explained by one Shia resident, that "it is the only party that provides security and services while remaining transparent."[39]

The sentiments toward Hamas are similar. Haim Malka wrote: "The centrality of welfare to Hamas's broad social agenda of Islamizing society has been Hamas's most effective form of activism."[40] An International Crisis Group (ICG) report also concluded that "the leaders of the movement themselves ascribe a significant if not primary role to Islamic social welfare activism in explaining the growth and enduring popularity of the Islamist movement."[41] In the immediate aftermath of the intensive fighting between Israel and Hamas in Gaza in late 2008 through early 2009, Hamas again distributed compensation and reconstruction assistance.

And during and after the uprisings in Tunisia and Egypt in 2011, opposition Islamist groups continued their decades-long roles as providers of basic social services. Interestingly, since Islamist parties have assumed power in both Tunis and Cairo, one of the most important questions is whether these long-standing opposition movements can continue to maintain their popular support now that they have to play the difficult job of politics, which inevitably involves compromise. Should economic conditions continue to darken,[42] will more radical Islamist factions increase their popularity and power in those rural communities that are inaccessible to the central government? Or will political failure pave the way for success at the polls by more secular-leaning groups?

These findings are not just relevant to the Arab Middle East—the results are similar in other parts of the world as well. Theodore Gerber and Sarah

Mendelson conducted surveys in the North Caucasus region and concluded, "Whoever gets there first and delivers social goods—the Russian government, the West, or radical Islamists—will shape the political trajectory of this region."[43] This model now seems to be spreading to new parts of Africa, including Chad, Mali, and Nigeria, where Islamist groups are increasing their power and capacity especially in marginalized parts of their countries.[44]

In Somalia, again according to the ICG, the fundamentalist movements owed "their rapid growth since 1990 less to genuine popularity than access to substantial external funding."[45] Mark Bradbury added that "the success of [the radical Somali Islamist group] al-Ittihaad has, in part, been based on investing in a social and economic welfare program that the West will not fund."[46] My interviews of Somalis and a review of the Somali press indicated that Somalis initially supported the radical Islamic Courts Union (ICU, which included the former al-Ittihaad organization) when it took over much of southern Somalia in mid-2006, because the ICU established security for the first time since the state collapsed in 1991 and because of the social services provided by affiliated charities.[47] Public support for the ICU was also intended as a rebuke of many of the warlords, who were deeply unpopular, responsible for numerous human rights abuses and extortion, and perceived as uncaring about the suffering of ordinary Somalis.

Although some Islamic charities in Somalia—such as those managed by al-Islah—may not support extremist violence, other Somali Islamists, notably al-Shabaab, a radical youth militia movement turned political insurgency, do advocate more fundamental changes to Somali society and endorse violence as a strategy to achieve their goals.[48] Therefore, much like in other parts of the world, providing the poor with social services helped to broaden the appeal of fundamentalist and violent interpretations of Islam inside Somalia for a time, though al-Shabaab seems to have squandered those gains due to its harsh social measures (for example, prohibiting Somalis from viewing soccer on television, preventing Somali women from wearing bras) and especially its suicide attacks in 2011 and 2012 that demonstrated massive disregard for civilian casualties.

Some observers have argued that extremist groups provide charitable services and other economic and social welfare goods in order to expand their political power base. A variation on this argument posits that many of the more radical Islamic organizations purposely link assistance with politics because the two are an inextricable part of their overall worldview, identity, and purpose (help for the poor is indeed core to all religions). Whatever the motive, it is clear that affiliated charities fulfill critical state functions in places where the state does not. The result may be that they successfully realign community loyalty in the direction of radicalism.

When an extremist nongovernmental organization (NGO) is the only service provider in an area and a beneficiary refuses to wear a head scarf, for example, she may not get any service at all. Even if a recipient complies only temporarily to receive the aid, such pressures can transform societies over the long term.[49] Significantly, this aid monopoly often results in members of the public being reluctant to speak out against terrorist acts in their communities or to help government authorities locate suspects.

Increased support for Somali, Algerian, or Pakistani terrorist groups does not necessarily imply that more Somalis, Algerians, or Pakistanis will themselves become terrorists. And there are enormous differences between the extreme Salafist and some radical Shia groups versus the Muslim Brotherhood, which has renounced terrorist acts against civilians, even if some of their platforms do concern some Western policymakers. But if the goal is to isolate terrorists and reduce their appeal, then effective provision of basic social services would be one way to do this. At the most basic level, it is often simply the dearth of government-provided services or international donor support that makes some people and communities vulnerable and susceptible to extremist ideology.[50]

The sad fact is that the extremist charities and other social service networks in many fragile, weak, and even autocratic states receive very little competition from national capitals, Western donors, and multilateral agencies. The ideological viewpoint espoused by a radical group may not be the primary draw for many recipient families, but the lack of alternatives for schooling or health care fuels the growth of extremist movements. Because many developing states do not have the capacity to provide basic services for their inhabitants today and may not for the foreseeable future, Western assistance providers need to take a deeper look at their own approaches and funding mechanisms and elaborate more creative alternatives, especially when dealing with the "poor performers."

THE ORDINARY FOOT SOLDIER

In many instances, the provision of social services to the poor has shaped the environment in which terrorists operate. Here the linkages between poverty and terrorism are indirect, but compelling. More direct connections between the two can be found when examining the drivers for *some* volunteers and recruits: poor education and indigence have influenced decisions to volunteer (or be recruited or duped) for suicide bombing missions and also to enlist (or be conscripted) as a low-level operative. The evolution of the terrorist threat into evermore impoverished parts of the world has also shifted the issue of poverty into sharper focus.

Education and the Madrassa

A poor education (or no education) has been linked to terrorism, but it also has been determined not to be a crucial factor. According to some researchers, children who are educated in extremist madaris (plural for *madrassa*) are cannon fodder for terrorist organizations.[51] To the contrary, argue others, they do not have the requisite basic skills to carry out a terrorist attack.[52]

Either the data are not conclusive enough, or both may be correct. The nineteen hijackers who committed the 9/11 atrocities and their spiritual father bin Laden were neither poor nor uneducated. Most members of the Muslim Brotherhood movement including its more radical offshoots emerged from secular universities in Egypt. Palestinian and Lebanese members of Hamas and Hezbollah also tend to come from the ranks of the educated rather than the impoverished.

At the same time, some extremist madaris have provided recruits from the ranks of the impoverished for terrorist and militant organizations. Most madaris are heavily subsidized or free of charge. In addition to tuition, children receive food, clothing, and books, at no cost to the family. Thus these schools are an attractive option for a poor family. In Pakistan alone, nearly two million children attend madaris.[53]

Not all madaris have an extremist agenda; many also teach secular subjects and middle-class children. Yet the children who attend the more radical madaris are taught from an early age a violent worldview and to despise "corrupting western influences."[54] According to Ali Riaz, "Children are taught that Muslims all around the world . . . are under siege from sinister forces which they must fight to the death."[55] It is primarily in South Asia (India, Pakistan, and Bangladesh) where these schools have been used to promote a political agenda—unlike in the Arab world where they do not play such a role.[56] Parts of Indonesia resemble the South Asia model rather than the Arab one, as do a growing number of regions in East and West Africa.

The Taliban leader Mullah Omar famously called on the Pakistani-based madaris to help with the fighting in Afghanistan during the Taliban takeover of the country in the late 1990s.[57] In response, in 1997 Maulana Sami ul-Haq shut down his renowned Haqqania madrassa in the North West Frontier Province of Pakistan, now Khyber Pakhtunkhwa, and sent all 2,800 students to the front line. The word *talib* itself means religious student, and indeed an estimated one-third of the original Afghan Taliban were educated in Pakistan's madaris.

Some may argue that the madrassa students were not attacking the West during the fight against the Soviets or during their national struggle against the Afghan warlords and other rebel leaders, and thus they are not relevant to a discussion of international terrorism. Since 9/11, however, these same madaris are sending students and graduates to kill NATO troops and civilians in

Afghanistan. Some are also targeting Pakistani and expatriate civilians inside Pakistan. Christine Fair adds, "Pakistan's madaris in FATA [Federally Administered Tribal Areas]—especially in North and South Waziristan—are deeply implicated in the recruitment of suicide attackers in both Afghanistan and Pakistan."[58] These madaris may also be providing short-term, "executive-level" education programs for European Muslims and other foreigners wishing to join the global jihad (the July 2005 London bombers allegedly spent time in a Pakistani madrassa). And radical madaris are expanding to new reaches— many members of the violent Nigerian Islamist group Boko Haram were recruited from the religious school started by the group's founder, Mohammed Yusuf, who was recently killed after a shoot-out with Nigerian police. For nearly ten years, children of poor Muslim families from across Nigeria and neighboring countries were sent to Yusuf's school to obtain a strict religious education free of any Western influence (loosely translated *Boko Haram* means "Western education is forbidden").[59]

On a more general level, very few students from the world's madaris will become terrorists, even if there are some notable exceptions (such as in Afghanistan and Pakistan, and parts of Africa). And many of those who become terrorists will not be as skilled as their educated counterparts, accounting, perhaps, for some failed suicide bombing attempts. And it should be noted that in many public schools in these same countries, students are also often offered a similarly violent worldview.

The madrassa has become the catchall for the debate on the root causes of terrorism, but as Fair and others point out, it is the quality of education—not whether it is religious or secular, public or private—that matters. As Fair explains, the available data suggest that in Pakistan's public schools, which educate 70 percent of Pakistan's children, "public school students have views only marginally more accommodating of domestic and external peace than those of madrassah counterparts. The same can be said of their teachers."[60] How many poorly educated public school students have joined terrorist groups is not known and should be an area of future inquiry.

Thus the data currently show that poverty and a lack of education can have a direct influence in some instances: some poor madrassa students do become terrorists. Poverty and lack of education also can play an indirect role: the nonterrorist, impoverished student with a substandard education will gain few practical skills to prepare him or her for working in modern society.[61] These students and graduates will populate the enabling environment. Therefore, educational reform should become a top priority for counter-radicalization programs in the appropriate countries. The story is similarly nuanced for volunteers (or recruits) for suicide attacks.

Suicide Bombers

Because the families of Muslim "martyrs" are compensated by a number of charitable organizations (often very generously), it has been argued that the financial reward is an incentive for a poor family. Some families of suicide bombers are indeed elevated to a higher status in their communities, and receive financial help to start businesses or build new homes. Jessica Stern found from her interviews with those involved in the Kashmir dispute that "wealthy Pakistanis would rather donate their money than their sons to the cause, [while] families in poor, rural areas are likely to send their sons to 'jihad' under the belief that doing so is the only way to fulfill this spiritual duty."[62] Peter Bergen also reported on fees paid to families of suicide bombers who carried out attacks in Afghanistan, some earning $500, which Bergen described as "a good sum of money in a part of the world where many laborers only make a couple of dollars per day."[63]

A study of suicide attacks in Afghanistan from 2001 to 2007 conducted by the United Nations Assistance Mission in Afghanistan (UNAMA) found that children were recruited from both Afghanistan and Pakistan, and "these young children may be uneducated, ignorant, impressionable, brainwashed, and seeking money for their families."[64] Although suicide bombers may be motivated by a mix of greed, grievance, and ideology, in recent years they have largely been drawn from the ranks of the poor. Whether they commit an act of terrorism for money or for belief is less relevant here than the fact that poverty led them into the hands of radicals in the first place. The UNAMA study concluded: "Poverty and lack of education figure in all but one [sic] the interviews of the confessed perpetrators."[65]

In Afghanistan and Pakistan, the connection appears to be direct. Evidence has also been found of indirect links. One study of the relationship among education, income, and support for suicide bombings in six Muslim countries (Indonesia, Jordan, Lebanon, Morocco, Pakistan, and Turkey) found that "increased education reduces the probability of support for suicide bombings . . . in the case of attacks on civilians, but not in the case of attacks on foreign forces and supporting civilians occupying Muslim lands."[66] Although this finding does not focus on the attackers themselves, it does fit into the enabling environment discussion and thus is also relevant. The researchers conclude that "educated Muslims identify and confront the moral dilemmas that come with the killing of civilians better than less educated ones. They are also more capable of dealing with the clear Islamic prohibition on suicide that some extremist Islamist ideologues have undermined by reinterpreting suicide as 'martyrdom.'"[67]

Another study carried out by researchers at the University of Jordan concurred with these results, though on a more general level. Polls carried out by the research team showed that the better educated were more likely to define groups that rely on suicide tactics such as Islamic Jihad, Hamas, al-Aqsa Martyrs' Brigades, and al-Qaeda as terrorist organizations. By contrast, the less educated were more likely to view these same organizations—notably al-Qaeda—as legitimate.[68]

On the other hand, some researchers have found conflicting results. Nasra Hassan discovered in her study of Palestinian suicide bombers that they were mostly educated, middle-class men.[69] Other reports seem to back her findings, though they tend to focus on longitudinal studies that stopped around 2001 or 2002 or only pertained to the Middle East.[70] Thus most of the research does not take into account the backgrounds of suicide bombers in Iraq after the U.S. invasion, the changing dynamics in Somalia and other parts of Africa, or the evolving situation in Pakistan and Afghanistan, where terrorists regularly attack Western interests, soldiers, and citizens as well as local civilians. Motivation for these "new terrorists" will likely be a mix of factors, with poverty relevant in some instances and grievances or ideology in others.

The Peasants Revolt!

The research on the role of poverty is complex and demonstrates that there is no prototype terrorist. For example, at the leadership level most research has concluded that the bosses are typically educated and relatively affluent. Recent changes in the terrorist threat, however, indicate that there are more and more exceptions. Most of the leaders of the forty-plus militias in the loose network that comprises Pakistan's Taliban (Tehrek-e-Taliban), parts of which are now working with al-Qaeda, come from humble backgrounds. Baitullah Mehsud, the recently deceased militia commander in South Waziristan and self-proclaimed head of the Pakistan Taliban, was himself from a poor peasant family, as is Mangal Bagh, the current militia head in Khyber Agency, who previously swept buses for a living.[71] Many other militant leaders in FATA, NWFP [North West Frontier Province/Khyber Pakhtunkhwa], and Balochistan also come from deprived backgrounds, as did Mullah Omar, the reclusive Afghan Taliban leader. Some would argue that warlords or militia heads should not be evaluated in the same way as terrorists, and yet today many of these leaders and groups have fused with al-Qaeda and are officially stamped with the terrorist label.

Although the leaders of terrorist organizations seem to come from both indigent and bourgeoisie backgrounds, that is not true of their humble servants. Strangely, most researchers recognize that poverty may be a factor among the lower ranks but do not include the foot soldiers in their research or when aggregating data.

Returning to South Asia, the ordinary volunteer or recruit in Pakistan and Afghanistan has typically been poor. Daniel Markey explains, "In Pakistan,

Taliban recruits are drawn from Afghan refugee camps and the network of extremist madrassas in the tribal areas. Taliban foot soldiers tend to be uneducated, poor Pashtuns with few other employment prospects."[72]

According to the UN study in Afghanistan, "Given the low development of FATA and paucity of employment opportunities, unemployed youth have joined these local militant groups as a way of both earning a livelihood and as a means of enhancing their social status."[73] Bergen learned that Taliban fighters were paid about $300 a month, "four times the wage of the average Afghan police officer."[74] Early indications are that at least one of the ten terrorists who committed the Mumbai attacks in November 2008 was motivated by poverty: the sole surviving gunman captured admitted that he joined LeT for the money.[75]

Deprivation seems to be a common factor among recruits elsewhere. The infamous impoverished town of Darnah in Libya sent a disproportionate number of young men to fight in Iraq, and an equally disproportionate number of them volunteered for suicide missions.[76] As Kevin Peraino explains, "There is no doubt that economic misery and its social consequences have scarred Darnah's young people."[77] And since the 2011 revolution in Libya many of these fighters have been actively and directly supporting violent Islamist insurgencies in neighboring and nearby countries including Chad and Mali.[78]

In Somalia and Nigeria—two other African countries that have witnessed an unfortunate increase in al-Qaeda–inspired terrorism—poverty has convinced some young people to join the violent jihadist groups al-Shabaab and Boko Haram. Here the motivation for membership at the foot soldier level appears to be more about dollars than dogma. There are not enough reliable data to draw on in Somalia because of the twenty-plus years of state collapse, or in Nigeria due to the deteriorating security situation, which also complicates efforts to disentangle the competing motivations for joining and leading such groups. The available evidence does indicate, however, that lack of governance and inadequate economic opportunities have been persuasive at the lower ranks of the violent movements in both of these countries. Moreover, although the motivations at the leadership level may be a mix of ideology, opportunism, personal political ambition, greed, and grievance, the leaders have exploited the issue of poverty in Somalia and Nigeria as part of their public rhetoric and to attract more recruits to their movement.

CONCLUDING REMARKS

Returning to the question posed at the outset, it appears that the research on the relationship between poverty and terrorism is by no means conclusive and, if anything, reveals a mixed and complex picture. Poverty plays a role in some instances and not in others. Certain terrorist movements have expanded their support base in the enabling environment by providing the poor with direct aid. Some volunteers for suicide missions and many ordinary foot soldiers come from impoverished backgrounds, and also attended the radical madaris. Thus poverty has played an indirect and a direct role in the recruitment of terrorists in some critical cases.

Moreover, many of the more privileged terrorists use the plight of the poor as one justification for committing violence and for broadening their appeal. They claim to speak on behalf of the poor, just as other middle-class, well-educated ideologues have done in the past. This claim allows them to broaden their constituencies to include many marginalized communities throughout the world. Thus it is too early to shut the book on this debate, especially because poverty appears to be more relevant in today's hottest terrorist theaters in Africa and southern Arabia, along with Afghanistan and Pakistan, which remain the primary Taliban and al-Qaeda sanctuaries, breeding grounds, and training centers.

Indeed, in recent years in Pakistan militant activity and violence have spread throughout the poorest parts of the country, from South and North Waziristan into all seven agencies of the FATA, into settled parts of the NWFP/Khyber Pakhtunkhwa, and into Balochistan, where Afghan Taliban leaders regroup from fighting. The writ of the central government and traditional authority has steadily eroded in FATA. This is not to say that the region is an "ungoverned territory" (an inappropriate term), but rather this extremely impoverished and undergoverned region has been infiltrated by violent extremists over the years, and these extremists have coerced, bribed, or killed local authorities when entrenching their authority.

Yet much like in Somalia and parts of Nigeria, Mali, and Yemen, and because few Westerners and Pakistanis visit most of FATA, Pakistani and American analysts and officials have only a rudimentary understanding of the complicated alliances, dynamics, and threats posed by the numerous groups operating in these areas, especially the Pakistan Taliban, the Afghan Taliban, al-Qaeda, and other militant groups.[79] Nor does anyone seem to have a good grasp of who the "foreigners" are, and the alliances among and between Pakistanis, Afghans, Arabs, and Central Asians (for example, the Uzbeks, Chechens, Tajiks, Kazaks, and Uighurs). The lack of reliable data and information on this region (and other "ungoverned spaces") may account for why these areas have not been integrated into previous studies on the relationship between poverty and terrorism.

When examining the research on the role of poverty in terrorism, it is therefore important to consider the areas excluded from the analysis and what creative tools can be used to learn more about these no-go territories so that they can be included in ongoing research. If these areas were factored in, more researchers would find that poverty is indeed an important concern in some of today's most pressing terrorist hot spots.

Much of the previous research that supposedly debunked the poverty-terrorism thesis concentrated on international terrorism and terrorism that targeted the West, not on nationally focused insurgencies. Yet as most researchers know, the al-Qaeda movement and network are extremely fluid and rapidly mutating. Over the last few years, many of the national and international groups have fused. For example, today Somalia's al-Shabaab, the Afghan Taliban, the Pakistani Taliban, Algeria's Armed Islamic Group, and Yemen's Ansar al-Sharia are very different creatures from their predecessors or earlier iterations. Such groups collaborate and learn from each other as well as from their counterparts in places such as Iraq, Chechnya, and even Colombia. Policymakers and researchers need to ensure that the debate and the response are also fluid, flexible, and able to adapt in real time.

Notes

1. President Bill Clinton, remarks to the Jordanian Parliament, Amman, Jordan, October 26, 1994, www.presidency.ucsb.edu/ws/index.php?pid=49373.
2. Transcription of *La Stampa* interview with James D. Wolfensohn, World Bank, December 7, 2001.
3. Quoted in Claude Berrebi, "Evidence about the Link between Education, Poverty and Terrorism among Palestinians," *Peace Economics, Peace Science and Public Policy* 13, no. 1 (2007): 2.
4. For Obama's full video statement see www.whitehouse.gov/blog/2010/01/02/weekly-address-fight-against-al-qaeda-0.
5. For background on the 9/11 hijackers, see National Commission on Terrorist Attacks upon the United States, *The 9/11 Commission Report* (New York: Norton, 2004), esp. chap. 5; and Terry McDermott, *Perfect Soldiers* (New York: HarperCollins, 2005).
6. Daniel Pipes, "God and Mammon: Does Poverty Cause Militant Islam?" *National Interest* (Winter 2001/2002); Alan Krueger and Jitka Maleckova, "Does Poverty Cause Terrorism?" *New Republic,* June 24, 2002.
7. World Health Organization, *World Health Statistics 2008* (Washington, D.C.: WHO, 2008).
8. Ching-Chi Hsieh and M. D. Pugh, "A Meta-Analysis of Recent Aggregate Data Studies," *Criminal Justice Review* 18, no. 2 (1993): 182–196.
9. James Fearon and David Laitin, "Ethnicity, Insurgency and Civil War," *American Political Science Review* 97, no. 1 (2003): 75–90.
10. Leif Ohlsson, "Livelihood Conflicts: Linking Poverty and Environment as Causes of Conflict," Swedish International Development Cooperation Agency, 2000.

11. Adam Przeworski, Michael Alvarez, Jose Antonio Cheibub, and Fernando Limongi, *Democracy and Development: Political Institutions and Well-Being in the World 1950 to 1990* (New York: Cambridge University Press, 2000); J. B. Londregan and K. Poole, "Poverty, the Coup Trap and the Seizure of Executive Power," *World Politics* 42, no. 2 (1990): 151–183.

12. Aristide R. Zolberg and Peter M. Benda, *Global Migrants and Global Refugees* (New York: Berghahn Books, 2001).

13. Ted Robert Gurr, *Why Men Rebel* (Princeton, N.J.: Princeton University Press, 1971).

14. See, for example, James A. Piazza, "Rooted in Poverty? Terrorism, Poor Economic Development and Social Cleavages," *Terrorism and Political Violence* 18 (2006): 219–237; Alberto Abadie, "Poverty, Political Freedom and the Roots of Terrorism," *American Economic Review* 96, no. 2 (2006): 159–177; Berrebi, "Evidence about the Link." Note, however, that Quan Li and Drew Schaub, in "Economic Globalization and Transnational Terrorism," *Journal of Conflict Resolution* 48, no. 2 (2004): 230–258, did find economically developed countries to be significantly less likely to experience terrorist attacks.

15. Figures derived from Shaohua Chen and Martin Ravallion, "How Have the World's Poorest Fared Since the Early 1980s?" *World Bank Research Observer* 19, no. 2 (2004): 141–169.

16. This figure was derived from the RAND-MIPT Terrorism Knowledge Base (TKB), a now-inactive database maintained by the Memorial Institute for the Prevention of Terrorism, a federal research institute established within the Department of Homeland Security after the 1995 Oklahoma City bombings.

17. United Nations Development Programme, *World Development Report* (various years).

18. The time-series line graphs for these data can be found in James A. Piazza, "Global Poverty, Inequality and Transnational Terrorism: A Research Note," *Perspectives on Terrorism* 1, no. 4 (2007).

19. Explanations for the Human Development Index and data tables are available at the United Nations Development Programme's website, http://hdr.undp.org/en/.

20. The results in Table 2-2 are made more dramatic by the inclusion of Iraq in the "Medium Human Development" category, a country that saw a dramatic increase in domestic terrorism after the United States toppled the Saddam Hussein regime in 2003. The most recent Human Development Index score available for Iraq, 1999, places it firmly in the "Medium" category. Even if Iraq is excluded from the data in Table 2-2, the overall results are the same: "Low Human Development" countries still produce the least transnational terrorism, sustain the lowest level of terrorism, and host the fewest terrorist groups.

21. The twenty countries are, in order from the most unequal, Namibia, Lesotho, Sierra Leone, the Central African Republic, Botswana, Bolivia, Afghanistan, Haiti, Colombia, Paraguay, South Africa, Brazil, Panama, Guatemala, Chile, Honduras, Ecuador, El Salvador, Peru, and the Dominican Republic.

22. For a full discussion of the Naxalites and their origins, see Dipak K. Gupta, "The Naxalites and Maoist Movement in India: Birth, Demise and Reincarnation," *Democracy and Security* 3, no. 2 (2007): 157–188.

23. Ken Menkhaus, "Quasi-States, Nation-Building and Terrorist Safe Havens," *Journal of Conflict Studies* 23, no. 2 (2003): 7–23.

24. Alan Krueger and Jitka Maleckova, "Education, Poverty and Terrorism: Is There a Causal Connection?" *Journal of Economic Perspectives* 17, no. 4 (2003): 119–144; Berrebi, "Evidence about the Link"; Charles A. Russell and Bowman H. Miller, "Profile of a Terrorist," *Studies in Conflict and Terrorism* 1, no. 1 (1977): 17–34.

25. Simon Haddad and Hilal Khashan, "Islam and Terrorism: Lebanese Muslim Views on September 11," *Journal of Conflict Resolution* 46 (2002): 812–828; Krueger and Maleckova, "Education, Poverty and Terrorism."

26. Edgar O'Ballance, *The Language of Violence: The Blood Politics of Terrorism* (San Rafael, Calif.: Presidio Press, 1979).

27. James A. Piazza, "Poverty, Minority Economic Discrimination and Domestic Terrorism," *Journal of Peace Research* 48, no. 3 (2011): 339–353; James A. Piazza, "Types of Minority Discrimination and Terrorism," *Conflict Management and Peace Science* 29, no. 5 (2012).

28. Christopher Hewitt, *The Effectiveness of Anti-Terrorism Policies* (Lanham, Md.: University Press of America, 1984).

29. Martha Crenshaw, "The Causes of Terrorism," *Comparative Politics* 13, no. 4 (1981): 379–399.

30. At the time of writing the first published version of this chapter, Karin von Hippel was the co-director of the Post-Conflict Reconstruction Project at the Center for Strategic and International Studies (CSIS). She currently serves as a deputy assistant secretary for operations in the State Department's Bureau of Conflict and Stabilization Operations. The views expressed in this chapter are her own.

31. See Alan Krueger, *What Makes a Terrorist* (Princeton, N.J.: Princeton University Press, 2007); Krueger and Maleckova, "Education, Poverty, Political Violence and Terrorism"; Piazza, "Rooted in Poverty?" 159–177; Tim Krieger and Daniel Meierrieks, "What Causes Terrorism?" Working Papers Series No. 2008–05, Center for International Economics, Paderborn, Germany, June 2008.

32. Krueger, *What Makes a Terrorist*, 12.

33. See "Poverty 'Fuelling Terrorism,'" BBC News, March 22, 2002, http://news.bbc .co.uk/hi/english/world/newsid_1886000/1886617.stm.

34. Speech before the Peterson Institute for International Economics, Washington, D.C., January 6, 2010.

35. Louise Richardson at Harvard University originally coined this term. Another useful term is *complicit society.*

36. Interestingly, some of the more successful Islamist political parties have a social service wing, whereas secular political parties do not.

37. See, for example, Ghaith Abdul-Ahad, "Al-Qaida's Wretched Utopia and the Battle for Hearts and Minds," *The Guardian,* April 30, 2012, www.guardian.co.uk/ world/2012/apr/30/alqaida-yemen-jihadis-sharia-law.

38. John Lancaster and Kamran Khan, "Extremists Fill Aid Chasm after Quake: Group Banned in Pakistan Dispenses Relief," *Washington Post,* October 16, 2005.

39. National Democratic Institute, "Findings of Lebanon Focus Groups," NDI, Washington, D.C., 2007, 8.

40. Haim Malka, "Hamas: Resistance and Transformation of Palestinian Society," in *Understanding Islamic Charities,* ed. Jon Alterman and Karin von Hippel (Washington, D.C.: Center for Strategic and International Studies, 2007), 100.

41. "Islamic Social Welfare Activism in the Occupied Palestinian Territories: A Legitimate Target?" ICG Middle East Report No. 13, International Crisis Group, Brussels, April 2, 2003, 27.

42. Hussein Ibish, "Was the Arab Spring Worth It," *Foreign Policy* (July/August 2012): 92–93.

43. Theodore P. Gerber and Sarah E. Mendelson, "Security through Sociology: The North Caucasus and the Global Counterinsurgency Paradigm," unpublished manuscript, November 2007.

44. Nicolas Pelham, "Is Libya Cracking Up?" *New York Review of Books,* June 21, 2012.

45. International Crisis Group, "Somalia: Countering Terrorism in a Failed State," ICG Africa Report No. 45, Brussels, May 23, 2002, 13.

46. Mark Bradbury, "Somalia: The Aftermath of September 11th and the War on Terrorism," Oxfam Great Britain Report, February 2002, 25.

47. This point is difficult to demonstrate more conclusively because there are no reliable polling or survey data for Somalia. In general, since the state collapsed in 1991 statistics have been difficult to accrue because of the insecurities on the ground, because of the lack of regular and reliable data collection, and because up to half of the population is nomadic. Different organizations—both Somali and international—gather data in different ways, with no agreed methodology or reliable means of accumulating information over time.

48. See Andre LeSage, "Islamic Charities in Somalia," in Alterman and von Hippel, *Understanding Islamic Charities.*

49. See Shawn Teresa Flanigan, "Charity as Resistance: Connections between Charity, Contentious Politics, and Terror," *Studies in Conflict and Terrorism* 29 (2006): 641–655.

50. See Karin von Hippel, "Aid Effectiveness: Improving Relations with Islamic Charities," in Alterman and von Hippel, *Understanding Islamic Charities.*

51. See Jeffrey Goldberg, "Inside Jihad U.: The Education of a Holy Warrior," *New York Times Magazine,* June 25, 2000.

52. See, for example, Peter Bergen and Swati Pandey, "The Myth of the Madrassa," *International Herald Tribune,* June 15, 2005.

53. Christopher Candland, "Pakistan's Recent Experience in Reforming Islamic Education," in *Education Reform in Pakistan: Building for the Future,* ed. Robert Hathaway (Washington, D.C.: Woodrow Wilson International Center for Scholars, 2005), 151–165.

54. See Craig Davis, "'A' is for Allah, 'J' is for Jihad," *World Policy Journal* (Spring 2002): 90.

55. Ali Riaz, "Global Jihad, Sectarianism and the Madrassahs in Pakistan," Working Paper 85, Institute of Defence and Strategic Studies, Singapore, August 2005, 20.

56. Uzma Anzar, "Islamic Education: A Brief History of Madrassas with Comments on Curricula and Current Pedagogical Practices," World Bank, Washington, D.C., March 2003, 17–18.

57. See Ahmed Rashid, *The Taliban: Islam, Oil and the New Great Game in Central Asia* (London: I. B. Taurus, 2002), 59, 72, 78.

58. C. Christine Fair, *The Madrassah Challenge: Militancy and Religious Education in Pakistan,* U.S. Institute of Peace, Washington, D.C., 2008, 7. See also United Nations Assistance Mission in Afghanistan, "Suicide Attacks in Afghanistan (2001–2007)," September 1, 2007, 6, 98.

59. Farouk Chothia, "Who are Nigeria's Boko Haram Islamists?" *BBC News,* January 11, 2012.

60. See, for example, Fair, *Madrassah Challenge,* 97–98.

61. See Jessica Stern, "Meeting with the Muj," *Bulletin of the Atomic Scientists* 57 (January/February 2001): 42–51.

62. Jessica Stern, "Pakistan's Jihad Culture," *Foreign Affairs* 79 (November/December 2000): 122.

63. Peter Bergen, "Afghan Spring," *New Republic,* June 18, 2007.

64. United Nations Assistance Mission in Afghanistan, "Suicide Attacks in Afghanistan (2001–2007)," 89.

65. Ibid., 79.

66. M. Najeeb Shafiq and Abdulkader H. Sinno, "Education, Income and Support for Suicide Bombings: Evidence from Six Muslim Countries," Indiana University Working Paper Series, July 2008, 1.

67. Ibid., 22.

68. Center for Strategic Studies, University of Jordan, "Revisiting the Arab Street Research from Within," Amman, February 2005, 75, 78–79.

69. Nasra Hassan, "An Arsenal of Believers," *New Yorker,* November 19, 2001, 36–41.

70. See, for example, Berrebi, "Evidence about the Link"; Krueger, *What Makes a Terrorist;* and Marc Sageman, *Understanding Terror Networks* (Philadelphia: University of Pennsylvania Press, 2004), 61–98.

71. Dexter Filkins, "Right at the Edge," *New York Times Magazine,* September 7, 2008.

72. Daniel Markey, "Securing Pakistan's Tribal Belt," CFR 36, Council on Foreign Relations, July 2008, 11.

73. UNAMA, "Suicide Attacks in Afghanistan (2001–2007)," 84.

74. Bergen, "Afghan Spring," 2007.

75. Vikas Bajaj and Lydia Polgreen, "Suspect Stirs Mumbai Court by Confessing," *New York Times,* July 20, 2009.

76. Kevin Peraino, "Destination Martyrdom: What Drove So Many Libyans to Volunteer as Suicide Bombers for the War in Iraq? A Visit to Their Hometown— The Dead-end City of Darnah," *Newsweek International,* April 28, 2008.

77. Ibid.

78. Ross Douthat, "Libya's Unintended Consequences," *New York Times,* July 7, 2012.

79. As diplomat Richard Holbrooke remarked in congressional testimony on May 7, 2008, "I don't have a clue what's going on in the FATA. And if anyone ever comes before this Committee and says so, you'd better ask twice, because it is one of the most elusive areas in the world."

can terrorism ever be justified?

NO: Terrorist violence is never justified.
Tamar Meisels, *Tel Aviv University*

YES: Terrorism is a just tool of the weak.
Ted Honderich, *University College London*

There is a famous scene in Gillo Pontecorvo's 1966 film *The Battle of Algiers* in which the recently captured leader of Algeria's National Liberation Front (FLN), Larbi Ben M'Hidi, is brought before international journalists at a press conference. The year is 1957 and the FLN, a group committed to Algeria's full independence from French colonial rule, had recently launched a series of deadly bombings in civilian locations in the European quarter of Algiers.

French reporter: "Mr. Ben M'Hidi, isn't it a filthy thing to use women's baskets to carry explosives for killing people?"

Ben M'Hidi: "Doesn't it seem even filthier to drop napalm bombs on defenseless villages, wreaking even greater havoc? It would be better if we too had planes. Give me the bombers, and you can have the baskets."

This exchange, in a nutshell, brings to life two of the most contentious and politically charged issues surrounding terrorism: how and why groups choose—and justify—the killing of innocents as a means of achieving their goals and how is it determined who has the "legitimate" right to use violence in the first place.

Terrorism, by any definition, involves the use of violence in furtherance of a political cause.[1] But definitions are one thing, justifications quite another. In the subjective world of terrorism, when it comes to justifying killing, much depends on *who is doing the justifying.* The FLN and its supporters justified indiscriminant killing as a necessary means of achieving what they believed to be a legitimate political goal—ending French colonial rule. Opponents of the FLN and its tactics (though not necessarily its goals) argued the opposite: that such killing was "filthy" and illegitimate.

In accusing the French government of even more widespread killing of innocents, Ben M'Hidi raises a larger point: how can the French government claim legitimacy in its use of violence to maintain control of its colony, while those seeking independence are morally condemned for doing the same? In other words, how is it that states can use force in furtherance of their political goals—or, in the parlance of the military strategist Carl von Clausewitz, as "a continuation of politics by other means"—while aggrieved groups within those states cannot?[2]

Tamar Meisels and Ted Honderich delve bravely into these issues. Meisels argues that it is the calculated targeting of civilians that separates terrorism from other forms of substate violence (for example, guerrilla warfare) and eliminates the right of terrorists to claim moral justification for their actions. Yes, states sometimes kill civilians in the course of military operations, but they are rarely if ever the primary target; this is not the case with terrorists. Mesiels also takes issue with the presumption, offered by many defenders of terrorism, that aggrieved groups often have "no other option" than indiscriminate killing in order to achieve their goals. Nonviolence often pays far greater dividends, she argues.

Honderich, using the example of Palestinian terrorism as his primary resource, addresses these issues from a very different plane of logic. What, for example, is an "innocent civilian"—surely not those who support (and benefit from) an unjust occupation, whether or not they wear a military uniform? In addition, who determines whether and in what ways the use of violence may be "legitimate"? It cannot simply be the side that has the biggest guns. And if the term *terrorist* is to be used pejoratively, should states escape such description simply because they are, in fact, states?

The important issues raised in this chapter will not be resolved here. Perhaps they will never be. Terrorism, by its very nature, is a highly social and emotional phenomenon—passionate differences on the basic questions of definition, description, and justification will linger as long as terrorism itself remains on the world scene.

NO: Terrorist violence is never justified.
Tamar Meisels, *Tel Aviv University*

Terrorism Can Never Be Justified

As terrorism penetrates liberal democracies, Western intellectuals, particularly left-leaning ones, seem increasingly confused, because traditional loyalties appear to pull in opposing directions. Liberals and leftists are accustomed to siding with the underdog and supporting the self-determination of peoples (most recently they are fervently committed to Palestinian independence). They customarily oppose violence and war and associate with peace movements. Most versions of modern liberalism include a complicated commitment to cultural pluralism and the toleration of cultures and societies, beliefs, and life choices, including those that appear dramatically alien to their own. Perhaps one man's terrorist is another's freedom fighter; one man's crime against humanity is another's resistance against oppression. Why, one might ask, are the desperate actions of militant groups dubbed illegitimate terrorism, while the military operations of established nation-states are considered legitimate warfare?

Such liberals often support a global application of equality standards, and they are therefore particularly sensitive to the plight of impoverished populations of developing nations. In the extreme, this sensitivity has led some to an overall antiglobalization stance or even to outright support of some forms of terrorism.

This essay looks at such questions of moral judgment, which have been thrust upon political philosophy by current events. Analyzing both the definition of terrorism and its possible justifications, the argument developed here calls for a unanimous liberal front against terrorism and its perpetrators.

IS TERRORISM EVER "RIGHT"?

There is a growing academic reluctance to define terrorism as a specific and fiendish deed. The considerable body of academic literature now available expresses sympathy, and at times outright justification, for Islamic (particularly Palestinian) terrorism. Among these apologetics of terrorism are well-known intellectual figures such as Noam Chomsky and the late French philosopher Jacques Derrida. Another such leading scholar who offers a vigorous defense of modern-day terrorism is the philosopher Ted Honderich.

In his controversial book *After the Terror,* Honderich takes up the linguistic challenge of defining *terrorism,* alongside the moral issues that flow from it. Setting out with more basic terms such as *violence* in general, and *political violence* in particular, Honderich ultimately refrains from defining *terrorism* independently.[3] Choosing to make no distinction between various forms of political violence, Honderich speaks of either terrorism or political violence as "violence with a political and social intention, whether or not intended to put people in general in fear, and raising a question of its moral justification— either illegal violence within a society or smaller-scale violence than war between states or societies and not according to international law."[4]

In defense of this inclusive definition, Honderich argues that making people in general fearful is not a significantly distinctive factor between forms of violence. He believes that "the main thing is getting political and social change," and this goal characterizes all forms of political violence. The idea that certain forms of political violence are directed specifically at innocent people (i.e., noncombatants), and that this notion ought to be viewed as part of their particular condemnation as "terrorism," is also raised in passing and similarly dismissed out of hand. This common intuition that there is a particular wrong involved in the *intentional* killing of noncombatants, and that such attacks in particular ought to be singled out as "acts of terror," is no more than momentarily considered and subsequently denied in the name of consistency.[5] After all, Western states kill innocents, too, and do not condemn the death of some innocents as loudly as we denounce the death of other (our) innocents.

Honderich's self-professed excuse for not singling out and condemning the specific sort of violence usually called "terrorism" is that it is actually more like all other forms of political violence than it is distinct from them. Whatever their particular mode of operation, all terrorists aspire to bring about (or preserve) a social and political end by means of inflicting harmful force. In his view, then, there is nothing unique or particularly condemnable about any one specific type of political violence, aside from the prima facie assumption of possible wrongfulness, which applies to the infliction of all injury and harm.[6]

This perspective bears clear normative implications, because it "does not by itself morally condemn in a final way anything that falls under it. It leaves open the possibility that there was justification of, say, the particular terrorism that led to the existence of the state of Israel. So with the attempt on Hitler's life and attempts to kill Osama Bin Laden in the years before September 11."[7]

Because Honderich's view of "terrorism" makes no distinction between various forms of political violence, it justifies the subsequent comparison between these examples and the case that appears to form the foundation of Honderich's agenda: that Palestinian terror against Israeli civilians is in fact justified. As Honderich puts it: "I myself have no doubt . . . that the Palestinians have exercised a moral right in their terrorism against the Israelis . . . and those who have killed themselves in the cause of their people have indeed sanctified themselves."[8]

As for the attacks of September 11, 2001, Honderich holds that "our definition of terrorism does not rule out the possibility that some terrorism could be justified as response to what others called structural violence." His overall political argument, developed throughout several publications, is that political violence, including terrorism, is justifiable in response to the wrongs done to individuals in the developing and Arab world—by the immoral omissions or direct commissions, particularly of the United States, associated with globalization, oil, and other capitalist interests and support of Israel.[9] For Honderich, "the conclusion is that there is no simple objection of a certain kind to terrorism against us, even the terrorism of September 11. We do not have a certain imagined moral high ground to stand on in condemning terrorism against us, in explaining our revulsion for the killers at the twin towers."[10]

Certainly, if terrorism is conceived so widely as to include all forms of political violence with no moral distinction between them, then that means "we are all terrorists," with the United States, Britain, and Israel leading a rotten bunch. Thus Noam Chomsky, who shares many of Honderich's assumptions, states clearly and repeatedly that the United States is a leading terrorist state.[11] Add to this the forms of "structural violence"—that is, America's alleged responsibility for the misfortunate lives in developing countries and among Arab populations—how then can one nonhypocritically oppose attacks against the United States by those harmed by its policies? On these question-begging assumptions, one cannot. Once terrorism is defined with a deliberate disregard for the element of fear—the literal terrorization of a civilian population—along with the element of targeting innocent noncombatants, the convenient outcome is inevitably going to be a striking formal similarity between killing soldiers, policemen, or officials, assassinating Adolf Hitler or targeting Osama bin Laden, and blowing up a café, a commuter bus, or a skyscraper. It would seem that, according to Honderich, these are "all in a good cause."

Nevertheless, Honderich regards the events of September 11, 2001, as wrong (as opposed to Palestinian terrorism aimed at Israelis), but only because they involved the use of violence *without any reasonable hope of achieving its justifiable goals,* understood as fighting off the effects of America's bad policies. Indeed, Honderich more than implies that if the attacks of 9/11 could reasonably have been conceived as an effective means of saving more misfortunate lives (say, in Africa) than the number of lives taken in New York, then such attacks would, in fact, have been justified. Furthermore, future attacks on

American civilians that would explicitly have antiglobalization and ending U.S. exploitation as their goals, with reasonable hope of achieving this end, would be justified, perhaps even commanded by Honderich's "humanitarian" principles.

Honderich, of course, is not a lone voice. In an engaging dialogue with Giovanna Borradori, Jacques Derrida presents a somewhat more subtle, yet not dissimilar, evaluation of the events of September 11. He, too, discredits the commonly attempted distinctions between terrorism and other types of violence.[12] Aside from the terrorist excesses of states during wartime and otherwise, Derrida suggests that causing fear, anxiety, panic, and even outright terror among the citizens of a state, far from being unique to any specific type of political violence, actually characterizes the very authority of law and exercising of state sovereignty. Partly in view of "state terror," Derrida's comments imply that the civilian-military distinction between wartime killing and terrorism is misplaced, although, like Honderich, he pays this distinction little attention, remarking only in passing and in a somewhat offhand tone that "the victims of terrorism are *assumed* to be civilians."[13] He also reminds readers of the undeniable fact that the predominant powers often use, and abuse, terminology and definitions opportunistically to suit their own partisan political advantage, and he attempts to move from this reminder to the disputable claim that terrorism therefore cannot be strictly defined. Derrida also reiterates the platitude "that terrorists might be praised as freedom fighters in one context . . . and denounced as terrorists in another," but without seriously scrutinizing this common aphorism.

In a similar vein as Honderich, Derrida then points out that both terrorists and states invoke self-defense as their excuse for exercising the type of violence that their adversaries regard as terrorism. And he alludes to the possibility that certain forms of Western-instigated "structural violence" associated with capitalism and globalization could in themselves be regarded by some observers as prior incidents of state terrorism. With this, Derrida joins Honderich in placing the distinctions between deliberate and unintentional actions as well as between acts and omissions in the philosophical wastepaper basket, alongside the earlier dismissal of the civilian-combatant distinction.[14] Thus he also questions whether terrorism need necessarily involve the deliberate act of killing, or whether the neglect of developing nations, for example, can in itself count as terrorism. As Derrida has said, "All situations of social or national structural oppression produce a terror."[15] Having "deconstructed" the notion of terrorism, Derrida's terminology is also deliberately inclusive, referring only to "violence" in a general fashion rather than to "war" or "terrorism." Ultimately, for these thinkers the normative evaluation of terrorism hinges on its prospects of success.

A DEADLY TRILOGY: GUERRILLA WARFARE, POLITICAL ASSASSINATION, AND TERRORISM

Furthering this discussion of general conceptions of terrorism, Michael Walzer's classic work *Just and Unjust Wars* offers a uniquely instructive (and contemporarily relevant) distinction between three categories of irregular warfare, each warranting a different moral attitude.[16] First, there are guerrillas, who are undeniably irregular in that they do not wear uniforms or other revealing dress (such as identifying badges or caps) and conceal their weapons and militant identity, and so remain unprotected by international laws of war. They also endanger civilian populations in a variety of ways, such as by hiding among them. Guerrilla warfare, however, does not itself subvert the war convention by attacks on civilians. Indeed, guerrillas draw a fine line between military and civilian targets. For the most part, guerrillas uphold the distinction between combatants and civilians, primarily targeting combatants either by direct ambush or by means of espionage and sabotage. As a rule, Walzer tells us, guerrillas do not target innocent civilians.[17] This distinguishing feature of guerrilla warfare indicates, at least intuitively, that, though nonconventional, this kind of warfare warrants some legitimacy, even though it does not render its participants eligible for the protection of international conventions and the war rights of soldiers specified in them. Guerrillas make distinctions and although they do at times kill civilians (as do antiguerrilla forces), civilians are not their primary targets. Guerrillas, then, may warrant moral respect, at least by those who identify with their cause. The French resistance to the German occupation in World War II is a classic case in point.

This vital distinction between modern terrorism and guerrilla warfare, along with its normative implications, was recently restated by Jürgen Habermas in slightly different terms. Habermas clearly distinguishes between "indiscriminant guerrilla warfare" and "paramilitary guerrilla warfare"—"the first is epitomized by Palestinian terrorism, in which murder is usually carried out by a suicide militant."[18] By contrast, only "the model of paramilitary guerrilla warfare is proper to the national liberation movements and is retrospectively legitimized by the formation of the state." Contra Derrida, then, indiscriminant guerrilla warfare cannot be retrospectively legitimized by political success. In Habermas's own words, "Palestinian terrorism . . . revolves around murder, around the indiscriminate annihilation of enemies, women and children—life against life. This is what distinguishes it from the terrorism that appears in the paramilitary form of guerrilla warfare."[19]

Next, political assassination, despite what Honderich would have people believe, is clearly distinguishable from terrorist strikes of the 9/11 type. When acting in the capacity of assassins, revolutionaries draw a moral distinction "between people who can and people who cannot be killed." Those who can be killed consist exclusively "of officials, the political agents of regimes, thought to be oppressive." Assassination, Walzer explains, necessarily involves "the drawing of a line that we will have little difficulty recognizing as the political parallel of the line that marks off combatants from non-combatants."[20] Crucially, assassins do not kill indiscriminately; ordinary private citizens remain immune from attack.[21] Although assassins cannot claim any of the soldiers' rights specified by international war conventions and treaties, they may gain some degree of respect simply because they do set limits to their actions. In his recent book *Terror and Liberalism,* Paul Berman makes a similar observation about the ethics of assassination. The "terrorists" of the past, such as the Russian anarchists who assassinated czarist officials, took care to avoid incidental innocent casualties; they "were morally fastidious," even "delicate."[22]

Terrorism more strictly conceived, however, is distinct from both guerrilla warfare and assassinations. It allows for no fusion of terms or the kind of confusion of the various forms of political violence attempted by Honderich and Derrida. In sharp contrast with guerrillas who (as a rule) confront armies and assassins who target particular officials, modern terrorists uphold no distinctions. Terrorists do not kill civilians by accident, as an unfortunate consequence of their military activity. All armed forces admit and profusely regret (whether cynically or sincerely) the killing of (at times many) innocent civilians in the course of military strikes or operations. For terrorists, however, the killing of noncombatants is not a regrettable by-product or side effect; innocent victims are not an "occupational hazard." Instead, they are the be all and end all of this form of belligerency.

THE TROUBLE WITH TERROR

What, then, is so wrong about terrorism in particular? Terrorism, Walzer explains, "breaks across moral limits beyond which no further limitation seems possible, for within the category of civilian and citizen, there isn't any smaller group for which immunity might be claimed. . . . Terrorists anyway make no such claim; they kill anybody."[23] For Walzer, this is a crucial point about terrorism: it is not aimed at particular people.

Berman's evaluation of modern terrorism is similar. He marks an important transition within revolutionary movements in the twentieth century, which he eloquently describes as the point at which "the fastidious yielded to the not fastidious."[24] Berman describes the loss of what the Russian revolutionary Boris Savinkov called a "terrorist conscience," which took care to aim at the victim. For modern-day terrorists, the murder is massive and anonymous, the nihilism unlimited, and the transgression total.

Crucially, terrorism is also a form of immoral free riding. All groups have at least some interest in upholding the distinction between civilian and military targets. It was precisely the growing realization of the dangers of war to civilian populations, probably more than any abstract moral principle, that pushed European statesmen in the nineteenth and twentieth centuries to negotiate and regulate the manners in which wars ought, and ought not, to be fought. As war became a more popular business, states were led, largely by the concern for the well-being of their own citizenry, to initiate international conventions and side with treaties that committed them to upholding distinctions between military and nonmilitary personnel, as well as between lawful and unlawful combatants, with the proviso that others do the same.

Such distinctions and codes of war, which are desirable for conventional armies and the states they represent, are in fact absolutely essential for terrorists and the success of their strategies. Terrorist tactics rely entirely on conventional armies maintaining these distinctions, while the terrorists themselves openly thwart them. Put differently, terrorism wholly depends on its opponents' upholding of a moral code that the terrorists themselves reject. Terrorists hitch a morally dubious free ride on their adversaries' moral code. If their adversaries were to match the terrorists' nihilism by denying the status of noncombatants and the distinction between belligerents and civilians, choosing to terrorize civilians with their superior force, they would once again have the upper hand, rendering the smaller-scale terrorism of the "underdog" totally ineffective.

In explaining why suicide terrorists almost exclusively target democracies, Robert Pape argues that "suicide terrorists . . . must also be confident that their opponent will be at least somewhat restrained. . . . [D]emocracies have generally been more restrained in their use of force against civilians, at least since World War II."[25] The Kurds, Pape points out, are a case in point:

> Although [pre-2003] Iraq has been far more brutal towards its Kurdish population than has Turkey, violent Kurdish groups have used suicide attacks exclusively against democratic Turkey and not against the authoritarian regime in Iraq. There are plenty of national groups living under authoritarian regimes with grievances that could possibly inspire suicide terrorism, but none have.[26]

To put all this more concretely, the instigators and perpetrators of 9/11 relied on the fact that the United States—for whatever its moral transgressions— would not retaliate by, for example, using atomic weapons against civilian Arab populations in the Middle East. Palestinian terrorists rely on the fact that Israel, while at times killing civilians, is nevertheless bound in a web of international and internal pressures alongside moral restraints that prevent it from striking back at Palestinians with all its might with no regard for civilian life. Terrorists also rely on a set of civil liberties, which they often hold in contempt but which enable them to operate more freely than they could in the absence of such civil liberties. Terrorism's very livelihood depends on a reversal of the Kantian imperative to "act only on that maxim through which you can at the same time will that it should become a universal law."[27] Terrorists must will, and be assured of, the precise reverse. They rely wholeheartedly on their maxim not being universalized. Where terrorists are pursued in kind—that is, by a military force that shares their disregard for human rights and moral codes—they have no hope of success.

All this is less true of guerrillas and assassins, who need not be free riders. As noted earlier, guerrillas customarily take advantage of the local terrain, or civilian surroundings. Admittedly, they depend on their enemies to respect the lives of civilians and consequently to refrain from pursuit in civilian settings. However, at least for the most part, guerrillas themselves uphold the very same distinctions and standards they expect their enemies to maintain. Unlike terrorists, guerrillas draw the same fine line that their opponents do between combatants and civilians. Their strategic advantage derives from a difference in circumstances (such as familiarity with the local topography and enjoying the sympathies of the local population) and not from the evasion of any moral code.

As for assassins, the success of their operations does not, as with terrorism, depend on their opponents refraining from similar tactics—two can play at this game. To take a familiar case, Israel's policy of targeting wanted arch-terrorists does not invalidate the effectiveness of Palestinian attacks on Israeli officials, such as the 2001 assassination of Israeli minister Rechavaam Zeevi. When viewed from conflicting points of view, or from a neutral standpoint, the Palestinian gunman displayed the same moral code as the one upheld by Israel's assassination policy—kill an (allegedly) guilty oppressor while refraining (as much as possible) from harming the innocent. Israel's frequent reference to the assassination of Minister Zeevi as "terrorism" is an unfortunate example of inaccurate political speech (though the culpable organizations are legitimately dubbed "terrorists" by virtue of some of their other actions). A terrorist, as opposed to an assassin or a guerrilla, is essentially a free rider on the moral codes and political liberties of others. Terrorists are, to say the least, free riders on the prohibitions to which civilized nations adhere.

LAST RESORT

One might respond to the preceding comments by observing that there are worse things in the world than free riding—oppression, persecution, occupation, and economic exploitation, to name just a few. Perhaps something further can be said along these lines in defense of terrorism, at least when it is employed in the pursuit of a "just cause." Honderich, who at least superficially renounces 9/11 (primarily for its predictable inefficiency), nevertheless defends "liberation-terrorism," understood as "terrorism to get freedom and power for a people when it is clear that nothing else will get it for them."[28]

This argument, whereby terrorism is justified as the only means of attaining particular political ends such as overthrowing repressive regimes, liberating oppressed peoples, and founding new nations, is not a new one. Terror apologists often point out that terrorism is a weapon of the weak. Terrorists are frequently portrayed by their sympathizers as the underdog, at times conjuring up images of the young biblical David. This comparative weakness, it is implied, can be overcome only through the use of unconventional tactics. Such arguments sometimes imply counterfactually that the only choice faced by disadvantaged groups engaged in conflict with a stronger power is between conventional warfare, at which they are inferior to their enemies, and terrorism. But, as just noted, this assertion is far from accurate. In *Just and Unjust Wars*, Walzer argues that the availability of alternative forms of irregular warfare— that is, guerrilla tactics and assassinations—attests to the falsity of this assertion.[29] Or, as Walzer put it more recently, following 9/11, "terrorism is a choice; it is a political strategy selected from among a range of options."[30]

Similarly, Habermas's distinction suggests that revolutionaries may resort to "paramilitary guerrilla warfare," which, unlike indiscriminant terrorism, is a proper course of action for a national liberation movement and is retrospectively legitimized with the formation of its state.[31] Paul Gilbert points out that, although "the militarily weaker side has little chance of obtaining victory by conventional military conflict, however justified its cause may be," still "there are several possible avenues open to it."[32] One such alternative is the use of guerrilla tactics, understood by Gilbert as well to be distinct from terrorism by virtue of its respect for the immunity of noncombatants. Freedom fighters have fastidious alternatives and are therefore unjustified in turning to terrorism under the pretenses of last-resort arguments.

Honderich's paradigmatic case, that of Palestinian terrorism against Israel, is particularly curious in this respect. Palestinians clearly have a variety of effective options. Aside from the occasional assassination, Palestinians regularly attack Israeli soldiers in operations that, despite Israeli rhetoric, are not, strictly speaking, terrorism, but rather guerrilla warfare to be judged on the merits of its political goals. There is no cause to believe that guerrilla tactics are less effective than terrorist strikes against civilians. In fact, guerrilla action bears the distinct advantage that it rarely warrants large-scale international condemnation, which often makes Palestinian terrorism appear counterproductive. In addition, quite apart from Walzer's, Gilbert's, and Habermas's alternative modes of nonconventional warfare, Palestinians have the option of falling back on internationally supervised peaceful negotiations. Indeed, in the wake of the Camp David meetings that emerged from the 1993 Oslo peace process, in which a fully functioning Palestinian state was offered, to continue to construe Palestinian terrorism against Israel as "liberation-terrorism" is rather peculiar. Berman well makes this point when he questions the logic of Palestinians rejecting U.S. president Bill Clinton's plan in favor of suicide attacks:

> Clinton and [Israeli prime minister Ehud] Barak had already offered a Palestinian state. Perhaps the purpose of the suicide attacks was to widen the borders of the proposed new state—though, in that case, Arafat might have haggled at Camp David for an extra slice or two, and the question of slightly wider borders would at least have been broached. Or maybe the purpose was to widen the proposed new borders by more than a slice, to obtain a Palestinian state on a different scale altogether. But the whole point of negotiating during the eight years of Israeli-Palestinian talks, beginning at Oslo, was to work out a compromise. Or maybe the purpose of the attacks was, as Hamas and Islamic Jihad forthrightly proclaimed, to abolish Israel altogether and establish the reign of Shariah in every corner of the land. But this was not within the realm of reality. Actually, none of the imaginable purposes had any chance of being realized, and especially not after 9/11. . . . Suicide terror against the Israelis was bound to succeed in one realm only, and this was the realm of death. [33]

In contrast, Honderich's example is telling. The sheer absurdity of celebrating Palestinian terror in the post-Clinton era as "terrorism to get freedom and power for a people when it is clear that nothing else will get it for them"[34] casts a dark shadow on his very notion of "liberation-terrorism," which the Palestinian illustration is intended to personify. Even if there were such a thing as "liberation-terrorism," which (unlike 9/11) could be justified as the *only* available realistic means of achieving an essential noble end, Palestinian terrorism is clearly not a case in point. An additional oddity in attempting to justify Palestinian terrorism on the grounds that it rightfully aims to "liberate" Palestinians from Israeli domination is the fact that Arab terrorism against Jews in Palestine began in the 1920s and was notoriously supported by the Nazis in the 1930s, long before

Jewish sovereignty was established over any of the land. The Palestine Liberation Organization (PLO) and Fatah, dedicated to the "liberation of Palestine" by terrorist means, were established in 1964 and 1965, respectively, several years before Israel won the "occupied territories" from Jordan in 1967.

Anyone contemplating "liberation-terrorism" also might find it interesting to consider the paradigmatic case of desperate liberation movements—such as the internal struggle against Nazism—in which nothing resembling Palestinian terror tactics was ever employed. As Israeli prime minister Benjamin Netanyahu likes to point out, "It is instructive to note, for example, that the French Resistance during World War II did not resort to systematic killing of German women and children, although these were well within reach in occupied France."[35] Some years earlier he had noted: "No resistance movement in Nazi-occupied Europe conducted or condoned terrorist attacks against German civilians, attacking military and government targets instead."[36]

Finally, as for the concerns of Honderich, Chomsky, Derrida, and others about the plight of developing nations and their populations, however miserable their lives or just their grievances, very little terror is actually emanating from sub-Saharan Africa. The attempt to tie terrorism to globalization, U.S. exploitation, and so forth is similarly problematic. Of course, these critiques of Western policies were formulated long before 9/11 by scholars such as Honderich, as well as by Chomsky, who is notorious for his criticism of the United States and its actions. Although those views are certainly respectable, one must wonder, as Walzer said of terror apologists immediately after 9/11, whether these critics now do not simply "see a chance to use Islamic terrorism as a kind of 'enforcer' for their own political agenda. They attribute their agenda to the terrorists (what else could terrorists have in mind but what Western Leftists have always advocated?)."[37]

Can terrorism ever be justified as essential to liberation? It has sometimes been argued that the type of state terror bombing carried out by Allied forces during World War II on cities such as Dresden and Hamburg, and later the atomic attacks on Hiroshima and Nagasaki, were justifiable last-resort terrorism of the essential liberating type. Certainly, many of the bombings meet the strict definition of terrorism, and as such many liberals remain unconvinced that they can be altogether justified. It is possible that in some rare instances in which no other form of military strategy would have been effective, arguments of overriding necessity could conceivably be invoked in their defense. But clearly this was not usually the situation in World War II, and in most instances the resort to terrorism was based on calculations of utility or on indifference to civilian life on the enemy side. Possibly some of the Allied terror bombings, while unjustifiable, may be retrospectively excusable, considering the uniquely diabolical nature of the enemy on the European front. But such hindsight would still not amount to a justification of terrorism of any kind, and I doubt any useful analogies can be drawn from it.[38]

TERROR AND LIBERALISM

Finally, to restate the obvious, terrorism, by definition, attacks the defenseless, the prohibition of which is perhaps the most basic rule of just war theory. This violation is not merely conventional, nor is it based solely on the utilitarian consideration to narrow the overall scope of suffering in war. Terrorism, as discussed in the previous section, defies a most basic standard of liberal-humanistic morality (at least since Immanuel Kant and up to John Rawls), which fundamentally forbids the use of human beings as means only and commands their treatment as ends in themselves.[39] Certainly, this imperative would categorically prohibit the arbitrary use, and intentional killing, of innocents as mere means toward attaining practical ends. Perhaps this logic is not purely Western. Berman cites the Islamist scholar Sayyid Qutb's understanding of the concept of jihad as containing a similar ethical dimension:

> He [Qutb] quoted Mohammed's successor, Abu Bakr, the first Caliph, who told his army "Do not kill any women, children or elderly people." Qutb quoted the Koran, which says: "Fight for the cause of God those who fight against you, but do not commit aggression. God does not love aggressors." Qutb thought that ethical commandments were crucial to military victory. Writing about Muhammad and his companions, he said, "These principles had to be strictly observed, even with those enemies who had persecuted them." Jihad did have its rules. It was fastidious.[40]

Be that as it may, among liberals there can be little dispute about the moral status of terrorism and terrorists. It is precisely the unequivocal Kantian "thou shalt not" invoked earlier, prohibiting the arbitrary use of rational beings, that requires Honderich to take great pains toward obscuring the distinction between terrorism and other forms of political violence that do not fall so clearly under this liberal commandment. It is not an incidental feature of his argument that it involves discrediting many of the distinctions that are basic to liberal philosophies, particularly Kantian-based ones.[41] Aside from downplaying the conventional distinction between killing belligerents versus innocent noncombatants, Honderich's disregard for the distinction between civilian casualties incurred in war and terrorist victims entails obscuring the relationship between intentions and consequences and the difference between deliberate action and unintentional effects. The extent of blame he attributes to the citizens of prosperous nations for the misfortunate lives of inhabitants of the developing world (with the implication that they had 9/11 coming to them) is largely pitted against the traditional moral distinctions between acts and omissions and between perfect and imperfect duties.[42] Rawls's version of liberalism, at least as it appears in *A Theory of Justice,* is reduced by Honderich to no more than "a philosophical celebration of America."[43]

In the end, Honderich's views on terrorism and its causes require him to do away with liberalism, from Kant to Rawls, almost entirely. Quite a high price to pay, one might think, for the defense of suicide bombers. Nevertheless, in this one respect Honderich's intuitions are quite correct: in the end, it must be either terrorism *or* liberalism. Honderich makes his choice, and ultimately everyone else must make theirs.

Once again, terrorism, properly distinguished and defined, is the intentional random murder of defenseless noncombatants, with the intent of instilling fear of mortal danger within a civilian population as a strategy designed to advance political ends. This understanding cannot be "deconstructed," nor can it be inclusively obscured. Terrorism is a particularly objectionable form of moral free riding because it relies inherently on the moral restraints of others, and it is a paradigmatic instance of the ruthless use of individuals as a mere means toward ends that they cannot conceivably share. Regardless of its professed cause, terrorism is diametrically opposed to the requirements of liberal morality and can be defended only at the expense of relinquishing the most basic of liberal commitments.

YES: Terrorism is a just tool of the weak.
Ted Honderich, *University College London*

Humanity, Terrorism in Palestine, Innocents

1. THE MORALITY OF HUMANITY

Plainly we are in our lives much concerned with right and wrong. The fact is not obscured by the extent to which our dim politicians and others talk a little vaguely and ambiguously of the *acceptable* and the *unacceptable*, and make use of other locutions. They proceed in this somewhat covert way, presumably, in order to try to conceal the uncertainty and vulnerability of judgments of right and wrong, theirs in particular, and to evade challenges to their judgments and themselves.[44]

In fact, to my mind, we are all yet more concerned with right and wrong than is shown by our overt and covert judgments. Right or wrong is not one option among several in thinking of what to do. Consider someone who gives as her reason for getting or keeping something that she is just "doing as everyone does," or that "everyone is selfish." Patently she is *justifying* her action, not opining about her society, not doing a little sociology or social psychology.

If we are to be confident about and persuasive in our judgments as to right and wrong, we need to be consistent and to show ourselves to be. In fact, to be inconsistent about something is to give and to have *no* reason for or against it. It is only by inconsistency that we actually fail to have reasons of right and wrong, but certainly we can do it. We do it a lot.

For consistency, we need a general principle of right and wrong. The principle, if it is to command respect and be useful, must be as literal, clear, specific, and therefore determinant as possible. Only then will it be resistant to self-interest and in particular to self-interest by way of self-deception.

One principle, the guiding principle of all or most of us in crucial circumstances where self-interest is not defeating our reason-giving natures, is the Principle of Humanity. Like *all* principles, despite an illusion to the contrary, it judges actions, policies, institutions, societies, and the like by the *consequences* of them. The principle is as follows:

> What is right is what, according to the best available information and judgment, is the rational means, which is to say the means that are effective and not self-defeating, to the end of getting and keeping people out of bad lives, with bad lives defined in terms of deprivation or frustration with respect to the great goods, the great desires of human nature—a decent length of conscious life, bodily or material well-being, freedom and power, respect and self-respect, the goods of relationship, and the goods of culture.[45]

It is, of course, a *maximizing* principle. It does not contemplate the monstrosity that there is nothing to choose between one and a thousand killings, torturings, or deaths by starvation or international sanctions because no individual suffers more than one of these. It is not the Principle of Utility or Greatest Happiness Principle, partly because it is particular and not abstract, partly because it prohibits exactly the victimization that the Principle of Utility sanctions.[46]

It is, of course, not the principle that the end justifies the means, if there is such a *principle,* since, as it states, the means must satisfy the requirement that what is done must not be likely to cause more distress than it prevents. Rather, it is a principle that the end *and* the means justify the means. It is a principle that does not make much difference between acts and omissions.[47] It is a principle that seeks to have the recommendation of decent philosophy, which is a concentration on ordinary logic.

It is clear and literal as against, say, Immanuel Kant's wholly uninstructive imperative that we are to treat each person never only as a means but also as an end. Can you treat someone in dire need as an end without giving the person real help? Who knows? The Principle of Humanity, more than any other moral principle, has foundations in our human nature. It has what truth the attitudes that are our moral principles and moral judgments can have.[48]

The most difficult part of judging right and wrong in many circumstances is the making of necessary judgments as to facts. It is often more difficult to judge these factual propositions than it was to establish a general moral principle in the first place. These propositions include some about the bad or good lives of people now, these being owed in part to their recent histories. They also include propositions as to the probability of the consequences of things, say of terrorism, and comparisons of alternative possible consequences, say of terrorism as opposed to peaceful negotiation.

The subject of this essay is Palestinian terrorism, a judgment in support of it, and objections to that judgment having to do with the killing of innocents.

We can begin with a summary of the circumstances of the Palestinians and the Israelis now, partly in terms of their histories in living memory. The summary is not only factual. It also contains my judgments of right or wrong entailed by the Principle of Humanity with respect to the founding of Israel and Palestinian terrorism.

2. PALESTINE AND ISRAEL, A SUMMARY

Jews lived in the society of another people, the Germans, and through their enterprise and other strengths succeeded in it. They were at least resented. Use was made of this. Millions were horribly killed. Their having a place of their own in compensation was a kind of necessity placed on us all. It was not seen as a possibility that they could have such a refuge formed out of a part of Germany, which indubitably ought to have happened.

Having no state of their own, the Palestinians could be taken to be less than a people, and thus not open to a certain great injury. In 1948 a homeland for the Jews was taken from the Palestinians with the agreement of the victors in the war against the Germans. This was four-fifths of the historic homeland of the Palestinians, the indigenous people. They had had nothing to do with the Holocaust. They were driven from their homes and otherwise violated in terms of the great human goods.

The defense of the new Jewish homeland within roughly the 1948 borders, the project of *Zionism* in a clear sense of the word, subsequently acquired the further justification that the lives of the Jewish people had become deeply rooted in a land.

In 1967 there began the project of *neo-Zionism*. This was the terrorism that took from the Palestinians at least their freedom in the last one-fifth of their historic homeland. It was resisted by them. Their terrorism and self-defense, the intifadas, gave evidence that in fact they *had* been a people in 1948. This is a further part of the fact that they have suffered a kind of Holocaust at the hands of descendants of people who suffered the first one.

The Palestinians have continued to resist the terrorism of neo-Zionism by the only means that has a possibility of success, their terrorism. They have resisted the vileness that is the ongoing ethnic cleansing of neo-Zionism. Their struggle is as much to be reverenced as are the existence and life of Israel within its 1948 borders.

Against the Palestinians has been not only neo-Zionism in Palestine but the superpower and kept-ignorant population that is the United States. Against them, as well, has been the existence of Semitism, a prejudice in favor of Jews in all things, owed in part to the greater prejudice of anti-Semitism. Despite this, the Palestinians have the possibility of achieving some goal of their terrorism. Their killing is not pointless. With respect to their goals, it is worth remembering the Jews who fought hopelessly to the death in the Warsaw ghetto. They fought for those who came after them.

Given these various propositions, beginning with those on Germany, the Palestinians have had and now have a moral right to their terrorism against the ethnic cleansing of neo-Zionism in all of historic Palestine, including Israel.[49]

3. REMARKS ON RIGHT AND WRONG, LIBERALISM, FREE RIDERS, SUMMARY

There are four lines of thought and feeling in Tamar Meisels's essay about which I shall only make brief remarks.

One line, not developed, is indicated by the use of quotation marks around the word *right* in her subheading "Is Terrorism Ever 'Right'?" Are the scare quotes an indication of some known and indeed common attitude to the effect that the question of Palestine is one of self-interest that is universal, or of legality, or of *realpolitik*, or of *facts*, or whatever? Something other than right or wrong? I don't know. Any such assumption, while tempting for many Israelis and others, could only pretend that the question is other than it is. It would also stand in flat contradiction with what follows in her essay—overt and covert moral condemnation of what has been done and is being done by Palestinians. We do not escape the question of right and wrong.

A second line of thought and feeling in her essay, certainly a main implication of it, is to the effect that we need to judge right and wrong in Palestine on the basis of the ideology or morality of liberalism.

Liberalism, in my view, is a congeries of stuff. It is about selected individual rights, self-serving liberties or freedoms, the state and a limited role for it, democracy, maybe the mixed economy, maybe the market, and more. Authoritative summaries disagree. At best, liberalism is some decency, some feeling for good lives and bad lives, but a decency and feeling not carried into clarity and resolution.[50]

The liberalism of John Stuart Mill, perhaps its founder, or John Rawls for that matter, certainly has no overwhelming or even great recommendation by way of its connection with our merely hierarchic democracy.[51] Liberalism is forgetful about much—for example, the truth that its talk of individual rights, say to bequeath property, has the effect of concealing the fact that equal or general or social rights, the rights of all, say to medical treatment, are no less the rights of precisely individuals.

Why is a better principle not produced by Meisels in order to help us, say, to make a choice between innocents? There are innocents killed on both sides in Palestine, of course. If you say that a principle will not make such things simple, that is readily agreed. But do you propose not to have any general and determinant means of being consistent, of satisfying that first requirement of argument and humanity? Will you judge only by your loyalties? If so, surely you rule yourself out of serious discussion.

That liberalism is indeed a congeries of stuff, by the way, is indicated by what is close to the *raison d'être* of Meisels's essay. That is the proposition that liberals are now unsure whether it is their commitment to support the Palestinians, because of what has been and is being done to them, or instead to condemn them because of their violence. Liberalism is not made clearer by the essay's implied declaration in the end that basically it is against all terrorism, presumably including terrorism thought to be somehow "legitimated" by the eventual formation of a state.

A third line in the essay is that the Palestinians are guilty of "free riding" in attacking and killing innocent people. That is to say they are not paying their way by limiting themselves, as it is supposed others do, and in particular their opponents, to attacks on non-innocents. Evidently the argument depends on what can be said in defense of or explanation of killing innocents in particular and awful circumstances.

There is a gulf between the case of something like a fair society where (1) people in general pay their way in various senses while (2) some others don't— that subject of liberal rumination—and the case of a conflict where (1) a vicious ethnicism is killing, depriving, and degrading a people, almost all of them innocents, indubitably the indigenous people of a land, and (2) some of them engage in "free riding" by fighting back in the only way they can. Who can really say seriously that the two cases are usefully judged by saying that the latter people in their self-defense against destruction are *not paying their way?* Shall we also judge what the Germans did in the Holocaust by saying they were *not paying their way?*

A fourth line in the Meisels essay is about the history of Palestine, partly the proposition that the Palestinians have in fact had an alternative to their terrorism, that it has not been and is not their last resort. In so doing, she questions my above summary of the history of Palestine.

The factual propositions in the summary, to my mind, are in several senses a true account, one that is widely agreed, certainly agreed by the so honorable and courageous Israelis who stand out to their cost against neo-Zionism and Semitism. It is possible to have confidence in the factual propositions in the summary despite also believing what was said earlier, that factual premises for conclusions of right and wrong are more difficult to establish than a general premise of right and wrong. Truth exists. Truth does not always or even often have two sides to it. There are real rapes.

One last general thought pertaining to my summary of Palestine has to do with any conflict between the rich and the poor, also the powerful and the weak, and a history of no success in peaceful negotiations between them. The rich and powerful side had so much more to give up. They could easily have made concessions. If they did not give anything up, they showed themselves to be at least self-concerned in a way that demonstrates the necessity of recourse by the poor and weak to means other than negotiation.

4. DEFINITIONS OF TERRORISM

Here is a definition of *terrorism* in general, the definition used by me and others in connection with the varieties of terrorism in historic Palestine: "Terrorism is (i) violence, (ii) smaller in scale than war, (iii) social and political in aim, (iv) illegal, and (v) *prima facie* wrong since it is indeed killing, maiming and destruction."[52]

The definition does not define *terrorism* as violence against innocent persons or the like. Nor does it define it as pursuing its aim by way of fear or terror caused by the killing, maiming, and destruction.[53]

The definition does, of course, include *state terrorism,* on account of the illegality of it and its also satisfying the four other requirements. It therefore covers Israeli state terrorism. It is worth noting that the definition goes with another one, of *terrorist war.* That is different from terrorism only in being larger in scale. Neo-Zionism unquestionably is and has been all of terrorism, state terrorism and terrorist war, again in terms of satisfying the requirements. You can argue neo-Zionism is *more* against international law, incidentally, especially in the form of United Nations resolutions, than is Palestinian terrorism.

Here is the different definition of terrorism offered by Meisels:

> terrorism . . . is the intentional random murder of defenseless noncombatants, with the intent of instilling fear of mortal danger within a civilian population as a strategy designed to advance political ends.

5. OBJECTIONS TO THE FIRST DEFINITION

Passages in the Meisels essay convey strong expressions of a familiar sort of objection to the first definition and others like it. For example, she says:

> There is a growing academic reluctance to define terrorism as a specific and fiendish deed. The considerable body of academic literature now available expresses sympathy, and at times outright justification, for Islamic (particularly Palestinian) terrorism.

A distinction is reported by Meisels between kinds of what is called irregular warfare. There are campaigns by guerrillas, whose primary targets are military personnel and not civilians. There are the actions and campaigns of political assassins, whose targets are political officials. There are, thirdly, those irregular fighters—terrorists in her definition—who target civilians.

Meisels argues that since my definition of terrorism makes no distinction between various forms of political violence, it somehow justifies or seeks to justify my proposition that the Palestinians have had a moral right to their terrorism—terrorism that kills Israeli civilians.

She says that "if terrorism is conceived so widely as to include all forms of political violence with no moral distinction between them, then that means 'we are all terrorists.' "

Ultimately relying on the Kantian "Thou shalt not" prohibiting the arbitrary use of rational beings, she reiterates what she speaks of as the necessity of including the intentional random murder of defenseless noncombatants in any proper definition of terrorism.

6. WHO ARE THESE INNOCENTS?

Any rigorous analysis of the subject of Palestinian terrorism against innocents calls out for more attention than it can have here—and could have in the Meisels essay. Still, two subjects can perhaps be treated more explicitly and fully here. They are of particular relevance to the essence of her objections above. One subject has to do with innocents, as they are usually called, and the other subject has to do with what it is to do something intentionally, in particular kill someone intentionally.

Is the first subject really *innocents?* Or is it *civilians?* Or *innocent civilians,* or *noncombatants,* or *innocent noncombatants,* or *citizens,* or *private citizens?* All are mentioned and run together by Meisels. This is careless, or useful in argument, or both.

Innocents are persons not guilty of a crime or offense, not responsible for an event yet suffering it, free from moral wrong. We can suppose an innocent in the present context is in some sense all of the three things. So innocents here are such in virtue of not doing or not having done something or certain things. That is why they call for special attention, which they get in all decent moralities, most certainly including the morality of humanity.

The good records of innocents, present and past, obviously may be lacked by civilians, noncombatants, citizens, and private citizens. Members of all four of these categories, for a start, can instigate killings. The conclusion must be that an objection to terrorism must have to do with innocents rather than civilians, noncombatants, citizens, and private citizens.

We still have a question. Who are these innocents? *What is it that they do not do?* They cannot possibly be understood simply to be persons who do not commit crimes or offenses according to an existing legal system. Someone who hid a Jewish child from the Nazis, against the law, was certainly not guilty in the sense now relevant to us, but innocent and better than that. It cannot conceivably be Israel's positive law, the law of the land, or any other such law that determines who are the innocents.

Nor are they to be understood as persons who do not kill or otherwise do violence to others. This understanding would for a start make all soldiers non-innocent, including Israeli soldiers.

Innocents, rather, are presumably persons who do not intentionally do other things, maybe kill under certain circumstances, or benefit from such killings. More generally, innocents do not act in or benefit from certain projects. What are the projects?

Needless to say, there is in the context of Palestine an answer that comes to many minds, and may be implied by Meisels herself, though she does not offer an explicit answer herself. She may be taken to imply that the innocents are persons not actively engaged in the Palestinian-Israeli conflict, more particularly Israelis not actively engaged in it. Innocents are people not themselves killing or wounding Palestinians. It is indicative that in her essay she regularly mentions noncombatants, and in fact it is noncombatants who are specified as the victims in her definition of terrorism quoted earlier.

But it will not conceivably do to understand innocents as just noncombatants. As any tolerable morality or law asserts, those who instigate killers, pay for them, defend them, profit from them, and so on are not innocents. I am not innocent if I choose to benefit from killings of Palestinians in the neo-Zionist cause. For a start, I thereby contribute to the probability or certainty of more killings by the movement on which my benefits continue to depend. I can be counted on not to condemn it.

The short answer in the present context to the question of who the innocents are, what it is that they do not do, must be along certain lines. The innocents are those who do not intentionally somehow take forward the project of neo-Zionism or choose to benefit from it when they could do otherwise.

I readily allow that there is much more to be said of innocents generally and of kinds of them.[54] Still, in sum, it is evident that there are greatly fewer such innocents than is ordinarily supposed, and is supposed by Meisels. Some are not very innocent.

It is my own present inclination, by the way, to take the innocents as not including people who refrain from absolutely and explicitly condemning neo-Zionism. Some of these speak of *understanding* neo-Zionism. Some take the problem of Palestine to be complicated or the claims of both sides to be controversial. But what is right is simple—that Israel, without condition, qualification, negotiation, delay, or any other such thing withdraws from and accords to the Palestinians their freedom in the last one-fifth of their homeland and otherwise recompenses them fully.[55]

7. INTENTIONAL ACTION

What is it intentionally to do something? The question arises not only in connection with our present discussion about innocents killed by terrorism, but also in another connection of importance having to do with war and the like.

A man's wife leaves him. He goes to the apartment he knows she is in, with glue for the door lock and gasoline. As he gets there, he sees someone else go in, a cleaning woman. He sticks to his plan. The two women might have got out of the burning apartment somehow, but they don't. In court he pleads guilty to only one murder, on the ground that he did not intend to kill the cleaning woman. The judge disdains his argument and convicts him of two murders. The husband sends a note of condolence and excuse to the family of the cleaning woman. They loathe him for it.

Can he change the mind of an appeal court or change the feelings of the family by establishing that he did not intend the killing of the cleaning woman since in a sense he *wanted* only to kill his wife? No, he cannot.

Can he change the mind of the appeal court, more particularly, by establishing that *if* he had had the option of killing only his wife, maybe at that time, without killing anyone else, he *would* have taken that option? No, he cannot. He cannot begin to establish to the satisfaction of judges and family that he did not intentionally kill both women in the only relevant sense. It does not matter much that if he could have killed only his wife, he would have.

Can he change the minds of the judges and family by convincing them that when he poured in the gasoline and threw in the matches he was then *thinking* only of his wife, that he had only her on his mind and in his feelings? No, he cannot.

Can he do so by saying in some vague sense that he was *targeting* only his wife—maybe a sense related to the one in which it is said an American soldier firing a rocket has one person in the crosshairs of the telescopic aiming device and not the person he sees or knows to be a yard away who is also about to be killed? No, the husband cannot save himself this way, any more than the American soldier.

Can the husband change the mind of the appeal court by convincing the judges that he had natural justice or religion on his side with respect to his wife, that he was taken up with that *personal conviction?* No, he cannot.

Can he change their minds by producing a philosopher's analysis of what it is to intend something—say an analysis beginning from the proposition that an intention is a predictive belief about a future event based in a certain way on an instrumental or causal belief and a want?[56] No, he certainly cannot.

The example of the husband is as good as any other in reminding us that what it is to intentionally do something in the relevant sense is *to act with the foreknowledge or reasonable belief that a thing will be the probable or certain consequence of the action.* No other idea carries any significant weight with respect to intention in any decent court or in the human life that is codified by decent law.[57]

No other doctrine will begin to persuade the Israeli mother of a dead child that the Palestine suicide bomber who saw the child near the Israeli border guard did not intentionally bring about the death of the child.

The subject of the intentional killing of innocents is therefore the subject of actions known to carry at least the probability of deaths of innocents. It is not any other subject. Meisels offers no alternative. In my view she cannot.

8. OBJECTIONS HAVING TO DO WITH DEFINITIONS

Meisels objects, as noted earlier, that I and others take up a definition of terrorism that covers three kinds of irregular warfare, and that this has the effect of somehow excusing or reducing the culpability of one of them by associating it with the other two. That is, the objectionable general definition of terrorism covers guerrilla war, and political assassination, and intentionally killing the innocent. The third of these, intentionally killing the innocent, by inclusion in the single general subject matter, is in effect excused or made less culpable by the inclusion of the first and second. They are less condemnable—despite the fact that guerrillas and political assassins only *for the most part* do not kill or endanger innocents.

Is the gravamen of the objections by Meisels that a certain factual mistake was made by many of us, including the U.S. Army, in defining terrorism without specifying that it is intentional killing of the innocent? That is, is the gravamen of the objections that a definition is chosen that goes against the ordinary use of the term, whatever does or does not follow from that supposed mistake? That a definition is chosen that goes against dictionaries, whatever does or does not follow from that? Well, the best dictionary I know, *The New Oxford Dictionary of English,* defines *terrorism* as "the use of violence and intimidation in the pursuit of political ends."

Also, Meisels is not fully convincing in facing an embarrassment. In the course of her argument or implication that her definition is true to usage and dictionaries, she finds herself allowing that one author with whom she is in sympathy differs from another in that he uses the term *terrorism* to *include* political assassination, which purportedly does not much involve killing innocents. He is not alone. So too do her own countrymen and women include political assassination in terrorism. As she reports, if judgmentally:

> Israel's frequent reference to this assassination of Minister Zeevi as "terrorism" is an unfortunate example of inaccurate political speech.

There can be little doubt that contemporary English usage, whether or not it is inaccurate political speech, does not regard terrorism as necessarily consisting only in the killing or attacking of innocents.

But I leave this matter of usage, which is of much less importance than others. Survey dictionaries to get a better answer if you want. Hire a lexicographer. The result, as I say, for reasons to be given in a moment in connection with any definition, will be unimportant.

Consider the fact of stipulation, that different definitions of terrorism, whatever their relation to usage, are to an extent stipulated or chosen. This is indeed the case with the two definitions we are contemplating, the first not mentioning the killing of innocents and the second doing so.

Meisels would agree, I am sure, that she does not intend something that is incredible in her objections about a definition. It is that those who use the

first definition of terrorism take themselves thereby to be able to do something like *deduce* that some terrorism is justifiable. Or, maybe slightly less
incredibly, they suppose their use of the first definition somehow *logically or
conceptually* removes an objection to terrorism as they define it—the objection that it includes killing the innocent. It might be contemplated that they
suppose this because they take a definition to specify *all* the properties of a
thing, every last one.

This is easily dealt with. My definition of an automobile does not include
every fact about one. More importantly, that my definition does not include the
fact that it can be used for murder does not remove part of my objection to
murder by automobile. Nor, patently, does a definition of terrorism that leaves
out the intentional killing of innocents remove anything at all of the objection
to terrorism that it includes intentional killing of innocents.

I note that despite having taken up a definition of terrorism that does not
mention killing the innocent, I have considered the objection that some terrorism is wrong, and more particularly that some Palestinian terrorism is wrong,
because it is the killing of innocents.[58] The largest thing of immediate relevance
to it, of course, is the circumstance that the killing of innocents seeks to change.

It may also be worth noting that there is no possibility whatever of Meisels
getting straight from her definition of terrorism to the conclusion that terrorism
is wrong. Let us assume that her including "intentional random murder" in her
definition does not go so far as condemning all terrorism as wrong—say including the terrorism that was a part of the founding of the state of Israel in 1948. So
there can be no logical step from the definition to any condemnation.

The general fact of this whole matter of definitions is that *any* definition of
terrorism, at least any not useless and inane in argument, logically or conceptually allows for *any* judgment for or against what is singled out by the definition.

9. INQUIRY, PREJUDICE, ADVOCACY

Inquiry, that which is found in university lectures, good books and articles, and
some exceptional journalism, directly relates to our discussion of definitions.
Inquiry is not to be confused with *prejudiced contention* or just *prejudice.*[59]

With respect to inquiry, it is possible to believe, indeed to know, that definitions do not matter. So I believed in the past. They make no substantial difference, even no significant difference, with respect to the conclusions drawn. In
particular, definitions do not matter in inquiry about terrorism, *thinking* about
terrorism. Certainly definitions can be inconvenient or otherwise, get in the
way of proceedings, give rise to confusion, and so on, but, as you know, they
do not determine outcomes.

Meisels's objections and also objections by Georg Meggle[60] have led me to a kind of change of mind. More particularly, their insistence on definitions that include killing of the innocent, however well supported their insistence, has led to this change of mind. It is also owed to my including Meisels, and certainly Meggle, in the class of inquirers.

The change of mind is not to the cynical proposition that there is no inquiry, that it does not exist, but to the proposition that there is a kind of inquiry that is not so pure as the rest of it. There is something other than *pure inquiry* in addition to prejudiced contention. It is what can be called *advocacy*.

It goes beyond reliance on logic as a means to factual truth and also the kind of truth or justification we can aspire to with respect to right and wrong. Advocacy aims to *influence*, notably by means of *persuasive definitions*.[61] Advocacy, which lies on a spectrum including pure inquiry, has the aim of getting a certain agreement of others with respect to right and wrong.

Evidently philosophers and others are sometimes engaged in advocacy. I have been engaged in it in the past, and am now. This essay is advocacy.

In this new realism, I am *more* content to persist in the definition of terrorism that does *not* include the killing of innocents. It would be contrary to my aim in my advocacy to do otherwise, an aim that has the distinction of having been made clear. To take up the definition that includes talk of innocents could have some effect in persuading you away from what I take to be an entailment of the Principle of Humanity having to do with justification of Palestinian terrorism. It could make you less ready to agree.

But since this is advocacy in which I am engaged, not prejudiced contention, I am also ready to give reasons in defense of my definition. As you may expect, and have heard already, they have to do with innocents and not-so-innocents, intentional killing, war, and also what is distinguished as guerrilla war and political assassination.

War intentionally kills innocents on an immeasurably greater scale than terrorism. In war, the deaths of innocents, often in very great numbers, are foreseeable probabilities. In our own lifetimes we needed only World War II as confirmation, but we have also had the American and British terrorist war on Iraq.

To come exactly to the point, the definition of terrorism in terms of killing innocents is motivated by and depends for its effect precisely on an explicit or inexplicit comparison with war and like things. The definition lives and breathes in that comparison. *It is a false comparison.* Terrorism is no worse than war in the given respect.

Given this consideration of war alone—forget about irregular warfare— there is full reason to persist in exactly the definition of terrorism that does not mention killing innocents. This is not the reason, of course, that this definition is at least as true to ordinary usage and dictionaries as the other one. It is that this definition serves the necessary and great purpose of advocacy of the morality of humanity.

You will recall that an additional item in the Meisels definition of terrorism is that it is what instills fear of mortal danger in a civilian population. I shall also persist in the definition not mentioning fear. The reason, you will know, is the same as with the killing of innocents. War does more to cause fear than terrorism ever did. The contrast is false, and against what it is right to do.

One final comment. If you were to persuade me to add the item about killing innocents to my definition, I would not add it alone. I would add other items. They would be as true to facts and would be no more questionable as items of advocacy or persuasion than mention of the killing of innocents.

One such addition, of course, would be to the effect that terrorism, in intentionally killing innocents, is not thereby different from war. A second addition would be that some terrorism, much of what the newspapers and politicians call terrorism, is a response to ethnic cleansing or another great violation of a people. A third addition would be that the terrorism that kills innocents and has the support of the Principle of Humanity is directed to the saving of other innocents as we ordinarily speak of them, more of them, and also innumerable other victims.[62]

OTHER INNOCENTS

Finally, let me bring together in a certain way the principal facts that must be the reality of any attempt to justify Palestinian terrorism.[63] They were touched on earlier, first in the summary of the circumstances of the Palestinians and the Israelis, then in connection with liberalism, and also a moment ago, but they can do with more explicit expression.

There is a necessary distinction to be made. It is between the innocents or innocent victims we have mainly had in mind so far and other innocent victims.

The innocent victims we have mainly had in mind are individuals killed or directly harmed by an explosion, a shooting, or another piece of violence. More particularly, we have been thinking about Israelis killed or directly harmed by Palestinian terrorism, Israelis not themselves advancing or intentionally benefiting from neo-Zionism.

There is also the category of their counterparts among the Palestinians— the innocent Palestinians killed or directly harmed by Israeli terrorism, including state terrorism, and also Israeli terrorist war. They are innocent in the sense that they are not themselves somehow engaged in resistance to neo-Zionism and not gaining from this resistance. There are more of these

Palestinian victims than Israeli victims, three or four times as many. This fact is important in several ways, but it is not the most important fact.

There is a category of innocents far larger than these two. It consists in Palestinian victims of neo-Zionism who have *not* been killed or been directly harmed by a piece of violence. They have not been shot by an Israeli soldier or settler. Rather, they have lost their lives or been indirectly harmed as a result of earlier events with general effects. They are victims of earlier neo-Zionist decisions to carry forward the ethnic cleansing of the last one-fifth of Palestine. They include victims whose lives have been degraded by the effective threat carried by earlier neo-Zionist killings and other actions. Some live in refugee camps. Some die for want of medical supplies stopped in neo-Zionist blockades.

These victims are exactly and absolutely as innocent as those we have had in mind up until this point. They are not engaged in resistance to neo-Zionism or gaining from this resistance. It is true that we do not immediately *call* them *innocent* victims. Maybe we do not *ordinarily* call them innocent victims. This is because of the absence of a particular piece of violence against an individual, or a few individuals, or because there is not a non-innocent victim on hand. This fact of language is nothing whatever to the point. They *are* innocent victims. A habit of the English language and maybe other languages does not even touch this fact.

The justification of Palestinian self-defense, their moral right to it, is most importantly this fact of these Palestinian innocent victims in their great numbers. The Palestinian people since 1967, to go back only that far, have been violated—they have been deprived by neo-Zionism of every great human good. All the Palestinians have been deprived of some or all of decent lengths of conscious life, bodily or material well-being, freedom and power, respect and self-respect, the goods of relationship, and the goods of culture. Means to these great goods have been transferred to Israelis since 1967.

It is a recommendation of the Principle of Humanity that it is explicit in what is allowed by almost every human moral or political doctrine or project, certainly Zionism and neo-Zionism. That is that the killing of innocents can be forced upon us. The morality of humanity is more concerned with innocents, so named or not, than any of the large alternatives to it.[64]

Notes

1. For a detailed discussion of definitions of terrorism, see Bruce Hoffman, *Inside Terrorism*, rev. and exp. ed. (New York: Columbia University Press, 2006), 1–41.
2. For a discussion of states as terrorists, see, for example, Noam Chomsky, "International Terrorism: Image and Reality," in *Western State Terrorism*, ed. Alexander George (New York: Cambridge University Press, 1991), 12–38.

3. Ted Honderich, *After the Terror* (Edinburgh: Edinburgh University Press, 2002).
4. Ibid., 98–99.
5. Ibid., 103. Noam Chomsky repeatedly makes similar points concerning the inconsistent and self-serving use of the term *terrorism* on the part of the United States, which he regards as a terrorist state. See, for example, Noam Chomsky, *9-11* (New York: Seven Stories Press, 2001), esp. 23, 40–54, 57, 73–74, 90–91.
6. Honderich, *After the Terror*, 97–99. Note, in contrast, the overall thesis of Paul Berman, *Terror and Liberalism* (New York and London: Norton, 2003), which involves the suggestion that real-world political or social change is not always the object of political violence.
7. Honderich, *After the Terror*, 99.
8. Ibid., 151.
9. In addition to *After the Terror*, see Ted Honderich, *Terrorism for Humanity—Inquiries in Political Philosophy* (London and Sterling, Va.: Pluto Press, 1989, 2003).
10. Honderich, *After the Terror*, 115.
11. Chomsky, *9-11*, 23, 40, 76, 84.
12. Jacques Derrida attempts to "deconstruct" the concept of terrorism in Giovanna Borradori, *Philosophy in a Time of Terror—Dialogues with Jürgen Habermas and Jacques Derrida* (Chicago and London: University of Chicago Press, 2003), 102–107, 152. Derrida died in 2004.
13. Ibid., 103 (emphasis added).
14. Honderich, *After the Terror*, 73–88, 97–99, 103.
15. Derrida in Borradori, *Philosophy in a Time of Terror*, 108.
16. Michael Walzer, *Just and Unjust Wars* (New York: Basic Books, 1977).
17. Ibid., 180. For a similar characterization of guerrilla warfare as opposed to terrorism, see Paul Gilbert, *New Terror, New Wars* (Edinburgh: Edinburgh University Press, 2003), 96–97.
18. Borradori, *Philosophy in a Time of Terror*, 56.
19. Habermas in Borradori, *Philosophy in a Time of Terror*, 33.
20. Walzer, *Just and Unjust Wars*, 198.
21. As Paul Gilbert puts it: "Assassination is, however, far from the worst offence against the prohibition on attacking civilians that we witness in new wars." Gilbert, *New Terror, New Wars*, 94.
22. Berman, *Terror and Liberalism*, 33–34.
23. Walzer, *Just and Unjust Wars*, 203.
24. Berman, *Terror and Liberalism*, 34.
25. Robert A. Pape, "The Strategic Logic of Suicide Terrorism," *American Political Science Review* 97 (August 2003): 350. See also 347–349.
26. Ibid., 350.
27. Immanuel Kant, *Groundwork of the Metaphysic of Morals*, trans. and analyzed by H. J. Paton (New York: Harper and Row, 1964), 88.
28. Honderich, *After the Terror*, 151.
29. Walzer, *Just and Unjust Wars*, 204.
30. Michael Walzer, "Five Questions about Terrorism," *Dissent* 49 (Winter 2002).
31. Habermas in Borradori, *Philosophy in a Time of Terror*, 56.
32. Gilbert, *New Terror, New Wars*, 97.
33. Berman, *Terror and Liberalism*, 132–133.

34. Honderich, *After the Terror*, 151.
35. Benjamin Netanyahu, *Fighting Terrorism* (New York: Farrar, Straus and Giroux, 2001), 9.
36. Benjamin Netanyahu, ed., *Terrorism—How the West Can Win* (New York: Farrar, Straus and Giroux, 1986), 204.
37. Walzer, "Five Questions about Terrorism."
38. For an illuminating discussion of the World War II terror bombings, see Walzer, *Just and Unjust Wars*, 109–106, 255–268.
39. See Kant, *Groundwork of the Metaphysic of Morals*, 96; and John Rawls, *A Theory of Justice*, 9th ed. (London: Oxford University Press, 1989), chap. 3, sec. 29, 179.
40. Berman, *Terror and Liberalism*, 98.
41. See, in particular, his section on liberalism in *After the Terror*, 46–50.
42. Honderich, *After the Terror*, esp. 73 88, 97–99, 103. Many of these classic distinctions are also called into question in connection with terrorism by Jacques Derrida in Borradori, *Philosophy in a Time of Terror*; see, for example, p. 108.
43. Honderich, *After the Terror*, 70.
44. I thank my wife, Ingrid Coggin Honderich, for her thoughtful and troubling objections to a draft of this essay. We remain in disagreement about the proposition that the Palestinians have a moral right to their terrorism.
45. Ted Honderich, *On Political Means and Social Ends* (Edinburgh: Edinburgh University Press, 2003), 103, 112–132; Ted Honderich, *Right and Wrong, and Palestine, 9/11, Iraq, 7/7 . . .* (New York: Seven Stories Press, 2006), 61.
46. Ted Honderich, "The Principle of Humanity and the Principle of Utility," in *Consciousness, Reality and Value: Essays in Honour of T. L. S. Sprigge*, ed. Pierfransesco Basile and Leemon B. McHenry (Frankfurt: Ontos Verlag, 2007).
47. Ted Honderich, *After the Terror*, 2nd ed. (Edinburgh: Edinburgh University Press, 2003), 73–88.
48. Honderich, *On Political Means*, 1–57; Honderich, *Right and Wrong*, 58–83.
49. For some recent writings on these matters, related but not the same in inclination, see Noam Chomsky, *Fateful Triangle: The United States, Israel and the Palestinians* (London: Pluto Press, 1999); Noam Chomsky, "Simple Truths, Hard Problems: Some Thoughts on Terror, Justice and Self-Defence," *Philosophy* 80 (2005): 5–28; Ghada Karmi, *In Search of Fatima: A Palestinian Story* (London: Verso, 2002); Karma Nabulsi, "Being Palestinian," www.ucl.ac.uk/~uctytho/Being_Palestinian. html; Ilan Pappe, *A History of Modern Palestine: One Land, Two Peoples* (Oxford, UK: Oxford University Press, 2004); Igor Primoratz, ed., *Terrorism: The Philosophical Issues* (Basingstoke, UK: Palgrave Macmillan, 2004); and essays by Noam Chomsky, Tomis Kapitan, G. A. Cohen, Ardon Lyon, William McBride, Tamar Meisels, Michael Neumann, and Timothy Shanahan in *Israel, Palestine and Terror*, ed. Stephen Law (London: Continuum, 2008). Many of the essays in this book comment on my opening essay, "Terrorisms in Palestine."
50. Honderich, *Right and Wrong*, 35–38.
51. Ibid., 38–58; Honderich, *After the Terror* (2003), 105–115; Honderich, *On Political Means*, 135–154.
52. Honderich, *After the Terror* (2003), 97–100; Honderich, *Right and Wrong*, 86–92.
53. Compare the good consideration of definitions of terrorism in C. A. J. Coady, "Defining Terrorism," in Primoratz, *Terrorism*.

54. For a more detailed discussion, see Honderich, *After the Terror* (2003), esp. 158–162.
55. Michael Neumann, "Terror and Expected Collateral Damage: The Case for Moral Equivalence," in Law, *Israel, Palestine and Terror*. G. A. Cohen and I are not in full agreement about Palestine and Israel. I do not mean to conscript him to a cause, but do recommend his "Casting the First Stone: Who Can, and Who Can't?" in Law, *Israel, Palestine and Terror*.
56. Ted Honderich, *Mind and Brain* (Oxford: Oxford University Press, 1990), 216–231.
57. Honderich, *Right and Wrong*, 155–159.
58. Ibid., 111–115, 155–159; Honderich, *After the Terror* (2003), 158–162.
59. *Inquiry* is informed and restrained by ordinary logic, which consists in the large contribution toward truth that consists in clarity, consistency and validity, and completeness. The truth being served by this logic is not only factual truth but also whatever truth or justification we can aspire to with respect to right and wrong. In contrast, the aim of *prejudiced contention*, the sort of thing that happens in the politics of our democracies, in most of their media, in second-rate books and articles, on so much of the Internet, paradigmatically in what was to me the moral stupidity of Bush and Blair, and so on, is not truth but something else. Its relation to truth is at best the relation of *selling* to truth. Ted Honderich, *Conservatism: Burke, Nozick, Bush, Blair?* (London: Pluto Press, 2005).
60. Georg Meggle, "What Is Terrorism?" in *Terrorism: Moral, Legal, and Political Issues, Filozofski Godisnjak* (edited by Jovan Babic) 19 (2006) : 11–24; Georg Meggle, "Terror and Counter-Terror: Initial Ethical Reflections," *Deutsche Zeitschrift fur Philosophie* 50 (2002): 149–162.
61. C. L. Stevenson, *Ethics and Language* (New Haven, Conn.: Yale University Press, 1944).
62. Honderich, *After the Terror* (2003), 1–29; Honderich, *Right and Wrong*, 94–105.
63. For greater discussions of the main parts of that advocacy, see Honderich, *After the Terror* (2003), 24–29, 155–186, 184; Honderich, *Right and Wrong*, 94–125; and Honderich, "Terrorisms in Palestine," in Law, *Israel, Palestine and Terror*.
64. Tamar Meisels is to be commended and has my admiration for not joining those who confuse or choose to confuse condemnation of neo-Zionism with anti-Semitism. She does not in this way give in to the prejudice of Semitism or too much defer to it. This just compliment to a philosopher is given more force by a comparison that perhaps understandably sticks in my mind in connection with my book she criticizes, *After the Terror*. When it was translated into German by the publisher Suhrkamp, having been recommended for translation by Jürgen Habermas, and known to have been recommended by him, he wrote a newspaper article on the charge of anti-Semitism against the book (www.ucl.ac.uk/~uctytho/BrumlikHabermastrans.html). Habermas, to his credit, affirmed the book was not anti-Semitic. But he did so in such an apologetic style, and with such additions, as to qualify his judgment and to be little defense of the book. Suhrkamp's decision the next day to "ban" the book as anti-Semitic was no surprise. The second German publisher of the book, Abraham Melzer, Jewish himself, was closer to truth and humanity.

does islam play a unique role in modern religious terrorism?

YES: Islam has a unique impact on modern terrorism.
Andrew C. McCarthy, *National Review Institute*

NO: Islam itself is not the problem in the current wave of global terrorism.
Fawaz A. Gerges, *London School of Economics*

Although terrorism in the name of religion has been around for millennia and had been growing as a phenomenon in recent decades, on September 11, 2001, religious terrorism exploded onto the world scene as never before.[1] Al-Qaeda, the group responsible for the 9/11 attacks, claimed to be acting on behalf of Islam, as guided by God. Shortly after the attacks, al-Qaeda leader Osama bin Laden said he had not expected the World Trade Center's twin towers to fully collapse, and credited God's will for the extra death and destruction.[2]

Despite the clear religious motives behind the attacks, President George W. Bush sought to quickly dispel any connections among the 9/11 terrorists, God, and the religion the attackers claimed to represent. In an address before a joint session of Congress on September 20, 2001, he said, "[Islam's] teachings are good and peaceful, and those who commit evil in the name of Allah blaspheme the name of Allah. The terrorists are traitors to their own faith. . . . We are not deceived by their pretenses to piety."[3] Bush later remarked, "All Americans must recognize that the face of terror is not the true face of Islam. Islam is a faith that brings comfort to a billion people around the world. . . . It's a faith based upon love, not hate."[4]

Seeking to downplay the religious component of the 9/11 attacks and the role of Islam in the al-Qaeda movement was certainly understandable, and accurate. After all, the vast majority of Muslims in America and around the world were outraged by the attacks, and even more so by claims that they were committed on their behalf.

Yet understanding the central role of religion—particularly militant branches of Islam—for al-Qaeda, its affiliated organizations, and their millions of supporters and sympathizers around the world is vital in order to diagnose correctly the current threat and fashion proper responses.[5] And, in the broader context of the history and evolution of terrorism, it will help explain how and why religion has come to play such an important role in modern terrorism.

The fact is that thirty-five years ago there were virtually no identifiable terrorist organizations motivated primarily by religion. Today, however, most of the world's active terrorist groups are religion-based, the vast majority of which are Islamist.[6]

What accounts for the tremendous upsurge in religious, predominantly Islamic, terrorism in recent decades? Geostrategic contributors include the 1979 Islamic revolution in Iran, which showed the power of religion to achieve major political goals; the 1979 Soviet invasion of Afghanistan, which gave the impression of Islam under attack; decades of self-serving American and Western policies in the Middle East; and general social and economic malaise in Muslim countries.

But what about the role of Islam itself? Since 9/11, a passionate debate has raged over the nature and depth of spiritual support for al-Qaeda and other violent Islamist movements. Is the world in the midst of a modern-day global religious war—an existential clash between Muslim and Western belief systems that the recent uprisings associated with the Arab Spring will only exacerbate? Or is Islamic terrorism merely an outgrowth of resentment felt across the Muslim world toward Western policies, corrupt governance, and economic backwardness—grievances that the Arab awakenings may well help ameliorate?

Andrew McCarthy says the answers lie within the religion of Islam. He argues that there are features unique to Islam that explain not just the current global outbreak of terrorism, but also its particularly vicious variety—filled with images of beheadings, suicide bombings, and mass-casualty attacks. He makes the case that the spiritual importance of violent jihad and martyrdom for tens of millions of adherents of militant Islam are not well understood by the West—or are conveniently papered over. And he says that this violent movement has been growing in strength for centuries; it is not simply an outgrowth of recent policies, and indeed the Arab Spring will only accelerate the spread of Islamism. The threat, McCarthy concludes, will cease only if the worldwide Muslim community redirects itself toward moderation and tolerance.

According to Fawaz Gerges, such moderation and tolerance already predominate in the Muslim worldview; most Muslims admire Western values and wish to coexist peacefully with the West. He says that Muslims (religious or otherwise) detest Americans and Westerners not for "who they are" but rather for "what they do"—their specific policies, which always seem to place their interests first and the interests of Muslims last. And the world is not in the midst of an existential religious war: only a tiny fraction of Muslims condone or engage in violence. He concludes that if the West would endeavor to better understand the Muslim world and craft more thoughtful policies—as Westerners have the opportunity to do in the wake of the Arab Spring—support for militant movements would quickly dry up.

Islam is certainly not the only religion of late to witness heinous acts of violence committed on its behalf—the 1995 Oklahoma City bombing, for example, was perpetrated by individuals inspired by America's Christian militia movement. However, the ubiquity and tremendous global reach of militant Islamist movements have come to define the terrorism threat of the modern era, and such movements present the most daunting global challenge for the West since the Cold War. Grasping the specific roles played by Islamic radicalism, on the one hand, and other sociopolitical factors, on the other, can only help better inform the policy choices of Western governments, and other governments around the world.

YES: Islam has a unique impact on modern terrorism.
Andrew C. McCarthy, *National Review Institute*

Islam's Unique Impact on Modern Religious Terrorism

Wasn't the "jihad" he was clamoring for just a spiritual camouflage for *terrorism*?[7] Omar Abdel Rahman, more notoriously known as the "Blind Sheikh," the man who would inspire the 1981 murder of Egyptian president Anwar Sadat, the 1993 World Trade Center bombing, and the atrocities of September 11, 2001, did not mince words:

> What kind of name is this? Why are we afraid of it? Why do we fear the word *terrorist*? If the terrorist is the person who defends his right, so we are terrorists. And if the terrorist is the one who struggles for the sake of God, then we are terrorists. We . . . have been ordered with terrorism because we must prepare what power we can to terrorize the enemy of Allah and your enemy. The Qur'an [said] "to strike terror." Therefore, we don't fear to be described with "terrorism." . . . They may say, "He is a terrorist, he uses violence, he uses force." Let them say that. We are ordered to prepare whatever we can of power to terrorize the enemies of Islam.

Omar Abdel Rahman was indeed proud to be a terrorist. He was relentless in the cause of annealing his large international following to this purpose. It was a cause he traced to a centuries-old summons to revive the "true Islam" of its founders. It was also the cause of a lifetime, ever since he'd lost his sight to juvenile diabetes in 1942 at the age of four. Reared in the tiny Nile Delta town of al-Gamalia, the sickly boy memorized the Qur'an and became a stellar academic, earning renown as a scholar who had graduated from Cairo's venerable al-Azhar University, where he earned a doctorate, with distinction, in Qur'anic studies.

Now serving a sentence of life imprisonment after his conviction for sundry terrorism crimes, Abdel Rahman is old and infirm. Because of his various maladies, he has never been known to help build or plant a bomb, to hijack an airplane, or even to fire a gun. He is no grand military tactician or even capable of plotting out (as opposed to authorizing) the activities of an urban guerrilla cell. And yet he has been a colossus in the world of international terrorism for three decades. Indeed, one attorney has been convicted for helping him continue to run his Egyptian jihadist organization, al-Gama'at al-Islamiyya, from his American jail cell. Osama bin Laden, the late leader of al-Qaeda, publicly credited him with having issued from that cell the fatwa (or religious edict) that authorized the 9/11 attacks. And in his first public speech after being elected president of Egypt in June 2012, the Muslim Brotherhood's Mohamed Morsi vowed to pressure Barack Obama's White House to release and repatriate Abdel Rahman—a top demand of Egyptian Islamists ever since his arrest in 1993. All of this stems solely from his undeniable status as a globally recognized authority on Islamic jurisprudence.

In the modern world, the common denominator of the most savage terrorism is an amalgam of fundamentalist Islamic ideologies (cutting across the Sunni/Shiite divide) assigned the Panglossian label of "radical Islam." Both doctrinally and popularly, it is much less aberrational than the term *radical* suggests. And in that framework, the catalyzing power of doctrine is such that a man who would otherwise be of utterly no use to a terrorist organization is a driving force of global terrorism. Which is to say: after all that has occurred in the last thirty-plus years, to have to ask whether Islam has a unique impact on modern terrorism is something like asking whether the sky is really blue. The question can be answered, but its very asking highlights the extent to which self-delusion prevails in a world where the fear of giving offense has become more dire than the fear of being rendered defenseless.

VANGUARD OF MODERN JIHAD

Trailing only Morocco's al-Karaouine among the world's oldest institutions of higher learning, al-Azhar University is the seat of the Sunni tradition vastly predominant among the world's 1.4 billion Muslims. In terms of influence, al-Azhar's grand imam is about as close a cognate as Islam has to the Roman Catholic papacy. The analogy, though, is far from perfect. Islam is bereft of a regimented clerical hierarchy, councils, or synods to provide standards of orthodoxy.[8] This omission, indeed, is the central challenge confronting Islamic moderates—that is, the hundreds of millions of Muslims who reject terrorism as barbaric and regard as libelous the perpetrators of terror who rely on Islam to justify themselves. Muslim terrorists *do* rely on scripture and Muhammadan tradition—scripture and tradition that they do not need to twist or pervert in order to serve the purpose. For argument's sake, suppose the moderates are right: jihadists like the Blind Sheikh are betraying the core principles of Islam. Even if this is true, Islam gives the moderates no vehicle by which to say this with authority so that it will be accepted as such by Muslims and non-Muslims throughout the world. Islam provides no hierarchical structure for marginalizing terrorists as heretics—and, in view of the alarming number of influential

Islamic scholars who actually contend that the terrorists are in the right, this challenge may be insuperable for the foreseeable future.

Instead of a hierarchy, Islam relies on a venerated consensus of its greatest *mujtahids,* the masters of its four established schools of thought. That consensus was set in stone even before al-Azhar's doors first opened in the middle of the tenth century. Although early Islam had enjoyed a tradition of *ijtihad*—free and independent inquiry into Islamic scripture by believers seeking to discern Allah's intended meaning—those authoritative schools determined by about 900 AD that all essential questions had been settled with finality. From then on, no one would be deemed qualified for independent reasoning. According to Joseph Schacht, "All future activity would have to be confined to the explanation, application, and, at the most, interpretation of the doctrine as it had been laid down once and for all."[9] The "gates of *ijtihad*" were closed.

It was to this task of interpretation that Abdel Rahman set himself. Never reaching the high station of grand imam, Abdel Rahman's accomplishments did include a prestigious stint as an al-Azhar lecturer, as well as the leadership of the vicious Egyptian terror organization al-Gama'at al-Islamiyya (Islamic Group), and great influence over the "Arab-Afghans," who joined the mujahidin resistance against the 1979 Soviet invasion of Afghanistan. As a result, he was dubbed the "pope of jihad" by some of the few Western investigators who followed such things in the early 1990s. Later it became clear, though, that "*emir* of jihad," employing the Arab term for "prince" or "commander," was the more apt and widely used honorific among the faithful.

The Blind Sheikh was undeniably a mufti, a specialist in Islamic law authorized to opine on points of doctrine and to issue fatwas.[10] His status as an emir, a position of high operational authority, did, however, evoke occasional dissent, including from a feisty young Ayman al-Zawahiri—his ally and sometime rival who would rise years later to become al-Qaeda's second-in-command, and now its current leader—when the two, detained together in an Egyptian prison after the Sadat murder, squabbled over a Qur'anic verse that casts the sightless as unfit for command.[11] Such dissent, however, was rare and muted, owing to the awe Abdel Rahman's religious erudition inspired and the practical impossibility of cleaving the spiritual from the operational in radical ideology.

SPIRITUAL UNDERPINNINGS OF MODERN JIHAD

Perhaps the most profound influence on Abdel Rahman's scholarship, and thus the intellectual font of radical Islam's modern iteration, was the fourteenth-century Sunni docent Taqi al-Din Ahmad Ibn Taymiyyah. A controversial scholar in his time, Ibn Taymiyyah championed a literal interpretation of scripture and the concept that the original Islamic communities forged during the Prophet Muhammad's Medinan period were the ideal to which all humanity must aspire.[12]

Muslim reverence for the Prophet is, of course, a given. The Qur'an endorses Muhammad as "an excellent model of conduct" (33:21), who exhibited an "exalted standard of character" (68:4). Obedience to him is repeatedly adjured—made, in fact, just as essential as obedience to Allah himself (4:80).[13] Ibn Taymiyyah's focus on the Medinan period, though, is of seismic significance. During this phase of Islamic development, Muslims were forced to flee from Mecca by powerful tribes, including the Prophet's native Quraysh, which refused to accept the new religion. This flight, the *Hijra*, is Islam's ground-breaking moment, the event by which time is marked.

In the preceding thirteen-year Meccan period, when Muhammad first endeavored to call converts to Islam, he had been highly solicitous of the existing tribes and their traditions. It should come as no surprise, then, that the more tolerant verses of the Qur'an can be traced to this early Meccan period, such as the injunction that there shall be "no compulsion in religion" (2:256)—the unparalleled favorite verse of moderates and Western elites bent on portraying Islam as "the religion of peace."

In Medina, things changed drastically. It was from there that Islam was principally spread not by intellectual persuasion but by the sword. The scriptures tending toward ecumenism and tolerance were superseded by divine commands that the Prophet "make war on the unbelievers and the hypocrites and deal rigorously with them. Hell shall be their home: an evil fate" (9:73). This command is not immediately apparent to the unschooled observer because the Qur'an is arranged not chronologically but according to the length of its *suras* (chapters). It is reflective, however, of the Islamic doctrine of *naskh* (abrogation), the concept that, as he sees fit, Allah refines or repeals his prior instructions.[14] Abrogation is essential to a proper understanding of the Medinan period and of the chasm between the Islam of Western fantasy and the one that actually exists.

The Muhammad of Medina—which is to say, the Muhammad of Ibn Taymiyyah—sought Islamic hegemony, not ecumenical coexistence. Enemy tribes that had tormented him were savaged, their leaders slain and decapitated, their pleas for mercy ignored.[15] Rejection of Islam was construed as an attack upon Islam to be met with brutal retribution, meted out more than once by the Prophet himself. For example, as jihad historian Andrew Bostom relates:

> According to Muhammad's sacralized biography by Ibn Ishaq, Muhammad himself sanctioned the massacre of the Qurayza, a vanquished Jewish tribe. He appointed an "arbiter" who soon rendered this concise verdict: the men

were to be put to death, the women and children sold into slavery, the spoils to be divided among the Muslims. Muhammad ratified this judgment stating that it was a decree of God pronounced from above the Seven Heavens. Thus some 600 to 900 men from the Qurayza were [led] on Muhammad's order to the Market of Medina. Trenches were dug and the men were beheaded, and their decapitated corpses buried in the trenches while Muhammad watched in attendance. Women and children were sold into slavery, a number of them being distributed as gifts among Muhammad's companions, and Muhammad chose one of the Qurayza women (Rayhana) for himself. The Qurayza's property and other possessions (including weapons) were also divided up as additional "booty" among the Muslims, to support further jihad campaigns.[16]

Jihad campaigns are, indeed, the phenomenon known today as Islamic radicalism. It being the preoccupation of many Muslim political activists and Western intellectuals to deny the patent nexus between Islamic doctrine and terror, a controversy naturally has developed over the "true" meaning of jihad—a controversy that is itself ill-conceived because the salient question is not which construers of the term have the better of the argument, but whether there is enough persuasive force in the militant construction that, even if arguably wrong (and I do not think it is), it is sure to convince a meaningful number of Muslims.

Today's moderates and their intellectual allies grudgingly acknowledge that jihad is a tenet of Islam—although, they imply, not all that important a tenet because it is not one of the five "pillars" of the faith.[17] But while Muhammad himself made jihad—militaristic jihad—Islam's doctrinal *ne plus ultra*, declaring that no deed on earth could equal it in God's favor, today's solons are determined to portray jihadists as heretics who have perverted the "true" faith, relieving us of any need to concern ourselves over the relationship between Islam and terror.

Thus is a fable assiduously advanced, pitting the good (or "greater") jihad against the bad (or "lesser") jihad. This school of thought finds a fine exemplar in Marc Sageman, a forensic psychiatrist and former case officer of the U.S. Central Intelligence Agency (from the late 1980s when the agency was underwriting the Afghan mujahidin's jihad against the Soviets). A frequent adviser to federal and state agencies, Sageman writes:

> Like other great, long established religions, Islam is full of contentious issues, especially about some of its core concepts, such as *jihad,* which translates roughly as "striving" but denotes any form of activity, either personal or communal, undertaken by Muslims in attempting to follow the path of God. No single doctrine is universally accepted.

> In a world full of iniquities, the greater jihad is the individual nonviolent
> striving to live a good Muslim life, following God's will. It includes adhering
> to the five pillars of Islam: profession of faith (*shahada*); praying regularly;
> fasting during Ramadan; being charitable; and performing the *hajj*, the
> pilgrimage to Mecca. It requires lifelong diligence and constant vigilance.[18]

How admirable, indeed. The "greater" jihad is the good jihad. That other
jihad—he is too nuanced to suggest it is altogether bad—is the "lesser" jihad.
Only this small subordinate species of the genus involves "the violent struggle
for Islam." It is a vestige of an antiquated *Weltanschauung* that simplistically
divided the world into "the land of Islam (*dar al-Islam*) and the land of conflict
(*dar al-Harb*)," and saw jihad as the Muslim *ummah's* (Muslim community's)
communal obligation "to expand dar al-Islam throughout the world so that all
humankind could benefit from living within a just political social order."[19]

That old world, Sageman claims, is no more. The purportedly lesser jihad
has been "diluted," he contends, by "one school of interpretation," which
introduced the concept of a "land of treaty (*dar al-Sulh*)" in which jihad was
forbidden in lands that had struck agreements with Muslims. Sageman conveniently glides by the rather obvious point that the existence of "one school
of interpretation" implies that there are other schools following different
interpretations—to say nothing of the facts that the Qur'an limits treaties to
ten years' duration and that Muhammad reserved the right to break them
whenever it was expedient to do so (since "war," as the Prophet observed, "is
deceit"). Instead, Sageman plows ahead with the suggestion that this "lesser"
jihad has been further marginalized by its division into "defensive" and
"offensive" strivings. Individual Muslims are required to fight only in the
former, which happens only if a Muslim land has been invaded and a competent authority has issued a fatwa declaring a "state of jihad."

MISREADING OFFENSE AND DEFENSE IN JIHAD

Self-defense, of course, is a natural human right and, by extension, a bedrock
of international law. Who, then, could argue with "defensive" jihad, if that is all
the "lesser" jihad is about? Well, even leaving aside the inconvenient fact that
what constitutes "defense" is often in the eye of the beholder, the concept of
"offensive" jihad remains. This, Sageman concedes, involves Muslims invading
infidel lands to impose sharia and spread the faith. Shouldn't such a possibility
raise concerns that many Muslims will feel validated in acting on what they
rationally see as a divine injunction? Not according to Sageman. He rational-
izes that "offensive" jihad is a *collective* obligation—that is, one in which only
Islamic governments, not individual believers, will involve themselves. Thus

scholars and others seem to think they can Jesuitically define out of existence the nexus between Islam and terror by asserting that "offensive" jihad cannot be performed by individuals, and therefore those individual terrorists must not be jihadists—QED, terrorism is un-Islamic.

Sageman is far from alone. In their invaluable account of al-Qaeda's rise, *The Age of Sacred Terror,* former Clinton administration National Security Council officials Daniel Benjamin and Steven Simon more accurately acknowledge that jihad grew up as "exclusively actual, physical warfare." They argue, however, that "the concept of jihad took on a new meaning" in the late eighteenth and early nineteenth centuries as Islam was beleaguered by the rise of imperial Western European powers and the decay of Ottoman Turkey. There was, they aver, a "domestication of jihad," rendering it "a struggle against evil impulses within the soul of a believer." The "greater jihad" became the internal struggle for personal betterment waged through "acts of charity, good works in society, and education." "Military jihad" fell in status.[20]

Benjamin and Simon forthrightly concede that this greater/lesser divide is a "modern-day distinction" that would have been unrecognizable to classical Muslim scholars such as Ibn Taymiyyah. Their argument is indistinguishable from that advanced by devotees of the "living Constitution," who contend, for example, that the Eighth Amendment's prohibition against "cruel and unusual punishments" operates to ban the death penalty notwithstanding several implicitly approving references to capital punishment elsewhere in the Constitution—that is, the Framers would not have understood themselves to be proscribing executions, but because we Americans (or at least some of us) have evolved, we should deem the Eighth Amendment to have evolved along with us. So too we should interpret jihad as reprogrammed to fit enlightened sensibilities, such that today's "real" jihads are noble efforts to rid societies of blights such as narcotics trafficking, hate speech, and intolerance.

This unmooring of *jihad* from its original meaning was taken to a new level by President Obama's top counterterrorism advisor John Brennan. In a May 2010 speech, Brennan purges not only the violent underpinnings of jihad but its status as a distinctly Islamic concept and obligation.[21] According to Brennan, jihad did not evolve into something wholly anodyne; it has always been precisely that: a "holy struggle" that merely means "to purify oneself or one's community." Therefore, the fairy tale goes, since there can be "nothing holy or legitimate or Islamic about murdering innocent men, women and children," don't blame jihad—there simply must be some other explanation.

Sadly, these new constructions are most persuasive to those desperate to be persuaded: Western intellectuals—many of whom look askance at religion and are insensitive to a believer's faith in what he takes to be transcendent, non-evolving values. In the ivory towers, the nexus between Islamic doctrine and modern terrorism can be whisked away by logic, enlightenment, and (mainly) the sheer desire that it disappear. Down here on planet earth, though, the exercise is futile. The Muslim world is not populated by Western intellectuals hardwired to nuance white into black by legalistic arcana and historical massaging. In large swaths of the *ummah*, there is rampant illiteracy, education consists of a myopic focus on the Qur'an, and intolerance (especially anti-Semitism) is so rudimentary a part of everyday life that any jihad rooted in "good works in society" would not conceivably reflect what Western progressives mean by that well-intentioned term.

Progressive moderate Muslims would no doubt like the concept of jihad to vanish altogether. They are in a battle for authenticity with fundamentalists, and jihad would be far easier to omit than it is to explain away. Jihad, however, will not go away. In every triumph of Islamic supremacist ideology, it rears its head. In October 2010, on the eve of the "Arab Spring"—an Islamist ascendancy camouflaged as a democratic revolution—the Supreme Guide of the Islamist vanguard, the Muslim Brotherhood's Mohammed Badi, called for violent jihad against the United States and Israel.[22] Specifically, he admonished Muslims to remember "Allah's commandment to wage jihad for His sake with [their] money and lives, so that Allah's word will reign supreme and the infidels' word will be inferior."[23] Applying this injunction, Badi exclaimed that jihad "is the only solution against the Zio-American arrogance and tyranny." On went the invective: the United States had been wounded by jihadists in Iraq and Afghanistan; thus, Badi gleefully surmised, America "is now experiencing the beginning of its end, and is heading towards its demise."

Jihad is a peculiarly Islamic form of triumphalism, and it is deemed obligatory by today's Islamist leaders just as it was by early Islamic conquerors. At all times, the objective of true jihad is the imposition of sharia. There would be no Muslim world without it. When it comes to jihad, authenticity is simplicity, and, simply stated, jihad is and has always been about conquest, principally military conquest—although submission without violence is always welcome. As explicated by the West's preeminent scholar of Islam, Bernard Lewis:

> Conventionally translated "holy war" [jihad] has the literal meaning of striving, more specifically, in the Qur'anic phrase "striving in the path of God" (*fi sabil Allah*). Some Muslim theologians, particularly in more modern times, have interpreted the duty of "striving in the path of God" in a spiritual and moral sense. The overwhelming majority of early authorities, however, citing relevant passages in the Qur'an and in the tradition, discuss jihad in military terms.[24]

In fact, the erudite former Muslim with the nom de plume Ibn Warraq points out that even

> the celebrated *Dictionary of Islam* defines *jihad* as "a religious war with those who are unbelievers in the mission of Muhammad. It is an incumbent religious duty, established in the Qur'an and in the Traditions as a divine institution, enjoined specially for the purpose of advancing Islam and of repelling evil from Muslims."[25]

It is no wonder that this should be so. The Qur'an repeatedly enjoins Muslims to fight and slay non-Muslims. "O ye who believe," commands Sura 9:123, "Fight those of the disbelievers who are near you, and let them find harshness in you, and know that Allah is with those who keep their duty unto him." It is difficult to spin that as a call to spiritual self-improvement. Likewise, Sura 9:5 instructs: "But when the forbidden months are past, then fight and slay the pagans wherever ye find them. And seize them, beleaguer them, and lie in wait for them in every stratagem (of war)," relenting only if they have accepted Islam.[26] The *hadith*, lengthy volumes recording the words and traditions of the Prophet, are even more explicit, as in Muhammad's teaching that "a single endeavor (of fighting) in Allah's cause in the afternoon or in the forenoon is better than all the world and whatever is in it."[27]

This is the jihad of Islamic scripture. It is the jihad on which Ibn Taymiyyah insisted. The caliphate's defeat and the suddenly dire straits of thirteenth-century believers stemmed from their deviation from the true Islam: the Islam of conquest, whose calling, whose *command*, was to bring about universal submission to Allah. For Ibn Taymiyyah, this divine mandate required both imposing the penalties of sharia (Islamic law) on Muslims who strayed and

> the punishment of recalcitrant groups, such as those that can only be brought under the sway of the Imam by a decisive fight. That then is the jihad against the unbelievers (*kuffar*), the enemies of God and his Messenger. For whoever has heard the summons of the Messenger of God, Peace be upon him, and has not responded to it, must be fought, "until there is no persecution and the religion is God's entirely."[28]

"Lawful warfare," Ibn Taymiyyah elaborated, "is essentially jihad." Because its purpose is to eradicate all obstacles to the obligatory spread of Islam (so that "the religion is God's entirely"), "those who stand in the way of this aim must be fought." Famously, Ibn Taymiyyah further inferred from this a duty to overthrow rulers who failed to govern in accordance with a fundamentalist construction of sharia—including rulers who were, at least nominally, Muslim.

Among the heirs of Ibn Taymiyyah's thought—those who "swoon of death" while their enemies, as Osama bin Laden scoffed, cling desperately to life—was Muhammad bin Abdul Wahhab, the eighteenth-century fundamentalist. His atavistic Sunni Islam, known today as Wahhabism, became the Saudi royal family's creed—and, in the twentieth century, its second best-known export. But Ibn Taymiyyah's influence was not confined to Sunnis. Iran's Grand Ayatollah Ali Khomeini, trailblazer of the most significant revolutionary movement in Shiite history, echoed Ibn Taymiyyah in this blistering critique of those who would bowdlerize the true jihad:

> Islam makes it incumbent on all [able] adult males ... to prepare themselves for the conquest of [other] countries so that the writ of Islam is obeyed in every country of the world. ... [T]hose who study Islamic Holy War will understand why Islam wants to conquer the whole world. ... Those who know nothing of Islam pretend that Islam counsels against war. [They] are witless. Islam says: Kill all the unbelievers just as they would kill you all! Does this mean the Muslims should sit back until they are devoured? Islam says: Kill them, put them to the sword and scatter [their armies]. ... Islam says: Whatever good there is exists thanks to the sword and in the shadow of the sword. People cannot be made obedient except with the sword! The sword is the key to Paradise, which can be opened only for Holy Warriors! There are hundreds of [scriptures] urging Muslims to value war and to fight. Does all that mean Islam is a religion that prevents men from waging war? I spit upon those foolish souls who make such a claim.[29]

SAYYID QUTB AND GLOBAL RELIGIOUS WAR

From across the Arabian Peninsula and the Sunni/Shiite divide, the Blind Sheikh admired the grand ayatollah and harbored dreams of an Egyptian replication of his Iranian coup d'état. Still, for Abdel Rahman, coming of age in a boiling cauldron of dissidence, the most striking of Ibn Taymiyyah's legatees was Sayyid Qutb. The intellectual father of modern jihadism and an iconic figure in the formidable Muslim Brotherhood, Qutb was "martyred" by Gamal Abdel Nasser's Egypt in 1966, when Abdel Rahman was twenty-eight years old.

Qutb was an education scholar who studied from 1948 until 1950 in the United States, where he was repulsed by what he saw as America's racism, debauchery, and vulgar materialism. Presaging Khomeini, he rejected the revisionism that depicts jihad as a personal struggle, a purely "defensive" obligation, or an antiquated concept confined to the time and circumstances of the early Muslims. Islam, he explained, was not merely intended for Arabs, and, plainly, there would not be what today is known as the "Islamic world" (*dar al-Islam*) unless Muslims had fought and conquered the preexisting regimes. "The religion," he wrote,

> is really a universal declaration of the freedom of man from servitude to
> other men and from servitude to his own desires, which is also a form of
> human servitude; it is a declaration that sovereignty belongs to God
> alone and that He is the Lord of all the worlds. It means a challenge to all
> kinds and forms of systems which are based on the concept of the sover-
> eignty of man; in other words, where man has usurped the Divine attri-
> bute. . . . [Thus it] addresses itself to the whole of mankind, and its sphere
> of work is the whole earth.[30]

It is crucial to grasp this Islamic notion of *freedom*, for it is the obverse of the Western conception. Reckless indifference to this fact has led to such follies as the grand project to democratize the Islamic world, as well as the failure to perceive the "Arab Spring" for what it is: the rise and rule of Islamic supremacism, even as sharia emerges before our very eyes. *Islam* means *submission* to God. *Freedom* in Islam must be understood in this context. It is not, as Westerners assume, free *choice*; it is the voluntary *surrendering of oneself* to Allah, unqualifiedly accepting the laws he has established (sharia). For, as Qutb instructed, "Legislation is a Divine attribute," so to concede it to other men is to "accept [them] as Divine," whether or not one actually considers them so, because the Qur'an equates obedience with worship. When Islam speaks of free will, as in Western intellectuals' much loved decree that there shall not be compulsion in religion, *this* is the sense of freedom it conveys. That freedom, Qutb taught, cannot be realized without establishment of the sharia system—the only system that removes all obstacles to the comprehension and, inexorably, the acceptance of the imperative to submit to Allah. It is thus no surprise that, in the closing days of the 2012 Egyptian presidential campaign, Mohamed Morsi, the Muslim Brotherhood candidate who continues to revere Qutb as among its most eminent thinkers, described his proposed governing program this way: "The sharia, then the sharia, and finally, the sharia."[31]

Indeed Qutb recognized that supplanting man's dominion with God's could never "be achieved only through preaching." Incumbent infidel regimes were plainly "not going to give up their power merely through preaching." Expelling them was the mission of jihad, highlighting its centrality as a core Islamic obligation, the *sine qua non* of, as Ibn Taymiyyah put it, making the religion God's entirely—of cementing Islam as universally supreme. The purpose of jihad is "to wipe out tyranny and to introduce freedom to mankind." Whenever Islam is obstructed by "the political system of the state, the socio-economic system based on races and classes, and behind all these, the military power of the government," the religion, according to Qutb, "has no recourse but to remove them by force so that when [Islam] is addressed to peoples' hearts and minds they are free to accept or reject it with an open mind." All such impediments hindering human beings from achieving their highest calling are seen as persecution, implicating the Qur'anic injunction to "fight in the cause of Allah those who fight you . . . and slay them whenever you catch them, and turn them out from where they have turned you out, for persecution is worse than slaughter."[32]

The logic of Qutb's construction is patently circular, and frightening. Sharia is the precondition necessary to ensure perfect "freedom," but sharia cannot be established without the violent overthrow of regimes that refuse to adopt it voluntarily. And—again foreshadowing Khomeini—the "freedom" extended by Islam is not liberty of conscience, for the purportedly "complete freedom to accept or reject" the religion's tenets "does not mean [people] can make their desires their gods, or that they can choose to remain in the servitude of other human beings, making some men lords over others." No, the system in which this "choice" takes place must be based "on the authority of God, deriving its laws from him alone."

Thus the "free" decision to submit is made in an atmosphere of intimidation, where the Islamic battalions have supplanted their opposition and installed the sharia system. In this system, the choices of nonbelievers are to convert "voluntarily," or to remain infidels with the consciously humiliating status of *dhimmitude* (they were compelled to pay a tribute, the *jizya* tax, aimed primarily at constantly reminding *dhimmis* of their subjugation), or to die. The descent of Egypt into sharia tyranny once the Muslim Brotherhood took power is a good example. In August 2012, religious minorities, secular democrats, and authentic Muslim moderates announced their intention to protest the Morsi government's seizure of dictatorial authority, its takeover of the media, the persecution of Coptic Christians, and so on. In response, Sheikh Hashem Islam, a member of the influential fatwa committee at al-Azhar University, immediately issued a fatwa ruling that it was a religious obligation to fight participants in any anti-Brotherhood demonstrations. Citing Islamic scripture, he concluded, "Resist them; if they fight you, fight back; if they kill you, you are in paradise; if you kill them, there is no blood money [i.e., required compensation]."[33]

While obsessed with establishing sharia societies, Islam is never content with them. Islamic history is an inevitable progression. At times, Muslims refrained from jihad for tactical reasons (such as when Muhammad was first attracting converts in Mecca). At other times, Muslims employed jihad defensively because they actually were under armed attack. Nevertheless, none of that can obscure Islam's sacred quest for hegemony—to expand *dar al-Islam*, the realm of the Muslims, throughout the world. For Qutb, history had reached

Does Islam Play a Unique Role in Modern Religious Terrorism?

this final phase of Islam's march, with war declared against all non-Muslims, in accordance with the command of Sura 9:29: "Fight those who do not believe in Allah nor the Last Day, nor hold that forbidden which hath been forbidden by Allah and His messenger, nor acknowledge the Religion of Truth from among the People of the Book, until they pay the *jizya* with willing submission, and feel themselves subdued."[34]

Echoing Ibn Taymiyyah, Qutb's jihad targeted not only declared nonbelievers but also those rulers who professed to be Muslim but did not adhere to the commands of the faith—the commands divinely required for the furtherance of "freedom." In many ways, such Muslims, particularly those in authority positions, were more responsible than declared infidels for the *ummah*'s descent into the dystopian condition of *jahiliyya*. This term, drawn from the Qur'an and Ibn Taymiyyah's theology, denoted the pre-Islamic phase of history, the dark pagan ignorance overcome by the incandescence of the Prophet's message. Qutb infused the concept with a connotation of oppressive, anti-Islamic corruption. The *jahiliyya* included all people, including Muslims, who failed to comport unflinchingly with sharia. There was but a single true Islam, which Allah had commanded his adherents to establish through jihad. Everyone and everything else was *jahiliyya*. By nature, they could not coexist with Islam. Therefore, in this the final phase of Islam's history there was a positive duty to eradicate them—not to wait for them to attack so that the jihad could be spun as "defensive," for their very existence was an affront to Allah.

This jurisprudence of jihad is crucial to grasping why the newfangled theories of the Obama administration's John Brennan and other like-minded officials are so wayward. They would create an Islam of their very own rather than deal with the Islam that exists. Yes, jihad—the mission to implement, spread, or defend sharia—is not exclusively violent; an army doesn't need to be violent if its enemies are willing to give ground. But jihad only means "to purify oneself or one's community" in a very narrow sense. It is not the syrupy quest to become a better person but the command to become *a better, more sharia-compliant Muslim*. It is not the smiley-face mission to "purify" one's community of crime but the command to cleanse one's community of influences that do not honor sharia mores.

The continuing and inextricable bond between jihad and sharia is easily explained in eras of Islamist ascendancy. In Islamic supremacist ideology, which is the dynamic ideology in the Middle East (i.e., the ideology whose proponents are winning landslide elections), sharia is the nonnegotiable foundation of Islamic society. Even in Islam's less threatening iterations, it is taken as a given that believers must call all of humanity to the faith. What separates

the true moderates from the Islamists and the violent jihadists are the lengths
to which one is willing to go in carrying out that injunction. That it *is* an
injunction, however, is not open to debate.

CONCLUSION

Because discussions of the nexus between Islamic doctrine and modern terrorism are so infected with timidity, passion, and demagoguery, it bears
emphasizing that there is no single Islam. There is a seemingly infinite variety
of Islamic sects, to say nothing of the prevalent phenomenon—quite familiar
to Westerners—of adherents who are at best culturally or nominally Muslim
but care little about theology and its demands. That said, however, it is whis-
tling past the graveyard to ignore or minimize the virulent strain of fundamentalist Islam that galvanizes jihadism. And it is positively fatuous to suggest
that it stems from poverty, alienation, wounded pride, American policies, or
whatever is the anything-but-Islam justification du jour.

It is simply not the case that a mere nineteen terrorists hijacked a peaceful
religion, as President George W. Bush hastened to assure Americans while
smoke billowed from the Pentagon and lifeless bodies were pulled from the
rubble of the World Trade Center. It is not the case, as the Clinton administration and its Justice Department were equally emphatic in mollifying the
public when the World Trade Center was first bombed in 1993, that a ragtag
handful of miscreants had "perverted" the "true Islam." The species of Islam
that has spurred these and other attacks has a long and distinguished pedigree. It is fourteen centuries old. It is rooted in the literal commands of the
scriptures. It is a project that has engaged high intellects. It is a belief system
that continues to win the allegiance of the educated and illiterate, rich and
poor, young and old, princes and peons. Yes, Islamic supremacists differ
intensely on tactics. There are severe disagreements about the appropriate-
ness of violence as a method for implementing sharia, especially in the West.
But it must be underscored: these disagreements are principally about tactics
and timing, about violent extortion or gradual pressure; they are not disagreements about goals. On the matter of goals, all Islamists, including the
subset of violent jihadists, concur on the imperative of installing the sharia
societal system.

It is that ideology, with classical, military sharia as the hard-power backbone
of an aggressive if often nonviolent campaign, that is the dynamic Islam of the
Middle East. In the West, it remains a minority construction of Islam, but
claims the allegiance of increasingly forceful pluralities.

We ignore this reality at our peril.

NO: Islam itself is not the problem in the current wave of global terrorism.
Fawaz A. Gerges, *London School of Economics*

What Osama bin Laden and George W. Bush Got Wrong about Muslims

After September 11, 2001, two questions dominated America's public debate: Why do Muslims hate Americans so much?[35] And where are the Muslim moderates? On the first question, commentators supplied easy, simplistic answers that appealed to the country's wounded egos and prejudices, not critical faculties and common sense. Americans were told that "they" (Muslims in general, not just the tiny militant minority) hated their freedoms and way of life, and were jealous of America's economic success, political influence, and international prestige. Americans had nothing to do with the twisted misperceptions of their country and foreign policy. In short, the root causes of anti-Americanism, asserted pundits, reveal more about the moral and political decay of Muslim societies than about American actions.

For many Americans, the answer to the second question was that there are not any moderates, that Osama bin Laden and the radicals were the exclusive representatives of Islam, and that the Muslim moderates were either a misnomer or a cowardly bunch who dared not challenge the bullies among them. Islam, it was believed, was a radical religion, with terrorist violence a natural outgrowth.

Political leaders and pundits reassured us that the United States neither played empire nor caused harm abroad; a beacon of light and catalyst for good, America was an innocent bystander in a cynical, jealous, and ungrateful world. Americans are hated because of who they are, not because of what their country did—that was the received wisdom after September 11.[36]

But a dozen years later, after embroiling itself in two wars in Muslim countries and with deep interests in political conflicts from Morocco to Egypt to Indonesia, it is worth pausing to ask whether this received wisdom is entirely correct. Of course, the landscape has changed. Iraq, in particular, became a new source of radicalization and a reason to hate American foreign policy. And under President Barack Obama drone strikes from 15,000 feet replaced Iraq and Guantánamo as the number-one recruiting tool for militant jihadist movements.[37] But the broader questions about what the world's one billion–plus Muslims think remain, and in many ways—with the advent of the Arab Spring uprisings in 2011 and 2012—are even more pertinent today than ever before. After all, to understand Islam today, one must understand what Muslims actually think and how that compares with both what we in the West believe and what al-Qaeda believes to be true. To those who assume that radical, violent interpretations of Islam inspire most Muslims, the answers will be most surprising.

MUSLIMS AND MODERATION

The very nature of the second question—where are the Muslim moderates?— is based on a fundamental misreading of Islam 101. Unlike, say, the Catholic Church, no organized, hierarchical clerical establishment exists in Islam. There is no intermediary—church or priest—between the believer and God. Religious scholars and leaders, then, derive their authority mainly by interpreting Islamic texts and jurisprudence. That authority is even contested with multiple interpretations and counterinterpretations. To be sure, Muslim puritans and radicals— and some of their Western counterparts—want those who study Islam to believe that it is a monolith, with a timeless essence. But it is a mistake to take their claims at face value, because the Muslim world is complex and fragmented, divided along ethnic, nationalist, and socioeconomic lines. The militant fringe claims as much legitimacy and authority in representing Islam and Muslims as do the political moderates, but scholars and others assume otherwise because they do not hear the latter as often, or as loudly.

Unfortunately, many U.S. commentators bought the rhetoric of bin Laden and his right-hand man, Ayman al-Zawahiri, who anointed themselves spokesmen for Islam and Muslims. Those commentators lost sight of the social and political turmoil shaking Muslim societies to their very foundation. Indeed, bin Laden the man, and bin Ladenism the ideology, represented not a new dominant Islam but a revolt inside it, directed as much against the clerical establishment as against the ruling elite. It was bin Laden and al-Zawahiri's aim to fill the vacuum of legitimate political authority in the Muslim world and challenge the unholy alliance between Muslim rulers and clerics. In other words, Muslims, not Americans, were intended to be the primary audience for the attacks of September 11.

The ensuing struggle was momentous—and completely ignored in the United States. Less than two weeks after September 11, I traveled to the Middle East and was pleasantly surprised by the almost universal rejection—from taxi drivers and bank tellers to fruit vendors and high school teachers—of al-Qaeda's terrorism. Everyone I met expressed genuine empathy with the American victims, even while highly critical of U.S. foreign policy.

The initial sympathetic Muslim response to September 11 received hardly any coverage in the U.S. media, which constantly replayed sensational images of a few Palestinian children and teens in refugee camps celebrating the fall of the twin towers.

If the "terrorism experts" had listened closely, they would have learned that, far from condoning the September 11 attacks, leading mainstream and, yes, radical clerics—such as Hassan al-Turabi, former head of the National Islamic Front and now with the Popular Congress Party in Sudan (in the early 1990s he hosted bin Laden) and Sayyid Mohammed Hussein Fadlallah, the spiritual founding father of Lebanon's Hezbollah—had condemned the 9/11 attacks, recognizing that they were harmful to Islam and Muslims.[38]

Yusuf al-Qaradawi, an influential Egyptian-born conservative cleric now based in Qatar, even issued a fatwa denouncing al-Qaeda's "illegal jihad" and expressed sorrow and empathy with the American victims. "Our hearts bleed because of the attacks that have targeted the World Trade Center, as well as other institutions in the United States," he wrote on his website just after the September 11 attacks. Nothing could justify the attacks, he wrote, including "the American biased policy toward Israel on the military, political, and economic fronts." That may be cold comfort to the victims, but it was also a significant challenge to bin Laden, and bin Ladenism.

To be fair, most political religious leaders did not criticize al-Qaeda's political ideology; they criticized only its terrorist methods. Bin Laden may have occasionally reverted to religious rhetoric, but it was his *political and ideological* rhetoric that truly resonates among Muslims of all persuasions and ranks who blame the United States for sustaining Israeli military occupation of Palestinian territories, as well as oppressive Arab autocrats. As countless polls show, and as I have found in my own research, the efficacy of al-Qaeda's anti-American (and anti-Western) message stems from politics and foreign policy, not culture and religion.

THE MYTH OF MONOLITHIC JIHAD

Equally important, September 11 opened up a wide cleavage between the local and global branches of the jihadist tribe. Contrary to the received wisdom, 9/11 did not turn out as bin Laden and al-Zawahiri had hoped. Far from reinvigorating and unifying jihadist ranks, taking on the United States widened the cleavages separating local jihadists from transnational jihadis, clear signs of the ongoing internal struggle tearing the jihadist family apart. Even with the upheavals spurred on by the Arab Spring uprisings, this war within has hardly been noticed, let alone critically examined, in the United States.

Instead of closing ranks against the "enemies of Islam," as bin Laden and al-Zawahiri had hoped, 9/11 put to rest any possibility of bridging the gulf between al-Qaeda's global jihadists and the army of deactivated local jihadists who far outnumber bin Laden's few thousand men. The bulk of local jihadists (numbering tens of thousands) refused to fight alongside al-Qaeda and condemned its reckless tactics. Neither the *ummah* (Muslim community worldwide) nor the army of decommissioned local jihadists was willing to join al-Qaeda's suicidal caravan, however much they empathized with its grievances against the international order and American foreign policy in particular.

Before the dust settled on the September 11 crime scenes, cracks appeared within the jihadist front. Top jihadists opposed what bin Laden had done, some even within his own wing of the movement. One of the first, Abu al-Walid al-Masri, a senior member of the al-Qaeda *shura* (consultative) who had been a leading theoretician of the network and participated in its most significant decisions, saw the attacks of September 11 as a calamity. He was among the most senior of the Arab Afghans to break with bin Laden over September 11 and take his grievances public. He publicly lambasted bin Laden's "catastrophic leadership" and his underestimation of American willpower.

Based in Kandahar, Abu al-Walid had worked closely with both Taliban leader Mullah Omar and bin Laden, and had supervised *The Islamic Principality*, a newsletter regarded as the mouthpiece of Mullah Omar. After the events of 9/11, he published a series of articles titled *The Story of the Arab Afghans: From the Entry to Afghanistan to the Final Exodus with Taliban in Asharq al-Awsat*, in which he paints a dark portrait of bin Laden as an autocrat, running al-Qaeda as he might a tribal fiefdom, and offers a stinging critique of bin Laden's vision of global jihad.

Abu al-Walid's withering criticism of bin Laden was echoed by others, including Egypt's al-Jamaah al-Islamiyah organization. Whereas at the height of its strength in 2001 al-Qaeda's membership numbered about 4,000, al-Jamaah fielded almost 100,000 fighters in the 1990s.

Of all the Islamists, al-Jamaah's senior leaders (most of whom had been in prison in Egypt since the 1980s and 1990s and were recently released) presented the most comprehensive critique of al-Qaeda's strategy and methods. Since early 2002, they have released more than a dozen manuscripts in Arabic, two of which deal specifically with the September 11 attacks. The first, authored by Mohammed Essam Derbala and reviewed and approved by the entire leadership, is titled "Al Qaeda Strategy: Mistakes and Dangers," and the other, authored by Nageh Abdullah Ibrahim, is titled "Islam and the Challenges of the Twenty-First Century." Both were serialized in the Egyptian newspaper *Asharq al-Awsat*. These vital historical documents shed light on the thinking of the biggest and most influential jihadist organization in the region. But neither of the manuscripts has been translated into English, and thus they have not received the attention they deserve.

At the time, Derbala, one of the leaders of al-Jamaah, was serving a life sentence in prison for his role in the 1981 assassination of Egyptian president Anwar Sadat. He drew on religious texts to show that al-Qaeda's attacks violated Islamic law, which "bans killing civilians" of any religion or nationality. Derbala and his associates denounced al-Qaeda for preaching that American and Muslim interests would never meet and that "the enmity is deeply embedded and the clash is inevitable." They cited several instances in the 1990s when the United States helped to resolve international conflicts, with results benefiting Muslims. For example, U.S. military and financial assistance in the Afghan war tipped the balance in favor of the mujahidin against the Russian occupiers; from 1990 to 1991 the United States helped Kuwait and Saudi Arabia expel Iraqi forces from Kuwait; in 1995 American military intervention put a stop to the persecution and massacre of Bosnian Muslims by Serbs; and in 1999 the United States led a North Atlantic Treaty Organization (NATO) military campaign to force Serbia to end ethnic cleansing of Muslims in Kosovo. All these examples showed clearly, al-Jamaah's senior leaders asserted, that there is nothing inevitable about a clash of cultures between Islam and the West; American and Muslim interests can and do meet.

Derbala, Ibrahim, and their imprisoned colleagues condemned bin Laden and al-Zawahiri's religious justification for attacking the Americans, reminding them that Islam has always practiced—not just taught—peaceful coexistence as a permanent way of life. Religious coexistence is a strategic, not a tactical, goal in Islam, particularly when Muslims migrate to foreign lands and are welcomed by native inhabitants. What makes the crime of the September 11 suicide bombers uniquely un-Islamic, Ibrahim wrote, is that the U.S. government had admitted them as guests. This was a betrayal of the most fundamental spiritual obligation, the one practiced in shops, cafés, and homes throughout the Arab world. Had the bombers read the *Sunnah* (containing the deeds of the Prophet—the second source of Islam after the Qur'an), they would have respected peaceful coexistence.

Al-Jamaah's critique of the 9/11 attacks is all the more powerful because the credibility and legitimacy of its leaders cannot be questioned, even by al-Qaeda. Derbala, Ibrahim, Karam Zuhdi, Osama Hafez, Assem Abdel-Maged, and the rest who signed and blessed these two documents were the founding fathers of a major wing of the jihadist movement. Indeed, the group's renunciation of violence paved the way for its participation in the democratic political process in Egypt following the fall of President Hosni Mubarak in 2011.

And these leaders of al-Jamaah were not alone in their criticism. The majority of key Islamists and jihadists have condemned al-Qaeda's internationalization of jihad and echoed al-Jamaah's view of September 11: that it was a catastrophic blunder.

Indeed by the mid to late 2000s the revolt against al-Qaeda's global jihad had escalated into all-out civil war. Former heavyweights in the bin Laden group began blaming him directly for the turmoil engulfing the Muslim world. And in an open letter written in September 2007, one of his prominent Saudi mentors, the preacher and scholar Salman al-Oadah, publicly reproached bin Laden for causing widespread mayhem and killing.[39] A few months later, in November 2007, al-Qaeda's former top ideologue and theorist, Sayyid Imam al-Sharif (known to those in the underground as Dr. Fadl, author of the dissenting manifesto *Rationalizing Jihad*), publicly criticized bin Laden and al-Zawahiri in another shattering blow to their authority. "Al Qaeda committed suicide on September 11," said Fadl.[40] Indeed, toward the end of his life bin Laden himself recognized the potential costs to his organization from its use of violent tactics. Contrary to common perceptions in the United States, the cache of letters and documents seized from bin Laden's hideaway in Abbottabad, Pakistan, show that the al-Qaeda leader was deeply troubled by an apparent loss of Muslim public support. In fact, a few months before his death, he considered changing the name of al-Qaeda to rebrand the group and allow it to better exploit the Arab uprisings of 2011.[41]

Unfortunately, the escalating war within jihadism and debates over use of violence have received hardly any coverage by the so-called terrorism experts, who still lump all Islamists together with al-Qaeda and its cohorts. Terrorism pundits look backward and pigeonhole Islamists and repentant local jihadists through the prism of al-Qaeda's global jihadists. Many invested little or no effort in analyzing the conceptual and operational differences and boundaries among mainstream (moderate) Islamists, local jihadis, and global jihadis such as al-Qaeda. Their stories blur the lines between *Islamist, radical, militant, extremist, jihadi,* and *terrorist,* and equate Islamists' offensive speech with jihadists' violent actions.

After September 11, terrorism pundits, eschewing scholarly analysis and balance, injected their commentaries with a heavy dose of ideology. They viewed themselves as foot soldiers in an existential struggle against terrorism and evil. In all fairness, an injured, angry America was not in the mood to examine nuances and differences within Islamism and jihadism, or to reflect on what went wrong with the country's foreign policy. Americans wanted bin Laden and his associates—those evildoers who visited horror and death on their shores—dead or alive.

Wittingly or not, after September 11 some observers and commentators endorsed the official agenda by portraying Islamism not just as jihadism but as a mortal threat to the West, an aggressive and totalitarian ideology dedicated to random destruction and global subjugation. Others advocated an all-out war against all manifestations of Islamism or political Islam. With ideological blinders clouding their vision, some of these experts fell prey to al-Qaeda's propaganda, while others let their ignorance of Middle Eastern languages and cultures distort their analysis. The result was half-baked truths deployed by the Bush administration to convince Americans of the urgency of expanding the war on terrorism worldwide.

Building on the consensus among independent observers and policy ideologues and ratcheting up the rhetoric, President Bush grouped all mainstream (moderate) and militant Islamists together under the name "Islamo-fascists" and called on Americans to be prepared for a global war on terrorism, the "inescapable calling of our generation."

The global war on terrorism, Bush said, will eradicate the threat of Islamic radical terrorism (a loose and incoherent term) and target rogue states that sponsor terrorism or offer safe haven to terrorists. Declaring an end to the post–World War II security system, Bush said the United States will no longer observe international treaties and institutions that constrain its ability to wage a long struggle on its own terms. Set in sweeping ideological terms, Bush and Vice President Dick Cheney's global war on terrorism set the stage for the American-led invasion and occupation of Iraq, but it is doubtful whether the Bush administration could have sold its ambitious war to the public without the complicity of the foreign policy and security establishment. And while President Obama ratcheted down the rhetoric—eliminating the phrase "war on terror" for one thing—and spent his first months in office reaching out to the Muslim world, his policies were eventually viewed even less favorably than his predecessor's in many Arab and Muslim nations.[42]

WHAT REALLY MOTIVATES MUSLIMS

It certainly does not help that Americans continue to know very little about Islam and Muslims, and what they do know is based more on stereotypes than on facts. For example, 44 percent of Americans say Muslims are too extreme in their religious beliefs. Less than half believe U.S. Muslims are loyal to the United States. Nearly one-quarter of Americans, 22 percent, say they would not want a Muslim as a neighbor. Thirty-two percent say they admire nothing about the Muslim world, and 25 percent admit they simply "don't know." Fifty-seven percent say they know either nothing or not much about the opinions and beliefs of Muslims.[43] Interestingly, the more Americans report knowing about Muslim societies, the more likely they are to hold positive views of those countries.

Fortunately, two recent evidence-based books, *Who Speaks for Islam? What a Billion Muslims Really Think* by John Esposito and Dalia Mogahed and *Al Qaeda in Its Own Words*, edited by Gilles Kepel and Jean-Pierre Milelli, shatter the conventional wisdom and set the record straight.[44]

Based on tens of thousands of hour-long, face-to-face interviews conducted by the Gallup Organization between 2001 and 2007 with residents of more than thirty-five predominantly Muslim nations, *Who Speaks for Islam?* lets the voices of a billion Muslims be heard. But it is more than a statistical research survey. Esposito—a leading scholar of Islam and the director of the Center for Muslim-Christian Understanding at Georgetown University—puts the data in context and makes sense of it. Few are as qualified as Esposito, who has written extensively on contemporary Islamic societies, to assess the findings and draw relevant public and foreign policy lessons.

Some of the findings will shock American readers. For example, according to the survey, only 7 percent of the respondents think the September 11 attacks were "completely" justified, and a majority of Muslims—including nine out of ten Muslims who are called "moderate"—condemned the killings on religious and humanitarian grounds. Forget what bin Laden and al-Zawahiri preach about jihad. For most Muslims, jihad—whether it means a struggle of the soul or the sword—must be a just and ethical struggle. It has only positive connotations, and does not sanction the killing of noncombatants.

Moreover, Esposito and Mogahed show clearly that many Western commentators assign too much weight to Islam and neglect the social and political factors that are the real drivers of both politically "moderate" and radicalized Muslims: to wit, according to the study, those 7 percent of respondents who condoned the attacks mentioned the West's politics, not its culture, its religion, or its way of life, as justification.

When asked what they admired most about the West, the politically radicalized and moderates alike most often mentioned three areas, all of which indicate admiration and respect for American values and way of life: (1) its achievements in technology; (2) its value system, including hard work, self-responsibility, rule of law, and cooperative ethic; and (3) its fair political system, democracy, respect of human rights, freedom of speech, and gender equality.[45] It is the third answer that offers the most hope for a positive future for the Arab awakenings, and helps explain the strong mass support for democratic institution building following the fall of dictators in Tunisia, Libya, Egypt, Yemen, and elsewhere.

Indeed, the interviews put to rest the popular hypothesis that Muslims hate American freedom and success. Contrary to the conventional wisdom that extremists are antidemocratic, a significantly higher percentage of the politically radicalized (50 percent versus 35 percent of moderates) said "moving toward greater governmental democracy" will foster progress in the Arab/Muslim world—a sentiment that was borne out with Islamist parties' embrace of democratic elections in North Africa and the Middle East in 2011 and 2012. More surprisingly, the politically radicalized were as likely as moderates, if not more so, to express interest in improving relations between the world of Islam and the Christian West (58 percent versus 44 percent of moderates).[46]

Again, instead of religion or religious extremism, it comes down to foreign policy. Although the American way of life is prized by Muslims, American foreign policy is loathed. When Esposito and his colleagues asked respondents in ten predominantly Muslim countries how they viewed a number of countries, the attributes they most associated with U.S. foreign policy were ruthlessness (68 percent), scientific and technological advancement (68 percent), aggressiveness (66 percent), conceit (65 percent), and moral decadence (64 percent). When asked what about America reflects these qualities, most respondents listed foreign policy such as the U.S. role in the Palestinian/Israeli conflict and America's support for Muslim dictators. Much of these attitudes seem to have developed since September 11. Clearly, then, the war on terrorism has damaged American standing and reputation in the Muslim world. In the poll, a substantial majority of Muslims believed that the United States was waging a "war against Islam" and that its goal is "to weaken and divide the Islamic world."[47] A majority of moderate and radical Muslims alike viewed Western, particularly American, political, economic, military, and cultural hegemony as a threat to Islamic identity and independence. Indeed, more than a year and a half after the outbreak of the Arab Spring, most Muslims perceive the United States as unsupportive of their democratic aspirations.[48] As Esposito correctly concludes, when Muslims believe their grievances are not being addressed, they are more willing to offer a sympathetic ear to radicals and terrorists.

In my own interviews with politically radicalized activists over the years, many cited Western intervention as a primary driver of their decision to join extremist groups. They said they wanted the West to stop meddling in their countries' internal affairs and pay them respect. When asked by Gallup interviewers what they wanted from the West, a plurality of Muslims cited concrete changes in certain aspects of foreign policy and greater respect for Islam. Esposito groups Muslim grievances against the United States along three dimensions—perceptions of cultural disrespect and denigration of Islam, political domination, and the reality of acute conflicts—all of which he finds filtered through a focus on U.S. foreign policy. Regardless of whether respect can be granted as opposed to earned, the important point is that Muslims do not demand that Westerners change who they are. As Esposito stresses, foreign policy grievances can be addressed if the United States and its Western allies possess the moral courage and proceed with caution, consistency, and respect.

THE MUSLIM WORLDVIEW

An important question remains: what sort of political worldview do Muslims hold? According to the Gallup survey, however diverse Muslim populations may be, a large majority (over 80 percent) of moderates and political radicals want sharia or Islamic law as a source of legislation in a democratic polity. Women are as likely as men to say that "religion is an important part of life" and that "attachment to spiritual and moral values is critical to their progress." Even in the "new" Iraq, 58 percent of Iraqi women opposed separation of religion from politics, and 81 percent said religious authorities should play a direct role in crafting family law.[49] Polling conducted—and election results—since the outbreak of the Arab Spring confirm these findings: Muslims want Islam in political life.[50]

But it would be wrong to read too deeply into these findings. Such views are not a call for theocracy. A majority of the politically radicalized and moderates said they did not want religious leaders to directly govern. Implementing sharia, according to many Muslims, would limit the power of rulers whom they regard as autocratic, "un-Islamic," and corrupt. And although many Western commentators and policymakers argue that sharia is antidemocratic, Muslims view it as a vehicle of liberation and counterweight against political authoritarianism at home and Western domination.

In short, the gaps between Western and Muslim worldviews are real, but they are bridgeable. Take the gulf between the perceptions of Westerners and Muslims of the status and plight of women in Muslim societies. Studies and surveys show that what Americans find most troubling about Islam is the "oppression of women" and that women readily accept second-class status. However, according to the Gallup survey, a majority of women in virtually every country surveyed say they deserve the same legal rights as men—to vote without influence from family members, to work at any job for which they are qualified, and to hold the highest executive position in government. In Saudi Arabia, one of the most religiously conservative Muslim countries, where women are not allowed to vote or drive, a majority of women say they should be able to drive a car by themselves (61 percent), vote without influence (69 percent), and choose the job for which they are qualified (76 percent).[51] In 2012 Saudi Arabia sent two women to compete in the Olympics for the first time in its history.

At the same time, although Muslim women challenge the entrenched patriarchal structure of their societies, the majority do not yearn to become like their Western counterparts. They favor gender parity, but they want it on their own terms and within their own cultural and religious contexts. They do not want to imitate the lifestyle of their Western feminist counterparts. They would like to have equality before the law but preserve their local traditions. Like their male counterparts, Muslim women say their most pressing priorities are economic development and political reforms, not gender issues. Moreover, the Gallup survey did not find that religiosity among Muslim men correlates with less egalitarian views toward women. In Lebanon, Morocco, and Iran, men who support women's rights tend to be more religious than those who do not support women's rights.[52] Plain old secular patriarchy, not Islamic principles— let alone Islamic extremism—accounts for the lagging status of women in much of the Muslim world.

As a result, for those seeking to understand women's issues within a Muslim context, what seems to be an intractable divide is, in fact, nothing of the kind. This holds true as well for similar gaps in understanding on issues such as religion, politics, and extremism.

Indeed, upon closer inspection such gaps are balanced by commonalities between the Muslim world and the West. A critical segment of both Americans and Muslims believe that religion is or ought to be a pillar of their society, informed and guided by the Bible or sharia. Both groups also emphasize the preservation of family values; are concerned about their economic futures, employment, and their abilities to support their families; and give high priority to human rights and broad-based political participation. Finally, both groups strongly support eradicating extremism and terrorism.[53]

UNDERSTANDING ISLAM

The possibility of better relations and mutual understanding is just that, a possibility, and one made less likely thanks to America's global war on terrorism. The Bush ideologues, in their zeal to defeat the "enemy," alienated the very Muslim majorities that are American allies in the struggle against religious extremism and global terrorism. The Obama administration, despite cursory attempts, has done very little to remake America's image in the Muslim world, and has in fact escalated many of the Bush-era counterterrorism strategies that Muslim countries find most troubling. The war on terrorism, or whatever one chooses to call it, continues to play into the hands of al-Qaeda and other militant Islamist groups who relentlessly portray themselves as the vanguard elite who speak for the *ummah* and defend it.

In *Al Qaeda in Its Own Words,* Gilles Kepel—a renowned French scholar on contemporary Islam who has written extensively on Muslim militancy at the Institute of Political Studies (IPS) in Paris—has collected and annotated selected extracts by four radical leaders: bin Laden, al-Zawahiri, Abu Musab al-Zarqawi (the al-Qaeda chief in Iraq), and Abdullah Azzam, leader of the Afghan Arabs in the 1980s. The insightful chapter on bin Laden by IPS researcher Omar Saghi argues convincingly that bin Laden gained ground not by appealing to a monolithic form of dogmatism that should apply to all Muslims; to the contrary, he claimed to tolerate multiple varieties of belief.[54] Rather, he justified his claim to being the exclusive representative of the *ummah* by insisting that only a vanguard like al-Qaeda can carry out jihad on behalf of the *ummah* and take upon itself the duty of applying God's laws and preserving the Muslim community from sin. Bin Laden and his successors claim a much bigger tent than Western analysts give them credit for.

This claim has not gone unchallenged. A significant majority of Muslims—more than 90 percent, according to the Gallup interviews—condemn al-Qaeda's terrorism on religious grounds and thus reject its claim as a representative of Islam and Muslims. Moreover, on the run from U.S. forces for nearly a decade, bin Laden, at the time of his death, was reduced to a static photo, a fading television image who fell victim to his own success.

As Saghi argues, al-Qaeda's large-scale, spectacular terrorism is a product of media consumption: "It is still a crime, but less and less effective as a political and military tool."[55] Meanwhile, al-Qaeda is increasingly being overshadowed by a galaxy of wannabes in Iraq, London, Spain, Lebanon, and Indonesia who call themselves al-Qaeda but have at best a tenuous connection to the group. Now, more and more Muslims view the bin Laden project through the monstrosity of killing of civilians around the world.

Al Qaeda in Its Own Words makes clear that the distinctions among the extremist groups typically lumped under the umbrella term *jihadists* are significant, and that understanding them is critical to assessing the relatively limited nature of the threat and constructing strategies to deploy the Muslim public in the struggle against extremists. For example, in his chapter on Azzam, Thomas Hegghammer, a Norwegian researcher who specializes in Muslim militancy, highlights the discontinuities between Azzam's radical ideas and those of bin Laden and al-Zawahiri.[56]

The conventional wisdom in the United States describes contemporary *Salafi* jihadism, or global Sunni jihad, as homogenous and historically continuous, beginning in Soviet-occupied Afghanistan and carried forth by Azzam's disciples bin Laden and al-Zawahiri after their mentor's 1989 assassination. In reality, the "global jihad movement" is a complex and fragmented political phenomenon that has witnessed radical ruptures and shocks since its inception. Although Azzam certainly influenced his two most famous acolytes, to equate his world-view with bin Laden's and now al-Zawahiri's total global war against "the alliance of Jews and crusaders," as many terrorism experts do, is to falsify history: Azzam opposed terrorism as a tool of war as well as aggression against noncombatants. His definition of *jihad* was the defense of Muslims under attack and occupation, not waging battle against Muslim rulers and the United States. In my interviews with Azzam's former lieutenants and confidantes, I was told that at the height of the Soviet occupation Azzam vetoed proposals by militants to attack Russian civilians, because it would tarnish the image of the mujahidin and jihad. Bin Laden and company, of course, have had no similar reservations.

WHY THE ARAB SPRING WILL BEAT GLOBAL JIHADISM

Even more than the killing of bin Laden, the Arab uprisings—in Egypt, Tunisia, Libya, Yemen, Syria, and Bahrain—have not only shaken the very foundation of the regional authoritarian order but unraveled the standard terrorism narrative. As the Arab revolts gathered steam, al-Qaeda was notably absent. Neither jihadist slogans and rituals nor its violent tactics found a receptive audience among the millions of Arab protesters.

Al-Qaeda offers no economic blueprint, no political horizon, and no vision for the future. While tens of millions of Arabs demand effective citizenship, genuine elections, and the separation of powers, al-Qaeda considers elections and democracy "heresy" and an "evil principle." Out of touch with the aspirations of the vast majority of Arabs calling for political emancipation, Abu Yahya al-Libi, a top al-Qaeda chief, lectured them against "wasting the fruits of liberation" and pursuing democracy, because it is a "road to hell."

Contrary to the call of al-Qaeda chiefs for jihad and violence as pathways to political change, the Arabs who flooded the streets have shown that politics matters and that peaceful protests are more effective at delivering change. The ballot box and parliamentarianism, not the sword and the caliphate, are their rallying cry—an utter rejection of what al-Qaeda stands for.[57]

It is true that religion-based activists—such as the Muslim Brotherhood in Egypt, Ennahda in Tunisia, and the Party of Justice and Development in Morocco—are assuming ownership of the seats of power in the Arab heartland. But these Islamic modernists have little in common with al-Qaeda, and most accept democratic values in shaping the future political trajectory of their societies. There is no Ayatollah Khomeini waiting in the wings to hijack the Arab revolts and seize power. Despite repeated claims by Arab autocrats such as Hosni Mubarak, Muammar Gaddafi, Ali Abdullah Saleh, and Bashar al-Assad, al-Qaeda not only did not spearhead the Arab uprisings but is distinguished by its absence.

Al-Qaeda leaders eventually embraced the uprisings and welcomed the downfall of their arch nemeses in Tunisia, Egypt, Libya, Yemen, and later Syria. And they would certainly like to ride the Arab revolts and take ownership of them. Among his final words bin Laden expressed his "happiness" and "delight" with the demonstrators, saying the *ummah* had been waiting for the revolution for decades. In his eulogy to bin Laden, al-Zawahiri celebrated the "the fall of corrupt and corrupting agents of America in Tunisia and Egypt, and the shaking of their thrones in Libya, Yemen, and Syria." He affirmed his support for the uprisings and called upon the people not to be "tricked" by American and Western support, particularly the NATO mission in Libya.

Yet the Arab awakenings have reinforced what many of us already knew: al-Qaeda's core ideology is intrinsically incompatible with the universal aspirations of Arabs—including human rights and dignity, social justice, free elections, peaceful transition of leadership, and separation of powers. The millions of protesters have neither burned American and Western flags nor blamed Western colonialism for their predicament. The key goal of the demonstrators was sociopolitical and economic transformation through the ballot box, as opposed to the bayonet and suicide bombing.[58]

In other words, the broadly based, peaceful Arab uprisings have demolished al-Qaeda's claim that the Islamist vanguard will spearhead revolutionary Qur'an-based change in Muslim societies. The Arab revolts have left bin Laden's vanguard behind. The terrorism narrative has suffered an equally hard blow. The question is no longer why Muslims so hate America, as the conventional wisdom would have it after the September 11 attacks, but why Western pundits and policymakers so underestimated the millions of Arabs and Muslims yearning for universal values such as human rights, the rule of law, effective citizenship, and open and pluralistic societies.

AN OPEN DOOR

By focusing so intently on al-Qaeda's violent ideology, the so-called terrorism experts have neglected the wider context that decisively shapes how ideology operates. It is only by studying the social conditions that give rise to violent ideologies that one can shed light on the drivers behind them.

The Arab Spring represents a fundamental challenge to the very conditions that fuel extremist ideologies. Time will tell if the Arab revolts will manage to fill the gap of legitimate political authority. If this happens, Arab opinion will deliver the final blow to al-Qaeda and its local branches.

Indeed the Arab awakenings offer a new chance to reach out to Muslim moderates, including newly elected Islamist parties in the Middle East. But doing so will require a more nuanced and subtle understanding of who they are and how they think. Policymakers must eschew ideology in favor of a more analytical and constructive approach, one that draws distinctions between the many faces of Islamism—a politico-religious ideology that accepts the rules of the political game—and jihadism—a tiny breakaway insurgent current that uses violence in the name of religion and seeks to seize power and Islamize society by autocratic fiat.

Notes

1. For overviews on the relationship between religion and terrorism, see David Rapoport, "Fear and Trembling in Three Religious Traditions," *American Political Science Review* 78 (September 1984): 658–677; and Jessica Stern, *Terror in the Name of God: Why Religious Militants Kill* (New York: HarperCollins, 2003).
2. "Pentagon Releases Bin Laden Videotape," National Public Radio, December 13, 2001, www.npr.org/news/specials/response/investigation/011213.binladen.tape.html.
3. President George W. Bush, address to joint session of Congress, September 20, 2001, http://archive.org/details/gwb2001-09-20.flac16.
4. For this and other George W. Bush quotes regarding Islam following the 9/11 attacks, see http://georgewbush-whitehouse.archives.gov/infocus/ramadan/islam.html.
5. For historical and contemporary background on militant Islamic movements, see John L. Esposito, *Unholy War: Terror in the Name of Islam* (New York: Oxford University Press, 2002).
6. Bruce Hoffman, *Inside Terrorism*, rev. and exp. ed. (New York: Columbia University Press, 2006), 85; U.S. Department of State, "Country Reports on Terrorism 2011," July 2012, chap. 6, "Terrorist Organizations," www.state.gov/j/ct/rls/crt/2011.
7. This essay is adapted in part from Chapter 3, "We Are Terrorists," of my book, *Willful Blindness: A Memoir of the Jihad* (New York: Encounter Books, 2008), and from my essay "The Jihad in Plain Sight" (May 6, 2008), which was commissioned by the Hudson Institute for its 2008 Bradley Symposium. The essay is available at www.hudson.org/index.cfm?fuseaction=publication_details&id=5567.
8. Bernard Lewis, *Islam and the West* (New York: Oxford University Press, 1993), 155; Ibn Warraq, *Why I Am Not a Muslim* (Amherst, N.Y.: Prometheus Books, 1995), republished in 2003.
9. Joseph Schacht, *An Introduction to Islamic Law* (New York: Oxford/Clarendon Press, 1982), 69–71; Robert Spencer, *The Politically Incorrect Guide to Islam (and the Crusades)* (Washington, D.C.: Regnery, 2006), 38.
10. Schacht, *Introduction to Islamic Law*, 73.
11. Lawrence Wright, *The Looming Tower* (New York: Knopf, 2006), 57, 138; see also Fawaz A. Gerges, *The Far Enemy—Why Jihad Went Global* (New York: Cambridge University Press, 2005), 100. As Wright recounts, Abdel Rahman is said to have tartly rebuked the younger al-Zawahiri, reminding him that the sharia also forbids a prisoner from being emir. Wright further describes how the rivalry between

Abdel Rahman and al-Zawahiri, who ran competing (though at times cooperating) Egyptian terrorist organizations, became especially heated when they accused each other of treachery while jockeying for leadership positions in Afghanistan during the 1980s. After the Blind Sheikh's conviction and sentencing to life imprisonment, however, al-Zawahiri joined Osama bin Laden in vowing revenge if he died in American custody. See, for example, "Inside Al-Qaeda: A Window into the World of Militant Islam and the Afghani Alumni," *Jane's*, September 28, 2001.

12. Ibn Taymiyyah is widely regarded as a theological eminence; see, for example, Schacht, *Introduction to Islamic Law*, 63, 72. For a decidedly contrary view, see Stephen Schwartz, *The Two Faces of Islam* (New York: Anchor Books, 2003), 60–62.

13. Robert Spencer, *The Truth about Muhammad—Founder of the World's Most Intolerant Religion* (Washington, D.C.: Regnery, 2006), 8.

14. Schacht, *Introduction to Islamic Law*, 115, 1n; Spencer, *Politically Incorrect Guide to Islam (and the Crusades)*, 24.

15. Serge Trifkovic, *The Sword of the Prophet—Islam: History, Theology, Impact on the World* (Salisbury, Mass.: Regina Orthodox Press, 2002), 37–54; Spencer, *Truth about Muhammad*, 89–145.

16. Andrew Bostom, "The Sacred Muslim Practice of Beheading," *FrontPage Magazine*, May 13, 2004, www.frontpagemag.com/Articles/ReadArticle.asp?ID=13371.

17. Annemarie Schimmel, *Islam—An Introduction* (Albany: State University of New York Press, 1992), 35.

18. Marc Sageman, *Understanding Terror Networks* (Philadelphia: University of Pennsylvania Press, 2004), 1–2.

19. Ibid.

20. Daniel Benjamin and Steven Simon, *The Age of Sacred Terror—Radical Islam's War against America* (New York: Random House, 2003), 54–55.

21. www.whitehouse.gov/the-press-office/remarks-assistant-president-homeland-security-and-counterterrorism-john-brennan-csi.

22. The Muslim Brotherhood perceives itself, justifiably, as the leader of a global mass movement whose goal is the implementation of sharia, Islam's legal system and social framework. In Islamist ideology, sharia is the necessary precondition to the Islamizing of society.

23. "Muslim Brotherhood Supreme Guide: 'The U.S. Is Now Experiencing the Beginning of Its End'; Improvement and Change in the Muslim World 'Can Only Be Attained Through Jihad and Sacrifice'" (Middle East Media Research Institute, Oct. 6, 2010), www.memri.org/report/en/0/0/0/0/0/0/4650.htm.

24. Bernard Lewis, *The Middle East: A Brief History of the Last 2,000 Years* (New York: Simon and Shuster, 1996), 233.

25. Ibn Warraq, *Why I Am Not a Muslim*, 12.

26. See Andrew Bostom, ed., *The Legacy of Jihad—Islamic Holy War and the Fate of Non-Muslims* (Amherst, N.Y.: Prometheus Books, 2005), 125–126 (collected Qur'anic verses commanding warfare).

27. Ibid., 136–137, quoting the Sahih Bukhari Collection of Hadith, vol. 4, bk. 52, nos. 42 and 48.

28. Ibid., 165, quoting Sura 2:193 and 8:39.

29. Amir Taheri, *Holy Terror* (Chevy Chase, Md.: Adler and Adler, 1987), 226–227; Ibn Warraq, *Why I Am Not a Muslim*, 12.

30. See Chapter 4, "Jihaad in the Cause of God," in Sayyid Qutb, *Milestones* (Cedar Rapids, Iowa: Mother Mosque Foundation, 1993), 57–58, 59–60. See also Bostom, *Legacy of Jihad,* 233, 235.

31. "Mohamed Morsi during Elections Campaign: Jihad Is Our Path, Death for the Sake of Allah Is Our Most Lofty Aspiration, the Shari'a Is Our Constitution" (Middle East Media Research Institute, May 13, 2012), www.memri.org/clip_tran script/en/3476.htm.

32. Qutb, *Milestones,* 58–59; see also Bostom, *Legacy of Jihad,* 234–237; and Benjamin and Simon, *Age of Sacred Terror,* 64–66. The passage, Sura 2:190–191, continues: "But fight them not at the Sacred Mosque, unless they first fight you there; but if they fight you, slay them. Such is the reward of those who reject faith."

33. "Al-Azhar Cleric Encourages Fighting Demonstrators, Sparks Controversy," *Egypt Independent,* August 15, 2012 (translated from *Al-Masry Al-Youm*), www.egyptin dependent.com/news/update-al-azhar-cleric-encourages-fighting-demonstrators-sparks-controversy.

34. Qutb, *Milestones,* 64; see also Bostom, *Legacy of Jihad,* 238.

35. An earlier version of this essay appeared in *Democracy: A Journal of Ideas* 9 (Summer 2008).

36. At a joint session of Congress on September 20, 2001, President George W. Bush asked, "Why do they hate us? They hate what they see right here in this chamber— a democratically elected government. They hate us for our freedoms—our freedom of religion, our freedom of speech, our freedom to vote, and assemble, and disagree with each other."

37. Jo Becker and Scott Shane, "Secret 'Kill List' Proves a Test of Obama's Principles and Will," *New York Times,* May 29, 2012.

38. For further elaboration on Muslim responses to 9/11, see the chapter "The Aftermath: The War Within," in Fawaz A. Gerges, *The Far Enemy.*

39. Fawaz A. Gerges, "His Mentor Turns on bin Laden," *International Herald Tribune,* September 21, 2007.

40. I have examined in depth Oadah and Imam's critiques of al-Qaeda in the chapter "Beyond the Far Enemy," in Gerges, *Far Enemy.*

41. According to the letters—of which only seventeen out of tens of thousands have been made public—bin Laden described the Arab Spring uprisings as a "tremendous event," and he suggested launching a media campaign to incite "people who have not yet revolted and exhort them to rebel against the rulers" while hoping to guide them away from "half solutions" like secular democratic politics. For a complete set of publically released letters, see U.S. Military Academy at West Point, Combating Terrorism Center, "Letters from Abbottabad," May 3, 2012, www.ctc .usma.edu/posts/letters-from-abbottabad.

42. Pew Research Center, "Global Opinion of Obama Slips, International Policies Faulted," Global Attitudes Project, June 13, 2012.

43. John L. Esposito and Dalia Mogahed, *Who Speaks for Islam? What a Billion Muslims Really Think* (Washington, D.C.: Gallup Press, 2008), 155.

44. Ibid.; Gilles Kepel and Jean-Pierre Milelli, eds., *Al Qaeda in Its Own Words* (Cambridge, Mass.: Harvard University Press, 2008).

45. Esposito and Mogahed, *Who Speaks for Islam?* 80–81.

46. Ibid., 81.

47. Ibid., 87.
48. Pew Research Center, "Most Muslims Want Democracy, Personal Freedoms, and Islam in Political Life," Global Attitudes Project, July 10, 2012.
49. Ibid., 101–102.
50. Pew Research Center, "Most Muslims Want Democracy, Personal Freedoms, and Islam in Political Life."
51. Ibid.
52. Ibid., 123.
53. Ibid., 154.
54. Omar Saghi, in ibid.
55. Ibid., 39.
56. Thomas Hegghammer, in Kepel and Milelli, *Al Qaeda in Its Own Words*.
57. Trying to jump on the bandwagon of the protesters and appeal to them, Ayman al-Zawahiri, al-Qaeda's current emir, reminded Egyptians that before he escaped from the country, he "had participated in many popular protests and demonstrations," including one "in Tahrir Square in 1971." Far from it: several of al-Zawahiri's contemporary associates have told me that he never believed in political activism as a means to overthrow the secular Egyptian regime and did not even use the mosque for recruitment or mobilization.
58. Of all militants, Anwar al-Awlaki, an American Yemeni militant preacher killed by a U.S. drone strike in 2011, was candid and realistic, conceding that al-Qaeda had nothing to do with the historical developments remaking the region. In an article titled "Tsunami of Change," which appeared in his *Inspire* magazine in May 2011, al-Awlaki said that "we do not know yet what the outcome would be, and we do not have to. The outcome doesn't have to be an Islamic government for us to consider what is occurring to be a step in the right direction."

5

is suicide terrorism an effective tactic?

Suicide terrorism is a pragmatic choice.
YES: Gordon H. McCormick and Lindsay Fritz,
Naval Postgraduate School

NO: Suicide terrorism is a political failure.
Max Abrahms, *Johns Hopkins University*

From the September 11, 2001, attacks on the United States, through the 2002 Bali nightclub bombings, the 2005 London transit bombings, the 2008 Mumbai attacks, and scores of other recent terror incidents across the Middle East, Central Asia, North Africa, and elsewhere, suicide attacks have come to symbolize the shockingly lethal terrorism of the modern age.

But has the ultimate sacrifice of hundreds of individual attackers and the deaths of thousands of innocent victims paid off in terms of suicide terror groups achieving, or moving closer to achieving, their stated goals?

This question cuts to the heart of long-standing academic and policy debates over whether terrorism itself is an effective means of achieving political objectives.[1] Although this broader concern remains far from resolved, a specific focus on suicide terrorism is a constructive way to test the utility of terrorism itself. Because suicide attacks are far deadlier and more fear-inspiring than conventional attacks—compare the failed conventional bombing of the World Trade Center in 1993 (six dead) with the successful suicide operation in September 2001 (nearly three thousand dead)—they are presumably more politically effective than conventional attacks as well. Indeed, terrorist groups adopt suicide tactics for a simple reason: they believe they will work.[2]

Ever since a series of Hezbollah suicide bombings drove the United States and France out of Lebanon in the early 1980s, a mythology of success has surrounded suicide terrorism, leading dozens of different terror groups to since adopt the tactic. And although the use of suicide terrorism parallels the modern rise of religious, particularly Islamic, terrorism, many prominent non–religion-based groups have also ubiquitously employed the tactic—including the secular Palestinian Fatah organization, and the separatist Tamil Tigers in Sri Lanka, which committed more suicide attacks between the mid-1980s and 2001 than any other group in the world.

The authors of both essays in this chapter agree that suicide terrorism is a more lethal and fear-provoking form of terrorism than conventional terrorism. And they agree that groups employ suicide attacks for reasons beyond purely instrumental goal attainment—for example, powerful individual and group solidarity benefits are gained from having members willing to commit the ultimate act of sacrifice for the cause. Suicide tactics are, therefore, an understandably attractive option for terrorist organizations. The authors strongly disagree, however, on the question of whether suicide tactics are an effective means of achieving political ends.

In the first essay, Gordon McCormick and Lindsay Fritz argue that terrorism is a tactic chosen by strategic actors who rationally calculate that it will maximize their chances of achieving objectives. Suicide attacks are employed for a similar reason: it is believed they offer a "higher return on investment" than conventional alternatives (the authors present eight factors that they say contribute to the greater utility of suicide terrorism). Terrorist groups do not always make perfect decisions (who does?), but, according to McCormick and Fritz, if we start from the empirically grounded proposition that terrorists make rational (context-dependent) strategic choices—including the choice to employ suicide attacks—it is possible to efficiently isolate key variables and ultimately better understand the nature of terrorist decision making, including decisions that may appear to deviate from rationality.

Max Abrahms, by contrast, believes that terrorism is a futile political strategy and that adding suicide attacks to the mix does nothing to alter its losing track record. Like McCormick and Fritz, he believes the choice of both terrorism and suicide tactics may be rational, but for reasons other than political goal attainment such as for ideological/organizational purposes. Indeed, Abrahms contends that suicide attacks against civilian populations tend to backfire, leaving groups further from, rather than closer to, their objectives. As for the question of whether terrorists are strategically rational political maximizers, Abrahms says there is little evidence that terrorist groups carefully weigh their strategic options; they often reflexively shun nonviolent avenues with stronger track records of eliciting political change. He concludes that political scientists and policymakers need to reexamine assumptions that suicide terrorist groups behave as rational political actors.

The use of suicide as a tactic of war or terrorism is not new. For example, during World War II thousands of Japanese kamikaze pilots attacked American ships and military outposts across the Pacific. And in the nineteenth century, Russian anarchists often employed suicide tactics against the royal family and other government targets.[3] What is new is the widespread use of suicide attacks as a form of mass-casualty terrorism. A tremendous amount of death and destruction has been wrought by suicide terrorists over the last twenty-five years. Determining whether this carnage has paid political dividends for groups employing the tactic is not simply an academic exercise; it will inform policymakers' understanding of future terrorist strategies and help determine strategies of response as well.

Suicide terrorism is a pragmatic choice.
YES: Gordon H. McCormick and Lindsay Fritz,
Naval Postgraduate School

A Strategic Perspective on Suicide Attack

O n a warm autumn morning in 2003, Hanadi Jaradat said goodbye to her parents in the West Bank city of Jenin. The twenty-nine-year-old apprentice lawyer had a reputation as an ambitious and independent young woman. She had grown up as the eldest daughter in a large family, studied law at Jerash University in Jordan, and aspired to one day open her own law office. Hanadi was so driven to succeed, her mother later claimed, that she had turned down a succession of suitors to pursue her studies and career. Her parents therefore detected nothing out of the ordinary when she hurriedly bid farewell that morning, rushing off with a smile to close a real estate deal for her law office.

Six hours later, Hanadi quietly entered Maxim's, a restaurant in Haifa many miles from Jenin and on the other side of the security zone that separated Israel from the West Bank. Like her parents, the diners of the crowded seaside establishment did not perceive anything out of the ordinary. Hanadi had left her home in traditional dress, but she entered the restaurant in fashionable black jeans with her hair pulled back in a ponytail framing what witnesses said was a pretty "heart-shaped" face. She looked like any other casual lunchtime customer. Upon sitting down, Hanadi ordered a meal. After finishing her meal, she calmly got up and walked to the most crowded part of the restaurant. Situating herself between two families, she then detonated the 22 pounds of explosives laced with ball bearings that she had concealed under her clothing.[4]

In an instant, body parts of diners were strewn across the room. Hanadi's victims—twenty-one in total—included women and children, Jews and Arabs. Each of the two families that Hanadi had made sure was within the lethal blast radius of her explosives lost five members. All that remained to identify the young Palestinian woman was her head. Her attack proved to be one of the deadliest suicide attacks of the Second Palestinian Intifada.

It is reasonable to ask how a young woman of such great promise could take her own life. How could she do so, furthermore, for the express purpose of carrying out such a merciless and calculated attack? The portrait that first emerged of Hanadi Jaradat and the scene of devastation that she left in her wake—what Haifa's chief of police called "a vision of hell"—seemed incongruous. Once all the facts surrounding the incident were uncovered, however, it was clear that her actions, though dramatic, were in no way unique. Hanadi's attack was one of over two hundred suicide operations carried out in Israel during the Second Intifada (2000–2004) and one of at least a dozen such actions carried out by Palestinian women, including wives, mothers, and students. Since 1983, over 3,500 suicide attacks have been carried out worldwide.[5] The circumstances that surround these actions reveal a common underlying logic.

To uncover this logic, we must distinguish between the reasons why individuals are willing to die to kill others and the reasons why the groups that train, equip, and send them on their way choose to solicit or otherwise accept their sacrifice. At the level of the individual, the reasons for martyrdom vary widely. These reasons can be found in the realm of individual and social psychology and are beyond the scope of this essay. The task of this essay is to examine the *strategic* basis of suicide attacks. To do this, we will evaluate these operations at the level of the group.

We begin with the observation that terrorism is not a strategy, per se, but a tactic that traditionally has been employed to support one of two alternative strategic programs: political coercion or political mobilization. We follow with a discussion of the specific nature and utility of suicide tactics. We conclude with a brief discussion of the meaning and limits of strategic behavior. Some of the confusion about the underlying strategic basis of terrorism begins with a prior misunderstanding of the nature of strategic action itself. A complete understanding of terrorist behavior requires a multilayered approach to terrorist decision making. The starting point for any such effort, however, must be the hypothesis that terrorist groups are rational agents that try to match means with ends to achieve their objectives.

TERRORISM, SIGNALING, AND STRATEGY

From a strategic perspective, terrorism can be thought of as a multistaged signaling game in which violent images are employed to communicate a group's ability and commitment to use violence in whatever form is necessary to achieve its goals.[6] The players in this game consist of a terrorist group and one or more target audiences. As in all signaling games, one or both sets of players act with incomplete information on the other. The terrorist group may or may not have a complete understanding of the relevant attributes of its target audiences, but its target audiences will always begin the game with an incomplete picture of the utility function, commitment, and capabilities of the group. It is this state of incomplete information that permits the group to manipulate external perceptions of its "type." The group can be seen as strong or weak. The targets of influence that the group wishes to impress evaluate its type based on what they see, which is what the group chooses to reveal through the "signals" it generates by its attacks. These attacks—as signals—are designed to shape audience perceptions of the payoff structure of the game in a way that advances the group's political agenda.[7]

Terrorism can be used to support two different strategic programs. The first is a strategy of political coercion or "dirty bargaining."[8] In such cases, terrorism is a means of gaining negotiating leverage over the state. The group begins by initiating attacks against high-value targets to establish that it is willing and able to continue its attacks into the foreseeable future. Having established its bona fides, the group then enters into (tacit or explicit) negotiations with the target government and offers to halt its campaign of violence in return for political concessions. Coercive campaigns are designed to convince the target regime that the costs of not complying with a group's wishes are greater than the costs of concession. Although the dynamics of dirty bargaining is a complicated subject in its own right, it is generally true that the degree of leverage a group will be able to exercise is directly related to the perceived level of damage it can threaten over time. This is a function, in turn, of the frequency, scale, and "media quality" of its attacks.

In the second strategic program, terrorism can play a significant role in supporting a strategy of political mobilization. Signaling attacks are designed to draw attention to the group's existence and purpose, sharpen popular views of the nature of the struggle, demonstrate the group's growing strength and the increasing weakness of the incumbent regime, and embolden people to begin to actively support the group's efforts to usher in a new political order. Such attacks are also regularly employed in the hope of provoking an extreme response. If successful, this strategy can have the effect of radicalizing and polarizing popular opinion, retroactively legitimating the group's use of violence, and making it easier for the group to mobilize popular support for its cause.[9] In contrast to a strategy of coercion, the ultimate objective of this program is not to gain a greater degree of leverage at the negotiating table, but to eventually displace the state altogether. To do so, a terrorist group must grow to the point that it can defeat the state on its own terms.

Each of these strategic programs is designed to shape the perceptions of a different primary audience. For a program of coercive bargaining to succeed, a terrorist group must establish itself as a plausible threat in the minds of state decision makers and their constituents, who must be made to believe that they will be subjected to an unacceptable level of continuing violence if a compromise settlement is not reached. In making this determination, state authorities will consider a number of factors that will bear on their decision, each of which is subject to manipulation. Is the group actually capable of carrying through on its threats? What would it cost the group to do so? Is it willing to incur these costs? Does it have the means to sustain a protracted campaign in the face of government countermeasures? What will these countermeasures cost? What costs will be incurred in defying the group's demands? What are the costs of compliance? The answers to these and related questions can be answered only after a group has begun to develop a track record for itself. Even at this point, the answers cannot be known with certainty. With this in mind, today's terrorists design their actions to magnify the state's perceptions of the threat it can expect to confront tomorrow.

The primary audience in a program of political mobilization is the group's own constituents. Violent opposition groups are generally composed of a hardcore minority and a much larger majority who are more or less committed to the cause. The much larger majority is made up of "conditional supporters"[10] whose willingness to back the opposition (and not the state) is based on their subjective estimates of the expected costs and benefits of their alternatives. These estimates, in turn, are based on their perceptions of the relative balance of power between the two players and their corresponding prospects. This process poses a mobilization challenge to violent opposition groups during the early days of their campaigns because of the state's obvious and overwhelming force advantage. Who would want to join such a high-risk enterprise? This challenge can be overcome through a program of symbolic violence designed to generate an exaggerated image of group strength and regime weakness. Terrorist actions, in this respect, are intended to create a self-fulfilling prophecy: if a group can convince enough people that it has the ability to effectively challenge the state, it can mobilize the support it needs to do so.[11]

Such efforts, as noted, are generally reinforced by a program of target provocation. High-profile attacks on the state and its constituents, in such cases, are carried out for the purpose of triggering indiscriminate counterattacks on a group's own political followers. The intention is to force the state into a Hobson's choice—either "retreat or unleash the struggle."[12] Regardless of what course of action it chooses, the state can be expected to improve the group's chances of expanding its base of support. In contrast to the demonstrative use of terrorism, which is designed to manipulate the *expectations* of the target audience, the provocative use of terrorism is designed to (indirectly) influence the *preferences* of that audience. As a practical matter, of course, many if not most terrorist actions serve both purposes at the same time. A series of terrorist attacks against high-value targets in the face of state efforts to keep such attacks from occurring will not only make the attacking group look strong and the government look weak, but also put increasing pressure on the state to use "every means at its disposal" to put an end to the violence. The provocative utility of such actions derives not from their popularity among a group's constituency "but from the unpopularity of the ensuing repression."[13]

To accomplish these goals, terrorist groups must create a perceptual or subjective effect that is greater than the sum of the physical consequences of their attacks. This approach places a premium on conducting operations that are newsworthy enough to be picked up and transmitted to a larger audience by the mass media. The media, in this respect, play an essential intermediate role in amplifying the signal a group transmits every time it carries out an attack.[14] By analogy, this is the same role played by the amplifier in one's home sound system, television, or computer. The function of an amplifier is to take an initially weak audio signal and boost it to the point that it is strong enough to drive a speaker. The audience, then, is listening not to the sound of the initial signal, but to that of an amplified signal strong enough to be heard. This is the function the media play in the aftermath of a terrorist attack. In the absence of a strong media boost, terrorist attacks have little or no effect beyond the immediate area of the event. With this boost, by contrast, they are international news. To paraphrase an old philosophical question: if a car bomb goes off in the forest and there is no one around to hear it, does it make any (political) noise? The answer, of course, is no. Terrorists, through their actions, either succeed in staying in the headlines or are out of the game.

As many observers have noted over the years, nothing is more likely to seize the headlines than a deliberately executed act of violence. Furthermore, the more graphic the violence is, the more prominently, broadly, and repeatedly it is likely to be reported.[15] To ensure the media boost they need to prevail, terrorist groups have a strong incentive to select targets and tactics that are as audacious as possible. Even violent acts of terrorism, however, can become routine. As they do so, their media value diminishes. To escape this trap, terrorist groups must continue to innovate and escalate to hold the attention of their target audiences over the course of their campaigns. As a practical matter, this tactic frequently results in greater levels of violence. Who is killed, how many are killed, the ways in which they are killed, and the frequency with which such killings take place—all influence the newsworthiness of a terrorist event. In an oft-quoted remark, terrorism expert Brian Jenkins claimed some years ago that "terrorists want a lot of people watching, not a lot of people dead."[16] The increasingly deadly nature of terrorism over the past decade, however, would appear to validate the counterclaim of McCormick's first corollary to Jenkins's rule: "If a lot of people are dead, a lot of *other* people are watching."

Regardless of the nature of its specific strategic program, every violent opposition group faces a similar challenge at the outset of its campaign: to "win," it must find a way to achieve an ambitious political agenda in the face of imposing resource constraints. This challenge is generally complicated by two competing requirements: the need to remain secure, on the one hand, and the need to continue to advertise itself, on the other.[17] In the first case, a group's small size makes it highly vulnerable to attack. Any significant breach in security can easily end the game before it starts. This factor places a premium on reducing a group's exposure to government counterattack by reducing its operating profile. However, this same constraint means that underground groups must make the most of the little they have. Should the group fail to maintain an effective presence before the state and in the minds of its constituents, it will not only result in a loss of influence, but also eventually destabilize the organization itself. The underground group, then, faces two ways to lose but only one way to win. To prevail, it must walk an often-fine line between two competing types of operational errors.

Terrorist groups, in this respect, face a dual paradox. To carry out their strategic program, they must appear to be strong, but they must do so from a position of weakness. To create an appearance of strength, they must operate in a way that signals strength rather than weakness in the minds of those they wish to influence. This goal must be accomplished, however, in a manner that minimizes the risk that the state will exploit a group's weakness to eliminate it from the game. This paradox helps explain why violent opposition groups turn to terrorism in the first place. Terrorism, as high-profile symbolic violence, offers a way of balancing the competing requirements of influence and security in the face of constrained resources. It appears to offer a way of achieving a lot with a little at a relatively small price. From this perspective, of course, terrorism is not an expression of strength but a sign of weakness. To overcome this contradiction, terrorist groups must appear to be much stronger than they are using the same violent tactics that mark them as weak actors. Their objective strength in the long run will be directly proportional to the illusion of strength they are able to create for their target audiences along the way.

THE TACTICAL UTILITY OF SUICIDE ATTACKS

Suicide attacks, as noted earlier, can be evaluated at two different levels of analysis: the individual and the group. At the individual level, there is no consistent pattern. When the circumstances surrounding Hanadi Jaradat's attack came to light, for example, it was found that the young Palestinian woman was motivated by revenge. Four months before her attack, her brother and fiancé had been shot and killed by an Israeli assassination squad while drinking coffee on the family's front porch. Both men, it was alleged, had ties to Islamic Jihad. The murder of her loved ones led her to offer herself to Islamic Jihad as a suicide bomber. Each case, however, is different. Although the desire for revenge is a common contributing factor in suicide attacks, it is by no means universal. Some individuals, it appears, are motivated by a sense of social and moral obligation, some make a deal with God, and still others are willing to trade their lives for a promise of financial support for their families. The reasons why people volunteer or allow themselves to be recruited for suicide attacks, in short, are as diverse, complex, and idiosyncratic as the individuals themselves.[18]

At the group level, which is what interests us here, the motivations underlying the use of suicide attacks are more consistent. The decision to employ suicide tactics at this level of analysis is a rational choice that can be evaluated through the same strategic lens that we have used to evaluate a group's decision to resort to terrorism in the first place. Both decisions are subject to a "logic of consequence," in which a group's strategic and tactical alternatives are evaluated in terms of their anticipated effects and potential utility.[19] Groups that employ suicide tactics under this logic do so because these attacks appear to offer a higher return on investment than their conventional alternative.

We have isolated eight key factors that explain the utility of suicide terrorism. First, suicide attacks are more lethal than their conventional counterparts. Conventional bombers depend on the unwitting cooperation of their targets to carry out their missions. The bomb itself is stationary. The target(s) of attack must come within the effective blast radius of the bomb before the explosion can have the intended effect. In the case of a timed detonation in particular, which constitutes the majority of bombings, the attacker has no control over who or how many are caught in the fragmentation pattern. The suicide attacker, by contrast, is a "smart bomb" with a "human guidance system."[20] He can vary the timing and vector of his attack to improve his chances of hitting his target and maximizing his intended effects. When Hanadi Jaradat got up from her table to move to a more crowded area of the restaurant, she did so to improve her chances of killing as many people as possible. This is not the exception but the norm in suicide operations. In one survey carried out several years ago, suicide attacks were estimated on average to be four times as deadly as conventional operations.[21] In 2011, suicide attacks accounted for only 2.7 percent of terrorist incidents, but 21 percent of all terrorism-related fatalities.[22]

Second, suicide operations have proven to be a highly effective way of gaining the spotlight, which is one of the reasons groups resort to terrorist tactics in the first place. The efficiency of suicide attacks stems not just from their greater average lethality, but also from the fact that the act itself is a newsworthy event in its own right. The self-destructiveness of these operations makes them attractive publicity stunts. At times, their inherent drama is further extended through a systematic follow-on program of symbolic exploitation. Most groups such as Hamas, Islamic Jihad, and al-Qaeda that employ suicide operations as a standard tactic glorify and immortalize the attacker in videos, audiocassettes, posters, graffiti, and group websites. The Palestinian groups, in particular, regularly videotape the last will and testaments of their martyrs and distribute these tapes to local and international media. During the period of the Second Intifada, a number of these groups are reported to have even circulated calendars that featured a "martyr of the month." The heroism and self-sacrifice of the martyr are discussed in mosques and madrassas. The attacks are reenacted in playgrounds and on the streets.[23] A single suicide action, in this respect, can generate a significant level of second-order attention.

Third, in enabling social circumstances, suicide attacks can be a way of building solidarity with one's political base. The decision to use suicide terrorism does not occur *ex nihilo*, but occurs in the context of a larger social and cultural environment that can either promote the use of suicide operations or restrict their use as a practical tactic. In the absence of facilitating social norms, suicide tactics would most likely be rejected by a group's own target audience. Indeed, the use of such tactics under these conditions is likely to do more harm than good, even assuming a group could find the recruits needed to carry out such attacks in the first place. In a facilitating environment, by contrast, a group finds not only ample recruits who are willing to die for the cause, but a ready audience for their sacrifice. A martyr's death, in this case, is a mutual loss for the group and the community that raised him. Honoring his memory requires honoring the cause and, by association, the group for which he sacrificed his life. This support, in turn, can be used as a means of building a stronger common bond between a terrorist group and its core supporters.

Fourth, and in a related vein, the use of suicide tactics can be a way of deflecting or reducing the possibility of backlash over civilian casualties. Terrorism by its nature is horrific—it is intended to be. Although suicide operations, as we have argued, can be useful, they also carry risks. One such risk is that a suicide operation will be rejected by the very people it is supposed to impress. This risk can be acute in the case of deliberately chosen civilian targets. The fact that the goals of a group have widespread popular support does not mean that the methods it employs to achieve its goals will receive the same level of acceptance. Disputes over tactics can divide a group from its own self-defined constituency. Suicide operations, paradoxically, can prove to be a more acceptable alternative than conventional terrorist attacks—even when they prove to be more lethal. The reason for this, it is argued, is their built-in act of atonement.[24] The self-martyr only kills others at the cost of his own life. His willingness to do so justifies the event. In the right social setting, once again, this willingness can turn an act of murder into a necessary sacrifice. To the degree it does so, it can give a group the political space it needs to conduct its program without losing the support of its own followers.

Fifth, suicide attacks can be a useful instrument of "auto-propaganda,"[25] which, in turn, can help motivate and unify a group's internal membership. Extremist elements within violent opposition groups often reflect the underlying emotions of the group as a whole. Their actions, if properly calibrated, can tap into these emotions, give them definition, and, in doing so, contribute to forging a group's collective identity. They also personify the group's mission and its ideology in its purest form. Their example can be used to remind others of who they are, why they fight, and how they must fight to win. Martyrdom operations, and the culti-vated ritual that almost universally surrounds these operations, serve this purpose admirably. Although those who are selected for suicide missions are typically marginal affiliates of their group in life, they are elevated into symbols of the group's purpose and motivation in death. Those who survive them are strength-ened by their shared image and memories of their dead heroes and their mutual responsibility to live by the example of those who died for their convictions.

Sixth, suicide terrorism can be employed as an instrument of interorganiza-tional competition, providing terrorist groups with a competitive advantage over their local rivals. Terrorists frequently compete for political market share. In such cases, suicide operations can be used as a means of signaling a group's relative attractiveness over groups that share the same or similar ideological goals but employ a more conventional tactical portfolio. This argument is sup-ported by the work of Mia Bloom, who has shown that Palestinian suicide operations, and the events in their aftermath, have resulted in an increase in popular support for martyrdom attacks and a reduction in support for the Palestinian Authority.[26] Similar findings have been generated by Dipak Gupta and Kusum Mundra,[27] who have illustrated the way in which intra-Palestinian rivalries have influenced the timing of suicide operations, and Scott Atran, who has observed that although Hamas's suicide campaign during the Second Inti-fada actually prompted Israel to reoccupy the Palestinian territories, the organi-zation's level of popular support increased substantially during the same time period, eventually eclipsing that of the Palestine Liberation Organization (PLO). The September 11 attacks, Atran suggests, represent a similar case. Though it ultimately resulted in a significantly greater level of foreign intervention in the Muslim world, the 9/11 operation dramatically bolstered al-Qaeda's reputation as a global jihadist organization and significantly increased its leverage over rival jihadist groups.[28]

Seventh, suicide operations are cheap. As with any operation, suicide attacks require a preexisting infrastructure to select, prepare, and equip new recruits. Once this is in place, however, the marginal cost of carrying out an attack is insignificant. The average improvised explosive device (IED) worn or carried by a suicide bomber, while increasingly sophisticated, probably still costs no more than $100 to $200 to produce.[29] Where explosives are plentiful, even vehicle-born IED attacks, which typically employ stolen vehicles, are a trivial expense. The bombers themselves are expendable assets. Often, as suggested earlier, they are not even members of the group, but individuals—like Hanadi Jaradat—who are recruited for the sole purpose of carrying out a single one-way mission. The costs of achieving the same effect with conventional means would often prove to be much higher. This was summarized nicely by a member of the Black Tigers, the suicide arm of the Liberation Tigers of Tamil Eelam (LTTE), who noted: "If we have a target and use conventional operations we normally lose 15 or 16 fighters. With self sacrifice we can achieve the same objective and only one dies."[30]

Finally, as economist Thomas Schelling observed years ago, it is sometimes rational to appear to be irrational. Many observers during the period in which suicide attacks first emerged as a terrorist tactic tended to classify them as irrational, or at least as nonrational, acts. They were considered to be the actions of individuals who had lost the capacity to reason and were "crazy for the cause." Rational actors, as we have noted, weigh the consequences of their actions in relation to their goals and select the course of action that appears to offer the highest expected return. This gives them a measure of predictability. It also gives their opponents a way of influencing their behavior, at least in principle. One has only to identify and manipulate their incentive structure to get them to change their ways. Irrational actors, by contrast, are not motivated by incentives. They are guided by impulse and emotion and, as a consequence, often act in ways that undermine their own interests. They are not subject to manipulation in the same way that rational actors are. All things being equal, this frame of mind makes them more dangerous and more difficult to deter. The group that can gain a reputation for being "a little bit crazy" can enhance its leverage at the negotiating table and its reputation as an effective counterweight to the state.[31]

THE (IMPERFECT) STRATEGIC TERRORIST

The strategic perspective on terrorist decision making in general, and the use of suicide tactics in particular, is not without its challengers. Terrorists, we are told, always lose, and a strategic actor would never adopt a course of action with a losing track record. The critics, therefore, conclude that terrorists are not strategic agents.[32] This argument has a number of shortcomings. The first is empirical. Terrorists, in fact, sometimes win. Three examples include the Irgun Zvai Leumi in Israel, the Ethniki Organosis Kyprion Agoniston (EOKA) in Cyprus, and the National Liberation Front (FLN) in Algeria. Each of these groups played a pivotal role in displacing a colonial occupier and establishing an independent political order. Terrorism was an important tool in each organization's larger strategic program. This conclusion is echoed by Robert Pape, who lists a series of successful or partially successful terrorist campaigns over the last twenty-five years that specifically employed suicide tactics. His examples include Hezbollah's campaign to force the United States and France out of Lebanon (1983), Hezbollah's efforts to force Israel's withdrawal from Lebanon (1983–1985), and Hamas versus Israel (1994–1995).[33] A recent RAND study focusing on how terrorist campaigns end found that roughly 10 percent of the 268 terrorist groups that have come and gone since 1968 disbanded after achieving all or some of their political objectives. A much larger percentage ended after being incorporated into the mainstream political process, which, for some of these groups, represented a partial victory in its own right.[34] In evaluating such cases we must recognize that the operative goals of terrorist groups are frequently more complex, differentiated, and nuanced than their public agendas might otherwise suggest.[35]

Some of the cases just cited, one might argue, are actually examples of guerrilla or insurgent organizations rather than terrorist groups, and therefore somehow do not count.[36] For the purposes of this discussion, this is a distinction without a difference. As suggested earlier, one of the principal ways violent opposition groups use terrorism is to jump-start the mobilization process by attempting to polarize society and reshaping popular images of the relative power and prospects of the opposition and the state. Most "insurgent" organizations, in this respect, initiate their campaigns with the liberal use of high-profile violence, much of it directed against nonmilitary and, often, explicitly civilian targets. Examples include such groups as the Viet Cong, Shining Path, Tupac Amaru Revolutionary Movement (MRTA), Farabundo Martí National Liberation Front (FMLN), the Tamil Tigers, and the contemporary Taliban, to name just a few. Many so-called terrorist groups, by the same token, remain hopeful of transforming their campaigns into a full-fledged insurgency. Terrorism, in such cases, is a means of "bootstrapping" themselves into a position of eventual strength by expanding their popular bases.[37] Most insurgent organizations, in short, begin their operational life as "terrorists," and many terrorist groups think of themselves as future "insurgents."

Strategic actors, furthermore, not only pursue long-range goals; they have short-range goals as well. These short-range, or proximate, objectives are intermediate goals that must be achieved to implement their larger strategic program. In the case of terrorist groups, such objectives include advertising a group's presence and political agenda; raising popular consciousness about the terms of the struggle; discrediting the target regime; revealing the "inner contradictions" of the state; creating fissures and confusion within the governing bodies of the state and between the government and its internal and external political constituencies; finding outside allies to support the inside struggle; and polarizing popular political attitudes and creating the conditions needed to mobilize popular support. As the record of the past fifty years has demonstrated, terrorism—including suicide terrorism—is a well-established means of achieving such goals. Even when a group ultimately fails, it frequently succeeds in achieving many of its intermediate objectives along the way. As with conventional strategic actors, these tactical achievements can give the illusion of strategic progress and motivate a group to continue the struggle long after the possibility of a final victory has faded.

A recent and dramatic example of such a situation is offered by al-Qaeda in Iraq (AQI), a group that has relied heavily on suicide attacks. Before his death, Abu Musab al-Zarqawi stated that one of his objectives was to incite widespread internecine violence between the Shiite and Sunni communities in Iraq as a means of expanding his own base of support within the Sunni population. "If we succeed in dragging the [the Shi'ia] into a sectarian war," he declared, it "will awaken the sleepy Sunnis who are fearful of destruction and death at the hands of the Shi'ia."[38] One of the single most provocative attacks he carried out to support this objective was the February 2006 bombing of the al-Askari mosque in Samarra.[39] Few targets could have been as well chosen to catalyze the polarization process that al-Zarqawi believed would enable him to grow his base. Within a week of the attack, hundreds of Sunnis and Shiites had been killed in spontaneous and orchestrated outbreaks of sectarian violence, and some two hundred Sunni mosques were reported to have been damaged or destroyed.[40] The incident marked the beginning of a brutal and highly destabilizing cycle of violence, fed by the continuing AQI conventional and unconventional attacks against Shiite population targets, which had the intended effect of further dividing Iraqi society and pushing the country to the brink of civil war.

The next six months leading up to al-Zarqawi's death in June were probably the high-water mark of AQI's strength. Growing Sunni fears about the consequences of a Shiite-dominated Iraq, due in part to the Shiite backlash catalyzed by al-Zarqawi's operations, resulted in an upsurge in Sunni-initiated violence throughout the country. The fact that, in the end, AQI did not succeed in carrying out its larger game plan is not evidence of a lack of strategic focus under al-Zarqawi's leadership. In fact, much of the support AQI was able to gather within the Sunni community was attributable to the very reason he foresaw. After his death, to be sure, AQI effectively lost its way as a unified organization, fragmenting into a series of poorly coordinated and locally motivated factions under second-tier commanders. This fragmentation, coupled with a series of bad tactical decisions (and corresponding good decisions by U.S. forces), led AQI into the situation in which it finds itself today: standing on the wrong side of many of its former allies.[41] Although AQI, in the end, made some poor choices that ultimately alienated many of its previous supporters within the Sunni community, it was the calculated use of violence that allowed it to achieve its position of influence in the first place.

AQI's rapid decline in the years after al-Zarqawi's death illustrates the essential role that strong central leadership plays in keeping a group on course. Terrorist groups, like every other organization, are made up of individuals and cliques with a wide range of interests, motives, and worldviews. Many if not most of these factors are likely to be in sync with, complementary to, or at least not incompatible with a group's objectives and planning assumptions. Others, however, will certainly contradict them. The presence of such internal contradictions represents a continual (if often hidden) challenge to a terrorist group's strategic program, as it does for all strategic actors. One of the roles of group leadership, in this respect, is to ensure that the diverse motives of a group's members are harnessed to its mission rather than allow its mission to be effectively defined by the individual motives of its members. As a rule, few strategic actors ever completely live up to this ideal. Equally few, however, end up at the other end of the spectrum and lose any semblance of strategic direction. Those groups that begin to drift in this direction, as AQI did in the wake of al-Zarqawi's death, either tend to disintegrate internally because of their own centrifugal forces or are otherwise eliminated from the game before they arrive.

This bounded view of terrorist rationality does not invalidate the argument that terrorism can be viewed as a strategic, or more specifically an instrumentally tactical, activity. A strategic choice is one that selects the best means of achieving specified ends. The strategic nature of the choice does not depend on the nature of these ends, whether the individual making the decision fully and accurately understands his environment, whether he appreciates what his alternatives are, or whether he understands what the consequences of his alternative courses of action might be in relation to his goals. It depends only on whether he selects the best course of action based on his beliefs. Beliefs, of course, are perceptually grounded and subject to error. To the degree that the assumptions underlying one's decisions are in error, any instrumental choices that follow from these assumptions are likely to be suboptimal. This situation does not make these choices any less strategic or rational. The strategic view of

terrorist decision making, in this sense, addresses not the outcome or consequences of group decisions, but the nature of the decision process itself.

Terrorist groups are imperfect strategic agents, just like everyone else. A complete understanding of why terrorists do what they do, at the level of the group
and certainly at the individual level, must account for organizational and psychological factors that are deliberately excluded by the strategic frame. The strategic
model, in this sense, is not an inaccurate depiction of terrorist decision making;
it is incomplete. It is one of a number of competing models that can be usefully
employed to evaluate terrorist events. All have their strengths and weaknesses,
based on what they include and what they exclude. In different situations, at different times, and in relation to different cases, one approach is likely to provide
greater insights into the decision processes of a group than others. In most cases,
however, each has something to contribute. As long as the nonstrategic factors
that influence terrorist choices follow a discernible pattern, they can be identified, weighted, and factored into a hybrid of terrorist behavior. Even in this case,
however, the strategic approach to terrorist decision making, including the tactical decision to employ suicide attacks, must serve as the baseline frame of reference to identify and evaluate any apparent deviations from rationality.

NO: Suicide terrorism is a political failure.
Max Abrahms, *Johns Hopkins University*

Dying for Nothing? The Political Ineffectiveness of Suicide Terrorism

Why do groups turn to suicide terrorism? Two competing explanations have shaped the debate. Steeped in the rationalist tradition of
microeconomics, political scientists generally assume that militant groups
employ a particular tactic for a purpose—to advance their stated political
goals.[42] Palestinian Islamic Jihad is thus said to practice suicide terrorism to
attain a Palestinian state, and the Kurdistan Workers' Party (PKK) supposedly does it for a Kurdish national homeland. The general public, by contrast,
typically views suicide terrorism not as an aggressive form of politically
motivated violence, but as deadly madness. According to this viewpoint
pervasive in the media, suicide terrorist groups do not aim to accomplish

anything at all. In the parlance of political science, their attacks are non-instrumental; suicide terrorism is simply an expression of craziness or fanaticism. Neither school of thought has much empirical support. The evidence suggests that suicide terrorism is an ineffective tactic for coercing government concessions. But members of suicide terrorist groups benefit from their actions in a variety of other ways. In short, suicide terrorism is politically useless, but quite useful for obtaining a range of nonpolitical ends.

In this essay, I make four main points in support of my argument. First, I show that suicide terrorism is a losing political tactic. Despite its added lethality, suicide terrorism is no more effective than conventional terrorism in forcing target countries to make political concessions. In fact, suicide terrorism tends to be politically counterproductive. Second, I explain why no suicide terrorist group has ever accomplished its political platform by attacking civilians. Third, I demonstrate that even though suicide terrorism is a losing tactic politically, groups that use it do not consistently seize alternative opportunities for political change. Fourth, I show how all members of suicide terrorist organizations—from leaders to foot soldiers—may benefit from their violence independent of the political outcome. I conclude by briefly exploring the policy implications of fighting a highly lethal terrorist enemy that is rational, albeit oftentimes surprisingly apolitical.

THE POLITICAL INEFFECTIVENESS OF SUICIDE TERRORISM

Political scientists typically assume that groups adopt terrorism for its effectiveness in coercing political concessions. This assumption is especially common for suicide terrorist groups. By deploying individuals who are indifferent to their personal fates, suicide terrorist groups tend to be extra lethal and difficult to stop. Compare the two attacks on the World Trade Center: the 2001 suicide attack was a far greater operational success than the 1993 conventional attack, largely because of the willingness of the perpetrators to martyr themselves. But destructiveness is one thing, political gain quite another. Does the use of suicide terrorism increase the likelihood of government compliance? The answer is a definitive no.

For decades, terrorism specialists have noted that terrorists are political losers. In the 1970s, Walter Laqueur published a paper titled "The Futility of Terrorism" in which he claimed that terrorist groups do not attain their political platforms.[43] In the 1980s, Martha Crenshaw likewise observed that terrorists do not obtain their given political ends, and "therefore one must conclude that terrorism is objectively a failure."[44] Similarly, RAND remarked that "terrorists have been unable to translate the consequences of terrorism into concrete political gains ... [I]n that sense terrorism has failed. It is a fundamental failure."[45] In the 1990s, Thomas Schelling proclaimed that "terrorism almost never appears to accomplish anything politically significant."[46] Virginia Held went even further, claiming that the "net effect" of terrorism may actually be counterproductive.[47]

A universally accepted definition of terrorism eludes resolution.[48] But a common distinction is between nonstate attacks on civilian targets and military ones. The former are generally labeled as terrorist attacks whereas the latter are often labeled as insurgent, guerrilla, or militant attacks.[49] Since 9/11, a series of large-*n* observational studies has shown that nonstate attacks on civilian targets in particular inhibit government compliance. This fact holds true regardless of whether the terrorists die in the operation. In this way, terrorism—including the suicide variety—is politically worthless.

My own research has confirmed these findings. In 2006, I published an article in *International Security* that was the first large-*n* study on terrorism's political effectiveness.[50] To test the effectiveness of terrorism, I analyzed the political plights of twenty-eight Foreign Terrorist Organizations (FTOs), as designated by the U.S. State Department. The analysis yields two main findings. First, the FTO success rate is far lower than other scholars had asserted. Robert Pape, for instance, states that terrorists—specifically suicide terrorists—achieve their strategic demands over 50 percent of the time, whereas I found that less than 10 percent prevailed politically.[51] In fact, the vast majority of FTOs have perpetrated terrorism for decades without any real signs of political progress. Second, the successful FTOs used terrorism only as a secondary tactic. Although nonstate actors are known to employ a hybrid of asymmetric tactics, all of the politically successful FTOs directed their violence against military targets, not civilian ones. By disaggregating the FTOs by target selection, I therefore helped to reveal the full extent to which terrorism—defined as nonstate attacks on civilian targets—has historically been a losing political tactic.

Seth Jones and Martin Libicki subsequently examined a larger sample, the universe of known terrorist groups between 1968 and 2006. Of the 648 groups identified in the RAND-MIPT Terrorism Incident database, only 4 percent obtained their strategic demands.[52] Audrey Cronin then reexamined the success rate of these groups, confirming that less than 5 percent triumphed.[53] These low figures actually exceed the coercion rate, as terrorists may accomplish their demands for reasons other than civilian pain. In fact, all of the studies conclude that terrorism does not encourage concessions. In my 2006 study, I argue that terrorism's poor success rate is inherent to the targeting of civilians. Jones and Libicki say that in the few cases in which terrorist groups have triumphed, civilian casualties "had little or nothing to do with the outcome."[54] Cronin finds that the victorious have achieved their demands "despite the use of violence against innocent civilians [rather] than because of it," and that "the tactic of terrorism might have even been counterproductive."[55] And two new studies—one by me and one by Page Fortna—show statistically that attacking civilian targets actually impedes militant groups from accomplishing their political demands.[56]

Suicide terrorist attacks are roughly ten times more lethal than conventional terrorist attacks,[57] but the extra punch does not help the perpetrators to achieve their political demands. In my 2006 study, suicide terrorist groups had a political success rate of 0 percent. And in the RAND and Cronin studies, none of the groups that happened to achieve their demands dispatched a single suicide terrorist. My statistical study in *Comparative Political Studies* isolates the impact of suicide terrorism on target countries; across models, the tactic is useless for promoting government compliance.

Famously, Pape contends that suicide terrorist campaigns are a chillingly effective way to compel political concessions. But his confirming examples are actually of guerrilla campaigns.[58] Defined precisely, terrorist campaigns are directed mainly against the target country's civilians, whereas guerrilla campaigns are directed mainly against its military.[59] As Jeff Goodwin points out, "It is a mistake, therefore, to refer to these [guerrilla] campaigns as 'terrorist' in nature, as Pape does."[60] In the accompanying essay, McCormick and Fritz make the same conceptual mistake, citing the anticolonial campaigns by the Irgun in Israel, the EOKA in Cyprus, and the FLN in Algeria as examples of politically successful terrorist campaigns. Yet those asymmetric campaigns also exacted concessions from the target countries by attacking their militaries, not their civilian populations. As Laqueur explains, the anticolonial campaigns used "little or no terrorism" against the occupiers, though "a great deal of guerrilla warfare, which is something quite different."[61]

Not only do aggrieved groups fail to advance their political platforms by targeting civilians, but governments tend to do the political *opposite* of whatever the terrorists demand. The political impact of terrorism is usually negative regardless of whether the perpetrators die in their violent acts. Al-Qaeda neatly illustrates the political perils of using suicide terrorism. Its leaders favor "the method of martyrdom operation" because it "is the most successful way of inflicting damage against the opponent."[62] But what is the political return? According to the late Osama bin Laden, the political purpose of the attacks of September 11, 2001, was fourfold: (1) to force the United States into withdrawing its troops from the Persian Gulf; (2) to deter the United States from supporting military interventions that kill Muslims; (3) to sever U.S. relations with pro-Western Muslim rulers; and (4) to destroy U.S.-Israeli relations. By his own scorecard, then, the 9/11 suicide attack was an unmitigated disaster.[63]

Instead of forcing a U.S. retreat from the Gulf, 9/11 provided the strategic rationale for Operation Iraqi Freedom and was the critical enabler for securing the support of the American public. The main selling point for regime change in Baghdad was not that Iraq would itself attack the United States or its allies; it was that, using Iraqi weapons of mass destruction, "the terrorists" could one day launch a mega-attack on the U.S. homeland. Even before September 11, 2001, President George W. Bush and top-level officials had considered removing Iraqi dictator Saddam Hussein from power. The American public, however, did not support the invasion until August 2002, when the administration began ratcheting up its rhetoric linking Saddam to terrorism. From this point until the invasion in March 2003, two-thirds of the American public supported Bush's Iraq policy in the context of the wider war on terrorism. In the absence of the attacks of 9/11, it is impossible to imagine that the United States would have increased its troop presence in the Gulf by a factor of fifteen.

Rather than protecting the global Muslim population (or *ummah*), the 9/11 attacks brought on the proverbial war on terrorism, which has killed countless innocent Muslims around the world. About four thousand Afghan civilians were killed in the course of Operation Enduring Freedom. In Iraq, the number of Muslim deaths has been orders of magnitude greater. Washington responded to the 9/11 attacks not only with an aggressive counterterrorism campaign that has inadvertently killed thousands of Muslim civilians; the Bush administration also broadened its definition of the terrorism threat. The catch-all slogans of the "global war on terror" and "global struggle against violent extremism" did not distinguish between terrorist enemies of the United States and asymmetric conflicts around the world of limited strategic importance to either the United States or al-Qaeda. With this expansive definition, the Bush administration turned a blind eye toward foreign governments engaged in localized crackdowns against their Muslim civilians, such as in Russia and India. The Bush administration dropped its demand for Moscow to reach a peaceful settlement with Chechnya, and it refrained from criticizing President Vladimir Putin when Russian forces flattened Grozny, the rebel stronghold. In the wake of 9/11, the Bush administration was likewise mum on the massacre of two thousand Muslims in Gujarat by Hindu rioters. As part of its global campaign on terrorism, the United States also assisted numerous Muslim countries in capturing and killing al-Qaeda–affiliated operatives, with untold civilian losses.

Quite the opposite of severing U.S. relations with pro-Western Muslim rulers, the Bush administration used the events of 9/11 to bolster them. Almost overnight, the governments of Algeria, Egypt, Jordan, Pakistan, and Saudi

Arabia became critical allies in the war on terrorism, sharing real-time intelligence on the movements of al-Qaeda and its affiliates. Because of this unprecedented strategic convergence, Washington increased both its dependence and its influence on these governments; in short, U.S. ties with al-Qaeda's so-called near enemy deepened. After the September 11 attacks, the Bush administration publicly attributed terrorism to autocratic regimes. But notwithstanding its newfound commitment to democracy promotion, the Bush administration only selectively pressured Muslim governments to reform. As realists would predict, leaders who supported the war on terrorism were exempt from making reforms that might threaten their survival. If anything, the events of 9/11 provided a disincentive for removing pro-American Muslim rulers. For the Bush administration, the fear of Taliban-like regimes assuming power across the globe was evidently more threatening than inflaming the Muslim street.

Finally, instead of breaking U.S.-Israeli relations, the 9/11 attacks strengthened the "special relationship." Bush suddenly granted the government of Ariel Sharon unprecedented leeway to reoccupy the West Bank, detain Yasser Arafat in his Ramallah compound, authorize targeted assassinations, and construct the security wall in the West Bank. The American public shared Bush's pro-Israel reaction. Before September 11, 2001, 41 percent of Americans expressed support for Israel and 13 percent for Palestinians. After the attack, 55 percent backed Israel, while support for Palestinians dropped by almost half, to 7 percent. Such high approval levels for Israel were unseen since 1991, when Saddam Hussein had launched dozens of Scud missiles at the Jewish state. Predictably, the American public also became less supportive of Washington engaging in the peace process. In other words, not only did 9/11 fail to end al-Qaeda's stated political grievances, but the suicide attacks actually exacerbated them.

As this important case study shows, along with the broader empirical evidence, aggrieved groups do not advance their political platforms by attacking civilians. Terrorism is not simply politically unprofitable; it steels target countries from granting concessions regardless of whether the perpetrators sacrifice themselves in the operation.

WHAT MAKES SUICIDE TERRORISM SO POLITICALLY INEFFECTIVE?

It is no mystery why suicide terrorism is so politically unproductive. Like conventional terrorism, the more lethal suicide variety tends to empower hardliners opposed to concessions. Studies on public opinion show that terrorism does not intimidate citizens of target countries into supporting more dovish politicians. Quite the opposite, terrorism systematically raises popular support for right-wing leaders opposed to appeasement. Claude Berrebi and Esteban Klor, for example, demonstrate that terrorist fatalities within Israel significantly boost local support for right-bloc parties opposed to accommodation, such as the Likud.[64] This trend is not specific to Israel, but the international norm. Polls show, for example, that after the Irish Republican Army attacked British civilians in conventional bombings, the British people became significantly less likely to favor withdrawing from Northern Ireland. The same trend was apparent after suicide attacks in Egypt, Indonesia, Jordan, the Philippines, and Russia.[65]

In the United States, the mere release of a bin Laden videotape the weekend before the 2004 presidential election boosted George W. Bush's electoral lead by two percentage points over his comparatively dovish opponent, Sen. John Kerry. Similarly, in the run-up to the 2008 presidential election, staffers for the Republican nominee, Sen. John McCain, acknowledged that another 9/11-type attack on the homeland would benefit their candidate, not the more gun-shy Democratic alternative, Sen. Barack Obama. That electorates tend to shift to the right in the face of terrorism goes a long way toward explaining why it does not work politically. In a summary of the literature, RAND remarks: "Terrorist fatalities, with few exceptions, increase support for the bloc of parties associated with a more-intransigent position. Scholars may interpret this as further evidence that terrorist attacks against civilians do not help terrorist organizations achieve their stated goals."[66]

Suicide terrorism is even more likely than conventional terrorism to turn electorates and their leaders against complying with terrorists' political demands. This is because the suicide variety is more lethal, and the most lethal terrorist attacks are the most counterproductive. A spate of recent studies shows that escalating against civilians only impedes groups from inducing government compromise. Within Israel, for example, we now know that the most lethal terrorist attacks are the most likely to boost electoral support for politically intransigent right-bloc parties.[67] Historically, this has also been true within France, Germany, Spain, the United Kingdom, and the United States.[68] This finding can explain why escalating against noncombatants tends to dissuade government concessions, and why suicide terrorism is hence even less politically effective than the standard variety.[69]

Suicide terrorist groups also engage in other politically self-defeating behaviors. Even more than conventional terrorist groups, they are notoriously poor at conveying their presumed policy preferences. In theory, spectacular terrorist acts highlight the group's policy demands so that the target country can then comply. Yet most terrorist attacks—particularly suicide attacks—are anonymous. Since 1968, 64 percent of worldwide terrorist attacks have been carried out by unknown perpetrators. Anonymous attacks have been rising in tandem with suicide terrorism, as three out of four terrorist incidents have gone unclaimed since September 11, 2001. Clearly, target governments are constrained from making concessions without knowing which group committed the attack. Furthermore, specific policy demands are rarely forthcoming even when the terrorist group divulges its identity to the target country. Writing in 1991, Schelling captured this point: "Usually there is nothing to negotiate. A soldier is killed in a disco in Germany. A bomb explodes in front of an Israeli consulate. Japanese Black Septembrists unpack automatic weapons in the Lod airport and start shooting. The perpetrators don't ask anything, demand anything."[70] This tendency for terrorist groups to refrain from issuing policy demands increased in the late 1990s with the ascendance of suicide terrorism, leading Bruce Hoffman to conclude that its political logic is "seriously flawed."[71] It is still unclear, for example, what political aspirations the suicide terrorists could have hoped to achieve by blowing up the three hotels in Amman, Jordan, in November 2005. It is not even known which government the violence was supposedly intended to pressure. People say the attacks were aimed at the Hashemite monarchy or the United States or Israel or the broader international community.

Not only is terrorism counterproductive for winning concessions, but even the weakest terrorist groups are known to issue wildly unrealistic demands. The Japanese Red Army, for example, had roughly six hard-core members in the 1970s, but that did not stop it from demanding the Japanese government to adopt Marxism. Compared with conventional terrorist groups, suicide terrorist groups tend to have even more ambitious, and thus unrealistic, demands.[72] The bulk of al-Qaeda's criticisms have focused on a handful of unpopular U.S. policies in the Muslim world. But bin Laden and his lieutenants also suggested at times that the endgame is to resurrect the caliphate—a single global state under *sharia* rule. Such maximalist pronouncements only dissuade countries from even contemplating concessions. Paul Wilkinson has found that in deciding whether to negotiate with terrorists, the target government first assesses whether the terrorist demands are "corrigible" or "incorrigible." When terrorists are deemed corrigible, the government is inclined to engage in a roots debate—an assessment of the pros and cons of negotiation. But when terrorists are seen as incorrigible, concessions are rejected outright because the demands are viewed as so extreme that they fall outside of the realm of consideration. In Wilkinson's terminology, incorrigible terrorists are not categorically implacable, but placating them would exact a prohibitive cost.[73] With their loose talk of resurrecting the caliphate, al-Qaeda and its affiliates are generally viewed as incorrigible.

This perception that terrorist groups are politically incorrigible is fueled by their tendency to abruptly shift their political rationales. This observation applies to conventional terrorist groups such as France's Action Directe, which from 1979 to 1986 altered its political rationale from opposing Israel to nuclear energy to the Catholic Church. Similarly, the Basque Fatherland and Liberty (ETA) claimed it was fighting to overturn Spain's dictatorship but, with its passing, proceeded to target the emergent democratic government—a progression similar to that followed by the Shining Path, Peru's most notorious terrorist organization.[74] Such political capriciousness is perhaps even more common in suicide terrorist groups. In her article "The Protean Enemy," Jessica Stern charts al-Qaeda's transitory political platform as the movement morphed rapidly and unpredictably from waging defensive jihad against the Soviets in Afghanistan to fighting local struggles in Bosnia, the Philippines, Russia, Spain, and Muslim countries to eventually targeting the American "far enemy" in the late 1990s.[75] Al-Qaeda members have frequently noted the inconsistency of their own organization's jihadist message. Al-Qaeda's military strategist Abu'l-Walid observed that with its "hasty changing of strategic targets," his organization was engaged in "random chaos."[76] Other al-Qaeda members have acknowledged that their organization espouses political objectives that seemingly "shift with the wind."[77] Cronin notes, "It is hard to conceive of al-Qaeda fully achieving its aims, in part because those aims have evolved over time."[78] Naturally, the "opportunistic" nature of al-Qaeda's political platform has led scholars to question the movement's dedication to achieving it. Al-Qaeda is hardly the only suicide terrorist group to rapidly overhaul its political rationale. The Kurdistan Workers' Party—Turkey's most dangerous contemporary suicide terrorist group—has vacillated between advocating jihad, a Marxist revolution, and a Kurdish homeland governed without Islamist or Marxist principles.[79] Similarly, Hezbollah remains a potent suicide terrorist group, despite the fact that its guerrilla attacks on the Israel Defense Forces succeeded in liberating southern Lebanon in May 2000, which was its stated goal for nearly twenty years. Today, Hezbollah's official goal is not to merely defend Lebanon, but also to destroy the "Zionist Entity" within Israel's own borders.

Finally, the target selection of terrorist groups often makes no sense for exacting the relevant political concessions. In the early years of the Algerian War, the National Algerian Movement and the National Liberation Front mainly attacked each other, not their French occupiers. Terrorist groups likewise undermined their political platforms by targeting each other more than their mutually declared enemies in the violent clashes in Aden between the Front for the Liberation of Occupied South Yemen and the National Liberation Front in 1967; in Argentina between Marxist terrorist organizations in the late 1970s; and in the Gaza Strip between Palestinian groups fighting for a common cause during the First Intifada.

Suicide terrorist groups follow the same apolitical pattern. The Tamil Tigers, for example, did not target the Sinhalese government in the mid-1980s. Instead, they engaged in a "systematic annihilation" of other Tamil organizations "espousing the same cause" of national liberation.[80] Pape concedes that the "apparent implication" of the Tigers' target selection is that the violence had "little to do with the political grievances of Tamil society or the relationship between the Tamils and their Sinhalese opponents."[81] Ami Pedahzur agrees: "In contrast to what might be expected from a guerrilla or a terrorist organization whose [expressed] goals were national liberation, the first violent actions initiated by the Tigers were not aimed at any army forces or Sinhalese politicians. . . . [T]he Tigers systematically liquidated leaders and sometimes activists of other [Tamil] organizations."[82] Similarly, in Iraq, the Mecca of suicide terrorism from 2003 to 2008, one would have expected the attacks to be directed against the occupying U.S. troops. In reality, though, the most lethal suicide attacks targeted Shiites, Kurds, and Sufis, ultimately uniting them against the terrorists. One of the biggest suicide attacks did not even take place within the country, but occurred when Iraqi terrorists crossed into Jordan to bomb civilians, again drying up local support for the terrorists. Indeed, in recent years suicide attacks have rocked Bangladesh, Indonesia, Morocco, Saudi Arabia, Turkey, and Uzbekistan, even though these countries are not "occupied," the supposedly key factor for analysts like Pape.[83] Together, these apolitical tendencies help to explain why conventional and suicide terrorist groups alike have such a poor record of advancing their political demands.

SUICIDE TERRORISTS AS POLITICAL UTILITY MINIMIZERS?

Political scientists like to say that terrorist groups are political utility maximizers; that is, they adopt terrorism because the political gains are superior to those from alternative forms of protest. In truth, not only is terrorism an unprofitable political instrument, but its practitioners inconsistently seize alternative avenues for inducing political change. Like conventional terrorist groups, the suicide variety does not even consistently survey its political options.

Terrorist groups never lack political alternatives.[84] Studies show that only the most oppressive totalitarian states have been immune from terrorism. The number of terrorist groups operating in a country is positively associated with its freedom of expression, assembly, and association—conditions conducive to effecting peaceful political change. Yet suicide terrorist groups seldom go out of the terrorism business by embracing national elections. Instead, they routinely toil alongside peaceful parties, refuse to lay down their arms after participating in elections, or sabotage open elections that would have yielded political gains, such as the Sunni suicide squads in postwar Iraq. In dismissing voting as apostasy, al-Qaeda leaders instruct their followers to abstain from a mechanism of altering the political status quo with a far better track record than that of terrorism; indeed it was free elections, not terrorist violence, that brought Islamist parties to power in both Tunisia and Egypt in 2011 and 2012. Furthermore, in electing to use suicide terrorism, these groups regularly abstain from nonviolent strategies such as symbolic protests, labor strikes, and economic boycotts that also have superior records at inducing government concessions. Unlike terrorism, nonviolent strategies do not tend to rouse target countries into going ballistic on the aggrieved group and digging in their political heels.[85]

As a rule, suicide terrorist groups also do not compromise with the target country. On the contrary, they characteristically derail negotiations by ramping up their attacks. This aversion to compromise is again not politically sensible. In many cases, these terrorist groups could have achieved their political platforms by entering into talks. The al-Aqsa Martyrs' Brigades, for example, claims to be motivated to establish a Palestinian state in the West Bank and Gaza Strip. Yet the group responded with an unprecedented wave of suicide terror to Israel's January 2001 offer of the Gaza Strip and nearly all of the West Bank. Predictably, the Martyrs ended up with no Palestine at all. Suicide terrorist groups with more openly extreme policy demands fail to accomplish even part of them because of this refusal to compromise. Hamas, for example, may oppose surrendering claims to all of historic Palestine. But the terrorist group still claims to value the West Bank and Gaza Strip. If acting to optimize its political platform, Hamas would therefore be expected to accept the Palestinian territories in exchange for peace. Hamas, however, acts as a spoiler, depriving its members of policy goals that the group purports to support. In summary, if suicide terrorist groups actually behaved as political utility maximizers, then they would compromise—even if that means securing only partial concessions over continued deadlock—but they rarely do.

Why do terrorist groups so often reject these political opportunities? This behavior is puzzling in light of terrorism's political inefficacy. A common answer of terrorism specialists is that these groups seem partial to violence—specifically, they possess "an innate compulsion" to engage in terrorism and an "unswerving belief" in its desirability over nonviolence.[86] This observation certainly applies to al-Qaeda and its affiliates. After the Soviets withdrew from Afghanistan in the late 1980s, jihadist leaders began exporting suicide terrorism around the globe without even considering nonviolent tactics.[87] As Peter Bergen concluded from his interviews with the al-Qaeda leader, "Bin Laden acts on impulse . . . paying little attention to the potential [political] consequences of his actions."[88]

SUICIDE TERRORISTS AS IRRATIONAL ACTORS?

It would be easy to conclude that suicide terrorists and their leaders are irrational. As I have argued, suicide terrorism is politically unprofitable behavior. When their civilians are attacked or even threatened, governments are no more likely to ameliorate the terrorist groups' professed political grievances. On the contrary, governments tend to do the opposite by rendering them more urgent as their electorates shift to the right. In many cases, the target government does not even know the putative political purpose of the attack. When the government does know what is demanded of it, the demands are often wildly unrealistic, such as to transform a liberal democratic country into a tyrannical Islamist regime. The perception that suicide terrorist groups are implacable is fueled by their tendencies to abruptly change the nature of their demands and to prey on citizens who have nothing to do with their given political problems. To be sure, suicide terrorism is a superb way to blow things up. But there is precious little empirical evidence that groups turn to suicide terrorism to maximize the political return. These groups are notorious for reflexively eschewing elections, compromise proposals, and other nonviolent avenues with a much stronger record than terrorism of eliciting political change. Clearly, political scientists need to reexamine their *a priori* assumption that suicide terrorists behave as rational political actors.

These facts do not imply that members of suicide terrorist organizations are irrational. Interviews with prospective suicide bombers and biographical information on operationally successful ones indicate that they do not have higher rates of psychopathology than the general population. The leadership actually vets out unstable terrorists for reasons of organizational security.[89] So how can suicide terrorists and their leaders be rational, and yet partake in politically inefficacious behavior at such seemingly high costs to themselves?

Suicide terrorism does not work politically, but that does not mean it accomplishes nothing at all. It is effective and thus rational for achieving countless nonpolitical ends. Ironically, suicide terrorism can help to preserve the organization. Suicide terrorist attacks are relatively cheap, requiring fewer personnel and resources because of the enhanced precision. Equally important, the suicide terrorist cannot be captured and then coerced into revealing organization-threatening secrets. Suicide terrorism's greater visibility also helps to "outbid" rival organizations and thereby win over new members.[90] Perpetuating the organization directly benefits the leadership by maintaining its prestige, legitimacy, and identity.

Even the suicide attackers themselves can benefit from their actions by

- enjoying the camaraderie and social solidarity of participating in a tight-knit group, even if temporarily;
- paying tribute to ideologies that are consistent with their worldviews, even if these will never be realized;
- avenging the mistreatment of kin, friends, or strangers with whom they empathize;
- relishing the violation of societal norms;
- receiving financial compensation, at least for their families;
- assuming positions of responsibility;
- gaining respect within their communities, whose members often appreciate their personal sacrifice;
- delighting in the attention that their violence will invariably attract, even if they are no longer around to witness the fallout;
- feeling closer to their god; and
- ending their personal state of despair.

CONCLUSION

Determining what makes terrorists tick is not simply an academic exercise; we cannot expect to cure a malady without understanding its underlying causes. If people participate in suicide terrorist groups for the social solidarity, then governments should promote nonviolent social outlets, such as moderate places of worship. If people participate out of vengeance, then governments should think twice before authorizing counterterrorism measures that are liable to harm the local population. If people participate for empowerment, then the media should resist elevating them with generous postattack coverage. If people participate to honor an idealized ideology, then the international community should discredit it by highlighting its pernicious real-world consequences. If people participate for the financial compensation to their family, then governments are presumably able to buy some of them off. If people participate to find their god, then moderate religious authorities need to underscore the relevant religious passages that condemn the taking of life, including their own. And if people participate to alleviate their depression, then the international community should invest in identifying and treating at-risk populations, particularly in cultures that value martyrdom. Clearly, continued research on the motives of suicide terrorist members is vital to formulating effective counterterrorism strategies. In all likelihood, terrorism is an equifinal phenomenon in that people gravitate to it for diverse reasons.[91]

Terrorist foot soldiers and their leaders surely derive different payoffs from suicide terrorism, but its political return is not one of them.

For this reason, the most common counterterrorism strategies have not worked on any systematic basis: within the policy community, it is assumed that suicide terrorists are mainly committed to achieving political concessions. The three most prevalent counterterrorism strategies therefore try to reduce terrorism by divesting it of its political utility. The predominant counterterrorism strategy is to deter terrorism by adopting a strict no-concessions policy. Like most heads of state, President George W. Bush believed that terrorism will end when its practitioners realize that "these crimes only hurt their [political] cause," a sentiment shared by the Barack Obama administration.[92] Although target governments rarely appease terrorists, the second most common strategy is to defuse them through political accommodation. Proponents of this strategy urge rekindling stalled peace processes, for example, to deny prospective political benefits from using terrorism. The third most common strategy is promoting democracy, which is designed to decrease terrorism's value by empowering citizens to peacefully address their country's political problems.

And yet all three counterterrorism strategies have poor track records. Suicide terrorist groups generally resist disbanding in the face of consistent political failure, when presented with promising alternatives for political gain, and even after their original political rationale has become moot because of factors unrelated to terrorism. Political solutions are not a panacea for suicide terrorism because it is manifestly not intended to achieve concrete political aims. If this were the point of participating in suicide terrorist groups, then their members would be profoundly irrational, especially those who traded their lives and ruined dreams for nothing.

Notes

1. See, for example, Alan M. Dershowitz, *Why Terrorism Works: Understanding the Threat, Responding to the Challenge* (New Haven, Conn.: Yale University Press, 2002); and Seth G. Jones and Martin C. Libicki, *How Terrorist Groups End: Lessons for Countering al Qa'ida* (Santa Monica, Calif.: RAND, 2008).
2. Ehud Sprinzak, "Rational Fanatics," *Foreign Policy* (September/October 2000): 66–73; Robert A. Pape, *Dying to Win: The Strategic Logic of Suicide Terrorism* (New York: Random House, 2005).
3. Indeed, Czar Alexander II was assassinated in 1881 by a suicide bomber dispatched by the group People's Will.
4. For details on Hanadi Jaradat's attack, see John F. Burns, "The Mideast Turmoil: The Attacker; Bomber Left Her Family with a Smile and a Lie," *New York Times*, October 7, 2003; John Ward Anderson and Molly Moore, "For 2 Families in Haifa,

3 Generations of Victims," *Washington Post,* October 6, 2003; and Robert Baer's documentary *The Cult of the Suicide Bomber 2,* Many Rivers Films, 2008.

5. Suicide Attack Database: 1983–Present, Department of Defense Analysis, Naval Postgraduate School, Monterey, Calif.

6. Earlier versions of some of the arguments presented in this chapter can be found in Gordon H. McCormick, "Signaling and the Logic of Suicide Terrorism," Occasional Paper, Department of Defense Analysis, Naval Postgraduate School, Monterey, Calif., May 2003; and Bruce Hoffman and Gordon H. McCormick, "Terrorism, Signaling, and Suicide Attack," *Studies in Conflict and Terrorism* 27, no. 4 (2004): 243–381.

7. For a general discussion, see Jeffrey S. Banks, *Signaling Games in Political Science* (New York: Harwood Academic Publishers, 1991). For an application to terrorism, see Harvey E. Lapan and Todd Sandler, "Terrorism and Signaling," *European Journal of Political Economy* 9 (August 1993): 383–397.

8. Hoffman and McCormick, "Terrorism, Signaling, and Suicide Attack," 245–246.

9. Gordon H. McCormick and Frank Giordano, "Things Come Together: Symbolic Violence and Guerrilla Mobilisation," *Third World Quarterly* 28, no. 2 (2007): 295–320.

10. Ibid., 306.

11. For further discussion, see Gordon H. McCormick and Guillermo Owen, "Revolutionary Origins and Conditional Mobilization," *European Journal of Political Economy* 12, no. 3 (1996): 377–402.

12. Ernesto Guevara, *Guerrilla Warfare* (Lincoln: University of Nebraska Press, 1985), 189.

13. Quoted in Nathan Leites, "Understanding the Next Act," *Terrorism* 3, no. 1–2 (1979): 1–46.

14. The relationship between terrorists and the media is, in this respect, a symbiotic one. Terrorist groups need someone to tell their story; the media, for their part, need a story to tell.

15. See, for example, the discussions in Brigitte Nacos, *Terrorism and the Media* (New York: Columbia University Press, 1996); and Brigitte Nacos, "Revisiting the Contagion Hypothesis: Terrorism, News Coverage, and Copycat Attacks," *Perspectives on Terrorism* 3, no. 3 (2009).

16. Brian Michael Jenkins, "International Terrorism: A New Mode of Conflict," in *International Terrorism and World Security,* ed. David Carlton and Carlo Schaerf (London: Croom Helm, 1975), 15.

17. This trade-off is examined in detail in Gordon H. McCormick and Guillermo Owen, "Security and Coordination in a Clandestine Organization," *Mathematical and Computer Modeling* 31 (2000): 175–192; and J. Bowyer Bell, "Revolutionary Dynamics: The Inherent Inefficiency of the Underground," *Terrorism and Political Violence* 2 (Summer 1990): 193–211.

18. For a good discussion of some of the individual motives that underlie suicide attacks, see Mohammed M. Hafez, *Manufacturing Human Bombs: The Making of Palestinian Suicide Bombers* (Washington, D.C.: U.S. Institute of Peace Press, 2006), 33–52; and Ariel Merari, *Driven to Death: Psychological and Social Aspects of Suicide Terrorism* (New York: Oxford University Press, 2010).

19. For a general discussion of this logic, see James March, *A Primer on Decision Making* (New York: Free Press, 1994), 2–3. This logic is applied to the problem of

terrorism in Gordon H. McCormick, "Terrorist Decision Making," *Annual Review of Political Science* 6 (June 2003): 481–486.

20. Suzanne Goldenberg, "The Men behind the Suicide Bombers," *Guardian,* June 12, 2002.
21. Bruce Hoffman, "The Logic of Suicide Terrorism," *Atlantic Monthly,* June 2003. According to Robert A. Pape, suicide attacks accounted for 3 percent of terrorist incidents from 1980 to 2003, but 48 percent of all fatalities, making an average suicide attack twelve times deadlier than other forms of terrorism. See Pape, *Dying to Win* (New York: Random House, 2005), 6.
22. The National Counterterrorism Center, Report on Terrorism, May 12, 2012.
23. Nasra Hassan, "Letter from Gaza: An Arsenal of Believers," *New Yorker,* November 19, 2001, 39.
24. Speaking of the People's Will, for example, Camus noted that "for them, as for all rebels before them, murder is identified with suicide. A life is paid for another life, and from these two sacrifices springs the promise of a value." Albert Camus, *The Rebel: An Essay on Man in Revolt* (New York: Vintage Books, 1956), 169.
25. Bonnie Cordes, "When Terrorists Do the Talking: Reflections on Terrorist Literature," *Journal of Strategic Studies* 10 (December 1987): 164.
26. Mia Bloom, *Dying to Kill: The Allure of Suicide Terror* (New York: Columbia University Press, 2005). For anecdotal evidence of Palestinian groups, see Barbara Victor, *Army of Roses* (New York: Rodale Books, 2003).
27. Dipak K. Gupta and Kusum Mundra, "Suicide Bombing as a Strategic Weapon: An Empirical Investigation of Hamas and Islamic Jihad," *Terrorism and Political Violence* 17 (Winter 2005): 573–598.
28. Scott Atran, "The Moral Logic and Growth of Suicide Terrorism," *Washington Quarterly* 29 (Spring 2006): 132.
29. See Christoph Reuter, *My Life Is a Weapon* (Princeton, N.J.: Princeton University Press, 2004), 87; and Hoffman, "Logic of Suicide Terrorism."
30. Quoted in Rosemarie Skaine, *Female Suicide Bombers* (London: McFarland, 2006), 85.
31. This statement is, of course, ironic. The implication is that the less open to incentive-based manipulation a terrorist group appears to be (that is, the "crazier" it seems), the more dangerous it will appear and the stronger the state's incentive will be to come to terms with it. Thus the less open a group is to a negotiated compromise, the more likely it is to be offered a compromise and the more attractive that compromise is likely to be.
32. In the companion piece to this essay, for example, Max Abrahms states that in 2006 he "conducted the first study to analyze a large number of terrorist groups in terms of their political accomplishments." The groups he examined were the twenty-eight organizations that were listed by the State Department as *active* terrorist groups in 2001. In 2006 these groups were still active. Based on the assumption that these groups had already had "ample time" to achieve their goals, he concludes that they must not be strategic actors. There must be something else that is motivating them. This argument is problematic. First, circumstances, rather than outside observers, determine how much time is necessary to achieve one's objectives, whatever these might be. It took the Chinese Communist Party (CCP) twenty-eight years to assume power in China in 1949. We would have been in error if we had stated in

1939 that Mao and the CCP were not strategic actors because they had already had eighteen years to achieve their goals and had not yet done so. Second, should we be surprised that terrorist groups that have not yet achieved their objectives are still in the fight? This is what you would expect from strategic actors who still believed that the game was worth the candle. If the author wishes to test his claim that those actors who use terrorism never achieve their goals, he needs to examine the list of groups that are *no longer active* to determine whether or not any have been successful, not look at the list of groups that have not yet been successful and are therefore still active. For the original discussion, see Max Abrahms, "Why Terrorism Does Not Work," *International Security* 31 (Fall 2006): 42–78.

33. Pape, *Dying to Win*, 64–65.

34. Jones and Libicki, *How Terrorist Groups End* (2008). This percentage, quite appropriately, is based on the outcome of terrorist campaigns that have "ended"; it does not consider ongoing campaigns—that is, those that have not yet ended. A recent study of how political insurgencies end has found that the success rate for insurgent campaigns, most of which employed various forms of terrorism, is slightly higher over a longer time frame. Just over 14 percent (*n* = 34) of the insurgent conflicts that came and went between 1945 and 2007 ended with either an outright insurgent victory or a nominal negotiated settlement with the incumbent government that codified its de facto defeat. See Gordon H. McCormick, Steven B. Horton, and Lauren A. Harrison, "Things Fall Apart: The Endgame Dynamics of Internal Wars," *Third World Quarterly* 28 (March 2007): 321–367.

35. In the end, of course, the success rate of groups that employ terrorism is ultimately irrelevant to the discussion of whether terrorism is strategically motivated. What is important is whether a group chooses to use terrorist tactics based on the belief that terrorism is a means to its ends and that the net expected benefits of pursuing such a course of action exceed those of its alternatives.

36. See, for example, the accompanying essay by Abrahms. How one labels a group— "terrorist" or "guerrilla"—of course, is again irrelevant to the point of this discussion, which focuses on the utility of terrorist tactics in the eyes of the organizations that employ these tactics, regardless of what one chooses to call these groups after the fact.

37. If terrorist groups grow in strength in relation to the state, their tactical options will increase accordingly. The mix of tactics they employ under these circumstances will become more diversified. Terrorists and insurgents, in this respect, do not generally employ different tactics; they tend to employ a different mix of tactics. As a historical matter, over the last fifty years few insurgent organizations have not employed terrorist tactics at some point in their life cycles, and few abandon such tactics completely as they grow.

38. Quoted in Mary Anne Weaver, "Inventing Al-Zarqawi," *Atlantic Monthly*, July/August 2006, 98.

39. The al-Askari mosque was ultimately attacked twice by AQI. The first attack, in February 2006, destroyed its golden dome and severely damaged its main structure. A second attack in June 2007 destroyed its two minarets.

40. See, for example, Patrick Cockburn, "Ten Imams Murdered in Iraq as Sectarian Killings Intensify," *Independent*, February 24, 2006.

41. AQI's fall from grace, so to speak, began when it tried to impose a social fundamentalism in its zones of control and challenge the traditional authority of Sunni

tribal leaders, many of whom had been among al-Zarqawi's strongest early allies. These errors were then compounded by the organization's efforts to enforce its dicta at the point of a gun. AQI's anti-Shiite attacks are not considered to be a reason for its decline in Sunni support. To the contrary, AQI was originally considered to be an important shield against Shiite domination because of its revealed willingness and ability to protect Sunnis against a Shiite majority. Al-Zarqawi successfully cultivated these fears and used them to expand AQI's influence.

42. I have labeled this school of thought the Strategic Model. For a more extensive description and critique of this model, see Max Abrahms, "What Terrorists Really Want: Terrorist Motives and Counterterrorism Strategy," *International Security* 32 (Spring 2008): 78–105.

43. Walter Laqueur, "The Futility of Terrorism," *Harper's Magazine* 252 (March 1976): 99–105.

44. Martha Crenshaw, "The Logic of Terrorism: Terrorist Behavior as a Product of Strategic Choice," in *Origins of Terrorism: Psychologies, Ideologies, Theologies, States of Mind*, ed. Walter Reich (Washington, D.C.: Woodrow Wilson, 1980), 15.

45. Bonnie Cordes, Bruce Hoffman, Brian M. Jenkins, Konrad Kellen, Sue Moran, and William Sater, *Trends in International Terrorism, 1982 and 1983* (Santa Monica, Calif.: RAND, 1984), 49.

46. Thomas C. Schelling, "What Purposes Can 'International Terrorism' Serve?" in *Violence, Terrorism, and Justice*, ed. R. G. Frey and Christopher W. Morris (New York: Cambridge University Press, 1991), 20.

47. Virginia Held, "Terrorism, Rights, and Political Goals," 70, in Ibid.

48. Alex P. Schmid and Albert J. Jongman, *Political Terrorism* (New Brunswick, N.J.: Transaction Books, 1998).

49. See, for example, Boaz Ganor, "Defining Terrorism: Is One Man's Terrorist Another Man's Freedom Fighter?" *Police Practice and Research: An International Journal* 3 (2002): 296; Jeff Goodwin, "A Theory of Categorical Terrorism," *Social Forces* 84 (2006): 2027–2046; Bruce Hoffman, *Inside Terrorism* (New York: Columbia University Press, 2006), 35; Alex P. Schmid and Albert Jongman, *Political Terrorism: A New Guide to Actors, Authors, Concepts, Data Bases, Theories, and Literature* (New Brunswick, N.J.: Transaction Publishers, 2005), 14; and Paul Wilkinson, *Terrorism and the Liberal State*, rev. ed. (London: Macmillan, 1986), 209.

50. Max Abrahms, "Why Terrorism Does Not Work," *International Security* 31 (2006): 42–78.

51. Robert A. Pape, "The Strategic Logic of Suicide Terrorism," *American Political Science Review* 97, no. 3 (2003): 13–14.

52. Seth Jones and Martin Libicki, *How Terrorist Groups End: Lessons for Countering Al-Qaeda* (Santa Monica, Calif.: RAND, 2008).

53. Audrey Kurth Cronin, *How Terrorism Ends*.

54. Jones and Libicki, *How Terrorist Groups End*, 32–33.

55. Cronin, *How Terrorism Ends*, 203.

56. Max Abrahms, "The Political Effectiveness of Terrorism Revisited," *Comparative Political Studies* 45 (March 2012): 366–393; and Page Fortna, "Do Terrorists Win? Rebels' Use of Terrorism and Civil War Outcomes," Working Paper, Columbia University, 2012.

57. Author's conversation with Nicholas Ayers, U.S. Military Academy at West Point.

58. Pape, *Dying to Win*, 40–41. For a discussion of the wider literature on terrorism's political effectiveness, see Max Abrahms, "Does Terrorism Really Work? Evolution in the Conventional Wisdom since 9/11," *Defense and Peace Economics* 22, no. 6 (2011): 583–594.

59. See fn. 8.

60. Jeff Goodwin, "A Theory of Categorical Terrorism," *Social Forces* 84 (2006): 317.

61. Walter Laqueur, "Left, Right, and Beyond: The Changing Face of Terror," in *Understanding the War on Terror*, ed. James F. Hoge Jr. and Gideon Rose (New York: Norton, 2005), 154.

62. Quoted in Abdel Bari Atwan, *The Secret History of Al Qaeda* (Los Angeles: University of California Press, 2006), 99.

63. For a lengthier analysis of how 9/11 backfired politically, see Max Abrahms, "Al Qaeda's Scorecard: A Progress Report on Al Qaeda's Objectives," *Studies in Conflict and Terrorism* 29, no. 5 (2006): 509–529. Al-Qaeda's supporters agree that 9/11 was politically counterproductive. See Fawaz A. Gerges, *The Far Enemy: Why Jihad Went Global* (New York: Cambridge University Press, 2005), 228.

64. Claude Berrebi and Esteban F. Klor, "Are Voters Sensitive to Terrorism: Direct Evidence from the Israeli Electorate," *American Political Science Review* 102 (2008): 279–301; Claude Berrebi and Esteban F. Klor, "On Terrorism and Electoral Outcomes: Theory and Evidence from the Israeli–Palestinian Conflict," *Journal of Conflict Resolution* 50, no. 6 (2006): 899–925.

65. John Mueller, *Overblown: How Politicians and the Terrorism Industry Inflate National Security Threats and Why We Believe Them* (New York: Free Press, 1996), 184; Paul Wilkinson, *Terrorism and the Liberal State*, 52.

66. Claude Berrebi, "The Economics of Terrorism and Counterterrorism: What Matters and Is Rational-Choice Theory Helpful?" In *Social Science for Counterterrorism: Putting the Pieces Together*, ed. Paul K. Davis and Kim Cragin (Santa Monica, Calif. RAND, 2009), 189–190.

67. Eric D. Gould and Esteban F. Klor, "Does Terrorism Work?" *Quarterly Journal of Economics* 125, no. 4 (2008): 1507.

68. Christophe Chowanietz, "Rallying Around the Flag or Railing Against the Government? Political Parties' Reactions to Terrorist Acts," *Party Politics* 2 (June 2010): 111–142.

69. Khusrav Gaibulloev and Todd Sandler, "Hostage Taking: Determinants of Terrorist Logistical and Negotiation Success," *Journal of Peace Research* 46, no. 6 (2009): 739–756.

70. Schelling, "What Purposes Can 'International Terrorism' Serve?" 24.

71. Bruce Hoffman, "Why Terrorists Don't Claim Credit," *Terrorism and Political Violence* 9, no. 1 (1997): 1.

72. James A. Piazza, "A Supply-Side View of Suicide Terrorism: A Cross-National Study," *Journal of Politics* 70, no. 1 (2008): 28–39.

73. Paul Wilkinson, "Security Challenges in the New Reality," lecture, Tufts University, Medford, Mass., October 16, 2002.

74. See Martha Crenshaw, "An Organizational Approach to the Analysis of Political Terrorism," *Orbis* 29, no. 3 (1985): 71.

75. Jessica Stern, "The Protean Enemy," *Foreign Affairs* 82, no. 4 (2003).

76. Quoted in Vahid Brown, "Cracks in the Foundation: Leadership Schisms in al-Qaeda from 1989–2006," Combating Terrorism Center Report (West Point, N.Y.: September 2007), 10.

77. Omar Nasiri, *Inside the Jihad: My Life with Al Qaeda, A Spy's Story* (New York: Basic Books, 2006), 295.

78. Audrey Kurth Cronin, "How al-Qaeda Ends: The Decline and Demise of Terrorist Groups," *International Security* 31, no. 1 (2006): 41–42.

79. See Ami Pedahzur, *Suicide Terrorism* (Cambridge, UK: Polity Press, 2005), 87, 89. See also Bloom, *Dying to Kill*, 112.

80. Shri D. R. Kaarthikeyan, "Root Causes of Terrorism? A Case Study of the Tamil Insurgency and the LTTE," in *Root Causes of Terrorism: Myths, Reality, and Ways Forward*, ed. Tore Bjorgo (New York: Routledge, 2006), 134.

81. Pape, *Dying to Win*, 139–140.

82. Pedahzur, *Suicide Terrorism*, 81–82.

83. Assaf Moghadam, "Suicide Terrorism, Occupation, and the Globalization of Martyrdom: A Critique of *Dying to Win*," *Studies in Conflict and Terrorism* 29, no. 8 (2006): 719.

84. Martha Crenshaw, "How Terrorists Think: What Psychology Can Contribute to Understanding Terrorism," in *Terrorism: Roots, Impact, Responses*, ed. Lawrence Howard (New York: Praeger, 1992), 71.

85. Maria J. Stephan and Erica Chenoweth, "Why Civil Resistance Works: The Strategic Logic of Nonviolent Conflict," *International Security* 33, no. 1 (2008): 7–44.

86. Bruce Hoffman, *Inside Terrorism*, 245; Cronin, "How al-Qaeda Ends," 11.

87. Jason Burke, *Al-Qaeda: The True Story of Radical Islam* (New York: I. B. Tauris, 2004), 290.

88. Quoted in Khalil Hasan, "Postcard USA: Osama bin Laden Unveiled," *Daily Times*, February 26, 2006.

89. Robert J. Brym and Bader Araj, "Suicide Bombing as Strategy and Interaction: The Case of the Second Intifada," *Social Forces* 84 (June 2006): 1970–1971.

90. Bloom, *Dying to Kill*.

91. Karen Rasler, "Review Symposium: Understanding Suicide Terror," *Perspectives on Politics* 5 (February 2007), 118.

92. Bush is quoted in "Pledge to 'Liquidate' Pearl Killers," BBC.com, February 22, 2002. For the Obama administration view, see White House, "National Strategy for Counterterrorism," June 2011, www.whitehouse.gov/sites/default/files/counterter rorism_strategy.pdf.

is nuclear terrorism
a real threat?

YES: The threat is very real.
Matthew Bunn, *Harvard University*

NO: The threat is overblown.
Susan B. Martin, *King's College London*

Prior to the attacks of September 11, 2001, the possibility of terrorists utilizing weapons of mass destruction, particularly the most potentially devastating weapon, a nuclear device, received a good deal of attention.[1] The conventional wisdom at the time, even among those who were warning of the growing danger, was that the possibility of a nuclear terrorist attack was a "low probability, high consequence" threat.[2] Nuclear terrorism was generally considered a low-probability threat because of issues related to supply, technical feasibility, and demand. It would be extremely difficult for a terrorist group to obtain materials for a tactical nuclear device. Successfully carrying out an attack meant leaping over another set of technical and logistical hurdles. And wouldn't a terrorist group create a counterproductive backlash against itself (and its cause) if it callously massacred hundreds of thousands of people?

After the events of 9/11, these purported constraints were urgently rethought. For one thing, the brazen and catastrophic nature of the 9/11 attacks (and many since) gave new credence to the idea that al-Qaeda and similarly inspired religious and millennial groups actively seek maximum casualties. In addition, with the growing global proliferation of nuclear materials and know-how, obstacles to filling in the supply and technical side of the equation have been greatly reduced. In 2005 Sen. Richard Lugar, chairman of the Senate Foreign Relations Committee, issued a report that estimated the likelihood of a nuclear terrorist attack somewhere in the world in the next ten years to be as high as 29 percent.[3] A 2008 presidential commission on the subject concluded that "it is more likely than not" that a biological or nuclear weapon of mass destruction will be used in a terrorist attack in the next five years.[4]

There is, however, another side to the story. Each year that passes without a nuclear terrorist attack breathes life into arguments that frightening predictions may be used simply as predictions to frighten.[5] The possibility of nuclear terrorism must, of course, be acknowledged, and efforts must be made to prevent it. But overstating and oversimplifying the threat may only make matters worse by, for example, increasing the incentives for terrorists to try to accomplish this bold act and by diverting valuable resources from other areas of diplomacy and counterterrorism.

Matthew Bunn and Susan Martin each bring their own unique professional insights (and predictions) into the debate over nuclear terrorism. Although careful not to overstate the threat, Bunn lays out in detail why he believes nuclear terrorism to be a real risk, based on technical plausibility and the mass-casualty motivations of some terrorist groups. Martin views issues of capabilities and motives through a different lens, arguing that the hurdles for a terrorist group to detonate a nuclear device remain prohibitively high in terms of both technical and political considerations. Although they may disagree on many core issues, there is one thing on which all can agree: that this debate will stay firmly in the realm of the hypothetical.

YES: The threat is very real.
Matthew Bunn, *Harvard University*

The Real Risk of Nuclear Terrorism

O n the night of November 8, 2007, two teams of armed men attacked the
Pelindaba nuclear facility in South Africa, where hundreds of kilograms
of weapons-grade highly enriched uranium (HEU) are stored. One of the teams
was reportedly chased off by site security forces, but the other team of four
armed men disabled the detection systems at the site perimeter, got through the
10,000-volt security fence without setting off any alarm, and went to the emergency control center and shot a worker there in the chest. The injured worker
raised the alarm for the first time. This team spent forty-five minutes inside the
secured perimeter without ever being engaged by site security forces, and then
disappeared through the same point in the fence where they entered. No one
on either team has been captured, and the identity of the organizers of the
break-in remains a mystery—though there are strong reasons to believe that
the intruders had information from insiders at the site.[6] South Africa has
upgraded security at the site substantially since this incident, with cooperation
from the United States, but has declined suggestions from the United States and
others that it blend the HEU at the site to low-enriched uranium that cannot be
used in a nuclear bomb, but can be used for reactor fuel.

Although it is not known whether the intruders were after the HEU (and
there is no evidence that they went near the area where the HEU is stored), this
incident is nevertheless a potent reminder of the kinds of highly capable adversaries that nuclear security systems must be designed to combat. The threat
that night included two groups of well-armed, well-trained individuals, capable
of disabling intrusion detectors, and apparently with insider information about
the site and its security systems. With the security upgrades in place, Pelindaba
is now better protected against such a threat—but the reality is that at nuclear
facilities in many countries, the security systems would not be enough to protect against such a threat.

INTRODUCTION: THE THREAT OF NUCLEAR TERRORISM

Nuclear terrorism poses a very real and urgent threat to U.S. and global security.[7] Mother Nature has been both kind and cruel in setting the laws of physics

that frame the nuclear predicament the world faces. She has been kind in that the essential ingredients of nuclear weapons, highly enriched uranium and plutonium, do not occur in significant quantities in nature and are quite difficult to produce. Making them is well beyond the plausible capabilities of terrorist groups. Thus if all of the existing stockpiles could be effectively guarded, nuclear weapons terrorism could be reliably prevented: no material, no bomb. (Because of this factor, nuclear weapons are quite different from chemical and biological weapons, whose essential ingredients can be found in nature.) Mother Nature has been cruel in that, although it is not easy to make a nuclear bomb, it is not as difficult as many believe once the needed materials are in hand. Most states, and even some particularly well-organized terrorist groups, could do it. Mother Nature has also been cruel in that HEU and plutonium, though radioactive, are not radioactive enough to make them difficult to steal and carry away, or to make them easy to detect when being smuggled across borders. Therefore, the best defense is keeping these items from being stolen in the first place.

Getting and using a nuclear bomb would be the most technically challenging operation any terrorist group has ever carried out. The *probability* of nuclear terrorism is surely far lower than the probability of many other types of terrorist attack. But the *risk* posed by nuclear terrorism—the probability multiplied by the immense consequences of such an attack—is unacceptably high. Fortunately, practical and affordable actions can be taken to drastically reduce the risk. In 2009, U.S. President Barack Obama launched a four-year international effort—since endorsed by the United Nations Security Council and two nuclear security summits—to secure all nuclear material worldwide. This effort is making significant progress—but it will certainly not be the case that at the end of 2013 all the world's stockpiles of weapons-usable nuclear material will be effectively and sustainably secured against the full spectrum of threats they face.[8]

Indeed, that progress is being slowed by widespread complacency about the threat. Many key policymakers and nuclear managers around the world simply do not believe that nuclear theft and nuclear terrorism are real dangers. Until they are convinced that nuclear theft and terrorism are real threats to *their* countries' security, worthy of a significant investment of their attention and resources, they are highly unlikely to take the actions needed to prevent nuclear terrorism. Some academics have contributed to this complacency—and thereby have increased the difficulty of reducing the risk—by making unfounded arguments that the threat of nuclear terrorism is vanishingly small.[9]

The answers to the following series of "frequently asked questions" will help to clarify the risk of nuclear terrorism. After exploring these questions, and their implications for the overall risk of nuclear terrorism, this essay concludes with a few thoughts on where the world should go from here.

NUCLEAR TERRORISM Q&A

1. Do terrorists want nuclear weapons?

For a small set of terrorists, the answer is clearly yes. By word and deed, al-Qaeda and the global movement it has spawned have made it clear they want nuclear weapons. Osama bin Laden called the acquisition of nuclear weapons a "religious duty,"[10] and al-Qaeda operatives have made repeated attempts to buy the nuclear material for a nuclear bomb and to recruit nuclear expertise. These attempts include the well-known case in which two extremist Pakistani nuclear weapons scientists met with bin Laden and his deputy Ayman al-Zawahiri in the summer of 2001 to discuss nuclear weapons, which reportedly included handing over a sketch of a nuclear bomb design and discussing other Pakistani scientists who might be recruited for the effort.[11] The sketch they provided reportedly included simple explosive lenses to increase the weapon's efficiency.[12]

In 2003, members of a Saudi cell of al-Qaeda attempted to purchase three items they believed were nuclear devices, and reportedly received authorization from key al-Qaeda leaders to make the purchase if a Pakistani expert working with the group confirmed they were real; the main plotter in this incident was the "steady companion" of the radical Saudi cleric who at around the same time issued a fatwa authorizing the use of nuclear weapons against American civilians. The plot was cut short by the arrest of the Saudi participants—but the Pakistani nuclear weapons expert in whom al-Qaeda leaders had such confidence has never been identified, and may still be working with al Qaeda.[13] In his 2008 book *Exoneration,* responding to critics of al-Qaeda's violent tactics, al-Zawahiri repeated all the arguments of the nuclear fatwa, citing the same authorities, while elaborating the arguments in places—conceivably representing a reaffirmation of the religious justification for escalating to the nuclear scale of violence.[14] The many defeats al-Qaeda has suffered in recent years—discussed below—may increase the group's desire to land a decisive blow against the infidels.

Nor does al-Qaeda pose the only nuclear terrorism problem. Before al-Qaeda, the Japanese terrorism cult Aum Shinrikyo also tried to obtain nuclear weapons, which, like al-Qaeda's efforts, included attempts to buy stolen nuclear warheads or nuclear material from the former Soviet Union.[15] This group was entirely homegrown—though it had extensive operations in Russia, the United States, and elsewhere—and it was not on anyone's radar screen as a weapons of mass destruction (WMD) threat until it carried out its 1995 nerve gas attack in the Tokyo subway. While the evidence with respect to Chechen terrorists is less conclusive, they have repeatedly threatened to sabotage nuclear facilities or to carry out radioactive dirty bomb attacks, and the balance of evidence suggests that they have pursued nuclear weapons as well. Russian officials have confirmed two cases of Chechen groups carrying out reconnaissance at nuclear weapons storage sites—and the Russian state newspaper reported two other cases of reconnaissance of nuclear weapon transport trains. There have also been a number of suggestions—none confirmed to date—of nuclear ambitions among Pakistan-based groups such as Lashkar-e-Taiba, some of whom have significant links to al-Qaeda.

As of mid-2012, both Aum and terrorist groups in the North Caucasus appear to be largely out of the nuclear terrorism picture, and the al-Qaeda threat has been greatly diminished. But with at least two and probably three groups having actively pursued nuclear weapons in the last fifteen years, others are likely to do so in the future.

2. Could a terrorist group plausibly get the materials needed for a nuclear bomb?

The answer here is also yes. Nuclear weapons or their essential ingredients can be found in hundreds of buildings in dozens of countries, protected by security measures that range from excellent to appalling. No specific and binding global standards specifying how these stockpiles should be secured exist.

No government or international organization has comprehensive knowledge of where all the nuclear stockpiles in the world are, what security measures are present at each location, and what kinds of threats target each site. The U.S. government has prepared an estimate of this global picture under the Nuclear Materials Information Program (NMIP), but many uncertainties remain.[16] Based on the information available in the public domain, the highest risks of nuclear theft today appear to be in Pakistan, in Russia, and at HEU-fueled research reactors around the world. In each of these three categories, significant progress toward greater nuclear security has been made in recent years. But in all three cases, significant dangers remain.

Pakistan

Pakistan maintains a small (though growing) nuclear stockpile, in a small number of locations, with extensive security measures. But with al-Qaeda's core leadership, a dangerous Taliban insurgency, and a range of highly capable terrorist groups with links to the Pakistani state all operating in the area, Pakistan's nuclear assets face a greater threat from extremists seeking nuclear weapons than any other stockpile on earth.

In the last decade, Pakistan has taken major steps to improve security and command and control for its nuclear weapons—often with secret U.S. assistance.[17] In 2010 President Obama stated he had confidence in Pakistan's nuclear security arrangements,[18] though subsequent leaks to the press suggest that many U.S. government officials continue to have grave concerns.[19] The extent of progress in improving nuclear security in Pakistan is unknown, but the following factors continue to make the country's stockpile a source of apprehension:

Growing extremist threats. Pakistan has seen a sharp rise in terrorist activity in recent years. Some attacks have shown worrisome levels of sophistication. In October 2009, militants wearing army uniforms attacked Pakistani Army headquarters in Rawalpindi using automatic weapons, rocket-propelled grenades, and explosives (apparently with insider knowledge of the layout of the base).[20] In May 2011, well-armed and well-trained militants attacked the Pakistani naval base at Mehran, reportedly wearing military fatigues and with insider knowledge of the base, and succeeded in holding off Pakistani military personnel for some fifteen hours.[21] Attacks such as these could pose a significant threat to nuclear weapon and nuclear material sites.

The insider threat. In at least two cases, Pakistani military officers working with al-Qaeda came within a hair's breadth of assassinating then–Head of State Pervez Musharraf. If military officers guarding the president cannot be trusted, how much confidence can we have in officers guarding the nuclear weapons? Will Pakistan's Strategic Plans Division, which controls nuclear weapons, be able to exclude all personnel with extremist sympathies?

The world's fastest-growing nuclear arsenal. Unclassified estimates suggest that Pakistan's stockpile has grown by an estimated 25 percent since 2009 and is currently thought to contain around one hundred warheads.[22] The country has two operating plutonium production reactors and two more under construction, which will increase bulk processing of fissile material—the stage in the life cycle of nuclear material that historically has proven the most vulnerable to insider theft.[23]

Growing U.S.-Pakistani tensions. Events such as the U.S. raid that killed bin Laden, the alleged effort by the Pakistani ambassador to the United States to get U.S. help for Pakistan's civilian government in its struggle with the Pakistani military, U.S. airstrikes that have killed Pakistani soldiers on the border with Afghanistan, simmering unease over the U.S. drone strikes in Pakistan, and U.S. concerns over Pakistani military links to extremist groups have led to a sharp downturn in U.S.-Pakistani relations. These tensions are likely to constrain what can be done in nuclear security cooperation.

A struggling government. The Pakistani government remains weak, and faces a daunting array of economic, political, and security challenges. While it remains highly unlikely that the Pakistani state will collapse, this scenario cannot be entirely ruled out.

The reality is that improved nuclear security measures can never address more than a part of the problem in Pakistan. If the threat is a modest group of outside attackers or one or two relatively low-level insiders, improved nuclear security measures can provide effective protection. But if the officers in command of a nuclear weapons base decide to provide their weapons to terrorists, the Pakistani state collapses, or extremists seize power, better fences and vaults are not going to solve the problem.

Russia

Russia possesses the world's largest stockpiles of nuclear weapons, plutonium, and HEU, located in the world's largest number of buildings and bunkers. Having recovered from the chaos following the collapse of the Soviet Union, Russia put in place dramatically improved security and accounting measures for its nuclear weapons and materials during the past two decades, with billions of dollars of U.S. assistance. But significant weaknesses remain: its security measures face substantial threats from both corrupted insiders and hostile outsiders; and the sustainability of its improved security measures is very much in doubt.

Insider theft is the biggest concern, as all cases of nuclear theft where the origins of the theft are known were perpetrated by or with the help of insiders. Corruption and insider theft are both rampant in Russia, a dangerous combination that may penetrate deep into Russia's nuclear complex. To take just one example, a general who once commanded a nuclear weapons base is now on trial for corruption, which reportedly included stealing money from U.S. assistance to upgrade security at nuclear sites.[24] Protections against such insider theft are improving, but are still insufficient: for example, the detailed analyses of anomalies in nuclear material accounting needed to catch thieves periodically stealing small bits of material are still not required in Russian regulations, and some sites are still using easily faked seals to indicate whether material has been tampered with.

The terrorist threat remains significant in Russia as well. Over the past decade, terrorists in Russia have shown the ability to organize and execute large-scale, no-warning attacks involving well-trained, well-armed attackers willing to die for their cause, in such incidents as the Moscow theater siege in 2002 and Beslan school massacre of 2004. Moscow's brutal crushing of the Chechen rebellion suppressed the ability of terrorists to organize such large-scale attacks, but in recent years the terrorist threat has again been on the rise: the movement has regrouped and spread, carrying out dozens of deadly attacks a year, with a new goal of establishing an Islamic caliphate throughout the North Caucasus.[25] Despite this threat, Russia continues to use poorly paid and poorly trained conscripts to guard some of its nuclear material sites. These conscripts would be no match for a well-armed, well-trained attack.[26]

Of equal concern, it remains uncertain how well Russia will sustain the improved nuclear security and accounting measures that have been put in place in recent years. Many Russian sites have limited resources to pay for nuclear security, and though the Russian government now has needed funds, it has not made nuclear security spending a priority.[27]

Research Reactors

Over the past two decades, weapons-usable nuclear material has been removed entirely from scores of sites, including many HEU-fueled research reactors that have been shut down or converted to use low-enriched uranium (LEU) fuels that cannot be used in a nuclear bomb. Some twenty-three countries have eliminated all the weapons-usable material on their soil. But there is a great deal still to be done. Roughly 120 research and training reactors worldwide still use HEU either as fuel or as targets for producing medical isotopes. Many of these facilities—some on university campuses—have only minimal security measures in place. While most research reactors do not have enough HEU on site for a bomb, some do. Two special types of reactors—called critical assemblies and pulsed reactors—often have hundreds of kilograms or even tons of weapons-grade HEU on site. While two-thirds of these special HEU-fueled reactors are in Russia, there are sites in other nuclear weapons states and civilian sites in Belarus, South Africa, and Japan that still have large amounts of weapons-usable nuclear material in forms that would require minimal chemical processing to fashion into a bomb.

Although stocks in Pakistan, in Russia, and at HEU-fueled research reactors are the three highest risk categories, virtually every country in possession of nuclear materials—including the United States—has more to do to ensure that these stocks are effectively protected against the kinds of threats that terrorists and criminals have shown they can pose. The recent incident in which an 82-year-old nun and two other pacifists successfully breached one of America's most secure nuclear weapons facilities is a stark reminder that effective nuclear security requires eternal vigilance.[28]

Not a Hypothetical Worry

Theft of HEU and plutonium is not a hypothetical worry; it is an ongoing reality. Since the end of the Cold War, there have been approximately twenty documented cases of theft and smuggling of plutonium or HEU, some in kilogram-plus quantities. One alarming recent case was a seizure of stolen HEU in Moldova in mid-2011, in which the smugglers claimed to have access to nine kilograms of HEU that they were willing to sell for $31 million. Moldovan officials report that "members of the ring, who have not yet been detained, have one kilogram of uranium." This case appears to involve a real buyer—still at large—and the possibility that there are kilograms of weapons-grade HEU in the smugglers' hands, making it potentially the most serious case in years.[29]

Though some believe nuclear theft or attacks on nuclear facilities are beyond the sophistication of common thieves or terrorists, successful assaults or covert thefts at well-secured non-nuclear facilities around the world—such as banks, military bases, and high-end jewelry facilities—suggest that existing nuclear security measures in many countries may be insufficient. Nuclear material is certainly not kept more securely than diamond caches, for example, yet there have been examples of highly sophisticated diamond heists in recent years.

Yet another unsettling factor is that the amounts of fissile material required for a bomb are small. The Nagasaki bomb contained some 6 kilograms of plutonium—a ball you could hold in the palm of your hand. A similar HEU bomb would require only about three times as much. For a simpler but less-efficient "gun-type" design, which simply slams two pieces of HEU together at high speed, roughly 50 kilograms of HEU would be needed—an amount that would fit in less than two 2-liter bottles.[30] In either case, the material for a nuclear bomb could easily be transported across borders in a variety of forms—including already manufactured parts that would be small and easy to hide, but that could be assembled in a matter of hours near the target.

3. Could a sophisticated terrorist group plausibly make a crude nuclear bomb if it was able to obtain HEU or separated plutonium?

Unfortunately, the answer here is also yes. Those who discount the threat of nuclear terrorism often fail to grasp a crucial fact: the most difficult part of making a nuclear bomb is acquiring the nuclear material. As one leading critic has argued, "Actually building [a crude nuclear weapon] is extremely difficult. A number of countries with vast resources and expertise, such as Iraq, have struggled unsuccessfully to produce one. It is difficult to imagine that a small terrorist group would find bomb-building any easier."[31] Similarly, the security chief of Russia's Federal Agency for Atomic Energy has publicly stated that "even having any nuclear material does not mean that an explosive device can be made [by terrorists]. This is absolutely impossible."[32]

These arguments are simply incorrect. They conflate the difficulty of producing the nuclear material—the key step on which Iraq spent billions of dollars—with the difficulty of making a bomb once the material is in hand. These critiques also fail to make the crucial distinction between the technical and scientific challenge of building safe, reliable, and efficient nuclear weapons suitable for delivery by a missile or a fighter aircraft and the far simpler task of making a single crude, unsafe, and unreliable terrorist nuclear explosive that might be delivered by truck or boat.

If a sophisticated terrorist group obtained HEU or plutonium, making at least a crude nuclear bomb might well be within its capabilities. According to one study by the (now-defunct) congressional Office of Technology Assessment, "A small group of people, none of whom have ever had access to the classified literature, could possibly design and build a crude nuclear explosive device ... Only modest machine-shop facilities that could be contracted for without arousing suspicion would be required."[33] Indeed, even before the revelations from seized al-Qaeda documents after the fall of the Taliban in Afghanistan, U.S. intelligence concluded that "fabrication of at least a 'crude' nuclear device was within al-Qa'ida's capabilities, if it could obtain fissile material."[34] Rolf Mowatt-Larssen, who was charged with tracking down al-Qaeda's nuclear, chemical, and biological efforts for U.S. intelligence after the 9/11 attacks, told Congress that an al-Qaeda nuclear bomb effort "probably would not require the involvement of more than the number of operatives who carried out 9/11" and would be "just as compartmented," making it extraordinarily difficult for the intelligence community to detect and stop.[35]

The simplest type of nuclear bomb that terrorists could build is the aforementioned gun-type bomb. The bomb that incinerated the Japanese city of Hiroshima, for example, consisted of a cannon that fired one piece of HEU against another.[36] In most cases, building such a bomb would require some ability to cast and machine uranium, a reasonable knowledge of the nuclear physics involved, and a good understanding of cannons and ballistics. An ability to undertake some chemical processing may also be needed (for example, to dissolve research reactor fuel containing HEU in acid, separate the HEU, and reduce the HEU to metal), but the chemical processing required is no more sophisticated than some of the processing criminals routinely undertake in the illegal drug industry.

It is impossible, however, to achieve a substantial nuclear yield with a gun-type bomb made from plutonium, because the neutrons emitted from plutonium will set off the nuclear chain reaction prematurely, causing the bomb to blow itself apart. Thus, if terrorists only had plutonium available, they would have to attempt the more challenging task of designing and building an implosion-type device, such as that used at Nagasaki, in which explosives arranged around nuclear material compress it to a much higher density, setting off the nuclear chain reaction. Although terrorists' likelihood of success in making such a bomb would be lower than for a gun-type bomb, the danger certainly cannot be ruled out.

If terrorists working to make a nuclear bomb were able to get help from someone with direct experience in matters such as machining uranium metal weapons components, their chances of succeeding would be higher. But repeated U.S. government studies have concluded that terrorists might well be able to make a crude bomb without such knowledgeable help. To slam two pieces of HEU together, unwritten "tacit knowledge" is not likely to be crucial, in contrast to more complex endeavors such as getting the many finicky pieces of a uranium enrichment centrifuge to work properly.

4. Could a terrorist group likely deliver a bomb to Washington, New York, or other major cities around the world?

Here, too, unfortunately, the answer is yes. If stolen or built abroad, a nuclear bomb might be delivered to the United States, intact or in ready-to-assemble pieces, by boat or aircraft or truck. The length of the U.S. border, the diversity of means of transport, the vast scale of legitimate traffic across national borders, and the ease of shielding the radiation from plutonium or especially from HEU all operate in favor of the terrorists. Building the overall system of legal infrastructure, intelligence, law enforcement, border and customs forces, and radiation detectors needed to find and recover stolen nuclear weapons or materials, or to interdict these as they cross national borders, is an extraordinarily difficult challenge. In particular, the radiation detectors currently at ports and border crossings worldwide cannot detect HEU metal that is shielded, and, in any case, it seems very likely that sophisticated terrorist operatives would choose one of the myriad possible routes for moving their nuclear material that did not pass through a monitored border crossing equipped with large, readily observable radiation detectors.

5. What would happen if terrorists set off a nuclear bomb in a U.S. city?

Here, the answers are nothing short of terrifying. A bomb with the explosive power of 10,000 tons of TNT—that is, 10 kilotons, roughly two-thirds the size of the bomb that obliterated Hiroshima—could easily be delivered in an ordinary truck. If set off in midtown Manhattan on a typical workday, such a bomb could kill half a million people and cause $1 trillion in direct economic damage.[37] Neither the United States nor any other country is remotely prepared to cope with the aftermath of such an attack—caring for tens of thousands of burned, wounded, and irradiated victims, evacuating hundreds of thousands of people in the path of the fallout, restoring essential services to a partly burned and irradiated city, and much more.[38]

Terrorists—either those who committed the attack or others—would certainly claim they had more bombs already hidden in U.S. cities (whether they did or not), and the fear that this might be true could lead to panicked evacuations of major U.S. cities, creating widespread havoc and economic disruption. If the bomb went off in Washington, D.C., large fractions of the federal government would be destroyed, and effective governance of the country would be very much in doubt.

Devastating economic aftershocks would reverberate throughout the country and the world—global effects that in 2005 UN Secretary-General Kofi Annan warned would push "tens of millions of people into dire poverty," creating "a second death toll throughout the developing world."[39]

Politically, confidence in the U.S. government would be profoundly, perhaps irrevocably, shaken, because no one could be certain that the government that had failed to protect its citizens from such a devastating attack would succeed in protecting them from another. Far more than after 9/11, U.S. policies on eavesdropping, handling of terrorist suspects, and the legitimacy of attacking foreign countries to prevent possible future attacks would change dramatically. America and the world would be transformed forever—and not for the better.[40]

NUCLEAR TERRORISM: THE RISKS

To understand the risks of nuclear terrorism, it is important to put these aspects of the real danger in a broader context, balancing both the bad news and the good news—and there is good news in this story as well.

The Good News

First, there is no convincing evidence that any terrorist group has yet acquired a nuclear weapon or the materials needed to make one, or that al-Qaeda has succeeded in pulling together the expertise needed to make a bomb. Indeed, to the contrary, there is some evidence of confusion and lack of nuclear knowledge by some senior al-Qaeda operatives.[41]

Second, as already noted, making and delivering even a crude nuclear bomb would be the most technically challenging and complex operation any terrorist group has ever carried out. The effort could fail at any one of many different points, and the obstacles may seem daunting even to determined terrorists, convincing them to focus more of their efforts on conventional (if nevertheless creative) tools of terror—as al-Qaeda appears to have done.[42] Both al-Qaeda and Aum Shinrikyo appear to have encountered a variety of difficulties in trying to fulfill their nuclear ambitions, demonstrating that building or acquiring a nuclear bomb is a difficult challenge, even for large and well-financed terrorist groups with ample technical resources.

Third, as described earlier, the overthrow of the Taliban, the disruption of al-Qaeda's old central command structure in Afghanistan, and the assassination of many in al-Qaeda's core leadership, including Osama bin Laden himself, certainly reduced the group's chances of pulling off such a complex operation.

Fourth, there is now a very real debate, even within the community of violent Islamic extremists, over the moral legitimacy of the mass slaughter of innocents. One of the founders of al-Qaeda, who wrote two of the books on which the organization has long relied for its ideological justification for violent jihad, has since reversed course with a book that argues that most forms of terrorism— and particularly the indiscriminate killing of bystanders—are forbidden by Islamic law, and that violent jihad is permissible only under very rare circumstances. "There is nothing that invokes the anger of God and His wrath like the unwarranted spilling of blood and wrecking of property," this key al-Qaeda ideologist argues.[43] Al-Qaeda was sufficiently concerned about this frontal assault by one of its founders that Ayman al-Zawahiri rushed out a 188-page response only two months after the book was released. Moreover, when al-Qaeda organized an electronic question-and-answer session with al-Zawahiri, many of the questions he chose to answer focused on bitter criticisms of al-Qaeda's killing of innocent people. He was at pains to argue that al-Qaeda fighters would kill innocents only when doing so was unavoidable, quoting bin Laden as instructing fighters to "make sure that their operations targeting the enemies are regulated by the regulations of the Shari'ah and as far as possible from Muslims."[44] A nuclear bomb, of course, is the apotheosis of indiscriminate mass slaughter, making no distinction between the innocent and the guilty, between Muslims and non-Muslims. These debates are not likely to convince al-Zawahiri, al-Qaeda's current leader, but the more the broader community of extreme Islamists views the nuclear level of mass slaughter as a moral crime, the more difficult it is likely to be for the organization to recruit experts and raise money to help it build a nuclear bomb.

Fifth, nuclear security is improving. Although a great deal has yet to be done, at scores of sites in Russia, in the rest of the former Soviet Union, and elsewhere security is dramatically better than it was fifteen years ago. Security upgrades were completed for most Russian nuclear warhead and nuclear material sites by the end of 2008. HEU is being removed from sites all around the world, permanently eliminating the risk of nuclear theft at those sites. An alphabet soup of programs and initiatives—the Cooperative Threat Reduction (CTR) effort, the Material Protection, Control, and Accounting (MPC&A)

Program, the Global Threat Reduction Initiative (GTRI), the Global Initiative to Combat Nuclear Terrorism (GICNT), the IAEA's Office of Nuclear Security, the Domestic Nuclear Detection Office (DNDO), and many more—is making real contributions.[45] Two nuclear security summits, in 2010 and 2012, attended by dozens of countries have elevated nuclear security to the level of presidents and prime ministers, which in turn has helped galvanize bureaucracies to take action. There can be no doubt that America and the world face a far lower risk of nuclear terrorism today than they would have had these efforts never begun.

Sixth, it is highly unlikely that hostile states would consciously choose to provide terrorist groups with nuclear weapons or the materials needed to make them. Such a decision would mean transferring the most awesome military power the state had ever acquired to a group over which it had little control— a particularly unlikely step for dictators or oligarchs obsessed with controlling their states and maintaining power. If the terrorists actually used the transferred capability against the United States or one of its allies, there would be a substantial chance that the source of the weapon or material would be traced back to the state that provided it, almost certainly provoking a government-destroying retaliation.

All of this good news comes with a crucial caveat: "as far as we know." The gaps in knowledge remain wide. Some intelligence analysts argue that the lack of hard evidence of an extensive current al-Qaeda nuclear effort simply reflects the group's success in compartmentalizing the work and keeping it secret. It is sobering to remember how little was known about Aum Shinrikyo before it launched its nerve gas attack in the Tokyo subway.

Probabilities

So, taking the good news with the bad, what are the chances of a terrorist nuclear attack? The short answer is that nobody knows. In 2006 I published a mathematical model that provided a structured, step-by-step way of thinking through the problem. A set of plausible illustrative values for the input parameters resulted in a 29 percent ten-year probability estimate—by coincidence, the same as the median estimate of the ten-year probability of a nuclear attack on the United States in a survey of national security experts by Sen. Richard Lugar's office a few years ago.[46] Because there are large uncertainties in each of those inputs, however, the real probability could well be either higher or lower. But even a 1 percent chance of nuclear terrorism over the next ten years would be enough to justify substantial action to reduce the risk, given the unimaginable scale of the consequences. No one in his right mind would operate a nuclear power plant upwind of a major city that had a 1 percent chance over ten years of blowing sky-high—the risk would be understood by all to be too great. But that, in effect, is what countries are doing—or worse—by managing the world's nuclear stockpiles as they do today, and by not doing nearly as much as they should to address the multifaceted threat of nuclear terrorism.

CONCLUSION

To motivate and guide the actions needed to prevent nuclear terrorism, policy-makers and nuclear managers around the world must understand the scope and urgency of the threat even in a post–bin Laden world. Complacency is the enemy of effective response.

The critical first step in an effective response is clear: do everything possible to ensure that *all* caches of nuclear weapons and the materials needed to make them, wherever they may be, are secured and accounted for to standards sufficient to ensure that they are defended, in ways that will work and will last, against the threats that terrorists and thieves have demonstrated they can pose. Improving nuclear security is the one step that will most reduce the overall risk of nuclear terrorism, because once a nuclear weapon or nuclear material has left the facility where it is supposed to be, it could be anywhere, and all the subsequent layers of defense are variations on looking for needles in haystacks.

But nuclear security is not all that must be done, for it will never provide perfect protection against nuclear theft, and some material has likely already been stolen and not recovered. The most critical elements of the next line of defense are police and intelligence measures; most of the past successes in seizing stolen nuclear material have arisen from conspirators informing on each other and from good police and intelligence work, not from radiation detectors. The United States and other concerned countries should undertake a substantially stepped-up effort to build international police and intelligence cooperation focused on stopping nuclear smuggling. This should include additional sting operations and well-publicized incentives for informers to report on such plots. The United States should also work with key nations to ensure that they put in place laws that make any participation in nuclear terrorism or in real or attempted theft or smuggling of nuclear weapons or weapons-usable materials crimes with penalties comparable to those for murder or treason.

Next, countries should focus on stopping the other elements of a nuclear plot—the recruiting, fund-raising, equipment purchases, and other activities that inevitably would be required. Because of the complexity of a nuclear effort, it might offer a bigger and more detectable profile than many other terrorist conspiracies. The best chances to stop such a plot lie not in exotic new detection technologies but in a broad approach to counterterrorism—targeting and disrupting those groups with the skills, ambitions, and financing to attempt nuclear terrorism.[47]

The international community can achieve the goal of effectively and lastingly protecting all stocks of nuclear weapons, HEU, and plutonium so that they never fall into the hands of terrorists. Doing so requires sustained high-level leadership, a sensible strategy, partnership-based approaches, adequate resources, and good information. The actions President Obama and other world leaders have already taken has led to real progress and opened new opportunities. Countries need to seize those opportunities and build a world in which there is virtually no chance that terrorists could acquire the means to build a nuclear bomb. This mission cannot be completed until the international community has a firm understanding of the real and urgent risk of nuclear terrorism.

NO: The threat is overblown.
Susan B. Martin, *King's College London*

The Threat of Nuclear Terrorism Is Overblown

The possibility of nuclear terrorism is real, but a terrorist attack using nuclear weapons is not inevitable and is in fact unlikely.[48] In this essay, I will explain how I arrive at this assessment of the probability of nuclear terrorism, and then address what the consequences of this are for policymaking in general on this issue.

The current debate on the risks of nuclear terrorism is heated, and the stakes are high. An underestimation of the risk can lead to inadequate polices that, in turn, may raise the risk of such an attack. But an overestimation of the risks can also be dangerous, and these dangers are too often ignored. An overestimation can lead to inappropriate and costly policies that can decrease instead of increase security, such as the 2003 war against Iraq. It can lead as well to an unfounded and harmful sense of fear and vulnerability. And it is also possible that the hyperbole surrounding nuclear terrorism makes it more likely through both demand and supply effects. The insistence that nuclear terrorism is only a matter of time suggests that there is a demand for fissile material, and this postulated demand might then create supply, encouraging those who are desperate or mercenary enough to try and steal it. In addition, the portrayal of nuclear terrorism both as inevitable and as the thing that frightens people most encourages terrorists to think that such an attack is both possible (I can imagine them thinking, "If someone can do it, why not us?" or "If someone is going to do it, it should be us") and necessary to have a major impact ("If this is what they are most afraid of, this is what we have to do").[49]

Participants in the current debate generally agree on the appropriate starting point for the discussion.[50] The risk of a nuclear terrorist attack is defined as a product of the probability of such an attack times its consequences. All agree that the consequences of a nuclear attack would be horrific. Estimates of the immediate fatalities from a 10-kiloton, Hiroshima-sized bomb range from thousands to hundreds of thousands, with the precise effects dependent on the size of the explosion and other characteristics of the attack, including the population density of the target area. Even here, though, hyperbole poses a danger. For example, some have warned that a terrorist nuclear attack, in addition to causing death and destruction, would "end American civil liberties."[51] But other experts have testified to Congress that a nuclear attack would affect only part of a major city, and it is clear that other sorts of effects, including on civil liberties, would depend not on the terrorists but on Americans themselves.[52]

The other component of risk, probability, is a function of motives and capabilities. The difficulty is that the probability of a nuclear terrorist attack is essentially unknowable. The possibilities and uncertainties seem endless. There are many levels of capability and many different paths to acquiring those capabilities. There are hundreds of different terrorist groups, and although only one or two may be discussed as likely candidates for a nuclear capability today, an estimation of probability unbounded by time has to include groups that might emerge or change in the future. Even if analysts tried to limit probability to the possibility of a nuclear attack by al-Qaeda in the next ten years, the unknowables are still immense. For example, estimates of the size and capability of al-Qaeda and its affiliates vary enormously today, particularly since the death of Osama bin Laden. Despite these difficulties, estimates of the probability of a terrorist nuclear attack can be and are made. But it is important to keep in mind the degree of fundamental uncertainty in these estimates.

In assessing the risk of a terrorist nuclear attack, I proceed by analyzing the probability of such an attack, looking first at capabilities and then at motives. I then conclude with a discussion of the policy dilemma posed by the uncertain threat of nuclear terrorism.

PROBABILITY OF A TERRORIST ATTACK WITH NUCLEAR WEAPONS

No one with knowledge of the subject argues that a terrorist attack with nuclear weapons is impossible, and few are willing to say that a terrorist attack with nuclear weapons will never happen.[53] Most analysts hedge a bit, with the doubters arguing that such an attack is unlikely.[54] Others, including Graham Allison and Matthew Bunn, argue that the consequences of such an attack would be so horrendous that the probability does not really matter.[55] And still others argue that such an attack is nearly inevitable.[56] I find the argument that such an attack is unlikely the most persuasive for reasons centered on both motives and capability. And I argue that this low probability does matter, and it should be taken into account when making policy decisions about how to respond to the threat.

The first task is to specify what is meant by a terrorist nuclear attack. The possibilities include food or water contaminated with nuclear material; a conventional bomb that disperses radioactive material, otherwise known as a radiological or dirty bomb; an attack on a nuclear power plant; an attack with a stolen nuclear weapon; or an attack with an improvised nuclear device (IND), a crude nuclear bomb that terrorists construct themselves.

Analysts generally, although not universally, agree that governments are deterred from giving a nuclear weapon to a terrorist group both by the fear that the weapon could be turned against the government or its interests and by the retaliation that would follow if the terrorist group used the weapon and its source was identified.[57] Analysts also acknowledge that a terrorist group would find it very difficult to steal or buy a nuclear weapon, and that, even if it managed to do so, the group would have to overcome additional difficult hurdles before it could use a purloined bomb.[58]

Other scenarios are more possible but also less alarming. There seem to be no large hurdles to terrorist acquisition of radioactive material that could be used to contaminate food or water or that could be used in a dirty bomb. But no open source examples of these sorts of attacks are available, suggesting that terrorists lack the motives to carry them out. A handful of non-nuclear attacks on food have taken place in the past, but they were not very effective, and contaminating food or water with radioactive materials would not cause mass casualties or create spectacular media images. A radiological dirty bomb would inflict a heavy economic toll and could cause great disruption, but the death toll would be small. Similarly, an attack on a nuclear power plant is likely to be within the capability of at least some terrorist groups, and such an attack is frightening in its environmental, economic, and long-term health costs. But the number of direct deaths caused by such an attack would be low, and the motive for such attacks appears to be small.[59]

This leaves the possibility of a terrorist attack with an IND. How does one estimate the probability of such an attack? Probability is a function of capability and motives, so the following sections will look at each of these in turn.

Capability

The two main categories of nuclear devices, gun type and implosion type, largely use two kinds of nuclear material, highly enriched uranium, or HEU, and plutonium. The simplest device is the gun type, which requires HEU. An implosion device is more challenging technically, and it can use either HEU or plutonium. Most analyses focus on a gun-type device using HEU as the simplest, and therefore most likely, path to a terrorist nuclear bomb, and because of space considerations I will do the same.[60]

There are two chief hurdles to the construction of any nuclear device: acquisition of the necessary fissile material and the specialized knowledge and expertise required to construct a bomb using that material. There is little agreement on the amount of fissile material a terrorist group would need to obtain for a nuclear device; in part, this is because the amount needed varies with the fissile material used, the desired explosive yield, and the technical sophistication of the bomb design.[61] The International Atomic Energy Agency (IAEA) identifies 25 kilograms of HEU as a "Significant Quantity (SQ)"—"the approximate amount of nuclear material for which the possibility of manufacturing a nuclear explosive device cannot be excluded."[62] The Federation of American Scientists (FAS) notes that "the six bombs built by the Republic of South Africa were gun-assembled and used 50kg of uranium enriched to between 80 percent and 93 percent in the isotope U-235," and the Union of Concerned Scientists (UCS) estimates that 40–50 kilograms of HEU enriched to 90 percent would be required to build a bomb.[63]

Acquiring the Fissile Material

No one expects a terrorist group to attempt to produce this material on its own; to construct a bomb a group would have to either steal the material or purchase it on the black market.[64]

The factors that suggest that such a theft or purchase is possible include the enormous amount of fissile material produced since 1945 and the lack of an accurate inventory or record of this material;[65] the lack of adequate security arrangements for much of the fissile material known to exist, which creates an opportunity for theft as well as the possibility that such theft will go undetected, at least for a time;[66] economic and political instabilities in countries, which can create both incentives (disaffection, economic hardship) and opportunity (corruption, criminal gangs) for theft; and the record of trafficking incidents since 1993.[67]

However, there are serious obstacles to the acquisition through theft or purchase of the fissile material necessary for an IND. The record of trafficking incidents is at least somewhat comforting on this score. None of the known incidents has come close to the quantity necessary for a gun-type device. The largest reported incident is a failed attempt to steal 18.5 kilograms of HEU from Russia in December 1998.[68] In an incident reported in 2007, 79.5 grams of uranium enriched to 89 percent were seized in Georgia.[69] Although the enrichment level of this material is alarming, and although the smuggler alleg-edly claimed to have 2–3 kilograms of this material, this amount is still far short of what would be required for a gun-type device. In addition, policies and clearinghouses have been and are being enacted and put into place to make the trafficking of nuclear materials more difficult now than it was in the past.[70]

Another obstacle to the theft of fissile material is the complicated nature of the task.[71] Theft of fissile material requires identifying a vulnerable source of HEU, stealing that material from what is likely to be at least a somewhat guarded site, and then transporting the material, most likely across interna-tional borders, to the location where the bomb will be constructed. As John Mueller has pointed out, this scenario will surely include some people who are not committed to the terrorists' cause (facility insiders or smugglers motivated only by money), and so the conspirators must maintain their silence, even in the face of the rewards offered for information on the theft of such materials or planned terrorist acts.[72] They also must avoid arousing the suspicions of others in the vicinity. To the extent that a series of such thefts is needed to accumulate the required amount of material, the same gauntlet of obstacles must be run each time. Mixing and matching different sources of uranium would also increase the technical challenge of constructing a bomb, because sophisticated analysis would be needed to identify the isotopes in each batch of uranium, and additional processing of the fissile material might be required.[73] Attempt-ing to steal the required amount in one go also would be difficult, however, because such an amount is less likely to go unnoticed and may give facilitators (such as facility insiders) pause.

All this applies if the terrorists themselves steal the material. Purchasing material requires that someone else undertake all the steps just described; that the seller and the buyer are able to find each other, avoiding any sting opera-tions; that they are able to negotiate a deal for the purchase; that the material for sale is actually fissile material and not fake goods; and that the deal is not discovered or reported for reward money.

Clearly, acquiring sufficient fissile material is a complicated, risky (and expensive) undertaking. Even though I do not think I can say with certainty that a terrorist group would *never* be able to achieve all of this, I do know that the acquisition of the required amount of fissile material by a terrorist group would be a very complicated undertaking, requiring careful planning and research, good management, and a lot of luck. And even if a terrorist group does succeed in acquiring the necessary material, it will find itself only partway toward achieving a usable nuclear device.

Building the Bomb

How likely is it that, having acquired the requisite amount of nuclear material, a terrorist group would be able to construct a nuclear device? In looking at this question, it is important to remember that I am examining the ability of a terrorist group to build one bomb, not its ability to build a sophisticated arsenal.

Analysts generally agree that it is within the realm of possibility that a subnational group could build a gun-type device, especially if the group is not concerned with the efficiency and reliability of the weapon.[74] In 1977 the U.S. Office of Technology Assessment (OTA) estimated that an improvised nuclear device could be built by a minimum of two people, and Anna Pluta and Peter Zimmerman agree that this is plausible, as long as the uranium is enriched to at least 50 percent.[75] When constructing a scenario of how a terrorist group would build a nuclear bomb, Peter Zimmerman and Jeffrey Lewis assume it would take nineteen people and argue that it would take them up to a year.[76]

But just because it is feasible that terrorists could construct a nuclear device does not mean that any particular group would be successful, or that the construction of a device by some group in the future is inevitable. Substantial hurdles are again involved. Even while arguing forcefully that a terrorist group could build a nuclear bomb, Matthew Bunn cautions that "making and delivering even a crude nuclear bomb would be the most technically challenging and complex operation any terrorist organization has ever carried out."[77] And the OTA also cautions against oversimplifying the construction of a gun-type device, arguing that

> although the gun assembly may be conceptually simpler [than an implosion device], the difficulty of actually constructing a nuclear explosive is roughly equivalent whether a gun or implosion assembly is used. The difficulties of the gun assembly are often not appreciated: a large mass of high density must be accelerated to a high speed in a short distance, putting quite unusual requirements on the gun design.[78]

This means that not just anyone can build a nuclear bomb. Furthermore, one cannot learn how to do so by reading a book. Tacit knowledge or learning by doing is important. No matter what blueprints have been obtained and what publications have been read, adjustments must be made when designing and building a bomb, which requires an ability to carry out experiments and to use the information gained from these experiments. But will terrorists be able to do this? And even if they can, there will be little room for learning by doing because both time and the necessary materials will be scarce.

The difficulty in assessing the likelihood of a terrorist nuclear attack is that one can spin scenario after scenario. Yes, it is possible that a terrorist group can figure out a way to acquire the necessary nuclear material. Yes, it is possible that a terrorist group can manage to recruit the people with the requisite knowledge and skills. Yes, it is possible to imagine that this group will be able to work together well, and that it will overcome the technical challenges, making all the necessary precise measurements and identifying any errors so that they can be corrected.

But how likely is it that all of this will happen at the right time without any discovery? How likely is it that the fissile material is acquired at the same time the group of experts is recruited? If there is a time lag, the risk of things going wrong increases—for example, the stolen material may be discovered (or may be stolen by someone else); one of the experts may have a change of heart or become unable to participate; someone from outside may discover or stumble upon the plot.

The bottom line is that, although it is certainly possible that a terrorist group could build a nuclear bomb, the chances of its doing so successfully are small. But even extremely difficult tasks can be accomplished if one is motivated enough, and so motives are the subject of the next section.

Motives

As noted earlier, analysts such as Graham Allison and Matthew Bunn argue that the consequences of a terrorist nuclear attack would be so horrendous that even an extremely low probability of such an attack does not decrease the risks. If one follows this logic, then the motives of a group to carry out such an attack become irrelevant. All that matters is that such an attack is possible, because the very possibility, given the consequences, is all that is required to justify action to prevent it. But I do not think motives can be dismissed so easily. After all, a strongly motivated group will be more likely to overcome the hurdles involved in building a bomb than a weakly motivated group, which may give it a try, but turn back at the first failure or obstacle.

It is clear that some terrorist groups have an interest in nuclear weapons. The Japanese group Aum Shinrikyo first tried to buy a nuclear weapon and then, when that attempt failed, recruited scientists and engineers to help in its pursuit of nuclear as well as chemical and biological weapons.[79] What is most significant about the Aum example, however, is not that the group tried to get nuclear weapons but that it failed. Due in part to the technological challenges—and despite the enormous financial and scientific resources available to this group, which dwarf those available to other known groups except perhaps al-Qaeda—its efforts to acquire nuclear weapons were unsuccessful. In addition to illustrating the difficulty of acquiring nuclear weapons, the Aum example is suggestive because of the light it sheds on motives for use. When the group decided to launch a chemical weapons attack on the Tokyo subway, using the sarin nerve gas that it was able to make, it did so in the pursuit of tactical aims and not to maximize destruction.[80]

There is also evidence that al-Qaeda has at least some interest in nuclear materials.[81] This evidence includes reported attempts by al-Qaeda operatives to purchase fissile material as well as past statements by Osama bin Laden. Perhaps the statement most cited is bin Laden's assertion that it is a "religious duty" for Muslims to acquire nuclear weapons. But note that in this statement bin Laden focuses on acquisition, not use, as the duty for Muslims and suggests that nuclear weapons could be used for the prevention of harm (perhaps deterrence):

> Acquiring weapons for the defense of Muslims is a religious duty. If I have indeed acquired these weapons, then I thank God for enabling me to do so. And if I seek to acquire these weapons, I am carrying out a duty. It would be a sin for Muslims not to try to possess the weapons that would prevent the infidels from inflicting harm on Muslims.[82]

Other statements, however, can be read as suggesting that al-Qaeda might try to justify the use of nuclear weapons on the United States by reference to Hiroshima and Nagasaki.[83] And indeed, from al-Qaeda's perspective, a nuclear attack could conceivably be "just," part of a defensive jihad against the West or a "preventive" attack, intended to prevent future attacks on Muslims.[84]

But it is difficult to use statements such as these from the late Osama bin Laden to gauge al-Qaeda's motives and intentions. These sorts of public announcements can serve different functions and be intended for different audiences. They may be intended to recruit Muslims to al-Qaeda's cause. They may also be intended to terrorize the West as part of al-Qaeda's strategy to generate fear. Thus they are not necessarily an accurate indication of al-Qaeda's aims and strategies.

The issue of strategy raises the question of whether a nuclear attack would be a rational choice for a terrorist group—that is, could such an attack serve its aims and objectives? This question assumes that terrorist groups are rational in the sense that they choose their means with an eye to their ends. And, indeed, this seems to be a reasonable assumption, because groups that fail to meet this limited definition of rationality would have a hard time organizing, managing, and completing a project to acquire nuclear weapons. In addressing the question of rational choice, I will focus on al-Qaeda as the most prominent terrorist group alleged to be pursuing nuclear weapons today. The general argument, however, would apply to other groups as well.

Al-Qaeda wants to punish the United States and to compel it to change its policies in the Middle East—to end its support of Israel and "corrupt" Arab governments, to withdraw its troops from the region, and to allow the establishment of sharia in Muslim lands. But it is unlikely that an al-Qaeda nuclear attack on the United States, which would be limited to one or two nuclear weapons, would accomplish these objectives. The Middle East and the oil it contains are a vital national security interest of the United States. A nuclear attack on the United States and the economic damage it would inflict would probably make it even more important that the United States not suffer another economic blow from a disruption to its oil supply. As a consequence, a terrorist nuclear attack is unlikely to compel the United States to withdraw from involvement in the Middle East. And even if a nuclear attack on the American homeland somehow led to the establishment of a regime and territory controlled by al-Qaeda, it would simply provide a target for retaliation by the United States.

There is no reason to think that after a nuclear attack the United States would be unwilling or unable to retaliate. Contrary to what bin Laden implied, America would not be in the situation of Japan in August 1945.[85] The nuclear attack in 1945 came after Japan had fought a long war and its military was close to defeat. By contrast, a terrorist nuclear attack would have no ability to destroy the military capabilities of the United States. In the aftermath of such an attack, the U.S. military, supported by the American people, would be determined to retaliate and to bring the perpetrators to justice.

Nor is there any reason to conclude that a nuclear attack would succeed in undermining liberal democracy in the United States, which is often stated as one of al-Qaeda's primary aims. How the United States responds and how that response affects the health of democracy are in the hands of American policymakers and the American people. Even if the first impulse is to sacrifice civil liberties in the name of security, such a response is not inevitable and will not necessarily be sustained in the long run.

In addition, any terrorist group that launched a nuclear attack would likely be the subject of the most intensive international effort to find and punish those responsible the world has ever seen. Nuclear weapons have not been used since 1945, and any group or state that breaks this tradition of nonuse would be shunned and outcast not just by the victim of the attack but also by people and states around the world. The tradition of nonuse is generally held to be in the interest of all; no one wants nuclear weapons to become a "normal" weapon of war. In addition, no state can afford to be seen harboring a terrorist group that launched a nuclear attack for fear that it would be held responsible. Again, unlike Japan in 1945, the United States and other states opposed to the use of nuclear weapons would be in a position to retaliate. Al-Qaeda has to ask itself if unleashing such a response is really in its interest.

To the extent that a group like al-Qaeda is interested in fueling divisions between Muslims and the West, the use of a nuclear weapon seems risky. If, as just argued, the nonuse of nuclear weapons is a common interest, not just in the West but around the world, then the use of nuclear weapons would unite most if not all the world into a coalition against the group. Al-Qaeda might hope that the retaliation provoked by its attack would weaken or shatter this coalition. Although this is possible, the nuclear character of the terrorist attack makes it unlikely. In addition, the 9/11 attacks demonstrate that there are easier means of creating divisions between Muslims and the West.

It is also possible to question whether a nuclear attack would serve other goals of terrorist groups, including recruitment and increased support from passive sympathizers. Although the use of a nuclear weapon may make the group seem powerful and attract some additional recruits, I believe the use of such a weapon would also make passive sympathizers and perhaps even potential recruits question the wisdom of supporting al-Qaeda.[86]

In a world of more than two nuclear powers, no state has been able to devise a strategy for the first use of nuclear weapons that serves its interests. It may be possible that some terrorist group will succeed where states have failed, but luckily I think this prospect is unlikely. Nuclear weapons are useful for deterrence, and perhaps when possessed but not used for "getting a seat at the table." But it is not clear how the first use of nuclear weapons can advance any substantive goals.

If terrorists are interested in inflicting pure destruction, they may be better off sticking with what they know. The empirical record thus far suggests that attacks with "weapons of mass destruction" have done less damage than more conventional attacks.[87] A successful terrorist nuclear attack is clearly the most destructive attack imaginable. But a failed nuclear attack, where much time, effort, and money are devoted to a failed effort to acquire or build a nuclear bomb, would be much less effective than that same amount of effort put into attacks using more accessible means.

This observation suggests that the motives for a terrorist nuclear attack are not nearly as strong as people in the West are often led to believe. Ironically, the strongest motivation for such an attack is probably the attention that the possibility of a terrorist nuclear attack receives in the West. To the extent that the West continues to portray the terrorist nuclear threat as the thing it fears most—to the extent that the West continues to portray it as inevitable and as only a matter of time—it nurtures the idea that a nuclear attack is what terrorists must do if they want to be taken seriously.

This is not to say that if the world ignores the possibility of nuclear terrorism it will go away—the possibility exists and needs to be addressed. But I do think that analysts and policymakers need to lower their rhetoric and approach the problem carefully so that they do not inspire the very attacks they are trying to prevent.

CONCLUSION

In view of the difficulties involved in terrorists' acquisition of a nuclear weapon, the paucity of motives for a nuclear attack, and the reasons why such an attack would not be in the interests of a terrorist group, I judge the probability of such an attack to be low.

But even if a terrorist attack with nuclear weapons is unlikely, the possibility cannot be ignored for two reasons. First, the consequences of such an attack would be catastrophic, so some effort to prevent it is justified. Second, many of the hurdles that terrorists face today in carrying out a nuclear attack flow from the various policies governments around the world have put in place to prevent nuclear terrorism.

The most important policies are those aimed at preventing the theft of fissile material and tracing and recovering that material if prevention fails.[88] In addition to securing sources of fissile material, reducing the potential sources of such material is important.[89] The costs of carrying out these policies are both financial and political. The financial costs are obvious. The political costs arise when cooperation from other countries is needed to implement these policies, as this may require compromise on other issues. Policies that are "international" rather than "American" or "Western" may help to lower these political costs, and the establishment of global standards for the security of stockpiles of fissile material, as suggested by Matthew Bunn, could be very helpful in this regard.

However, tensions between policies that address the terrorist nuclear threat and other policies will still exist, which is where the policy dilemma arises. How does one determine the best policy to counter such an uncertain threat? And how does one weigh the possible benefits of a policy to decrease the likelihood of a terrorist nuclear attack against the benefits of policies to counter other more likely threats? After all, states do not possess unlimited resources, and therefore they must trade off one policy against others.

Analysts such as Matthew Bunn and Graham Allison emphasize the possibility of a nuclear attack in order to overcome what they see as the complacency of governments. There are sensible, effective policies that should be enacted to increase the difficulty of a terrorist nuclear attack, but these policies require government activity and financing and may be neglected if the possibility of a terrorist nuclear attack is not emphasized.

Other analysts such as John Mueller and William Arkin emphasize the low probability of an attack in an effort to counter what they see as an overreaction to the threat. In the extreme, this overreaction can contribute to events such as the 2003 war against Iraq, which served to increase, not decrease, the terrorist threat.[90] An overreaction can also contribute to a lack of preparedness to meet other threats (whether natural disasters such as Hurricane Katrina or other military threats) and results in fewer resources for other needs (e.g., job creation, health care, environmental protection, education).[91] These sorts of trade-offs are less acute for the most developed countries, but they have to decide how much of their limited diplomatic capital should be spent on encouraging international cooperation against nuclear terrorism versus other policy goals.

Caught on the horns of the policy dilemma are the policymakers who are responsible for making the decisions and who have to act even in the face of the uncertainties. They are also the ones who will be held to account if a terrorist nuclear attack does occur, and this political reality is a contributing factor to overreaction.

In all likelihood, nations will continue to be both over- and underprepared for a terrorist nuclear attack. Overreaction may occur if the threat is overhyped or if it is manipulated in order to serve other interests. Underreaction may occur if sensible but relatively unexciting policies such as increasing the security of fissile material are underfunded. A way must be sought between these two dangers, which requires continued scholarly analysis and debate as well as informed discussion among both policymakers and the general public. The possibility of a terrorist nuclear attack is real, but the likelihood of such an attack and the efficacy and costs of proposed policies to counter that threat demand careful analysis and thorough discussion.

Notes

1. See, for example, Richard Falkenrath, Robert Newman, and Bradley Thayer, *America's Achilles' Heel: Nuclear, Biological, and Chemical Terrorism and Covert Attack* (Cambridge, Mass.: MIT Press, 1998).
2. Ibid., 2. Also see Ashton Carter, John Deutch, and Philip Zelikow, "Catastrophic Terrorism: Tackling the New Dangers," *Foreign Affairs* 77 (November/December 1998): 80 94.
3. Sen. Richard Lugar, "The Lugar Survey on Proliferation Threats and Responses," Office of U.S. Senator Richard Lugar, Washington, D.C., June 2005, http://lugar.senate.gov/nunnlugar/pdf/NPSurvey.pdf.

4. Commission on the Prevention of WMD Proliferation and Terrorism, *World at Risk: The Report of the Commission on the Prevention of WMD Proliferation and Terrorism* (Washington, D.C.: Commission on the Prevention of WMD Proliferation and Terrorism, December 2008).

5. See, for example, John Mueller, "Radioactive Hype," *National Interest* (September/October 2007): 59–65.

6. The South African police arrested three individuals, but soon released them without charge. See "60 Minutes: Assault on Pelindaba," *CBS News,* November 23, 2008; Rob Adam, "Media Briefing: Security Breach at NECSA on 08 November 2007," Nuclear Energy Corporation of South Africa, Pelindaba, November 13, 2007; Graeme Hosken, "Officer Shot as Gunmen Attack Pelindaba," *Pretoria News,* November 9, 2007; Graeme Hosken, "Two Gangs of Armed Men Breach Pelindaba Nuclear Facility," *Pretoria News,* November 14, 2007; and Joel Avni, Gertrude Makhafola, and Sibongile Mashaba, "Raid on Site Planned," *Sowetan,* November 14, 2007.

7. This essay focuses on terrorist use of an actual nuclear explosive—either detonating a nuclear weapon from a state stockpile or making a crude bomb from weapons-usable nuclear materials. It does not address, for example, sabotage of major nuclear facilities intended to disperse large quantities of radioactive material, or dispersal of radioactive material in a so-called dirty bomb. For a discussion of these other nuclear-related types of terrorism, see, for example, Charles D. Ferguson and William C. Potter, with Amy Sands, Leonard S. Spector, and Fred L. Wehling, *The Four Faces of Nuclear Terrorism* (Monterey, Calif.: Center for Nonproliferation Studies, Monterey Institute of International Studies, 2004). Nor does this essay address other terrorist options for causing catastrophic harm, many of which would be less challenging for terrorists than a nuclear attack. But the massive, assured, instantaneous, and comprehensive destruction of life and property that would result may make nuclear weapons a priority for terrorists despite the diffi-culties. A substantial literature on the danger of nuclear terrorism is now available. For one comprehensive (and alarming) look, see Graham T. Allison, *Nuclear Terrorism: The Ultimate Preventable Catastrophe* (New York: Times Books/Henry Holt, 2004). For a less alarming examination, see Michael Levi, *On Nuclear Terrorism* (Cambridge, Mass.: Harvard University Press, 2007).

8. For a summary of progress in improving nuclear security since 2009, see Matthew Bunn, Eben Harrell, and Martin B. Malin, *Progress on Securing Nuclear Weapons and Materials: The Four-Year Effort and Beyond* (Cambridge, Mass.: Project on Managing the Atom, Harvard University, March 2012), www.nuclearsummit.org/files/security_progress_report_2_482949862.pdf.

9. See, for example, John Mueller, *Atomic Obsession: Nuclear Alarmism from Hiroshima to Al-Qaeda* (Oxford: Oxford University Press, 2010), 161–234; and Robin M. Frost, *Nuclear Terrorism After 9/11,* Adelphi Papers (London: International Institute for Strategic Studies, 2005). For replies to some of the myths of the nuclear terrorism skeptics, see Matthew Bunn and Anthony Wier, "Debunking Seven Myths of Nuclear Terrorism and Nuclear Theft," in *Securing the Bomb: An Agenda for Action* (Cambridge, Mass., and Washington, D.C.: Project on Managing the Atom, Harvard University, and Nuclear Threat Initiative, 2004); Anna M. Pluta and Peter D. Zimmerman, "Nuclear Terrorism: A Disheartening Dissent," *Survival* 48 (Summer 2006); and Peter Zimmerman, "Do We Really Need

to Worry? Some Reflections on the Threat of Nuclear Terrorism," *Defence Against Terrorism Review* 2, no. 2 (Fall 2009), www.coedat.nato.int/datr4.htm.

10. Rahimullah Yusufzai, "World's Most Wanted Terrorist: An Interview with Osama bin Laden," *ABC News*, December 22, 1998, http://gtrp.haverford.edu/aqsi/aqsi/statements/worlds-most-wanted-terrorist-interview-osama-bin-laden.

11. George Tenet, *At the Center of the Storm: My Years at the CIA* (New York: HarperCollins, 2007), 263–268; and Rolf Mowatt-Larssen, *Al Qaeda Weapons of Mass Destruction Threat: Hype or Reality?* (Cambridge, Mass.: Belfer Center for Science and International Affairs, Harvard Kennedy School, January 2010), 18–19, http://belfercenter.ksg.harvard.edu/files/al-qaeda-wmd-threat.pdf. See also Kamran Khan and Molly Moore, "2 Nuclear Experts Briefed Bin Laden, Pakistanis Say," *Washington Post*, December 12, 2001; Peter Baker, "Pakistani Scientist Who Met Bin Laden Failed Polygraphs, Renewing Suspicion," *Washington Post*, March 3, 2002.

12. Matthew Bunn, Yuri Morozov, Rolf Mowatt-Larssen, Simon Saradzhyan, William Tobey, Victor I. Yesin, and Pavel S. Zolotarev, *The U.S.-Russia Joint Threat Assessment of Nuclear Terrorism* (Cambridge, Mass.: Belfer Center for Science and International Affairs, Harvard Kennedy School, and Institute for U.S. and Canadian Studies, June 2011), http://belfercenter.ksg.harvard.edu/publication/21087.

13. Tenet, *At the Center of the Storm*, 272–273; Mowatt-Larssen, *Al Qaeda WMD Threat*, 26–27. For an English translation of this fatwa, see Nasir Bin Hamd al-Fahd, "A Treatise on the Legal Status of Using Weapons of Mass Destruction against Infidels," May 2003, www.carnegieendowment.org/static/npp/fatwa.pdf.

14. Rolf Mowatt-Larssen, *Al-Qaeda's Religious Justification of Nuclear Terrorism* (Cambridge, Mass.: Belfer Center for Science and International Affairs, Harvard Kennedy School, November 2010), http://belfercenter.ksg.harvard.edu/publication/20518.

15. For a summary of the al-Qaeda and Aum Shinrikyo efforts, see Sara Daly, John Parachini, and William Rosenau, *Aum Shinrikyo, Al Qaeda, and the Kinshasa Reactor: Implications of Three Case Studies for Combating Nuclear Terrorism* (Santa Monica, Calif.: RAND, 2005).

16. For a discussion of NMIP, see testimony of Rolf Mowatt-Larssen, then director of the Office of Intelligence and Counterintelligence at the U.S. Department of Energy, in Homeland Security and Governmental Affairs Committee, *Nuclear Terrorism: Assessing the Threat to the Homeland*, U.S. Senate, April 2, 2008. Many might assume that the International Atomic Energy Agency (IAEA) keeps track of all the world's nuclear material, but in fact IAEA safeguards cover mainly nuclear material in non–nuclear weapons states, most of which have modest stocks; more than 95 percent of the world's HEU and more than half of the world's separated plutonium is not under any form of international monitoring. Moreover, IAEA "safeguards," despite the name, are only tangentially related to either safety or guarding—they are inspections to confirm that the state has not removed material for military use, and would do little to prevent thieves from taking it in the weeks that go by between inspections.

17. For an unclassified overview of Pakistan's nuclear security arrangements, see International Institute for Strategic Studies, *Nuclear Black Markets: Pakistan, A. Q. Khan and the Rise of Proliferation Networks: A Net Assessment* (London: IISS, 2007), 112–118.

18. See Ravi Khanna, "President Obama Calls Nuclear Security Summit Day of Great Progress," *Voice of America News,* April 14, 2010, www.voanews.com/english/news/usa/ President-Obama-Calls-Nuclear-Security-Summit-Day-of-Great-Progress–90868504 .html.

19. See Jeffrey Goldberg and Marc Ambinder, "Nuclear Negligence," *National Journal,* November 4, 2011.

20. Jane Perlez, "Pakistani Police Had Warned Army About a Raid," *New York Times,* October 11, 2009. See also Hassan Abbas, "Deciphering the Attack on Pakistan's Army Headquarters," *Afpak Channel, Foreign Policy,* October 11, 2009, http://afpak .foreignpolicy.com/posts/2009/10/11/deciphering_the_attack_on_pakistan_s_ army_headquarters.

21. Syed Shoaib Hasan, " 'New Kind of Militant' Behind Pakistan Karachi Attack," *BBC News,* May 23, 2011, www.bbc.co.uk/news/world-south-asia-13508864.

22. Hans M. Kristensen and Robert S. Norris, "Nuclear Notebook: Pakistan's Nuclear Forces, 2011," *Bulletin of the Atomic Scientists* 67, no. 4 (July/August 2011): 91–99; David Sanger and Eric Schmitt, "Pakistani Nuclear Arms Pose Challenge to U.S. Policy," *New York Times,* January 31, 2011.

23. Almost all of the known thefts of HEU and plutonium have been of bulk material, such as powders, and were committed without anyone knowing the material was missing until it was seized.

24. See "Russian General Dips into U.S. Taxpayers' Pockets," *Nezavisimaya Gazeta,* December 27, 2010; and Russian Legal Information Agency, "General Discharged for False Income Disclosure Took $333K in Bribes," release, February 20, 2012.

25. Simon Saradzhyan, "Russia's North Caucasus: The Terrorism Revival," *International Relations and Security Network* (online), December 23, 2010, http://belfercenter .ksg.harvard.edu/publication/20636.

26. Interviews with U.S. and Russian participants in nuclear security cooperation, 2010–2012. For an account of the weakness of these defenders from a senior Russian nuclear security official, see Igor Goloskokov, "Refomirovanie Voisk MVD po Okhrane Yadernikh Obektov Rossii (Reforming MVD troops to guard Russian nuclear facilities)," *Yaderny Kontrol* 9, no. 4 (Winter 2003): 39–50, www.pircenter .org/data/publications/yk4-2003.pdf.

27. The legal basis for U.S.-Russian cooperation on nuclear security expires in 2013, and renewal is uncertain. It should be noted, however, that Congress has extended the legal authority for U.S. programs to cooperate on nuclear security in Russia through 2017. See *National Defense Authorization Act for Fiscal Year 2011,* Public Law 111–383, Section 3119.

28. See Matthew Wald and William Broad, "Security Questions Are Raised by Break-in at a Nuclear Site," *New York Times,* August 8, 2012.

29. U.S. Congress, Senate, Committee on Foreign Relations, *Enhancing Non-Proliferation Partnerships in the Black Sea Region: A Minority Staff Report* (Washington, D.C.: U.S. Government Printing Office, 2011); Desmond Butler, "Officials Say Crime Ring Has Uranium," *Associated Press,* September 27, 2011; and Nick Amies, "US Concerns Over Nuclear Smuggling Between Europe, North Africa," *Deutsche Welle,* May 10, 2011, www.dw.de/us-concerns-over-nuclear-smuggling-between-europe-north-africa/a-15434811-1.

30. This is especially disconcerting when considering that the world's stockpiles of separated plutonium and HEU amount to 1,800–2,100 tons—enough to manufacture over 150,000 nuclear weapons. See International Panel on Fissile Materials, *Global Fissile Material Report 2011: Nuclear Weapons and Fissile Material Stockpiles and Production* (Princeton, N.J.: Program on Science and Global Security, Princeton University, 2011), www.ipfmlibrary.org/gfmr11.pdf.

31. Karl-Heinz Kamp, "Nuclear Terrorism Is Not the Core Problem," *Survival* 40, no. 4 (1998): 168.

32. Aleksandr Khinshteyn, "Secret Materials," Russian Center TV, November 29, 2002.

33. Office of Technology Assessment, *Nuclear Proliferation and Safeguards* (Washington, D.C.: OTA, 1977), 140.

34. Commission on the Intelligence Capabilities of the United States Regarding Weapons of Mass Destruction, *Report to the President* (Washington, D.C.: WMD Commission, 2005), 276. For discussions of official assessments of the complexity of the operation and the number of people required, see Matthew Bunn and Anthony Wier, "Terrorist Nuclear Weapons Construction: How Difficult?" *Annals of the American Academy of Political and Social Science* 607 (September 2006): 133–149. For a particular scenario involving a cell of nineteen people working for roughly a year (probably more than is actually required for some types of crude bomb), see Peter D. Zimmerman and Jeffrey G. Lewis, "The Bomb in the Backyard," *Foreign Policy* 157 (November/December 2006): 32–39.

35. Mowatt-Larssen, testimony in *Nuclear Terrorism: Assessing the Threat to the Homeland.*

36. For a more detailed discussion of the difficulty of making a crude nuclear bomb, see Bunn and Wier, "Terrorist Nuclear Weapons Construction." Scientists working on the Manhattan Project were so certain of success using this mechanism that they did not bother to test it before its use over Japan.

37. See Matthew Bunn, Anthony Wier, and John Holdren, *Controlling Nuclear Warheads and Materials: A Report Card and Action Plan* (Cambridge, Mass., and Washington, D.C.: Project on Managing the Atom, Harvard University, and Nuclear Threat Initiative, 2003), 15–19.

38. Ashton B. Carter, Michael M. May, and William J. Perry, *The Day After: Action in the 24 Hours Following a Nuclear Blast in an American City* (Cambridge, Mass., and Palo Alto, Calif.: Preventive Defense Project, Harvard and Stanford Universities, May 2007).

39. Kofi Annan, "A Global Strategy for Fighting Terrorism," Madrid, March 10, 2005, http://english.safe-democracy.org/keynotes/a-global-strategy-for-fighting-terrorism .html.

40. For a meditation arguing that such an attack would leave the very notion of the sovereignty of nation-states in tatters, see Stephen D. Krasner, "The Day After," *Foreign Policy* 146 (January/February 2005): 68–70.

41. For example, both Khalid Sheikh Muhammad and Abu Zubaydah reportedly believed that uranium, which is only weakly radioactive, would be a good material for a dirty bomb. See U.S. Department of Defense, *Summary of José Padilla's Activities with al-Qaeda* (Washington, D.C.: DOD, 2004), http://news.findlaw.com/ nytimes/docs/padilla/pad52804dodsum5.html.

42. For the most comprehensive available account of this argument, see Levi, *On Nuclear Terrorism*.

43. The book is from Sayyid Imam al-Sharif, sometimes known as "Dr. Fadl," an original member of the al-Qaeda ruling council. See Lawrence Wright, "The Rebellion Within," *New Yorker*, June 2, 2008, 37–53.

44. "The Open Meeting with Shaykh Ayman al-Zawahiri," As-Sahab Media, 1429–2008. As-Sahab is al-Qaeda's media arm.

45. For a detailed discussion of these programs, see Matthew Bunn, *Securing the Bomb* (Cambridge, Mass. and Washington D.C.: Project on Managing the Atom, Belfer Center for Science and International Affiars, Harvard Kennedy School and Nuclear Threat Initiative, 2008).

46. Lugar, "Lugar Survey on Proliferation Threats and Responses."

47. For a detailed agenda to prevent nuclear terrorism, see Matthew Bunn, *Securing the Bomb 2010: Securing All Nuclear Materials in Four Years* (Cambridge, Mass.: Project on Managing the Atom, Harvard University, and Nuclear Threat Initiative 2010), www.nti.org/securingthebomb, 91–112.

48. I wish to thank James Acton, Wyn Bowen, Chris Hobbs, and Stuart Gottlieb for their valuable comments and suggestions.

49. That discussions in the West can have such effects is suggested by a memo on an al-Qaeda computer found in Afghanistan. The memo states that al-Qaeda "only became aware of [chemical and biological weapons] when the enemy drew our attention to them by repeatedly expressing concern that they can be produced simply." See Alan Cullison et al., "A Computer in Kabul Yields a Chilling Array of al-Qaeda Memos," *Wall Street Journal*, December 31, 2001.

50. Key works in this debate include Allison, *Nuclear Terrorism*; Bunn and Wier, "Seven Myths of Nuclear Terrorism"; Bunn and Wier, "Terrorist Nuclear Weapon Construction"; Robin Frost, *Nuclear Terrorism after 9/11* (London: Routledge/ International Institute for Strategic Studies, 2006); Brian Michael Jenkins, *Will Terrorists Go Nuclear?* (New York: Prometheus Books, 2008); William Langewiesche, *The Atomic Bazaar: The Rise of the Nuclear Poor* (New York: Farrar, Straus and Giroux, 2007); Levi, *On Nuclear Terrorism*; John Mueller, "The Atomic Terrorist: Assessing the Likelihood" (paper prepared for presentation at the Program on International Security Policy, University of Chicago, January 15, 2008), http://polisci. osu.edu/faculty/jmueller/APSACHGO.PDF; John Mueller, *Atomic Obsession: Nuclear Alarmism from Hiroshima to Al-Qaeda* (Oxford: Oxford University Press, 2009); Christoph Wirz and Emmanuel Egger, "Use of Nuclear and Radiological Weapons by Terrorists?" *International Review of the Red Cross* 87 (September 2005).

51. Lee H. Hamilton, director of the Woodrow Wilson International Center for Scholars in Washington, D.C., is one person who has warned that a nuclear terrorist attack could end civil liberties. See "There's No End to the Threat from Terrorist Weapons," *Indianapolis Star*, January 31, 2005. For other examples of hyperbole about the effects of a terrorist nuclear attack, see Mueller, "Atomic Terrorist."

52. On the physical effects of a nuclear attack, see "Lieberman, Collins Survey Consequences of Terrorist Nuclear Attack," press release, Office of Senator Joseph Lieberman, April 15, 2008, www.hsgac.senate.gov/media/majority-media/lieber man-collins-survey-consequences-of-terrorist-nuclear-attack. See also "Nuclear Attack on D.C. a Hypothetical Disaster," *Washington Times*, April 16, 2008; and

Kevin O'Neill, "The Nuclear Terrorist Threat," Institute for Science and International Security (August 1997), www.isis-online.org/publications/terrorism/threat.pdf.

53. William Arkin is one exception, arguing that after the events of September 11, 2001, terrorists will not be able to acquire the materials necessary to build a nuclear weapon. See William M. Arkin, "The Continuing Misuses of Fear," *Bulletin of Atomic Scientists* (September/October 2006): 43.

54. Examples here include Karl-Heinz Kamp, "Nuclear Terrorism: Hysterical Concern or Real Risk?" *Aussenpolitik: German Foreign Affairs Review* 46, no. 3 (1995): 211–219; Frost, *Nuclear Terrorism after 9/11;* Gavin Cameron, "Nuclear Terrorism Reconsidered," *Current History* 99 (April 2000): 154–157; Langewiesche, *Atomic Bazaar;* and Mueller, "Atomic Terrorist."

55. Graham Allison, "The Failure of Imagination," *Bulletin of Atomic Scientists* (September/October 2006): 36; Matthew Bunn's essay in this chapter.

56. See Graham Allison, "Nuclear Attack a Worst-Case Reality?" *Washington Times,* April 23, 2008; Rob Edwards, "Top Police Officer Warns that Nuclear Attack Is Inevitable," *Sunday Herald* (Scotland), November 25, 2007.

57. Although it is not universally agreed that states will not pass nuclear weapons to terrorists—the George W. Bush administration was a notable exception—even those such as Matthew Bunn who worry about terrorists' use of nuclear weapons argue that states are unlikely to supply them. See his accompanying essay in this chapter.

58. On the hurdles in using a stolen weapon, see Mueller, "Atomic Terrorist"; Wirz and Egger, "Use of Nuclear and Radiological Weapons by Terrorists?" 502; Robin Frost, "Nuclear Terrorism Post 9/11: Assessing the Risks," October 2003, www.cda-cdai .ca/cdai/uploads/cdai/2009/04/frost03.pdf.

59. This does not mean that there has been no interest in these sorts of attacks. For example, the *Washington Post* reported that in 2003 Canada arrested nineteen people who allegedly planned to destroy a nuclear power plant. Cited in Charles D. Ferguson and William C. Potter, *The Four Faces of Nuclear Terrorism* (New York: Routledge, 2005), 2.

60. For background on nuclear weapons and materials, see the overview provided by the International Panel on Fissile Materials and Nuclear Weapons, www.fissilema terials.org/ipfm/pages_us_en/fissile/fissile/fissile.php; Gary T. Gardner, *Nuclear Nonproliferation: A Primer* (Boulder, Colo.: Lynne Rienner, 1994); Office of Technology Assessment, *Technologies Underlying Weapons of Mass Destruction,* OTA-BP-ISC-115 (Washington, D.C.: U.S. Government Printing Office, December 1993), www.fas.org/ ota/reports/9344.pdf; Peter D. Zimmerman, "Technical Barriers to Nuclear Proliferation," *Security Studies* 2 (Spring/Summer 1993): 345–355; and Randall Forsberg et al., *Nonproliferation Primer* (Cambridge, Mass.: MIT Press, 1996).

61. See Thomas B. Cochran and Christopher E. Paine, "The Amount of Plutonium and Highly-Enriched Uranium Needed for Pure Fission Weapons" (Washington, D.C.: Natural Resources Defense Council, April 13, 1995), 5, www.nrdc.org/nuclear/fis sionw/fissionweapons.pdf.

62. IAEA Safeguards Glossary, 2001 edition, International Nuclear Verification Series no. 3, 23, www-pub.iaea.org/MTCD/publications/PDF/nvs-3-cd/PDF/NVS3_scr .pdf. But also see Cochran and Paine who argue an implosion device would need much less than this.

63. FAS, "Nuclear Weapon Design," www.fas.org/nuke/intro/nuke/design.htm; UCS, "Weapons Material Basics," www.ucsusa.org/nuclear_weapons_and_global_secu rity/nuclear_terrorism/technical_issues/fissile-materials-basics.html. See also Owen R. Cote Jr., "Appendix B: A Primer on Fissile Material and Nuclear Weapon Design," in *Avoiding Nuclear Anarchy: Containing the Threat of Loose Russian Nuclear Weapons and Fissile Material*, ed. Graham T. Allison, Owen Cote Jr., Richard A. Falkenrath, and Steven E. Miller (Cambridge, Mass.: MIT Press, 1996), 203–228. As a point of comparison, Little Man, the gun-type device dropped on Hiroshima, used 60 kilograms of HEU enriched to 80 percent.

64. A state would have as little reason to supply a terrorist group with fissile material as it would to supply it with a nuclear weapon.

65. See Siegfried S. Hecker, "Toward a Comprehensive Safeguards System: Keeping Fissile Materials Out of Terrorists' Hands," *Annals of the American Academy* 607 (September 2006): 121–132; and David Albright and Mark Gorwicz, "Tracking Civil Plutonium Inventories: End of 1999," *ISIS Plutonium Watch* (October 2000).

66. The attack on Pelindaba, described by Matthew Bunn in this chapter, is a vivid example of vulnerable security arrangements. See also the National Intelligence Council's "Annual Report to Congress on the Safety and Security of Russian Nuclear Facilities and Military Forces," December 2004, www.dtic.mil/cgi-bin/Get TRDoc?AD=ADA511744.

67. See William C. Potter and Elena Sokova, "Illicit Nuclear Trafficking in the NIS: What's New? What's True?" *Nonproliferation Review* (Summer 2002): 112–120. See also the website of the IAEA Illicit Trafficking Database, www-ns.iaea.org/security/ itdb.htm, and of the Nuclear Threat Initiative's Newly Independent States (NIS) Nuclear Trafficking Abstracts Database, www.nti.org/db/nistraff/index.html.

68. Reported in Pluta and Zimmerman, "Nuclear Terrorism," 58. They describe this amount as "nearly enough for a nuclear bomb," but that is true only if the bomb in question is a far more complex implosion device.

69. See Elena Sokova, William C. Potter, and Cristina Chuen, "Recent Weapons Grade Uranium Smuggling Case: Nuclear Materials Are Still on the Loose," CNS Research Story, January 26, 2007, http://cns.miis.edu/stories/070126.htm; and IAEA Staff Report, "Georgian Authorities Report Seized Illicit Nuclear Material," www.iaea .org/newscenter/news/2007/georgia_material.html.

70. Examples here include the voluntary commitments made by states at the 2010 and 2012 Nuclear Security Summits; the Convention on the Physical Protection of Nuclear Material and its 2005 amendment, UN Security Council Resolution 1540 (2004); the International Convention for the Suppression of Acts of Nuclear Terrorism (2005); the Nuclear Threat Initiative's Nuclear Materials Security Index; the Global Initiative to Combat Nuclear Terrorism; the G-8 Global Partnership Against the Spread of Weapons and Materials of Mass Destruction; and Cooperative Threat Reduction. Indeed, programs to promote nuclear security have become so numerous that there are calls for a global, framework convention that would not only unite these efforts but also make action on nuclear security more transparent and verifiable. But this is not without controversy, as there is little agreement inter- nationally on the relative importance of the nuclear terrorism issue, especially rela- tive to other nuclear issues—proliferation, existing stockpiles of weapons, and, in the wake of Fukushima, nuclear safety. For arguments and information see, for

example, Kenneth C. Brill and Kenneth N. Luongo, "A Security System Commen-
surate with the Risk of Nuclear Terrorism," *Bulletin of Atomic Scientists*, April 16,
2012; Mark Fitzpatrick and Jasper Pandza, "Maintaining High-Level Focus on
Nuclear Security," Working Paper, US-Korea Institute at SAIS 2012, www.fmwg
.org/USKI_NSS2012_FitzPandza[1].pdf; Wyn Q. Bowen, Matthew Cottee, and
Christopher Hobbs, "Multilateral Cooperation and the Prevention of Nuclear
Terrorism: Pragmatism over Idealism," *International Affairs* 88, no. 2 (2012):
349–368; IAEA, *Combating Illicit Trafficking in Nuclear and Other Radioactive
Material*, IAEA Nuclear Security Series No. 6. (Vienna: IAEA, 2008), www-pub
.iaea.org/books/IAEABooks/7806/Combating-Illicit-Trafficking-in-Nuclear-and-
Other-Radioactive-Material; Gloria Duffy, "Cooperative Threat Reduction in
Perspective," in *Dismantling the Cold War: US and NIS Perspectives on the
Nunn-Lugar Cooperative Threat Reduction Program*, ed. John M. Shields and
William Potter (Cambridge, Mass.: MIT Press, 1997), 23–29; and Rose E.
Gottemoeller, "Cooperative Threat Reduction beyond Russia," *Washington
Quarterly* 28 (Spring 2005): 145–158.
71. This section draws on John Mueller's "The Atomic Terrorist," which provides a very
useful breakdown of all the obstacles that would have to be overcome for a terrorist
group to build a nuclear weapon.
72. The U.S. "Rewards for Justice" program is one example of the rewards offered for
information on terrorist activities. See www.rewardsforjustice.net for further information on this program.
73. The point is not that this sort of processing is necessarily beyond the capabilities of
a terrorist group, but that the need for this additional step requires additional skills
and knowledge and so is just one more hurdle for the group to overcome.
74. *Efficiency* refers to the efficiency with which a bomb uses the fissile material in the
resulting explosion; *reliability* refers to whether the bomb would produce the
expected force when exploded.
75. See Office of Technology Assessment, *Nuclear Proliferation and Safeguards*, 17,
140–141; Pluta and Zimmerman, "Nuclear Terrorism."
76. Zimmerman and Lewis, "Bomb in the Backyard." Note that Pluta and Zimmerman
estimate that a terrorist group could build a gun-type IND in as little as sixty days.
Pluta and Zimmerman, "Nuclear Terrorism," 64.
77. See Matthew Bunn, "The Risk of Nuclear Terrorism—and Next Steps to Reduce the
Danger," testimony to the Senate Committee on Homeland Security and
Governmental Affairs, 110th Cong., 2nd sess., April 2, 2008.
78. Office of Technology Assessment, *Nuclear Proliferation and Safeguards*, 142. See
also Mueller's discussion in "The Atomic Terrorist," where he quotes Steven M.
Younger on the difficulty of designing and constructing a nuclear device. Younger
is former head of the Defense Threat Reduction Agency and former senior fellow
at Los Alamos National Laboratory, where he was in charge of nuclear weapons
research and development. Younger's arguments can also be found in his book
Endangered Species: How We Can Avoid Mass Destruction and Build a Lasting Peace
(New York: Ecco, 2007).
79. On Aum Shinrikyo's attempt to obtain nuclear weapons, see Sara Daly, John
Parachini, and William Rosenau, *Combating Nuclear Terrorism: Lessons from Aum
Shinrikyo, Al Qaeda and the Kinshasa Reactor* (Santa Monica, Calif.: RAND, 2005).

For a more general discussion of Aum, see David E. Kaplan, "Aum Shinrikyo (1995)," in *Toxic Terror: Assessing Terrorist Use of Chemical and Biological Weapons,* ed. Jonathan B. Tucker (Cambridge, Mass.: MIT Press, 2001), 207–226.

80. On the tactical nature of Aum's attack, see Jonathan B. Tucker, "Chemical and Biological Terrorism: How Real a Threat?" *Current History* 99 (April 2000): 150.

81. For an overview of al-Qaeda's nuclear attempts, see Jack Boureston, "Assessing Al Qaeda's WMD Capabilities," *Strategic Insight* (Center for Contemporary Conflict), September 2, 2002; and Daly et al., *Combating Nuclear Terrorism.*

82. "Interview with *Time Magazine,* December 23, 1998: 'Wrath of God: Osama bin Laden Lashes Out against the West,'" *Time Magazine,* January 11, 1999, www.time .com/time/world/article/0,8599,2054517,00.html. See also Hamid Mir, "Osama Claims He Has Nukes: If US Uses N-arms It Will Get Same Response," *Dawn Internet Edition* (Karachi, Pakistan), November 10, 2001. In this interview, bin Laden states explicitly that al-Qaeda has chemical and nuclear weapons "as a deterrent."

83. For example, see the quote from bin Laden that appeared in the October– November 1996 issue of *Nida'ul Islam* magazine, as reported in "Calls to Action," *Washington Post,* August 23, 1998. See also the transcript of a May 1998 bin Laden interview with John Miller, www.pbs.org/wgbh/pages/frontline/shows/binladen/ who/interview.html.

84. Osama bin Laden was careful to portray al-Qaeda's attacks as a response to previous attacks by the West on Muslims—as part of a defensive jihad. See John Stone, "Al-Qaeda, Deterrence and Weapons of Mass Destruction," *Studies in Conflict and Terrorism* 32 (September 2009): 1–13, for a discussion of bin Laden's attempt to justify his actions to the global Muslim community and the way in which this may have limited the types of attacks that al-Qaeda undertook.

85. See Steve Coll, "What Bin Laden Sees in Hiroshima," *Washington Post,* February 6, 2005.

86. Even al-Qaeda's conventional violent tactics have been the subject of debate and condemnation. See, for example, Rich Gardella, "Insurgent Groups Condemn al-Qaeda Tactics," *NBC Nightly News,* October 16, 2007, www.msnbc.msn.com/ id/21267335.

87. John V. Parachini, "Comparing Motives and Outcomes of Mass Casualty Terrorism Involving Conventional and Unconventional Weapons," *Studies in Conflict and Terrorism* 24 (2001): 389–406.

88. That there is still much to be done to enhance nuclear security is clearly seen from the July 2012 successful break-in at a Tennessee nuclear weapons facility by three peace activists. See Douglas P. Guarino, "Democrats: Y-12 Break-in Highlights Dangers of Nuclear Agency Reform Bill," *Global Security Newswire,* August 8, 2012, www.nti.org/gsn/article/democrats-y-12-break-highlights-dangers-nnsa-reform-bill.

89. One important example here is the ongoing effort to replace research reactors that use HEU with research reactors that use less dangerous fissile material. See Nuclear Threat Initiative, "Past and Current Civilian HEU Reduction Efforts," www.nti.org/ db/heu/pastpresent.html.

90. Director of National Intelligence, Declassified Key Judgments of the National Intelligence Estimate "Trends in Global Terrorism: Implications for the United States," April 2006.

91. See Arkin, "Continuing Misuses of Fear," for a discussion of these and other dangers of an overzealous focus on the terrorist nuclear threat.

counterterrorism strategies: do we need bombs over bridges?

NO: There is a need to focus more on building bridges.
Brigitte L. Nacos, *Columbia University*

YES: More creative military strategies are needed.
Michael Rubin, *American Enterprise Institute and Naval Postgraduate School*

Upon taking office in January 2009, President Barack Obama engaged in an unprecedented campaign of outreach to Muslims around the world. The new president chose the Arabic satellite television station al-Arabiya for his first formal televised interview, where he called for a "new partnership" between America and the Muslim world "based on mutual respect and mutual interest." This interview was followed by speeches in Turkey and Egypt, where he quoted verses from the Qur'an and promised Muslims worldwide that the United States would "listen carefully, bridge misunderstanding, and seek common ground."

During his presidency President Obama also authorized dozens of targeted executions of suspected Islamic terrorists in Afghanistan, Pakistan, Yemen, and elsewhere. The strikes, usually by unmanned drone aircraft using guided missiles, have killed scores of terrorist leaders and lower-level operatives. The diplomatic price, however, has been tremendous: wives, children, and hundreds of innocent bystanders have also been killed or maimed in the strikes, provoking mass outrage and protests across Pakistan and other Muslim countries.[1]

Though these two examples might appear to be contradictory, what they in fact show is that counterterrorism is rarely an either/or proposition. Effectively confronting a robust terrorist movement requires the deployment of a whole range of options and initiatives, some of which may seem in direct opposition.[2]

At its core, the goal of counterterrorism is to weaken the strike capacity of terrorist organizations and to undercut their base of support. Although both hard power (such as military force) and soft power (such as diplomatic endeavors) will play a role in any comprehensive counterterrorism strategy,[3] choices of emphasis will inevitably be made: Is the threat best handled in a more warlike fashion, where the elimination of terrorist leadership, destruction of physical bases of operation, and direct confrontation with state sponsors form the basis of the approach? Or should emphasis be placed on more diplomatic efforts, such as global law enforcement cooperation, aid and outreach to affected communities, and direct negotiations with state sponsors and possibly terrorist organizations themselves?

Both approaches have their benefits, and potential pitfalls. Hard-line tactics can put terrorist leaders on the run and weaken their organizations, but if relied upon too heavily such tactics can inflame and alienate local populations, possibly laying the foundation for another round of fighting. Softer approaches can win legitimacy and the moral upper hand, but savvy terrorist groups will spin such efforts as signs of weakness, creating a potential boon for terrorist recruiters.

And both approaches have their passionate supporters among counterterrorism experts and professionals, each armed with facts and evidence to show that their preferred strategies are more likely to lead to the reduction or elimination of the terrorist threat.

Brigitte Nacos and Michael Rubin recognize the need for balance in counterterrorism policy—effectively confronting modern terrorism will require an ability to build bridges as well as the wherewithal to occasionally blow some up. They strongly disagree, however, on the strengths and weaknesses of hard power versus soft power in counterterrorism, and especially on which approach should guide the effort.

Nacos believes that the use of hard power—for example, missile strikes against terrorist camps or commando raids to free hostages—tends to accomplish only limited objectives; hard power tactics are unlikely to destroy a terrorist organization or dry up its support. She argues that such tactics should be a rarely used adjunct to a broader strategy based on "traditional diplomatic mechanisms and soft power approaches." Specifically, she supports the use of multilateral economic and political sanctions against state sponsors of terrorism and cooperative policing against terrorist groups as the most effective means of destroying those groups and networks. In addition, she promotes aggressive public diplomacy and generous foreign aid as the most promising tools to steal hearts and minds away from terrorist groups.

Rubin does not disagree that hearts and minds can be won through direct political, economic, and humanitarian assistance. But he argues that such efforts are doomed to fail or to backfire unless besieged communities feel secure from terrorist violence—security that can come only from the defeat of the terrorist groups in their midst. Rubin says that reliance on soft power strategies aimed at state sponsors and terrorist groups will only perpetuate terrorist movements. Indeed, he says it will bring back the 1990s mindset in which prosecution and punishment after attacks were the main objective of counterterrorism policy. In this age of catastrophic terrorism, preventing attacks—not responding after the fact— must be the primary goal, and this can be accomplished only when aggressive military and intelligence efforts are leading the way.

The rise of modern mass-casualty terrorism has placed a tremendous existential premium on crafting effective counterterrorism strategies. Although there is no such thing as perfect security against terrorism, reducing the scale and scope of attacks and weakening or eliminating groups require skillful and thoughtful policymaking. Success will depend on a mixture of both hard and soft strategies—strong enough to disrupt and deter terrorist groups and their sponsors and temperate enough to secure global allies and win hearts and minds. As the essays in this chapter make clear, finding the right balance is one of the most critical —and challenging— aspects of any counterterrorism initiative.

NO:
There is a need to focus more on building bridges.
Brigitte L. Nacos, *Columbia University*

Soft Power Trumps Hard Power in Counterterrorism

October 7, 2001

Less than a month after the September 2001 terrorist attacks on the United States, American and British forces launch military operations against targets in Afghanistan. The declared goal of the invasion is the removal of the Taliban regime that allowed Osama bin Laden and his organization to establish headquarters and training camps inside Afghanistan and, of course, the destruction of al-Qaeda. Though the initial military operations ended the Taliban's rule, tore down al-Qaeda's camps in Afghanistan, and forced al-Qaeda to flee into Pakistan, the Taliban as well as al-Qaeda's central organization regrouped in the tribal regions along the Afghanistan-Pakistan border.[4]

March 1, 2008

A predawn air strike by the Colombian military against a jungle camp of the Revolutionary Armed Forces of Colombia (FARC) just inside neighboring Ecuador kills Raul Reyes, one of the most influential leaders and the most prominent spokesperson of FARC. Sixteen other members, among them Reyes's female partner, are also killed in the air raids. The well-planned and well-executed military move strikes the core of one of the most durable and most dangerous terrorist organizations.

July 28, 2008

A U.S. drone missile strike against an al-Qaeda compound in Pakistan's South Waziristan region kills Abu Khabab al-Masri, a top commander of the terrorist organization. Three other members of al-Qaeda Central die along with al-Masri, the mastermind of the terrorist attack on the USS *Cole* eight years earlier. The strike "neutralizes" a terrorist with a $5 million bounty on his head from the United States.

May 1, 2011

U.S. Special Operations forces led by the Navy's SEAL Team Six raid Osama bin Laden's secret compound in Abbottabad, Pakistan, killing bin Laden and securing a treasure trove of al-Qaeda documents and other intelligence.

September 30, 2011

A U.S. drone strike in southeastern Yemen kills Anwar al-Awlaki, a U.S.-born radical preacher and a leader of al-Qaeda in the Arabian Peninsula (AQAP). The strike illustrates the broad expansion of U.S. drone attacks from the tribal regions of Pakistan and Afghanistan to other parts of the world.

W hether responding to domestic and transnational terrorism carried out by nonstate actors or dealing with states that sponsor terrorists, governments should not exclude military options altogether. Just as military force and the mere threat of force are factors in international politics, hard power has a place in counterterrorism.[5] The opening summaries of actions against FARC and al-Qaeda operatives and the Taliban regime are cases in point. And yet successful attacks against terrorist camps, missiles fired from unmanned drones, commando raids to free hostages, and even invasions tend to meet only limited objectives (the destruction of training camps, the decimation or displacement of a group's or regime's leadership, the freeing of hostages). They are far less likely to destroy terrorist organizations or dry up community or state support for terrorism.

The distinct differences between terrorist organizations and state sponsors of terrorism require different counterterrorism approaches. In this essay, I will therefore discuss first counterterrorism options vis-à-vis state supporters of terrorist violence and thereafter responses to the terrorist groups themselves. It is my argument that both are more effectively dealt with using the traditional diplomatic mechanisms and "soft power" approaches rather than the more aggressive, military-dominant measures.

DEALING WITH STATE SPONSORS OF TERRORISM

Both the George W. Bush and Barack Obama administrations, in their respective 2008 and 2012 national defense strategies, made it clear that as a last resort the U.S. military must be prepared to use force against state sponsors of terrorism, rogue states, and any other state-based threats to U.S. national security.[6] To be sure, retaliatory or preventive military actions with and without formal declarations of war are options in the most serious of conflicts between two or more states. When it comes to state sponsors of terrorism, the problem is that neither all-out war nor limited attacks guarantee a reduction in terrorist activities; indeed, they can have the opposite effects. The Iraq War, sold by the Bush administration as a preemptive move against a state sponsor of terrorism that was accused of being in bed with al-Qaeda, is an instructive case. No doubt,

Saddam Hussein and his government supported terrorists and their violence. For many years, the Baghdad regime provided safe harbor for Abu Abbas, Abu Nidal, and other leaders of secular Palestinian terrorist groups; it also promised and paid out substantial sums of money to the families of Palestinians that committed deadly suicide attacks against Israelis. Furthermore, Iraq hosted and supported the Mujahidin-e-Khalq, a large group that opposed the Islamic Republic of Iran and carried out terrorist attacks on Iranian targets.

However, even though it was supporting anti-Israeli and anti-Iranian terrorism and harboring some prominent Palestinian terrorists, Iraq was not a breeding ground of terrorists and did not allow foreign extremists from all over the Arab world to enter the country and unleash lethal violence against civilians. In stark contrast, during the years after the fall of Saddam Hussein, Iraqi and foreign militants carried out waves of terrorist attacks—not only against members of the occupation forces but most of all against the civilian population in many parts of the country. If Iraq was indeed the most important front in the so-called global war on terrorism, as the Bush administration claimed, it stemmed directly from the resentment and anger in the Arab and Muslim world triggered and nourished by the military invasion and occupation of Iraq. In 2007, for example, more than 6,000 (43 percent) of the more than 14,000 terrorist incidents worldwide occurred in Iraq, and more than 13,000 (60 percent) of the more than 22,000 persons killed by terrorists around the globe died in terrorist attacks in that country.[7]

While the U.S. troop surge and so-called Anbar Awakenings in 2007 and 2008 helped reduce violence by more than 90 percent, since the withdrawal of all U.S. troops in early 2012 Iraq has witnessed a dramatic upsurge in al-Qaeda–related violence.[8] One of the goals of the Iraq War was to show that hard power can thwart terrorism; it ended up showing nearly exactly the opposite.

Prior to the Iraq War, U.S. military actions against nation-states in the name of counterterrorism were typically immediate responses to specific terrorist incidents—such as the U.S. strikes against al-Qaeda camps in Afghanistan following the 1998 embassy bombings in Africa—not in the name of prevention or preemption. Indeed Washington has traditionally utilized both hard and soft power against states, with the latter more effective than the former, as seen in the case of Libya.

Disengaging and Reengaging State Sponsors of Terrorism: The Case of Libya

In the summer of 2008, twenty-eight years after the United States and Libya broke off diplomatic relations and five years after some diplomatic ties were reestablished, the two countries were ready to restore full diplomatic relations. Actually, Libya was removed from the U.S. State Department's list of state sponsors of terrorism in 2003, when its leader, Muammar al-Qaddafi, agreed to give up his weapons of mass destruction (WMD) program and any involvement in international terrorism and promised to compensate the families of victims who perished in Libya-sponsored terrorist incidents. By settling outstanding lawsuits on behalf of American families against the Libyan government and by Libyan civilians killed during U.S. air raids on Tripoli and Benghazi in 1986, the U.S. and Libyan governments removed the final obstacle on the way to full diplomatic relations. Indeed it was this improved relationship that led the United States and some European states to initially doubt the wisdom of supporting the anti-Qaddafi uprisings in Libya in early 2011.

During the 1980s and beyond, the U.S. government considered Libya one of the most flagrant sponsors of international terrorism. After intercepted phone calls implicated Libyan agents in the 1986 bombing of the La Belle Disco in Berlin, a favorite of American GIs stationed in the then-divided city, President Ronald Reagan ordered the retaliatory bombing of two Libyan cities. Forty-one Libyans, including Qaddafi's adopted daughter, were killed, but the attacks did not persuade Qaddafi to end Libya's involvement in terrorism. Instead, Libya continued to support terrorists and was behind one of the most lethal acts of terrorism in history: the downing of Pan Am Flight 103 over Lockerbie, Scotland, just days before Christmas 1988. All 259 persons on board and 11 more on the ground died.

What eventually convinced Qaddafi to abandon his support for terrorism and his ambition to develop WMDs were not actual and threatened military measures but concerted American, European, and United Nations sanctions that isolated Libya economically and politically. In one expert's judgment, "Libya represents probably the best case of sanctions helping to shape a state sponsor's behavior on terrorism-related matters."[9]

The families of the Pan Am Flight 103 victims also played an important role in Libya's metamorphosis from a sponsor of terrorism to a state willing to shed its pariah status. By relentlessly lobbying the U.S. government and the United Nations to pressure Qaddafi into admitting his government's role in the Pan Am Flight 103 bombing by handing over two incriminated Libyan agents to the Scottish High Court, they kept the limelight on Qaddafi's misdeeds and reinforced the rationale for tough sanctions against Libya.

Disengaging a state sponsor of terrorism from important players in the political and economic community of nations and reengaging the state's leadership in direct diplomacy worked in the case of Libya.

Enticing Other State Sponsors

Joint diplomatic efforts, not military might, brought North Korea, another longtime member of the State Department's list of terrorism sponsors, to the

negotiating table as well during the Bill Clinton and George W. Bush administrations. As a result of the "six-party talks" by the United States, China, Japan,
Russia, and South Korea, Pyongyang took its first small steps toward dismantling its Yongbyon nuclear reactor and promised a long-delayed declaration of
its nuclear program and acceptance of a verification regime. In turn, the United
States pledged to lift economic sanctions, remove North Korea from its list of
terrorist sponsors, and open the door for international aid once the verifiable
denuclearization process was in place. In October 2008, after North Korea was
indeed scratched from the State Department's terror list, Helene Cooper of the
New York Times wrote:

> The decision to remove North Korea from the terror list was a dramatic
> moment for President Bush, who had called the country part of an "axis
> of evil" and had only reluctantly ordered administration officials to
> engage in negotiations, saying that the United States had made deals with
> the nation's leaders before without winning enough concessions. That
> calculus changed in 2006, when North Korea exploded a nuclear device.[10]

Although it was far from clear whether North Korea would ever agree to give
international inspectors full access to its nuclear facilities and eventually abandon its nuclear weapons, a difficult and protracted negotiation process had
brought about some positive results. As Secretary of State Condoleezza Rice
put it, "The North Koreans took 30 years to get a nuclear weapons program, I
think it might take more than a couple to unravel it."[11]

Indeed, in April 2009, less than three months into the Obama presidency,
North Korea expelled the inspectors of the International Atomic Energy
Agency and announced that it was reactivating all of its nuclear facilities. This
step came in reaction to the UN Security Council's criticism of North Korea's
several missile launches and the adoption of a tougher sanction regime
against Pyongyang. That same month, North Korea arrested two American
journalists, Laura Ling and Euna Lee, for allegedly entering its territory across
its border with China. But after trying and sentencing the women to twelve
years of hard labor, North Korea signaled in August 2009 once again a desire
for diplomacy by freeing the two Americans during former president Bill
Clinton's visit in Pyongyang where he met with Kim Jong-il and his top
nuclear negotiator, Kim Kye-gwan.[12]

But traditional diplomacy is not the whole story in the changing relationship
between Washington and Pyongyang. Just as "ping-pong diplomacy" in the
early 1970s opened the door for President Richard Nixon's China visit in 1973
and the eventual normalization of diplomatic relations between the two countries, cultural diplomacy in the form of the New York Philharmonic's concert

in Pyongyang in early 2008 was a prelude to North Korea's subsequent reengagement in six-party talks.

The death of longtime leader Kim Jong-il in December 2011 led to a great upheaval in relations between North Korea and the United States, as well as with South Korea and China. The anointing of Mr. Kim's youngest son, Kim Jong-un, as successor in early 2012 coincided with a mixture of militaristic antagonism and possible outreach for improved relations. In February 2012, North Korea agreed to suspend nuclear weapons tests and uranium enrichment in return for new shipments of American food aid. By summer Pyongyang had violated this agreement by testing an advanced satellite that could assist in the development of intercontinental ballistic missiles, and resuming its work at the Yongbyon nuclear complex.[13] Nonetheless, the continuing dance of hard-edged diplomacy is much preferred to the alternative, and remains the best chance to achieve mutually beneficial relations.

The stick-and-carrot tactic of traditional diplomacy does not guarantee immediate wholesale behavioral changes on the part of state sponsors of terrorism, but it does offer the best possibility of small victories one at a time. For example, in 1994, under pressure from U.S. and UN sanctions, the Sudanese government allowed French agents to fly Ilich Ramirez Sanchez, better known as Carlos the Jackal, from his hideaway in Khartoum to Paris, hoping that the United States would reward this cooperative act by removing Sudan from its list of terrorism sponsors. Instead, Washington continued to pressure the Sudanese government to deny safe haven to terrorists, among them Osama bin Laden.[14]

At the request of the Sudanese government, bin Laden and his closest aides left Khartoum in 1996 and relocated in Afghanistan. Unlike in the case of Carlos the Jackal, when French agents were invited to take custody of one of the most notorious terrorists of the 1970s and 1980s, Khartoum did not arrange for U.S. agents to arrest bin Laden. Nevertheless, in the following years the Sudanese government was less hospitable to terrorists and actually signaled its willingness to counter transnational terrorism.

In 2001 the UN Security Council lifted terrorism-related sanctions against Sudan. Washington, too, has recognized a sea change in Sudan's policies with the exception of the government's continued support for the Palestinian groups Hamas and Islamic Jihad, which has kept Sudan on the list of state sponsors of terrorism. According to the State Department's "Country Reports on Terrorism" for 2010:

> Sudanese officials have indicated that they view continued cooperation with the United States as important . . . [and] the Government of Sudan worked actively to counter al-Qa'ida operations that posed potential threats to U.S. interests.[15]

And what about Iran? Since the Islamic revolution in 1979, the Iranian government has been the most flagrant sponsor of terrorism in the region. The Tehran government was instrumental in the establishment of the Lebanese Hezbollah and has supported the organization ever since. Hamas has been another beneficiary of Iran's support for terrorists, as have groups in Africa and elsewhere. At a time when several terrorist organizations are trying hard to get their hands on WMDs, the Iranian government's nuclear program has raised alarms in Washington, Jerusalem, and the capitals of several Arab countries. The question was and remains how to discourage the mullahs in Iran from developing nuclear weapons and how to dissuade their support for regional and global terrorist groups.

Since the Nixon presidency, American administrations have insisted that they will not negotiate or make deals with terrorists and state sponsors of terrorism like Iran. But in reality, they have conducted negotiations and struck deals with state sponsors even during ongoing terrorist incidents, typically through third parties. One of the most obvious examples was the deal by the U.S. and Iranian governments—negotiated by Algerian diplomats—to end the Iranian hostage crisis. It secured the release of fifty-two Americans in January 1981 after 444 days of captivity in the U.S. embassy in Tehran.

Throughout his presidency, George W. Bush sent contradictory signals on Iran. For example, in a May 2008 speech to the Israeli Knesset, after mentioning Iranian president Mahmoud Ahmadinejad, Bush said:

> Some seem to believe that we should negotiate with the terrorists and radicals, as if some ingenious argument will persuade them they have been wrong all along. We have heard this foolish delusion before. As Nazi tanks crossed into Poland in 1939, an American senator declared: "Lord, if I could only have talked to Hitler, all this might have been avoided." We have an obligation to call this what it is—the false comfort of appeasement, which has been repeatedly discredited by history.[16]

Yet two months after the president categorically nixed suggestions to open a dialogue with Iranian leaders and attacked those who recommended direct talks, the U.S. State Department's third-ranking official, William J. Burns, traveled to Geneva to participate, along with representatives of the European Union, in talks with Iran's nuclear negotiator, Saeed Jalili. Although the Geneva meeting ended without any tangible results, there were reports that the Bush administration and the Iranian government were considering opening interest sections in each other's capitals. Comments in Washington and Tehran on the possibility of informal diplomatic representations were in oubstance and tone a marked respite from President Ahmadinejad's and President Bush's usually combative rhetoric and Vice President Dick Cheney's long practice of saber rattling.

In fact, before Secretary of State Condoleezza Rice met with Libya's Qaddafi in early September 2008 to discuss common interests, State Department officials had expressed the hope that Iran and North Korea would take note of the changed U.S.-Libyan relationship. According to one of her deputies, Rice was eager to demonstrate "that even sworn enemies who have inflicted pain on Americans can reap dividends by conclusively changing their ways."[17]

For decades, Iran has been a model of the limits of economic and political sanctions against state sponsors of terrorism. Indeed, as sanctions against Iran have demonstrated, authoritarian rulers in particular can simply ignore even the harmful effects of measures meant to inflict pain and change behavior. Even the tough new sanctions imposed by the United States and its European allies in the summer of 2012, meant to compel Iran to cease uranium enrichment, have been met with limited results at best.[18] Like Iraq under Saddam Hussein, Iran under the mullahs has not changed its support for terrorists because of sanctions. Nor has it shown a willingness to give up its nuclear ambitions. Thus, short of military conflict that could destabilize the whole region, the advantages of top-level negotiations in such cases are twofold: first, there is always a chance that common ground can be found—not in one single meeting but during ongoing exchanges; second, if talks ultimately fail in spite of serious efforts by the party seeking to engage a state sponsor of terrorism, the failure may well work in favor of the rejected side. As one expert in favor of negotiations with Iran suggested, "If Tehran rebuffs an opportunity to have meaningful talks with Washington, it will increase its own isolation and put itself under greater international pressure, while the United States will improve its own standing."[19] After four years of Obama administration efforts to extend an open hand to Tehran, and being continually rebuffed, this is the very outcome that is developing.

DEALING WITH TERRORIST GROUPS

Dealing with nonstate terrorist entities is far more difficult than responding to state sponsors both for hard and soft power. Unlike states that sponsor or harbor terrorists, terrorist organizations are difficult targets for military action—especially if they are small or geographically dispersed. Even if a sizable guerrilla or terrorist organization controls a chunk of real estate, these fighters are not easily defeated by traditional military force as the examples of FARC in Colombia and the Tamil Tigers in Sri Lanka attest.

In one military expert's view, "most of the tools and expertise developed for fighting military organizations will have limited utility in fighting al-Qaeda and similar groups, until and unless they are fixed in place geographically."[20] If there is reliable intelligence on training camps, hideouts, or other locations frequented by terrorists, surgical air strikes or commando operations can be successful. One proponent of what he calls "offensive action and offensive military capabilities" argues that "even unsuccessful offensive actions, which force terrorist units or terrorist cells to stay perpetually on the move to avoid destruction, will help reduce their capability," and that the "threat of offensive action is critical to exhausting the terrorists, whether they are with units in the field in Afghanistan or hiding out in cities and empty quarters across the world."[21]

But targeting terrorists who fight within larger military units—not exactly typical for terrorist organizations—is very different from using offensive military force against terrorists or insurgents who hide among civilians in cities, towns, or villages. One of many tragic examples of high-risk offensive actions against terrorists or insurgents during the war on terrorism was an August 2008 ground operation by U.S. Special Operations forces backed by air strikes in the Afghan village of Azizabad. When the dust settled, more than ninety civilians—most of them women and children—were dead along with three dozen or so insurgents.[22] The damage to America's reputation in the Afghan village, in all of Afghanistan, and in the international community was once again far greater than the benefit of eliminating a few terrorists or insurgents. Military actions, especially when they involve the death of innocent bystanders, tend to rally supporters and recruit new ones, and, as with the drone strike that killed the al-Qaeda leader al-Masri, are often followed by a surge in violence by the Taliban and other al-Qaeda allies.

President Obama not only continued the Bush administration's drone strike and targeted killings policy; he dramatically expanded the practice to the point where it came to define his counterterrorism policy.[23] While the hundreds of covert strikes have decimated the leadership of al-Qaeda in Afghanistan, Pakistan, and elsewhere, the human costs, and costs to America's "soft power," have been unacceptably high. As noted by the Pulitzer Prize–winning journalist David Rohde, "Missile strikes that kill members of al Qaeda and its affiliates in Pakistan and Yemen do not strengthen economies, curb corruption, or improve government services."[24]

Recognizing the inherent negative utility of this "shoot first" approach, one leading counterterrorism expert promotes a softer terrorism-as-crime understanding rather than the aggressive terrorism-as-war paradigm:

> Terrorism is a phenomenon that is global in its range, constant in its presence, and inevitably involves the commission of crime. Any national or

international mechanism to counter it must be predicated on that understanding. Liberal democracies have well-developed legislation, systems,
and structures to deal with crime; consequently, the criminal justice system should be at the heart of their counterterrorism efforts.[25]

Over time, conventional criminal justice work or policing has been far more
successful in weakening and destroying terrorist groups than offensive military
actions. Italy's Red Brigade, Germany's Red Army Faction, the United States'
Weather Underground, and similar groups in the West ended because their
leaders and many rank-and-file members were arrested, tried, and imprisoned.

A recent study of all terrorist groups active worldwide from 1968 through
2006 found that 7 percent ceased to exist because of military force, 40 percent
because of policing, and 10 percent because they realized their typically very
limited objectives. According to the same research, 43 percent of these organizations terminated their violence because of political solutions or settlements.[26]
In other words, traditional criminal justice approaches and efforts to bring
terrorist groups into the political process were far more successful in ending
terrorism than military actions.

Engaging Group Leaders in Negotiations

In the past, negotiations with terrorist groups were most likely during hostage
situations, when governments were under pressure to free their citizens and
save their lives. Most governments, however, are reluctant to admit they ever
negotiate with terrorists. In the negotiated release of the Iranian hostages, for
example, both the Carter administration and the Iranian authorities pretended
that an autonomous group of students took over the U.S. embassy in Tehran
and held Americans captive rather than a group with direct links to the new
radical regime in power. Later, the arms-for-hostages deal pursued by the Reagan
White House was justified as a transaction with Iranian officials who had contacts and influence with but not control over the Hezbollah hostage-holders in
Lebanon. Many governments and many corporations have struck deals with
terrorists to free hostages without admitting such bargains. The practice continues to this day.

I am not in favor of negotiating with terrorists who hold hostages and offering them something tangible in return for the release of their captives: history
has shown that such bargains encourage further hostage taking by the same
groups or by other organizations. But negotiating the abandonment of terrorism and bringing groups into the domestic or international political process
are another story. Northern Ireland is an excellent example. After decades of
bloody violence and a long, protracted peace process, Northern Ireland finally

turned the corner in early 2007 when Sinn Féin, the political wing of the Irish Republican Army (IRA), and the Democratic Union Party, representing the Protestant majority, formed a government in which Ian Paisley, the longtime Protestant opponent of any meaningful political role for the Catholic minority, became the first minister and Martin McGuinness, a former IRA commander, the deputy first minister. In June 2012 the world witnessed what was once deemed impossible: a smiling handshake between Mr. McGuinness and Queen Elizabeth II of Great Britain.[27]

As the case of Northern Ireland demonstrates, negotiated peace agreements rarely hold after the first try; instead, it is far more likely that the road to peace is paved with broken accords and renewed outbreaks of violence. Cease-fire agreements between the Sri Lankan government and the Tamil Tigers, between Spain's government and the Basque Fatherland and Liberty (ETA), and between the Israeli government and Hamas have been repeatedly negotiated and broken. Yet in view of the poor track record of military actions in ending terrorism, the criminal justice approach and the negotiation route are the most promising options.

However, the goals and the ideologies of terrorist organizations determine whether there are opportunities for common ground and compromises. Separatist groups may be inclined to settle for a significant degree of political, economic, and social autonomy short of full independence if only because such a compromise satisfies their supporters. By contrast, organizations with uncompromising objectives will not compromise on their ultimate goals. Although it was possible in the 1970s and 1980s to negotiate with Marxist militants such as the Baader-Meinhof terrorists in Germany about the release of hostages in return for freeing some of their imprisoned comrades, it would have made little sense to talk about the group's final solution: the destruction of capitalism and democracy in Germany and elsewhere in the West.

Religious terrorists, too, tend to have absolute demands and goals that defy compromise—they also have far greater longevity than nonreligious groups. Although 62 percent of all terrorist organizations ended between 1968 and 2006, only 32 percent of religious groups ceased to exist, and not one of them realized its objectives.[28] A comparison between Yasser Arafat's secular Palestinian Fatah, a terrorist organization before—at least officially—abandoning terrorism, and the religious Palestinian Hamas is instructive. Even though Fatah has been open to a compromise two-state solution with Israel, Hamas has stuck to its ultimate objective—the violent removal of Israel from the map of the Middle East.

What, then, are the prospects for persuading groups such as al-Qaeda to forsake terrorism through negotiations? On this issue, I side with those who reject talks with the leadership of al-Qaeda because of the organization's non-negotiable goals. As one observer wrote:

> There is no sign that al Qaeda has changed its thinking on the utility of violence. And it is hard to conceive of a viable process of primary negotiations in which al Qaeda could be included. Al Qaeda has global aspirations and no firm territorial base, and there is no clearly defined territory in which its aims could be satisfied through constitutional means. Under these conditions, opening negotiations would be a counterproductive move: it would provide al Qaeda with political legitimacy.[29]

But opposing viewpoints deserve consideration as well. Noting that her take on this is unpopular, Louise Richardson favors negotiations with al-Qaeda for the following reasons:

> By overcoming our reluctance to talk, we could discover a great deal about our adversaries, the importance they assign to particular goals, about how they make decisions, and about their assessment of their own position. Such talks do not have to be public, nor do they have to be direct. They could be conducted through intermediaries, but it is very difficult to know your enemies if you don't try to engage them.[30]

It should be noted that this advice has been heeded by U.S. officials in Afghanistan: part of America's exit strategy entails negotiations with "moderate" elements of the Taliban, for the purposes of isolating the more radical factions and forging new relationships for the future.[31]

An even more promising course of action, one that Richardson recommends as well, would concentrate on weakening support and sympathies among those Arabs and Muslims in whose name al-Qaeda, its affiliates, and like-minded groups claim to act. Terrorists need community support to sustain their activities. When that support fades, terrorists' support lines and recruitment reservoirs dry up. The most effective way to engage in this endeavor would be to focus attention and resources on effective public diplomacy.

PUBLIC DIPLOMACY AND COUNTERTERRORISM

Even though the Bush administration relied heavily on military force in its war on terrorism, the Bush Pentagon's 2008 *National Defense Strategy* recognized the limits of hard power in response to terrorism:

> The use of military force plays a role, yet military efforts to capture or kill terrorists are likely to be subordinate to measures to promote local

participation in government and economic programs to spur development, as well as efforts to understand and address grievances that often
lie at the heart of insurgencies.[32]

Although it is far from clear that democratic participation and economic
development prevent or decrease terrorism, public diplomacy may well be the
best hope to diminish terrorists' natural reservoirs of recruits, supporters, and
sympathizers. The three pillars of American public diplomacy during the Cold
War era—the spread of information via foreign language broadcasts into the
communist world, cultural exchanges, and educational exchanges—should be
adapted to the global realities of the twenty-first century.[33] In the age of information, when a multitude of global television and radio networks and the
wireless Internet provide instant news, information, and communication,
the successful broadcast strategies of the past will no longer work. There are
more vehicles for and opportunities to reach and engage larger audiences overseas than ever before—but only by means of innovated programs conceived,
produced, and presented by professionals who speak the languages and know
the cultures of the target audiences and, of course, the public relations goals of
the United States.

To date, American public diplomacy efforts via television, radio, and Internet have not been success stories. For example, although well financed, the U.S.
government's Arab-language television network, al-Hurra, and radio station,
al-Sawa, have neither displayed the excellence of their Cold War predecessors,
such as Voice of America or Radio Free Europe, nor found promising new
approaches for a completely different media and communication environment.
Established by George W. Bush to cultivate a positive image of the United
States in the Arab world, al-Hurra and al-Sawa were overseen by bosses who
either did not speak Arabic or had no experience in broadcasting. As a result,
they made incredible blunders, such as airing "anti-American and anti-Israeli
viewpoints" and showcasing pro-Iranian policies and giving "air time to a
militant who called for the death of American soldiers in Iraq."[34]

An investigation by the media watchdog *ProPublica* and CBS News's
60 Minutes found that the two outlets had "an untrained, largely foreign staff
with little knowledge of the country whose values and policies they were hired
to promote. There appeared to be little oversight of the daily operations."[35]
Certainly not a recipe for effective public diplomacy.

As for the Internet, Robert Gates, U.S. Secretary of Defense under both
George W. Bush and Barack Obama, was right on target when he said:

> Public relations was invented in the United States, yet we are miser-
> able at communicating to the rest of the world what we are about as

a society and a culture, about freedom and democracy, about our policies and our goals. It is just plain embarrassing that al-Qaeda is better at communicating its message on the Internet than America. As one foreign diplomat asked a couple of years ago, "How has one man in a cave managed to out-communicate the world's greatest communication society?" Speed, agility, and cultural relevance are not terms that come readily to mind when discussing U.S. strategic communications.[36]

A modernized public diplomacy model must focus on the Internet's ample opportunities for virtual cultural and educational exchanges, but it should not do so at the expense of direct physical, cultural, and educational exchanges. Most important, the United States has a big opportunity to influence the attitudes of foreign publics if Washington decision makers, not just in the Department of State, are committed to developing new approaches to public diplomacy and making them part of their policy deliberations.

And while President Obama placed better outreach to the Muslim world at the top of his list of foreign policy priorities, there has been surprisingly little progress on these fronts—certainly nowhere near the effort his administration placed on hard power operations like drone strikes.[37] This is most unfortunate when considering that in the Arab and Muslim world, public opinion polls in Pakistan, Saudi Arabia, Indonesia, and several other countries reveal that the strong support for al-Qaeda has a soft underbelly and could be softened more so with the right public diplomacy approaches. Kenneth Ballen, president of the organization Terror Free Tomorrow, which has conducted extensive surveys in Muslim countries, found significant resentment toward the United States and yet the potential for a dramatic turnaround in favor of America without drastic policy adjustments.[38]

Take the example of Pakistan, where 80 percent of respondents in a June 2008 survey said that al-Qaeda's top goal was "standing up to America," and 57 percent agreed with that objective. The same survey revealed that only one-third of Pakistanis had a favorable opinion of bin Laden and al-Qaeda. When asked what would improve their opinion of the United States, the vast majority pointed to educational scholarships and visas to the United States, free trade between the two countries, and American disaster relief, medical aid, and resources to build schools and train teachers. The most surprising result was that a larger percentage of al-Qaeda supporters than of nonsupporters reacted positively to U.S. measures deemed likely to improve Pakistanis' attitudes toward America and Americans.

Or take Indonesia, where public opinion became much more favorable toward the United States and much less positive toward al-Qaeda after the

American-led relief efforts in the wake of the deadly tsunami of 2005. With these and similar results in other Muslim countries in mind, Ballen wrote:

> What our surveys uncovered is that the U.S. would witness dramatic improvements in the view of the United States among the overwhelming majority of Muslims, including those who express support for al Qaeda and Bin Laden, if we demonstrate respect and caring for people in their daily lives through practical, relatively achievable steps such as increasing direct humanitarian assistance (medical, education, food), visas and better trade terms.[39]

CONCLUSION

Although military actions against state sponsors and terrorist groups are appropriate in certain circumstances, they tend to be stopgap measures. As the Iraq War demonstrated, massive military force can result in a recruiting bonanza for terrorists. And as ground and air operations against al-Qaeda and Taliban figures in Pakistan's tribal region have shown, such strikes can trigger further waves of terrorist attacks and increased popular support for terrorist movements.

In the long run, widely supported economic and political sanctions against state sponsors and policing against terrorist groups are the most hopeful approaches to ending state sponsorship of terrorism and destroying terrorist groups and networks. In addition, soft power in the form of new public diplomacy initiatives as well as generous disaster relief and targeted foreign aid are the most promising tools for depriving terrorists of their lifeblood: the popular support and breeding grounds among those in whose interest they claim to act.

More creative military strategies are needed.
YES: Michael Rubin, *American Enterprise Institute and Naval Postgraduate School*

Military Tactics Are Essential for Fighting Terrorism

Anti-Americanism peaked under President George W. Bush. The administration's global war on terrorism, its supposed unilateralism, and its reflexive reliance on military means all fueled hatred of the United States.

Though President Barack Obama entered the White House promising a new beginning and reaffirming the traditional idea that diplomacy and criminal prosecutions of terrorists could best counter terrorism, he shifted in office not only to embrace Bush's tactics, but also to pursue the war on terrorism with renewed vigor. Simply put, Obama learned in office that lofty diplomatic ideals are best left to relations among Western capitals, but when it comes to terrorists, military tools are the most effective.

The fact is soft power and police investigations are not effective counter-terrorism strategies absent intelligence and force. Obama's initial belief that "our courts and juries . . . are tough enough to convict terrorists" was naïve.[40] Convictions require evidence available only after attacks; they are meaningless to prevention, the essence of effective counterterrorism. In short, Obama, like many U.S. policymakers in the wake of the 9/11 attacks, concluded we should eschew theory and recognize the reality: military tactics are the best means to counter terrorist threats.

THE NATURE OF TERRORISM CUES STRATEGIES FOR RESPONSE

Terrorism is a tactic; it is not simply an asymmetric strategy or an approach used by the "weak" against the "strong." State sponsors use terrorism to amplify force.[41] For example, Soviet sponsorship of the Baader-Meinhof Gang in West Germany or the National Liberation Army of Bolivia was not a replacement for its military buildup. Algerian support for the Polisario Front in the 1970s and 1980s was simply one more way for it to challenge the Moroccan army. Only when these groups lose sponsors are they "weak." The Kurdistan Workers' Party (PKK) is only David to Turkey's Goliath if the supply and support of Greece, Syria, and Iraqi Kurdistan are ignored. Without the support of Venezuela, it is doubtful that the Revolutionary Armed Forces of Colombia (FARC) would pose a serious threat.

Like state sponsors, political movements employ terrorism to achieve aims. They engage in terrorism because it can maximize gain at relatively little cost. Even minor military deployments by states are expensive. Each M1 Abrams battle tank carries a replacement cost of $4.1 million, and each UH-60L Black Hawk helicopter costs $5.9 million. Flying an F-18 costs thousands of dollars an hour in fuel alone. By contrast, Matthew Levitt, a former terrorism finance analyst at the U.S. Treasury Department, placed the cost of a November 2001 Palestinian gunmen's attack on the Afula central bus station in northern Israel at just $31,000, while the July 2002 bombing of a Hebrew University cafeteria that killed seven, including five Americans, cost just $50,000.

Andrew Garfield, an influence operations specialist with experience in both Iraq and Afghanistan, places the production cost of terrorists' martyrdom videos at only $2,000.[42]

Modern media amplify the effectiveness of terror. The proliferation of satellite television networks wins terrorists a global audience for every hijacking, bombing, or kidnapping, and can undercut a target's will to fight. In the 1990s, Chechen units operated in cells of five: four armed fighters and one whose only responsibility was to film exploits to amplify perceptions of effectiveness. Terrorist violence in Iraq—especially videos depicting the murders of kidnapped foreigners—undercut public support for Operation Iraqi Freedom, which translated into an earlier end to the conflict. In Afghanistan, too, terrorists employ the media to undercut the morale of the population of the country deploying armed forces. Not only is terrorism cheap, but, by enabling its sponsors plausible deniability, it also allows them to avoid costly accountability while they reap the benefits of diplomatic legitimacy that soft power too often bestows.

A fuller understanding of the nature of terrorism, its cost-effectiveness, and its support structures leads to one conclusion: whether the target is state sponsorship or the terrorists themselves, reliance on soft power and diplomacy only perpetuates terrorism.

THE SOFT POWER FALLACY

Proponents of soft power argue that military force alone cannot effectively counter terrorism. Joseph S. Nye Jr., a Harvard political scientist who coined the phrase in 1990, later revisited the topic in the context of the war on terrorism. "The United States cannot confront the new threat of terrorism without the cooperation of other countries," he wrote. "Of course, other governments will often cooperate out of self-interest. But the extent of their cooperation often depends on the attractiveness of the United States."[43] As for Islamic terrorism, Nye adopted the metric articulated by Secretary of Defense Donald Rumsfeld in February 2003: "Are we capturing, killing or deterring and dissuading more terrorists every day than the madrassas and the radical clerics are recruiting, training and deploying against us?" The key to success, Nye argued, is to appeal more to moderate Muslims so that they gain the upper hand against extremists.

Nye's approach is naïve. Countering terrorism is not a popularity contest. As the 2006 "Quadrennial Defense Review" stated, "This is both a battle of arms and a battle of ideas," not one or the other.[44] As I wandered through the Taliban's Afghanistan in March 2000, ordinary Afghans told me they chafed under Taliban rule. However, because the Taliban had monopolized force, they could do little. Iraqis living under Muqtada al-Sadr's grip in Najaf likewise had little ability to express their views freely as long as his Mahdi militia retained its local dominance. Only after the U.S. and Iraqi armies routed al-Sadr's militia in November 2004 did moderate Iraqis emerge from hiding. Hezbollah in Lebanon and Hamas in Gaza pursue similar reigns of terror.

Soft Approaches to the Root Causes of Terrorism

Too often, Western officials seek to address terrorism by speculating about root causes. Misidentifying these, however, undercuts any soft power antidote. For example, as Taliban fighters advanced on Buner, just sixty miles from the Pakistani capital, on April 22, 2009, Secretary of State Hillary Clinton declared, "The government of Pakistan must begin to deliver government services, otherwise they are going to lose out to those who show up and claim that they can solve people's problems."[45] This statement indicates that the secretary had misread the Islamist threat. Should Pakistan embark on land reform, the Taliban would simply switch to a new talking point to distract local attention while they pursue centuries-old ideological aims with force of arms.

As discussed in an earlier chapter of this volume, the notion that poverty breeds terrorism lacks evidence. Indeed, sub-Saharan African countries are among the poorest on earth, but they are not the major incubators of terrorism; rather, Saudi Arabia, Pakistan, and Libya are. The well-educated and middle class are more likely than the poor to pursue terrorism. The 9/11 hijackers, for example, had university educations and lived comfortable lives. Elite Palestinian institutions such as the Islamic University of Gaza and Birzeit University in the West Bank serve as breeding grounds. Likewise, British security services reports suggest that in the United Kingdom, universities (and not soup kitchens) are incubators of extremism.

Basing counterterrorism on economic development and poverty eradication, as was tried in Sri Lanka, is counterproductive, even though such assistance is the chief weapon in the soft power arsenal. Not only is foreign aid ineffective in battling terrorism; it often exacerbates the problem. In 2000 the Palestinian Authority launched its second intifada, a decision that led to a 40 percent drop in government revenue. Rather than hold the Palestinian leadership accountable for its decision to pursue its aims through violence rather than diplomacy, the international community doubled direct financial assistance. As Palestinian Authority chairman Yasser Arafat began to realize that the international community would not allow his constituents to suffer as a result of his decisions, the violence increased. Between 1999 and 2006, international assistance to the Palestinian Authority and incidences of terrorism were directly proportional.[46] In May 2009, the U.S. Government Accountability Office reported that it was unable to certify that U.S. taxpayer dollars did not subsidize Palestinian terror-ists or underwrite their propaganda.[47]

Even if foreign aid does not pad terrorists' coffers, prioritization of develop-ment over security wastes funds. In numerous reports between 2004 and 2009, the special inspector general for Iraq reconstruction detailed how security concerns constrained the multibillion-dollar reconstruction effort. When ter-rorists undermine stability, development aid at best is ineffective and at worst encourages corruption.

"Understanding" Terrorists' Grievances

If targeting economic development does little to reduce (and in fact may exac-erbate) terrorism, what about addressing directly the demands and grievances that terrorists say underpin their actions? Soft power strategies to address demands and grievances are counterproductive for two reasons. First, diplo-matic outreach or responding to terrorists' demands incentivizes terror. The core of the Iran-Contra affair, for example, was the Reagan administra-tion's attempt to trade arms for American hostages held by Iranian proxies in Lebanon. At first, it seemed to work: between June 9, 1985, and September 9, 1986, these militias kidnapped no Americans. But as soon as the Reagan administration delivered its last shipment of spare parts, kidnappers seized three more Americans.[48] William Quandt, a Middle East aide in the Nixon and Carter administrations, acknowledged as much: "This provides a perverse incentive to Iran to keep some hostages."[49]

The second reason seeking to address grievances is ineffective is that declared complaints do not always correlate with goals. The PKK used the cause of realizing Kurdish cultural rights and an independent state as justifi-cation for its bloody struggle in Turkey. However, throughout the entire con-flict, the PKK staged more attacks on fellow Kurds than on Turkish soldiers. The goal of its leader, Abdullah Öcalan, was power, not freedom. In March 1987, for example, Öcalan ordered some Kurdish villages in Turkey to be burned in order to subjugate the region to his authority. No amount of "out-reach" or "understanding" of the PKK's purported grievances has reduced PKK terrorism. Indeed, since the Turkish government again began speaking to PKK delegates in 2011, and enacting social reforms, PKK terrorism has increased.

Furthermore, terrorists' objectives expand as they achieve aims; they do not discard effective tools. Hezbollah demonstrates the tendency of terrorists to manufacture grievances once they fulfill initial goals. On May 24, 2000, Israel pulled its forces out of southern Lebanon, a withdrawal that the UN secretary-general subsequently certified complete. Israel's occupation of southern Lebanon was the reason for Hezbollah's birth in 1982, and yet rather than disband, Hezbollah asserted new claims to the Shebaa Farms and seven villages in Galilee in order to justify its continued existence.

The primary problem with soft solutions is that the ideologies that spark terrorism—be they Islamism, Maoism, or some other totalitarian creed—are often so extreme that they allow no solution other than surrender or victory. Sometimes, there are simply no alternatives to military solutions. A Vietnamese invasion, not a donors' conference, ended Pol Pot's reign of terror in Cambodia; a Tutsi invasion, not the United Nations, ended the Rwandan genocide. Terrorist groups often operate in such a world of extremes. In an October 22, 2002, speech, Hezbollah Secretary-General Hassan Nasrallah declared, "If they [Jews] all gather in Israel, it will save us the trouble of going after them worldwide."[50] When the solution to grievance is genocide, compromise is untenable. Bush recognized this after the 9/11 attacks on New York and Washington. Addressing a joint session of Congress on September 20, he declared, "The terrorists practice a fringe form of Islamic extremism. . . . The terrorists' directive commands them to kill Christians and Jews, to kill all Americans and make no distinctions among military and civilians, including women and children."[51]

Many scholars and academics resist the idea that ideology or religion actually motivates terrorism. Robert Pape, a University of Chicago political scientist, challenged the idea in his 2005 book *Dying to Win: The Strategic Logic of Suicide Terrorism*, which asserts that pragmatic grievance—specifically resistance to occupation—motivates suicide bombers.[52] His assumption that all terrorism shares common core motivations is problematic. Indeed, his theory does not conform to radical Muslims' own statements of motivation voiced in martyrdom videos and last wills.[53]

Terrorist successes—the multinational peacekeepers' withdrawal from Beirut in 1983 after a series of devastating bomb attacks; the U.S. withdrawal from Somalia after the "Black Hawk down" incidents in 1993; Israel's withdrawal from Lebanon in 2000; Israel's unilateral disengagement from Gaza in 2005; and America's precipitous withdrawal from Iraq—have only emboldened terrorist groups. A willingness to turn the other cheek and not respond militarily to terrorism does little to break cycles of violence. The U.S. refusal to respond militarily to an al-Qaeda attack on the World Trade Center in 1993 did nothing to prevent that group's attack on U.S. embassies in Tanzania and Kenya five years later. Nor did the lack of military response to the 2000 USS *Cole* attack prevent the group from striking again on 9/11. Only when countries show commitment to denying and defeating the terrorists can counterterrorism strategies succeed.

HARD POWER: RAISING THE COST

The key to an effective counterterrorism strategy is to raise the price of terrorism for its perpetrators and sponsors so that its costs outweigh its benefits. Even if material resources are unlimited, conducting terrorist attacks is never a cost- or risk-free enterprise. Any terrorist attack—whether a rocket strike, an improvised explosive device, or a suicide bombing—leaves forensic evidence. Rocket trajectories can be calculated, components traced, and suicide bombers' associates identified. By striking at terrorists and their sponsors militarily, states amplify the cost to any group or government seeking to achieve its aims through terrorism.

The experience of Israel is instructive. Rather than accept Israel's independence, its neighbors pursued a policy of attrition and harassment, providing safe haven to terrorists who would strike across the border. In the 1950s, Israeli Prime Minister David Ben-Gurion and Chief of Staff Moshe Dayan embraced a disproportionate military response to induce Israel's neighbors to restrain Palestinian terrorists in their territories. For example, an October 14, 1953, Israeli raid on the West Bank town of Qibtiyah quieted the Jordanian front for two-and-a-half years. And although the Egyptian-controlled Gaza Strip was a hotbed of *fidayin* activity through the early 1950s, Israel's 1956 Sinai campaign stopped all terrorist attacks launched from Egypt and the Gaza Strip for more than a decade. Retaliation did not end terrorism, but it did raise the cost of sponsorship.

More recently, Israel's targeted strikes against Palestinian terrorists and the U.S. drone missile attacks on insurgents in Iraq, Taliban targets in Afghanistan and Pakistan, and al-Qaeda leaders in Pakistan and Yemen offer a template for effective hard power counterterrorism strategies aimed at weakening terrorist organizations and denying them bases of operation from which to strike.

Targeted Killings

In the 1970s, Israel began to assassinate terrorists such as those who massacred Israel's Munich Olympic team in 1972. Future Prime Minister Ehud Barak gained fame when, dressed as a woman, he led a squad to assassinate Arafat's deputy in the heart of Beirut. The April 1988 raid on Tunis that killed Khalil al-Wazir, the Palestine Liberation Organization's second-in-command, convinced Arafat that distance did not bring security. Diplomats might have wrung their hands over cycles of violence, but it was Israel's ability to make Palestinian leaders face a personal cost for terrorism that opened a window for diplomacy. Had the Israeli military not crushed the First Intifada (1987–1993), it is doubtful that Arafat would have acceded to the Oslo peace process. The

Palestinian leadership chose diplomacy only after the costs of terrorism became too great to bear.

In September 2000, the Palestinian Authority launched the Second Intifada, seeking to gain through force what it could not gain at the negotiating table. In the months that followed, Palestinian terrorists launched hundreds of attacks against Israeli civilians. The Israeli government responded by using aircraft to assassinate terrorist leaders. The international community condemned the practice, but Jerusalem's policy was effective: terrorist attacks inside Israel declined by over 90 percent. It is a strategy upon which Obama has capitalized. Not only did he order a targeted assassination to kill al-Qaeda leader Osama bin Laden, but he ordered more drone hits against terror masters in his first year as president than Bush did during his entire two terms.

It is a fallacy that terrorist recruitment from an antagonized population negates the benefit of killing terrorist leaders. As recent success rolling back al-Qaeda shows, striking at terrorist leaders undercuts group effectiveness. Because most terrorist groups organize in cells, killing organizers can disrupt both hierarchical and lateral communications. Prior to his death, bin Laden had become so fearful that he relied only on couriers to communicate, a method that hampered his ability to control and coordinate the organization he founded. Repeated assassinations—often executed only after receiving information from informants—also spread paranoia among terrorist leaders, hampering their effectiveness. Time spent on their own security (for example, seeking the next safe house) is energy diverted from operations.[54]

In addition, elimination of recruiters and trainers degrades effectiveness, and in a desire for revenge terrorists may rush attacks, making detection easier. For example, after Israel commenced targeted assassinations, Israeli bus drivers and guards encountered terrorists who, lacking complete psychological preparation, exposed themselves by sweating or fumbling with wiring, enabling denial of access to the target.

Denial of Safe Havens

Although the debate over counterterrorism strategies can strike partisan rancor, there is a bipartisan consensus that denial of safe haven is central to effective counterterrorism. As the 9/11 Commission concluded, "Terrorists should no longer find safe-haven where their organizations can grow and flourish."[55] The question then becomes how best to deny safe haven, especially in failed states. In theory, foreign assistance can prevent states from descending into failure, but, in reality, the track record of foreign ministries and nongovernmental organizations is poor. Few have any strategy other than to cocoon themselves amidst lawlessness. In 1994, as genocide loomed in Rwanda, Kofi Annan, then head of

UN peacekeeping, ordered his forces to stand down. Eighteen years later, in 2012, Annan has shown himself equally ineffective amidst Syria's descent into chaos. Intervention and occupation provides an alternative, but military deployments, whether to Haiti or Somalia or East Timor, are expensive and cannot be undertaken without governments' willingness to fund their militaries adequately and sanction the use of force. For example, no matter how much the United Nations condemned the al-Qaeda–affiliated al-Shabaab attacks on the recognized government in Somalia, it was only Ethiopia, Kenya, Uganda, and Burundi's willingness to deploy troops that forced the extremists to scatter. Unlike direct intervention, targeted military strikes enable states to deny safe haven to terrorists without costly deployments. Taliban officials in Pakistan acknowledged in 2009 that the only counterterrorism strategy they feared was drone attacks, because they negated the safe haven they enjoyed.[56]

Preventing the Proliferation and Use of WMDs by Terrorists

Al-Qaeda and other apocalyptic terrorist organizations have a clear desire and willingness to kill on a massive scale. The 9/11 attacks convinced national security experts that they could no longer assume that terrorists' lack of advanced delivery systems offered protection from weapons of mass destruction (WMDs). If terrorist groups could use airplanes as missiles, then they could just as easily use hijacked container ships or airplanes as delivery systems for WMDs. A jihadist on one militant Islamist forum explained, "You can, in any European village, make up a gas canister, and go and put it in a bomb or parachute or fire truck, and you go and blow it in a stadium that has 120,000 spectators, and get 70,000 dead. This is called terrorism."[57]

Proponents of soft power solutions argue that the fight against terrorism is more appropriately left to the police, but there is a huge difference between threats to kill a few people and threats to wipe out tens of thousands. Chemical, biological, and nuclear weapons are military threats, not criminal justice concerns. Indeed, the Clinton administration underscored this conclusion when, on August 20, 1998, a U.S. cruise missile strike destroyed the Shifa factory in Khartoum, Sudan. Debate continues about whether the factory produced chemical weapons, but, by ordering the strike, Bill Clinton showed that the deciding factor should be military suspicion rather than criminal proof. Regardless of whether U.S. intelligence was accurate, the Sudanese government's subsequent compliance on terrorism matters suggested that it understood that there would be costs for even the appearance of involvement with terrorism and unconventional weapon development.

The recognition that the confluence of terrorism and technology had created a new paradigm infused the 2002 U.S. "National Security Strategy." "The

gravest danger our Nation faces lies at the crossroad of radicalism and technology," President Bush wrote in his introduction to the document, explaining,
"As a matter of common sense and self-defense, America will act against such
emerging threats before they are fully formed."[58] It was this broader concept of
preemption—not simply allegations of Iraqi ties to al-Qaeda—that motivated
the White House to topple the Iraqi government when it would not cooperate
with international inspections of its decades-old WMD programs.

Some critics fear that whatever the risks of WMDs falling into the wrong hands,
accepting preemption undercuts international law and justifies interventions like
the 2003 U.S.-led invasion of Iraq. This view is simplistic. UN Secretary-General
Ban Ki-moon, speaking to students at the 2009 commencement of the Johns
Hopkins University School of Advanced International Studies, emphasized the
importance of timing: "If we can intercede early to prevent conflict, we save lives
and forestall the need for a vastly more expensive peacekeeping mission down the
road," he explained, while also asserting the simultaneous need for diplomacy.[59]
Waiting until threats develop magnifies the costs of intervention. It is best to
intervene early against WMD threats, as Israel did against Iraq in 1981 and
against Syria in 2007, than to wait for threats to grow. The North Korean
and Iranian examples illustrates the other extreme. North Korean officials played
first Clinton and then Bush for fools, pursuing nuclear weapons against the back-
drop of diplomacy. In October 2011, Iran's former nuclear negotiator admitted
Iranian diplomacy was tactical, meant only to avert sanctions and create more
space for Tehran to advance its nuclear program.[60]

ONLY HARD POWER CAN LAY THE FOUNDATION FOR EFFECTIVE SOFT POWER

Soft power strategies have utility, but they are ineffective absent hard power.
Here, the case of Iraq is instructive. On January 11, 2007, President Bush
announced that the United States would deploy additional military forces to
Iraq. The "surge" occurred at the same time as diplomatic engagement with
Sunni Arabs in al-Anbar, Iraq's insurgency-ridden western province. The subsequent decline in violence surpassed expectations. The opposite is also true.
Violence increased in Iraq when the U.S. precipitously withdrew all of its forces
in early 2012, and when it signaled its unwillingness to confront the states
sponsoring insurgency in Iraq.

Because of the success of the surge, critics of the Bush administration argued
that its earlier refusal to diplomatically engage Baathists and insurgents exacerbated violence. "If the compromises accepted later by the Bush administration had been accepted when a rapprochement was first broached by the

Sunnis, in 2004, some 2,000 Americans and thousands more Iraqis might not have died," wrote David Rose, a British journalist.[61]

The problem with such a conclusion, however, is that it employs anachronism. Sunni attitudes did not remain constant over time. Rose ignores earlier engagement initiatives that undercut his thesis. After Sunni fighters ambushed four American contractors and mutilated their bodies on March 31, 2004, in Fallujah, a hotbed of insurgency, U.S. forces surrounded the city. Rather than seize the city and risk collateral damage, U.S. Marine General James Conway crafted a deal to lift the siege of Fallujah and empower the Fallujah Brigade, a unit of former Baathists and insurgents, to restore order. It backfired. Islamists interpreted the deal as a victory over the United States. Minaret-mounted loudspeakers lauded "victory over the Americans." The cost to innocent Iraqis of the outreach was devastating. Between April 6 and April 30, 2004, the period of siege, there were five bombings in Fallujah. In the twenty-four days after the creation of the Fallujah Brigade, there were more than thirty bombings, killing and wounding hundreds.

Gen. David Petraeus also preached reconciliation throughout his tenure in Iraq, during which he served as the commanding general of the multinational force. Eventually, he was successful, but not on his first tries. "The coalition must reconcile with a number of the thousands of former Ba'ath officials . . . giving them a direct stake in the success of the new Iraq," he declared on April 7, 2004.[62] While commanding the 101st Airborne in Mosul, Petraeus appointed senior Baathists to high positions in defiance of both the Iraqi government and the Coalition Provisional Authority. For example, he assigned Gen. Mahmud Muhammad al-Maris to lead Border Police units guarding the Syrian border, and he appointed another Baathist general, Muhammad Khairi Barhawi, as chief of police. Both used their positions to undermine security. Al-Maris facilitated terrorist infiltration from Syria into Iraq, and only after Mosul erupted in insurgency in November 2004 did Petraeus learn that Barhawi had organized insurgent cells in the city. So why did the Sunnis accept reconciliation in 2007? Becoming the prime target of U.S. military force convinced them that the costs of armed struggle were too great to bear. Only after Iraqi Sunni leaders concluded that they would gain little through bombs and boycotts did they agree to participate in Iraq's political reconstruction. The willingness by the White House to deploy additional troops to Iraq despite significant opposition inside the United States convinced many holdouts that they simply could not outlast U.S. willpower.

Across the globe, from Peru to Sri Lanka, military force has succeeded where soft power has failed. Through the 1980s, the Shining Path, a Maoist group, waged a bloody campaign against the Peruvian government, killing between thirty and seventy thousand people. By 1991 the Shining Path controlled much of the countryside in central and southern Peru, and had begun to strike in the heart of Lima. Peru was on the brink. The tide turned only when President Alberto Fujimori launched a military response. On September 12, 1992, Peruvian police captured the Shining Path's leaders. Within weeks, the group collapsed.

In Colombia, too, military force succeeded where diplomacy could not. For forty-five years, Colombia has battled a FARC insurgency. The Colombian government sought negotiation, but to no avail. On November 7, 1998, President Andrés Pastrana granted FARC a 16,200-square-mile safe haven—an area larger than Switzerland—as a confidence-building measure. But instead of reducing the violence, the compromise encouraged FARC to ramp up pressure. It was only when President Álvaro Uribe abandoned diplomacy and resorted to military measures that Colombia not only contained the terrorist threat, but also created a cascade of momentum that unraveled decades of FARC gains. On July 2, 2008, Colombian soldiers raided a FARC camp, freeing fifteen hostages, including a former Colombian presidential candidate and three American contractors, some of whom had been held for six years. Military force succeeded where diplomacy and soft power failed.

Sri Lanka underlines this conclusion. From 1976 to 2009, the Liberation Tigers of Tamil Eelam (LTTE), or Tamil Tigers, waged a bloody insurgency and terrorist campaign marked by suicide attacks, rape, impressments, bombings of buses and trains, and ethnic cleansing, altogether killing more than seventy thousand people. Throughout this period, the international community sought to mediate. Norwegian mediation failed after the LTTE broke its 2001 cease-fire. The same pattern was repeated in 2005 and 2006. What diplomats hailed as chances for peace the Tamil Tigers saw as tactical pauses to regroup and resupply. In 2008 the Sri Lankan government ordered its military to advance. Amid hand-wringing and condemnation by both UN agencies and the U.S. government, the Sri Lankan army pushed forward, routing the LTTE and eliminating its leadership. The next year, brute military force ended a thirty-three-year civil war. Had the Sri Lankan government listened to UN officials, European diplomats, or the White House, thousands more might have perished in a prolonged LTTE terrorist campaign. Obama even sought to withhold $1.9 billion in International Monetary Fund assistance unless the Sri Lankan government accepted a cease-fire that would have only allowed the Tamil Tigers to live to fight another day. Ironically, Joseph Nye had cited Sri Lanka as a test case for soft power.[63] Reconstruction and reconciliation are important, but they do not ameliorate conflict; they are effective only after its conclusion.

Military strategies need not be violent. The value of military force is that its demonstration—and the adversary's belief that the threat is credible—is often enough to coerce a change of behavior. Many proponents of diplomacy, including Brigitte Nacos, like to cite Libyan leader Qaddafi's decision to abandon terrorism and his WMD program as a triumph for diplomacy. The *Washington Post* even ran the headline "Two Decades of Sanctions, Isolation Wore Down Gaddafi." To credit diplomacy for Tripoli's agreement, however, is a stretch. As columnist Charles Krauthammer observed,

> By amazing coincidence, Gaddafi's first message to Britain—principal U.S. war ally and conduit to White House war councils—occurs just days before the invasion of Iraq. And his final capitulation to U.S.-British terms occurs just five days after Saddam is fished out of a rat hole.[64]

> Indeed, while diplomats and other proponents of soft power credit sanctions for Qaddafi's about-face, Qaddafi's own advisers say American military might have swayed the mercurial Libyan strongman.[65] While Qaddafi's attacks against his own people against the backdrop of the Arab Spring show rogues never truly change, Qaddafi's behavior also suggests that fearful rogues may think long and hard about again targeting Americans.

CONCLUSION

Despite the high-minded rhetoric of the United Nations and other international bodies, coercion—the threat of force and, if necessary, its use—remain a critical element of counterterrorism. It may be comforting to believe that diplomacy with state sponsors of terrorism and with terrorist groups themselves can alone alter their behavior, but such wishful thinking is dangerous. The United States has learned this lesson. In 1996, the Clinton administration engaged the Taliban. Over subsequent years, the militant group "indicated a willingness to negotiate with the opposition and agreed on the need for a broad-based government.... They repeated their pledge to prevent terrorists from using Afghanistan to launch attacks on others."[66] Hindsight may be 20/20, but the Taliban's insincerity has always been clear. Had the Clinton administration preempted the terrorist threat rather than pursued engagement, perhaps bin Laden would have lost his safe haven and 9/11 would have been averted. The symbolism of a one-time missile strike in 1998 against empty camps—the harshest of Clinton's actions—is not enough to defeat terrorists or ensure security; only eradication of terrorists by any means necessary is. If the Obama administration has made negotiation with "moderate Taliban" a cornerstone of their Afghan withdrawal strategy, then the price will likely be paid with American lives. The Taliban themselves underlined this fact in October 2011, when they attacked both the U.S. embassy and a hotel frequented by foreigners.

Secretary of State Hillary Clinton acknowledged that diplomats had sat down and talked with the very groups who subsequently targeted American civilians.[67] So how then should counterterrorism strategies be crafted? U.S. military academies teach that every strategy should have diplomatic, informational, military, and economic components. Recognizing the necessity to confront terrorists with military force does not mean dispensing with diplomacy. Diplomacy is important because transnational terrorists respect no boundaries. It is always preferable to win other countries' cooperation through diplomacy, thereby minimizing cost. But diplomacy itself should not be an excuse for inaction. As Qaddafi's surrender of his nuclear ambitions shows, sometimes it is the willingness to use military force rather than simply engage that enables diplomacy to succeed.

A military-based strategy also does not mean eschewing aid and development. While Bush is remembered first and foremost for the invasion of Iraq, he also formulated the Millennium Challenge Account. But even though aid and development have a role, absent security they are counterproductive. As the United Nations discovered in Somalia, dispatching aid to insecure zones bolsters warlordism, not rule of law. It is all well and good for Europeans to build schools in Afghanistan, but if they flee when fired upon, they help no one and, indeed, can make matters worse.

Police investigate crimes; militaries preempt and neutralize threats. As technology advances and access to it increases, terrorism becomes a more deadly phenomenon. Police pursuit might have contained the Weather Underground, the Baader-Meinhof Gang, and the Red Army Faction, but transnational masscasualty terrorists enjoying safe haven and advanced weapons pose a far deadlier threat, one that only a robust strategy centered on military force can counter.

Notes

1. David Kilcullen and Andrew McDonald Exum, "Death from Above, Outrage Down Below," *New York Times,* May 17, 2009.
2. For an excellent overview of the basic instruments of counterterrorism policy—diplomacy, criminal justice, military force, intelligence, and financial controls—see Paul R. Pillar, *Terrorism and U.S. Foreign Policy* (Washington, D.C.: Brookings, 2003), chap. 4.
3. See, for example, White House, "National Strategy for Combating Terrorism," September 2006, http://georgewbush-whitehouse.archives.gov/nsc/nsct/2006.
4. For years the Afghanistan war was widely hailed as a success story in the fight against terrorism, even though neither the Taliban nor al-Qaeda was mortally wounded. As the United States shifted its interest and military assets from Afghanistan to Iraq, Taliban and al-Qaeda forces were able to regroup in hiding places across the border with Pakistan and to mastermind violent attacks in Afghanistan and elsewhere.

5. For excellent overviews and examples of "hard" and "soft" counterterrorism strategies, see Pillar, *Terrorism and U.S. Foreign Policy*; and Audrey Kurth Cronin and James M. Ludes, eds., *Attacking Terrorism* (Washington, D.C.: Georgetown University Press, 2004). For a classic discussion of "soft power" in international relations, see Joseph S. Nye Jr., *Soft Power: The Means to Success in World Politics* (New York: Public Affairs, 1994).

6. U.S. Department of Defense, *National Defense Strategy* (Washington, D.C.: DOD, June 2008); U.S. Department of Defense, *Defense Strategic Guidance* (Washington, D.C.: DOD, January 2012).

7. According to the *2007 Report on Terrorism* (Washington, D.C.: National Counterterrorism Center, June 2008).

8. "Six Months after US Withdrawal, Surge in Violence Spurs Fears Iraq Will Be Unstable for Years," *Associated Press*, June 30, 2012.

9. Pillar, *Terrorism and U.S. Foreign Policy*, 167. For an in-depth account of the role of diplomacy versus force in America's relations with Libya over twenty-five years, see Bruce Jentleson and Christopher Whytock, "Who 'Won' Libya? The Force-Diplomacy Debate and Its Implications for Theory and Policy," *International Security* 30 (Winter 2005/2006): 47–86.

10. Helene Cooper, "U.S. Declares North Korea Off Terror List," *New York Times*, October 23, 2008.

11. Roger Runningen and Mark Drajem, "Talks on North Korea's Nuclear Program to Be Held," Bloomberg, November 23, 2008, www.bloomberg.com/apps/news?pid=20601089&sid=aAu80wL_lvCw.

12. I was among those who did not applaud Bill Clinton's humanitarian mission to Pyongyang because the former president's visit offered North Korea's leadership the opportunity for a major propaganda coup. It had rejected a less prominent special envoy's visit and insisted on the former president to meet with Kim and others. For more on this, see my post at www.reflectivepundit.com/reflectivepundit/2009/08/bill-clinton-and-the-freed-hostages-a-win-win-for-the-us-and-north-korea.html?cid=6a00d8341ca8e553ef017c317c2486970b.

13. Choe Sang-Hun, "North Korea Said to Resume Work on Nuclear Reactor," *New York Times*, May 17, 2012.

14. Saudi Arabia, too, pressured Sudan's government to stop supporting bin Laden. For more on this, see Simon Reeve, *The New Jackals* (Boston: Northeastern University Press, 1999), chap. 9.

15. The U.S. Department of State's "Country Reports on Terrorism" for 2010 is available at www.state.gov/j/ct/rls/crt/2010/index.htm.

16. The transcript of President George W. Bush's speech on May 15, 2008, is available at http://georgewbush-whitehouse.archives.gov.

17. Howard LaFranchi, "Rice's Visit to a Changed Libya," *Christian Science Monitor*, September 4, 2008.

18. Annie Lowrey and David Sanger, "U.S. Bets New Oil Sanctions Will Change Iran's Tune," *New York Times*, June 30, 2012.

19. Richard Holbrooke, "The Next President: Mastering a Daunting Agenda," *Foreign Affairs* 87 (September/October 2008): 18.

20. Timothy Hoyt, "Military Force," in Cronin and Ludes, *Attacking Terrorism*, 173.

21. Barry R. Posen, "The Struggle against Terrorism: Grand Strategy, Strategy, and Tactics," *International Security* 26 (Winter 2001/2002): 47.

22. Carlotta Gall, "Evidence Points to Civilian Toll in Afghan Raid," *New York Times*, September 9, 2008.

23. David Rohde, "The Obama Doctrine: How the President's Secret Wars Are Backfiring," *Foreign Policy* (March/April 2012): 64–69.

24. Ibid, 69. Also see Ibrahim Mothana, "How Drones Help Al Qaeda," *New York Times*, June 13, 2012.

25. Lindsay Clutterbuck, "Law Enforcement," in Cronin and Ludes, *Attacking Terrorism*, 141.

26. Seth Jones and Martin Libicki, *How Terrorist Groups End: Lessons for Countering al Qa'ida* (Santa Monica, Calif.: RAND, 2008), chap. 2.

27. Alan Cowell, "Clasping Hands, Ex-Guerilla and Queen Bridge a Divide," *New York Times*, June 27, 2012.

28. Jones and Libicki, *How Terrorist Groups End*, 36.

29. Peter Neumann, "Negotiating with Terrorists," *Foreign Affairs* 86 (January/February 2007): 136.

30. Louise Richardson, *What Terrorists Want* (New York: Random House, 2006), 214.

31. David Ignatius, "Negotiations with the Taliban Find Some Momentum," *Washington Post*, February 27, 2012.

32. U.S. Department of Defense, *National Defense Strategy*, 8.

33. For public diplomacy in the information age, see Geoffrey Cohen and Amelia Arsenault, "Moving from Monologue to Dialogue to Collaboration: The Three Layers of Public Diplomacy," in "Public Diplomacy in a Changing World," ed. Geoffrey Cohen and Nicholas J. Cull, *The Annals* 616 (March 2008): 46–52.

34. Dafna Linzer, "Lost in Translation: Alhurra—America's Troubled Effort to Win Middle East Hearts and Minds," *ProPublica*, June 22, 2008.

35. Ibid.

36. The remarks were made during the Landon Lecture at Kansas State University, November 26, 2007, www.defenselink.mil/speeches/speech.aspx?speechid=1199.

37. David Ignatius, "An Embassy Asks, Drones or Diplomacy?" *Washington Post*, June 20, 2012.

38. For survey summaries and news accounts about them, see Terror Free Tomorrow's website, www.terrorfreetomorrow.org.

39. Kenneth Ballen, "Even al Qaeda Supporters Can Be Won Over," *Los Angeles Times*, June 14, 2008.

40. Barack Obama, "Remarks by the President on National Security," delivered at the National Archives, Washington, D.C., May 21, 2009.

41. Stephen Sloan, "Terrorism and Asymmetry," in *Challenging the United States Symmetrically and Asymmetrically*, ed. Col. Lloyd Matthews (Carlisle Barracks, Pa.: U.S. Army War College, Strategic Studies Institute, 1998), 176.

42. Matthew Levitt, *Hamas: Politics, Charity, and Terrorism in the Service of Jihad* (New Haven, Conn.: Yale University Press, 2006), 55; Andrew Garfield, "Winning the War of Ideas: Cultural Understanding, and Influence Operations," Lecture at I Corps headquarters, Ft. Lewis, Wash., April 29, 2008.

43. Joseph S. Nye Jr., "The Decline of America's Soft Power," *Foreign Affairs* 83 (May/June 2004): 16–20.

44. U.S. Department of Defense, "Quadrennial Defense Review," February 3, 2006, 22.

45. "Pakistan Giving Up to Militants: Hillary," *Dawn.com* (Karachi), April 23, 2009.

46. Steven Stotsky, "Does Foreign Aid Fuel Palestinian Violence?" *Middle East Quarterly* 15 (Summer 2008): 23–30.

47. U.S. Government Accountability Office, "Foreign Assistance: Measures to Prevent Inadvertent Payments to Terrorists under Palestinian Aid Programs Have Been Strengthened, but Some Weaknesses Remain," GAO-09-622, May 2009, 15–19.

48. *The Tower Commission Report* (New York: Bantam, 1987), 47–48.

49. Quoted in Bernard Gwertzman, "Why President Ended Silence on Iran Policy," *New York Times,* November 14, 1986.

50. *Daily Star* (Beirut), October 23, 2002.

51. White House, "President George W. Bush's Address to a Joint Session of Congress Concerning the Sept. 11, 2001 Terrorist Attacks on America," September 20, 2001.

52. Robert Pape, *Dying to Win: The Strategic Logic of Suicide Terrorism* (New York: Random House, 2005).

53. Jonathan Fine, "Contrasting Secular and Religious Terrorism," *Middle East Quarterly* 15 (Winter 2008): 59–69.

54. Gal Luft, "The Logic of Israel's Targeted Killing," *Middle East Quarterly* 10 (Winter 2003).

55. National Commission on Terrorist Attacks Upon the United States, *The 9/11 Commission Report,* July 22, 2004, 364, www.gpoaccess.gov/911/Index.html.

56. Jane Perlez and Pir Zubair Shah, "Porous Pakistani Border Could Hinder U.S.," *New York Times,* May 4, 2009.

57. Transcript provided by SITE Intelligence Group, no. 2008052701, May 27, 2008.

58. George W. Bush, Introductory Letter, in White House, "The National Security Strategy of the United States of America," September 2002, http://georgewbush-whitehouse.archives.gov/nsc.

59. Ban Ki-moon, "Global Leadership in a Time of Crisis," Commencement Address at the Paul H. Nitze School of Advanced International Studies, Washington, D.C., May 21, 2009.

60. "Nagoftaha-ye Hassan Rowhani as Diplomasi Hasteh-ye Dureh Eslahat az Europa qol Vatave Tareh-i Amrika ra Gerefteh Budam," *Etemaad* (Tehran), October 24, 2011.

61. David Rose, "Heads in the Sand," *Vanity Fair,* May 12, 2009.

62. Gen. David Petraeus, "Lessons of the Iraq War and Its Aftermath," Washington Institute for Near East Policy, April 9, 2004.

63. "Joseph Nye on Smart Power," John F. Kennedy School of Government, website interview, July 3, 2008.

64. Charles Krauthammer, "Aftershocks of War," *Washington Post,* December 26, 2003.

65. Målfrid Braut-Hegghammer, "Libya's Nuclear Turnaround: Perspectives from Tripoli," *The Middle East Journal* (Winter 2008).

66. "Afghanistan: Meeting with the Taliban," State Department cable no. 231842, December 8, 1997. Republished in the National Security Archives website, www.gwu.edu/~nsarchiv/NSAEBB/NSAEBB97/tal24.pdf.

67. Indira A. R. Lakshmanan, "Clinton Says U.S. Met with Militants who Later Attacked Embassy in Kabul," Bloomberg, October 21, 2011.

can spreading democracy help defeat terrorism?

NO: Democracy promotion is problematic as a counterterrorism priority.
F. Gregory Gause III, *University of Vermont*

YES: Promoting democracy can help combat terrorism.
Jennifer L. Windsor, *Georgetown University*

In the early morning of January 26, 2006, Secretary of State Condoleezza Rice was enjoying her regular workout on an elliptical trainer while watching the morning news on television. Suddenly, the news crawl at the bottom of the screen reported something that caused her to halt her workout: "In wake of Hamas victory, Palestinian cabinet resigns." As the *New York Times* reported on the episode:

> "I thought, 'Well, that's not right,'" Ms. Rice recalled. When the crawl continued, she got off the elliptical trainer and called the State Department.
> "I said, 'What happened in the Palestinian elections?'" Ms. Rice recalled. "And they said, 'Oh, Hamas won.' And I thought, 'Oh my goodness, Hamas won?'"[1]

The 2006 Palestinian elections had been heralded by the administration of George W. Bush as a symbol of the stirrings of democracy in the Middle East, and as a way to counteract extremist groups like Hamas that engage in terrorism. Instead, the Hamas landslide victory over Mahmoud Abbas's moderate Fatah party became an important illustration of the frustrating complexity encountered in trying to combat extremism and terrorism through the spread of democracy.

Indeed, the promotion of democracy as a means of addressing the important root causes of terrorism in the Arab world—corrupt autocratic regimes and disenfranchised, disaffected populations that fuel the popularity of radical religious groups—was a vital part of the Bush administration's post-9/11 national security and counterterrorism strategies, both of which promoted the spread of freedom and democracy as a "long-term antidote to the ideology of terrorism."[2]

Yet as the wars in Afghanistan and Iraq showed, fashioning democracies through direct military intervention and occupation is rife with cost and controversy, leaving the final outcomes, at best, uncertain (although, in fairness, the primary justification for those wars was not the creation of democracy).

And as revealed by the 2006 Palestinian election, and more recent post–Arab Spring elections in countries including Morocco, Tunisia, and Egypt, Islamist parties—some with current or historic ties to active terrorist groups—often fare very well. Should Saudi Arabia and Jordan permit free and fair elections, the results would also likely be Islamist, and anti-American, governments.

So, although the idea of transforming countries that generate terrorism into democracies may be attractive in theory, in practice it remains a very uncertain long-term proposition.

But perhaps that is the point. Perhaps it is the very *process* of opening up political systems in the Arab and Muslim world—with all of the uncertainty this often entails—that will eventually lay a path for stable, legitimate political structures that can marginalize radical groups. There are certainly examples of former terrorist movements becoming moderated by inclusion in open political processes—including the Irish Republican Army in Northern Ireland and the African National Congress in South Africa. And there are examples of radical Islamist parties faring very poorly in elections in Muslim countries, including Indonesia.

As the United States rethinks its policies toward the Middle East in light of the Arab Spring, a debate has reemerged over the utility of democracy promotion as a tool of combating radicalism and terror. Should any or all of the Bush administration's much-maligned "freedom agenda" be resurrected? Should other democracy promotion initiatives toward the Middle East be developed?

Gregory Gause answers no to all such questions. He argues that promoting democracy in the Arab world has always been counterproductive, and that the Arab awakenings have done nothing to alter this reality. Not only have democratic governments in general not been shown to reduce or eliminate terrorism, but groups such as al-Qaeda have declared democracy promotion a new tool of Western imperialism, and they use such outside meddling to draft new recruits. Indeed, Gause contends that even if free elections took place across the Arab world, the types of governments they would produce would likely be more anti-American than they are now, as the 2012 election in

Egypt explicitly shows. If the United States cannot cease all pro-democracy efforts, then at a minimum, he suggests, it should shift its emphasis away from elections that will simply bring Islamists to power and toward encouraging the development of secular political organizations that may one day compete for power in the region.

Jennifer Windsor agrees that democracy is not a panacea for social unrest and possible terrorist activities. But, she argues, democratic governments are far more responsive to their citizens and far more capable of ameliorating conditions that breed violence than autocracies. In the Arab and Muslim world, she believes democratization can address conditions that facilitate radical Islamist movements: governments that support human rights and the rule of law, and encourage political participation, will drain the recruitment pool for groups like al-Qaeda. Although Americans may not celebrate the outcome of every election, Windsor says holding regular, lawful elections offers a slow but sure way to ease the development of moderate political and social institutions. Yes, the Arab Spring contains a degree of peril, but it also holds tremendous promise. She concludes that assisting emerging democracies with innovative aid packages and support in building accountable political institutions will place the United States firmly on the right side of history regarding its policies toward the Middle East.

Debates over the relationship between democracy and global peace and security have been around since at least the days of Immanuel Kant. The role of democracy in addressing terrorism is a much more recent policy paradigm, and one that has only been energized by the recent political awakenings in the Middle East. As the authors of the essays in this chapter make clear, the stakes in this ongoing debate are high—not only for U.S. counterterrorism policy, but also for citizens of the Arab and Muslim world.

NO: Democracy promotion is problematic as a counterterrorism priority.

F. Gregory Gause III, *University of Vermont*

Democracy, Terrorism, and American Policy in the Arab World

Much has changed since the heady days of 2003 and 2004, after the fall of Saddam Hussein's regime in Iraq and of the notion that the United States could remake the Middle East.[3] The initial enthusiasm of the George W. Bush administration and its supporters for democratic change in the region as a central element of "draining the swamp" that produced the terrorism of September 11, 2001, was eventually tempered by the realities of Islamist victories at Arab polls, a trend reinforced by the elections coming after the Arab Spring of 2011. Still, the American debate about the Middle East remains characterized by the belief that democratic reform will ameliorate the root causes of terrorism. Because it was not just President Bush who held these ideas, and because the democratic trend in the Arab world has accelerated as a result of the Arab Spring, it is useful to consider both the theoretical argument about the relationship between democracy and terrorism more generally and the effects of real democratic reform in the Arab world for American interests there.

Two questions present themselves in this context. First, is there a relationship between terrorism and democracy such that the more democratic a country becomes, the less likely it is to produce terrorists and terrorist groups? In other words, is the security rationale for democracy promotion in the Arab world based on a sound premise? Second, what kind of governments would likely be generated by democratic elections in Arab countries? Would they be willing to cooperate with the United States on important policy objectives in the Middle East, not only in curbing terrorism but also on Arab-Israeli, Gulf security, and oil issues?

Unfortunately, the answer to the first of these questions appears to be no. Although the state of scholars' knowledge about terrorism is admittedly incomplete, and thus subject to revision as more research is done, the data available now do not show a strong relationship in general between democracy and an absence of or reduction in terrorism. It seems that terrorism stems much more from specific political and social factors than from regime type. When it comes to the current opponents of the United States in the global struggle against terrorism, it is even clearer that democratization would not end their violent campaign against the United States and its allies. Al-Qaeda and like-minded groups are, of course, not fighting for democracy in the Muslim world; in fact, they have declared the promotion of democracy a new tool of Western imperialism. Instead, they are fighting to impose their notions of an Islamic state. They oppose democracy on both doctrinal and practical grounds. Democratic change in Arab countries will not change their course, as al-Qaeda's violent resurgence in Iraq in 2012 demonstrates. Whether such change would reduce the number of potential recruits to al-Qaeda and similar organizations is a matter of speculation. But, if the Arab democracies that the United States wants to encourage pursue foreign policies amenable to Washington—if they cooperate with American military operations, host American military forces, make peace with Israel, and generally follow the American foreign policy line—then there will be ample incentives for anti-American terrorist organizations to continue to be able to recruit followers in Arab societies.

On the second question, we now have a good idea of what kinds of governments would be produced in the first elections in real Arab democracies. Based on Arab public opinion surveys and recent elections in the Arab world, democratic elections are likely to produce Islamist governments. This was true of Iraq and Palestine before the Arab Spring and has been true of Tunisia and Egypt since the Arab Spring. Such governments are less likely to cooperate with the United States than their authoritarian predecessors on a whole range of issues, including the global struggle against terrorism.

The answers to these two questions should lead to a rethinking of democracy promotion strategies toward the Arab world. My preference would be to drop these efforts altogether, both on the principled grounds that the United States should not be interfering in the domestic affairs of other countries and out of the prudential concern that U.S. meddling in the domestic affairs of others usually turns out very differently than intended. On these same principles, Washington should also not oppose democratic openings resulting from popular mobilizations against authoritarian rulers, as we have seen in the Arab Spring. The United States should just not do anything to encourage them. Washington cannot micromanage political change in countries that it only imperfectly understands. If the United States must promote democracy in the Middle East, it should shift its emphasis toward encouraging the development of secular, nationalist, and liberal political organizations that can compete on an equal footing with Islamist parties.

TERRORISM AND DEMOCRACY

President Bush was absolutely clear about why the promotion of democracy in the Muslim world generally and the Arab world more specifically is not only consistent with American values, but also central to American interests. He laid out that logic in an address in March 2005 at the National Defense University:

> Our strategy to keep the peace in the longer term is to help change the conditions that give rise to extremism and terror, especially in the broader Middle East. Parts of that region have been caught for generations in the cycle of tyranny and despair and radicalism. When a dictatorship controls the political life of a country, responsible opposition cannot develop and dissent is driven underground and toward the extreme. And to draw attention away from their social and economic failures, dictators place blame on other countries and other races and stir the hatred that leads to violence. This status quo of despotism and anger cannot be ignored or appeased, kept in a box or bought off.[4]

President Bush's analysis of the link between the lack of democracy in the Arab world and terrorism is shared across the political spectrum in the United States. In 2004 the Democratic presidential candidate, John Kerry, also highlighted the need for greater political reform in the Middle East as an integral part of the war on terrorism.[5] *New York Times* columnist Thomas Friedman, one of America's leading commentators on foreign affairs, has done more to propound this logic to the attentive American public than anyone else.[6] In a prominent mea culpa published in 2002, Martin Indyk, a senior Middle East policymaker in the Clinton administration, said that the strategy President Bill Clinton pursued of focusing on Arab-Israeli peace while downplaying democracy in the region was a mistake and urged a new American policy focused on political reform. Morton Halperin, the director of policy planning in the Clinton State Department, is the lead author of a 2004 book that argues that the roots of al-Qaeda are in the poverty and educational deficiencies of Saudi Arabia, Egypt, and Pakistan. These deficiencies arose from the authoritarian nature of those states and can be overcome only by their democratization.[7] The argument underlying the Bush administration's emphasis on political reform in the Middle East as a necessary part of the struggle against terrorism is widely accepted in Washington, and it has not disappeared since Bush and the neoconservatives left office.[8]

Terrorism and Democracy: The Empirical Evidence

The academic literature on the relationship between terrorism and other sociopolitical indicators such as democracy is surprisingly scant. Very good case studies of terrorists and terrorist organizations and overall surveys of the phenomenon are available, but few try to answer the question posed earlier: does democracy lead to less terrorism? Analysts are hamstrung, in particular, by the quality of the data available. There is a bias in the data toward international terrorist incidents—attacks that have a cross-border element and tend to be reported more completely in the Western press—and away from homegrown terrorist attacks in developing countries that might not make it into the *New York Times*. The most widely used data sets tend to identify the location of a terrorist incident, but they are not as reliable or complete in identifying the perpetrator. If an attack occurs in a democracy but is perpetrated by people from a nondemocratic country or countries, as were the 9/11 attacks, analysts would want to know more about the countries of origin of the attackers than about the target country to test whether nondemocratic political systems are more likely to produce terrorists than democratic political systems.

Because of these data constraints, only preliminary conclusions from the academic literature are possible. However, those conclusions call into question the close link between terrorism and lack of democracy that underpinned the Bush administration's justification of the democracy initiative in the Arab world. In their widely cited study of terrorist events in the 1980s, William Eubank and Leonard Weinberg found that during that period the most common type of terrorist incident was one that occurred in a democracy, and one in which both the victims and the perpetrators were citizens of democracies.[9] In a more recent look at the same data set for the period between 1975 and 1997, Quan Li found that although higher levels of democratic political participation correlate negatively with terrorist attacks, the kinds of restraint on executive power associated with liberal democracy seem to encourage terrorist actions.[10] In *Dying to Win: The Strategic Logic of Suicide Terrorism*, Robert Pape finds that democracies are almost always the targets of suicide bombers, but that the motivations of the groups behind those bombings is to fight against military occupation and for self-determination. It is not the lack of democracy that drives suicide terrorism, but opposition to what is seen as foreign domination.[11]

A quick look at the numbers published by the U.S. government also does not appear to bear out a close link between terrorism and the lack of democracy. Between 2000 and 2003, based on the State Department's annual *Patterns of Global Terrorism*, 269 major international terrorist incidents occurred in countries classified as "Free" in Freedom House's *Freedom in the World* annual report; 119 occurred in countries classified as "Partly Free"; and 138 occurred in countries classified as "Not Free."[12] This is not to argue that free countries are more likely to produce terrorists than other countries. Rather, it seems that terrorist incidents are distributed somewhat proportionately according to the number of people governed by countries in the three categories, or perhaps even randomly, indicating no necessary relationship between terrorism and the degree of freedom enjoyed by citizens. These numbers certainly do not indicate that democracies are substantially less susceptible to terrorism than other forms of government.

But, of course, terrorism is not distributed randomly. Only a few countries account for the vast majority of terrorist incidents, according to the official U.S. government data. Terrorist incidents in India account for fully 75 percent of all terrorist incidents in free countries (as defined by Freedom House) in the four years surveyed. It is fair to assume that some of those terrorist incidents, particularly in Kashmir, are perpetrated by groups based in Pakistan, though clearly not all of the terrorist attacks in India are foreign in origin. A significant number of the terrorist incidents in the country are far from Kashmir, reflecting other local grievances against the central government. A vibrant democracy with the full range of political rights available to its citizens, India has rightly been held up as an example of the possibility of democracy outside the context of wealthy Western countries. And yet as strong as Indian democracy is, one Indian prime minister was assassinated (Indira Gandhi, by a Sikh extremist), and a former prime minister campaigning to regain the office was assassinated (her son, Rajiv Gandhi, by Tamil extremists). If democracy reduces the prospects for terrorism, India's numbers should not be so high. It is also interesting to note that in 2003 two countries classified as "Not Free" by Freedom House accounted for 50 percent of the international terrorist incidents reported in *Patterns of Global Terrorism* in "Not Free" countries—Iraq and Afghanistan. At least for that year, movement toward democracy did not lessen the incentives for terrorists to operate in those countries; indeed, Iraq witnessed a tremendous spike in terrorist incidents over the next four years even as real democratization accelerated. Unfortunately, neither Afghanistan nor Iraq has seen an end to terrorist attacks—quite the contrary—even as both have sustained their democratic development in the decade since U.S. military operations brought down the Taliban and Saddam Hussein.

The comparison between India, the world's most populous democracy, and China, the world's most populous authoritarian state, highlights the difficulty in assuming that democracy can solve the terrorism problem. The *Patterns of Global Terrorism* data for 2000–2003 report 203 international terrorist incidents in India and none in China. A more comprehensive list of terrorist incidents between 1976 and 2004 compiled by the Memorial Institute for the Prevention of Terrorism in its Global Terrorism Database contains over four hundred incidents in India and only eighteen in China.[13] If the relationship between authoritarianism and terrorism were as strong as the Bush administration implied, the discrepancy in terrorist incidents between China and India would run the other way.

More anecdotal evidence also calls into question a necessary relationship between regime type, particularly democracy, and terrorism. In the 1970s and 1980s, democratic countries generated some brutal terrorist organizations: the Red Brigades in Italy, the Provisional Irish Republican Army in Ireland and the United Kingdom, the Japanese Red Army, and the Red Army Faction (Baader-Meinhof Gang) in West Germany. The transition to democracy in Spain did not eliminate the terrorism perpetrated by the Basque Fatherland and Liberty (ETA). Turkish democracy suffered through a decade of mounting political violence from the late 1960s through the late 1970s. The strong and admirable democratic system in Israel has been the subject of terrorist assault, but it also has produced its own terrorists, including the assassin of Prime Minister Yitzhak Rabin. Norway, a model democracy, experienced a mass domestic terrorist shooting incident in 2011. And then there is the memorial in Oklahoma City testifying to the fact that U.S. democracy has not been free of domestic terrorism.

All in all, there is no solid empirical evidence of a strong link between democracy, or any other regime type, and terrorism, in either a positive or a negative direction. In the first edition of Bruce Hoffman's widely quoted survey of the phenomenon, *Inside Terrorism*, published in 1998, the word *democracy* does not even appear in the index.[14] Jessica Stern, in her highly praised post-9/11 study of religious militants, *Terror in the Name of God*, argues that "democratization is not necessarily the best way to fight Islamic extremism," because that transition to democracy "has been found to be an especially vulnerable period for states across the board."[15] Terrorism springs from sources other than form of government. There is, therefore, no reason, based on this evidence, to believe that a more democratic Arab world will, simply by virtue of being more democratic, generate fewer terrorists.

Terrorism and Democracy: Logic, Theory, and al-Qaeda

Logical and theoretical problems, as well as these empirical problems, surround the argument bolstering the American push for democracy as part of the struggle against terrorism. The logic underlying the assertion that democracy will reduce terrorism is the belief that, if able to participate openly in competitive politics and have their voices heard in the public square, potential terrorists and terrorist sympathizers will not feel the need to resort to violence to achieve their goals. Even if they lose in one round, the confidence that they will be able to win in the future will inhibit the temptation to use extra-democratic means. To put it another way, the habits of democracy will ameliorate extremism.

Well, maybe. But it is just as logical to assume that terrorists, who rarely represent political agendas that could mobilize electoral majorities, would reject the very principles of majority rule and minority rights on which liberal democracy is based. If they cannot achieve their goals through democratic politics, why should it be assumed that they will privilege the democratic process over those goals? It seems more likely that, having been mobilized into politics by a burning desire to achieve a goal, a desire so strong that they are willing to take up arms and kill and maim defenseless civilians, terrorists and potential terrorists will attack democracy and its processes if those processes do not produce the desired result. Respect for American democracy did not stop Southern slaveholders and their supporters from taking up arms in 1861. Respect for the nascent democracy in Iraq, despite very successful elections in January 2005, December 2005, and January 2010, has not stopped Iraqi and foreign terrorists from their campaign against the new political order in that country. If the goal is important enough, it will trump democracy for some militants, who, in turn, might become terrorists.

Another factor is that the primary terrorist organizations that threaten the United States and its allies are not mass-based; they are small and secretive. And they are not organized or based on democratic principles; they revolve around strong leaders and a cluster of committed followers, willing to take actions from which the vast majority of people, even people who might support their political agendas, would rightly shrink. It seems unlikely that simply being outvoted would deflect them from their path.

America's major foe in the struggle against terrorism, al-Qaeda, certainly would not close up shop if every Muslim country in the world were to become a democracy. Osama bin Laden was very clear about democracy—he did not like it. His political model was not democratic; it was the early years of the Muslim caliphate. The Taliban regime in Afghanistan was the closest in modern times to that model in bin Laden's view. In an October 2003 "message to Iraqis," bin Laden castigated those in the Arab world who are "calling for a peaceful democratic solution in dealing with apostate governments or with Jewish and crusader invaders instead of fighting in the name of God." He referred to democracy as "this deviant and misleading practice," and "the faith of the ignorant."[16] His view of American democracy is equally negative: "The majority of you [Americans] are vulgar and without sound ethics or good manners. You elect the evil from among you, the greatest liars and the least decent."[17] Bin Laden's ally in Iraq, the late Abu Musab al-Zarqawi, was even more direct in his reaction to the Iraqi election of January 2005: "The legislator who must be obeyed in a democracy is man, and not God. . . . That is the very essence of heresy and polytheism and error, as it contradicts the bases of the faith and monotheism, and because it makes the weak, ignorant man God's partner in His most central divine prerogative—namely, ruling and legislating."[18] Bin Laden's successor as head of al-Qaeda, Ayman al-Zawahiri, has continued his predecessor's approach toward democracy. While praising the revolts against Arab authoritarians in the Arab Spring, he called for governments based on Islamic law, not on democracy, to replace them.[19]

There is absolutely no reason to believe that a move toward more democratic Arab states will deflect al-Qaeda and its affiliates from their course. There is also no reason to believe that they will not be able to recruit followers in more demo cratic Arab states, as long as those more democratic Arab states continue to have good relations with the United States, make peace with Israel, and generally behave in ways that Washington hopes they will. It is the American agenda in the Middle East, as much as if not more than democracy itself, to which al-Qaeda objects. Even though Washington hopes that a democratic Middle East will be a Middle East that continues to accept a major American agenda, it is simply foolish to think that democracy will dry up support for al-Qaeda, as will be demonstrated in the next section.

When it works, liberal democracy is the best form of government. It affirms the dignity of each person in the right to vote. It provides the check of popular elections on those in power, along with other constitutional and legal barriers to the abuse of power. It provides for an independent judiciary to guarantee those rights and curb the abuses that inevitably come with great power. There is much to recommend it. But there is no evidence that it reduces terrorism or prevents terrorism. There is strong evidence, however, that the current opponents in the struggle against terrorism will not be placated by democracy in their home countries. Thus a fundamental assumption of the push for democracy in the Arab world as part of this struggle is seriously flawed.

ARAB DEMOCRACY: WHAT TO EXPECT

Would democratically elected Arab governments be as cooperative with the United States as the current authoritarian incumbents? That is highly unlikely. To the extent that public opinion can be measured in these countries, the polls reveal that Arabs are very supportive of democracy, a support manifested tangibly in the popular demonstrations of the Arab Spring. When they have a chance to vote in real elections, they generally turn out in percentages far greater than Americans. However, many elements of American policy remain distinctly unpopular in the Arab world. If Arab governments were to reflect more accurately their public opinion, they would be more anti-American, not less. Moreover, in recent free elections in the Arab world the Islamists have done very well. Moves toward Arab democracy will, at least for the foreseeable future, most likely generate Islamist governments that will be less likely to cooperate with the United States on important American policy goals, including American basing rights in the region, peace with Israel, and the campaign against terrorism. And above all there is no evidence that it will reduce terrorism within countries or the region.

Arab Public Opinion: Yes to Democracy, No to the United States

Arabs in general do not have any problem with democracy, though some Islamist ideologues do. In polling since the Arab Spring, between 80 and 90 percent of Arabs believe that democracy would be the best form of government for their countries, though they divide fairly evenly on whether Islam should play a major role in their democracy.[20] This is not a new phenomenon. The Pew Global Attitudes Project conducted public opinion surveys in several Arab countries in 2003, asking whether "democracy is a Western way of doing things that would not work here" or whether "democracy would work" in that country. In Kuwait, 83 percent said democracy would work there, and only 16 percent thought it would not. In Jordan, 68 percent said democracy would work there; 25 percent disagreed. In the Palestinian Authority, 53 percent thought democracy would work there, but 38 percent disagreed.[21] In a 2002 poll by Zogby International, majorities of those polled in five Arab states—Egypt, Kuwait, Lebanon, Saudi Arabia, and the United Arab Emirates (UAE)—had a favorable attitude toward American freedom and democracy, even while holding very unfavorable attitudes toward U.S. policy in the Arab world.[22]

These positive views toward democracy are borne out on the ground. Turnout in Arab states for real elections is regularly very high. Despite the boycott by most Sunni Arabs (roughly 20 percent of the population) and threats of violence, Iraqi turnout for the January 2005 parliamentary elections was 53 percent of registered voters. Turnout in the December 2005 Iraqi elections, with the Sunni boycott lifted, was much higher—nearly 80 percent of registered voters. Algerians turned out at a rate of 58 percent for their April 2004 presidential election. Official figures put Palestinian turnout for the January 2006 parliamentary election at 78 percent of registered voters. In 2003, 76 percent of eligible Yemeni voters cast their ballots in the legislative elections; 59 percent of Jordanian voters did the same in their 2003 parliamentary elections.[23] Turnout rates in the first post–Arab Spring elections were not as high as these previous elections, but were still impressive given the upheavals these societies recently experienced: about 50 percent of eligible voters participated in the Tunisian parliamentary elections of October 2011; 54 percent in the Egyptian parliamentary elections of December 2011–January

2012; 50 percent in the runoff round of the Egyptian presidential election in June 2012; and 61 percent in the Libyan parliamentary elections of July 2012.[24] In general Arabs are enthusiastic about voting and elections.

The problem for the United States in promoting democracy in the Arab world is not that Arabs do not like democracy; it is that Washington will probably not like the governments that Arab democracy would produce. If it is assumed that more democratic Arab governments will be more affected by public opinion than the incumbent Arab regimes, Arab democracy should produce more anti-American foreign policies. In the 2012 Pew Global Attitudes Project survey, none of the four Arab countries in which polling was done showed a favorable rating for the United States of over 50 percent. In Egypt, where the United States has provided billions of dollars in foreign aid and supported the political transition from the Mubarak dictatorship in 2011, only 19 percent of those polled had a favorable view of the United States. In Jordan, recipient of hundreds of millions of dollars of American aid, the figure was 12 percent. It was higher in Tunisia (45 percent), a country much less central to American Middle East interests, and Lebanon (48 percent), with its substantial Christian population.[25]

These numbers are not an artifact of the Arab Spring: unfavorable attitudes toward the United States in the Arab world long predate recent events. In a February–March 2003 poll conducted in six Arab countries by Zogby International and the Anwar Sadat Chair for Peace and Development at the University of Maryland, overwhelming majorities held either a very unfavorable or a somewhat unfavorable attitude toward the United States. The overall favorable rating of the United States in Egypt was 13 percent, in the United Arab Emirates 10 percent, in Morocco and Jordan 6 percent, and in Saudi Arabia 4 percent.[26] A March 2008 poll by Zogby International found America's unfavorability to be over 80 percent in Egypt, Saudi Arabia, and Jordan, and over 70 percent in Lebanon, Morocco, and the UAE.[27]

Although the available poll data do not allow analysts to pinpoint the precise sources of anti-American feeling in the Arab world, there are indications that it is American policy in the region, not rejection of American ideals, that drives Arab anti-Americanism. In the February–March 2003 poll by the Sadat Chair at the University of Maryland and Zogby International, those polled in every Arab country except the UAE said that their attitudes toward the United States are based more on American policy than on Americans' values. In Egypt, 46 percent identified American policy as the source of their feelings; 43 percent identified Americans' values. In the other countries polled—Saudi Arabia, Morocco, Lebanon, and Jordan—no fewer than 58 percent said their views on America were based on American policy.[28] No poll is needed to know that

American policy on Arab-Israeli questions is very unpopular in the Arab world. Arab governments more in tune with their public opinion, as democratic governments must be, will feel enormous pressure to distance themselves from the United States.

Arab Elections: The Recent Record

The Arab Spring, from an electoral standpoint, has proven (with an important exception) to be an Islamist Spring. The success of Islamist parties in Morocco, Tunisia, and Egypt in post–Arab Spring elections should not, however, be surprising. In real democratic elections in the Arab world before the Arab Spring, Islamists also did very well. This brief survey of Arab elections demonstrates the power of Islamist parties at the ballot box:

- In the Egyptian presidential election of 2012, Muslim Brotherhood candidate Mohamed Morsi was the leading vote-getter in the multicandidate first round, with almost 25 percent of the vote, and he won the runoff election against a former prime minister from the Mubarak era with 51 percent of the vote.[29] The Brotherhood's Freedom and Justice Party won 45 percent of the seats in the Egyptian parliamentary elections of December 2011–January 2012; the *salafi* Islamist coalition led by the Nour Party won another 25 percent of the seats.[30]

- In Tunisia's parliamentary elections of October 2011, the Ennahda Party, a moderate Islamist group similar to the Muslim Brotherhood, won 42 percent of the seats. Its closest competitor, the secular Congress for the Republic, won 14 percent.[31]

- In the Libyan parliamentary elections of July 2012, the Muslim Brotherhood did not do as well as in Egypt, winning only 17 of the 80 seats elected on a party list basis, while the more secular list headed by former Prime Minister Mahmoud Jibril (though he rejected the secular label) won 39 seats. However, 120 parliamentary seats were filled in district elections where candidates with Islamist sympathies did well.[32]

- Morocco's parliamentary election of October 2011 saw the moderate Islamist Justice and Development Party win 27 percent of the seats, nearly double its nearest competitor.[33] The party leader, Abdelilah Benkirane, was subsequently appointed prime minister by King Mohammed VI.

- After major successes for Islamist groups, both Shiite and Sunni, in the Iraqi parliamentary elections of December 2005, the Iraqi elections of 2010 saw something of a reversal at the ballot box. Two party lists that ran on less sectarian and more nationalist platforms, the State of Law list of Prime Minister Nouri al-Maliki and the Iraqiyya list of former Prime Minister Iyad Allawi, dominated the voting. Iraqiyya won 91 seats (of 325), and State of Law won 89. Despite their relative similarity in platforms, however, the two leaders refused to cooperate with each other. Al-Maliki, in order to retain the prime minister's office, turned to Shiite Islamist and Kurdish parties to form a majority, assisted by support from Iran for the narrower, more Islamist and sectarian coalition.[34]

• In the January 2006 Palestinian parliamentary elections, Hamas—the political wing of the Palestinian Muslim Brotherhood—won a stunning victory against the long-dominant Fatah, the Palestinian nationalist movement founded by Yasser Arafat. Hamas carried 56 percent of the seats against Fatah's 34 percent and 7 percent for liberal, leftist, and other nationalist parties.[35]

• In a number of free or semi-free elections in Egypt, Jordan, Yemen, Bahrain, and Kuwait in the 2000s, Islamist parties and groups established themselves as the major opposition formation against governing parties (Egypt, Yemen) or as substantial players in nonpartisan elections (Jordan, Bahrain, Kuwait).

The trend in Arab elections is absolutely clear. Islamists do very well in the first free elections after a change of regime. They do well in other elections, in more normal circumstances. They do not always win, as the Iraqi election of 2010 demonstrates, but they remain important forces on the political scene even when they do not win. Perhaps the Islamist wave in Arab electoral politics will be short-lived. Iraq's 2010 result shows that Arab voters can turn against Islamists if they do not deliver the goods once in power. Certainly the Persian Iranians seem to have soured on their Islamist government, though the Iranian example also shows that, once in power, Islamists (like other political trends) can use the prerogatives of office to consolidate their political control in non-democratic ways. But for the near future, we can expect Islamists to do very well in Arab elections.

CONCLUSION

It is hard to avoid the conclusion that an American push for democracy in the Arab world is unlikely to have much effect on its anti-American terrorism, but such a push could help bring to power governments that will be much less cooperative with the United States on a whole range of issues—including assistance in the struggle against terrorism, the Arab-Israeli peace process, and military-strategic issues. An American democracy initiative can be defended as an effort to spread American democratic values, whatever the cost, or as a long-term gamble that the realities of governance will either moderate Islamists or lead to public disaffection from them once they are in power, which may be happening in Iran. However, the emphasis on electoral democracy cannot be said to serve immediate American interests either in the campaign against terrorism or in other important policy areas in the region.

If Washington continues down the road of promoting democracy in the Arab world, at least it can take a lesson from the variety of electoral experiences briefly reviewed here. Where there are strongly rooted non-Islamist parties, such as in Morocco, Islamists have a harder time dominating the field. This is also true in non-Arab Turkey, where the Islamist political party has moderated its message over time to contend with the power of the secular army and with the well-established, more secular Turkish parties. Likewise, the confessional mix in Lebanon will prevent Hezbollah and other Islamists from dominating elections there. Conversely, where non-Islamist political forces have been suppressed, such as in Bahrain, Islamist parties and candidates can dominate the field.

It was not only the focus on elections that was troubling in the Bush administration's democracy initiative in the Arab world. Equally troubling was the unjustified confidence that Washington could predict, and even direct, the course of domestic politics in other countries. No one in the administration would sign on, at least in public, to the naïve view that Arab democracy would produce governments that would always cooperate with the United States. But there was precious little appreciation for the likelihood that democratic Arab governments would actively oppose American policy on important issues, including the Arab-Israeli conflict and the campaign against terrorism. That is why the Hamas victory in the 2006 Palestinian elections so shocked Washington. Likewise, the success of Islamist parties in the post–Arab Spring elections led to trepidation in the Obama administration, though it has been more accepting of those results than the Bush administration was of the Hamas victory in Palestine.

Those who advocate democracy seem to assume that Arab transitions will be like those in Eastern Europe, Latin America, and East Asia that produced governments friendly to the United States. However, in those areas the major ideological challenge to liberal democracy and market capitalism—Soviet-style communism—was thoroughly discredited. In the Arab world, there is a real ideological competitor to liberal politics: the movement that claims as its motto "Islam is the solution." The hubris that says America can direct the domestic politics of foreign countries should have been exploded in Iraq, where even the presence of 140,000 U.S. troops could not guarantee that politics would go the way the policymakers back home wanted. The lack of humility in the Bush administration's approach to the democracy initiative bespoke a lack of reality about the extent to which the United States can control the political future of societies about which it knows very little. The Obama administration, faced with the upheavals of the Arab Spring, has shown more humility about its ability to direct the politics of the Arab world but no less confusion about how to deal with Islamists in power.

YES: Promoting democracy can help combat terrorism. Jennifer L. Windsor, *Georgetown University*

Democratization in the Middle East: Revisiting the Democracy and Terrorism Debate

The last several years have witnessed dramatic political changes in the Middle East. The "Arab awakening," which began in December 2010, led to unprecedented—and unpredicted—civic mobilizations and demonstrations in countries including Tunisia, Egypt, Bahrain, Libya, and Yemen. Demonstrators demanded not only economic improvements but also democratic rights and freedoms. Several longtime authoritarian leaders were ousted or forced to step down, and many more face a future of uncertainty. In 2011 and 2012, elections considered to be the region's most open and credible in recent history were held in Morocco, Tunisia, Egypt, and Libya.

Washington has reverberated with vigorous discussions about America's role in and reaction to the momentous changes. Events in the region have been seen by some as vindication for President George W. Bush's much maligned policy of supporting democratization in the Middle East, with supporters of Bush's vision charging that President Barack Obama had not done nearly enough to support democracy in the region.[36] The Obama White House, by contrast, pointed out that many experts believed that under the Bush administration U.S. democracy efforts had been "contaminated" by its linkage to the U.S. war in Iraq and the "war on terror."[37] Because of the legacy of this "contamination," there was a need for President Obama to clearly distinguish his policy approaches from those of President Bush. Indeed, Obama's Cairo speech a few months after entering office was seen by many as an attempt to establish a new tone and approach to the Middle East, including on issues relating to political freedom.[38]

As an advocate of U.S. support for democracy, I believe there is much to praise and criticize in both administrations. President Bush's use of the presidential bully pulpit to speak out for the right of all people to enjoy fundamental freedoms was groundbreaking. The Bush administration's decision to no longer exclude the Middle East from U.S. democracy promotion efforts was the right one. On the other hand, the Bush White House hurt the cause of democracy by linking it to an unpopular war in Iraq and by engaging in many practices—in the name of fighting terrorism—that violated international human rights standards.[39] And while stating that the promotion of freedom would contribute to the war against terror, the Bush administration in practice turned a blind eye to the human rights violations of other countries that were perceived (and justified) as necessary to combat terrorism. The gap between rhetoric and action increased even more following the election win by Hamas in the Palestinian territories in 2006 and the strong electoral showing by Hezbollah in Lebanon in 2005; even former Bush officials admit that the administration's interest in pursuing democracy in the Middle East significantly waned following these disappointing election results.[40]

In 2009 Barack Obama entered office disinclined to continue many of the policies of President Bush, with the aim of restoring America's reputation around the world. Unfortunately, that translated into reluctance by the administration to identify democracy promotion as a U.S. foreign policy goal for much of its first two years in office. As a result, the Obama White House stumbled in its reactions to several major events in the Muslim world, such as its initial silence in the face of the Iranian popular uprisings in the summer of 2009, and its initial statements of strong support for Egyptian President Hosni Mubarak as mass protests began exploding in Egypt's Tahrir Square in January 2011.[41] The Obama administration also never went beyond relatively tepid support for human rights in Bahrain (home to the U.S. Fifth Fleet) and waived congressional requirements for progress toward democracy in Egypt before unilaterally releasing billions of dollars in U.S. military assistance to Cairo.

On the positive side of the ledger, the Obama administration's National Security Strategy, released in May 2010, did include democracy, although the wording was carefully chosen to be quite different from the sweeping rhetoric of the Bush administration.[42] And in the Middle East, the Obama administration eventually changed its policy toward Egypt, and explicitly and repeatedly called for President Mubarak to step down in the face of ongoing popular demonstrations. The administration also negotiated an exit for Yemen's authoritarian leader, Ali Abdullah Saleh, and supported North Atlantic Treaty Organization-led military efforts to remove Muammar al-Qaddafi in Libya (although it characterized the Libyan intervention not as "support for democracy" but to prevent the imminent slaughter of innocent civilians by the al-Qaddafi regime). In May 2011, President Obama declared that support for democracy in the Middle East "is not a secondary interest . . . it is a top priority that must be translated into concrete actions, and supported by all of the diplomatic, economic and strategic tools at our disposal."[43] And these assurances were met with action—the Obama administration maintained the same baseline spending on democracy assistance as the Bush administration, and indeed committed considerable new funds to support political transition processes in Tunisia, Egypt, and Libya. It also proposed a new $770 million incentive fund for the region beginning in 2013 to help encourage democratic progress.[44]

LURKING DANGERS OF THE ARAB SPRING?

Beyond the debates over whether the Obama administration has done enough to support democratization in the Middle East, scant attention has been paid to another line of criticism and caution: whether the United States, under any president, should be involved in providing support of any kind for democratic transitions in the region. Indeed the Arab awakenings have reenergized the so-called democracy skeptics, particularly realists in the Middle East studies scholarly community, who seem to always view the status quo, no matter how repressive, as better for American national interests. The continued instability and the rise of new political actors in the region are seen by a number of these experts as extremely problematic, if not outright dangerous, for U.S. policy goals. The success of Islamist candidates in elections in Morocco, Egypt, and Tunisia, for example, reinforced the beliefs of some that democratization would produce more supporters of Islamic extremism as well as governments that would be more anti–United States.[45] Others noted that al-Qaeda and other violent extremists have already capitalized on the instability and uncertainty in the region to make headway into new areas of recruiting.[46]

Others have disagreed. Daniel Byman, for example, noted that the Arab awakening may bring about lasting changes that would reduce the attractiveness of radical ideologies and terrorist movements that thrived under the previous repressive regimes.[47] The triumph of nonviolent "people power" and the popular demand for greater political freedom in the Middle East was a massive ideological defeat for al-Qaeda and its affiliates, who had claimed for decades that entrenched corrupt authoritarian regimes could only be removed by violence. Indeed, recent political changes seem to have only accelerated the declining popularity of and support for al-Qaeda and its violent methods in the Middle East, according to the Pew Global Attitudes Project.[48]

In short, the Arab awakening has awakened, once again, debates about the relationship between democracy and terrorism, and the compatibility of democratization with the fight against terrorism. Regardless of the preferences of the White House, events have compelled the United States to involve itself with the dramatic changes occurring in the Arab world. As such, understanding the relationship between two fundamental American goals—promoting democracy and fighting terrorism—has never been more important. The purpose of this essay is to reexamine the relationship between democracy and terrorism and to reassess the relationships between the two policy goals. Before doing so, it is important to briefly go back to basics and define the key terms. Surprisingly, even after decades of American support for democratization, there still seems to be a need to reiterate what democratization is, and to clarify what constitutes a "democracy" and what U.S. support for democracy abroad entails.

DEFINING DEMOCRATIZATION AND ITS PROMOTION

The process of democratization is aimed at increasing a government's accountability to the governed. Therefore, it is about regular elections and all that is necessary for an electoral process to be fair and meaningful, including but not limited to freedom of association, freedom of speech, genuine political choices for the people, and access to independent news media. Beginning with the 1948 Universal Declaration of Human Rights and reinforced by subsequent regional and global covenants and agreements, the international community has largely accepted that progress on all of these fronts must be part of becoming a democratic and rights-abiding society. The process of democratization is not just about elections, however. It also involves establishing a broader range of vital institutions that hold governments accountable after elections: an independent judiciary, a viable parliament, security forces that defer to the authority of elected civilian leaders, and protections against the diversion of public resources for private gain. In addition to these processes and institutions, democratization requires the majority of citizens to accept the overall rules of the "political game" and to embrace fundamental democratic principles such as the preservation of minority rights in the face of majority rule, tolerance of diversity (ethnic, religious, linguistic, political), and fair application of the law to all members of society.[49]

No country ever becomes perfectly democratic, but there has been substantial progress in the world over the last quarter-century. Governments have become more transparent, more accountable, more representative, and more respectful of individual freedoms and the rule of law. This tremendous growth in freedom has proven that no culture or society is impervious to citizens' yearnings for justice and the ability to exercise fundamental freedoms of expression, association, and belief. Over the years, almost every region in the world—including Asia, Africa, Latin America, and the Middle East, which are home to societies shaped by religious traditions including Catholicism, Confucianism, and Islam—have been considered inhospitable to democratic progress. Yet in each of these regions notable advances have been made—most recently in the Middle East and North Africa.[50]

The United States and other governments have traditionally used a variety of tools to encourage more respect for human rights and to support those who are committed to establishing or strengthening a democratic system, whether from inside or outside the existing power structure. Diplomatic pressure (through both private and public statements) can be applied to urge the adoption of laws and behavioral changes that result in greater respect for human rights and a more open political space. Incentives can come in the form of sticks (e.g., targeted sanctions against leaders, bans on military training or equipment) or carrots (e.g., the linkage of valuable U.S. foreign assistance to democratic performance). That said, the United States and other governments cannot "compel" any country to become democratic.

Democratization can also be supported through targeted democracy-support assistance programs. The U.S. government, private foundations, and other donors have funded such programs to assist democratic reformers within countries for more than thirty years. These programs involve training, citizen and academic exchanges, facilitation of the flow of information and expertise between democracy activists within and between societies, on-site advice and encouragement, visible demonstrations of solidarity, and emergency humanitarian and legal assistance for local activists and human rights defenders who face repression by their governments. The underlying premise of such assistance is that even though democracy can ultimately be brought about and maintained only by a country's own citizens, external support that is properly designed and applied can make a significant difference.[51]

Only rarely (and unsuccessfully) has democratization been supported through the use of force. As the 2003 Iraq War once again demonstrates, militaries can remove dictators, but they cannot build the institutions, processes, and values needed to sustain a democratic system of governance.

THE EVOLUTION OF U.S. COUNTERTERRORISM STRATEGY

In its 2006 National Security Strategy, the Bush administration described its counterterrorism strategy as a "battle of arms and a battle of ideas." The enemy in this "battle" was defined as terrorists of "global reach."[52] In countering the threat of transnational terrorism, the Bush administration primarily used U.S. military assets to eradicate terrorist enclaves; employed surveillance and law enforcement mechanisms to identify, kill, or capture suspected terrorists and their collaborators; and restructured the international financial system in order to monitor and choke off the flow of funding to terrorist groups.[53] But such "hard power" tactics were by no means the only methods identified and utilized by the Bush White House in fighting terrorism. In presidential speeches and in its National Security Strategies of both 2002 and 2006, the administration expansively laid out how the spread of democracy was a critical part of a long-term strategy to combat terrorism, arguing that functioning democratic systems can help to allay the sense of alienation and "festering grievances" that terrorist organizations may utilize to expand their membership and appeal.

It was this direct linkage by the Bush administration between its counterterrorism goals and democracy promotion that engendered such criticism from inside and outside the democracy community. While certainly wanting democracy promotion to be a U.S. foreign policy priority, the democracy community has traditionally wanted democracy support to become an instrument not to achieve other goals, but rather as an end in itself. By connecting democracy to the war on terror, the Bush administration was seen to have undermined U.S. democracy policies and programs, especially those carried out by nongovernmental organizations.[54] Others, outside the democracy community, contrarily criticized the Bush administration for believing that the spread of democracy would have any positive relationship to a decline in terrorism. A spate of scholarly analyses emerged that relied on statistical correlations and different data sets to criticize the Bush administration's approach.[55] Indeed the administration found itself caught in the crossfire between realists and Wilsonian progressives.

The Obama administration did its best to reframe, clarify, and narrow the goals of U.S. counterterrorism strategy, and more carefully articulate its linkage with democracy. In its 2011 National Strategy for Counterterrorism, the administration argued that the fight against terrorism is a fight not against "Islam" or "Islamic radicalism" or the "tactic of terrorism," but against "a specific organization"—al-Qaeda and its affiliates.[56] The strategy recognizes the importance of encouraging "representative, responsive governance" as a way to diminish popular discontent and "the associated drivers and grievances that al-Qaida actively attempts to exploit."

While being more cautious and precise in its language, the Obama administration actually continued much of what the Bush White House started in the values-driven areas of counterterrorism. Indeed, it did more than its predecessor to operationally connect and integrate its counterterrorism strategy with programs to support democracy and development. For example, in 2011 the administration requested that the U.S. Agency for International Development (USAID) produce a detailed policy paper on how its programs can contribute to reducing the drivers of violent extremism and terrorism.[57] Interestingly, the democracy and human rights community has not been as vocal in its distress about the linkages between the two strategies as it was under the Bush administration.

WHAT DEMOCRACY CAN AND CANNOT DO IN COUNTERING TERRORISM

Democracy is not a vaccine against terrorism. Democracy in India prevented neither the 2008 attacks in Mumbai nor the ongoing violence in Kashmir. Violent extremists have also emerged within democracies, including in alienated Muslim communities in Western Europe. Many individuals involved in transnational terrorist networks grew up or were even born in democracies (although one could plausibly assert that they felt excluded from the power structures of their societies). Of course, no matter what protections for human rights or mechanisms for political input are in place in democracies, there will always be men and women who are consumed with hatred and committed to killing innocents to prove a point. And yet, even though Timothy McVeigh, the perpetrator of the 1995 Oklahoma City bombing, and violent groups such as the Irish Republican Army and Basque Fatherland and Liberty (ETA) do emerge from or persist in democratic systems, their appearance is relatively rare because of the availability of numerous alternatives and often more successful means for addressing grievances and achieving political aims.

Functioning democracies provide an outlet for participating, channeling dissent, debating policies, and seeking peaceful resolution of grievances. They offer mechanisms for the regular exercise of citizen choice and changes of government. Within repressive systems, by contrast, individuals have no clear and effective recourse for their frustrations. Such governments cut off legitimate and peaceful forms of political dissent, with no allowance for public debate. The primary goal of an undemocratic regime is to maintain its monopoly on power at all costs. Civil society and peaceful political opposition are typically weakened by severe legal restrictions and coercive methods. Politics is driven underground. Although it is arguably effective in the short term, the use of brutal repression can also help to further radicalize individuals, swell the ranks of extremists, and marginalize or destroy the moderate elements within society. As USAID notes in its aforementioned report, "the harsher and more widespread the repression . . . the greater the push to embrace violent extremism."[58]

This has certainly been true in the broader Middle East, where transnational terrorist networks like al-Qaeda have profited from the combustible mix of lack of socioeconomic opportunities, political stagnation, and repression that is so prevalent throughout the region. Recruiters for extremist groups play effectively on the sense of humiliation, injustice, and powerlessness felt by those—especially the younger generation—who lack a voice and perceive that they have no ability to make their own future.[59] Repressive, unaccountable, and unresponsive systems create an enabling environment and can generate drivers for violent extremism.[60] And for generations, the Middle East has been the most repressive region in the world, and it remains so today, despite the recent stirrings and changes.[61]

Indeed it is within this deeper context—a volatile mixture of religious extremism and repression—that the recent processes of political uprising and democratization in the Middle East have been taking place. We know that the stakes are high. And we know that the moment is not without risks, as the "democracy skeptics" and others have been warning. Antidemocratic forces continue to hold many advantages over pro-democracy reformers in the current landscape. Generations of often-brutal repression in the Middle East forestalled the emergence of any effective organized democratic forces, especially in the political arena. Parties, if they existed at all, had little political space in which to operate and few opportunities to hone their skills or to translate their largely intellectual platforms into popular political messages. Islamist movements, however, were able to continue to function even under the most repressive conditions, and they have done a far better job of shepherding their message and organizations, frequently without the complications and compromises that come with full participation in the political process or government. This explains the runaway success of Islamist parties in the Tunisian and Egyptian elections in 2011 and 2012; secular parties have literally just begun to get their footing.

Despite using the language of democracy, and abiding new electoral processes, new political parties controlled by former Islamist opposition movements in Tunisia, Egypt, and elsewhere have certainly not yet demonstrated that they would be willing to accept and adhere to the rules of a democratic system over the long term. As evidenced by other parts of the world, nascent democracies are particularly vulnerable to elites that appeal to religious or ethnic differences to mobilize support and possibly thwart the democratic process itself.[62] There is no reason to believe the Middle East will be immune from these pressures.

But the moment is also one of tremendous promise. Not every revolution in the Middle East will instantly produce a functioning democracy—and some may never do so. But the political openings and increased popular participation offer a real pathway forward for the region, a pathway where differences may be settled at the ballot box and in parliaments rather than through calls to arms.

WILL DEMOCRACY HELP OR HARM EXTREMISM IN THE MIDDLE EAST?

So the big question is, what do the political openings in the Middle East mean not only for the quality of life of the citizens of the region, but also for the radical Islamist ideologies that underpin al-Qaeda's terror network and other extremist movements? Will elections simply bring Islamists to power, replacing one form of repression with another, and offering an ideological safe haven for radical groups? Or, will moderation prevail, and with it more stable and legitimate political institutions free from extremism? It is certainly too soon to tell whether the changes in the Middle East will have permanence. But it is not too soon to dispel some incorrect negative assumptions about elections in the Middle East—and offer a more hopeful assessment of what the future may hold.

Let's first state the obvious: genuinely free and fair elections in many societies in the world may produce leaders who prove problematic. In worst-case scenarios, leaders use democratic elections to gain power and then systematically attempt to dismantle the institutions that facilitated their ascent. Echoing Fareed Zakaria's admonitions about "illiberal democracies," Gause and others have argued that premature elections in the Middle East will just advance political gains by Islamist extremists who will be against U.S. interests. Elections, they argue, should be delayed until the rule of law and a liberal democratic culture are established and an organized, viable secular democratic alternative emerges in the region.[63]

The Arab awakening has clearly demonstrated that the United States has little control over when other countries choose to have elections. Elections will happen, regardless of whether we or others believe that a country or region is "ready" for them. And in terms of outcomes, Islamist political gains are not *caused* by elections. Elections are the occasion to measure the sentiments of society; they are not the cause of the unpopularity of current leaders or of the popularity of political groups within a society. The 2006 Palestinian elections are not to blame for the ascension of Hamas. The blame lies squarely on Fatah and the Palestinian Authority, which was widely seen as corrupt, unresponsive, and ineffective in addressing the real needs of the population. Likewise, the 2012 election of the Muslim Brotherhood's Mohamed Morsi as Egypt's president was as much about symbolically breaking from the past as it was about supporting the brotherhood's political agenda. Interestingly, despite bringing an Islamist to power, the holding of the most credible election in Egyptian history in itself was a disaster for al-Qaeda propagandists who promised for decades that it was only through violent jihad that Arab dictators could be toppled. And while Morsi's commitment to a genuine democratic transition in Egypt is uncertain at best, it is wrong to assume that the rise of Islamists to power will be accompanied by greater support for violent extremists and terrorists. As Byman argues, the "greater role for Islamists may be good news" for counterterrorism, given the "bad blood between the Brotherhood and al-Qaeda."[64]

None of this means, of course, that new leaders may not be suspicious of America if not outright anti-American. In general, democratization can encourage the emergence of executive and legislative leaders who are less pliable and more complex in their dealings with the United States and other Western states than a single autocrat who can, for example, approve a foreign military base with the stroke of a pen. On the other hand, the Islamist governments in Tunisia and Egypt do not seem to be reflexively anti–United States; they seem to be more pragmatically inclined, and have reached out to administration officials in the White House as well as to Western institutions like the International Monetary Fund.[65] The relationship between the United States and the new leaders of the Middle East will be determined partly by the actions of the current (and future) American governments, and our willingness to strategically engage with the new Islamist regimes.[66]

And for those who look wistfully back to supposedly better times in the past, maintaining the status quo in the Middle East was not only unsustainable; it was not necessarily beneficial to U.S. national interests. Authoritarian governments in the Middle East, including in Iran, Iraq, Syria, and Saudi Arabia, actively backed violent transnational movements to advance their own domestic interests and foreign policy goals in the region for decades. For example, long before the rise of al-Qaeda and the 9/11 attacks, the Egyptian and Saudi regimes regularly highlighted their opposition to Islamist extremism in order to maintain American support while simultaneously coddling Islamist groups. And a treasure trove of documents captured in Iraq after 2003 illustrated the great extent to which Saddam Hussein went in examining whether enhanced relations with extremist groups could serve Iraqi interests.

We must caution, however, that despite progress, no Arab country in the greater Middle East is yet a democracy. To date, only Tunisia has met the minimum requirements to be called an electoral democracy. Elections alone, as has been repeatedly affirmed, do not constitute democratization. Democratization requires strengthening the institutions—legislatures and independent judicial systems—that counter excessive executive powers. And it requires more freedom of expression and association—that is, a freer environment in which a society can generate alternatives to oppressive governments and aspiring authoritarians. And it requires a strengthened civil society, with members of that society playing key roles in civic education, raising awareness of human rights, and helping to cultivate more tolerant political attitudes.

And, of course, it also requires elections: it will be through regularly held free and fair elections—the defining mechanism by which citizens of a democracy choose their governments and hold them accountable—that lasting positive change may emerge in the region. Secular political parties cannot strengthen their organizational base and improve their appeal among the population without regular opportunities to do so.

The biggest dangers in the wake of the Arab awakening would arise from a stalling or hijacking of the nascent processes of political reform, by Islamists or other antidemocratic forces. The false starts of political openings that waxed and waned in the Middle East prior to the Arab Spring actually increased violent extremism in many countries in the region, as the relative moderates within Islamist movements were edged out by radicals who argued that they had no real shot at influencing the political system by peaceful means.[67] Should democratization fail in these countries, al-Qaeda may very well find a new lease on life.[68]

A WAY FORWARD

Recognizing that the world is currently living through a historic era of change in the Middle East that contains both peril and promise, where do we go from here? At a minimum the United States, while learning from the mistakes of the past, must reawaken its call for the advancement of democracy and human rights as a core part of its grand strategy. But Washington and other concerned actors need to move forward with equal parts caution, candor, and creativity.

Caution, in that there certainly are radical Islamist movements and other violent groups that will seek to take full advantage of the chaos and uncertainty that has arisen in parts of the Arab world. Candor, in that the Arab openings will not be an easy process, and that there will be setbacks along the way. This could include attempted Islamist power grabs, military pushback, crackdowns on pro-democracy nongovernmental organizations, and the development of weak political institutions that may invite a return of authoritarianism.

And finally, creativity. The United States and other advanced democracies need to develop innovative diplomatic approaches as well as robust assistance programs directed toward the Arab world in light of the new circumstances. Washington needs to convince new leaders (and their citizens) that we support their right to determine their own destinies, and to convey in a coherent and convincing fashion that the United States is on the right side of history in supporting democratic change. We must do this while also relentlessly highlighting al-Qaeda's opposition to democracy and its unwillingness to recognize the power of peaceful change.

Assistance programs can prove invaluable in providing incentives and rewarding positive steps toward democracy. The proposed Middle East and North Africa Incentive Fund mentioned earlier would be a step in the right direction. The Incentive Fund draws on some of the best practices of the U.S. response to the post–Cold War changes in Central and Eastern Europe—providing targeted assistance, setting up enterprise funds, and other elements to encourage and support democratic transitions. The United States needs to increase its support for traditional and new media and other communication, encouraging the flow of accurate information to counter the misinformation and propaganda supported by violent extremists. Assistance to new governments must not be provided at the expense of independent civic groups, however, as successful democratic transitions require an effective government but also one that is held accountable. Civic groups need to be truly independent, and Washington should use its diplomatic and other forms of leverage to convince governments like the one in Egypt that they cannot control which groups are able to receive outside assistance.

Most importantly, moving forward it will be vital to keep an eye on the big picture: it may take decades to establish functioning democratic systems in the Middle East. We should be prepared for the instability, back steps, and political jockeying that will be a part of the transition process. It is in America's direct interest that out of these struggles better political systems are born.[69] The more the United States and the West come to be seen as honest brokers in assisting the Arab world's development of fair, legitimate, and stable political institutions, the better the chances for mutually beneficial relations in the future.

In November 2012, Americans went to the polls and reelected a president. Despite an unusually bitter campaign, the public—including President Obama's opponent, Mitt Romney—accepted the results. American democracy may have its flaws, but we do have the right to elect our own leaders, and those leaders are given the chance to govern. At this critical juncture in Middle East history, the United States has a unique opportunity to reaffirm that everyone should have the right to freely elect *their* own leaders. The U.S. government should do all that it can to support the advance of democracy around the world. After all, it is the right of all individuals, no matter where they live, to live in freedom.

Notes

1. Elisabeth Bumiller, "Behind Rice's Shift on Leading Mideast Peace Efforts," *New York Times,* November 26, 2007.

2. The White House, "National Strategy for Combating Terrorism," September 2006, 1, http://georgewbush-whitehouse.archives.gov/nsc/nsct/2006. Also see the 2002 and 2006 versions of the "National Security Strategy of the United States of America" at http://georgewbush-whitehouse.archives.gov/nsc/nss/2002/index.html and http://georgewbush-whitehouse.archives.gov/nsc/nss/2006.

3. This essay is a revised and updated version of F. Gregory Gause III, "Can Democracy Stop Terrorism?" *Foreign Affairs* 84 (September/October 2005): 62–76.

4. President George W. Bush, remarks at National Defense University, March 8, 2005, www.presidentialrhetoric.com/speeches/03.08.05.html.

5. Candidate Kerry said, "We must support the development of free and democratic societies in the Arab and Muslim worlds to win the war of ideas. . . . In a Kerry Administration, America will be clear with repressive governments in the region that we expect to see them change, not just for our sake but for their own survival," www.4president.us/websites/2004/issues/kerry2004/kerryedwards2004nationalsecurity.htm.

6. For example: "Because if it is impossible for the peoples of even one Arab state to voluntarily organize themselves around a social contract for democratic life, then we are looking at dictators and kings ruling this region as far as the eye can see. And that will guarantee that this region will be a cauldron of oil-financed pathologies and terrorism for the rest of our lives." Thomas Friedman, "The Country We've Got," *New York Times,* January 6, 2005.

7. Martin Indyk, "Back to the Bazaar," *Foreign Affairs* 81 (January/February 2002): 75–88. Morton H. Halperin, Joseph T. Siegle, and Michael M. Weinstein, *The Democracy Advantage: How Democracies Promote Prosperity and Peace* (New York: Routledge for the Council on Foreign Relations, 2004), chap. 5. Halperin says, "In short, even as new security threats emerge in the twenty-first century, one thing remains constant: authoritarian governments are at the source" (121).

8. President Obama has not explicitly linked democracy and reduction in terrorism in the same way that President Bush did, but he has frequently emphasized American support for democratic change in the Middle East, both before and after the Arab Spring. See, for example, Obama's speech in Cairo in June 2009, where he disavowed any intention to impose democracy on the Middle East, but immediately added "that does not lessen my commitment, however, to governments that reflect the will of the people," www.whitehouse.gov/the-press-office/remarks-president-cairo-university-6-04-09. In May 2011, as the Arab Spring gained momentum, Obama made this commitment more explicit, saying that "it will be the policy of the United States to promote reform across the region, and to support transitions to democracy," www.whitehouse.gov/the-press-office/2011/05/19/remarks-president-middle-east-and-north-africa.

9. William Eubank and Leonard Weinberg, "Terrorism and Democracy: Perpetrators and Victims," *Terrorism and Political Violence* 131 (Spring 2001).

10. Quan Li, "Does Democracy Promote or Reduce Transnational Terrorist Incidents?" *Journal of Conflict Resolution* 49 (April 2005).

11. Robert Pape, *Dying to Win: The Strategic Logic of Suicide Terrorism* (New York: Random House, 2005). Pape's findings are summarized in Robert Pape, "Blowing Up an Assumption," *New York Times,* May 18, 2005.

12. Calculations from U.S. Department of State, *Patterns of Global Terrorism,* 2000–2003, www.state.gov/j/ct/rls/crt/; and Freedom House, *Freedom in the World* (Washington,

D.C.: Freedom House, 1999–2000, 2000–2001, 2001–2002, 2003), www.freedom house.org. I excluded from this count terrorist incidents that occurred in Israel, because they were overwhelmingly perpetrated by Palestinians, not Israelis (or Israeli Arabs), and would have skewed the count of incidents in democratic countries. I also excluded the September 11, 2001, attacks on the United States from the count, because they were not perpetrated by Americans.

13. The Memorial Institute for the Prevention of Terrorism was established by Congress after the Oklahoma City bombing of 1995. The Global Terrorism Database can be found at www.start.umd.edu/gtd/.

14. Bruce Hoffman, *Inside Terrorism* (New York: Columbia University Press, 1998).

15. Jessica Stern, *Terror in the Name of God: Why Religious Militants Kill* (New York: HarperCollins, 2003), 287–288.

16. Message broadcast on Al Jazeera television, October 19, 2003.

17. From a message broadcast on Al Jazeera television on October 18, 2003.

18. Middle East Media and Research Institute, Special Dispatch Series, No. 856, February 1, 2005.

19. "9/11 Anniversary: Al-Qaeda Video Marks Attack Date," BBC News, September 13, 2011, www.bbc.co.uk/news/world-us-canada-14895727.

20. Mark Tessler, "Popular Views about Islam and Politics in the Arab World," *II Journal*, University of Michigan, Fall 2011, www.lsa.umich.edu/UMICH/ii/Home/II%20Journal/Documents/2011fall_iijournal_article1.pdf. Tessler directs the Arab Barometer polling project (www.arabbarometer.org).

21. Pew Global Attitudes Project, "Iraq Vote Mirrors Desire for Democracy in Muslim World," February 3, 2005, www.pewglobal.org/2005/02/03/iraqi-vote-mirrors-desire-for-democracy-in-muslim-world.

22. James J. Zogby, "What Arabs Think: Values, Beliefs and Concerns," Zogby International and the Arab Thought Forum, September 2002, 63–64.

23. International Foundation for Electoral Systems (IFES), "Election Guide" Web site, various country pages, www.electionguide.org.

24. On turnout rates, see Wafa Ben Hassine, "Improving Voter Participation: Difficulties and Opportunities," *tunisialive*, March 22, 2012, www.tunisia-live.net/2012/03/22/improving-voter-participation-difficulties-and-opportunities; "Muslim Brotherhood Tops Egyptian Poll Result," *Al Jazeera*, January 22, 2102, www.aljazeera.com/news/middleeast/2012/01/2012121125958580264.html; "Al-Masry Al-Youm's Count: Morsy Wins Presidency with 51.13 Percent of Poll," June 18, 2012, www.jadaliyya.com/pages/index/6064/al-masry-al-youms-count_morsy-wins-presidency-with; and "Election: 1.7 Million Libyans Voted," *Libya Herald*, July 8, 2012, www.libyaherald.com/?p=10788.

25. www.pewglobal.org/database/?indicator=1&survey=14&response=Favorable&mode=chart.

26. "Arab Public Opinion Survey" public opinion poll conducted by Shibley Telhami, Anwar Sadat Chair for Peace and Development, University of Maryland, in cooperation with Zogby International, February 19–March 11, 2003.

27. See James Zogby, "Arab Opinion of the U.S. Declined in 2008," March 2008, www.arabamericannews.com/news/index.php?mod=article&cat=Opinions&article=1048.

28. "Arab Public Opinion Survey."

29. "Al-Masry Al-Youm's Count: Morsy Wins Presidency with 51.13 Percent of Poll," June 18, 2012, www.jadaliyya.com/pages/index/6064/al-masry-al-youms-count_morsy-wins-presidency-with.

30. Carnegie Endowment for International Peace, "Guide to Egypt's Transition," http://egyptelections.carnegieendowment.org/2012/01/25/results-of-egypt%E2%80%99s-people%E2%80%99s-assembly-elections.

31. "Tunisia Election Results Tables," October 24, 2011, www.tunisia-live.net/2011/10/24/tunisian-election-results-tables.

32. "Libya Election Success for Secularist Jibril's Bloc," BBC News, July 18, 2012, www.bbc.co.uk/news/world-africa-18880908.

33. Souad Mekhennet and Maia de la Baume, "Moderate Islamist Party to Lead Coalition Government in Morocco," New York Times, November 27, 2011.

34. For a comprehensive account of Iraqi politics since the 2010 election, see International Crisis Group, "Déjà vu All Over Again? Iraq's Escalating Political Crisis," Middle East Report No. 126, July 30, 2012.

35. "Palestinian Elections," Congressional Research Service, February 9, 2006, p. CRS-10, www.fas.org/sgp/crs/mideast/RL33269.pdf.

36. See, for example, Judy Keen, "Rice Reflects on Bush Tenure," USA Today, October 30, 2011; Walter Russell Meade, "W Gets a Third Term in the Middle East," Via Meadia Blog, August 22, 2011, http://blogs.the-american-interest.com/wrm/2011/08/22/w-gets-a-third-term-in-the-middle-east. Jackson Diehl of the Washington Post asserts that prior to the Arab Spring "Democracy in the Arab world . . . was largely written off by Obama's team as a fantasy of George W. Bush." See "South Sudan Shows What Obama Can Do When He Leads," Washington Post, July 3, 2011.

37. See Thomas Carothers, "Democracy Promotion under Obama: Finding a Way Forward," Policy Brief No. 77, Carnegie Endowment for International Peace, Washington, D.C., 2009; and Larry Diamond, "Supporting Democracy: Refashioning U.S. Global Strategy," in Democracy in U.S. Security Strategy: From Promotion to Support, ed. Alexander Lennon (Washington, D.C.: Center for Strategic and International Studies, 2009), 24.

38. President Obama, "A New Beginning," June 2009, www.whitehouse.gov/video/President-Obama-Speaks-to-the-Muslim-World-from-Cairo-Egypt#transcript. While the president did not mention democracy explicitly, he did indicate that the U.S. supported "governments that reflect the will of the people."

39. See Jennifer Windsor, "Advancing the Freedom Agenda: Time for a Recalibration?" Washington Quarterly 29 (Summer 2006): 21–34; and Thomas Carothers, "The Backlash against Democracy Promotion," Foreign Affairs 85 (March/April 2006): 55–68.

40. See remarks of Elliott Abrams at the Foreign Policy Institute's discussion of "Democracy Promotion: The Bush Doctrine in the Age of Obama," September 9, 2009, http://foreignpolicyi.org/advancing-and-defending-democracy/democracy-promotion-the-bush-doctrine-in-the-age-of-obama.

41. Thomas Carothers, "Democracy Promotion under Obama: Revitalization or Retreat?" (Washington, D.C.: Carnegie Endowment for International Affairs, January 2012), http://carnegieendowment.org/2012/01/11/democracy-policy-under-obama-revitalization-or-retreat.

42. See White House, "U.S. National Security Strategy 2010," www.whitehouse.gov/sites/default/files/rss_viewer/national_security_strategy.pdf.

43. See President Obama, "Remarks on the Middle East," May 19, 2011, www.white house.gov/the-press-office/2011/05/19/remarks-president-middle-east-and-north-africa. Secretary of State Hillary Clinton made an even more comprehensive speech on the importance of democracy in November 2011. See "Keynote Address at the National Democratic Institute's 2011 Democracy Awards Dinner," www.state.gov/secretary/rm/2011/11/176750.htm.

44. For an analysis of the Obama administration's allocation of aid for democracy in the Middle East, see Project on Middle East Democracy, "The Federal Budget and Appropriations for Fiscal Year 2013: Democracy, Governance, and Human Rights in the Middle East & North Africa," July 2012, http://pomed.org/wordpress/wp-content/uploads/2012/07/FY2013-Budget-Report-web.pdf.

45. See, for example, Greg Gause's essay in this volume; Bret Stephens, "Who Lost Egypt?" *Wall Street Journal,* June 25, 2012; and David Schenker, "Egypt's Islamist Future," *Los Angeles Times,* July 4, 2012.

46. See, for example, Bruce Reidel, "Al-Qaeda's Arab Comeback: Capitalizing on Chaos in Syria, Mali," *The Daily Beast,* July 30, 2012.

47. See Daniel Byman, "Terrorism after the Revolutions: How Secular Uprisings Could Help (or Hurt) the Jihadists," *Foreign Affairs* (May/June 2011): 48–54. Also see Omar Ashour, "From 9/11 to the Arab Spring" (Washington, D.C.: Brookings Institution, 2011).

48. "Most Muslims Want Democracy, Personal Freedoms and Islam in Political Life," Pew Global Attitudes Poll, July 2012, www.pewglobal.org/2012/07/10/most-muslims-want-democracy-personal-freedoms-and-islam-in-political-life.

49. Freedom House has a long-standing, well-established methodology for measuring freedom that includes a broad array of measures of political rights and civil liberties. A country cannot make it into the "Free" category only by holding elections that are considered free and fair. It must also meet clear standards related to accountable governance and respect for fundamental rights, including freedoms of expression, association, and religious belief, and show a commitment to the rule of law. See the methodology at www.freedomhouse.org.

50. For the latest findings see, *Freedom in the World 2012,* www.freedomhouse.org/report/freedom-world/freedom-world-2012. While advances in Tunisia led the country to be moved to the ranks of electoral democracies, and to the "Partly Free" status, it remains as the only Arab electoral democracy in the region. (Neither Iraq nor Morocco is considered to be an electoral democracy, despite holding elections.)

51. The U.S. Agency for International Development recently spent millions of dollars trying to prove that U.S. aid has an impact on democratization; see http://transition.usaid.gov/our_work/democracy_and_governance/publications/pdfs/SORA_pitt_vandy4pager_FINAL.pdf.

52. White House, "National Security Strategy of the United States of America 2006," http://georgewbush-whitehouse.archives.gov/nsc/nss/2006. Also see the original 2002 document at http://georgewbush-whitehouse.archives.gov/nsc/nss/2002.

53. White House, "National Strategy for Combating Terrorism" (September 2006), http://georgewbush-whitehouse.archives.gov/nsc/nsct/2006.

54. See Thomas Carothers, "U.S. Democracy Promotion during and after Bush" (Washington, D.C.: Carnegie Endowment for International Peace, 2007).
55. See Greg Gause's essay in this volume for a summary of some of these studies. For an interesting critique of Gause's argument see Shaded Hamid and Steven Brooke, "Promoting Democracy to Stop Terror, Revisited," *Policy Review* 159 (February 1, 2010), www.hoover.org/print/publications/policy-review/article/5285.
56. See White House, National Strategy for Counterterrorism (June 2011), www.white house.gov/sites/default/files/counterterrorism_strategy.pdf.
57. USAID, "The Development Response to Violent Extremism and Counter-Insurgency Policy," September 2011, http://transition.usaid.gov/our_work/policy_ planning_and_learning/documents/VEI_Policy_Final.pdf.
58. Ibid.
59. Jessica Stern, *Terror in the Name of God* (New York: HarperCollins, 2003).
60. For more in-depth treatment of this point, see Karin von Hippel's essay in Chapter 2 of this volume. In addition, see USAID, "Guide to the Drivers of Violent Extremism," February 2009.
61. Of the eighteen countries in the Middle East and North Africa, Freedom House rates ten as "Not Free," which means they have severely limited rights and political per-secution. In 2012, Tunisia moved into the "Partly Free" category, and was the first Arab country to be included in the list of electoral democracies. (While elections have been held in Jordan, Morocco, Iraq, and elsewhere, they are not seen as meet-ing even the minimum standards as electoral democracies.)
62. See, for example, Jack Snyder, *From Voting to Violence: Democratization and Nationalist Conflict* (New York: Norton, 2000).
63. See Fareed Zakaria, *The Future of Freedom: Illiberal Democracy at Home and Abroad* (New York: Norton, 2004); and Nathan Sharansky, "The Price of Ignoring Palestinian Needs," *International Herald Tribune*, February 1, 2006. For an incisive critique of the "sequencing" argument and a defense of the reasonable amount of funding that the U.S. government has actually put toward elections, see Thomas Carothers, "The Sequencing Fallacy," *Journal of Democracy* 19 (January 2007): 12–27.
64. See Byman, "Terrorism After the Revolutions"; and Daniel Byman, "Can Al Qaeda Capitalize on Unrest in Egypt and Syria?" (Washington, D.C.: Brookings Institution, December 1, 2011).
65. Kareem Fahim, "Egypt Requests $4.8 Billion from I.M.F.," *New York Times*, August 22, 2012.
66. See Shadi Hamid, "Prioritizing Democracy: How the Next President Should Re-orient U.S. Policy in the Middle East" (Washington, D.C.: Brookings Institution, 2012), www.brookings.edu/research/papers/2012/06/20-middle-east-hamid.
67. Dalia Dassa Kaye et al., "More Freedom, Less Terror? Liberalization and Political Violence in the Arab World" (Santa Monica, Calif.: RAND Corporation, 2008), www.rand.org/pubs/monographs/MG772.
68. On this point, see Byman, "Can Al Qaeda Capitalize on Unrest in Egypt and Syria?"
69. Reuel Marc Gerecht, "The Islamist Road to Democracy," *Wall Street Journal*, April 22, 2012; James Kitfield, "Rise of the Islamists," *National Journal*, June 14, 2012.

can international organizations make a difference in fighting terrorism?

NO: International organizations are limited in their ability to combat terrorism.
Zachary C. Shirkey, *Hunter College, City University of New York*

YES: International organizations are necessary for fighting international terrorism.
Bruce Cronin, *City College of New York*

On December 15, 1999, the United Nations Security Council adopted a unanimous resolution demanding that Afghanistan's Taliban government close all terrorist training camps, stop providing sanctuary for international terrorists, and arrest and extradite Osama bin Laden and other indicted al-Qaeda members to countries where they could be brought to justice.[1] This resolution was followed on December 19, 2000, by an even more strongly worded condemnation and threats of new international sanctions against the Afghan government for noncompliance with the first resolution.[2]

Less than nine months later, on September 11, 2001, Afghanistan served as the springboard for the most destructive terrorist attack in history.

As this example illustrates, the ability of global organizations—including the world's premier multilateral institution, the United Nations—to directly combat terrorism has shortcomings. If the UN could not act effectively against a known international terrorist group that for years was openly plotting and planning from within a member state, could it ever do so? And if the UN cannot directly confront terrorism, what hope is there for other global organizations with a stake in fighting terrorism, such as the International Criminal Court and the World Bank?

This assessment, however, may not be entirely fair. After all, the UN and other international organizations (IOs) were created not to replace states as the primary actors in world politics, but rather to help facilitate interstate cooperation and compliance with international obligations and best practices. So shortcomings in the ability of IOs to directly address global security threats such as terrorism are built into the system.

Acknowledging structural limitations in the ability of the UN and other IOs to lead counterterrorism efforts should certainly temper expectations about IO-based solutions. But it is also true that some IOs have undermined their own ability to play a credible role. For example, despite decades of trying, the UN has yet to agree on a common definition of *terrorism*. States can, then, pick and choose which terrorist groups or state sponsors they will act against and which they will not. And the UN's track record of objectivity in dealing with terrorism is spotty at best: in 1974 the UN granted the Palestine Liberation Organization "observer status" in the General Assembly, despite the assertions by Israel and other member states that the group was a terrorist organization.

After the 9/11 attacks, the UN and other IOs found themselves in a novel position in relation to terrorism. The advent of globalized terrorism in the form of al-Qaeda—a group with footholds and financiers in dozens of countries and that targets dozens more—called out for action by the world's leading political, security, and financial organizations.

Indeed, since the events of 9/11 the UN, for example, has strived to become a more effective player in combating terrorism. It has passed several aggressive Security Council resolutions, such as Resolution 1373 (September 28, 2001) that requires member states to adopt strict regulations against terrorism and enhance their own counterterrorism readiness. It also has created new bodies, such as the Counter-Terrorism Committee, to monitor and assist counterterrorism efforts by member states. And in 2006 the General Assembly adopted its first Global Counter-Terrorism Strategy, which pulls together all preexisting UN counterterrorism resolutions and treaties into one approved framework.

Other IOs such as the World Bank, the International Monetary Fund, and the International Criminal Police Organization (Interpol) have also since 9/11 postured themselves far more aggressively to combat the terror threats faced by their member states.

So does this mean that IOs have become key players in the global fight against terrorism?

Not according to Zachary Shirkey, who argues that, despite laudable efforts, the UN and other IOs remain hamstrung by their inherent shortcomings: failure to create a commonly acceptable definition of terrorism and corresponding legal frameworks that states will take seriously; failure to punish noncompliance with IO mandates on priorities such as sanctioning terrorist groups and their financiers; and failure to solve collective action problems on key issues related to terrorism such as intelligence gathering and sharing. Shirkey recognizes that terrorism can be countered successfully only through coordinated global action. And he believes that IOs play an important role in international politics. But he says that when it comes to terrorism—an acute security challenge often involving parochial passions—states will inevitably need to take the lead.

Bruce Cronin does not disagree that individual states are responsible for their own security, and that they will take the lead in counterterrorism. But he differs sharply with Shirkey over the importance of IOs in assisting these efforts. Indeed Cronin argues that modern international terrorism poses a special challenge to the system of state sovereignty, and that only IOs can coordinate action against this systemic challenge. This, he says, is in the direct national interest of individual states: international and regional security organizations like the UN and the Organization for Security and Co-operation in Europe (OSCE) are functionally superior to either unilateral action or ad hoc alliances in providing security from terrorism. It is only through the collective power and legitimacy of global organizations, asserts Cronin, that the global challenge of terrorism may be adequately addressed.

The UN and other international organizations are valuable global players that help the world deal with a plethora of challenges in the twenty-first century. If they are to play effective roles in combating terrorism, their member states need to both balance their expectations and boost areas where IOs can best contribute. The authors in this chapter offer a road map in this direction.

International organizations are limited in their ability to combat terrorism.

NO:

Zachary C. Shirkey, *Hunter College,*
City University of New York

Why IOs Are Ill Suited to Help Defeat Terrorism

T errorism, especially global terrorist movements like al-Qaeda, can be successfully confronted only through international cooperation. States must
work together on collecting intelligence, capturing and extraditing terrorists,
tracking and stanching the flow of terrorist funding, and even military actions
designed to curb terrorism. Without such cooperation, counterterrorism
efforts will be much more difficult, take longer to work, and be far less effective. For example, without cooperation states may fail to learn of impending
attacks as terrorists plot against them from foreign lands, or they may watch as
terrorist suspects remain free because of lack of extradition agreements or
sharing of evidence. And without cooperation, terrorist financial networks
would remain fluid and robust as groups simply play off different states with
varying and uncoordinated degrees of financial oversight and enforcement.

Because sustained bilateral and multilateral cooperation is needed to avoid
such undesirable scenarios, it seems logical that states would turn to international organizations (IOs) to overcome the free riding and coordination problems inherent in such multilateral efforts.[3] Although claims about the benefits of
institutions are not unchallenged,[4] institutions such as the United Nations (UN),
World Bank, International Monetary Fund (IMF), World Health Organization,
and European Union (EU) have been used widely in attempts to overcome the
problems that generally bedevil international cooperation. It follows, then, that
states also should turn to such organizations to help coordinate counterterrorism
efforts and that IOs may well be essential to winning the war on terrorism.

Surprisingly, such a conclusion is wrong. The reason, in part, is that broad-
based cooperation in security matters is difficult to achieve. Narrower security
cooperation through alliances such as the North Atlantic Treaty Organization
(NATO) is common, but broad-based cooperation is much rarer. Even in such
narrower settings, counterterrorism cooperation has been beset by free riding
problems and diverging interests as is seen by the limited role NATO members
outside of the United States, Canada, and the United Kingdom have played in

the NATO mission in Afghanistan.[5] Additionally, though al-Qaeda assets in Afghanistan have been significantly damaged and Osama bin Laden has been killed, the mission has not succeeded in stabilizing Afghanistan or eliminating al-Qaeda's Taliban ally. Given that NATO is arguably the world's most unified, coordinated, and powerful multilateral security organization, how can there be much optimism that the average action by an international institution will not be bedeviled by far greater conflicts of interest, lack of proper planning, and lack of deployable assets?

This is not to claim that organizations that seek broad-based cooperation are failed or useless. Yes, such organizations have their share of flaws and would benefit from reform, but they have helped the international community cope with issues as diverse as economic crises, interstate and civil wars, refugee flows, and human rights violations. It would be difficult to argue that greater cooperation or better results would have been achieved had these problems been tackled by states alone. Why then are these institutions poorly equipped to bring about cooperation for the specific purpose of combating terrorism?

To answer this question, it is necessary to think about what IOs could conceivably do to fight terrorism. First, they could enhance law enforcement efforts by providing a common legal framework, aid in the apprehension of terrorists worldwide, and prosecute suspected terrorists. Second, they could lead international cooperative efforts to stanch the flow of terrorist financing. Third, they could overcome free riding by coordinating interstate cooperation in intelligence gathering and synthesis and by synchronizing states' individual tactical responses to terrorism. In practice, though, each of these three approaches has serious flaws. First, the legal approach is problematic due to a lack of shared definitions, legal authority, and institutional capacity. Second, IOs have had limited success stanching financial flows to terrorists because their member states often lack the capacity or will to carry out the proposed measures. Third, IOs would likely be incapable of facilitating counterterrorism cooperation because, despite the widely shared interest in fighting the phenomenon of terrorism, states often do not share an interest in fighting specific terrorist groups. This essay will delve into these three areas of possible efforts by IOs in fighting terrorism and discuss in detail each of their shortcomings.

WHY INTERNATIONAL ORGANIZATIONS CANNOT ENHANCE LEGAL EFFORTS

Couldn't IOs help by coordinating the international legal efforts against terrorism? After all, the UN is capable of creating binding international law, and its court, the International Court of Justice (ICJ), is the most prestigious body in the realm of international jurisprudence. Additionally, the International Criminal Court (ICC) is designed to try and punish individuals who commit crimes against humanity. Furthermore, international police organizations like Interpol can foster coordination among police forces internationally, an ability that seemingly could be used to counter terrorist groups more effectively. And yet, despite these apparent capacities, international institutions are ill suited to aid the legal battle against terrorism because successful legal action requires at least three things: reasonably clear definitions of what is legal and what is not; a means of apprehending suspected perpetrators; and a body to adjudicate competing claims and convict the guilty. The UN lacks all three; the ICC lacks them in relation to terrorism; and international police organizations lack either the authority or the resources to directly apprehend perpetrators. The difficulties of these various organizations will be explored in turn.

The UN's Inability to Provide a Legal Framework

First, the UN has yet to even define terrorism.[6] The failure to take this necessary first step arises because every state naturally wants UN policy to first benefit its interests rather than any common good. Thus states that back groups whose actions could potentially be labeled as terroristic would want to define terrorism in order to exclude those groups. This is the old saw "one man's terrorist is another man's freedom fighter" in action. For example, Hugo Chavez of Venezuela has consistently rejected the notion that the Revolutionary Armed Forces of Colombia (FARC) is a terrorist organization or that its actions are in any way illegitimate.[7] Similarly, Iran certainly would resist any attempt to have its clients Hezbollah and Hamas labeled as terrorist groups. States that face guerrilla insurgencies would want such movements classified as terroristic, whereas many Arab states would want to include actions by states and not just groups, in order to label Israel as engaging in terrorism. Whether states truly believe their own claims about who is or is not a terrorist, or simply make them out of self-interest, is irrelevant. Because of their reluctance to have groups they support labeled as terrorists, and thus violators of international law, it is extremely difficult, if not impossible, to achieve a broad-based international consensus on how terrorism should be defined.

As far back as the failed effort of the League of Nations in 1937, such conflicting interests have paralyzed repeated efforts to define *terrorism*.[8] Since 1997, the UN General Assembly has failed repeatedly to pass resolutions that would define terrorism, such as Resolution 51/210 in 1999.[9] Debates in the General Assembly on a definition in the immediate post-9/11 period also went nowhere, so discouraging Secretary-General Kofi Annan that he urged the Assembly to give up the search for legal precision.[10] Again in 2005, even after the shocking attack by a Chechen group on a school in Beslan, Russia, the Assembly made no headway in its attempt to define terrorism, largely because of opposition from states in the Organization of the Islamic Conference.[11] Nor is it defined in the UN's Global Counter-Terrorism Strategy (2006).[12] Even narrow UN bodies focused specifically on global security have failed. Most notably, Security Council Resolution 1373 (2001), which created the UN's main counterterrorism committee, does not define terrorism.[13]

Worse than the definitional impasse is the fact that many UN members have been willing to tolerate terrorist groups, provided their goals are seen as admirable. Perhaps the most striking example of this was the success of the Palestine Liberation Organization (PLO) in obtaining observer status at the UN in the early 1970s, at a time it was clearly viewed by many as a terrorist organization. Thus even if the UN was to agree on a definition, many UN members would probably decline to denounce terrorism itself as always being illegitimate. If universal condemnation cannot be achieved, it will be impossible to target terrorism generally, and the notion of equality before the law will be undermined. It is not at all clear how the UN can impose legal constraints on terrorist activity if it cannot even agree on what it is trying to make illegal or that all terrorist activity is inherently wrong.

Second, the UN currently has no body to act as a law enforcement agency or police force, and it is unlikely to create such a body. The UN could call on member states to provide such forces on an ad hoc basis, but it is not clear how such an arrangement would be more effective than states simply acting without UN involvement. In fact, to the extent that UN involvement would add another layer of bureaucracy to the process, it might slow and reduce the effectiveness—secrecy is often required—of such actions. Thus even if the UN could pass effective laws, enforcement would, by necessity, be left to member states. This would not be an improvement over the status quo.

Finally, the UN lacks a body to rule on terrorism cases. The ICJ accepts only *states* (not institutions, businesses, individuals, or terrorist groups) as parties to a case.[14] Raising the profile of terrorist groups to the level of a state so that the ICJ could address them would be counterproductive, because it would give groups the attention, prestige, and legitimacy they desperately seek. Thus the ICJ cannot actually deal with terrorism, except in the case of a suspected state sponsor. Even then, the ICJ lacks the means to enforce its decisions. Although the ICJ charter says that the opinions of the ICJ are "final and without appeal," it is completely silent on how compliance is to be brought about. In practice, compliance occurs when states wish to be seen as playing by the rules. But because state sponsors of terrorism are already often operating outside of the normative and often-legal rules of the international system, such considerations are unlikely to compel them to comply. In any event, under the UN Charter the ICJ cannot directly impose sanctions. In cases in which states fail to voluntarily comply with a ruling, the aggrieved party can ask the Security Council to enforce the decision under Article 94(2) of the UN Charter, but the Security Council is not required to take such action. The Security Council's track record in dealing with state sponsors of terrorism, however, is spotty at best. Worse, many states refuse to accept the ICJ's jurisdiction in any matter involving national security: the United States and France, for example, have refused to comply with ICJ rulings affecting national security based on other states' refusal to admit jurisdiction over such matters.[15]

Not surprisingly, the UN has made little headway in its attempts to combat terrorism by imposing binding mandates on members. The UN's main effort has centered on creating two permanent committees within the Security Council: the 1267 Committee and the Counter-Terrorism Committee (CTC), created, respectively, by Resolutions 1267 (October 15, 1999) and 1373 (September 28, 2001). The UN's more recent effort, its Global Counter-Terrorism Strategy (2006), essentially enjoins member states to comply with previous UN statutes on terrorism and pledge to try to create more effective measures in the future.[16] Thus it effectively adds nothing new to the UN's counterterrorism tool kit. The 1267 Committee specifically targets individual members of al-Qaeda and the Taliban and forbids states from providing funding, safe haven, or weapons to any of some five hundred members whose names appear on the proscribed list. Although this interdiction may sound impressive, al-Qaeda alone has over four thousand known members, and no other terrorist groups are targeted by the committee.[17] Thus most terrorists escape UN sanctions. Furthermore, new names can be added only with the unanimous consent of the Security Council, a condition that has rarely been met except in the immediate aftermath of the 9/11 attacks, as illustrated by the fact that nearly half of the names on the list were added in September 2001.[18]

Even as it pertains to the listed members, the effectiveness of the 1267 Committee is unclear. Although terrorist groups' finances may have been interrupted to some degree, there is little evidence that the safe haven travel ban has been enforced, suggesting that rules passed by the 1267 Committee have little, if any, bite. The 1267 Committee's own monitoring group observed that "there have been no reports yet from any State that a designated individual has sought entry into or has been stopped from entering or transiting their country."[19] Worse, the committee has no mandate to bring any of these listed members to justice, and fully one-third of UN members have not even bothered to report whether they are in compliance with the committee's requirements.[20]

The CTC's efforts have not been much more successful. It is charged with confronting terrorism in general and has issued binding rules for UN members to follow when dealing with terrorist groups. However, because no UN body has created a global list of terrorist groups, member states retain great latitude in which groups they consider to be terrorists.[21] It is not clear, then, what sort of requirements CTC mandates actually place on UN member states. Like the 1267 Committee, the CTC has no actual enforcement powers, though at least it has moved most of the work on terrorism from the General Assembly to the Security Council. Beyond providing expert legal advice on tightening national antiterrorism laws, the CTC has no authority to punish state sponsors, identify terrorist groups, or prosecute actual terrorists.[22] The CTC's data gathering, though useful, in part duplicates work already being done by the United Nations Office on Drugs and Crime.[23]

This tendency to duplicate the efforts of other agencies both within the UN and in other IOs plagues many UN efforts.[24] Even here, the frequency of reporting to the CTC by member states has declined over time.[25]

Shortcomings of the ICC and International Police Organizations

If the UN can do little on the legal front in the battle against terrorist groups, perhaps an independent international body like the ICC would fare better. Certainly, the ICC has potential advantages over the UN and ICJ. Most importantly, unlike the ICJ, the ICC is designed to deal with individuals who break international law and has the authority—though not necessarily the capacity—to indict, apprehend, convict, and punish individuals. This concern about the ICC's capacity is very real, for while it can put individuals on trial and convict them, like the UN it lacks an ability to apprehend them. For example, indicted war criminals have been able to long avoid being brought before the ICC: former Bosnian Serb military leader Ratko Mladić eluded the ICC and its predecessors for years and Sudanese president Omar al-Bashir has been able to avoid trial to this day. Although Mladić was ultimately captured, he was apprehended by the Serbs themselves, rather than by the ICC. Even allowing that the ICC could rely on others to apprehend and hand over suspected terrorists, it would face a host of difficulties if it were to take up counterterrorist efforts. Most notably, the United States is not, nor soon likely to be, a member. This absence reduces the organization's capabilities and legitimacy. Additionally, the ICC and the various ad hoc human rights and war crimes tribunals that preceded it have often moved at a snail's pace—if at all. The slow pace may be acceptable in some issue areas, but terrorism is not one of them, because inaction or slow action may cost many lives, even if terrorists are ultimately brought to justice.

Indeed, the ICC actually lacks the authority to prosecute terrorists.[26] This authority was deliberately excluded during negotiations over the ICC's charter in 1995 as the United States feared including the authority to prosecute terrorists would not only be ineffective but would reduce states' legal abilities to prosecute terrorists themselves.[27] If U.S. concerns have merit, it is possible that granting the ICC authority to prosecute terrorists would be counterproductive. Of course, any effort to add terrorism to the ICC's jurisdiction would face the same definitional debates that have stymied the UN. Thus, the ICC lacks both the capacity and the authority to deal with terrorists.

What then of the international police cooperative known as Interpol? Remarkably it also lacks the capacity to apprehend terrorists. Interpol has four main functions: to be a central exchange for police queries; to serve as a library of information for common problems (e.g., examples of counterfeit money); to promote universal standards and norms; and to provide a forum for meetings.[28] While these are all useful functions, Interpol actually is specifically prohibited from participating in operational activities.[29] Thus, it is barred from arresting anyone, including terrorists. Additionally, to the extent Interpol can help fight terrorism through promoting common standards and information, that is already being done—Interpol has had counterterrorism resolutions on its books since the 1970s.[30] Thus, while Interpol may play a small role, it is likely already doing all it can, and little additional help should be expected from this quarter.[31]

True, other international police organizations, such as Europol, the Southeast European Cooperative, and the Southern African Development Community do have greater operational authority, though in each case this authority is relatively recent.[32] The challenge these organizations continue to face is a lack of capacity. This can be seen explicitly in Europol, the most developed of the regional police cooperatives. So far, Europol has played a very limited role in counterterrorism, despite having potentially large statutory powers. This is because European governments do not fully trust Europol and have therefore given it few resources and have been reluctant to share intelligence with it.[33] The result is that in practice Europol has limited operational abilities and relies heavily on liaison officers working with national police forces.[34] To argue that EU members should increase Europol's effectiveness by increasing funding, as some suggest, completely misses the point as states' inherent distrust of Europol's ability to limit their sovereignty and work toward goals they do not share causes them to intentionally limit Europol's effectiveness. Thus Europol, like the ICC, Interpol, and the UN, is unlikely to become an effective counterterrorism organization.

WHY INTERNATIONAL ORGANIZATIONS STRUGGLE TO STANCH TERRORIST FINANCING

Terrorist groups often rely on international networks to finance their operations. Indeed, such financing is often the lifeblood of terrorist groups. For this reason, attacking these financial networks is crucial to counterterrorism efforts. Certainly, the UN has attempted to do this—countering terrorist financing is an area of emphasis of both the aforementioned 1267 Committee and the CTC—but has struggled for the reasons outlined earlier as to why the UN cannot create a legal framework.[35] However, might not other organizations such as the IMF and World Bank, which have greater experience dealing with international financial flows and interact directly with banks and governmental financial organs on a daily basis, be better suited to the task? Unfortunately, these organizations also fall short.

Both the IMF and the World Bank have created training guides advising states on how to root out terrorist financing.[36] Though not useless, such guides do not create capacity. Less-developed states often lack the resources to implement the recommendations, some states lack the will, and those states that possess both often already possessed the know-how and were deeply involved in writing the recommendations, thus gaining little from the guides. To their credit, the IMF has also created counterterrorism programs, and the World Bank has provided some technical assistance to member states to implement those programs.[37] Unfortunately, the programs have serious limitations. For example, the main IMF and World Bank initiative, the Financial Action Task Force on Money Laundering (FATF), created to fight terrorism-related financial activities, can only implement "soft law" as opposed to "hard law."[38] Additionally, all of the FATF's actions are built on the UN's International Convention for the Suppression of the Financing of Terrorism—a General Assembly resolution passed in 1999—despite the fact that dozens of states have yet to even sign or ratify, let alone implement, that act.[39] Even getting wealthy American allies to agree to adopt and implement FATF standards has proven difficult, with most EU governments delaying and foot-dragging implementation for years.[40] Indeed, no money was allocated to implement the convention until 2009, and even then only $31 million was allocated to 29 states scattered through Asia, Africa, Eastern Europe, and Latin America—hardly enough to significantly increase state capacity.[41] By the body's own assessment, many states fall short of its recommendations.[42] For example, to this day few governments audit charities or financial institutions to look for terrorist transactions, and instead rely entirely on self-reporting, which is useless if the charity or financial institution is knowingly complicit in funding terrorists.[43] Self-reporting may still fail even if such institutions, while honest, lack the capacity or incentives to ferret out terrorist finances. Thus, existing IMF and World Bank counterterrorism programs have been of only limited effectiveness.

Another problem with using IOs to combat terrorist financing is that such cooperation is often made public by requiring states to ratify agreements and submit reports to international bodies. Yet many states may be willing to cooperate only if such cooperation is covert. The United States and other states that are targeted by terrorist groups are often unpopular to the publics in non-Western states where some terrorist groups are based or operate; such governments will be reluctant to publicize their cooperation with U.S.-led bodies. Additionally, Western publics may be reluctant to embrace counter-terrorism policies that increase government intrusion into their private financial transactions. For example, European publics reacted with outrage to the revelation in 2006 that, at the request of the United States, European governments were examining private electronic financial transactions, as part of a top secret cooperative called the Terrorist Finance Tracking Program.[44] The public uproar ultimately led the EU parliament to ban such monitoring practices. Interestingly, the program was resurrected in 2010, through a series of bilateral agreements between the United States and European governments, rather than through the institution. Forcing such cooperation into the light of day may be consistent with democratic accountability, but it is likely to reduce the effectiveness of counterterrorism cooperation.

Finally, much terrorist financing avoids formal banking channels that IOs like the IMF can monitor and instead goes through more informal networks such as Hawala, a traditional Islamic system of money transfers. Such systems often do not use electronic means and are incredibly difficult to monitor. And, as with electronic means of transferring money, the vast majority of money being moved is legitimate, making the tracing of illicit informal transfers a game of hide and seek. Because such transfers do not pass through banks, IOs have little to no leverage over such networks and would have to rely entirely on local state will and capacity. This essentially removes IOs from the "informal terror financing" equation.

THE DIFFICULTIES OF COUNTERTERRORISM CAPACITY BUILDING AND COORDINATION

Even if states wanted to comply with international counterterrorism mandates or confront terrorism on their own, many lack the capacity to do so. It has been suggested that IOs could provide expertise and capacity-building tools to countries that are willing but unable to fight terrorism—and that such efforts would be more politically palatable coming from such organizations rather than, say, the United States.[45] The UN is often looked to as the IO best suited to coordinate state action, solve free rider problems, and enhance overall state capacity to engage in counterterrorism. This is partly due to the fact that the UN is the broadest global institution; but it is also partly due to the clear failure of other organizations that have attempted to coordinate counterterrorism efforts. For example, the G8's Counter-Terrorism Action Group (CTAG) lacks both a permanent secretariat to act on any of its policies and legitimacy beyond the eight states that compose the G8.[46] A U.S. State Department official was quite clear as to CTAG's failure, stating that the group had "yet to devise a consistent [multilateral] framework to effectively address the numerous gaps that continue to exist between what we can do and what we need to do."[47] Thus the UN, with its permanent secretariat and some existing frameworks for dealing with terrorism, is ahead of many IOs. However, the UN also faces serious and likely insurmountable difficulties in coordinating and enhancing effective counterterrorism efforts—difficulties that are typical of established IOs with broad memberships. Specifically, the UN has little by way of capacity to lend to states. Beyond this, the main obstacle to successful cooperation and coordination in counterterrorism efforts remains not free riding, but a lack of shared state interests.

To the extent that the UN has tried to build counterterrorism capacity, it has been the work of the CTC, whose efforts have met with little success. The reason, in part, is that it is not clear in what sort of capacity building the CTC could engage. As mentioned earlier, the UN lacks its own policing or enforcement mechanisms. Therefore, it cannot lend that capacity to states. In addition, the CTC is not authorized to provide direct financial assistance to states; it can only put states in contact with donors and other providers of assistance.[48] Thus even in the unlikely event that the CTC's funding situation improved, it would not be able to provide direct financial aid to states.

One area in which the CTC could engage in state capacity building might be intelligence. Many states lack sufficient, actionable counterterrorism intelligence. Perhaps this deficit could be overcome if the UN acted as a clearinghouse for intelligence gathered by its member states, which could be done without having to create new UN intelligence assets. However, it is unlikely that the CTC or any other organ of the UN would be able to share intelligence with states to help them fight terrorism because most actionable counterterrorism intelligence is closely guarded by the states that gather it (they want to protect their sources and their ongoing counterterrorism operations). The same would be true of any international organization; as mentioned above, the reluctance of EU states to share intelligence with Europol is telling.

Proponents of an intelligence clearinghouse might argue that the International Atomic Energy Agency (IAEA), a UN-affiliated body, has been able to collect a good deal of information on the nuclear programs of states, and thus a similar agency could be created to deal with terrorism. Unfortunately, the tasks faced by the IAEA and counterterrorism intelligence organizations are quite different. The IAEA relies heavily on voluntary information and voluntary compliance, elements not common to counterterrorism intelligence gathering. Thus intelligence does not seem to be an area in which the UN can have much success at building state counterterrorism capacity.[49]

Aside from the admittedly difficult task of state capacity building, even the more limited goal of simply trying to coordinate state responses is problematic because of the public nature of UN action. As discussed above, regarding the challenges faced by IOs trying to stop terror financing, many states may wish to keep their cooperation with other countries against certain terrorist groups from becoming public. For example, governments of states in which terrorists maintain some popular support may well refuse to cooperate unless their actions remain secret or at least receive minimal publicity. Joint UN actions are, almost by definition, highly visible. To the extent that this visibility would reduce governments' willingness to collaborate against terrorist groups, the UN's involvement would, if anything, be counterproductive.

Generally speaking, IOs involved with fighting terrorism tend to promulgate global standards and recommend best practices for engaging in counterterrorism efforts, but can do little more. If member states ultimately adopt and implement these standards and practices, this would certainly be of some use. Member states, however, often lack the capacity, political will, or both to do so and instead simply adopt policies in name only.[50] The lack of capacity is often so severe in less developed regions of the world that states struggle to even keep up with IOs' reporting requirements.[51]

Capacity building and enhancing policy coordination are certainly major challenges for IOs seeking to assist in the global fight against terrorism. But perhaps the biggest problem for IOs lies in the assumption that all states share an equal interest in combating terrorism. Most IOs do not require unanimity to act, but do require broad consensuses to be effective.[52] Leaving aside the serious problem of state sponsors, it is extremely difficult to form broad coalitions to fight terrorism because states are threatened not by terrorism in general, but rather by specific terrorist groups. For example, Colombia certainly would be interested in measures that would help combat FARC, but it probably would have little interest in using its limited resources to combat radical Islamic groups such as al-Qaeda, which do not currently target the Colombian government. Pakistan may support measures targeting the Pakistani Taliban that seeks to overthrow its government, but that would certainly not extend to the Haqqani Network, Pakistan's close ally in neighboring Afghanistan. These divisions logically should limit the efforts of IOs to commissioning studies and issuing recommendations rather than targeting actual terrorists, because these kinds of actions would be the only ones that coincide with widely shared interests. Not surprisingly, these are exactly the kind of limited measures in which IOs actually engage.[53]

Lack of shared interests being an obstacle to cooperation is not confined to terrorism, but is apparent in other—though not all—security issues, such as efforts to halt Iran's nuclear program or Iraq's violation of UN resolutions in the decade following the Persian Gulf War.[54] There is no reason why concerns about terrorism would bring about more unity of action than security issues involving weapons of mass destruction. Inevitably, states will, as always, look to their own interests first, limiting the amount of cooperation they will offer against terrorism.

CONCLUSIONS

IOs have and will continue to have great difficulty in aiding counterterrorism efforts. In attempting to construct an international legal framework to fight terrorism, insuperable challenges exist as global institutions lack the authority and/or capacity to apprehend or deal with terrorists, leaving such institutions dependent on member states to enforce their dictates. Conversely, states that have the capacity to apprehend terrorists will generally want to prosecute the terrorists themselves, while states that lack the capacity to do so are of no help to IOs. Even where capacity exists, problems still exist due to definitional problems and legal uncertainties, as recent difficulties in determining how and where to try captured Somali pirates—an issue area, unlike terrorism, where customary international law has existed for centuries—have shown.[55] And frequently the interests of member states differ in their relations with terrorist groups, bedeviling the ability of states to cooperate through IOs.

These limitations do not stem primarily from funding constraints. Funding is certainly inadequate, but even if they had unlimited funding, the ICC, Interpol, and UN agencies would still be limited by their mandates in what they can do. Indeed, the deep divisions among member states about which terrorists groups to target, as illustrated by the debates on defining terrorism, ensure that restrictions on the actions of IOs are not likely to be removed. They exist because a sufficiently broad consensus on fighting terrorism does not exist—states focus on specific groups that impact them rather than on the phenomenon as a whole.

The failure of existing IOs to overcome the challenges they face in crafting effective counterterrorism policies has led even supporters of such efforts to call for the creation of a new, international counterterrorism organization.[56] While it is theoretically possible that a new organization could be an effective plank in global counterterrorism efforts, past failures suggest that it is not probable. Any such organization would still have to deal with the lack of capacity in many weaker states, the challenges of legal definitions and authorities, and differences of interests among member states when it came to actual terrorist groups. Thus, the problem is not solely that existing organizations were not designed to address terrorism—though that is obviously a serious issue—but also that the nature of the terrorist challenge may prevent broad-based efforts at institutional-level cooperation from succeeding.

This argument is not one against IOs in general. International organizations can help solve many problems. Similarly, it is not an argument against cooperative efforts in counterterrorism. Quite the contrary. Whenever possible, states should and must form coalitions dedicated to combating specific terrorist groups, including coalitions that take advantage of existing, more narrowly focused organizations and alliances, though as discussed earlier NATO's experience in Afghanistan suggests that even more narrowly tailored organizations face serious institutional challenges. Rather, it is an argument against putting too much hope into combating terrorism through IOs. Such efforts may produce some results, but the resources employed to get those results may well go further if used in the more traditional state-centered ways. Whatever tasks IOs undertake, they should be adjuncts to, rather than central planks in, global counterterrorism strategies.

International organizations are necessary for
YES: fighting international terrorism.
Bruce Cronin, *City College of New York*

Why IOs Are Needed to Help Defeat Global Terrorism

International terrorism can only be effectively challenged by the collective power of the international community, a power that is represented by international and regional security organizations. Although each state will continue to be primarily responsible for providing its own security, international terrorism presents a special challenge to the system of state sovereignty, and only international organizations can provide the legitimacy, legal framework, coordination, and state-building assistance necessary to meet this challenge.

This essay first offers an overview of the types of threats faced by states and the international system from terrorism, and the options states have for confronting the threat. It then lays out the invaluable functions played by global and regional institutions in helping states achieve their counterterrorism goals.

Options for Confronting International Terrorism

The use of political violence by nonstate actors is not a new phenomenon. Since the beginning of the nation-state system, insurgents, private militias, revolutionary organizations, secessionists, and loose networks of individuals have waged campaigns of violence and intimidation against established authorities and state institutions.[57] Such campaigns have included attacks on both military and civilian targets, and have been directed at both people and property. The underlying motives have embraced a wide range of factors such as political ideology, nationalism, and religion. When such violence occurred outside of an armed conflict or a civil war—and the aim was to spread fear and intimidation—political leaders and analysts considered it to be terrorism.

During the late nineteenth century, for example, anarchist movements in the United States and Europe engaged in high-profile political violence against state property and public officials that included assassinations, bombings, and orchestrated rioting.[58] Similarly, during the late 1960s and early 1970s, European revolutionary organizations such as the Italian Red Brigades and the German Red Army Faction employed political violence against the state in an effort to overthrow the existing political orders in their countries.[59] Throughout the second half of the twentieth century, nationalist movements such as the Irish Republican Army (IRA), the Turkish Kurdistan Workers' Party (PKK), and the Basque Fatherland and Liberty (ETA) targeted both civilian and military facilities in an effort to secede from their parent countries and create states of their own.[60] Similarly, after World War II, national liberation movements in Africa and Asia used coercive political violence against the colonial powers in countries such as Algeria, Kenya, and South Africa.[61]

Governments addressed these challenges by employing their own domestic political, legal, military, and judicial resources, with little support from international or regional security organizations. The reason for this was simple: political violence by nonstate actors has been traditionally viewed as a domestic issue outside the purview of global or regional institutions. International and regional security organizations are designed to protect states from external aggression, not governments from their domestic opposition. In each of the cases cited above, violence was largely confined to a specific territory, targeted against the authorities or populations that governed or controlled that territory, and perpetrated by organizations or political movements composed primarily if not solely of residents or citizens of the particular polity. While international or regional organizations occasionally provided diplomatic assistance to mediate agreements between the conflicting parties, any other involvement was beyond the scope of their mandates.

This changed with the rise of international terrorism beginning in the early 1970s.[62] Unlike domestic political violence, international terrorism is employed under one or more of the following conditions: (a) it is targeted against foreign authorities, populations, or property; (b) it occurs in international space, such as airplanes that cross national borders or ships traveling on the high seas; (c) the perpetrators represent a transnational organization or network comprising citizens from more than one country; and (d) the targets are international in character, such as the facilities of an intergovernmental organization or the Olympic Games.[63] Since international terrorism transcends national boundaries, it is outside the territorial jurisdiction of any specific state.

States have essentially three options for addressing foreign security threats, all of which are available in challenging international terrorism: self-help, collective defense, and collective security. A successful security policy requires that political leaders determine the proper balance among them, based on the nature of the specific threat. All three are relevant to combating terrorism; however, as I argue below, given the nature of transnational terrorism, collective security must rank among the top choices.

Self-help, also known as unilateralism, involves political, economic, or military action undertaken without significant consultation or coordination with other states. With this approach, the government defines threats, exploits opportunities, and charts its own course of action, although once initiated it may choose to seek the support of others. Governments generally adopt this approach in cases where the threat is limited and specifically directed at their own state. Thus, for example, the United States responded to al-Qaeda's 1998 bombings of U.S. embassies in Tanzania and Kenya by launching retaliatory missile attacks against the organization's facilities in Afghanistan and suspected facilities in Sudan.[64]

This response is known as a reprisal. Under customary international law and diplomatic practice, reprisals are acts that would otherwise be illegal, but are authorized (or at least tolerated) as one-time responses to a particular hostile action undertaken by another.[65] A reprisal permits a state to take extraordinary measures against an aggressor in response to a prior illegal act of the violator. Reprisals are therefore acts of self-help on the part of an injured state, seeking the cessation of the wrongful act and/or compensation or reparation for it.[66]

When the threat is perceived to be ongoing and sustained, governments may employ self-help in a more concerted way, for example, declaring war or initiating an ongoing series of military actions or economic and diplomatic sanctions against the perceived adversary. Thus, in response to the 2001 terrorist attacks on the World Trade Center and Pentagon, Congress passed an authorization for use of military force to respond to the attacks.[67]

A second method for confronting security threats is through collective defense (also known as an alliance), whereby self-selected states provide for their mutual protection against predefined adversaries by pooling their resources through a formal agreement. Unlike self-help, the members of the alliance collectively define what constitutes a security threat and decide how to act in concert to confront such threats.[68] Such associations are restrictive inasmuch as they are only required to protect their own members and do not need to consult with or cooperate with other states outside of the alliance in determining their courses of action. At the same time, in joining a collective defense arrangement, the individual states cede some of their right to self-help—at least within the scope and domain of the alliance—when they sign a legally binding treaty that establishes the association.

The North Atlantic Treaty Organization (NATO), a remnant of the Cold War, is the world's largest and most powerful alliance, with twenty-eight member states across North America and Europe. Many recent terrorist attacks have been directed against members of NATO. NATO membership greatly restricts the ability of states to act unilaterally when operating within the alliance's domain, primarily Europe. At the same time, the establishment of NATO has enabled the United States, Britain, and France to share the burdens of providing security, particularly after the end of the Cold War. Following the 2001 attacks against the United States, NATO invoked Article 5 of the North Atlantic Treaty—which stipulates that an armed attack against any alliance member will be considered an attack against them all—for the first time in its history. While the members activated the alliance in large part to support one of their own who had been the victim of an armed attack, the action was also initiated to ensure that the United States would not act unilaterally in its response. Indeed, they wanted to make sure that any action taken by the alliance or one of its members would not be launched without specific additional consultation and decision from the governing council.[69] For this reason, the current war in Afghanistan is technically being fought by NATO even if most of the troops and weapons are American.

Finally, the third way that states can confront threats is through collective security. Collective security is an institutional arrangement at either the regional or the global level that deems threats to be the concern of all, and promotes a collective response to acts of aggression and breaches of the peace. By participating in a collective security organization, states agree to significantly restrict their option to unilaterally use force. In return, they may tap the collective resources of the regime to help protect themselves against an aggressor.

Although the idea of collective security has existed for millennia, it was not until the creation of the United Nations and regional security organizations that states had means and potential to put their goals into practice. Within the

UN, the Security Council is the body that is primarily responsible for addressing security threats. The council was not specifically created to protect individual states from attack by other states, although it does occasionally do this. Rather, it was designed to provide for general security throughout the world. In essence, the council acts as a global "security manager," much like the Concert of Europe a century earlier.[70] As a body comprising the world's most dominant and influential states—as well as representatives from each of the world's regions—it has the means to establish and implement a wide range of policies regarding international peace and security, broadly defined. When its members pool their military and economic resources, it represents the strongest combination of states in the history of the nation-state system.[71]

This, of course, does not preclude the right of individual states to defend themselves when attacked—a right that is firmly embedded in customary international law and acknowledged by Article 51 of the UN Charter—nor does it prevent states from employing regional alliances and other security arrangements when the threat is of a regional or local nature (as permitted under Article 52). At the same time, the founders of the UN never intended for the right to self-defense to be unlimited.[72] Rather, they conceived it to be a temporary measure that allows for immediate state action when the Security Council is unable or unwilling to act, not a means of circumventing the obligations to bring matters involving international peace and security to the world body.

Prior to the 9/11 attacks, the Security Council had been very active in mobilizing diplomatic, political, and economic resources to oppose international terrorism in general and al-Qaeda in particular. In addition to levying economic sanctions against states supporting or sponsoring terrorist activity, the body focused particular attention on trying to disrupt al-Qaeda's operations. For example, Resolution 1333 (2000) ordered the closure of all camps where terrorists are trained, and Resolution 1267 (1999) levied sanctions against the Taliban regime in Afghanistan and demanded the surrender of Osama bin Laden to stand trial for the 1998 bombings of the U.S. embassies in Kenya and Tanzania. Clearly these measures did not prevent the September 11 attacks—or those subsequently in London, in Madrid, and elsewhere—but of course neither did the use of self-help by any of the affected states.

THE VALUE OF COLLECTIVE SECURITY IN FIGHTING MODERN GLOBAL TERRORISM

In choosing which of these three options—self-help, collective defense, or collective security—should be employed to address the threat of terrorism, states must first define the nature of the adversary and tailor the response to the threat. While domestic violence directed against specific governments will continue to remain primarily an internal issue for each state, international terrorism presents three unique challenges that require the active involvement of international organizations in the form of collective security.

First, contemporary international terrorism represents a challenge to state sovereignty, a principle that has provided the foundation for the nation-state system since the seventeenth century. Under this principle, all political space in the world is controlled and administered by a centralized state, which holds exclusive jurisdiction and supreme political authority over its defined territory and population.[73] All other authorities (such as religious or economic) are subordinate to the state, at least in political matters, and only the state can legitimately employ military force in the pursuit of its political, economic, or social goals. Thus, the mobilization of violence—either internationally through warfare or domestically through law enforcement—has been the monopoly of the state.[74] This has long been confirmed through international law and diplomatic practice.

Traditionally, those employing terrorism as a political/military tactic have done so within the framework of sovereign statehood. Groups engaged in terrorism did not challenge the principle of state sovereignty, but rather sought either to win state power—by overthrowing the existing political order or creating a new state of their own—or to force a ruling government to make major policy or structural changes. As such the challenges had been levied at specific governing authorities rather than at the system of sovereign statehood.

Over the past two decades, many analysts and political leaders have argued that the recent growth of nonstate actors using political violence across borders has created an international security threat directed against the system as a whole. For example, according to a U.S. government panel, "the enemy in the Global War on Terror is one neither the United States nor the community of nations has ever before engaged on such an extensive scale. These far-reaching, well-resourced, organized, and trained terrorists are attempting to achieve their own ends. Such terrorists are not of a nation state such as those who are party to the agreements which comprise the law of war. Neither do they conform their actions to the letter or spirit of the law of war" or any other aspect of international law or diplomatic practice.[75] Unlike the political violence used by traditional revolutionary or insurgent groups, contemporary international terrorism is often perpetrated by loose transnational networks of individuals that lack both a centralized leadership and a coherent political program or ideology.[76]

From this perspective, it is neither the use of violence nor the targeting of civilians that differentiates terrorist groups from other security threats—the overwhelming source of terror and political violence against civilians and military personnel alike is still the nation-state—but their very existence challenges the status of the state as the presumed sole authority with the right to wage war or employ political violence at the international level. As transnational actors, they do not represent a territory or population and cannot be deterred with traditional military threats. International terrorism is therefore a challenge to the nation-state itself, and as a result requires a collective response by the international community of states as a whole.

Second, contemporary international terrorism usually flourishes in areas where the state has lost the ability to control its own territory, provide security, or supply basic public services, and whose institutions lack the legitimate authority to govern. This is particularly acute in parts of North Africa and Central and South Asia, where the end of the Cold War system in the early 1990s led to widespread civil conflict and the collapse of central governing institutions in such countries as Afghanistan, Sudan, Somalia, and Yemen, producing what have become known as "failed" states.[77]

According to the journal *Foreign Policy*, as of July 2012 there were twenty failed states, with another nineteen labeled as "in danger."[78] Another recent study concluded that states plagued by chronic state failures are statistically more likely to (1) host terrorist groups that commit transnational attacks, (2) have their nationals commit transnational attacks, and (3) be targeted by transnational terrorists themselves.[79] Thus, for example, according to the Congressional Research Service, the increase in violent pirate attacks off the Horn of Africa is directly linked to continuing insecurity and the absence of the rule of law in war-torn Somalia.[80] In this context, the only solution to the issue of failed states is to develop either alternative forms of political organization (such as a decentralized clan-based or tribal system that is capable of administering the population and territory) or what has been commonly referred to as "state-building" or "nation-building" projects. This requires the active participation of international institutions, since the allocation of political space is a property of the international system. Moreover, as argued below, individual states have a dismal record of success in this endeavor.

Third, unlike traditional campaigns of terrorism—which are almost always targeted at specific authorities or populations—contemporary transnational violence tends to be directed against a wide variety of states and societies in many regions around the world; the foci of these terrorists' actions are often diffuse and indirect. Since these groups are transnational in membership, they do not share a common national or cultural bond with any particular society, nor do they have a stake in any long-term political or social development.[81] Such attacks defy traditional political alignments, such as East-West or North-South.

Over the past decade, for example, transnational organizations have used political violence against targets in Saudi Arabia, Jordan, Indonesia, the Philippines,
Britain, the United States, France, Russia, Morocco, India, Turkey, Spain,
Sri Lanka, and Ethiopia.[82] Since the security threat posed by contemporary
terrorist organizations is not confined to any particular state—or even a specific region—no single state or coalition can claim to be acting in its own self-
defense in prosecuting a campaign to eliminate international terrorism. Clearly
this is an issue of global security, which makes it one to be addressed by the
international community. The members of the UN Security Council clearly
understood this when they passed Resolution 1368 on September 12, 2001,
stating that the body regarded the 9/11 attacks "like any act of international
terrorism, as a threat to international peace and security"[83] and thus within the
jurisdiction of the United Nations.

The above discussion suggests that individual states lack both the competence and the legal authority to wage a generalized campaign against international terrorism. While states will continue to be primarily responsible for
responding to attacks against their territory, citizens, and interests, any
effort to confront the problem at its root will require a collective effort.
International organizations can assist such an effort by providing legitimacy,
a legal framework, coordination, and technical assistance.

Legitimacy

States are primarily guided by national policy, national self-interest, and their
histories of relations with specific countries that may become the targets or
supporters of terrorist violence. Individual states cannot therefore be trusted
or relied upon to challenge international terrorism as a general threat. This is
particularly true inasmuch as there are few checks against the ambitions of an
individual state—particularly a great power—that decides to launch unilateral
action in the furtherance of its self-defined interest under the guise of antiterrorism. While diplomatic practice, international customary law, and the UN
Charter have long maintained the right of states to act in self-defense when
their security is threatened, no state has the legal or political authority to initiate a generalized international war against an unnamed enemy without regard
to geographic location. The potential for abuse is obvious.

For example, the George W. Bush administration initiated a self-defined
global "war on terrorism" by expanding the concept of self-defense to include
any potential threats that may emerge from any general source anytime in the
unnamed future. In declaring this "war," the administration refused to limit the
conflict to any specific adversaries, establish any geographic or temporal
boundaries, define the limits of how this war would be prosecuted, or specify

the conditions under which the war would end. Rather, it created an open-ended commitment that claimed the right of the United States to pursue all terrorists and their unnamed state sponsors anywhere in the world.[84] As the U.S. invasion of Iraq demonstrated, this definition is so general that it can potentially encompass any and all states and organizations, regardless of whether they are linked to terrorist activity against the United States.[85] Less egregious but still significant, the Barack Obama administration asserted the position that once a state is engaged in an armed conflict with an armed non-state organization, the conflict follows the members of that group wherever they go, as long as the group's members continue to engage in hostilities against that state.[86]

Such an approach makes it very difficult to maintain a global consensus against international terrorism. Consider, for example, the differences between the international reaction to NATO's 2001 attack on the Taliban in Afghanistan and the U.S. invasion of Iraq in 2003. Following the 9/11 attack, the UN Security Council voted to affirm three key principles that justified a retaliatory response by the United States: First, terrorist violence can constitute an armed attack against the target state (affirming that the United States was the victim of an armed attack). Second, any facilitation of, support for, or assistance with such acts by a state constitutes a breach of that state's obligations under international law (legitimizing the designation of the Taliban as a party to the conflict). Third, the right to retaliate against both the terrorist organization and the specific state is inherent.[87] As such, there was no significant international opposition to the initial U.S. attack against the Taliban in 2002.

Now consider Iraq. Despite tremendous pressure and coercion by the United States, the UN Security Council refused to support the 2003 invasion, and many of America's traditional allies actively opposed it. The lack of a Security Council mandate prompted both the Turkish and Indian parliaments to deny the United States support (and, in the case of Turkey, permission to deploy troops).[88] It also reversed most of the support Washington had gained in its campaign against international terrorism in the wake of the September 11 attacks. Similarly, the U.S. policy of unilaterally engaging in targeted assassinations of suspected terrorists in Pakistan, Yemen, and elsewhere has made it more difficult for such countries to cooperate in antiterrorism efforts, has further harmed America's global image, and has led to political instability in many regions, creating new safe havens for international terrorist organizations.[89]

This strongly suggests that unilateral action or campaigns by "coalitions of the willing" will always be inconsistent in their application, undermining any effort to build a global consensus against international terrorism and confront the organizations engaged in that practice. For this reason, any global campaign that hopes to mobilize the support and participation of a broad group of states must receive the legitimation of international and/or regional security organizations. Otherwise individual states have no incentive to oppose terrorism except when it specifically affects their own interests.

The UN provides an obvious first step to legitimize efforts to combat international terrorism. No other international organization or coalition enjoys the UN's level of legal authority and political legitimacy. At the global level, the UN is the only organization in history that can boast universal membership; every state in the world has signed the UN Charter, which has the status of a multilateral treaty under international law. The General Assembly is contentious and its resolutions are nonbinding, yet it is the largest continuous diplomatic forum that has ever existed. Although it is often politically divided, it represents the only forum on earth where every state participates on a regular basis. The UN Charter invests a considerable amount of authority in the Security Council, and the requirements of UN membership impose a substantial level of obligation on the states to follow council mandates. It is this authority that enables the council to act on behalf of the international community, rather than simply the self-interest of its members.[90]

At the same time, many states—particularly those in the developing world—are very suspicious of international action initiated by the great powers and other militarily advanced states. The history of colonialism and of great power domination that dates back to the dawn of the nation-state system encourages smaller states to place the protection of sovereignty over international security. For that reason, in certain cases, regional organizations offer an alternative form for collective action in challenging international terrorism. Every region of the world has a security organization that represents virtually all of its states, for example, the Organization of American States, the African Union, the Organization for Security and Co-operation in Europe, the Arab League, and the East Asia Summit. Like the UN, these bodies are based on some concept of collective security and impose various levels of legal and political obligations on their members. The localization of collective action removes some of the fears that smaller states might have of great power intervention initiated by the UN Security Council.

Legal Framework

International law is the primary mechanism for establishing standards of behavior that regulate the activities of states across borders. Like most forms of cooperation, it is an institution designed to achieve common goals and provide for stable and predictable relationships between governments. Unlike other cooperative institutions, however, it is based on generalized principles of conduct that are both authoritatively binding and applicable in a wide variety of circumstances. Following these rules is not simply a policy choice for political leaders, but an obligation that is fundamental for international coexistence and domestic legitimacy.[91] States may sometimes violate the rules—and when they do there may be few coercive mechanisms to sanction them; however, other states expect them to meet their obligations, and there are often political and diplomatic consequences when they do not. In fact, in most cases, political leaders regard those who flagrantly violate these rules to be committing a hostile act not only against a particular state or group of states, but against the international community as a whole.[92]

Since the middle of the twentieth century, multilateral treaties have been the primary mechanism for creating new legal norms, and global and regional organizations have been in the forefront of virtually every new international agreement. In particular, they have created a broad legal regime to combat international terrorism. Since 1971, for example, the UN General Assembly has drafted twelve counterterrorism treaties, including conventions designed to suppress hostage taking, terrorist bombings, terrorist financing, nuclear terrorism, and airplane hijacking. These agreements have broad support within the international community. Following the UN's lead, regional organizations have also been active in creating a legal regime, resulting in the following agreements: Organization of American States (OAS) Convention to Prevent and Punish Acts of Terrorism; European Convention on the Suppression of Terrorism; South Asian Association for Regional Cooperation (SAARC) Convention on Suppression of Terrorism; Arab Convention on the Suppression of Terrorism; Convention of the Organisation of the Islamic Conference on Combating International Terrorism; Organization of African Unity (now the African Union) Convention on the Prevention and Combating of Terrorism; and the Association of South East Asian Nations (ASEAN) Convention on Counter Terrorism.

In addition to the formal treaties, the UN Security Council has created new legal obligations concerning international terrorism. Under the UN Charter, council resolutions passed under Chapter VII are legally binding on all member states. The council greatly expanded the reach of the twelve treaties by approving Resolution 1373 (2001), which directs all states to criminalize assistance for terrorist activities, deny financial support and safe haven to terrorists, and share information about groups planning terrorist attacks.[93] This is the first time the council passed a binding Chapter VII resolution directed at *all* states, not just those involved in a specific conflict. In approving this unprecedented resolution it created legal obligations that bind even those states that have not signed or ratified the above treaties. The council subsequently updated and strengthened these measures in 2004 with Resolution 1526, and again in 2005, when the council took the extraordinary act of mandating that the member states pass laws prohibiting the incitement to commit a terrorist act, deny safe haven to accused terrorists, and work to strengthen the security of their international borders.[94] It also required states to submit reports on their compliance with these various resolutions.

Finally, in 2004 the council passed Resolution 1540, which requires states to prevent nonstate actors from acquiring both weapons and related materials of mass destruction. This is clearly in the interests of all states, since even countries that provide assistance to terrorists would never trust them with highly lethal weapons. Significantly, this resolution combines separate bans on chemical, biological, and nuclear weapons into one blanket prohibition on weapons of mass destruction, streamlining existing international law and overcoming gaps in earlier nonproliferation regimes by covering all UN member states.

Thus, although the UN member states have not yet concluded a general anti-terrorism treaty that would encompass all aspects of international terrorism, taken in total, the twelve UN-sponsored agreements, seven regional treaties, and four council resolutions provide both a legal and a political foundation for a multilateral campaign to stop the spread of international political violence by nonstate actors.

Coordination

International organizations can facilitate coordination and collaboration among states that share a common set of goals and, in particular, overcome dilemmas of common interests and common aversion.[95] Without formal cooperation that is usually facilitated by international organizations, states often end up with suboptimal results even when they agree with each other, due to problems of collective action, lack of transparency, an absence of procedures, and lack of common rules.[96]

In an effort to oversee and coordinate global efforts to combat international terrorism, the Security Council in 2001 established a fifteen-member Counter-Terrorism Committee (CTC) and in 2004 added a Counter-Terrorism Committee Executive Directorate (CTED). Although the CTC does not have the authority to target specific terrorists or respond to specific acts, it builds and strengthens the infrastructure needed to fight terrorism and coordinates the efforts of the member states in pursuing this task.[97] The CTED, in turn, serves as a "switchboard," facilitating the provision of technical assistance to countries needing help to implement counterterrorism mandates, and coordinates the counterterrorism efforts of a wide range of international, regional, and subregional organizations within and beyond the UN system.[98]

Many analysts consider CTC efforts to collect information from governments on counterterrorism capacity and implementation to be at least moderately successful. UN member state compliance with CTC reporting requests has been extraordinarily high, far greater than for any previous Security Council mandate. All 191 UN member states submitted first-round reports to the CTC explaining their efforts to comply with Resolution 1373.[99] The requirements for implementing 1373 often involve substantial levels of training, the development of new administrative systems, and the purchase and installation of technically sophisticated equipment. The CTC has received numerous requests from governments for assistance in these areas. As of 2004 (the most recent statistics available), 58 states requested assistance from the committee in drafting antiterrorism legislation. In addition to requesting counterterror training, 50 states requested police and law enforcement training; 37, counterterror finance training, including banking supervision; 20, immigration and border control training; and 19, immigration and border control equipment.[100] The CTC has also made important strides in encouraging regional organizations to strengthen their counterterrorism capacity. Many regional organizations have created their own counterterrorism units, especially in Europe, the Asia-Pacific region, and Latin America.[101] In Latin America, for example, the OAS has developed a vigorous regional counterterrorism program, in cooperation with the CTC and the UN.

In addition to its recent activities, the council has drawn from a pre-9/11 resolution that created a "sanctions committee," requiring all states to freeze the financial assets of al-Qaeda and other related networks, and impose a travel ban on its members.[102] As part of this measure, the council created a "committee of the whole"—the so-called 1267 Committee—to monitor compliance and maintain the list of terrorist suspects. The list comprises names that are submitted to the committee by the UN member states, and all council members must approve each name for it to be included. The sanctions regime has been modified and strengthened by subsequent resolutions, including Resolutions 1333 (2000), 1390 (2002), 1455 (2003), 1526 (2004), 1617 (2005), 1735 (2007), and 1822 (2008), so that the sanctions (assets freeze, travel ban, and arms embargo) now cover individuals and entities associated with al-Qaeda, Osama bin Laden, and/or the Taliban wherever located.

In 2006, the UN General Assembly approved a Global Counter-Terrorism Strategy that seeks to enhance national, regional, and international efforts to counter terrorism. This is the first time that all member states agreed to a common strategic approach to fight international terrorism by resolving to take practical steps individually and collectively to prevent and combat it. The strategy consists of four "pillars" that include measures to address the conditions conducive to the spread of terrorism, prevent and combat terrorism, build states' capacity to prevent and combat terrorism, and ensure respect for human rights for all and the rule of law as the fundamental basis of the fight against terrorism.[103]

Along with the UN, other global organizations such as the World Bank and International Monetary Fund (IMF) have developed and refined their own specialized approach to combating terrorism, particularly in the area of financial transactions. Like other areas of modern terrorism, finance crosses international borders and global banking systems every day. The collaborative efforts of states working within the World Bank and IMF are among the least publicized but most productive antiterrorism efforts since 9/11.[104]

State Building/Nation Building

If, as suggested above, international terrorism tends to flourish within territories where the state has lost the ability to control its own territory, provide security, or supply basic public services, one of the most important tasks in challenging transnational political violence is to help these territories develop the institutional and political structures necessary to maintain territorial security, facilitate economic development, and provide for the general welfare of the population. Equally important, state building means developing a governing structure with the legitimacy and competence to pass laws, enforce social order, and adjudicate disputes. This requires creating administrative agencies and specialized personnel that can extend control over consolidated territory and maintain a centralized and autonomous state that holds the monopoly of violence within the legally constituted territory.[105]

Individual states, particularly the great powers, have an atrocious record in this regard. State-building projects initiated by individual states—for example, Iraq, Afghanistan, Haiti, and Somalia—have failed to produce stable institutions that can win the loyalty of the population and create an effective central government.[106] Iraq continues to be badly divided by sectarian conflict, and the governments in Afghanistan and Somalia do not have any functional authority outside of the capital cities of Kabul and Mogadishu, respectively. Haiti remains mired in corruption and internal conflict. This is in part because the foreign powers that have tried to impose such a project lack the legitimacy to implement a workable governance structure on a foreign population and in part because they lack the will and competence to do so even if the local populations agreed.

International and regional organizations can help to fill this gap. The UN's lack of a sustained military force makes it difficult for the organization to become involved in peace enforcement, a task that involves disarming militias and defeating recalcitrant parties to a civil conflict. However, once the conflict is settled (often with the diplomatic assistance of global and regional security organizations), intergovernmental bodies are far more likely to be successful in rebuilding the political infrastructure of the country. According to a study by the RAND Corporation, the UN has the ability to compensate for its deficit in military power with international legitimacy and local impartiality, and as a result, UN projects in such areas as Congo, Namibia, El Salvador, Cambodia, Mozambique, Sierra Leone, and East Timor have been largely successful.[107] The study concludes that "the U.S. (or any great power) does not have such advantages in situations where America itself is a part to the conflict being terminated, or where the United States has acted without an international mandate." For this reason, "the United States would be well advised to leave the small footprint, low profile approach to the United Nations."[108]

CONCLUSION

Efforts to confront transnational political violence will continue to draw from state, regional, and international resources. While each state will continue to be primarily responsible for its own security, modern international terrorism cannot be adequately challenged without mobilizing the collective resources of the international community. In practical terms, this means employing international and regional organizations.

Notes

1. See UN Security Council Resolution 1267. S/RES/1267, 1999.
2. See UN Security Council Resolution 1333. S/RES/1333, 2000.
3. For a sampling of the vast literature on how institutions can help foster cooperation, see Kenneth A. Oye, ed., *Cooperation under Anarchy* (Princeton, N.J.: Princeton University Press, 1986); Elinor Ostrom, *Governing the Commons* (Cambridge, UK: Cambridge University Press, 1990); and Robert O. Keohane and Lisa M. Martin, "The Promise of Institutional Theory," *International Security* 20 (Summer 1995): 39–51.
4. See, for example, Joseph M. Grieco, "Anarchy and Limits of Cooperation: A Realist Critique of the Newest Liberal Institutionalism," in *Neorealism and Neoliberalism: The Contemporary Debate,* ed. David A. Baldwin (New York: Columbia University Press, 1993); and John J. Mearsheimer, "The False Promise of International Institutions," *International Security* 19 (Winter 1994/1995): 5–49.
5. Helene Cooper, "NATO Allies Wary of Sending More Troops to Afghanistan," *New York Times,* January 27, 2007.
6. Kennedy Graham, "The Security Council and Counterterrorism: Global and Regional Approaches to an Elusive Public Good," *Terrorism and Political Violence* 17 (2005): 37–65. Graham highlights many of the issues that have bedeviled the UN's attempts to create an overarching definition of terrorism that can serve as the basis for UN actions.
7. Jenny Carolina González and Simon Romero, "Marches Show Disgust with a Colombian Rebel Group," *New York Times,* February 4, 2008.

8. See www.un.org/News/Press/docs/2005/gal3276.doc.htm; www.aljazeera.com/indepth/features/2010/11/20101124114621887983.html; and Ben Saul, "The Legal Response of the League of Nations to Terrorism," *Journal of International Criminal Justice* 4, no. 1 (2006): 78–102.

9. Ibid. Also see Chantal de Jonge Oudraat, "The Role of the Security Council," in *Terrorism and the UN: Before and After September 11*, ed. Jane Boulden and Thomas G. Weiss (Bloomington: Indiana University Press, 2004); and M. J. Peterson, "Using the General Assembly," in Boulden and Weiss, *Terrorism and the UN*.

10. Jayantha Dhanapala, "The United Nations' Response to 9/11," *Terrorism and Political Violence* 17, no. 1 (2005): 17–23.

11. Joshua Muravchik, "The U.N.'s Terrorism Gap," *Los Angeles Times,* September 18, 2005.

12. United Nations, "UN Action to Counter Terrorism," www.un.org/terrorism/strategy-counter-terrorism.shtml.

13. Eric Rosand, "Security Council Resolution 1373, the Counter-Terrorism Committee, and the Fight against Terrorism," *American Journal of International Law* 97, no. 2 (2003): 733–741.

14. Richard J. Goldstone and Janine Simpson, "Evaluating the Role of the International Criminal Court as a Legal Response to Terrorism," *Harvard Human Rights Journal* 16 (Spring 2003): 13–26.

15. For example, see *U.S. Statement of January, 1985*, 24 I.L.M. 246 (1985), related to its dispute with Nicaragua, or the French position in the *Nuclear Test Cases* (Austl. v. Fr.; N.Z. v. Fr.), 1973 I.C.J 99, 135 (June 22); 1974 I.C.J. 253, 257 (December 20).

16. de Jonge Oudraat, "The Role of the Security Council"; United Nations, "UN Action to Counter Terrorism."

17. Eric Rosand, "The Security Council's Efforts to Monitor the Implementation of Al Qaeda/Taliban Sanctions," *American Journal of International Law* 98, no. 4 (2004): 745–763.

18. Ibid.

19. Security Council Resolution 1455, Second Report, *Supra* note 33, at 5.

20. Rosand, "Security Council's Efforts."

21. Graham, "Security Council and Counterterrorism."

22. Rosand, "Security Council Resolution 1373."

23. Dhanapala, "United Nations' Response to 9/11."

24. Alistair Millar and Eric Rosand, *Allied Against Terrorism: What's Needed to Strengthen Worldwide Commitment* (New York: Century Foundation, 2006).

25. Thomas J. Bierstecker, Sue E. Eckert, and Peter Romaniuk, "International Initiatives to Counter the Financing of Terrorism," in *Countering the Financing of Terrorism*, ed. Thomas J. Bierstecker and Sue E. Eckert (New York: Routledge, 2008), 235–259.

26. Johan D. van der Vyver, "Prosecuting Terrorism in International Tribunals," *Emory International Law Review* 24, no. 2 (2010): 527–547.

27. Ibid.

28. Jonathan M. Winer, "The Growing Role of International Institutions in Counter-terrorism and Law Enforcement," Council on Foreign Relations, November 5, 2003, www.cfr.org/world/growing-role-international-institutions-counterterrorism-law-enforcement/p6585.

29. Ibid.
30. Mathieu Deflem, "International Police Cooperation against Terrorism: Interpol and Europol in Comparison," in *Understanding and Responding to Terrorism*, ed. H. Durmaz, B. Sevinc, A. S. Yayla, and S. Ekici (Amsterdam: IOS Press, 2007), 17–25.
31. Sandler, Arce, and Enders argue that Interpol actions are beneficial, but their research method shows only that arresting terrorists through police work is better than doing nothing or engaging in purely passive counterterrorism strategies, rather than showing that money spent on Interpol's counterterrorism efforts is as effective as or more effective than money spent on national police forces' counter-terrorism efforts. See Todd Sandler, Daniel G. Arce, and Walter Enders, "An Evaluation of Interpol's Cooperative-based Counterterrorism Linkages," *Journal of Law and Economics* 54, no. 1 (2011): 79–110.
32. Mathieu Deflem, "International Police Cooperation Against Terrorism: Interpol and Europol in Comparison"; Winer, "The Growing Role of International Institutions in Counterterrorism and Law Enforcement." In each case the authority was granted in 2003.
33. Oldrich Bures, "Europol's Fledgling Counterterrorism Role," paper presented at the WISC Second Global International Studies Conference, Ljubljana, 2008; Davide Casale, "Institutional and Legal Aspects of EU Counter-Terrorism," in *Legal Aspects of Combating Terrorism:* (Amsterdam Center of Excellence Defense Against Terrorism, 2008), 115–130. The inability to produce results is used to justify paltry funding for Europol.
34. Christian Kaunert, "Europol and EU Counterterrorism: International Security Actorness in the External Dimension," *Studies in Conflict and Terrorism* 33, no. 7 (2010): 652–671.
35. de Jonge Oudraat, "The Role of the Security Council."
36. Sener Dalyan, "Combating the Financing of Terrorism: Rethinking Strategies for Success," *Defense Against Terrorism Review* 1, no. 1 (2008): 137–153.
37. Ibid.
38. Michael Brzoska, "The Role of Effectiveness and Efficiency in the European Union's Counterterrorism Policy: The Case of Terrorist Financing," *Economics of Security Working Paper Series,* no. 51 (2011): 1–22. "Soft law" lacks the binding force of traditional "hard law" and is instead a statement of norms, guidelines, and recommendations that states are strongly encouraged to follow. "Soft law" is often aspirational in nature and can, but need not, evolve into "hard law."
39. See www.fatf-gafi.org/media/fatf/documents/FATF%20Standards%20-%2040%20 Recommendations%20rc.pdf and www.fatf-gafi.org/topics/fatfrecommendations/ documents/ixspecialrecommendations.html.
40. Brzoska, "The Role of Effectiveness and Efficiency in the European Union's Counterterrorism Policy." It took until 2009 for all twenty-seven bilateral U.S.-EU member state implementation agreements to be concluded.
41. Financial Action Task Force, "The 40 Recommendations"; IMF, "The IMF and the Fight Against Money Laundering and the Financing of Terrorism," 2012, www.imf.org/external/np/exr/facts/aml.htm; IMF, "Anti-Money Laundering/ Combating the Financing of Terrorism," 2009, www.imf.org/external/np/otm/ 2009/anti-money.pdf.

42. Ibid.

43. Bierstecker, Eckert, and Romaniuk, "International Initiatives to Counter the Financing of Terrorism."

44. Eric Lichtblau and James Risen, "Bank Data Is Sifted by US in Secret to Block Terror," *New York Times,* June 23, 2006.

45. See, for example, Shashi Tharoor, "Why America Still Needs the United Nations," *Foreign Affairs* 82, no. 5 (2003): 67–80.

46. Millar and Rosand, *Allied Against Terrorism.*

47. Ibid.

48. Dhanapala, "United Nations' Response to 9/11."

49. To be fair, the IAEA has had some success in tracking down loose nuclear material, which reduces the odds of radiological terrorism. See Miles A. Pomper and Michelle E. Dover, "The Seoul Nuclear Summit," *National Interest* 117 (January–February 2012): 47–54.

50. Bierstecker, Eckert, and Romaniuk, "International Initiatives to Counter the Financing of Terrorism."

51. Ibid.

52. The operation of the UN's CTC is typical in this regard (Millar and Rosand, *Allied Against Terrorism*).

53. Rosand, "Security Council Resolution 1373"; Rosand, "Security Council's Efforts."

54. Rick Fawn and Raymond A. Hinnebusch, eds., *The Iraq War: Causes and Consequences* (Boulder, Colo.: Lynne Reiner, 2006); Karen DeYoung, "Iranian Defiance of U.N. Detailed; Nuclear Enrichment Continues, Report Says," *Washington Post,* May 24, 2007.

55. Aprille Muscara, "Trying Pirates Often as Tricky as Catching Them," *Inter Press Service,* August 25, 2010.

56. Millar and Rosand, *Allied Against Terrorism.*

57. For an overview of this phenomenon, see Walter Laqueur, *A History of Terrorism* (New Brunswick, N.J.: Transaction Publishers, 2001). See also Eric Hobsbawm, *Primitive Rebels: Studies in Archaic Forms of Social Movement in the 19th and 20th Centuries* (New York: W. W. Norton, 1965).

58. See, for example, Richard Bach Jensen, "Daggers, Rifles and Dynamite: Anarchist Terrorism in Nineteenth Century Europe," *Terrorism and Political Violence* 16, no. 1 (Spring 2004): 116–153.

59. See Alessandro Orsini, *Anatomy of the Red Brigades: The Religious Mind-Set of Modern Terrorists* (Ithaca, N.Y.: Cornell University Press, 2011); and Stefan Aust, *Baader-Meinhof: The Inside Story of the RAF,* revised edition (New York: Oxford University Press, 2009).

60. See, for example, Richard English, *Armed Struggle: The History of the IRA* (Oxford: Oxford University Press, 2004); Robert P. Clark, *The Basque Insurgents: ETA, 1952–1980* (Madison: University of Wisconsin Press, 1984); and Aliza Marcus, *Blood and Belief: The PKK and the Kurdish Fight for Independence* (New York: New York University Press, 2009).

61. See, for example, Wunyabari Maloba, *Mau Mau and Kenya: An Analysis of a Peasant Revolt* (Bloomington: Indiana University Press, 1998).

62. See Bruce Hoffman, *Inside Terrorism* (New York: Columbia University Press, 2006), chap. 3.

63. See, for example, Gus Martin, *Understanding Terrorism: Challenges, Perspectives, and Issues* (London: Sage, 2012), 248–253.

64. Barton Gellman and Dana Priest, "U.S. Strikes Terrorist-Linked Sites in Afghanistan, Factory in Sudan," *Washington Post*, August 21, 1998.

65. See Andrew D. Mitchell, "Does One Illegality Merit Another? The Law of Belligerent Reprisals International Law," *Military Law Review* 170 (December 2001).

66. International Committee of the Red Cross, *Commentary, Convention (IV) Relative to the Protection of Civilian Persons in Time of War. Geneva, 12 August 1949* (Geneva, 1958).

67. See "S.J. Resolution 23—Authorization for Use of Military Force (Enrolled Bill); September 18, 2001." Available at http://avalon.law.yale.edu/sept11/sjres23_eb.asp.

68. See Stephen Walt, *The Origin of Alliances* (Ithaca, N.Y.: Cornell University Press, 1990).

69. Edgar Buckley, "Invocation of Article 5: Five Years On," *NATO Review* (Summer 2006).

70. Robert Hilderbrand, *Dumbarton Oaks: The Origins of the United Nations and the Search for Postwar Security* (Chapel Hill: University of North Carolina Press, 1990).

71. Bruce Cronin and Ian Hurd, "Introduction," in *The UN Security Council and the Politics of International Authority,* ed. Bruce Cronin and Ian Hurd (New York: Routledge, 2008), 1.

72. Josef Kunz, "Individual and Collective Self-Defense in Article 51 of the Charter of the United Nations," *The American Journal of International Law* 41, no. 4 (October 1947).

73. See John Ruggie, "Continuity and Transformation in the World Polity: Toward a Neorealist Synthesis," in *Neorealism and Its Critics,* ed. Robert Keohane (New York: Columbia University Press, 1986), 143.

74. See Max Weber, "The Profession and Vocation of Politics," in *Weber: Political Writings,* ed. Peter Lassman and Ronald Speirs (Cambridge: Cambridge University Press, 1994).

75. James R. Schlesinger et al., "Final Report of the Independent Panel to Review DoD Detention Operations" (August 2004), 81.

76. See Russell Howard, "Understanding Al Qaeda's Application of the New Terrorism," in *Terrorism and Counterterrorism: Understanding the New Security Environment,* ed. Russell Howard and Reid Sawyer (New York: McGraw-Hill/Dushkin, 2002).

77. On the concept of failed states in Africa, see Robert Bates, *When Things Fell Apart: State Failure in Late-Century Africa* (Cambridge: Cambridge University Press, 2008).

78. www.foreignpolicy.com/failed_states_index_2012_interactive.

79. James A. Piazza, "Incubators of Terror: Do Failed and Failing States Promote Transnational Terrorism?" *International Studies Quarterly* 52, no. 3 (2008).

80. Lauren Ploch et al., "Piracy Off the Horn of Africa," *Congressional Research Service Report for Congress* (April 27, 2011), 5.

81. Bruce Hoffman, *Inside Terrorism* (New York: Columbia University Press, 2006), chap. 9.

82. See United Nations Security Council, Counter-Terrorism Committee, www.un.org/en/sc/ctc/resources/st-press.html.

83. United Nations Document S/RES/1368 (2001).

84. The White House, *National Strategy for Combating Terrorism* (Washington, D.C., February 2003).

85. In 2002, Defense Secretary Donald Rumsfeld told the Senate Armed Services Committee that a war against Iraq would be a key part of the American war on terror. See Jim Garamone, "Iraq Part of Global War on Terrorism, Rumsfeld Says," U.S. Department of Defense, American Forces Information Service, September 19, 2002.

86. Ashley S. Deeks, "Pakistan's Sovereignty and the Killing of Osama bin Laden," *Insights* (Journal of the American Society of International Law) 15, no. 11 (May 5, 2011).

87. Jose Alvarez, *International Organizations as Law-Makers* (Oxford: Oxford University Press, 2006), 208–209.

88. Dexter Filkins, "Turkish Deputies Refuse to Accept American Troops," *New York Times*, March 2, 2003.

89. Paul Harris, "Drone Attacks Create Terrorist Safe Havens, Warns Former CIA Official," *The Guardian*, June 5, 2012; Ibrahim Mothana, "How Drones Help Al Qaeda," *New York Times*, June 13, 2012.

90. See Ian Hurd, "Legitimacy, Power and the Symbolic Life of the UN Security Council," *Global Governance* 8, no. 1 (2002).

91. The authority of international law goes well beyond obligations owed to other states. In most cases, states incorporate international law into their domestic legal systems, thereby creating legal liabilities for governments through their own judicial institutions. See Antonio Cassesse, *International Law* (Oxford: Oxford University Press, 2005), chap. 12.

92. See, for example, J. L. Brierly, *The Outlook for International Law* (Oxford: Oxford University Press, 1946).

93. United Nations Document S/RES/1373 (2001).

94. United Nations Document S/RES/1624 (2005).

95. A dilemma of common interest arises when independent actions by individual states fail to lead to an outcome that all of the individual parties desire, while a dilemma of common aversion occurs when independent actions result in an outcome that all wish to avoid. See Arthur Stein, "Coordination and Collaboration: Regimes in an Anarchic World," *International Organization* 36, no. 2 (Spring 1982).

96. See, for example, Kenneth W. Abbott and Duncan Snidal, "Why States Act Through Formal International Organizations," *Journal of Conflict Resolution* 42, no. 1 (February 1998): 3–32; and Lisa L. Martin and Beth A. Simmons, *International Institutions: An International Organization Reader* (Cambridge: MIT Press, 2001).

97. Eric Rosand, "Security Council 1373, the Counter-Terrorism Committee, and the Fight Against Terrorism," 337.

98. Nicholas Rostow, "Before and After: The Changed UN Response to Terrorism Since September 11," *Cornell International Law Journal* 35, no. 3 (Winter 2002): 482–485.

99. Eric Rosand, *Current Developments: Security Council Resolution 1373, the Counter-Terrorism Committee, and the Fight Against Terrorism,* 97 American J.I.L., no. 2, 337, 332–341 (April 2003).

100. David Cortright, "A Critical Evaluation of the UN Counter-Terrorism Program: Accomplishments and Challenges," paper presented at Global Enforcement Regimes: Transnational Organized Crime, International Terrorism and Money Laundering, Transnational Institute (TNI), Amsterdam (April 28–29, 2005), 12.

101. Cortright, "A Critical Evaluation of the UN Counter-Terrorism Program," 13.

102. United Nations Document S/RES/1267 (1999).

103. See www.un.org/terrorism/strategy-counter-terrorism.shtml.

104. See, for example, World Bank, International Monetary Fund, and United Nations Office on Drugs and Crime, Counter Terrorism Implementation Task Force, "Final Report of the Working Group on Tackling the Financing of Terrorism," January 2009, http://siteresources.worldbank.org/FINANCIALSECTOR/Resour ces/wg5-financing.pdf.

105. See Charles Tilly, "Western-State Making and Theories of Political Transformation," in *The Formation of National States in Western Europe*, ed. Charles Tilly (Princeton, N.J.: Princeton University Press, 1975).

106. James Dobbins, John G. McGinn et al., *America's Role in Nation-Building from Germany to Iraq* (Santa Monica, Calif.: RAND Corporation, 2003).

107. James Dobbins, Seth G. Jones et al., *The UN's Role in Nation-Building from the Congo to Iraq* (Santa Monica, Calif.: RAND Corporation, 2005).

108. Ibid., xxx. Parenthetical added.

10

is an outright ban the best way to eliminate or constrain torture?

YES: Torture violates U.S. and international law and should never be allowed.
Michael H. Posner, *U.S. Department of State*

NO: There is a need to bring an unfortunate practice within the bounds of law.
Alan M. Dershowitz, *Harvard Law School*

In April 2009, President Barack Obama sparked an impassioned national debate on torture when he released four previously top secret memos drafted by Bush administration lawyers that offered guidelines for "enhanced interrogations" by the Central Intelligence Agency (CIA) of al-Qaeda operatives in the wake of the attacks on the United States on September 11, 2001.[1] The release of the memos followed Obama's earlier executive order banning harsh interrogation practices and requiring all U.S. personnel, including CIA agents, to abide by the *Army Field Manual*'s noncoercive guidelines.

The Obama administration's reason for releasing the memos and its justification for banning coercive interrogations centered on three points. First, torture violates American law and values. Second, it hurts America's image abroad. And, third, such practices are unnecessary because, according to Obama, "we can effectively obtain the intelligence we need" without resorting to torture.

However, soon after the release of the Bush memos, a controversy erupted when a private internal memo written by Obama's director of national intelligence, Dennis Blair, was leaked to the press. The memo stated: "High value information came from interrogations in which those [coercive] methods were used and provided a deeper understanding of the al Qa'ida organization that was attacking this country."[2]

Blair quickly issued a public statement to clarify his words: "The bottom line is these techniques have hurt our image around the world, the damage they have done to our interests far outweighed whatever benefit they gave us and they are not essential to our national security."

Therein lies the policy dilemma over the use of torture. On the one hand, many if not most national security professionals recognize that harsh interrogations can glean actionable intelligence and will likely be used in extreme cases. Indeed, President Obama himself ordered a secret task force to determine whether the CIA may require "additional or different guidance" on interrogations in the event of special circumstances.[3] On the other hand, it is equally clear that the use of torture incurs tremendous strategic costs in terms of a nation's reputation.

The classic case of the 1957 Battle of Algiers bears this out. Relying on brutal interrogation tactics, the French army was able to destroy the hardened National Liberation Front (FLN) in Algiers in a matter of months. Yet at the same time, the legitimacy of France to maintain its Algerian colony was left in tatters, contributing to France's loss of Algeria just a few years later.

The bottom-line question on torture is this: if any sitting president should find himself in the position of facing an imminent terrorist attack and having suspects with possible knowledge of the plot in custody, should he—indeed, would he—refrain from ordering coercive efforts to extract information? Put differently, would knowledge of the long-term strategic costs of engaging in a nefarious practice that violates America's laws and values outweigh the tactical imperative to do everything possible to prevent a potentially catastrophic attack?

Michael Posner offers a morally and legally consistent answer to this question. He argues that under no circumstances should the use of torture or cruel, inhuman, or degrading treatment in interrogations be accepted as a matter of policy, law, or practice. His "zero-tolerance" approach applies equally to "ticking bomb" scenarios—which he says are "rare or almost nonexistent"— through stressful battlefield conditions where there may be a strong temptation to use rough tactics to glean quick operational intelligence. According to Posner, any use of torture under any circumstances will ultimately undermine America's security. Not only does torture often evoke false or misleading information, but its use makes Americans less safe by emboldening their enemies and alienating their allies. Thus an outright ban is required not simply on grounds of law and morals, but also on grounds of security.

Alan Dershowitz approaches the question from a more policy-centered perspective. He agrees with Posner that torture should be illegal and never be used by a democracy committed to the rule of law. But he also argues that it is unrealistic to expect a president to refrain from utilizing some form of torture if he believes it might prevent an imminent mass-casualty attack. Dershowitz believes that the standard approach by democracies—declare torture illegal, but, in the words of torture opponent Sen. John McCain, "do what you have to do" in extreme cases—actually weakens the rule of law and makes the use of torture more likely. He proposes ending this dangerous "off-the-books" approach by enacting a "torture warrant statute," authorized by Congress and sanctified by the courts, that would permit the president to temporarily suspend the prohibition against torture in extreme cases. This way, he says, an age-old tension between fundamental values and necessities of security can be resolved within a rule-of-law framework.

Both authors of this chapter have identical goals in mind: upholding the rule of law and keeping the country safe. The fact that they view torture so differently is indicative of the legal and moral complexities of this important issue. Yet the real debate over the use of torture will not take place in the pages of a book during a time of relative calm. Should the United States enter another period like that surrounding 9/11, urgent decisions on the treatment of terror suspects will be required, and the thoughtful arguments of these authors will be front and center.

Torture violates U.S. and international law
YES: and should never be allowed.
Michael H. Posner, *U.S. Department of State*

The Case for an Outright Ban on Torture

M ore than a decade after the attacks of September 11, 2001, the United States continues to debate a wide range of national security policies.[4] Perhaps no issue has stirred greater debate and controversy than the adoption of policies authorizing the use of torture and other coercive interrogation techniques to gather intelligence. And no other aspect of the George W. Bush administration's counterterrorism policies was more damaging to America's internal commitment to uphold the rule of law and to its reputation and standing in the world. From the very beginning of his presidency, Barack Obama strongly signaled his intent to ensure an absolute ban on torture and cruel treatment when he signed an executive order banning all forms of torture and cruel treatment.[5] The administration lived up to that commitment in policy and practice and the last four years have demonstrated the fallacy of the claim that banning torture would impede our ability to gather intelligence and protect our national security interests at home and abroad. Nonetheless, questions regarding the use of torture continue.[6]

The debate on this issue is set in a broader context, one in which the government has employed security measures to prevent or greatly reduce the risks of future attacks. Preventive measures are essential. The U.S. government has the right, indeed the duty, to protect its people. Since the attacks on 9/11, the government, mindful of this obligation, has devoted significant resources and attention to enhancing airport security and increasing financial and other support for America's front line defenders—police, firefighters, and emergency medical providers. It has taken a series of measures to step up inspections of shipping containers coming into this country. The government also has adopted additional means of protecting other aspects critical to the national infrastructure, such as nuclear power facilities, electrical grids, the water supply, and America's food production and distribution system.

On a parallel track, officials have made efforts to improve and better coordinate intelligence gathering by federal and state governmental entities, having realized that better intelligence can prevent attacks and save lives. The federal government aided this effort by creating a new post, the director of national intelligence. These measures and more were examined by the 9/11 Commission, an independent, bipartisan group established by the president and Congress. The commission made a series of useful recommendations for enhancing the safety of Americans that were prudent, thoughtful, practical, and wise. Everything recommended was rights-neutral and clearly within the bounds of the law.[7]

Reliance on coercive interrogations by the CIA and other agencies has harmed America's reputation in the world. Rather than enhancing intelligence gathering, it has undermined these efforts. Rather than increasing the nation's security, this reliance has emboldened America's enemies, strained relations with its closest allies, and put its troops around the world at greater risk. The relaxation of rules on interrogations has undermined discipline within the military. As a consequence, the introduction of official cruelty as government policy has made the United States weaker and more vulnerable to attack.

To fully restore America's reputation and image, to support its troops, and to reaffirm relations with its allies, the U.S. government must, as directed by President Obama, adopt a zero-tolerance approach, ensuring an end to all forms of torture and cruelty. The use of torture or cruel, inhuman, or degrading treatment in interrogations should never be tolerated, regulated, or justified as a matter of official policy, law, or practice.

THE PRECEDENT FOR TREATING PRISONERS HUMANELY

The United States has a proud history of requiring the humane treatment of all enemy prisoners, a tradition dating back to Gen. George Washington. In January 1777, Washington ordered his troops to treat captured British soldiers "with humanity," writing, "Let them have no reason to complain of our copying the brutal example of the British army."[8]

Washington's admonition to his troops reflected a broader commitment by the Founders to set a high ethical standard and to adhere to the rule of law. As Thomas Jefferson later wrote to James Madison, "It has great effect on the opinion of our people and the world to have moral right on our side."[9]

This commitment has been reinforced at key junctures in U.S. history. In the Civil War, Lincoln appointed Columbia law professor Francis Lieber, under sponsorship of the army's general-in-chief, Henry Halleck, to develop a set of minimum standards for the military that forbade suffering, disgrace, cruel imprisonment, want of food, mutilation, death, or other barbarity. The Lieber Code, as it came to be known, required Union forces to treat prisoners of war "with humanity" and to "be strictly guided by the principles of justice, honor, and humanity—virtues adorning a soldier even more than other men, for the very reason that he possesses the power of his arms against the unarmed."[10]

The Lieber Code served as a basis for the development of the law of armed conflict, which the U.S. military has taken a leading role in developing and promoting on the international stage. Influenced by the Lieber Code, Theodore Roosevelt urged at the time of the Philippine-American War that "determined an unswerving effort must be made to find out every instance of barbarity on the part of our troops, to punish those guilty of it, and . . . to prevent the occurrence of all such acts in the future."[11]

The Lieber Code also guided those U.S. officials who, after World War II, took a lead in the international negotiations that led to the promulgation of the Geneva Conventions of 1949. Each of the four Geneva Conventions contains an identical provision, Common Article 3, which specifically prohibits "violence to life and person, in particular murder of all kinds, mutilation, cruel treatment and torture" and "outrages upon personal dignity, in particular humiliating and degrading treatment."[12]

In 1950 Secretary of Defense George Marshall spelled out the application of the humane treatment standard to U.S. officials in a book titled *The Armed Forces Officer*. In it, he lists twenty-nine propositions that govern American conduct at war, explaining that

> the United States abides by the laws of war. Its Armed Forces, in their dealings with all other peoples, are expected to comply with the laws of war, in the spirit and to the letter. In waging war, we do not terrorize help-less non-combatants, if it is within our power to avoid doing so. Wanton killing, torture, cruelty or the working of unusual hardship on enemy prisoners or populations is not justified under any circumstances. Like-wise respect for the reign of law, as that term is understood in the United States, is expected to follow the flag wherever it goes.[13]

Consistent with General Marshall's words, the U.S. military applied the humane treatment standard of the Geneva Conventions to all prisoners in its custody, even those like the Viet Cong who neither recognized nor abided by the Geneva Conventions and did not qualify as prisoners of war under the Geneva Conventions.

Members of the military still hold to these precedents. In recent years, some retired senior U.S. military leaders and Defense Department officials have become increasingly outspoken critics of U.S. interrogation practices. In September 2006, about fifty members of this group wrote a letter to the Senate

Armed Services Committee in favor of strict adherence to Common Article 3 in the interrogation of al-Qaeda prisoners:

> The framers of the Geneva Conventions, including the American representatives in particular, wanted to ensure that Common Article 3 would apply in situations where a state party to the treaty, like the United States, fights an adversary that is not a party, including irregular forces like al Qaeda. The United States military has abided by the basic requirements of Common Article 3—even to enemies that systematically violated the Geneva Conventions themselves.[14]

THE CASE AGAINST TORTURE AND COERCIVE TACTICS: WHY AN ABSOLUTE BAN IS ESSENTIAL

The case against torture and official cruelty is clear. For starters, these techniques are an ineffective and even counterproductive way to gather intelligence. As experienced interrogators from the military and intelligence agencies have said repeatedly, these techniques are not the best way to obtain actionable intelligence. Joe Navarro, a twenty-year veteran of the Federal Bureau of Investigation (FBI) with wide experience in counterterrorism investigations, said, "The only thing torture guarantees is pain. It never guarantees the truth. It's a technique that we in the FBI have never used, we don't need . . . [M]ost of the military interviewers that I've worked with don't subscribe to it."[15]

Navarro teaches interrogators at the CIA and FBI that torture results in fear, contempt, and resistance. Although prisoners may occasionally volunteer useful information when tortured, they will not cooperate in the long run, and far more vital information will then be lost. Instead, an interrogator should "convince an informant to release information, not threaten," and remember "that acts of kindness help to build informants' confidence in the interrogator."[16]

As images and stories of torture and mistreatment by U.S. officials spread and gained currency since the events of 9/11, potential sources of intelligence and even America's close allies in the world turned and refused to cooperate with its intelligence-gathering efforts, making America less safe. Reacting to the U.S. government's recent reliance on harsh interrogations, fifteen senior interrogators, interviewers, and intelligence officials in the U.S. military, FBI, and CIA issued a public statement on this matter in June 2008. They concluded that

> the use of torture and other inhumane and abusive treatment results in false and misleading information, loss of critical intelligence, and has caused serious damage to the reputation and standing of the

United States. The use of such techniques also facilitates enemy recruitment, misdirects or wastes scarce resources, and deprives the United States of the standing to demand humane treatment of captured Americans.[17]

Torture and coercive interrogation practices also run counter to the fundamental principles upon which the United States was founded and betray its citizens' religious and ethical ideals as a people. Those who have experienced torture at the hands of their enemies are often the most passionate advocates on this point. For example, Sen. John McCain, who was imprisoned and tortured by the North Vietnamese during the Vietnam War for almost six years, led the fight in Congress in 2005 against the Bush administration's coercive interrogation policy.[18]

As mentioned earlier, torture and cruel treatment also violate U.S. national and international law obligations. The Geneva Conventions are complemented by a set of human rights standards, including a provision in the International Covenant on Civil and Political Rights that bars all forms of torture and cruel, inhuman, and degrading treatment.[19] The Convention Against Torture and Other Cruel, Inhuman or Degrading Treatment or Punishment, which entered into force in 1987 and was ratified by the United States in 1994, elaborated on this standard.[20] All of these international standards serve as a minimum baseline, a floor beneath which the U.S. government cannot sink, and conform with and reinforce U.S. law.

Torture and mistreatment carried out by U.S. soldiers or intelligence agents also invite retaliatory treatment when U.S. citizens are detained abroad. The U.S. military has been a staunch advocate of the Geneva Conventions because these standards protect American soldiers in the field. If the U.S. government adopts policies that sanction "enhanced interrogation techniques," how can the United States object when similar policies are applied to its own citizens?[21]

Reliance on cruelty also engenders a broader climate of lawlessness and ill discipline by those who engage in such practices. An effective military relies on discipline and adherence to the rules. When commanders begin to relax these rules, especially on something as basic as the treatment of prisoners, soldiers will inevitably take it upon themselves to stretch the meaning of other rules as well. This is a prescription for a breakdown of discipline and control.

The resort to torture also has profound international implications. Because the United States is such a powerful country and has long presented itself to the world as a leader on human rights, a U.S. retreat from those standards has had a devastating effect on others—a ripple effect that provided a convenient excuse for others around the world to follow. To cite just two examples:

- Former president of Georgia Eduard Shevardnadze stated in October 2002, after being criticized for colluding with Russia in violating the human rights of Chechens, that "international human rights commitments might become pale in comparison with the importance of the anti-terrorist campaign."[22]

- In September 2003, Malaysia's justice minister, Rais Yatim, defended detaining more than one hundred alleged terrorists without trial by citing the U.S. government's detention of individuals at Guantánamo Bay.[23]

In a similar vein, opportunistic governments expressed support for the fight against terrorism after the 9/11 attacks, while presenting their own domestic insurgencies as conflicts perpetrated by terrorist groups analogous to al-Qaeda. For example, both Syria under Bashar al-Assad and Egypt under Hosni Mubarak encouraged the United States to emulate their "successful" strategies for fighting terrorism. Syria's minister of information, Adnan Omran, declared that Syria was "ahead [of the United States] in fighting terrorism," and al-Assad invited the United States to "take advantage of Syria's successful experiences."[24] Similarly, Egypt's former prime minister, Atef Ebeid, responded to criticism of his country's use of torture by rejecting criticism of Egypt's rights record and linking Egypt's challenges to those of the United States:

> The U.S. and U.K., including human rights groups, have, in the past, been calling on us to give these terrorists their "human rights." You can give them all the human rights they deserve until they kill you. After these horrible crimes committed in New York and Virginia, maybe Western countries should begin to think of Egypt's own fight against terror as their new model.[25]

America's longtime pursuit of human rights around the world was tarnished by prisoner abuses, particularly the use of coercive interrogations, in the years after 9/11. Intangible but vitally important assets—such as U.S. standing in the world, its soft power, and its moral authority to lead—was severely damaged. This was put most eloquently by Sen. John McCain:

> We are Americans. We hold ourselves to humane standards of treatment no matter how terribly evil or awful they [enemy combatants] may be. To do otherwise undermines our security, and it also undermines our great-ness as a nation. We are not simply any other country. We stand for a lot more than that in the world: a moral mission, one of freedom and

democracy and human rights at home and abroad. . . . The enemy we fight has no respect for human life or human rights. They don't deserve our sympathy. But this is not about who they are. . . . It is about who we are. These are values that distinguish us from our enemies.[26]

JUSTIFICATION FOR TORTURE AND COERCIVE INTERROGATIONS: THE BUSH ADMINISTRATION'S GLOBAL WAR ON TERRORISM

James Madison once wrote, "War is in fact the true nurse of executive aggrandizement."[27] His admonition was borne out by the Bush administration's assertions that in a new "global war on terror," war trumps law, and laws become a luxury, not a necessity, binding on the executive.

In the aftermath of the 9/11 attacks, the Bush administration shifted U.S. policy to allow coercive interrogations in national security cases. This shift was part of what Vice President Dick Cheney called the "new normalcy," a concept he believed reflected an "understanding of the world as it is."[28] In an interview five days after the 9/11 attacks, the vice president asserted that to obtain information about al-Qaeda and to prevent future attacks, the U.S. government would

> have to work, though, sort of the dark side, if you will. We've got to spend time in the shadows of the intelligence world. A lot of what needs to be done here will have to be done quietly, without any discussion. . . . [I]t's going to be vital for us to use any means at our disposal, basically, to achieve our objective.[29]

By using this framework and asserting that it was fighting a new kind of enemy, the administration asserted that existing laws were impediments to fighting this new war. The thrust of the government's approach to the public was essentially this: "Trust us—we will do what is necessary to keep you safe."

In 2002 White House Counsel Alberto Gonzales provided a legal underpinning to the administration's approach to interrogations. He instructed the Office of Legal Counsel in the Justice Department (DOJ) to provide a legal definition of torture in order to give legal cover to interrogators from the CIA and other agencies who were fearful that their reliance on "enhanced interrogation techniques" could lead to future criminal prosecutions. In August 2002, the DOJ presented its memo, authored by Jay S. Bybee. It concluded that to constitute torture, an act "must inflict pain that is difficult to endure . . . equivalent in intensity to the pain accompanying serious physical injury, such as organ failure, impairment of bodily function or even death."[30]

Four months later, Secretary of Defense Donald Rumsfeld took his cue from the Bybee memo. Frustrated by the military's failure to obtain good intelligence from detainees at Guantánamo,[31] Rumsfeld authorized a series of harsh techniques, including the use of dogs, to intimidate detainees and to get better information. In the spring of 2003, he authorized twenty-four new interrogation methods for prisoners at Guantánamo, part of the administration's gloves-off approach to interrogations.[32] Rumsfeld subsequently authorized the extension of these harsh, often illegal techniques for use in the interrogation of prisoners in Afghanistan and Iraq.

On a parallel track, the CIA developed what President Bush called "an alternative set of procedures," which were intended to give the CIA greater latitude in questioning high-value detainees in its custody.[33] These "enhanced interrogation techniques," more aggressive and often more abusive, were carried out in secret detention facilities under the CIA's control and reportedly included painful stress positions, temperature manipulation, forced nudity, sexual humiliation, sleep deprivation, physical abuse, and, in some cases, a form of simulated drowning known as waterboarding.

The combination of these interrogation rules and secret detentions led to serious abuses. These abuses became front-page headlines in the spring of 2004 when the news media released photographs showing the abuse and humiliation of prisoners at Abu Ghraib prison in Baghdad.[34] But these photos only revealed a small slice of the problem. A 2006 study conducted by Human Rights First revealed that more than one hundred prisoners have died in U.S. custody in Iraq, Afghanistan, and other places. The Pentagon has classified thirty-four of those one hundred cases as criminal homicides. Of those thirty-four, none occurred at Guantánamo, and only one occurred at Abu Ghraib. Human Rights First also documented that eleven of the one hundred cases were prisoners who literally were tortured to death.[35]

Both Congress and the Supreme Court attempted to check the Bush administration, but they met intense resistance. In 2005 Congress overwhelmingly passed the Detainee Treatment Act with a provision that explicitly prohibits any cruel, inhuman, or degrading treatment of detainees in U.S. custody.[36] Although the president signed the bill into law, he included a signing statement that stripped it of its essential meaning, asserting that there would be compliance with the law so long as it did not compromise national security.[37]

In June 2006, the Supreme Court entered the debate, ruling in *Hamdan v. Rumsfeld* that all detainees in U.S. custody are entitled to humane treatment, as defined by Common Article 3 of the Geneva Conventions.[38] The administration, however, rejected the Court's ruling by proposing the Military Commissions Act (MCA) in September 2006. Though ostensibly aimed at bringing the procedures of Guantánamo's military commissions into conformity with the *Hamdan v. Rumsfeld* (2006) decision, the MCA included a provision that exempted the CIA, granting it latitude to continue using "enhanced interrogation techniques." At a press conference announcing this new initiative, President Bush made the case for circumventing the Court's decision, claiming that he was simply proposing "that there be clarity in the law so that our professionals will have no doubt that that which they are doing is legal . . . [and so that] our professionals [cannot] be held to account based upon court decisions in other countries."[39]

Although there was pushback from Congress, which principally came from Republican senators John Warner, John McCain, and Lindsey Graham, all former military servicemen, Congress ultimately passed the MCA, adding a requirement for the president to issue an executive order spelling out how the CIA would comply with Common Article 3.[40] The administration ignored the intent of the congressional directive. An executive order, issued by the president in July 2007, asserts that the CIA program "fully complies" with Common Article 3, but significantly limits the circumstances in which acts of abuse are strictly prohibited and only prohibits other forms of cruel, inhuman, or degrading conduct if the purpose of such abuses is to humiliate or degrade.[41] Commenting on this provision, Gen. P. X. Kelley, retired U.S. Marine Corps commandant, and Prof. Robert Turner wrote, "The president has given the CIA carte blanche to engage in 'willful and outrageous acts of personal abuse.'"[42]

Responding to the executive order, Congress passed in 2007 a provision as part of the Intelligence Authorization Act for Fiscal Year 2008 that would have required the CIA to follow the army standard. Although the provision passed both chambers of Congress, yet again the administration recoiled, and the president vetoed the bill in March 2008.[43] President Obama explicitly revoked this executive order on January 22, 2009.[44]

In December 2008, a month before Obama took office, the Senate Armed Services Committee released a report placing responsibility for abuses committed in Guantánamo, Abu Ghraib, and other detention centers squarely on the shoulders of top Bush administration officials, including Secretary Rumsfeld. Issued jointly by Senators Carl Levin and John McCain, the report states:

> Secretary of Defense Donald Rumsfeld's December 2, 2002 authorization of aggressive interrogation techniques and subsequent interrogation policies and plans approved by senior military and civilian officials conveyed the message that physical pressures and degradation were appropriate treatment for detainees in U.S. military custody. What followed was an erosion in standards dictating that detainees be treated humanely.[45]

TICKING BOMBS AND RED HERRINGS: WHY TORTURE IS NEVER LEGITIMATE

Despite the sound advice of many senior military officers and national security experts and practitioners, some policymakers, academics, and others continue to make the case for some form of officially sanctioned torture or abuse.[46] One such proponent is Prof. Alan Dershowitz. In a series of articles and books in recent years, he has argued that because coercive questioning will inevitably occur in the new national security environment, it should be regulated through the use of torture warrants.[47] Professor Dershowitz believes that torture warrants would not only limit torture but also ensure openness and accountability because oversight and monitoring would be built into the system.[48] His argument for these warrants is based on the notion that in a war against terrorists, it is no longer sufficient for the United States to be on the defensive. Thus he argues, as he did in a March 2003 interview, that the U.S. government needs to have at its disposal a series of aggressive measures, including coercive interrogation techniques, to prevent terrorist acts:

> We should never under any circumstances allow low-level people to administer torture. If torture is going to be administered as a last resort in the ticking-bomb case, to save enormous numbers of lives, it ought to be done openly, with accountability, with approval by the president of the United States or by a Supreme Court justice.[49]

Professor Dershowitz frequently cites this ticking bomb hypothetical to make his point. In such cases, he argues, a torture warrant would actually be a form of protection because it

> puts a heavy burden on the government to demonstrate by factual evidence the necessity to administer this horrible, horrible technique of torture. I would talk about nonlethal torture, say, a sterilized needle underneath the nail, which would violate the Geneva Accords, but you know, countries all over the world violate the Geneva Accords . . . secretly and hypothetically. . . . If we ever came close to doing it, and we don't know whether this is such a case, I think we would want to do it with accountability and openly and not adopt the way of the hypocrite.[50]

The logic behind the use of torture warrants as a protective measure is fundamentally flawed. As a threshold matter, the argument is premised on the belief that torture is inevitable—a premise rejected by the Obama administration and contradicted by three-plus years of successful national security policy where strict prohibitions have been imposed against the use of coercive interrogation techniques. Furthermore, as a theoretical matter, it is irrefutable that coercive interrogations tarnish the legal right to a presumption of innocence. With a presumption of guilt instead of innocence comes poor treatment and conditions, and the burden of proof is shifted to the detainee. In these situations, the detainee has the burden of providing information to his interrogators in order to stop the maltreatment. Torture warrants also promote and sustain an environment of hysteria and fear and open the door to more abuse, not less.

Professor Dershowitz has also theorized, "We won't know if he is a ticking-bomb terrorist unless he provides us information, and he's not likely to provide information unless we use certain extreme measures."[51] On its own terms, this logic leads to the inevitable conclusion that even the most stringent safeguards are unlikely to prevent serious abuse. If interrogators believe that the only way to know whether an individual has time-sensitive information is to torture him, then interrogators will be inclined to torture anyone who could possibly possess such information. For this and other reasons, national security experts warn against using this scenario as a basis for making official policy.

It is also important to emphasize that the ticking bomb scenario, while perhaps interesting as a law school exercise, is rare or almost nonexistent. As such, it is not a sound basis for making law or policy. As Stephen Holmes, a professor at New York University School of Law, writes:

> Although neither realistic nor representative, the hypothetical [ticking bomb] is nevertheless revealing. For one thing, the idea that authorities might get a dangerous terrorist into their custody, after he has planned an attack but before he has executed it, is a utopian fantasy. The elusiveness of these criminal conspirators is intensely frustrating and naturally gives rise, among counter-terrorism officials, to daydreams of superman-style rescues. To set policies on the basis of such far-fetched scenarios would be folly.[52]

However, viewed from the battlefield, stressful situations akin to the ticking bomb seem to occur every hour of every day. As retired major general Paul Eaton testified before Congress:

> The argument, the "ticking time bomb," Jack Bauer, the program "24 Hours" gets a lot of press for his solutions to the threats of our Nation. Recently, his performance under the pressure of the ticking time bomb scenario was favorably received by many people, with criminal behavior excused for the greater good. . . . [S]quad leaders in Iraq are faced with a ticking time bomb scenario every day. The question is: Do we want our soldiers and Marines to play Jack Bauer?[53]

These stresses of combat, however, rarely if ever lead to situations in which a single interrogation leads to the discovery and dismantling of a ticking time bomb, though movies and television shows like *24* would have us believe otherwise. In Jack Bauer's world on *24,* he and other interrogators often are presented with a detainee or suspect, and the evidence makes it seem as if he has time-sensitive information. That is the world of entertainment; in the real world, the choices are never so clear or simple.

Thus, according to two retired U.S. marine generals, Charles Krulak and Joseph Hoar, it is important for hard-and-fast rules to be established for interrogations and the battlefield so that interrogators and military personnel know how to react and what they can and cannot do. In 2007 General Krulak, former commandant of the U.S. Marines, and General Hoar, former commander in chief of the U.S. Central Command, wrote: "Complex situational ethics cannot be applied during the stress of combat. The rules must be firm and absolute; if torture is broached as a possibility, it will become a reality."[54]

Along these same lines, in September 2006 forty-eight retired generals, admirals, and other senior military leaders wrote a public letter to members of the Senate Armed Services Committee warning that "a flexible, sliding scale that might allow certain coercive interrogation techniques under some circumstances, while forbidding them under others . . . will only create further confusion."[55] If torture is sanctioned, allowed, or even winked at by a high-ranking official, including the president or a Supreme Court justice, there will be a trickle-down effect with disastrous results—one need only look at Abu Ghraib and its aftermath to see how information and practices can flow down the chain of command, become distorted, and then lead to undesirable, unforeseen results.[56]

Finally, military experts and other national security professionals reject the notion that because other countries or violent extremist groups rely on torture, the United States can too. As Rear Admiral John Hutson, a former judge advocate general of the U.S. Navy, testified to Congress in 2005:

> We must not be deterred just because our enemy in a war on terror doesn't comply with the [Geneva] Conventions. Our unilateral compliance will aid in the peace process. Moreover, it should have been understood that violations of the Conventions, or ignoring them, doesn't help bring an end to the war. To the contrary, as we have seen, this only adds ferocity to the fighting and lengthens the war by hardening the resolve of the enemy. Our flagrant disregard for the Conventions only serves as a recruiting poster for this enemy and for our enemies for generations to come.[57]

The experiences of other democratic societies such as Israel and Britain support Admiral Hutson's warning. In 1987 the Landau Commission examined interrogation methods of General Security Services (GSS), a department of the Israeli government that investigates individuals suspected of committing

crimes against the security of the country. The commission found that interrogation methods used against those suspected of "hostile terrorist activity"
would be allowed so long as the methods were not lied about. Specifically, the
commission wrote:

> The means of pressure should principally take the form of non-violent
> psychological pressure through a vigorous and extensive interrogation,
> with the use of stratagems, including acts of deception. However, when
> these do not attain their purpose, the exertion of a moderate measure of
> physical pressure cannot be avoided.[58]

A study conducted by B'Tselem, a human rights group based in Jerusalem,
found that the GSS interrogated 1,000–1,500 Palestinians a year and that
85 percent of those, about 850, were tortured.[59] Such figures and hundreds
of petitions to the Supreme Court by detained Palestinians who complained of
physical force and psychological pressure led to a change in policy. In September
1999, twelve years after the Landau Commission was appointed, the Israeli
Supreme Court banned the use of torture and cruel treatment during interrogations.[60] In its order, Prime Minister Ehud Barak wrote on behalf of the Court,
"Indeed, violence directed at a suspect's body or spirit does not constitute a
reasonable investigation practice."[61]

Similarly, there has been a shift in thinking in the United Kingdom where, during the height of the troubles in Northern Ireland, coercive interrogation methods
were used against suspected members of the Irish Republican Army and others.
In recent years, UK officials have relied on noncoercive methods, a shift in policy
that has served Britain well. According to terrorism analyst Louise Richardson,
who has studied British interrogation practices in-depth, the United States has
much to learn about interrogation: "The U.S. is repeating the same mistakes that
other democracies [like Britain] have made. They overreact initially by relying on
force and over time learn that force is not the most productive response."[62]

PREVENTING THE SLIPPERY SLOPE: PROGRESS MADE UNDER THE OBAMA ADMINISTRATION

In the long run, the struggle against al-Qaeda or other terrorist groups will not
be won by resorting to torture and abuse. To the contrary, such methods make
Americans less safe and are likely to actually prolong the struggle. As Generals
Krulak and Hoar wrote:

> This war will be won or lost not on the battlefield but in the minds of
> potential supporters who have not yet thrown in their lot with the enemy.

> If we forfeit our values by signaling that they are negotiable in situations
> of grave or imminent danger, we drive those undecideds into the arms of
> the enemy.[63]

In its first days in office, the Obama administration took bold and decisive steps to begin restoring America's reputation. The series of executive orders issued by the administration embraced strong, effective counterterrorism policies, which include the establishment of a single interrogation standard based on humane treatment and the closure of secret prisons, policies that are consistent with the nation's core civil liberties precepts.

Since then, as the Obama administration has acted to implement these directives and formulate policy in this important area, its actions have been guided in part by the findings of the Special Task Force on Interrogations and Transfer Policies. Chaired by the attorney general, the task force concluded that the *Army Field Manual* provides appropriate guidance on interrogation for military interrogators and that no additional or different guidance was necessary for other agencies. These conclusions rested on the task force's unanimous assessment, including that of the intelligence community, that the practices and techniques identified by the *Army Field Manual* or currently used by law enforcement provide adequate and effective means of conducting interrogations.

In addition, the task force evaluated and made recommendations to ensure that U.S. practices related to the transfer of individuals to other nations comply with domestic laws, international obligations, and policies of the United States and do not undermine the commitment to ensure humane treatment of individuals in its custody or control. These included a recommendation that the State Department be involved in evaluating assurances in all cases; a recommendation that agencies obtaining assurances from foreign countries insist on a monitoring mechanism, or otherwise establish a monitoring mechanism, to ensure consistent, private access to the individual who has been transferred, with minimal advance notice to the detaining government; and a recommendation that the inspector generals of the Departments of State, Defense, and Homeland Security prepare annually a coordinated report on transfers conducted by each of their agencies in reliance on assurances. The president reviewed and accepted the recommendations of the task force, and they are being implemented.

These steps will serve to enhance national security and to ensure the protection of basic civil liberties. In so doing, they will go a long way toward restoring America's moral standing in the world. As President Obama stated in his remarks at the National Archives Museum in May 2009, we Americans "cannot keep this country safe unless we enlist the power of our most fundamental values."[64]

NO: There is a need to bring an unfortunate practice within the bounds of law.
Alan M. Dershowitz, *Harvard Law School*

Why an Absolutist Approach toward Torture Is Bad for Democracy

I n this essay, I will first identify the points of agreement and disagreement between the absolutist approach represented by Michael Posner to reducing or eliminating torture and my own quite different approach. I will then describe and defend the idea of requiring torture warrants, and explain why the enactment of a torture warrant statute will minimize instances of torture and strengthen America's democratic values.

POINTS OF AGREEMENT

There are many areas of agreement between the most vocal advocates of an absolute ban on torture and myself. We agree that torture is bad and should not be used by democracies committed to the rule of law. We agree that under current law—both domestic and international—all forms of torture are prohibited under all circumstances. We agree that torture should be defined broadly to include waterboarding (a form of simulated drowning) and other physical measures that induce pain, cause injury, or risk death. We agree that it is important not to legitimate any form of torture. We agree that all nations should take whatever steps are necessary to eliminate or reduce torture. We agree that it would be a much better world if torture were no longer practiced or even considered as an option by civilized nations or individuals.

I am sure we also agree that torture is currently practiced by many, if not most, countries in the world, including many American allies such as Egypt, Jordan, the Philippines, and Pakistan. It is also practiced by the Palestinian Authority, Hamas, Iran, and other rogue nations and groups. I doubt we would disagree that torture has been employed by the United States not only during the Bush administration but also during the Vietnam War, the Korean War, the Second World War, the First World War, and probably other periods in U.S. history. I think we would also agree that if there ever were a situation perceived by the administration to be a real ticking bomb case involving a captured terrorist who had information that could prevent a mass-casualty attack, some form of torture would *in fact* be used if it was thought likely to save numerous lives, regardless of the law.

Nor would torture be resorted to in the ticking bomb situation only by Republican, conservative, or "bad" presidents. Consider what former president Bill Clinton said when asked by National Public Radio, as someone "who's been there," whether the president needs "the option of authorizing torture in an extreme case":

> Look, if the president needed an option, there's all sorts of things they can do. Let's take the best case, OK. You picked up someone you know is the No. 2 aide to Osama bin Laden. And you know they have an operation planned for the United States or some European capital in the next . . . three days. And you know this guy knows it. Right, that's the clearest example. And you think you can only get it out of this guy by shooting him full of some drugs or waterboarding him or otherwise working him over. If they really believed that that scenario is likely to occur, let them come forward with an alternate proposal.
>
> We have a system of laws here where nobody should be above the law, and you don't need blanket advance approval for blanket torture. They can draw a statute much more narrowly, which would permit the president to make a finding in a case like I just outlined, and then that finding could be submitted even if after the fact to the Foreign Intelligence Surveillance Court.[65]

Clinton was then asked whether he was saying there "would be more responsibility afterward for what was done." He replied: "Yeah, well, the president could take personal responsibility for it. But you do it on a case-by-case basis, and there'd be some review of it." Clinton quickly added that he did not know whether the ticking bomb scenario "is likely or not," but he did know that "we have erred in who was a real suspect or not."

In the interview, Clinton summarized his views in the following terms:

> If they really believe the time comes when the only way they can get a reliable piece of information is to beat it out of someone or put a drug in their body to talk it out of [him], then they can present it to the Foreign Intelligence Court, or some other court, just under the same circumstances we do with wiretaps. Post facto. . . .
>
> But I think if you go around passing laws that legitimize a violation of the Geneva Convention and institutionalize what happened at Abu Ghraib or Guantanamo, we're gonna be in real trouble.

I have little doubt—as a matter of *fact,* not *law* or *morality*—that presidents would condone some forms of torture if they truly believed it was the only option available to prevent an act of mass-casualty terrorism. Nor do I have much doubt that intelligence operatives on the ground would resort to torture under such circumstances. No law or proclamation would change this cruel reality.

Some people have argued that the entire debate about torture is foolish and unnecessary because torture never works, because it always produces false and useless information from suspects who will say anything to stop the pain.

It is in my view dishonest, though politically correct, to claim, as an empirical matter, that torture *never* works—that it *never* produces reliable and useful real-time information that could save lives. It can certainly be argued, though subject to empirical testing, that torture *rarely* works, that it *generally* produces false information, that there are *better* ways to secure such information, or that *on balance* any good it accomplishes is more than offset by the evil it produces. All of these are reasonable, and perhaps even true, statements.

But it defies history, science, common sense, logic, and what is known about human behavior to deny that under *some* circumstances *some* people will produce *some* useful and truthful information that could in fact save lives. Indeed, in numerous instances torture has produced truthful information.[66] It is not a question of seeking to use the fruits of torture to convict someone of a crime based on his own confession. Nor is it a question of merely verbal pronouncements of a person under torture. It is a question of the torturer who insists that his victim take him to where the bomb is hidden or take some other action that is self-proving. Too many brave men and women—in the French Resistance and other such organizations—disclosed the location of friends, loved ones, and even relatives under torture to doubt its effectiveness under some circumstances.

I do not believe that there is much room for disagreement with any of the above. Although Michael Posner argues in this chapter that torture and coercive interrogation tactics are "an ineffective and even counterproductive way to gather intelligence,"[67] he does not deny that it could, in some instances, produce truthful and self-proving information that could prevent a mass-casualty terrorist attack. The important point, however, is not whether Mr. Posner or I believe this, but whether the person who must make the decision to authorize or employ torture—the president or an intelligence official on the ground—might believe or be persuaded that in a given case torture is the best—or least worst—option available.

POINTS OF DEPARTURE

The major point of disagreement between my approach and the approach represented by Mr. Posner is about means, not ends. We both want to prevent any recurrence of what happened at Abu Ghraib. We both want to put an end to what happened under the Bush administration: publicly proclaiming that torture would never be used, while quietly encouraging "whatever it takes" to get intelligence information deemed necessary to prevent another act of mass-casualty terrorism. We both want to see torture ended, or—at the very least—reduced as much as humanly possible.

Mr. Posner believes that the best way to accomplish these admirable goals is by a blanket, unqualified, absolute prohibition on all torture, "adopt[ing] a zero-tolerance approach." More specifically, he insists that "the use of torture or cruel, inhuman, or degrading treatment in interrogations should never be tolerated, regulated, or justified as a matter of official policy, law, or practice."

I would agree—if I believed that this approach would work. But that is precisely the approach the United States has used for more than a century, and it has failed miserably. The twentieth century was the century in which the laws of virtually every nation and international body followed the Posner approach. And yet the twentieth century can fairly be characterized as the "Torture Century" in which torture was used extensively throughout the world, not only by evil nations such as Hitler's Germany, Hirohito's Japan, Stalin's Soviet Union, Mao's China, Castro's Cuba, and Pol Pot's Cambodia, but also by Britain, France, the United States, Israel, and other democracies.

Mr. Posner cites George Washington, Thomas Jefferson, James Madison, Abraham Lincoln, Theodore Roosevelt, George Marshall, and others in support of the myth that throughout American history the U.S. military has refrained from abusing prisoners of war. Although it is true that Americans have talked the talk of refraining from employing torture, the reality is that the U.S. military has tortured captured enemy soldiers to obtain real-time intelligence in every war it has fought. During the Vietnam and Korean Wars, torture was routine and pervasive, and these wars were fought after the enactment of the Geneva Conventions outlawing all forms of torture under all circumstances.

Saying they are against all forms of torture under all circumstances—even when it is believed that torture may be the only way to save thousands of innocent lives—makes Americans feel good. Announcing such a policy may make them look good. But the reality is that all democracies will close their eyes to torture in some extreme circumstances. In my view, that is an unacceptable option for a democracy. If torture is ever to be used—and it will be—it must be authorized as an explicit exception to the general law and with democratic accountability.

The strongest argument against my preference for candor and accountability is the claim that it is better for torture—or any other evil practice deemed necessary during emergencies—to be left to the low-visibility discretion of low-level functionaries than to be legitimated by high-level, accountable decision makers. Judge Richard Posner makes this argument:

> Dershowitz believes that the occasions for the use of torture should be regularized—by requiring a judicial warrant for the needle treatment, for example. But he overlooks an argument for leaving such things to executive discretion. If rules are promulgated permitting torture in defined circumstances, some officials are bound to want to explore the outer bounds of the rules. Having been regularized, the practice will become regular. Better to leave in place the formal and customary prohibitions, but with the understanding that they will not be enforced in extreme circumstances.[68]

The classic formulation of this argument was offered by Supreme Court Justice Robert Jackson in his dissenting opinion in one of the Japanese detention camp cases stemming from World War II:

> Much is said of the danger to liberty from the Army program for deporting and detaining these citizens of Japanese extraction. But a judicial construction of the due process clause that will sustain this order is a far subtler blow to liberty than the promulgation of the order itself. A military order, however unconstitutional, is not apt to last longer than the military emergency. Even during that period a succeeding commander may revoke it all. But once a judicial opinion rationalizes such an order to show that it conforms to the Constitution, or rather rationalizes the Constitution to show that the Constitution sanctions such an order, the Court for all time has validated the principle of racial discrimination in criminal procedure and of transplanting American citizens. The principle then lies about like a loaded weapon ready for the hand of any authority that can bring forward a plausible claim of an urgent need. Every repetition imbeds that principle more deeply in our law and thinking and expands it to new purposes. All who observe the work of courts are familiar with what Judge Cardozo described as "the tendency of a principle to expand itself to the limit of its logic." A military commander may overstep the bounds of constitutionality, and it is an incident. But if we review and approve, that passing incident becomes the doctrine of the Constitution. There it has a generative power of its own, and all that it creates will be in its own image.[69]

Experience has not necessarily proved Justice Jackson's fear or Judge Posner's prediction to be well founded. The very fact that the Supreme Court expressly validated the Japanese detentions contributed to its condemnation by the verdict of history. Today, the Supreme Court's decision in *Korematsu* stands alongside decisions such as *Dred Scott, Plessy v. Ferguson,* and *Buck v. Bell* in the high court's Hall of Infamy. Though never formally overruled, and even occasionally cited, *Korematsu* serves as a negative precedent—a mistaken ruling not ever to be repeated in future cases. Yet had the Supreme Court merely allowed the executive decision to stand without judicial review, a far more dangerous precedent might have been established: that executive decisions during times of emergency will escape review by the Supreme Court. That far broader and more dangerous precedent would then lie about "like a loaded weapon" ready to be used by a dictator without fear of judicial review. That comes close to what happened during the Ronald Reagan, George H. W. Bush, and George W. Bush administrations. Those administrations denied they were acting unlawfully, while aggressively resisting any judicial review of their actions.

TORTURE WARRANTS AS THE BEST MEANS OF MINIMIZING TORTURE

My own belief is that a warrant requirement, if properly enforced, would probably reduce the frequency, severity, and duration of torture. I cannot see how it could possibly increase it, since a warrant requirement simply imposes an additional level of prior review. Two examples demonstrate why I think there would be less torture with a warrant requirement than without one. Recall the case of the alleged national security wiretap being placed on the phones of Martin Luther King Jr. by the Kennedy administration in the early 1960s. This was in the days when the attorney general could authorize a national security wiretap without a warrant. Today, no judge would issue a warrant in a case as flimsy as that one. When al-Qaeda suspect Zacarias Moussaoui was detained a month before the 9/11 attacks after trying to learn how to fly an airplane without wanting to know much about landing it, the government did not even seek a national security wiretap because its lawyers believed that a judge would not have granted one. If Moussaoui's computer could have been searched without a warrant, it almost certainly would have been.

It should be recalled that in the context of searches the Framers of the Fourth Amendment to the U.S. Constitution opted for a judicial check on the discretion of the police by requiring a search warrant in most cases. In *Johnson v. United States* (1948), the Supreme Court explained the reason for the warrant requirement as follows: "The informed and deliberate determinations of magistrates . . . are to be preferred over the hurried actions of officers." Justice Robert Jackson, who delivered the opinion of the Court, then elaborated:

> The point of the Fourth Amendment, which often is not grasped by zealous officers, is not that it denies law enforcement the support of the usual inferences, which reasonable men draw from evidence. Its protection consists in requiring that those inferences be drawn by a neutral and detached magistrate instead of being judged by the officer engaged in the often-competitive enterprise of ferreting out crime. Any assumption that evidence sufficient to support a magistrate's disinterested determination to issue a search warrant will justify the officers in making a search without a warrant would reduce the Amendment to nullify and leave the people's homes secure only in the discretion of police officers.[70]

Although torture is very different from a search, the policies underlying the warrant requirement are relevant to whether there would likely be more torture or less if the decision were left entirely to field officers, or if a judicial officer had to approve a request for a torture warrant.

The major downside of any warrant procedure would be its legitimization of a horrible practice. But in my view it is better to legitimate and control a *specific* practice that will in fact occur than to legitimate a *general* practice of tolerating extralegal actions so long as they operate under the table of scrutiny and beneath the radar screen of accountability. Judge Posner's "pragmatic" approach would be an invitation to widespread (and officially—if surreptitiously—approved) lawlessness in "extreme circumstances." Moreover, the very concept of "extreme circumstances" is subjective and infinitely expandable. Jordan, which denies that it ever uses torture, has, in fact, tortured the innocent relatives of suspected terrorists. And when U.S. agents captured 9/11 mastermind Khalid Sheikh Muhammad, they reportedly also took into custody his two elementary school-age children—and let him know that they had them.

There is a difference in principle, as Jeremy Bentham noted more than two hundred years ago, between torturing the guilty to save the lives of the innocent and torturing innocent people. A system that requires an articulated justification for the use of nonlethal torture and approval by a judge is more likely to honor that principle—and other important ones—than a system that relegates these decisions to low-visibility law enforcement agents whose only job is to protect the public from terrorism.

Strengthening Democratic Principles

Several important values are pitted against each other in this conflict over the role of torture in national security and counterterrorism policy. The first is

the safety and security of a nation's citizens. Under the ticking bomb scenario, this value may argue for the use of torture if that were the only way to
prevent the ticking bomb from exploding and killing large numbers of civilians. The second value is the preservation of civil liberties and human rights.
This value requires that Americans not accept torture as a legitimate part of
their legal system.

In my debates with two prominent civil libertarians—Floyd Abrams and
Harvey Silverglate—both acknowledged that they would want nonlethal torture to be used if it could prevent thousands of deaths, but they did not want
torture to be officially recognized by the U.S. legal system. As Floyd Abrams
put it: "In a democracy sometimes it is necessary to do things off the books and
below the radar screen."

The former presidential candidate Alan Keyes has taken the position that
although torture might be *necessary* in a given situation, it could never be *right*.
He suggested that a president *should* authorize the torturing of a ticking bomb
terrorist, but that this act should not be legitimated by the courts or incorporated
into the legal system. He argued that wrongful and indeed unlawful acts might
sometimes be necessary to preserve the nation, but that no aura of legitimacy
should be placed on these actions by judicial imprimatur. Prof. Jean Elshtain
makes a similar point. Although she strongly favors the use of nonlethal torture
in certain extreme cases, she does not want "a law to cover such cases." Indeed,
she characterizes my proposal for a torture warrant as "a stunningly bad idea."
She prefers instead to have each individual "grapple with a terrible moral
dilemma" rather than have any open debate and then codify its results.[71]

This understandable approach is in conflict with the third important value:
open accountability and visibility in a democracy. Off-the-books actions
"below the radar screen" are antithetical to the theory and practice of democracy. Citizens cannot approve or disapprove of government actions of which
they are unaware. Indeed, the lesson of history teaches that off-the-books
actions can produce terrible consequences. President Richard Nixon's creation
of a group of "plumbers" led to the Watergate affair, and President Reagan's
authorization of an off-the-books foreign policy in Central America led to the
Iran-Contra scandal. And these are only the ones everyone knows about!

Perhaps the most extreme example of this hypocritical approach to torture
comes—not surprisingly—from the French experience in Algeria. The French
army used torture extensively in seeking to prevent terrorism during France's
brutal war between 1955 and 1957. An officer who supervised this torture, Gen.
Paul Aussaresses, wrote an account of what he had done and seen, including the
torture of dozens of Algerians. "The best way to make a terrorist talk when he
refused to say what he knew was to torture him," Aussaresses boasted.[72]

Although the book was published decades after the war was over, the general was prosecuted—but not for what he had *done* to the Algerians. Instead, he was prosecuted for *revealing* what he had done and seeking to justify it.

In a democracy governed by the rule of law, its citizens should never want their soldiers or president to take any action that they deem wrong or illegal. A good test of whether an action should or should not be done is whether those undertaking the action are prepared to have it disclosed—perhaps not immediately, but certainly after some time has passed. No legal system operating under the rule of law should ever tolerate an off-the-books approach to necessity. Even the defense of necessity must be justified lawfully. The road to tyranny has always been paved with claims of necessity made by those responsible for the security of a nation. The U.S. system of checks and balances requires that all presidential actions, like all legislative or military actions, be consistent with governing laws. If it is necessary to torture in the ticking bomb case, then the governing laws must accommodate this practice. If Americans refuse to change their laws to accommodate any particular action, then their government should not take that action. Requiring that a controversial, even immoral, action be made openly and with accountability is one way of minimizing resort to unjustifiable means.

Carefully Choosing Security

Only in a democracy committed to civil liberties would a triangular conflict of this kind exist. Totalitarian and authoritarian regimes experience no such conflict, because they subscribe to neither the civil libertarian nor the democratic values that come in conflict with the value of security. The hard question is, which value is to be preferred when a clash occurs? One or more of these values must inevitably be compromised in making the tragic choice presented by the ticking bomb case. If the United States does not torture, it compromises the security and safety of its citizens. If the country tolerates torture, but keeps the decisions to torture off the books and below the radar screen, it compromises principles of democratic accountability. If it creates a legal structure for limiting and controlling torture, it compromises its principled opposition to torture in all circumstances and creates a potentially dangerous and expandable situation.

In 1678 the French writer François de La Rochefoucauld said that "hypocrisy is the homage that vice renders to virtue." In this case, there are two vices: terrorism and torture. There are also two virtues: civil liberties and democratic accountability. Most civil libertarians I know prefer hypocrisy, precisely because it appears to avoid the conflict between security and civil liberties. But by choosing the way of the hypocrite these civil libertarians compromise the value of democratic accountability. Such is the nature of tragic choices in a complex world. As Bentham put it more than two centuries ago: "Government throughout is but a choice of evils." In a democracy, such choices must be made, whenever possible, with openness and democratic accountability, and subject to the rule of law.

Consider another terrible choice of evils that could easily have been presented on September 11, 2001, and may well be presented in the future: a hijacked passenger jet is on a collision course with a densely occupied office building, and the only way to prevent the destruction of the building and the killing of its occupants is to shoot down the jet, thereby killing its innocent passengers. This choice now seems easy because the passengers are certain to die anyway and their somewhat earlier deaths will save numerous lives. The passenger jet must be shot down. But what if it were only *probable*, not certain, that the jet would crash into the building? Say, for example, cell phone transmissions indicate that the passengers are struggling to regain control of the hijacked jet, but it is unlikely they will succeed in time. Or say there is no communication with the jet and all that is known is that it is off course and heading toward Washington, D.C., or some other densely populated area. Under these more questionable circumstances, the question becomes *who* should make this life-and-death choice between evils—a decision that may turn out tragically wrong?

No reasonable person would allocate this decision to a fighter jet pilot who happened to be in the area or to a local airbase commander—unless, of course, there was no time for the matter to be passed up the chain of command to the secretary of defense or the president. A decision of this kind should be made at the highest level possible, with visibility and accountability.

Why is this not also true of the decision to torture a ticking bomb terrorist? Why should that choice of evils be relegated to a local policeman, FBI agent, or CIA operative rather than to a judge, the attorney general, or the president?

It may be better to have each individual "grapple with a terrible moral dilemma" in a philosophy class. In a democracy, such grappling must occur in the open and be made by those accountable to the demos, not to the professorate.

Basically, four options are available to a democracy faced with what its leaders honestly believe is a ticking bomb situation that can be prevented only by torture. The first is to bravely do "the right thing": do not torture and accept responsibility for not having prevented the possibly preventable murders of thousands of innocent civilians. I might wish it were otherwise, but I am certain, as a matter of fact, that no democratic leader would knowingly accept that option.

The second option is to lie and claim that torture *never* works, that is why it was not tried, and that is why the president is not responsible for not having prevented the murder of thousands of civilians. No president would do that because the public would not believe him—and for good reason. They would insist that it should have been tried.

The third option has been called "the way of the hypocrite." The president would not "authorize" torture, but neither would he prevent its use. He would give himself—or his staff would give him—"plausible deniability." He would stick his head in the proverbial sand and engage in "willful ignorance." This is the option most presidents probably would prefer, because they can have their cake and eat it too. But in a democracy, such evasion of accountability in choosing among evil decisions raises profoundly disturbing questions.

The fourth option is for the president to declare that the nation is in a situation of dire necessity requiring temporary suspension of the absolute prohibition against torture. Such a declaration would have to be authorized by Congress (just like suspension of the writ of habeas corpus). It would have to be based on pre-existing law and justified by evidence. Criteria would have to be spelled out in advance by Congress and then found to exist by a justice of the Supreme Court. All three branches of government would have to agree. All three branches would have to dirty their hands by participating in this terrible choice of evils. But that is how democracy requires those who live under it to confront and choose between or among horrible evils.

A related example, not too distant from the torture of captured terrorists to prevent future acts of terrorism, is the targeted killing of suspected terrorists to prevent future acts of terrorism. The Obama administration condemns all forms of nonlethal preventive torture but employs lethal targeting of suspected terrorists. Some may argue that killing is worse than nonlethal torture. Others will answer that targeted killing is arguably lawful, at least under certain circumstances, whereas nonlethal torture is always illegal under both U.S. domestic law and international humanitarian law. However one comes out on this debate—and as a moral matter, it's awfully hard to argue that nonlethal torture is always worse than killing—the fact that there are considerable similarities is beyond dispute.

In a lengthy article in the *New York Times* on May 29, 2012, the process by which President Obama orders targeted killing is laid out in great detail.[73] He alone makes the decision, based on recommendations from his national security experts, but without articulated criteria that are available for public scrutiny. Critics of the Obama program, including the American Civil Liberties Union and the *New York Times*, have called for what essentially amounts to a "targeted killing warrant," similar to the proposal I have made with regard to torture. The arguments they make in support of articulated criteria and judicial review are also similar to the arguments I have made in the context of torture: democratic accountability, articulated criteria, and some sort of judicial review. The question

is posed, therefore: if it's good enough to justify the killing of suspected terrorists, why is it not good enough in the context of the nonlethal preventive torture
of suspected terrorists?

Notes

1. These memos are available at www.aclu.org/safefree/general/olc_memos.html.
2. Peter Baker, "Banned Techniques Yielded 'High Value Information,' Memo Says,"
   New York Times, April 22, 2009.
3. "Close the Torture Loophole," *Los Angeles Times*, April 18, 2009.
4. The author wishes to thank Emily Stanfield for her extensive research assistance.
   He also wishes to thank Devon Chaffee, Sharon Kelly, Elisa Massimino, and Gabor
   Rona for their helpful suggestions. Views expressed are those of the author and do
   not necessarily represent official views of the U.S. Department of State.
5. President Obama signed three executive orders on January 22, 2009, that put a halt
   to the CIA's "enhanced" interrogation program; ended secret detentions; guaranteed Red Cross access to prisoners; imposed a one-year deadline for closing the
   detention facilities at Guantánamo Bay, Cuba; and set a single U.S. standard for all
   prisoners in U.S. custody—a standard that is contained in the *Army Field Manual
   on Human Intelligence Collector Operations*. The executive order on lawful interrogations makes clear that every person in U.S. custody must be treated humanely
   and not subjected to torture or any other forms of cruel, humiliating, or degrading
   treatment. See White House, "Executive Orders to Date," January 23, 2009, www
   .whitehouse.gov/blog/2009/01/23/executive-orders-date.
6. Charlie Savage, "Election Will Decide Future of Interrogation Methods for
   Terrorism Suspects," *New York Times*, September 28, 2012.
7. National Commission on Terrorist Attacks upon the United States, *The 9/11 Commission Report: Final Report* (Washington, D.C.: Government Printing Office, 2004).
8. David Hackett Fischer, *Washington's Crossing* (New York: Oxford University Press,
   2006), 379.
9. Jefferson to James Madison, Monticello, April 19, 1809, in *The Works of Thomas
   Jefferson, Federal Edition*, Vol. 11, ed. Paul Leicester Ford (New York: G. P. Putnam's
   Sons, 1905), 107.
10. Frances Lieber, *Instructions for the Government of Armies of the United States in the
    Field* (Washington, D.C.: Government Printing Office, 1898), sec. 111, art. 76, and
    sec. 1, art. 4. These instructions were promulgated by Abraham Lincoln as General
    Orders No. 100, April 24, 1863. See Dietrich Schindler and Jiří Toman, eds., *The
    Laws of Armed Conflicts* (Boston: Martinus Nihjoff, 1988), 3–23.
11. President Theodore Roosevelt, speaking on May 30, 1902, to veterans at Arlington
    National Cemetery. See Joseph Bucklin Bishop, *Theodore Roosevelt and His Time
    Shown in His Own Letters* (New York: Charles Scribner's Sons, 1920), 192.
12. "Geneva Convention Relative to the Treatment of Prisoners of War," United
    Nations, Geneva, 1949.
13. U.S. Office of Information for the Armed Forces, U.S. Department of Defense, *The
    Armed Forces Officer* (Washington, D.C.: Armed Forces Information Service, 1975), 191.

14. Gen. John Shalikashvili et al., letter to Sen. John Warner and Sen. Carl Levin, September 12, 2006, www.americanprogress.org/wp-content/uploads/issues/2006/09/letter_geneva_threat.pdf.

15. "'Hardball with Chris Matthews' for November 22," msnbc.msn.com, November 23, 2005, www.msnbc.msn.com/id/10175425.

16. "Treating Terrorists with Respect," Talkradionews.com, June 2008, www.talkra dionews.com/newscommentary/2008/06/18/treating-terrorists-with-respect.html.

17. Human Rights First, "Top Interrogators Declare Torture Ineffective in Intelligence Gathering," June 24, 2008, www.humanrightsfirst.org/2008/06/24/top-interrogators-declare-torture-ineffective-in-intelligence-gathering/.

18. In November 2005, Senator McCain wrote, "Our enemies didn't adhere to the Geneva Convention. Many of my comrades were subjected to very cruel, very inhumane and degrading treatment, a few of them even unto death. But every one of us . . . knew and took great strength from the belief that we were different from our enemies, that we were better than them, that we, if the roles were reversed, would not disgrace ourselves by committing or countenancing such mistreatment of them." See John McCain, "Torture's Terrible Toll," *Newsweek,* November 21, 2005.

19. "International Covenant on Civil and Political Rights," United Nations, New York, 1966, part 3, art. 7.

20. American Civil Liberties Union, "FAQ—The Convention Against Torture," April 27, 2006, www.aclu.org/national-security/faq-convention-against-torture.

21. In a letter to members of the Senate Armed Services Committee in September 2006, a group of retired military leaders wrote: "If degradation, humiliation, physical and mental brutalization of prisoners is decriminalized or considered permissible [by the United States] under a restrictive interpretation of Common Article 3, we will forfeit all credible objections should such barbaric practices be inflicted upon American prisoners." See Shalikashvili et al., letter to Sen. John Warner and Sen. Carl Levin.

22. Naomi Klein, "Bush's War Goes Global," *Globe and Mail* (Toronto), August 27, 2003.

23. Human Rights First, "Defending Security: The Right to Defend Rights in an Age of Terrorism" (preliminary draft), Human Rights First, New York, 2004, 8, http://secure.humanrightsfirst.org/defenders/hrd_global/Defending_Security_Draft.pdf.

24. Human Rights First, *A Year of Loss: Reexamining Civil Liberties since September 11* (New York: Human Rights First, 2002), 42.

25. Ibid., 43. Egyptian president Hosni Mubarak claimed in 2001 that U.S. policies implemented after September 11 "prove that we were right from the beginning in using all means" to combat terrorism.

26. National Defense Authorization Act for Fiscal Year 2006, H.R. 1815, 109th Cong., 1st sess., Congressional Record 102 (July 25, 2005): S 8792.

27. Alexander Hamilton and James Madison, "Helvidius Number IV," in *The Pacificus-Helvidius Debates of 1793–1794: Toward the Completion of the American Founding,* ed. Morton J. Frisch (Indianapolis, Ind.: Liberty Fund, 2007).

28. White House, "Vice President Cheney Delivers Remarks to the Republican Governors Association," October 25, 2001, http://georgewbush-whitehouse.archives .gov/vicepresident/news-speeches/speeches/vp20011025.html.

29. White House, "The Vice President Appears on Meet the Press with Tim Russert," September 16, 2001, http://georgewbush-whitehouse.archives.gov/vicepresident/news-speeches/speeches/vp20010916.html.

30. Jay S. Bybee, memorandum to Albert R. Gonzales, counsel to the president, August 1, 2002, www.justice.gov/olc/docs/memo-gonzales-aug2002.pdf.

31. Commenting on the insulation of these practices from court review, a member of the "working group" assembled by the vice president and his attorney David Addington during the aftermath of September 11 called Guantánamo "the legal equivalent of outer space"—a "lawless" universe. See Michael Isikoff and Stuart Taylor Jr., "The Gitmo Fallout," *Newsweek*, July 17, 2006.

32. Donald Rumsfeld, memorandum to the commander, U.S. Southern Command, April 16, 2003, www.gwu.edu/~nsarchiv/NSAEBB/NSAEBB127/03.04.16.pdf.

33. White House, "President Discusses Creation of Military Commissions to Try Suspected Terrorists," September 6, 2006, http://georgewbush-whitehouse.archives.gov/news/releases/2006/09/20060906-3.html.

34. "Abu Ghraib," Times Topics, *New York Times*, http://topics.nytimes.com/top/news/international/countriesandterritories/iraq/abu_ghraib/index.html.

35. Human Rights First, *Command's Responsibility: Detainee Deaths in U.S. Custody in Iraq and Afghanistan* (New York: Human Rights First, 2006), 1.

36. Eric Schmitt, "House Backs McCain on Detainees, Defying Bush," *New York Times*, December 15, 2005.

37. The signing statement stated specifically: "The executive branch shall construe these sections in a manner consistent with the constitutional authority of the President." See White House, "President's Statement on Signing of H.R. 2863, the 'Department of Defense, Emergency Supplemental Appropriations to Address Hurricanes in the Gulf of Mexico, and Pandemic Influenza Act, 2006,'" http://georgewbush-whitehouse.archives.gov/news/releases/2005/12/20051230-8.html.

38. Linda Greenhouse, "Justices, 5–3, Broadly Reject Bush Plan to Try Detainees," *New York Times*, June 30, 2006.

39. White House, "Press Conference of the President," September 15, 2006, http://georgewbush-whitehouse.archives.gov/news/releases/2006/09/20060915-2.html.

40. *Military Commissions Act of 2006*, Public Law 109-366, 109th Cong., 2nd sess. (October 17, 2006), 2632, 2637.

41. The language of Executive Order 13440 specifically reads: "willful and outrageous acts of personal abuse done for the purpose of humiliating or degrading the individual in a manner so serious that any reasonable person, considering the circumstances, would deem the acts to be beyond the bounds of human decency, such as sexual or sexually indecent acts undertaken for the purpose of humiliation, forcing the individual to perform sexual acts or to pose sexually, threatening the individual with sexual mutilation, or using the individual as a human shield; or acts intended to denigrate the religion, religious practices, or religious objects of the individual." See White House, "Executive Order: Interpretation of the Geneva Conventions Common Article 3 as Applied to a Program of Detention and Interrogation Operated by the Central Intelligence Agency," July 20, 2007, http://georgewbush-whitehouse.archives.gov/news/releases/2007/07/20070720-4.html.

42. P. X. Kelley and Robert F. Turner, "War Crimes and the White House: The Dishonor in a Tortured New 'Interpretation' of the Geneva Conventions," *Washington Post*, July 26, 2007.

43. In a statement to the U.S. House of Representatives, the president wrote, "I am returning herewith without my approval . . . the 'Intelligence Authorization Act for Fiscal Year 2008.' The bill would impede the United States Government's efforts to protect American people effectively from terrorist attacks and other threats because it imposes several unnecessary and unacceptable burdens on our Intelligence Community." He went on to write: "Section 327 of the bill would harm our national security by requiring any element of the Intelligence Community to use only the interrogation methods authorized in the Army Field Manual on Interrogations. It is vitally important that the Central Intelligence Agency (CIA) be allowed to maintain a separate and classified interrogation program. . . . [M]y concern is the need to maintain a separate CIA program that will shield from disclosure to al Qaeda and other terrorists the interrogation techniques they may face upon capture." See www.fas.org/irp/congress/2008_cr/veto.html.

44. For the full text of President Obama's executive order revoking the Bush order, see www.whitehouse.gov/the_press_office/EnsuringLawfulInterrogations.

45. "Senate Armed Forces Committee Inquiry into the Treatment of Detainees in U.S. Custody," December 11, 2008, www.levin.senate.gov/issues/treatment-of-detainees-in-us-custody. The report pointedly rejects the administration's notion that using these coercive interrogation techniques keeps the country and its troops safe.

46. For a defense of the Bush administration's post-9/11 interrogation policy, see George Tenet, *At the Center of the Storm* (New York: HarperCollins, 2007).

47. Alan Dershowitz, "Want to Torture? Get a Warrant," January 22, 2002, www.alandershowitz.com/publications/docs/torturewarrants2.html.

48. Ibid.

49. "Dershowitz: Torture Could Be Justified," CNN.com, March 3, 2003, www.cnn.com/2003/LAW/03/03/cnna.Dershowitz.

50. Ibid.

51. Ibid.

52. Stephen Holmes, "Is Defiance of Law a Proof of Success? Magical Thinking in the War on Terror," in *The Torture Debate in America*, ed. Karen J. Greenberg (New York: Cambridge University Press, 2006), 127–128.

53. Senate Committee on Foreign Relations, "Extraordinary Rendition, Extraterritorial Detention and Treatment of Detainees: Restoring Our Moral Credibility and Strengthening Our Diplomatic Standing," hearing, 110th Cong., 1st sess., www.fas.org/irp/congress/2007_hr/rendition2.pdf.

54. Charles C. Krulak and Joseph P. Hoar, "It's Our Cage, Too; Torture Betrays Us and Breeds New Enemies," *Washington Post*, May 17, 2007.

55. Shalikashvili et al., letter to Sen. John Warner and Sen. Carl Levin.

56. Alberto Mora, former general counsel to the U.S. Navy from 2001 to 2005 and a principled dissenting voice on these issues, stated in an interview with *Vanity Fair* magazine, "I will also tell you that there are general-rank officers who've had senior responsibility within the Joint Staff or counterterrorism operations who believe that the number-one and number-two leading causes of U.S. combat deaths in Iraq have been, number one, Abu Ghraib, number two, Guantanamo, because of the effectiveness of these symbols in helping recruit jihadists into the field and combat against American soldiers." See Cullen Murphy and Todd S. Purdum, "Farewell to All That: An Oral History of the Bush White House," *Vanity Fair*, February 2009.

57. "Testimony of John D. Hutson before the United States Senate Committee on the Judiciary Concerning the Nomination of Alberto Gonzales for Confirmation as Attorney General of the United States," January 6, 2005, www.gpo.gov/fdsys/pkg/CHRG-109shrg99932/html/CHRG-109shrg99932.htm.

58. "Background on the High Court of Justice's Decision," www.btselem.org/english/Torture/Background.asp.

59. Ibid.

60. "Israel Supreme Court Bans Interrogation Abuse of Palestinians," CNN.com, September 6, 1999.

61. Barak, "Text of Israeli Supreme Court Decision on GSS Practices," Totse.com, September 6, 1999, www.jewishvirtuallibrary.org/jsource/Politics/GSStext.html.

62. Quoted in Josh Meyer, "CIA Should Tape More, Experts Say," *Los Angeles Times*, December 23, 2007.

63. Krulak and Hoar, "It's Our Cage, Too."

64. Remarks of President Barack Obama, National Archives Museum, Washington D.C., May 21, 2009, www.whitehouse.gov/the_press_office/Remarks-by-the-President-On-National-Security-5-21-09.

65. National Public Radio, *Morning Edition,* September 21, 2006.

66. For several such examples, see Alan Dershowitz, *Why Terrorism Works* (New Haven, Conn.: Yale University Press, 2002), chap. 4.

67. Posner cites Joe Navarro, a twenty-year FBI veteran, for the proposition that on balance torture is far less useful than other tactics. He also quotes a statement by fifteen senior interrogators that torture results in "false and misleading information" and "loss of critical intelligence."

68. Richard Posner, "The Best Offense," *New Republic,* September 2, 2002.

69. *Korematsu v. United States,* 323 U.S. 214 (1944), www.law.cornell.edu/supct/html/historics/USSC_CR_0323_0214_ZD2.html.

70. *Johnson v. United States,* 333 U.S. 10 (1948), http://supreme.justia.com/us/333/10/case.html.

71. Sanford Levinson, ed., *Torture: A Collection* (New York: Oxford University Press, 2004), 84.

72. Paul Aussaresses, *Battle of the Casbah: Terrorism and Counter-terrorism in Algeria, 1955–1957,* trans. Robert L. Miller (New York: Enigma, 2002).

73. Jo Becker and Scott Shane, "Secret 'Kill List' Proves a Test of Obama's Principles and Will," *New York Times,* May 29, 2012.

counterterrorism and the constitution: does providing security require a trade-off with civil liberties?

YES: The United States needs to reasonably limit civil liberties and bolster executive powers.
John Yoo, *University of California at Berkeley School of Law*

NO: Respecting civil liberties and preventing executive overreach are critical to preserving America's security and its ideals.
David Cole, *Georgetown University Law Center*

In 1864 Abraham Lincoln was unexpectedly reelected president of the United States amidst the savagery of the Civil War. Though best known for freeing the slaves and saving the Union, during the war Lincoln came under fire for his aggressive use of presidential powers, including suspending habeas corpus in defiance of the Supreme Court, ordering the incarceration of thousands of citizens without charges, and blockading Southern ports without congressional authorization.

Aware of the contradictions inherent in his actions to both preserve and when necessary limit liberty, Lincoln sought in his 1864 election victory speech to offer an explanation. He opened by saying, "It has long been a grave question whether any government, not too strong for the liberties of its people, can be strong enough to maintain its own existence, in great emergencies."

Ever since the attacks of September 11, 2001, one of the most important public policy questions confronting Americans parallels the one that so tested the country during the time of Lincoln: what is the proper balance between safety and civil liberties in times of national threat? Indeed, it is a question that spans the life of the republic itself. In 1775 Ben Franklin framed one answer, saying, "Those who would give up essential liberty to purchase a little temporary safety, deserve neither liberty nor safety." Nearly two hundred years later, Supreme Court Justice Robert Jackson framed a very different answer when he warned a Supreme Court majority that unless it tempered its notion of absolute rights with "a little practical wisdom," it risked converting the Constitution "into a suicide pact."

In fact, the tendency in U.S. history has been for wartime presidents to do what Lincoln did—assume vast executive powers that often run roughshod over civil liberties and test the very bounds of the Constitution. Witness President Woodrow Wilson's signing of the Espionage and Sedition Acts and the subsequent mass arrests during and after World War I. And then there is President Franklin Roosevelt's internment of tens of thousands of U.S. citizens of Japanese descent during World War II and his blatant violations of America's Neutrality Acts leading up to the war.

What differentiates past conflicts from the current threat of terrorism, however, is that the earlier ones were of limited duration—extraordinary executive powers quickly receded after the wars. Modern terrorism has created a potentially open-ended challenge to American democracy, threatening the delicate balance of power between branches of government and between government and citizen. Supreme Court Justice Sandra Day O'Connor, though generally supportive of robust presidential wartime powers, noted the perilous circumstances: "Have we ever had a situation like this, where presumably this status, warlike status, could last 25 years? 50 years? Whatever it is?"[1]

Justice O'Connor's warning of the inherent danger to individual rights in the age of terrorism—that the government in general, and the executive branch in particular, might use the threat to justify continued expansion of its powers at the expense of civil liberties—was certainly apt. But there is an equally acute second danger: that after years without another major domestic attack, pressure will mount to return to some variation of pre-9/11 policies that were highly deferential toward civil liberties, but proved insufficient against an enemy like al-Qaeda.[2]

John Yoo and David Cole both recognize the enormous stakes in this debate. And, as in the previous debate over torture, both have the safety and security of the nation foremost in mind. Yet they agree on little else.

Yoo says that because the United States is at war with al-Qaeda, the president is constitutionally obligated to protect the nation using all necessary tools. And unlike previous wars on traditional battlefields, this conflict has a significant domestic dimension, with covert cells seeking to infiltrate the country to kill on a mass scale. This means, Yoo argues, that aggressively gathering and acting on intelligence are critical priorities—executive branch functions that, in wartime, will inevitably butt up against individual rights. Yes, civil liberties must be protected, but Yoo says that compared with prior national emergencies, the post-9/11 policies—developed by George W. Bush and continued by Barack Obama—were measured and tempered. And though Congress should be consulted, the executive must maintain its flexibility to act swiftly and decisively in order to prevent another attack, the aftermath of which would certainly be evermore devastating for civil liberties.

Cole rejects outright this "preventive paradigm" developed under George W. Bush, which he says offers a lesson in how not to fight terrorism. By employing aggressive anticipatory actions—seizing private records under the USA Patriot Act, wiretapping Americans without a warrant, engaging in preemptive war—the administration turned the law's traditional approach to state coercion (responding after specific wrongdoing has occurred) on its head. Worse, it substantially compromised U.S. security. Shirking the rule of law led to discrimination against Muslims, CIA "black sites," torture, Abu Ghraib, and the Iraq War, thereby creating a loss of legitimacy that made allies less cooperative, spawned new enemies, and inspired those already against Americans to adopt more radical tactics. Cole outlines ways to aggressively fight terrorism and abide by the rule of law at the same time—an approach he says Obama has successfully nurtured.

The 9/11 attacks revealed to one and all that a crafty enemy could orchestrate heinous acts of violence using the architecture of America's openness—liberal visitor and immigration laws, unfettered freedom of communication, unrestricted domestic travel, and open financial networks. In the wake of 9/11, it was inevitable that some individual and collective freedoms would be tempered and that some warfare measures would be adopted. Finding the delicate balance of which Lincoln spoke—a government not too strong for the liberties of the people, but strong enough to safeguard the nation—remains the great test of American democracy, as well as other liberal democracies around the world.

YES: The United States needs to reasonably limit civil liberties and bolster executive powers. John Yoo, *University of California at Berkeley School of Law*

Executive Power, Civil Liberties, and Security: Constitutional Trade-offs in Fighting Global Terrorism

After the September 11, 2001, terrorist attacks, the United States went to war against the al-Qaeda terrorist organization. On that day in September, al-Qaeda operatives hijacked four commercial airliners and used them as guided missiles against the World Trade Center towers in New York City and the Pentagon in the nation's capital. Resisting passengers brought down a fourth plane that appeared to have been headed toward either the Capitol or the White House. The attacks sent about three thousand people to their death, disrupted air traffic and communications within the United States, and drained billions of dollars from the economy. Both the president, in his military order of November 13, 2001, and Congress, in its September 18, 2001, authorization to use military force, agreed that these attacks marked the beginning of an armed conflict between the United States and the al-Qaeda terrorist network. Indeed, al-Qaeda's attack amounted to a classic decapitation strike designed to eliminate the political, military, and financial leadership of the country.

The unconventional nature of the war, and of the enemy, had called upon the U.S. government to undertake a full spectrum of domestic and international responses.[3] In previous modern American conflicts, hostilities were limited to foreign battlefields, and the U.S. homeland remained safe behind the distances of two oceans. In this conflict, the strict division between the front and the home front has blurred. Al-Qaeda has not only taken to the international battlefield against the United States in somewhat conventional warfare, but also sought to infiltrate covert cells of operatives into the United States—such as in Buffalo, New York, Portland, Oregon, and Chicago, Illinois—to carry out surprise attacks on civilians. Al-Qaeda operatives launched the initial salvo against the United States from within U.S. borders, and it shows no inclination to lessen its efforts to pull off another attack within the United States on the scale of September 11.

The distinctive international dimension of the conflict has been the offensive role the U.S. armed forces and U.S. intelligence agencies have played abroad to destroy the terrorist network. In response to the 9/11 attacks by the al-Qaeda terrorist group, the United States under the administration of George W. Bush responded by overthrowing the Taliban regime in Afghanistan, launching the 2003 invasion of Iraq, and starting a global campaign against terrorism. As a part of the worldwide war on terror, the Bush administration began gathering intelligence through Internet and banking networks, preemptively capturing, interrogating, and detaining suspected terrorists, trying terrorist leaders in military courts, and using unmanned drone aircraft to assassinate terrorists in nations such as Pakistan and Yemen.

On the domestic side, perhaps the most important aspect of the Bush administration's efforts to combat terrorism was in the area of intelligence gathering. In 2001 Congress enacted legislation, the USA Patriot Act, to enhance the powers of the Federal Bureau of Investigation (FBI) and the intelligence community to collect and share intelligence on international terrorists within the United States. Most of these statutory changes modified and improved the Foreign Intelligence Surveillance Act (FISA) of 1978, which requires the FBI to seek a warrant from a special federal court when it wishes to intercept the electronic communications of a target inside the United States suspected of links to terrorist groups. By 2005 Congress had created a new Department of Homeland Security to consolidate domestic agencies with responsibilities for domestic security, and a new director of national intelligence to consolidate the more than a dozen separate federal intelligence agencies. Along with these legislative changes, the president issued an executive order directing the National Security Agency (NSA) to engage in an expanded surveillance effort, without going through the FISA warrant process, to intercept suspected terrorist communications entering the United States from abroad.

These modest and reasonable adjustments to policy—based on a clear and present security threat—led to widespread criticism, sometimes bordering on hysteria. Critics said that the Constitution was in crisis; that a presidential dictatorship was arising; and that the Bill of Rights and civil liberties were being trampled. And yet the record now is clear: the aggressive but necessary post-9/11 policies have prevented another successful and disastrous al-Qaeda attack and have done so without any reduction in civil liberties. In many ways individual rights and freedoms emerged from the decade stronger than before. The government did not censor the media, sabotage political opposition, or seize the economy. No dictatorship arose. As the Constitution intends, the executive, legislative, and judicial branches freely used all of their powers to struggle for influence over national security policy. Five bitterly contested national elections (the true check on any abuse of power) switched control of the presidency once, the Senate once, and the House of Representatives twice. Meanwhile, new technologies and social networking have created an expanding space for political activity and organization unlike anything seen in our history.

But the greatest evidence of both the constitutionality and the prudence of the post-9/11 policies is that the administration of Barack Obama kept, and even enhanced, the operations capabilities built by the Bush administration: the intelligence-gathering infrastructures and the special forces teams and drones that can strike with stealth and accuracy, halfway around the world, at a moment's notice.

Ironies certainly abound. In 2008 candidate Obama campaigned on narrowing presidential wartime power, closing Guantánamo Bay, trying terrorists in civilian courts, ending enhanced interrogation, eliminating warrantless wiretapping, and moving away from a wartime approach to terrorism toward a criminal-justice approach. Once in office Mr. Obama attempted to follow through on these promises, but the real-world demands of governing (and several near-attacks during his first year in office) compelled him back to the Bush template of aggressive prevention. Most ironically the one promise Obama consistently claims to have kept—supposedly "ending torture"—has been offset by a grotesque policy of killing rather than capturing and interrogating terrorists.[4] In fact, the Obama administration has not captured a single high-ranking al-Qaeda leader since taking office. With total reliance on drone attacks that kill rather than capture terrorists, more people die—not just al-Qaeda leaders but nearby innocent civilians—and we lose the valuable information they might provide us to preempt their attacks on U.S. soil. After ceaseless promises to abide a law enforcement approach to terrorism, Obama avoided these vexing issues simply by depriving terrorists of all of their rights—by killing them.[5]

Critics have challenged the policy merits, legality, and morality of almost all of these decisions, though perhaps less vociferously under Obama. Their basic claim attacks the president's authority to carry out these policies either on his own authority acting alone, or when inconsistent with congressional statutes. They argue that Congress must authorize the president's actions in wartime, the president cannot act inconsistently with statutes or treaties or international law, and post-9/11 counterterrorism policy has violated basic individual rights and civil liberties. The NSA surveillance program during the Bush years and the expanded targeted killings policy during the Obama years are typically identified as the clearest examples for two reasons. First the government's intelligence gathering did not comply with FISA's requirement for a judicial warrant when conducting electronic surveillance within the United States. Second the "kill list" for targeted assassinations—including those of U.S. citizens like Anwar al-Awlaki—has been undertaken with no due process other than the president and his staff. In this essay, I will explain that these critics have it wrong. Instead of an imperial presidency, the executive branch under both the Bush and Obama administrations has acted within its constitutional authorities—indeed, it fulfilled the purpose of its original design by taking action to protect the citizens and territory of the United States from attack. Furthermore, instead of acting in violation of basic rights and liberties, the Bush administration's initial exercise of executive power in the wake of 9/11 was measured and tempered—especially when compared with the actions of presidents during prior periods of national emergency.

FOUNDATIONS OF EXECUTIVE AUTHORITY

As commander in chief, the president has the constitutional power and the responsibility to wage war in response to a direct attack upon the United States. During World War II, the Supreme Court recognized that once war has begun, the president's authority as commander in chief and chief executive gives him access to the tools he needs to effectively wage war. The president has the power "to direct the performance of those functions which may constitutionally be performed by the military arm of the nation in time of war" and to issue military commands using the powers to conduct war "to repel and defeat the enemy."[6] In the wake of the September 11 attacks, even Congress agreed by enacting a law that declared "the President has authority under the Constitution to take action to deter and prevent acts of international terrorism against the United States."[7] This statement recognizes the president's authority to use force, and any powers necessary and proper to that end, to respond to al-Qaeda.

The shift of power to the executive branch in wartime is not just an inference from the constitutional text and structure, but a lesson of history. In the Civil War, for example, President Lincoln raised an army, withdrew money from the Treasury, and launched a blockade on his own authority in response to the Confederate attack on Fort Sumter—moves that Congress and the Supreme Court later approved.[8] Presidents of both political parties have waged war numerous times, in places ranging from Korea to Kosovo to Libya, on their own constitutional authority without congressional authorization. Past wartime presidents have also exercised tremendous unilateral powers within the borders of the country, including the suspension of habeas corpus, creation of military tribunals, and broad spying on private communications.

Even legal scholars who argue against this historical practice concede that once the United States has been attacked, the president can respond with force on his own.[9] The ability to direct military operations, detain the enemy, and collect intelligence is intrinsic to the use of military force. It is inconceivable that the Constitution would vest in the president the power of commander in chief and chief executive and give him the sole responsibility to protect the nation from attack, but then disable him by preventing him from using the means most effective to defeat the enemy. The Framers understood the Constitution to grant the government every ability to meet a foreign danger. James Madison wrote in *Federalist* No. 41 that "security against foreign danger is one of the primitive objects of civil society." Therefore, the "powers requisite for attaining it must be effectually confided to the federal councils."[10] As the Supreme Court declared after World War II, "This grant of war power includes all that is necessary and proper for carrying these powers into execution."[11]

During the writing of the Constitution, some Framers believed that the president needed to manage intelligence because only he could keep secrets. Several Supreme Court cases have recognized that the president's role as the sole organ of the nation in its foreign relations and as commander in chief must include the power to collect intelligence.[12] These authorities agree that intelligence rests with the president because the office's structure allows it to act with unity, secrecy, and speed.

Take the issue of surveillance. Presidents have ordered electronic surveillance without any judicial or congressional participation. More than a year before the Pearl Harbor attacks, but with war looming with the Axis powers, President Franklin Roosevelt authorized the FBI to intercept any communications, whether wholly inside the country or international, of persons "suspected of subversive activities against the Government of the United States, including suspected spies."[13] FDR was concerned that "fifth columns"—those people believed to be loyalists who clandestinely undermine the nation—could wreak havoc on the war effort. "It is too late to do anything about it after sabotage, assassinations and 'fifth column' activities are completed," FDR wrote in his order.[14] FDR ordered the surveillance even though a Supreme Court decision and a federal statute at the time prohibited electronic surveillance without a warrant.[15] FDR continued to authorize the interception of electronic communications even after Congress rejected proposals for wiretapping for national security reasons.[16]

Until FISA, presidents continued to monitor on their own authority the communications of national security threats, even in peacetime.[17] If presidents in time of peace could order surveillance of spies and terrorists, as President Roosevelt did in 1940, or as presidents from Truman through Carter did during the Cold War, then executive authority is all the more certain now, after the events of September 11. This is a view that justice departments have held not just under President Bush; the Clinton Justice Department held a similar view of the executive branch's authority to conduct surveillance outside the FISA framework.[18] And in his confirmation hearing before the Senate Judiciary Committee, President Obama's attorney general, Eric Holder, agreed that the president's constitutional authority to engage in intelligence surveillance may not be subject to limitation by statute, including FISA, which set the stage for the Obama administration's continuation of the Bush-era's NSA wiretapping program.[19]

Courts have never opposed a president's authority to engage in warrantless electronic surveillance to protect national security. When the Supreme Court first considered this question in 1972, it held that the Fourth Amendment required a judicial warrant if a president wanted to conduct surveillance of a purely domestic group, but it refused to address surveillance of foreign threats to national security.[20] In the years since, every federal appeals court to address the question, including the FISA appeals court, has "held that the President did have inherent authority to conduct warrantless searches to obtain foreign intelligence information."[21] In 1980 in *United States v. Truong Dinh Hung,* the Fourth Circuit observed that "the needs of the Executive are so compelling in the area of foreign intelligence, unlike the area of domestic security, that a uniform warrant requirement would, following *Keith,* 'unduly frustrate,' the President in carrying out his foreign affairs responsibilities."[22] The Fourth Circuit held that the government is relieved of the warrant requirement when the surveillance involves both a foreign power and a foreign intelligence motive. First, warrants are not required when the object of the search or surveillance is a foreign power, its agents, or its collaborators, because such cases are "most likely to call into play difficult and subtle judgments about foreign and military affairs." Second, "when the surveillance is conducted 'primarily' for foreign intelligence reasons," warrants are unnecessary for two reasons: first, "once surveillance becomes primarily a criminal investigation, the courts are entirely competent to make the usual probable cause determination," and, second, "individual privacy interests come to the fore and government foreign policy concerns recede when the government is primarily attempting to form the basis for a criminal prosecution."[23] The factors favoring warrantless searches for national security reasons are compelling under the current circumstances created by the war on terrorism. After the attacks on September 11, 2001, the government's interest in conducting searches related to fighting terrorism were perhaps of the highest order—the need to defend the nation from direct attack. As the Supreme Court pointed out in 1981, "It is 'obvious and unarguable' that no governmental interest is more compelling than the security of the Nation."[24]

It is true that the NSA program might be unusual in its reliance on the president's power alone. And for some other counterterrorism initiatives, the president could plausibly rely on Congress's support in the September 18, 2001, Authorization for Use of Military Force (AUMF). It is sweeping; it has no limitation on time or place; it authorizes the president to pursue al-Qaeda and those connected to the 9/11 attacks. Its passage was proof that the president and Congress fully agreed that military action would be appropriate. Congress's support for the president cannot just be limited to the right to literally use force, but to all the necessary subcomponents that permit effective military action. Congress's tacit approval of the killing of al-Qaeda operatives must obviously include the tools to locate them in the first place.

Indeed, a primary argument of critics is that post-9/11 measures such as indefinite detention, warrantless surveillance, and targeted killings are illegal violations of individual rights because the AUMF did not explicitly mention detentions, wiretapping, or executions. But even though the AUMF does not mention detentions and surveillance, U.S. courts including the Supreme Court later upheld the right of the president to control these policies. And now, with the upsurge in targeted killings under Obama, some are demanding a greater role for Congress and the courts in supervising these operations.[25]

Critics essentially argue that Congress must enact a grocery list of specific powers, and that, otherwise, the president cannot fight a war. However, in the AUMF Congress authorized the president "to use all necessary and appropriate force" against those "he determines" were involved with the 9/11 attacks, or those who aid, support, or harbor those involved to "prevent any future acts of international terrorism against the United States." The power to use force impliedly *includes* powers such as surveillance and targeted killings to avert future attacks.

Congress cannot legislate in anticipation of every circumstance that may arise in the future. That is one of the reasons, along with the executive branch's advantages in expertise and structural organization, why Congress delegates authority. Those who consider themselves legal progressives generally support the administrative state and vigorously defend broad grants of authority from Congress to the agencies of the executive branch. Agencies such as the Federal Communications Commission or the Environmental Protection Agency exercise powers over broad sectors of the economy under the incredibly vague and broad congressional mandate that they regulate in the "public interest." These agencies make decisions with enormous effects, such as which parts of the radio spectrum to sell or how much pollution to allow into the air, all with little explicit guidance or thought from Congress.

Yet when Congress delegates broad authority to the president to defend the nation from attack, critics demand that Congress list everything. Although the threats to individual liberty may be greater otherwise, those threats must be balanced against the potentially tragic cost of insufficiently safeguarding the homeland. Americans would expect and want Congress to delegate power to the branch that is best able to act with speed to threats to national security—the executive branch. War is too difficult to plan for with fixed, antecedent legislative rules, and war also is better run by the executive, which is structurally designed to take quick, decisive action.

EXECUTIVE INITIATIVE IN TIMES OF WAR AND NATIONAL EMERGENCY

Even accepting, for the moment, the claim that executive policies in the war on terrorism are in conflict with the wishes of Congress and civil libertarians, this acceptance does not make the former illegal, and it does not mean there is a practical alternative to decisive executive action. Everyone would prefer that the president and Congress agree on war policy; it was one of the reasons the Bush administration sought the AUMF in the first place. The nation will wage war more effectively if the executive and legislature share a unified purpose.

But conflict between the branches of government is commonplace. The president and Congress have pursued conflicting war policies many times. Congress passed the Neutrality Acts of 1935, 1937, and 1939 before World War II in a largely futile effort to restrain Franklin Roosevelt from assisting the Allies. Vietnam, Nicaragua, and Kosovo are just the most recent examples of wars in which Congress tried to frustrate or micromanage executive war policy.[26]

The Constitution not only anticipated this struggle—it was written to ensure it. The Framers did not give the president or the Congress complete control over war, foreign policy, and national security, but instead designed each branch differently and gave each a different set of powers that could be used to cooperate or fight. The president is the commander in chief and chief executive, while Congress has the power over funding, legislation, the creation and discipline of the military, and the power to "declare war." The power over national security is dramatically unlike other government powers, such as passing a statute, appointing a judge, or making a treaty, for which the Constitution sets out a precise, step-by-step process for the roles of the different branches of government.

Critics of executive wartime policy appeal to the Constitution as it works in peacetime when Congress authorizes a policy and the president carries it out. They imagine that the Constitution requires the president to check back with Congress on every strategy and tactic in the war on terrorism to, among other things, ensure that basic rights and liberties are protected. The NSA program, indefinite detentions, and targeted killings are illegal, they say, because President Bush neglected to get yet another law approving them. It

is true that Congress offers more transparency and perhaps greater accountability to the public. But it should also be clear that, over time, the presidency
has gained the leading role in war and national security because of its superior ability to take the initiative in response to emergencies. Indeed, the
Framers designed the executive branch precisely so that its powers could
grow to protect the country in times of crisis from external threat.

The Framers well understood that war's unpredictability makes unique
demands for decisive and often secret action. They rejected extreme republi-
canism, which concentrated power in the legislature, and created an executive
with its own independent powers to manage foreign affairs and address war
and emergencies. The power to protect the nation, Alexander Hamilton wrote
in *Federalist* No. 23, "ought to exist without limitation," because "it is impossible to foresee or define the extent and variety of national exigencies, or the
correspondent extent & variety of the means which may be necessary to satisfy
them."[27] It would be foolhardy to limit the constitutional power to protect the
nation from foreign threats. "The circumstances that endanger the safety of
nations are infinite; and for this reason no constitutional shackles can wisely be
imposed on the power to which the care of it is committed."

The Framers located the responsibility to respond to emergency and war in
the presidency because of its functional advantages. Hamilton, for example,
observed that "decision, activity, secrecy, and dispatch will generally character-
ize the proceedings of one man, in a much more eminent degree, than the
proceedings of any greater number." He went on to say: "Energy in the executive is essential to the protection of the community against foreign attacks."[28]
Wartime, that most unpredictable and dangerous of human endeavors, therefore ought to be managed by the president. "Of all the cares or concerns of
government, the direction of war most peculiarly demands those qualities
which distinguish the exercise of power by a single hand."[29]

If ever there were an emergency that Congress could not prepare for, it was
the war brought upon the United States on September 11, 2001. FISA, for
example, was a law written with Soviet spies working out of their embassy in
Washington, D.C., in mind. The Geneva Conventions of 1949 were adopted
when there were two types of conflicts—international wars between nation-
states and civil wars. No one in 1949 or 1978 anticipated war with an international terrorist organization wielding the destructive power of a nation. The
presidency was the institution of government best able to respond quickly to
the 9/11 attacks and to take measures to defeat al-Qaeda's further efforts.
Although the certainty and openness of a congressional act would certainly be
desirable, the success of counterterrorism policies depends on secrecy and
agility, two characteristics that Congress as an institution lacks.

But, critics respond, Congress foresaw that war might increase the demands for domestic wiretapping or military commissions or detentions and interrogation, and still did not authorize (or even prohibited) the president from taking those measures. Why should not Congress's view here, as in any other domestic question, particularly those of such basic sensitivity, prevail?

It is simply not the case that the president must carry out every law enacted by Congress. The Constitution is the supreme law of the land, and neither an act of Congress nor an act of the president can supersede it. If Congress passes an unconstitutional act, such as a law ordering the imprisonment of those who criticize the government, the president must give force to the higher law, that of the Constitution. Thomas Jefferson did just that regarding the Alien and Sedition Acts that were passed in 1798 during an undeclared naval war with France. He took the position that he, "believing the law to be unconstitutional, was bound to remit the execution of it, because that power has been confided to him by the constitution."[30] That does not mean that the president "is above the law"; it only means that the Constitution is above the Congress and the president. FISA might be unconstitutional if it were read to forbid the president from gathering information necessary to prevent attacks on the United States in wartime.

If the critics are right and presidents are duty bound to obey any and all acts of Congress, Congress could have ordered FDR not to attempt an amphibious landing in France in World War II, Truman to attack China during the Korean War, or JFK to invade Cuba in 1962. But presidents such as Jefferson, Jackson, Lincoln, and FDR believed they had the right to take action, within their own constitutional authorities, to follow their interpretation of the Constitution rather than the views of Congress or the Supreme Court, especially in their role as commander in chief.

Although Congress has the sole power to declare war, neither presidents nor Congresses have acted under the belief that a declaration of war must come before military hostilities abroad. And both the president and Congress generally agree that the legislature should not interfere in the executive branch's strategic and tactical decisions. Congress attempted to prevent presidents from using force abroad in the Nixon-era War Powers Resolution by prohibiting the insertion of troops into hostile environments abroad for more than sixty days without legislative approval. But the resolution has been a dead letter. Presidents and Congresses alike have since realized that the War Powers Resolution made little practical sense, and instead represented congressional overreaching into presidential expertise and constitutional authority in foreign affairs.

Presidential leadership has always included control over the goals and means of military campaigns. As the Supreme Court has observed, the president has the authority to "employ the armed forces in the manner he may deem most effectual to harass and conquer and subdue the enemy."[31] President Lincoln did not seek a law from Congress on whether to defend Washington, D.C.; President Roosevelt did not ask Congress whether he should make the war in Europe a priority over the war in the Pacific; President Truman did not seek legislative permission to drop nuclear bombs on Japan. The same applies to the application of presidential authority at home—from ordering conscription to directing private industries to support the war effort. Obviously, presidents should not ignore congressional leaders—a wise president will consult with them at the right time—but the Constitution does not force the president to get a letter from Congress every time he makes an important decision about wartime strategy or tactics, at home or abroad.

Nor is Congress powerless. It has ample powers to block wartime initiatives. It has total control over funding and the size and equipment of the military. If it disagrees with wartime strategy, it can cut off funds, reduce the size of military units, or refuse to provide supplies. War would be impossible without Congress's cooperation or at least acquiescence. This is even more so in the age of modern warfare, whose demands require constant congressional budgetary support.

Critics claim that Congress ought to have the upper hand in war to prevent military adventurism, to check war fever, to guarantee political consensus, and to safeguard values and rights. This sounds plausible, but it neglects the benefits of executive action during time of foreign threat, and it downplays Congress's faults, such as delay, inflexibility, and lack of secrecy. World War II clearly demonstrates that presidential initiative has been critical to the protection of American national security. When Europe plunged into war, Congress enacted a series of Neutrality Acts designed to keep the United States out of the conflict. In 1940 and 1941, FDR recognized that America's security would be threatened by German control of Europe, and he and his advisers gradually attempted to bring the United States to the assistance of Britain and the Soviet Union.[32] FDR stretched his authority to cooperate closely with Britain in protecting convoys in the North Atlantic and providing the British with fifty "obsolete" destroyers, among other things. Administration pressure on Japan to withdraw from China helped to trigger the war in the Pacific, without which America's entry into World War II might have been delayed by at least another year, if not longer.[33] With what they now know, most Americans would agree that earlier U.S. entry into World War II would have been much to the benefit of the United States and to the world.

Legislative deliberation can breed consensus in the best of cases, but it also can stand in the way of speed and decisiveness. Terrorist attacks are more difficult to detect and prevent than those posed by the conventional armed forces of nations; and In the age of weapons of mass destruction (WMDs), they may inflict devastation that once only could have been achievable by a nation-state.[34] To defend itself from this threat, the United States will have to use force earlier and more often than at the time when nations generated the primary threats. To forestall a WMD attack or to take advantage of a window of opportunity to strike at a terrorist cell, the president needs the flexibility to act quickly. By acting earlier, perhaps before WMD components have been fully assembled or before terrorist operatives have left for the United States, the executive branch might also be able to engage in a more limited, more precisely targeted use of force.

Ultimately, claims that terrorism policies amount to a presidential violation of the Constitution appeal to concerns not about law but about politics. Such critics worry that if the president is waging a war and the war has slipped into the United States itself, terrorism policies will centralize too much power in the presidency over domestic affairs. The response to 9/11, however, does not signal that the constitutional system of separation of powers has failed.

Instead, the other branches of government have powerful and important tools to limit the president should his efforts to defeat terrorism slip into domestic oppression. Congress has total control over funding and significant powers of oversight. It could do away with the NSA or the Central Intelligence Agency (CIA) as a whole; it could close any detention facility—including Guantánamo Bay. Congress need not engage in anything as drastic as doing away with the NSA, of course. At any point in the past twelve years Congress could have easily eliminated surveillance, detention, and interrogation programs themselves—on which congressional leaders of both parties were secretly briefed no fewer than thirty times in the months and years after 9/11—simply by cutting off funding. And it could similarly stop drone strike operations at any time. It could also link approval of administration policies in related areas to agreement on changes to terrorism policies. Congress could refuse to confirm cabinet members, sub-cabinet members, or military intelligence officers unless its wishes prevail. It could hold extensive hearings that bring to light perceived abuses, backed up by the power of subpoena, and require officials to appear and be held to account. So far, Congress, under both Republican and Democratic leadership, has not taken any of these steps.

Courts can also exercise their own check on presidential power, although it is one that is not as comprehensive as Congress's. Any effort to criminally prosecute an al-Qaeda member or a terrorism suspect within the United States will require the cooperation of the federal courts. If federal judges believe that terrorism policies are unconstitutional, they can grant a writ of habeas corpus to any detainee not properly held as an enemy combatant. In fact, the Supreme Court has taken steps to expand the habeas corpus jurisdiction of the courts over the detainees held at Guantánamo Bay, and demanded that Congress explicitly authorize military commissions (which it swiftly did).[35] Although they have not yet ordered the release of any detainees, and have been overruled by Congress twice, the courts retain limited measures to frustrate counterterrorism policies. Even in areas such as the NSA surveillance program or military commissions, the courts can maintain a check by refusing to admit any evidence gathered in violation of the Fourth Amendment and to order the release of any detainees convicted by military courts that have used unconstitutional procedures.

THE SYSTEM WORKS

The claims of an unchecked imperial presidency have been vastly overblown. Throughout American history, times of crisis have called forth broad uses of presidential power, episodes invariably accompanied by loud protests that the president arrogated the powers of a king. Yet history portrays such moments as times of challenge and presidential greatness. In the darkest depths of the Civil War, Lincoln took extraordinary measures to raise and fund an army without congressional appropriations, used military force against the seceding states, suspended habeas corpus, and instituted military trials for civilians suspected of working with the Confederacy. He was dogged throughout his presidency by harsh criticism that he was seeking "absolute power" with acts "subversive of liberty and law, and quite as certainly tending to the establishment of despotism."[36] Civil liberties did suffer, and perhaps he went too far at times, but Lincoln saved the Union, freed the slaves, and ended the Civil War.

The same is true for Franklin Roosevelt, whose creative use of executive power is credited with pulling the nation out of the Great Depression and putting it on the path to victory in World War II. Yet FDR also tested the very bounds of presidential authority, as with his secret executive order directing the internment of tens of thousands of American citizens of Japanese descent.

Exercises of presidential power can go badly wrong, of course. Culminating with Richard Nixon's Watergate scandal, the presidencies of Nixon, Lyndon Johnson, and John Kennedy came to symbolize an "imperial presidency" grown out of control during the 1960s and 1970s, to the point that it seemed to fundamentally threaten American liberty.

Yet post–Watergate efforts to restrict the executive branch have not made the American president less central to the political universe. This is particularly true in the realm of national security: the threats of the modern age—most notably the threat of catastrophic terrorism—require tremendous executive flexibility and decisive executive action. To those who argue that this is an unacceptable trade-off—that the robust exercise of executive power in times of war comes at too great an expense to fundamental rights and values—I would ask them to consider the potentially tremendous costs of restricting such action.

President Obama received justified congratulations for his administration's flawless execution of the operation that killed Osama bin Laden in May 2011. But buried in the stories of the raid in Abbottabad was perhaps the most illuminating example of Obama's shift from leading critic of the Bush administration's war on terror policies to its leading beneficiary. According to government sources, the al-Qaeda courier who led our intelligence agents to bin Laden was a protégé of Khalid Sheikh Muhammad (KSM), the architect of the 9/11 attacks who was captured in 2002, was subjected to enhanced interrogation methods, and yielded a trove of intelligence on al-Qaeda. These sources admit that interrogation of al-Qaeda leaders, presumably by the CIA, yielded the identity of the courier. That identity was then combined into a mosaic of other information from other detainee interrogations, electronic intercepts, and sources in other countries, to eventually identify bin Laden's hideout.

It is important to note that Obama's embrace of the Bush policies was certainly reluctant. He spent more than a year (and endangered America's national security) trying to follow through on his reckless promise to "reverse" Bush's policies, as best illustrated by his administration's failed effort to put KSM on trial in a civilian court in Manhattan. Indeed the Obama White House's initial loss of focus on national security priorities almost cost the country dearly: only the bravery of individual passengers stopped Umar Farouk Abdulmutallab from blowing up Northwest Airlines Flight 253 over Detroit on Christmas Day 2009. And if not for a failed detonator, Faisal Shahzad would have succeeded in exploding a car bomb in New York City's crowded Times Square in May 2010.

Obama deserves credit for eventually coming to the realization that the threats of the modern age—most notably the threat of catastrophic terrorism—require tremendous executive flexibility and decisive executive action. But this was not some new and novel realization: despite what the post-9/11 critics of America's war on terrorism would have you believe, the broad exercise of presidential power is not unique to the twentieth or twenty-first century, but represents the growth over two centuries of the constitutional powers of the office. It started with the Framers' efforts to avoid executives who might slip into monarchy or dictatorship. By the time of the Constitution's ratification, however, the Framers' views had evolved in favor of an independent, forceful president. The Framers devoted much of their attention to listing the powers of Congress, whereas they deliberately paint the president's powers in broad strokes. The nation's greatest presidents, from George Washington on, have filled in these sketchy outlines in the ways in which they have met national challenges, both foreign and domestic. Presidential power has grown as the nation's power has grown, both in constitutional law and in prestige and substantive power. It is that power that has allowed presidents to respond forcefully to challenges like the 9/11 attacks, and will allow future presidents, if they so choose, to rapidly change course as well.

NO: Respecting civil liberties and preventing executive overreach are critical to preserving America's security and its ideals.
David Cole, *Georgetown University Law Center*

Securing Liberty in the Face of Terrorism

> In order to fight and to defeat terrorism, the Department of Justice has added a new paradigm to that of prosecution— a paradigm of prevention.
>
> —U.S. Attorney General John Ashcroft, speech to the Council on Foreign Relations, February 10, 2003

As President Barack Obama took office in January 2009, he rejected "as false the choice between our safety and our ideals," and proclaimed that he would not sacrifice fundamental American values "for expedience's sake."[37] That message marked a departure from his predecessor's approach to the "war on terrorism," in which some of the nation's—and indeed the world's—most cherished ideals were abandoned in the name of security. The Bush administration authorized waterboarding and other forms of torture to interrogate suspects; "disappeared" others for years at a time into secret CIA prisons, known as "black sites," where they were held incommunicado and brutally abused; claimed the power to hold anyone labeled an "enemy combatant" indefinitely without abiding by the most basic protections guaranteed by the laws of war, including a fair hearing and humane treatment; asserted the right to violate federal criminal statutes outlawing torture and warrantless wiretapping of Americans; and "rendered" suspects to countries with long records of torture to be interrogated with even more extreme tactics than our own agents were authorized to employ. All of this was done in the name of the "war on terror," which President Bush defined as a war against all terrorist organizations of potentially global reach.

On his second day in office, President Obama sought to change course, issuing executive orders that halted the CIA's use of cruel, inhuman, and degrading interrogation tactics; closed the CIA's secret prisons; and committed to closing the military detention center at the Guantánamo Bay naval base within a year. Four years later, Guantánamo remains open, but many of the Bush-era practices have ceased. The black sites remain closed; there have been no reports of rendition used for purposes of torture; President Obama abandoned his predecessor's claim of uncheckable authority to violate federal laws when acting as commander in chief; there have been few if any reports of coercive interrogation; and warrantless wiretapping has been codified by federal statute with new oversight authorities. President Obama's record is far from perfect, of course. He has continued to rely on overly broad assertions of the "state secrets" privilege to block attempts to vindicate the rights of torture victims; he has successfully blocked judicial review of detentions at Bagram Air Force base in Afghanistan; he has radically increased targeted killing with unmanned drones and has declined to release the legal guidance that assertedly justifies that practice; and he has resisted calls for a commission to hold accountable those, like my adversary in this chapter John Yoo, who authorized torture and other war crimes. Still, President Obama staked out a very different approach to fighting terrorism from that of his predecessor: where Bush sought to thrust law aside in the name of security, Obama sought to fight terror within the law.[38]

Indeed, the central premise of the Bush administration's approach to fighting terrorism was that harsh preventive measures were necessary and appropriate to keep the United States secure. The Bush administration pursued what Attorney General John Ashcroft dubbed a "paradigm of prevention." Ashcroft and Bush argued that when one faces an enemy like al-Qaeda, the nation is justified in employing highly coercive and intrusive measures—warrantless wiretapping, detention, coercive interrogation, even war itself—preemptively, not based on hard evidence of past or current wrongdoing, but on the basis of predictions about future threats. All of these measures were said to be warranted by the need to prevent a future terrorist attack—as was the Iraq War, launched on claims that Saddam Hussein had weapons of mass destruction and might deliver them to terrorists who might use them against the United States at some unspecified point in the future.

This preventive approach, as applied by the Bush administration, entailed widespread sacrifices in prior commitments to fundamental values. Ideals such as due process and the right not to be subjected to inhumane treatment, the government's defenders argued, were not absolutes, and at the end of the day the nation's survival required a recalibration of the balance between its ideals and its security. As federal judge and conservative law scholar Richard Posner reminded Americans in a book defending this approach, the Constitution is "not a suicide pact."[39]

The challenge for any democracy facing the threat of terrorism is how best to counter that threat without unduly compromising the ideals that form the foundation of the rule of law. A review of the Bush administration's "preventive paradigm," and of the Obama administration's record during its first term, provides an important object lesson in the most appropriate and effective ways to fight terrorism. Abandoning the nation's ideals not only is normatively flawed but also undermines its security in the long run. Whatever else the Bush administration accomplished, it surely demonstrated that claims that respecting basic liberties necessarily undermines the nation's security are grossly reductive. In fact, hewing to basic rights may increase the nation's security in the long run. The nation appears to be no less safe under the law-abiding approach of President Obama—who if anything made dramatic progress in reducing al-Qaeda's threat—than it was under the law-defying approach of President Bush.

THE PREVENTIVE PARADIGM AND RULE OF LAW VALUES

In isolation, neither the goal of preventing future attacks nor the tactic of using coercive measures is particularly novel or troubling. All law enforcement, after all, seeks to prevent crime, and coercion is a necessary element of state power. The force of law depends in part on the threat that violations will trigger a coercive response such as arrest, prosecution, and punishment. But the rule of law generally requires that the state restrict its use of such measures to situations in which it has established through fair processes that a specific wrong has been committed. The Bush administration's "preventive paradigm," by contrast, employed anticipatory state violence—that is, preventive measures were undertaken before any wrongdoing had actually occurred and often without good evidence for believing that any wrongdoing would in fact occur. That approach not only placed tremendous stress on the ideals that the nation and the world associate with the rule of law, but also compromised the nation's security.

The preventive rationale made thinkable tactics that have long been unthinkable in the United States. No one defends coercive interrogation, disappearances, and renditions as permissible forms of investigation or punishment for past crimes; rather, they are invariably defended with some version of the familiar "ticking bomb" hypothetical, in which extreme measures such as torture are said to be warranted to defuse a bomb and thereby save thousands of lives. What would be unacceptable as punishment suddenly becomes acceptable, at least to some, when information is urgently needed to forestall some future hypothetical catastrophe.

The Bush administration even invoked the preventive paradigm to alter the grounds for starting a war. Established international law permits individual nations to go to war only in self-defense, meaning in response to an armed attack or an imminent armed attack. In its 2002 "National Security Strategy," the Bush administration pronounced this standard too constraining in an era of suicide terrorists and weapons of mass destruction, and maintained that the country is justified in going to war even when it has not been attacked and faces no threat of imminent attack.[40] An "emerging" threat is enough, the document insists. The administration relied on this theory to justify the attack on Iraq in 2003, at a time when Iraq had neither attacked the United States nor posed any threat of imminent attack.

This strategy of employing force anticipatorily, either at home or abroad, before there is evidence of wrongdoing and before wrongdoing occurs, turns the law's traditional approach to state coercion on its head. With narrow exceptions, the rule of law generally reserves invasions of privacy, detention, punishment, and use of military force for those who have been shown—on the basis of sound evidence and fair procedures—to have committed some wrongful act in the past. The police can invade privacy by tapping phones or searching homes, but only when there is probable cause to believe that a crime has been committed and that the search is likely to uncover evidence of the crime. Arrest, too, requires probable cause of crime. People can be preventively detained pending trial, but only when there is both probable cause of past wrongdoing and concrete evidence that they pose a danger to the community or are likely to abscond if left at large. Individuals can be punished only upon proof of guilt beyond a reasonable doubt. And nations may use military force unilaterally only in response to an objectively verifiable attack or threat of imminent attack. Meanwhile, the rule of law absolutely prohibits other forms of state coercion—such as disappearances and torture—even when it can be shown without a doubt that an individual has broken the law.[41]

The preventive paradigm rejects these constraints on coercive state intervention into people's lives. In the USA Patriot Act, the Bush administration obtained expanded powers to demand private records on suspects without showing a judge that there was probable cause to suspect the individual of criminal activity. It authorized a sweeping warrantless wiretapping program, run by the National Security Agency (NSA), that gathered up international phone calls between American citizens living in the United States and other persons thought to be living abroad—again without establishing probable cause or seeking judicial approval.

The preventive paradigm requires so many compromises in fundamental principles of legality that it renders the rule of law virtually unrecognizable. The rule of law, after all, is designed to subject state power to careful checks, to scrupulously enforce the line between guilt and innocence, and to hold government officials accountable to clear rules. These ideals mix uneasily with the strategies of the preventive paradigm, which generally demand sweeping executive discretion, eschew questions of guilt or innocence (because no wrong has yet occurred), and substitute secrecy and speculation for accountability and verifiable fact. Where the rule of law insists on objective evidence of wrongdoing, the preventive paradigm relies on predictions about future behavior. Such predictions generally cannot be proved true or false; frequently rest on questionable assumptions, stereotypes, and preconceptions; and are especially vulnerable to pretextual manipulation. In times of crisis, moreover, the increased fear of a false negative—allowing a real terrorist to go free—becomes so great that high rates of false positives—detaining or punishing innocents or attacking countries that do not intend to attack us—are deemed increasingly acceptable.

Where the rule of law demands fair and open procedures, the preventive paradigm employs truncated processes that are often conducted in secret, denying suspects a meaningful opportunity to respond to the charges against them. The need for preemptive action is said to justify the secrecy and the shortcuts, whatever the cost to targeted individuals. Where the rule of law demands that people be held accountable only for their own actions, not for their ethnic identity or religious or political views, the preventive paradigm paints in broad brushstrokes, frequently employing guilt by association and ethnic profiling to target suspected future wrongdoers. And where the rule of law absolutely prohibits torture and disappearances, the preventive paradigm maintains that these measures should be viewed as lesser evils to defuse the proverbial ticking bomb. In short, the preventive paradigm treats the rule of law's most fundamental commitments as luxuries that the nation cannot afford in the face of a catastrophic threat.

The impetus toward prevention is understandable. All other things being equal, preventing a terrorist act is preferable to responding after the fact—all the more so when the threats include weapons of mass destruction and adversaries are difficult to detect, are willing to kill themselves, and seemingly are unconstrained by any considerations of law, morality, or human dignity. There is nothing wrong with prevention itself as a motive or a strategy; think, for example, of preventive medicine. And plenty of preventive counterterrorism initiatives do conform to the rule of law such as more protective measures at borders and around vulnerable targets, institutional reforms designed to encourage better analysis of data and information sharing among the many government agencies responsible for the country's safety, prosecutions for conspiracies to engage in terrorist acts, and even military force and military detention when employed in self-defense. The real problems arise when the state seeks to inflict highly coercive measures—depriving individuals of their life, liberty, or property or going to war—on the basis of speculation about the future, without adhering to the processes long seen as critical to regulating and legitimating such force.

THE FAILURE OF THE PREVENTIVE PARADIGM

Abandoning the rule of law is not just wrong as a matter of principle. It is wrongheaded as a practical matter of security. The Bush administration's turn to preventive coercion appears to have made the United States more vulnerable to attack, not more secure. Even if one were to accept as a moral or ethical matter the "ends justify the means" rationales advanced for the preventive paradigm, the paradigm fails its own test: there is little or no evidence that the Bush administration's coercive preemptive measures made the United States safer, and there is substantial evidence that they exacerbated the dangers the nation faced.

Consider the most costly example of the administration's preventive paradigm: the war in Iraq. Precisely because the preventive doctrine turns on speculation about nonimminent events, it permitted an administration—which for its own reasons had persistently sought to topple Saddam Hussein—to turn its focus from al-Qaeda, the organization that actually attacked the United States, to Iraq, a nation that did not. The Iraq War has, by virtually all accounts, made the United States, the Iraqi people, many U.S. allies, and for that matter much of the world more vulnerable to terrorists. By targeting Iraq, the Bush administration not only siphoned off massive resources and expertise from the struggle against al-Qaeda, but also played into al-Qaeda's hands by reinforcing its anti-American propaganda and by creating a golden opportunity to inspire, recruit, and train terrorists to attack U.S. and allied targets. In February 2005, CIA Director Porter Goss told Congress that "Islamic extremists are exploiting the Iraqi conflict to recruit new anti-U.S. jihadists."[42]

Although Iraq had nothing to do with the so-called war on terrorism before the United States attacked it, the invasion and U.S. occupation turned Iraq into the world's premier training ground for terrorists. As Goss admitted, "Those who survive will leave Iraq experienced and focused on acts of urban terrorism. They represent a potential pool of contacts to build transnational terrorist cells, groups, and networks."[43] For years, the insurgents in Iraq repeatedly attacked the U.S. and Iraqi military and police forces. These attacks were often videotaped and disseminated worldwide via the Internet to inspire those in the widely dispersed diaspora who might take the initiative to commit their own atrocities—as the world witnessed in the Madrid bombing in 2004 and the London bombing in 2005. In terms of direct costs, over four thousand Americans and roughly one hundred thousand Iraqi civilians were killed in Iraq between the start of the war in March 2003 and the withdrawal of all U.S. troops in January 2012. And after a reduction in the level of insurgent violence between 2008 and 2011, the withdrawal of U.S. troops was followed by a dramatic spike in terror attacks. It is impossible to argue that the war has made the United States more safe.

What is less widely recognized is that the preventive paradigm in other aspects of the war on terrorism has been no more effective. According to U.S. figures, terrorist attacks worldwide increased by 300 percent between 2003 and 2004.[44] In 2005 alone, there were 360 suicide bombings, resulting in three thousand deaths, compared with 472 such attacks spread over the five preceding years.[45] Total terrorist attacks worldwide rose from 11,156 in 2005 to roughly 14,500 in 2006 and in 2007, and deaths as a result of terrorism rose from 14,616 in 2005 to 20,872 in 2006 and 22,685 in 2007.[46] These figures hardly constituted progress in the global war on terrorism during the Bush years.

Still, Bush administration supporters frequently noted that, other than the anthrax mailings in 2001, there was not another terrorist attack in the United States during the more than six years it served after 9/11. The real question, though, is whether the administration's coercive preventive measures can be credited for that fact. After all, eight years passed between the first and second attacks on the World Trade Center. Stationing U.S. troops in Baghdad where they could be blown up by suicide bombers may have *diverted* terrorist attacks, but their presence could hardly be said to have *prevented* terrorism. In fact, there is little reason to believe that the preventive paradigm worked. Take Guantánamo, once said to house the "worst of the worst." A 2006 study of the Defense Department's own findings on the detainees held at Guantánamo revealed that only 8 percent of the detainees held at that time were even *alleged* to be fighters for al-Qaeda or the Taliban, and fewer than half of the detainees were alleged to have engaged in any hostile act against the United States.[47]

As for terrorist cells at home, by February 2005 the FBI admitted that it had yet to identify a single al-Qaeda sleeper cell in the entire United States.[48] The Justice Department under President Bush claimed to have charged more than four hundred persons in "terror-related" cases, but its own inspector general criticized these figures as inflated and inaccurate. The vast majority of the cases involved no charges of terrorism whatsoever—only minor nonviolent offenses such as immigration fraud, credit card fraud, or lying to an FBI agent.[49] Many of the administration's most highly touted "terrorism" cases disintegrated under close scrutiny, most notably those against Capt. James Yee, a Muslim chaplain at Guantánamo initially accused of being a spy; Sami al-Arian, a computer science professor acquitted on charges of conspiracy to kill Americans; Sami al-Hussayen, a Saudi student acquitted on charges of aiding terrorists by posting links on a website; and Yaser Hamdi and José Padilla, the two U.S. citizens held for years as enemy combatants, but released from military custody when the government faced the prospect of losing in court.[50]

In preventive paradigm immigration initiatives, the Bush administration called in more than eighty-two thousand foreign nationals to be fingerprinted, photographed, and registered, simply because they came from predominantly Arab or Muslim countries. It sought out another eight thousand young men from the same countries for FBI interviews, and placed more than five thousand foreign nationals in preventive detention in just the first two years after 9/11. Yet apart from a conviction overturned on appeal, the Bush administration convicted none of these individuals of a terrorist crime. The government's record, in what is surely the biggest campaign of ethnic profiling since the Japanese internment of World War II, is zero for ninety-five thousand.[51]

One might object that this is the wrong way to measure success. If the Bush administration's measures succeeded in preventing terrorism, there would not be terrorist convictions because the terrorism itself will never occur. It is possible that some of these preventive paradigm measures deterred would-be terrorists from attacking the country, or perhaps helped to foil terrorist plots before they could come to fruition. But if real plots had been foiled and real terrorists identified, one would expect to see, at a minimum, corresponding criminal convictions for conspiracy or attempt to engage in terrorism. Thus, when FBI agents successfully foiled a plot by Sheikh Omar Abdel Rahman (popularly known as the "Blind Sheikh") and others to bomb bridges and tunnels around Manhattan in the 1990s, it convicted the plotters and sent them to prison for life.[52]

President Bush boasted that his administration foiled many terrorist plots after 9/11, but identified remarkably few terrorists brought to justice for these purported plots. The administration's claims of success were often questioned by people with inside knowledge. In October 2005, for example, President Bush claimed that the United States and its allies had foiled ten terrorist plots.[53] Later, however, the *Washington Post, Los Angeles Times,* and *USA Today* each reported that intelligence experts seriously questioned President Bush's claims.[54]

One of the most frequently heard criticisms of the FBI in the wake of 9/11 was that it was too "backward-looking," overly concerned with amassing evidence in order to try alleged criminals for crimes already committed and not sufficiently intelligence-focused, or "forward-looking." But this criticism ignores the fact that traditional measures of law enforcement investigation are often forward-looking and backward-looking at the same time, and that traditional tools are perfectly capable of disrupting plots and bringing would-be bombers to justice before bombs go off. It is traditional law enforcement methodology, for example, to conduct surveillance on a group of suspected criminals for an extended period of time before arresting them in order to assess the scope of the threat the individuals pose, to identify others who may pose even greater threats, and to develop sufficient evidence so that once individuals are apprehended they can be successfully prosecuted and incapacitated. It was just such traditional police work, for example, that enabled British authorities in the summer of 2006 to avert an alleged plot to explode numerous aircraft traveling from Britain to the United States and bring the asserted perpetrators to trial, three of whom were convicted and sentenced to thirty years to life in prison in September 2009. And it was such police work that led to the capture and 2012 conviction (and life sentences) for members of a three-man cell who were plotting a suicide attack against the New York City subway in 2009. There have, in the past ten years, been several convictions for attempting to engage in terrorist attacks, but they have generally been thwarted by old-fashioned police work.

Wars against countries that do not pose a threat and broad-brush measures that sweep up thousands of people who have nothing to do with terrorism consume scarce financial and human resources. Just as the U.S. military would have been put to better use had it concentrated on al-Qaeda in Afghanistan and the border regions of Pakistan, the law enforcement agents and resources used to track down ninety-five thousand Arabs and Muslims in the United States, none of whom were terrorists, would have been more effectively deployed had they targeted those from whom there was some reason to believe a threat was actually posed—beyond their mere ethnicity or religion. Registering eighty-two thousand people whose only connection to terrorism is that they are Arab and Muslim immigrants was a colossal waste of resources. So, too, apparently, was the NSA's warrantless wiretapping program, which, according to frustrated FBI agents, generated thousands of leads that were virtually all "dead ends or have led to innocent Americans."[55]

Because the Bush administration was so focused on swaggeringly aggressive and coercive forms of prevention, it devoted insufficient resources and attention to less glamorous but more effective preventive initiatives. It spent more in a day in Iraq than it did annually on some of the most important defensive initiatives here in the United States.[56] In December 2005, the bipartisan 9/11 Commission gave the Bush administration failing or near-failing grades on many of the most basic homeland security measures, including assessing critical infrastructure vulnerabilities, securing weapons of mass destruction, screening airline passengers and cargo, sharing information between law enforcement and intelligence agencies, ensuring that emergency first-responders have adequate communications, and supporting secular education in Muslim countries.[57] These measures were plainly not the Bush administration's priority.

COLLATERAL CONSEQUENCES

The preventive paradigm also had other collateral consequences. When the government chose to "disappear" al-Qaeda suspects into secret prisons and to use waterboarding to compel them to talk, it is certainly conceivable that it might have obtained useful intelligence, although we can never actually know whether the same information might have been obtained through lawful means. But we can know with certainty that such tactics foreclosed any real possibility of bringing the suspects to justice for their alleged crimes, because evidence obtained in a "black site" would taint any attempt to prosecute. The Bush administration was repeatedly stymied in its attempts to obtain convictions for war crimes against Guantánamo detainees. The head of military prosecutions at Guantánamo specifically ordered a high-profile prosecution dismissed because she concluded that the defendant, Mohammed al-Qahtani, suspected of being the "twentieth hijacker" on 9/11 had been tortured by military interrogators acting under Defense Secretary Donald Rumsfeld's orders. There is debate about whether torture ever results in reliable intelligence—but there can be no debate that it radically curtails the government's ability to bring a terrorist to justice.

The goal of protecting innocent civilians from terrorist violence is indisputably legitimate. When laudable goals are pursued through dubious means, however, the legitimacy of the entire enterprise is compromised. That loss of legitimacy makes potential allies less eager to work with the United States, creates new enemies, and inspires those already arrayed against America to adopt more radical tactics. Assuming that the principal terrorist threat at this juncture comes from a violence-prone fundamentalist strain of Islam and that the "enemies" in this struggle are largely composed of Arab and Muslim men, it is all the more critical that the United States develop close positive ties with Arab and Muslim communities here and abroad. We Americans need their eyes and ears if we are going to find the small number of persons actually planning to use violence against us. And we need their support if we are to succeed in isolating al-Qaeda from the wider circle of potential supporters. When we impose on these communities measures that we would not tolerate for ourselves, measures that fail to treat them with the respect and dignity owed all human beings, we sow distrust and enmity that impede the communication and cooperation we need and simultaneously fuel the anti-Americanism that we cannot afford.

Nothing could more perfectly meet the recruitment needs of al-Qaeda and its supporters than the abuse U.S. forces meted out to prisoners at Abu Ghraib prison, the legal black hole that is Guantánamo, the policy of rendering foreign nationals to third countries for torture, the practice of "disappearing" suspects into a network of secret CIA detention centers, or the war in Iraq. Defense Secretary Rumsfeld identified the critical question in an October 2003 internal Pentagon memo: "Are we capturing, killing or deterring and dissuading more terrorists every day than the madrassas and the radical clerics are recruiting, training and deploying against us?"[58] Although there is no certain metric for answering Rumsfeld's question, there can be little doubt that the preventive tactics adopted by the Bush administration were a boon to terrorist recruitment throughout the world.

One telling sign of the damage to America's image was that after the report of CIA black sites surfaced in November 2005, Russia, among several other countries, promptly issued a press release claiming that it had nothing to do with the sites.[59] When Russia feels the need to distance itself from the United States out of concern that its human rights image might be tarnished by association, we Americans know we have fallen far. The fact that European nations may have housed some of the black sites and cooperated in renditions has caused a firestorm of controversy in that region and will undoubtedly complicate future cooperation. Italy and Germany, for example, indicted CIA agents for their part in the kidnapping and rendition of their residents.[60] And Spain's national security court opened a formal criminal investigation of Bush administration attorney John Yoo, former White House counsel and attorney general Alberto Gonzales, former counsel to the vice president David Addington, and the former general counsel to the Department of Defense for their part in authorizing torture of a Spanish citizen at Guantánamo.[61]

In short, under the Bush administration's preventive paradigm the United States went from being the object of the world's sympathy immediately after the events of 9/11 to being the country most likely to be hated the world over. The Bush administration squandered all the support Americans had in the wake of the attacks, and its tactics caused anti-Americanism to climb to all-time highs. In some countries, Osama bin Laden had a higher approval rating than the United States.[62] Once widely admired for its record of safeguarding civil liberties and human rights, the United States under President Bush became the object of sweeping condemnations by the United Nations Human Rights Committee, international nongovernmental organizations, and judges and political leaders across the globe. These developments are linked; much of the anti-Americanism was tied to the perception that the United States pursued its war on terrorism in an arrogant, unilateral fashion, defying the very values that the nation had long championed.

PREVENTION WITHIN THE RULE OF LAW

Because the rule of law is a central element of popular conceptions of justice, those who adhere to it are likely to gain legitimacy and support in the all-important struggle for hearts and minds. But that is not how the Bush administration saw it. In March 2005, the Pentagon warned in its National Defense Strategy that "our strength as a nation state will continue to be challenged by those who employ a strategy of the weak using international fora, judicial processes, and terrorism."[63] The proposition that judicial processes and international accountability—the very essence of the rule of law—were to be dismissed as a strategy of the weak, aligned with terrorism itself, makes clear that the Bush administration viewed the rule of law as an obstacle, not an asset, in its effort to protect citizens from the threat of terrorist attack. Such an attitude can only breed still more anti-Americanism, and still more terrorists willing to sacrifice their lives in striking a blow against the United States.

The Obama administration sought to change course, recognizing that the long-term security of the United States does not require illegal spying on Americans; locking up thousands of "suspected terrorists" who turn out to have no connection to terrorism; forcing suspects to bark like dogs, urinate and defecate on themselves, and endure sexual humiliation; unilaterally attacking countries that have not threatened to attack America; or claiming that the president as commander in chief can ignore congressional and constitutional restrictions on his authority.[64] As President Obama stated in a May 2009 speech on national security at the National Archives, security rests not on exceptionalism and double standards but on a renewed commitment to fairness, justice, and the rule of law.[65] And under President Obama we witnessed just such a renewal: not only has he ended torture and released previously secret memos, he has also achieved greater legislative and judicial buy-in to issues such as detentions and military commissions, largely by insisting that he would act within rather than above the law. Under President Obama's more law-abiding approach to fighting terrorism, the United States has made great strides in neutralizing the al-Qaeda threat without engendering near-universal resentment against U.S. policies. He succeeded in bringing the Iraq War to a close, taking out Osama bin Laden, killing scores of al-Qaeda leaders and operatives (which is permitted in wartime), and setting a firm time line to end the war in Afghanistan. He has done so, moreover, while insisting that the United States must abide by its commitments not only to domestic but also to international law. As noted earlier, Obama has been far from perfect. But the difference between his regime and his predecessor's in terms of attitudes toward the rule of law could not be more stark. There is no evidence that Obama's approach has left the nation less safe in terms of tactical security, while the country is clearly stronger in terms of fundamental values.

A nation abiding by the rule of law has many options available for preventing terrorism. But it will succeed only if it sees the rule of law values as an asset in that campaign, not an obstacle. Aharon Barak, former president of Israel's Supreme Court, said it best in a case forbidding the use of "moderate physical pressure" in interrogating Palestinian terror suspects:

> A democracy must sometimes fight terror with one hand tied behind its back. Even so, a democracy has the upper hand. The rule of law and the liberty of an individual constitute important components in its understanding of security. At the end of the day, they strengthen its spirit and this strength allows it to overcome its difficulties.[66]

The preventive paradigm, by jettisoning fundamental commitments to the rule of law, compromised the nation's spirit, strengthened its enemies, and left the United States simultaneously less free and less safe. As the Obama administration aptly demonstrated, there is a way forward—through, rather than in spite of, a recommitment to the rule of law.

Notes

1. Oral arguments of Sandra Day O'Connor in *Hamdi v. Rumsfeld* (542 U.S. 507), April 28, 2004. In her lead opinion to this case she called for clear safeguards to prevent executive overreach in the fight against terrorism. See Justice O'Connor's controlling opinion in *Hamdi v. Rumsfeld*, June 28, 2004.
2. National Commission on Terrorist Attacks on the United States, *The 9/11 Commission Report* (New York: Norton, 2004), chap. 3.
3. An earlier version of this essay appeared as chapter 5 of John Yoo, *War by Other Means* (New York: Grove Atlantic, 2006). All rights reserved c/o Writers Representatives LLC, New York, N.Y.
4. Steve Coll, "Kill or Capture," *New Yorker.com*, August 2, 2012, www.newyorker .com/online/blogs/comment/2012/08/kill-or-capture.html.
5. While I agree with the constitutionality of targeted killings, the Obama administration's dependence on execution instead of interrogation has cost the United States dearly in actionable intelligence from foreign threat theaters. See John Yoo, "Obama, Drones and Thomas Aquinas," *Wall Street Journal*, June 7, 2012.

6. *Ex Parte Quirin*, 317 U.S. 1, 28 (1942).

7. Authorization for Use of Military Force, Public Law 107–40 (September 18, 2001).

8. *Prize Cases*, 67 U.S. 635, 670 (1863).

9. See, for example, Louis Fisher, *Presidential War Power* (Lawrence: University of Kansas Press, 1995), 11; and Michael J. Glennon, *Constitutional Diplomacy* (Princeton, N.J.: Princeton University Press, 1991), 17. But also see John Yoo, *The Powers of War and Peace: The Constitution and Foreign Affairs after 9/11* (Chicago: University of Chicago Press, 2005), 143–160.

10. Alexander Hamilton, James Madison, and John Jay, *The Federalist Papers*, intro. Clinton Rossiter (New York: New American Library, 1961).

11. *Johnson v. Eisentrager*, 339 U.S. 763, 788 (1950).

12. See, for example, *United States v. Curtiss-Wright Export Corp.*, 299 U.S. 304 (1936); and *Chicago & S. Air Lines v. Waterman S.S. Corp.*, 333 U.S. 103, 111 (1948). In a post–Civil War case, recently reaffirmed, the Court ruled that President Lincoln had the constitutional authority to engage in espionage. The president "was undoubtedly authorized during the war, as commander-in-chief . . . to employ secret agents to enter the rebel lines and obtain information respecting the strength, resources, and movements of the enemy." *Totten v. United States*, 92 U.S. 105, 106 (1876). On *Totten's* continuing vitality, see *Tenet v. Doe*, 544 U.S. 1, 0–11 (2005).

13. Franklin D. Roosevelt, President, Confidential Memorandum for the Attorney General, May 21, 1940, reprinted in Appendix A, *United States v. United States District Court*, 444 F.2d 651, 669–670 (6th Cir. 1971).

14. Id.

15. See *Nardone v. United States*, 302 U.S. 379 (1937), interpreting Section 605 of the Federal Communications Act of 1934 to prohibit interception of telephone calls.

16. See Robert H. Jackson, *That Man: An Insider's Portrait of Franklin D. Roosevelt* (New York: Oxford University Press, 2003), 68–69.

17. Foreign Intelligence Surveillance Act of 1978: Hearings on H.R. 5764, H.R. 9745, H.R. 7308, and H.R. 5632 Before the Subcommittee on Legislation of the House Committee on Intelligence, 95th Cong., 2nd sess., 15, 1978 (statement of Attorney General Griffin Bell).

18. Most notably, Clinton Deputy Attorney General Jamie Gorelick testified before Congress that the Justice Department could carry out physical searches for foreign intelligence purposes even though FISA at the time did not provide for them. Amending the Foreign Intelligence Surveillance Act: Hearings Before the House Permanent Select Comm. on Intelligence, 103rd Cong., 2nd sess., 61, 1994. Clinton's Office of Legal Counsel issued a legal opinion that the president could order the sharing between the Justice Department and intelligence agencies of electronic surveillance gathered through criminal wiretaps, even though this sharing was prohibited by statute. Sharing Title III Electronic Surveillance Material with the Intelligence Community, OLC Preliminary Print, 2000 WL 33716983, October 17, 2000.

19. See Executive Nomination of Eric Holder, Hearing Before the Senate Judiciary Committee, January 15, 2009. In an exchange, Republican senator Orrin Hatch of Utah asked Holder if he believed "that the President has . . . inherent authority under Article II of the Constitution to engage in warrantless foreign intelligence surveillance, or, in your opinion, does FISA trump Article II?" Holder replied,

"Well, the President obviously has powers under the Constitution that cannot be infringed by the legislative branch."

20. *United States v. United States District Court* ("Keith"), 407 U.S. 297 (1972).
21. *In re Sealed Case*, 310 F.3d 717, 742 (For. Intel. Surv. Ct. Rev. 2002) (footnote omitted).
22. 629 F.2d 908, 913 (4th Cir. 1980).
23. Id. at 915.
24. *Haig v. Agee*, 453 U.S. 280, 307 (1981).
25. "When the Government Kills," *Los Angeles Times*, July 29, 2012.
26. See, generally, John Yoo, "Kosovo, War Powers, and the Multilateral Future," *University of Pennsylvania Law Review* 148 (2000): 1673.
27. Hamilton, *Federalist* No. 23, 147.
28. Hamilton, *Federalist* No. 70, 471.
29. Hamilton, *Federalist* No. 74, 500. James Iredell (later an associate justice of the Supreme Court) argued in the North Carolina ratifying convention that "from the nature of the thing, the command of armies ought to be delegated to one person only. The secrecy, despatch, and decision, which are necessary in military operations, can only be expected from one person." "Debate in the North Carolina Ratifying Convention," in *The Debates in the Several State Conventions on the Adoption of the Federal Constitution*, Vol. 4, 2nd ed., ed. Jonathan Elliot (Manchester, N.H.: Ayer Company Publishers, 1987 [1888]), 107. See also Joseph Story, *Commentaries on the Constitution of the United States* (Buffalo, N.Y.: William S. Hein, 1994 [1833]), 341, arguing that in military matters, "unity of plan, promptitude, activity, and decision, are indispensable to success; and these can scarcely exist, except when a single magistrate is entrusted exclusively with the power."
30. Letter from Thomas Jefferson, President, to Mrs. John Adams (September 11, 1804), in *The Writings of Thomas Jefferson*, Vol. 8, ed. Paul L. Ford (New York: Putnam's Sons, 1892–1899), 310–311. President Andrew Jackson expressed the same view in 1832, vetoing a bill that he regarded as unconstitutional even though the Supreme Court had upheld it as constitutional. "It is as much the duty of the house of representatives, of the senate, and of the president to decide upon the constitutionality of any bill or resolution, just as with the Supreme Court when the law arises in a case before them," he wrote. Andrew Jackson, "Veto Message (July 10, 1832)", in *A Compilation of the Messages and Papers of the Presidents, 1789–1897*, Vol. 2, ed. James D. Richardson (Washington, D.C.: Government Printing Office, 1896–1899), 582. Abraham Lincoln, in the aftermath of the case of the slave Dred Scott, famously announced in his first inaugural that henceforth he would not follow the rule that a slave would not be free once in Northern territory, though he chose to obey the Supreme Court's order in the *Dred Scott* case itself. See "First Inaugural Address of Abraham Lincoln (March 4, 1861)," in *Abraham Lincoln, Speeches and Writings, 1859–1865*, ed. Don E. Fehrenbacher (New York: Literary Classics, 1989), 221.
31. *Fleming v. Page*, 50 U.S. (9 How.) 603, 615 (1850).
32. For a standard historical source on the period. see Robert Dallek, *Franklin D. Roosevelt and American Foreign Policy, 1932–1945* (New York: Oxford University Press, 1979). See also Robert Divine, *Roosevelt and World War II* (Baltimore: Johns Hopkins University Press, 1969); Gaddis Smith, *American Diplomacy during the Second World War* (New York: Wiley, 1965); Frederick W. Marks III, *Wind over*

Sand: The Diplomacy of Franklin Roosevelt (Athens: University of Georgia Press, 1988); and Warren F. Kimball, *The Juggler: Franklin Roosevelt as Wartime Statesman* (Princeton, N.J.: Princeton University Press, 1991).

33. Marc Trachtenberg, "The Bush Strategy in Historical Perspective," in *Nuclear Transformation: The New U.S. Nuclear Doctrine*, ed. James Wirtz and Jeffrey Larson (New York: Palgrave Macmillan, 2005).

34. National Commission on Terrorist Attacks on the United States, *9/11 Commission Report*, 361–362.

35. See, for example, *Rasul v. Bush*, 542 U.S. 466 (2004); *Hamdan v. Rumsfeld*, 548 U.S. 557 (2006); *Boumediene v. Bush*, 128 S. Ct. 2229 (2008).

36. See "To Erastus Corning and Others, June 12, 1863," in *The Collected Works of Abraham Lincoln*, Vol. 6, ed. Roy P. Basler (New Brunswick, N.J.: Rutgers University Press, 1953), 261.

37. Much of this essay is adapted and updated from David Cole and Jules Lobel, *Less Safe, Less Free: Why America Is Losing the War on Terrorism* (New York: New Press, 2007).

38. For an expansion on this argument, see David Cole, "Obama and Terror: The Hovering Questions," *New York Review of Books*, July 12, 2012.

39. Richard Posner, *Not a Suicide Pact: The Constitution in a Time of National Emergency* (New York: Oxford University Press, 2006).

40. White House, "National Security Strategy of the United States of America," September 17, 2002, http://georgewbush-whitehouse.archives.gov/nsc/nss/2002.

41. The Convention against Torture and Other Cruel, Inhuman or Degrading Treatment or Punishment prohibits torture under all circumstances and provides that "no exceptional circumstances whatsoever" can justify it. The prohibition on disappearances has been recognized as having the status of *jus cogens*, similar to torture, and similarly permitting no exceptions. See *Forti v. Suarez-Mason*, 694 F. Supp. 707 (N.D. Cal. 1988).

42. Senate Select Committee on Intelligence, Hearing on Current and Projected National Security Threats to the United States, 109th Cong., 1st sess., February 16, 2005.

43. Ibid.

44. Susan B. Glasser, "Global Terrorism Statistics Debated," *Washington Post*, May 1, 2005.

45. David Sands, "Suicide Bombing Popular Terrorist Tactic," *Washington Times*, May 8, 2006.

46. U.S. Department of State, "Country Reports on Terrorism 2007," April 30, 2008, www.state.gov/documents/organization/105904.pdf.

47. Mark Denbeaux and Joshua Denbeaux, "Report on Guantánamo Detainees: A Profile of 517 Detainees through Analysis of Department of Defense Data," Seton Hall Public Law Research Paper No. 46, February 2006, http://papers.ssrn.com/sol3/papers.cfm?abstract_id=885659; Corine Hegland, "Who Is at Guantánamo Bay?" *National Journal*, February 3, 2006.

48. "Secret FBI Report Questions Al-Qaeda Capabilities," *ABC News*, March 9, 2005, http://abcnews.go.com/WNT/Investigation/story?id=566425&page=1.

49. Dan Eggen and Julie Tate, "U.S. Campaign Produces Few Convictions on Terrorist Charges," *Washington Post*, June 12, 2005.

50. In 2004 the Justice Department released Hamdi to Saudi Arabia on the face-saving but unenforceable promise that he surrender his U.S. citizenship and stay in Saudi Arabia, where he also held citizenship. In January 2008, after a civilian criminal trial, Padilla was sentenced to seventeen years in prison for conspiracy and material support of terrorism overseas. Padilla was never tried for his alleged role in any plot to engage in terrorism in the United States.

51. See David Cole, *Enemy Aliens: Double Standards and Constitutional Freedoms in the War on Terrorism,* 2nd ed. (New York: New Press, 2004), xx–xxiii, 25.

52. *United States v. Rahman,* 189 F.3d 88 (2nd Cir. 1999).

53. See Peter Baker and Susan Glasser, "Bush Says 10 Plots by Al-Qaeda Were Foiled," *Washington Post,* October 7, 2005; "Mueller: More Than 100 Terror Attacks Foiled Worldwide," CNN.com, March 4, 2003, www.cnn.com/2003/ALLPOLITICS/03/04/terror.war.congress/; U.S. Department of Justice, "Waging the War on Terror," www.justice.gov/archive/ll/subs/add_myths.htm#s.

54. Josh Meyer and Warren Vieth, "Scope of Plots Bush Says Were Foiled Is Questioned," *Los Angeles Times,* October 8, 2005; Sara Kehaulani Goo, "List of Foiled Plots Puzzling to Some," *Washington Post,* October 23, 2005; John Diamond and Toni Locy, "White House List of Disrupted Terror Plots Questioned," *USA Today,* October 26, 2005.

55. Lowell Bergman, Eric Lichtblau, Scott Shane, and Don Van Natta Jr., "Spy Agency Data after September 11 Led F.B.I. to Dead Ends," *New York Times,* January 17, 2006.

56. Matt Brzezinski, "Red Alert," *Mother Jones,* September–October 2004, www.motherjones.com/news/feature/2004/09/08_400.html.

57. "The 41 Grades of the Failing Report Card on 9/11 Commission Recommends," available at http://usliberals.about.com/od/homelandsecurit1/a/ReportCard.htm.

58. Memorandum from Donald Rumsfeld to Dick Myers et al., "Re: Global War on Terrorism," October 16, 2003, www.globalsecurity.org/military/library/policy/dod/rumsfeld-d20031016sdmemo.htm.

59. Dana Priest and Josh White, "Policies on Terrorism Suspects Come under Fire," *Washington Post,* November 3, 2005.

60. Tracy Wilkinson, "Italy Issues Arrest Warrants for 3 CIA Officers in 'Rendition' Case," *Los Angeles Times,* July 6, 2006; Mark Landler, "German Court Confronts U.S. on Abduction," *New York Times,* February 1, 2007.

61. Scott Horton, "Bush Torture Lawyers Targeted in Criminal Probe," *Harper's Magazine Online,* March 28, 2009, www.harpers.org/archive/2009/03/hbc-90004640.

62. See Thomas Powers, "Bringing 'Em On," *New York Times,* December 25, 2005 (reports a 65 percent approval rate for Osama bin Laden in Pakistan); and Pew Research Center for the People and the Press, "A Year after Iraq War: Mistrust of America in Europe Ever Higher, Muslim Anger Persists," March 16, 2004 (reports that only 21 percent of Pakistanis had a favorable opinion of the United States), http://people-press.org/reports/pdf/206.pdf.

63. U.S. Department of Defense, *National Defense Strategy* (Washington, D.C.: DOD, March 2005), www.globalsecurity.org/military/library/policy/dod/nds-usa_mar2005_ib.htm.

64. In this chapter, John Yoo defends an expansive view of presidential power during wartime. While a lawyer in the Office of Legal Counsel after 9/11, Yoo wrote

numerous memos asserting similarly expansive theories. Those memos have been widely repudiated, including by subsequent heads of the Office of Legal Counsel under President Bush. See Jack Goldsmith, *The Terror Presidency: Law and Judgment inside the Bush Administration* (New York: Norton, 2007), which describes Yoo's August 1, 2002, memo on the CIA's use of coercive interrogation tactics as "wildly broader than was necessary," "tendentious [in] tone," and lacking "care and sobriety." Also see U.S. Department of Justice, Office of Legal Counsel, Memorandum "Re: Status of Certain OLC Opinions Issued in the Aftermath of the Terrorist Attacks of September 11, 2001," www.usdoj.gov/opa/documents/memo statusolcopinions01152009.pdf, in which OLC head Steven Bradbury notes the "doubtful nature" of many propositions about executive power in Yoo's memos.

65. White House, Office of the Press Secretary, Remarks by the President on National Security, May 21, 2009, available at www.whitehouse.gov/the-press-office/remarks-president-national-security-5-21-09.

66. *Public Committee Against Torture v. State of Israel*, HCJ No. 5100/94, July 15, 1999, 27, http://elyon1.court.gov.il/files_eng/94/000/051/A09/94051000.a09.htm.

conclusion: is the threat of terrorism being overstated?

YES: The threat of terrorism is overblown and more manageable than suspected.
John Mueller, *The Ohio State University*

NO: The threat is profound and will remain so for some time.
Walter Laqueur, *Center for Strategic and International Studies*

Most of the essays in this volume, though differing in important ways, operate under the assumption that terrorism poses a significant threat to nations and the international community, requiring thoughtful and assertive responses. This assumption was clear in Part I, which debates the nature of terrorist organizations; the root causes, motivations, and tactics of traditional and modern terrorism; and the possibility that terrorists might use weapons of mass destruction. And it has been a core component of Part II, which covers a range of issues related to counterterrorist responses—hard versus soft approaches; different international strategies; and how the rule of law fits in.

But is the underlying premise of the book correct, that terrorism is a high-priority issue, requiring a great deal of intellectual attention and policy action? In other words, are analysts and others accurately assessing the threat of terrorism itself? After all, as history tells us, misidentifying threats can lead to unfortunate policy outcomes.

In the book's final debate, John Mueller and Walter Laqueur review the terrorism and counterterrorism issues discussed and debated throughout the volume, and, with an eye toward the future, develop very different assessments of terrorist threats and the nature and necessity of government responses.

Mueller says the tendency in government is to overinflate national security threats, and there is no clearer example of this than the current take on terrorism. He believes any honest evaluation of today's terrorism, including that of al-Qaeda, leads to one conclusion: the threat is far less than meets the hype. Mueller points out that the probability of an American dying in a terrorist attack in any given year is about one in 3.5 million, while the chance of dying in an automobile accident is about one in eight thousand. Terrorism, then, is hardly the "existential threat" that is often portrayed. Indeed, for Mueller, the real threat comes not from terrorism, but from what he calls the "terrorism industry"—politicians, bureaucrats, journalists, and risk entrepreneurs who, for their own parochial reasons, stoke public fears by exaggerating the threat, leading to irrational government overreaction. He concludes that overwrought counterterrorism policies have proven far costlier than anything terrorists will likely ever be capable of doing.

Laqueur tackles the question from a very different vantage point. The issue, he says, is not the cost of overstating terrorist threats, but the risk of underestimating them. Reviewing the root causes, motivations, and global landscape of contemporary terrorism, Laqueur sees the threat as real, tangible, and, at least in the short to medium term, growing. Indeed, he believes the advent of "megaterrorism" (apocalyptic groups plus weapons of mass destruction) has not yet arrived. He agrees with Mueller that overreacting to terrorist threats is costly. But so is underreacting: nothing inspires violent global movements as much as perceptions of weakness in their enemies. Although democracies may be good at many things, Laqueur points out that dealing with violent asymmetric actors is, unfortunately, not one of them. Whereas terrorists abide by no laws and rules whatsoever, democratic states are bound by them. The tendency therefore, according to Laqueur, is to understate terrorist threats and the necessity of strong responses—that is, until the next major attack occurs.

These final essays bring home the point that terrorism, in one form or another, is destined to remain on the world scene. Like other age-old violent human phenomena—such as war and murder—there is no end in sight for terrorist violence. Yet the impact of terrorism now and into the future will depend on ever-shifting factors—the emergence and capacity of terror organizations; the lethality of specific acts of terrorism; threat perceptions and government responses. Understanding and addressing the complexities of terrorism will remain difficult, and imperfect. Continuing to research, analyze, disagree, and debate will remain the best tools for developing ways to meet the challenge.

YES: The threat of terrorism is overblown and more manageable than suspected.
John Mueller, *The Ohio State University*

Fear and Overreaction: Terrorism's Most Damaging Effects

With the benefit of hindsight, it strongly appears that there has been a tendency to inflate national security threats and then, partly in consequence, to overreact to them. For example, Americans have experienced anxieties over domestic and foreign communism, fears about the imminence of thermonuclear war, apprehensions over challenges posed by various "rogue states" or devils *du jour* (most of whom eventually faded into insignificance—remember Nasser, Sukarno, Qaddafi, Castro?), insecurities engendered by the Iran hostage crisis and the Japanese economic challenge of the 1980s, and worries about the "ethnic warfare" that was supposedly going to engulf the world in the 1990s. Not all concerns that could have been seized upon have evoked anxiety and overreaction, but it does appear that every threat to U.S. foreign policy in the last several decades that has come to be accepted as significant has then eventually been greatly inflated.[1]

Americans seem to be at it again lately with terrorism. And this has led to policies that have often been unwise, costly, and unnecessary, and sometimes been massively counterproductive.

The rhetoric of alarm about terrorism has been maintained at a high pitch. In a best-selling 2004 book, Michael Scheuer, formerly of the Central Intelligence Agency (CIA), repeatedly assured Americans that their "survival" is at stake and that they are engaged in a "war to the death," and by 2008 then–Homeland Security czar Michael Chertoff proclaimed the "struggle" against terrorism to be a "significant existential" one—carefully differentiating it, apparently, from all those insignificant existential struggles Americans have waged in the past—even as the *New York Times* editorial board was assuring its readers that "the fight against al-Qaeda is the central battle for this generation."[2] In 2009, an adviser in Barack Obama's administration, Bruce Riedel, joined the chorus by declaring the al-Qaeda threat to the country to be "existential."[3]

THE SCOPE OF THE THREAT

Like crime, terrorism can be carried out by a single individual or by a very small group and can never be completely expunged from the human experience. It is important, however, to assess the capacities of international terrorism to inflict damage. It is certainly true that it presents problems, but the "struggle" against it hardly seems existential, and any threat it may present appears to have been vastly overblown.

On May 1, 2011, nearly ten years after the 9/11 terrorist attacks, a costly and determined manhunt culminated in Pakistan with the killing of Osama bin Laden, a chief author of the attacks and one of history's most storied and cartooned villains. Taken away with his bullet-shattered body were massive amounts of written documents and electronic information stored on five computers, ten hard drives, and more than one hundred thumb drives, DVDs, and CD-ROMs. This, it was promised, was a "treasure trove" of data about al-Qaeda—"the mother lode," said one U.S. official eagerly—that might contain plans for pending attacks.[4] Poring through the material with great dispatch, however, a task force soon discovered that al-Qaeda's members were primarily occupied with dodging drone missile attacks, complaining about the lack of funds, and watching a lot of pornography.[5]

The 9/11 attacks were by far the most destructive in history—no terrorist act before or since has killed more than a few hundred people. But the tragic event seems increasingly to stand as an aberration, not as a harbinger, and it is surely time to consider that, as Russell Seitz put it in 2004, "9/11 could join the Trojan Horse and Pearl Harbor among stratagems so uniquely surprising that their very success precludes their repetition," and accordingly that "al-Qaeda's best shot may have been exactly that."[6]

To assess the danger presented by terrorists seeking to attack the United States, we can examine the fifty cases of Islamist extremist terrorism that have come to light since the September 11 attacks, whether based in the United States or abroad, in which the United States was, or apparently was, targeted.[7] These cases comprise (or generate) the chief terrorism fear for Americans.

The case studies can be used to assess the quality of the terrorists or would-be terrorists out there. Authors of the studies, with remarkably few exceptions, describe their subjects with such words as *incompetent, ineffective, unintelligent, idiotic, ignorant, inadequate, unorganized, misguided, muddled, amateurish, dopey, unrealistic, moronic, irrational,* and *foolish.*[8] And in nearly all of the cases where an operative from the police or from the Federal Bureau of Investigation (FBI) was at work (nearly half of the total), the most appropriate descriptor would be *gullible.*

In 2009, the U.S. Department of Homeland Security (DHS) issued a lengthy report on protecting the homeland. Key to achieving such an objective should be a careful assessment of the character, capacities, and desires of potential terrorists targeting that homeland. Although the report does contain a section dealing with what its authors call "The Nature of the Terrorist Adversary," the section devotes only two sentences to assessing that nature:

> The number and high profile of international and domestic terrorist attacks and disrupted plots during the last two decades underscore the determination and persistence of terrorist organizations. Terrorists have proven to be relentless, patient, opportunistic, and flexible, learning from experience and modifying tactics and targets to exploit perceived vulnerabilities and avoid observed strengths.[9]

This description may apply to some terrorists somewhere, including at least a few of those involved in the September 11 attacks. However, as the case studies suggest, it scarcely describes the vast majority of those individuals picked up on terrorism charges in the United States since 9/11. The inability of the DHS to consider this diversity even parenthetically in its fleeting discussion is rather amazing and illustrates its single-minded preoccupation with the extreme.

It is also worth noting that, although it is commonly held that terrorists target the United States because they oppose its values, almost none of the terrorist characters in the cases had any problem with American society even though many (but certainly not all) were misfits, suffered from personal identity crises, were friendless, came from broken homes, were often desperate for money, had difficulty holding jobs, were on drugs, were petty criminals, experienced various forms of discrimination, and were "losers." However, they do display plenty of outrage at U.S. foreign policy in the Middle East—the wars in Iraq and Afghanistan in particular and the country's support for Israel in the Palestinian conflict. They did not wish to spread sharia law or to establish caliphates—indeed few would likely even be able to spell either word. Rather they wanted to protect their religion against what was commonly seen to be a concentrated war upon it in the Middle East by the U.S. government and military.[10]

In all, as Shikha Dalmia has put it, would-be terrorists need to be

> radicalized enough to die for their cause; Westernized enough to move around without raising red flags; ingenious enough to exploit loopholes in the security apparatus; meticulous enough to attend to the myriad logistical details that could torpedo the operation; self-sufficient enough to make all the preparations without enlisting outsiders who might give them away; disciplined enough to maintain complete secrecy; and—above all—psychologically tough enough to keep functioning at a high level without cracking in the face of their own impending death.[11]

The case studies certainly do not abound with people with such characteristics.

Some of the plotters in the cases targeting the United States did harbor visions of toppling large buildings, destroying airports, setting off dirty bombs, or bringing down the Brooklyn Bridge. But these were all nothing more than wild fantasies, far beyond the plotters' capacities however much they may have been encouraged in some instances by FBI operatives. Indeed, in the nearly twelve years since September 11 no Islamist terrorist has been able to detonate even a primitive bomb in the United States. The only method by which terrorists have managed to kill anyone at all has been through gunfire—inflicting a total of perhaps sixteen deaths over the period.[12] This limited capacity is impressive because at one time small-scale terrorists in the United States were quite successful in setting off bombs. Noting that the scale of the September 11 attacks has "tended to obliterate America's memory of pre-9/11 terrorism," Brian Jenkins reminds us (and we clearly do need reminding) that the 1970s witnessed sixty to seventy terrorist incidents, mostly bombings, on U.S. soil every year.[13]

In 2004, Walter Laqueur, one of the top gurus in terrorism studies, deemed the short-term danger from terrorism to be "acute" and that it "may, in fact, grow," and he further suggested that "Europe is probably the most vulnerable battlefield."[14] But, except for bombings on the London transport system in 2005, there have been almost no terrorist attacks of any magnitude in Europe or anywhere else in the developed world since that article was published. And Michael Kenney, who has interviewed dozens of government officials and intelligence agents and analyzed court documents in Europe, has found that, in sharp contrast with the boilerplate characterizations favored by the DHS and with the imperatives listed by Dalmia, Islamist militants there are as operationally unsophisticated, short on know-how, prone to make mistakes, poor at planning, and limited in their capacity to learn as their counterparts in the United States.[15]

Then there is al-Qaeda Central, now holed up in Pakistan. It is not clear that this tiny group of one hundred or so has done much of anything since September 11 except issue videos filled with empty and self-infatuated threats. It does appear to have served as something of an inspiration to some Muslim extremists, may have done some training, has contributed a bit to the Taliban's far larger insurgency in Afghanistan, and may have participated in a few terrorist acts in Pakistan.[16] In an examination of the major terrorist plots against the West since September 11, Mitchell Silber finds only two that could be said to be under the "command and control" of al-Qaeda Central (as opposed to ones suggested, endorsed, or inspired by the organization), and there are questions about how full its control was even in these two instances.[17]

Other terrorists and terrorist groups around the world affiliated or aligned or otherwise connected to al-Qaeda may be able to do intermittent damage to people and infrastructure, but nothing that is very sustained or focused. In all, extremist Islamist terrorism—whether associated with al-Qaeda or not—has claimed two to four hundred lives yearly worldwide outside war zones. That's two to four hundred too many, of course, but it is about the same number as bathtub drownings in the United States.[18]

In addition, as Patrick Porter notes, al-Qaeda has a "talent at self-destruction."[19] With the 9/11 attacks and subsequent activity, the late bin Laden and his various followers and sympathizers have mainly succeeded in uniting the world, including its huge Muslim portion, against their violent global jihad.[20] These activities have also turned many radical Islamists against them, including some of the most prominent and respected.[21]

No matter how much states around the world might disagree with the United States on other issues (most notably on its decision in 2003 to go to war with Iraq), there is a compelling incentive for them to cooperate to confront any international terrorist problem emanating from groups and individuals connected to, or sympathetic with, al-Qaeda. Although these multilateral efforts, particularly by such Muslim states as Libya, Pakistan, Sudan, Syria, and even Iran, may not have received sufficient publicity, these countries have felt directly threatened by the militant network, and their diligent and aggressive efforts have led to important breakthroughs against the group.[22]

In addition, the mindless brutalities of al-Qaeda-affiliated combatants in Iraq—staging beheadings at mosques, bombing playgrounds, taking over hospitals, executing ordinary citizens, performing forced marriages—eventually turned the Iraqis against them, including many of those who had previously been fighting the U.S. occupation either on their own or in connection with the group.[23]

"Al-Qaeda is its own worst enemy," notes Robert Grenier, a former top CIA counterterrorism official. "Where they have succeeded initially, they very quickly discredit themselves."[24] Grenier's improbable company in this observation is Osama bin Laden who was so concerned about al-Qaeda's alienation of Muslims that he argued from his hideout that the organization should take on a new name.[25]

This record suggests that Glenn Carle, former deputy national intelligence officer for transnational threats for the CIA, was right in 2008 when he warned, "We must not take fright at the specter our leaders have exaggerated. In fact, we must see jihadists for the small, lethal, disjointed and miserable opponents that they are." Al-Qaeda "has only a handful of individuals capable of planning, organizing and leading a terrorist organization," and although the group has threatened attacks, "its capabilities are far inferior to its desires."[26]

If dealing with enemies like that is this generation's "central battle," it would seem it is likely to come out quite well.

WEAPONS OF MASS DESTRUCTION AND THE ATOMIC TERRORIST

For the number of terrorism casualties to change radically, terrorists would have to become *vastly* more capable of inflicting damage, and many (though not all) of those proclaiming the struggle against, and the threat presented by, al-Qaeda to be "existential" hinge their alarm on the prospect that the group could obtain weapons of mass destruction.

Actually, the terrorists would have to acquire an atomic arsenal and the capacity to deploy and detonate it. Chemical arms do have the potential, under the appropriate circumstances, for panicking people; killing masses of people in open areas, however, is beyond their modest capabilities. Gas accounted for much less than one percent of the fatalities in World War I where it was used prodigiously, and to produce heavy casualties among unprotected people in an open area of one square kilometer requires the controlled dispersion of a full ton of nerve gas or five tons of mustard gas—hardly an easy task for a small group. Biological weapons have greater destructive potential, but they are extremely difficult to deploy and to control. Explosive methods of dispersion may destroy the organisms, and, even if refrigerated, most of the organisms have a limited lifetime. "Dirty bombs"—conventional explosives laced with radioactive material—would spread potentially harmful radiation over a limited area, but would not kill anybody who walked away from the area.[27]

By contrast, nuclear weapons can inflict massive destruction, and warnings about the possibility that small groups could fabricate nuclear weapons have been uttered repeatedly at least since 1946. But there is extrapolation of delusionary proportions in the common observation that, because terrorists were able, mostly by thuggish means, to crash airplanes into buildings, they might therefore be able to construct a nuclear bomb. Brian Jenkins has run an Internet search to discover how often variants of the term *al-Qaeda* appeared within ten words of *nuclear*. There were only 7 hits in 1999 and 11 in 2000, but the number soared to 1,742 in 2001 and to 2,931 in 2002.[28] By 2008, Defense Secretary Robert Gates was assuring a congressional committee that what keeps every senior government leader awake at night is "the thought of a terrorist ending up with a weapon of mass destruction, especially nuclear."[29]

However, these cries of alarm have obviously so far proven to be much off the mark. The issue is discussed in greater length elsewhere in this volume, but it may be useful to note here that making a nuclear weapon is an extraordinarily difficult task. As the Gilmore Commission, a special advisory panel to the president and Congress, stresses, building a nuclear device capable of producing mass destruction presents "Herculean challenges."[30] The process requires a lengthy sequence of steps, and if each is not fully met, the result is not simply a less powerful weapon, but one that cannot produce any significant nuclear yield at all or cannot be delivered. After assessing this issue in detail, physicists Christoph Wirz and Emmanuel Egger conclude that fabricating a nuclear weapon "could hardly be accomplished by a subnational group" because of "the difficulty of acquiring the necessary expertise, the technical requirements (which in several fields verge on the unfeasible), the lack of available materials and the lack of experience in working with these."[31] And Stephen Younger, former head of nuclear weapons development at Los Alamos, considers the notion that terrorists working in isolation could fabricate an atomic weapon to be "far-fetched at best."[32]

Few of the sleepless, it seems, found much solace in the fact that an al-Qaeda computer seized in Afghanistan in 2001 indicated that the group's budget for research on weapons of mass destruction (almost all of it focused on primitive chemical weapons work) was some $2,000 to $4,000.[33] In the wake of the 2011 killing of Osama bin Laden, officials had many more al-Qaeda computers, and nothing in their content appears to suggest that the group had the time or inclination, let alone the money, to set up and staff a uranium-seizing operation, as well as a fancy, super-high-technology facility to fabricate a bomb. This is a process that requires trusting corrupted foreign collaborators and other criminals, obtaining and transporting highly guarded material, setting up a machine shop staffed with top scientists and technicians, and rolling the heavy, cumbersome, and untested finished product into position to be detonated by a skilled crew—all the while attracting no attention from outsiders.[34]

A common concern envisions a newly nuclear country palming off a bomb or two to friendly terrorists for delivery abroad. However, this situation is exceedingly improbable because there would be too much risk, even for a country led by extremists, that the ultimate source of the weapon would be discovered before or after detonation, or that it would be exploded in a manner and on a target the donor would not approve—including on the donor itself. Nor is it likely that a working nuclear device could be stolen and detonated. "A theft," note Wirz and Egger, "would involve many risks and great efforts in terms of personnel, finances, and organization," while safety and security systems on the weapons "ensure that the successful use of a stolen weapon would be very unlikely."[35]

It was in 1996 that Walter Laqueur contended that some terrorist groups "almost certainly" will use weapons of mass destruction "in the foreseeable future."[36] Presumably, any future foreseeable in 1996 is now history, but in contrast to that confident assertion, terrorists in effect seem to be heeding the advice found in a memo on an al-Qaeda laptop seized in Pakistan in

2004: "Make use of that which is available . . . rather than waste valuable time becoming despondent over that which is not within your reach"—that is, keep it simple, stupid.[37]

And, in fact, it seems to be a general historical regularity that terrorists tend to prefer weapons that they know and understand, not new exotic ones. Indeed, the truly notable innovation for terrorists over the last few decades has not been in qualitative improvements in ordnance at all, but rather in a more effective method for delivering it: the suicide bomber.

If the miscreants in the American cases have been unable to create and set off even the simplest conventional bombs, it stands to reason that none of them were very close to creating, or having anything to do with, nuclear weapons— or for that matter biological, radiological, or chemical ones. In fact, with perhaps one exception, none seems to have even dreamed of the prospect. And the exception is José Padilla who apparently mused at one point about creating a dirty bomb or even possibly an atomic one. His idea about isotope separation was to put uranium into a pail and then to make himself into a human centrifuge by swinging the pail around in great arcs.[38]

Moreover, in 2010, top counterterrorism officials announced that the "likelihood of a large-scale organized attack" (certainly including atomic ones) has actually gone down. They creatively add, however, that this means that al-Qaeda franchises are now able "to innovate on their own" (presumably developing small-scale disorganized attacks), with the result that the threat "in some ways" is now the highest it has been since September 11.[39]

REACTING TO THE THREAT

There are, then, several key facts for the American public to consider in evaluating how to respond to the terrorism challenge:

- There have been no al-Qaeda attacks whatsoever in the United States since 2001.
- No true al-Qaeda cell (nor scarcely anybody who might even be deemed to have a "connection" to the diabolical group) has been unearthed in the country.
- The homegrown "plotters" who have been apprehended, while perhaps potentially somewhat dangerous at least in a few cases, have mostly been flaky or almost absurdly incompetent.
- The total number of people killed worldwide by al-Qaeda types, maybes, and wannabes outside of war zones since 9/11 stands at some three hundred or so a year.

- Unless the terrorists are somehow able to massively increase their capacities—something that appears highly improbable—the likelihood a person living in the United States will perish at the hands of an international terrorist is about 1 in 3.5 million per year. To put this number in context, an American's yearly chance of becoming a victim of homicide is 1 in 22,000; of being killed in an automobile accident, 1 in 8,000; of dying from cancer, 1 in 500.[40]

The American public apparently continues to remain unimpressed by this set of inconvenient observations. It has come to pay less attention to terrorism as other concerns—the wars in the Middle East and, more lately, the economy—have dominated its responses to questions about the most important problem facing the country. However, polls suggest that people—or at any rate Americans—remain concerned about becoming the victims of terrorism, and the degree of worry does not seem to have changed all that much since 2001, even though no terrorism whatsoever has taken place in the country since that year.

Other poll data tell a similar story. Worries about flying because of the risk of terrorism registered at the same level in 2010 as in 2002. If anything, respondents felt that the country was less safe from terrorism in 2010 than they did in 2003 or 2004. Confidence that the government could protect them from terrorism was the same in 2012 as in 2002. Moreover, estimates of the likelihood of "another terrorist attack causing large numbers of Americans to be lost" stood a few months after bin Laden's death in 2011 at essentially the same level as in late 2001, with more than 70 percent of respondents deeming such a dire event to be very or somewhat likely. The same held for a question about which side was winning the war against terrorism.[41]

The public appears to have chosen, then, to wallow in a false sense of insecurity (to apply a phrase suggested by the philosopher Leif Wenar), and it apparently plans to continue to do so. As anthropologist Scott Atran aptly summarizes the situation, "Perhaps never in the history of human conflict have so few people with so few actual means and capabilities frightened so many."[42] Accordingly, the public will likely continue to demand that its leaders pay due deference to its insecurities and will uncritically approve as huge amounts of money are shelled out in a quixotic and mostly symbolic effort to assuage those insecurities—expenditures in the United States on domestic homeland security alone (that is, excluding overseas expenditures like those on the wars in Iraq and Afghanistan) have expanded by a total of over $1 trillion since 9/11.[43] And this has been done, notes a National Academy of Sciences report, without any serious analysis of the sort routinely carried out by DHS for natural hazards such as floods and hurricanes.[44]

In response to this apparent demand, something that might be called the "terrorism industry" has sprung up. This group consists of politicians, bureaucrats, journalists, and risk entrepreneurs who benefit in one way or another from exacerbating anxieties about terrorism.

Politicians and bureaucrats find it—or believe it—expedient to exaggerate and to inflate, desperate not to be thought soft on terrorism, and the interactive, if somewhat paradoxical, process is crisply described by Ian Lustick: the government "can never make enough progress toward 'protecting America' to reassure Americans against the fears it is helping to stoke."[45] It is a situation in which, as Bart Kosko points out, "government plays safe by overestimating the terrorist threat, while the terrorists oblige by overestimating their power."[46]

The media also play an important role. As has often been noted, the media appear to have a congenital incapacity for dealing with issues of risk and comparative probabilities—except, of course, in the sports and financial sections.

Risk entrepreneurs form the final layer of the terrorism industry. The monied response to 9/11 has swelled the industry's ranks, and its members would be out of business if terrorism were to be back-burnered. Accordingly, they have every competitive incentive (and they are nothing if not competitive) to conclude it to be their civic duty to keep the pot boiling. As "a rising tide lifts all boats," suggests Lustick, "an intractable fear nourishes all schemes."[47] And as it turns out, many of the agile risk entrepreneurs just happen to have stuff to sell, such as data mining software, antiradiation drugs, detention center bed space, and cargo inspection systems. Moreover, dependent as they are on public acceptance for status and recognition, notes Jeffrey Rosen, terrorism experts have an "incentive to exaggerate risks and pander to public fears."[48] Like other members of the terrorism industry, then, they are truly virtuosic at pouring out, and poring over, worst-case scenarios—or "worst-case fantasies," as military strategist Bernard Brodie once labeled them in a different context.[49]

Thus far at least, terrorism is rather rare and, appropriately considered, not generally a terribly destructive phenomenon. But there is a danger that the terrorism industry's congenital (if self-serving and profitable) hysteria could become at least somewhat self-fulfilling should extensive further terrorism be visited upon the Home of the Brave.

Ultimately, then, the enemy, in fact, is us. As military analyst William Arkin points out forcefully, although terrorists cannot destroy America, "every time we pretend we are fighting for our survival we not only confer greater power and importance to terrorists than they deserve but we also at the same time act as their main recruiting agent by suggesting that they have the slightest potential for success."[50] The physical, psychic, and economic costs of terrorism arise less from terrorist explosions than from the fear and from the hasty, ill-considered, expensive, and overwrought responses that terrorism too often inspires. The economic costs of the reaction to the 9/11 attacks have been much higher than those inflicted by the terrorists even in that record-shattering episode, and considerably more than three thousand Americans have died because, out of fear, they drove in cars rather than flew in airplanes, or because they were swept into wars made politically possible by the terrorist events. As Osama bin Laden once gleefully noted, fear, alarmism, and overreaction suit the terrorists' agenda just fine because they create the damaging consequences the terrorists seek but are unable to perpetrate on their own.[51]

All societies are "vulnerable" to tiny bands of suicidal fanatics in the sense that it is impossible to prevent every terrorist act. But the United States is hardly "vulnerable" in the sense that it can be toppled by dramatic acts of terrorist destruction, even extreme ones. A key element in a policy toward terrorism, therefore, should be to control, to deal with, or at least to productively worry about the fear and overreaction that terrorism so routinely inspires and that generally constitutes its most damaging effect.

NO: The threat is profound and will remain so for some time.
Walter Laqueur, *Center for Strategic and International Studies*

The Risks of Underestimating the Threat of Terrorism

A dozen years have passed since the twin towers fell in New York City and the United States declared its global "war on terrorism."[52] The president who spearheaded the initial phases of this endeavor has long since left the White House, and the president (from another party) who replaced him is now in his second term.

Terrorism, nonetheless, remains high atop the national and international agenda and the subject of ceaseless comment and controversy. It also remains one of the most emotionally charged topics of public debate, though quite why this should be the case is not entirely clear, because the overwhelming majority of participants do not sympathize with terrorism.

Confusion prevails, but confusion alone does not explain the emotions. There is always confusion when a new international phenomenon appears on the scene. This was the case, for example, when communism first appeared, and also fascism. But terrorism is not an unprecedented phenomenon; it has been around since as far back as recorded history.

Sometimes, terrorism has wrought tremendous global tribulations, even sparking great wars such as World War I. At other times, it has receded into the background noise of world politics.

Something of a cottage industry has formed of late, mainly in academic departments, urging a wholesale reevaluation of terrorism; the thinking goes that the threat of terrorism is overblown and being overhyped. Some point out that death by lightning strike is far more likely than death by terrorism.

That may be true, but if a lightning strike were substituted with a devastating attack on a major Western city, perhaps with a weapon of mass destruction, the ramifications would be profound, likely altering the course of human history.

This is not to overstate the threat, merely to point out the costs of understatement.

In any event, it is quite fair to ask: what is the current state of the terrorist threat, and is it being assessed correctly? Misdiagnosing the threat almost certainly means misapplying the responses.

To best understand present and future challenges, one must first try to make sense of the traditional misunderstandings that have prevailed in the study of terrorism, a field as beholden to passion, emotion, and confusion as any other.

PASSIONATE MISCONCEPTIONS OVER ROOT CAUSES

Some of the misunderstandings about the nature of terrorism are rooted in ideology. In the 1970s, when terrorism was predominantly left wing in inspiration—or at least in rhetoric—it was probably not surprising that commentators belonging to the same political persuasion would produce explanations that were, at the very least, not unsympathetic as far as the terrorists were concerned. Thus it was argued that terrorism always occurred when there was intolerable oppression, social or national, and that the terrorists had genuine, legitimate grievances. Thus the conclusion was that if these grievances were eradicated, terrorism would also disappear.

Terrorism was seen as a revolutionary phenomenon; it was carried out by poor and desperate human beings and therefore had to be confronted with sympathetic understanding.

The argument stressing the left-wing character of terrorism is no longer widely heard except perhaps among members of certain sects trying to establish a popular front with Islamists in whom sect members see a powerful ally in the struggle against imperialism, even if they do not agree with the Islamists' fundamentalist doctrine, which they may find primitive and sometimes embarrassing. But the belief in a fatal link between poverty and violence has persisted. Whenever a major terrorist attack takes place, one hears appeals from high and low to provide financial help, to deal at long last with the "true causes of terrorism," the "roots" rather than their symptoms and outward manifestations. And these roots are believed to be poverty, unemployment, backwardness, and inequality.

As developed earlier in this volume, investigations have shown that poverty does not cause terrorism and prosperity does not cure it. Most terrorists are not poor and do not come from poor societies. In the Indian subcontinent, terrorism has occurred in the most prosperous (Punjab) and the most egalitarian (Kashmir) regions. By contrast, the poorest regions such as North Bihar have been relatively free of terrorism. In Arab countries such as Egypt and Saudi Arabia and also in North Africa, the terrorists have originated not in the poorest and most neglected districts, but from places with concentrations of radical preachers. The backwardness, if any, has been intellectual and cultural, not economic and social.

These findings have had only a limited impact on public opinion and politicians, and it is not difficult to see why there has been resistance to accepting them. There is the general feeling that poverty and backwardness are bad and that there is an urgent need to do more about them.

Reducing poverty in the developing world may be a moral as well as a political and economic imperative, but to expect decisive change from it in the foreseeable future as far as terrorism is concerned is unrealistic. Such an expectation ignores both the causes of backwardness and poverty and the motives for terrorism. Poverty combined with youth unemployment does create a social and psychological climate in which Islamism and various populists and religious sects flourish. That climate, in turn, provides some of the foot folk for violent groups in internal conflicts. According to some projections, the number of young unemployed in the Arab world and North Africa—despite the best hopes of the "Arab Spring"—could reach fifty million in coming decades.

Such a situation will not be conducive to political stability. It will increase the demographic pressure on Europe, because, according to polls, a majority of these young people want to emigrate there. Politically, the populist discontent will be directed against the rulers—the Islamists in Iran and the moderates in countries such as Egypt, Jordan, or Morocco. But how to help the failed economies of the Middle East and North Africa? What are the reasons for the backwardness and stagnation in that part of the world? The countries that have made substantial economic progress, such as China and India, South Korea and Taiwan, Malaysia and Turkey, did so without massive foreign assistance.

All of this points to a deep malaise and even an impending danger, but not to a direct link between the economic situation and international terrorism. There is a negative correlation: terrorists will not hesitate to bring about a further aggravation in the situation by, for example, causing great harm to the tourist industries in North Africa, Egypt, and Bali. Terrorism has spread to the Maldives in the Indian Ocean not because of poverty (it has the highest per capita gross national product in Southeast Asia thanks to its tourism industry), but because Islamic preachers of violence were permitted to act freely. One of the main targets of terrorism in Iraq has been the oil industry.

Sometimes it is argued that resolving religious, nationalist, and ethnic grievances would eradicate terrorism. If the issue at stake is the conflict over a certain territory or the demand for more autonomy, a compromise through negotiations seems a possibility. But recall that al-Qaeda was founded and 9/11 occurred not because of a territorial dispute or the feeling of national oppression but because of a religious commandment—the establishment of sharia through jihad.

As in the war against poverty, the initiatives to solve local conflicts are overdue and should be welcomed. Easing these conflicts would probably bring about a certain reduction in the incidence of terrorism. But the conflicts are many, and even if some of them have been defused in recent years, new ones have emerged. Nor are the issues usually clear-cut or the bones of contention easy to define—let alone solve.

And there should be no illusions about the wider effects of a peaceful solution of one conflict on another. To give but one obvious example: peace (or at least the absence of war) between Israel and the Palestinians would be a blessing for those concerned. However, the assumption that the solution of a local conflict (even one of great symbolic importance) would have a dramatic effect in other parts of the world is unfounded. The late Osama bin Laden did not go to war because of Gaza and Nablus; he did not send his warriors to fight in Palestine. Even the disappearance of the "Zionist entity" would not have a significant impact on his supporters, except perhaps to provide encouragement for further action.

Such a warning against illusions is called for because there is much wishful thinking and naïveté in this respect—a belief in quick fixes and miracle solutions. Some say, if only there could be peace between Israelis and Palestinians, all the other conflicts would become manageable. But the problems are as much in Europe, Asia, and Africa as in the Middle East; there is a great deal of free-floating aggression that could (and probably would) easily turn in other directions once one conflict has been defused.

Tackling these supposed sources of terrorism, even for the wrong reasons, will do no harm and may bring some good. But it will not bring analysts any closer to a comprehensive understanding of the sources of terrorism, let alone a capacity to respond effectively.

NATURE OF THE THREAT: NOW AND INTO THE FUTURE

It is always risky to make predictions about the future of terrorism, even more so than about political trends in general. It is certain, however, that terrorism will not disappear from the earth: at a time when full-scale war has become too dangerous and too expensive, terrorism has become the prevailing mode of conflict. As long as conflict persists among groups of human beings, so will terrorism.

Today, nearly all attention is focused on Islamic terrorism, but it is useful to remember from time to time that this has not always been the case—even less than thirty-five years ago—and that a great many conflicts, perceived oppressions, and other causes are calling for radical action in the world, which also may lead to terrorism in the years to come. These need not be even major conflicts in an era in which small groups will have access to weapons of mass destruction.

Islamic terrorism has certainly not yet run its full course, but it is unlikely that its present fanaticism will last forever; religious-nationalist fervor does not constantly burn with the same intensity. There is a phenomenon known in Egypt as "Salafi burnout," the mellowing of radical young people, the weakening of the original fanatical impetus. Like all other movements in history, messianic groups are subject to routinization, to the circulation of generations, to changing political circumstances, and to sudden or gradual changes in religious belief. This could happen as the result of either victory or defeat. One day it might be possible to appease militant Islamism—though hardly in a period of burning aggression when confidence and faith in global victory have not yet been broken.

The terrorist impetus is likely to decline as the result of setbacks. Attacks will continue, and some will be crowned with success, perhaps spectacular success, but many will not. When Alfred Nobel invented dynamite, many terrorists thought that it was the answer to their prayers. But theirs was a false hope. The trust put today in that invincible weapon suicide terrorism may in the end be equally misplaced. Even the use of weapons of mass destruction might not be the panacea some terrorists believe it will be. Perhaps the effect of such a weapon will be less deadly than anticipated; perhaps it will be so destructive as to be considered counterproductive. Statistics show that in the terrorist attacks over the past decade, considerably more Muslims were killed than infidels. Because terrorists do not operate in a vacuum, this situation is bound to lead to dissent among their followers and even among the fanatical preachers.

In brief, a united terrorist front, if ever established, may not last. It is unlikely that the followers of bin Laden will be frontally challenged on theological or ideological grounds, but there has been criticism for political and tactical reasons such as the attacks against Muslim civilians, both Sunni and Shiite, and the failure to anticipate the massive retaliation of the West following the attacks of 9/11.

Some leading students of Islam have argued that radical Islamism reached its peak years ago and that its downfall and disappearance are only a question of time, perhaps not much time. Although some societies have been exposed to the rule of fundamentalist fanatics (such as Iran) or to radical Islamist attacks (such as Algeria), many Muslim countries have yet to undergo such firsthand experience; for them, sharia rule and the restoration of the caliphate are still brilliant dreams.

These, then, are the likely perspectives for the more distant future. But in a shorter-term perspective the danger remains acute and may, in fact, grow. Where and when are terrorist attacks most likely to occur? They will not necessarily be directed against the greatest and most dangerous enemy perceived by the terrorist leaders. Much depends on where the terrorists are strong and believe the enemy to be weak. That terrorist attacks are likely to continue in the Middle East goes without saying; other primary danger zones are central Asia, particularly Pakistan, and, more recently, nearly all of Western Europe.

Pakistan certainly remains at risk. Its madrassas continue to serve as breeding grounds for jihad fighters, and radical leaders can count on certain sympathies in the army and intelligence services. A failed Pakistan with nuclear weapons at its disposal would be a major nightmare.

Yet Europe is perhaps the most vulnerable battlefield, having become over the years the main base of terrorist support groups from the Middle East, North Africa, and Pakistan. This process has been facilitated by the growth of Muslim communities (and growing tensions with the local population), which have provided a reservoir of new recruits. The freedom of action for radicals to organize and indoctrinate in Western Europe is considerably greater than in the Arab and Muslim world. True, there were some arrests and closer controls after the events of 9/11 and the attacks in Madrid, London, and Toulouse, but because of the legal and political restrictions under which European security services labor, effective counteraction remains exceedingly difficult.

For decades, Western European governments have been frequently criticized for not doing enough to integrate Muslim communities, but cultural and social integration is not what many immigrants want, and their preachers have constantly warned against it. Immigrants have wanted to preserve their political, cultural, and religious identities and their ways of life, and have resented interference by secular authorities. And yet the vast majority of first-generation immigrants simply wanted to live in peace and quiet and make a living for their families. But today they no longer have much control over their more radical offspring.

The radicalization of second-generation immigrants is a common phenomenon in general, and is certainly the case in Western Europe. This generation has been superficially acculturated, speaking fluently the language of the land, and yet feeling resentment and hostility more acutely. It is not necessarily the power of the fundamentalist message that inspires many of the younger radical activists or sympathizers; they are by no means the most pious believers when it comes to carrying out all the religious commandments. The British suicide bombers in 2005, for example, were not known for their religious orthodoxy; most of them did not pray regularly. Rather, it is the feeling of deep resentment because, unlike immigrants from other parts of the world, Muslim immigrants in Europe often find themselves unable to compete successfully in the classroom or the workplace. Feelings of being excluded, sexual repression (a taboo subject in this context), and other factors have led to free-floating aggression and higher rates of criminal behavior directed against the authorities and the neighbors.

As a result, non-Muslims in Europe have felt threatened in the streets they could once walk without fear. They have come to regard the new immigrants as antisocial elements who wanted to impose on non-Muslim Europeans their way of life. Pressure on the European governments has been growing from all sides, right and left, to stop immigration and restore law and order.

This, in brief, is the milieu in which Islamist terrorism and terrorist support groups in Western Europe have developed. There is little reason to assume that this trend will change fundamentally in the near future. On the contrary, the more the young generation of immigrants asserts itself, the more violence occurs in the streets, and the more terrorist attacks take place, the greater will be the anti-Muslim resentment of the rest of the population. The rapid demographic growth of the Muslim communities further strengthens the impression among original residents that they are being deprived of their rights in their own homeland, not even entitled to speak the truth about the prevailing situation (such as revealing how many prison inmates have Muslim backgrounds). Thus violent reactions to Muslims are on view in even the most liberal European countries such as the Netherlands, Belgium, Denmark, and Norway.

True, the number of extremists is still quite small. Among British Muslims, fewer than 20 percent have expressed sympathy and support for terrorist attacks. But this percentage still translates into several hundred thousand, far more than is needed for staging a terrorist campaign. Furthermore, such statistics do not take into account the growth of Muslim communities and Western Europe's continuing need for immigrants because of their low and declining birthrates. There is already great pressure on southern and western Europe to absorb the growing legions of unemployed in North Africa and the Middle East.

If acculturation and integration have been a failure in the short run, prospects are less hopeless from a long-term perspective. Young Muslims cannot be kept forever in hermetically sealed ghettos, even if their preachers make a valiant effort to do so. The young people are disgusted and repelled by alcohol, loose morals, general decadence, and all the other wickedness of the society surrounding them—as indoctrinated by their preachers—but at the same time they are fascinated and attracted by them. As one Berlin imam put it: the road to the mosque is long, and the temptations are many. This environment is bound to affect young people's activist fervor, and they will be exposed to not only the negative aspects of the society around them but also its values. Other religions had to face these temptations over the ages and often fought a losing battle.

It is frequently forgotten that only a relatively short period passed from the primitive beginnings of Islam in the Arabian Desert to the splendor and luxury (and learning and poetry) of Harun al-Rashid's Baghdad—from the austerity of the Qur'an to the not-so-austere Arabian Nights. The pulse of contemporary history is beating much faster, but is it beating fast enough? For it is a race against time. The advent of megaterrorism and the access to weapons of mass destruction are dangerous enough, but coupled with fanaticism they generate scenarios unpleasant even to contemplate.

RESPONDING TO THE THREAT

There can never be a final victory in the fight against terrorism, for terrorism (rather than full-scale war) is the contemporary manifestation of conflict, and conflict will not disappear from earth as far as one can look ahead.

But the history of counterterrorism does offer certain lessons, and it will be within the power of policymakers to make life for terrorists and potential terrorists much more difficult.

I have always felt uneasy about the term *war on terrorism*. Obviously, the military needs to play certain roles in this context, especially when dealing with countries that have failed to function and have become terrorist havens. The military may also be needed to deliver blows against terrorist concentrations. But these are not the most typical or frequent terrorist situations, and the military's role must remain limited.

As far as terrorism is concerned, there can be no overall military doctrine similar to the regular warfare philosophy developed by Clausewitz, Jomini, and others. An airplane or a battleship does not change its character wherever it operates, but the character of terrorism depends largely on the motivations of those engaging in it and the conditions under which it takes place. In this age of asymmetric warfare, the key response roles should be played by the intelligence and security services, which may sometimes only require the assistance of relatively small specialized military units.

The fact is, the use of massive force is frequently unpopular at home and, in any event, will be applied only in extreme cases when the core interests of the state are involved. To give but one example, the Russian government could deport the Chechens (or a significant proportion), thereby solving its problem with them in a Stalinist style. If the Chechens were to threaten Moscow or St. Petersburg or the fuel supply of the Russian state, there is little doubt but that such measures would be taken. But as long as the threat remains marginal and peripheral, the price to be paid for the application of massive force will be considered too high.

So what about softer power? Its utility ought to be maximized, and may be important in some cases, but it has its limitations as well. Joseph Nye has described soft power as based on culture and political ideas as influenced by the seductiveness of democracy, human rights, and individual opportunity. This is a powerful argument, and it is true that Washington has seldom used all its opportunities: the public diplomacy budget is about one-quarter of one percentage point of the defense budget.

But the question to be asked is, how seductive are Western values and ideas in the Muslim world? Cultural propaganda (public diplomacy) had an effect in Europe and even behind the Iron Curtain during the Cold War. But soft power will have no impact on radical Islamists who abhor democracy, who believe that human rights and tolerance are imperialist inventions, and who do not want any ideas circulating except those that appear in the Qur'an—as they interpret it.

At a minimum, Western radio and television would have to be beamed to an audience of which 70 percent firmly believes that the 9/11 attacks were carried out by the Israeli Mossad. Such an audience will not be impressed by exposure to Western pop culture or a truthful, matter-of-fact coverage of the news.

The why-do-they-hate-us question can be raised in this context, along with the question of what could be done about it. Disturbing figures have been published about the low (and falling) popularity of America abroad, despite the election of President Barack Hussein Obama. Yet it is too often forgotten that international relations is not a popularity contest and that since the days of the Assyrians and the Roman Empire powerful countries have always been feared, resented, and envied; in short, they have not been loved. Neither the Ottoman nor the Spanish Empires, neither the Chinese nor the Russian Empires, were ever popular. British sports were emulated in the colonies, and the French culture impressed the local elites in North Africa and Indochina, but the emulation did not lead to political support, let alone identification with the rulers. Had there been public opinion polls in the days of Alexander the Great (let alone Genghis Khan), the results, one suspects, would have been quite negative.

Big powers will never be loved, but in the terrorist context it is essential that they be respected. As bin Laden's declarations prior to 9/11 show, it was lack of respect for America that made him launch his attacks. He felt certain that the risk he was running was small, for the United States was a paper tiger, lacking both the will and the capability to strike back. After all, after only a few attacks the Americans ran from Beirut in the 1980s and from Mogadishu in 1993, and there was every reason to believe that they would do so again.

ADAPTING TO THE RULES OF THE GAME: OPPORTUNITIES AND CHALLENGES

In contemplating a response to terrorism, it is most important to remember that terrorists abide by no doctrine other than that which they believe to be effective, whereas states largely adhere to the rules and laws of war that have been developed over centuries. Terrorists cannot possibly accept these rules. It would be suicidal from their point of view if, to give but one example, they were to wear uniforms or other distinguishing marks. The essence of their operations rests on hiding their identities. On the other hand, they and their well-wishers insist that when captured, they should enjoy all the rights and benefits accorded to belligerents, that they be humanely treated and released after the end of hostilities.

When regular soldiers do not stick to the rules of warfare, killing or maiming prisoners, carrying out massacres, taking hostages, or committing crimes against the civilian population, they will be treated as war criminals. If terrorists obeyed these rules, they would have little if any chance of success; the essence of today's terrorist operations is indiscriminate attacks against civilians. But governments defending themselves against terrorism are widely expected not to behave in a similar way but to adhere to international law as it developed in conditions quite different from those prevailing today.

Terrorism does not accept laws and rules, whereas governments are bound by them. This, in briefest outline, is asymmetric warfare. If any government were to behave in a similar way, not feeling bound by existing rules and laws such as those against the killing of prisoners, it would be bitterly denounced.

When Syrian president Hafez al-Assad faced an insurgency (and an attempted assassination) by the Muslim Brotherhood in the city of Hama in 1980, his soldiers massacred some twenty thousand inhabitants. This put an end for three decades to all ideas of terrorism and guerrilla warfare in Syria. After it ceased to be effective as a deterrent, the Syrian civil war broke out.

Such behavior on the part of democratic governments would be denounced as barbaric, a relapse into the practices of long-gone pre-civilized days. But if governments accept the principle of asymmetric warfare, they will be severely, possibly fatally, handicapped. They cannot accept that terrorists are protected by the Geneva Conventions, which would mean, among other things, that they should be paid a salary while in captivity.

The problem will not arise if the terrorist group is small and not very dangerous. In this case, normal legal procedures will be sufficient to deal with the problem (but even this is not quite certain as weapons of mass destruction become more readily accessible). Nor will the issue of shedding legal restraint arise if the issues at stake are of marginal importance—if, in other words, no core interests of the governments involved are concerned. But if the very survival of a society is at stake, it is most unlikely that governments will be impeded in their defense by laws and norms belonging to a bygone (and more humane) age.

Antiterrorist action in the West is an obstacle race, not so much because of the ingenuity of the terrorists but because of the very nature of democratic societies. Many terrorists or suspected terrorists have been detained in America and in Europe, but only a handful have been put on trial and convicted because inadmissible evidence was submitted or the authorities were reluctant to reveal the sources of their information. As a result, many who were almost certainly involved in terrorist operations were never arrested, while others were acquitted or released from detention.

As for those who are still detained, there have been loud protests against the violation of their elementary human rights. Activists have argued that the real danger is not terrorism (the extent and the consequences of which, they say, have been greatly exaggerated) but the war against terrorism. Should free societies so easily give up their freedoms, which have been fought for and achieved over many centuries?

Some scholars have foretold the coming of fascism in America (and to a lesser extent in Europe); others have predicted an authoritarian regime gradually introduced by governments cleverly exploiting the present situation for their own antidemocratic purposes. And it is quite likely indeed that among those detained there have been and are innocent people and that some of the controls introduced have interfered with human rights. However, there is much reason to think that to combat terrorism effectively considerably more stringent measures will be needed than those presently in force.

But these measures can be adopted only if there is overwhelming public support, and it would be unwise even to try to push them through until the learning process about the danger of terrorism in an age of weapons of mass destruction has made further progress. Time will tell. If devastating attacks do not occur, stringent antiterrorist measures will not be necessary. But if they do happen, the demand for effective countermeasures will be overwhelming. One could perhaps argue that further limitations of freedom are bound to be ineffective because terrorist groups are likely to be small or very small in the future and therefore likely to slip through safety nets. This is indeed a danger—but the advice to abstain from safety measures is a counsel of despair unlikely to be accepted.

It could well be that, as far as the recent past is concerned, the danger of terrorism has been overstated. In World Wars I and II, more people were killed and more material damage was sustained on certain days than through a decade of terrorist attacks. I said as much in my *History of Terrorism* written in the 1970s, and it is certainly flattering to find this insight rediscovered three decades later. But I also noted that our societies are becoming more vulnerable and far more sensitive to the loss of life. The real issue at stake is not the attacks of the past but the coming dangers. Megaterrorism has not yet arrived; even 9/11 was a stage in between traditional terrorism and the shape of things to come: the use of weapons of mass destruction.

For the first time in human history, very small groups have, or will have, not just the motivation but also the potential to cause immense destruction. There will continue to be small groups of terrorists who will be interested in negotiated settlements, satisfied with less than the annihilation of the enemy. But there will be always more radical elements eager to continue the struggle. They are not necessarily rational actors, and their motivation may not be political but apocalyptic.

Perhaps this scenario is too pessimistic; perhaps the weapons of mass destruction, for whatever reason, will never be used. But it would be the first time in human history that such arms, once invented, had not been used.

In 1932, when Albert Einstein attempted to induce Sigmund Freud to support pacifism, Freud replied that there was no likelihood of suppressing humanity's aggressive tendencies. If there was any reason for hope, it was that people would turn away on rational grounds—that war had become too destructive, that it was no longer an endeavor of honor based on the old ideals.

Freud was partly correct: war (at least between great powers) has become far less likely for rational reasons. But his argument does not apply to terrorism motivated not mainly by political or economic interests, based not just on aggression but also on fanaticism with an admixture of madness.

Terrorism, therefore, will continue—not perhaps with the same intensity at all times, and some parts of the globe may be spared altogether. But there can be no victory, only an uphill struggle, sometimes successful, at other times not.

Notes

1. John Mueller, *Overblown* (New York: Free Press, 2006).
2. Michael Scheuer, *Imperial Hubris: Why the West Is Losing the War on Terror* (Dulles, Va.: Brassey's, 2004); Shane Harris and Stuart Taylor Jr., "Homeland Security Chief Looks Back, and Forward," March 17, 2008, GovernmentExecutive. com; "All the Time He Needs," *New York Times*, April 16, 2008.
3. Lehrer NewsHour, PBS, October 16, 2009.
4. Alison Gendar and Helen Kennedy, "U.S. Commandos Find 'Mother Lode' of Material on Al Qaeda inside Osama Bin Laden's compound," *New York Daily News*, May 4, 2011.
5. Greg Miller, "Bin Laden Documents Reveal Strain, Struggle in al-Qaida," *Washington Post*, July 1, 2011; and Scott Shane, "Pornography Is Found in Bin Laden Compound Files, U.S. Officials Say," *New York Times*, May 13, 2011. See also David Ignatius, "The bin Laden Plot to Kill President Obama," *Washington Post*, March 16, 2012.
6. Russell Seitz, "Weaker Than We Think," *American Conservative*, December 6, 2004. See also John Mueller, "Harbinger or Aberration?" *National Interest*, Fall 2002.
7. See John Mueller, ed., *Terrorism Since 9/11: The American Cases* (Columbus: Mershon Center, The Ohio State University, 2012), polisci.osu.edu/faculty/jmuel ler/since.html.
8. See also Bruce Schneier, "Portrait of the Modern Terrorist as an Idiot," June 14, 2007, schneier.com; Daniel Byman and Christine Fair, "The Case for Calling Them Nitwits," *Atlantic* (July/August 2010).
9. Department of Homeland Security, *National Infrastructure Protection Plan* (Washington, D.C.: Department of Homeland Security, 2009), 11.
10. See also Robert A. Pape and James K. Feldman, *Cutting the Fuse* (Chicago, Ill.: University of Chicago Press, 2010), 76–79; Stephen M. Walt, "Why They Hate Us (II): How Many Muslims Has the U.S. Killed in the Past 30 Years?" November 30, 2009, foreignpolicy.com; Peter Bergen, "Five Myths about Osama bin Laden," May 6, 2011, washingtonpost.com; James Fallows, *Blind into Baghdad: America's War in Iraq* (New York: Vintage, 2006), 142. Although the tiny number of people plotting terrorist attacks in the United States display passionate hostility to U.S. foreign policy, there is, of course, a far greater number of people who share much of the same hostility, but are in no sense inspired to commit terrorism to express their deeply held views.
11. Shikha Dalmia, "What Islamist Terrorist Threat?" Reason.com, February 15, 2011.
12. See also Risa A. Brooks, "Muslim 'Homegrown' Terrorism in the United States: How Serious Is the Threat?" *International Security* 36 (Fall 2011): 39.

13. Brian Michael Jenkins, *Would-Be Warriors: Incidents of Jihadist Terrorist Radicalization in the United States Since September 11, 2001* (Santa Monica, Calif.: RAND, 2010), 8 9.

14. Walter Laqueur, "The Terrorism to Come," *Policy Review* 126 (August 1, 2004). Also see Laqueur's opposite essay in this chapter.

15. Michael Kenney, "'Dumb' Yet Deadly: Local Knowledge and Poor Tradecraft among Islamist Militants in Britain and Spain," *Studies in Conflict & Terrorism* 33 (October 2010): 911–932.

16. See Marc Sageman, *Leaderless Jihad: Terror Networks in the Twenty-first Century* (Philadelphia: University of Pennsylvania Press, 2008); and David Ignatius, "The Fading Jihadists," *Washington Post*, February 28, 2008.

17. Mitchell Silber, *The Al Qaeda Factor: Plots against the West* (Philadelphia: University of Pennsylvania Press, 2012).

18. Anthony H. Cordesman tallies "major attacks by Islamists" outside of Iraq: 830 fatalities for April 2002 through July 2005, Cordesman, *The Challenge of Biological Weapons* (Washington, D.C.: Center for Strategic and International Studies, 2005), 29–31. Brian Michael Jenkins tallies "major terrorist attacks worldwide" by "jihadist extremists" outside Afghanistan, Iraq, Israel, Palestine, Algeria, Russia, and Kashmir: 1,129 fatalities for October 2001 through April 2006, Jenkins, *Unconquerable Nation* (Santa Monica, Calif.: RAND, 2006), 179 184. IntelCenter tallies "most significant attacks executed by core al-Qaeda, regional arms and affiliate groups excluding operations in insurgency theaters": 1,632 fatalities for January 2002 through July 2007, IntelCenter, "Jihadi Attack Kill Statistics," August 17, 2007, www.intelcenter.com, 11.

19. Patrick Porter, "Long Wars and Long Telegrams: Containing Al-Qaeda," *International Affairs* 85 (March 2009): 300.

20. Joby Warrick, "U.S. Cites Big Gains against Al-Qaeda," *Washington Post*, May 30, 2008. See also Fawaz A. Gerges, *The Far Enemy: Why Jihad Went Global* (New York: Cambridge University Press, 2005), chap. 5; and Gerges's essay in *Chapter* 4 of this volume.

21. Peter Bergen and Paul Cruickshank, "The Unraveling: The Jihadist Revolt against bin Laden," *New Republic*, June 11, 2008; Lawrence Wright, "The Rebellion Within," New Yorker, June 2, 2008; and Fawaz Gerges, *The Rise and Fall of Al-Qaeda* (New York: Oxford University Press, 2011).

22. Gerges, *The Far Enemy*, 232, and, for a tally of policing activity, 318–319. See also Paul R. Pillar, *Terrorism and U.S. Foreign Policy* (Washington, D.C.: Brookings Institution Press, 2003), xxviii–xxix; Marc Lynch, "Al-Qaeda's Media Strategies," *National Interest* (Spring 2006): 54–55; Sageman, *Leaderless Jihad*, 149; Juan Cole, Engaging the Muslim World (New York: Palgrave Macmillan, 2009), 163; Max Abrahms, "Does Terrorism Really Work? Evolution in the Conventional Wisdom Since 9/11," *Defence and Peace Economics* 22 (2011): 583–594.

23. Bob Woodward, "Why Did Violence Plummet? It Wasn't Just the Surge," *Washington Post*, September 8, 2008; and Frederic Wehrey, "The Iraq War: Strategic Overreach by America—and Also by al Qaeda," in *The Long Shadow of 9/11: America's Response to Terrorism*, ed. Brian Michael Jenkins and John Paul Godges (Santa Monica, Calif. RAND, 2011), 47–55.

24. Quoted in Warrick, "U.S. Cites Big Gains against Al-Qaeda." See also Peter Bergen and Paul Cruickshank, "Self-Fulfilling Prophecy," *Mother Jones*, November December,

2007; Brian Michael Jenkins, *Will Terrorists Go Nuclear?* (Amherst, N.Y.: Prometheus, 2008), 191; and Gerges, *The Rise and Fall of Al-Qaeda.*

25. Ignatius, "The bin Laden Plot."
26. Glenn L. Carle, "Overstating Our Fears," *Washington Post*, July 13, 2008.
27. See John Mueller, *Atomic Obsession: Nuclear Alarmism from Hiroshima to Al Qaeda* (New York: Oxford University Press, 2010), 11–13.
28. Brian Jenkins, *Will Terrorists Go Nuclear?* 250–251.
29. Quoted in Bob Graham, *World at Risk: The Report of the Commission on the Prevention of WMD Proliferation and Terrorism* (New York: Vintage, 2008), 43.
30. Gilmore Commission (Advisory Panel to Assess Domestic Response Capabilities for Terrorism Involving Weapons of Mass Destruction), "First Annual Report: Assessing the Threat," RAND, Santa Monica, Calif., December 15, 1999.
31. Christoph Wirz and Emmanuel Egger, "Use of Nuclear and Radiological Weapons by Terrorists?" *International Review of the Red Cross*, September 2005.
32. Stephen M. Younger, *The Bomb: A New History* (New York: Ecco, 2009), 146.
33. Anne Stenersen, *Al-Qaida's Quest for Weapons of Mass Destruction: The History behind the Hype* (Saarbrücken, Germany: VDM Verlag Dr. Müller, 2008), 35–36.
34. For the extended argument that the likelihood of atomic terrorism is vanishingly small, see Mueller, *Atomic Obsession*, chaps. 12–15. See also John Mueller, "The Truth about al Qaeda: Bin Laden's Files Revealed the Terrorists in Dramatic Decline," Foreignaffairs.com, August 2, 2011; Jenkins, *Will Terrorists Go Nuclear?*
35. Wirz and Egger, "Use of Nuclear and Radiological Weapons."
36. Walter Laqueur, "Postmodern Terrorism: New Rules for an Old Game," *Foreign Affairs* 75 (September/October 1996).
37. Craig Whitlock, "Homemade, Cheap and Dangerous," *Washington Post*, July 5, 2007.
38. Garrett M. Graff, *The Threat Matrix: The FBI at War in the Age of Global Terror* (New York: Little, Brown, 2011), 366.
39. Richard A. Serrano, "U.S. Faces 'Heightened' Threat Level," *Los Angeles Times*, February 10, 2011. For commentary on this phenomenon, see Heather MacDonald, "The Ever-Renewing Terror Threat," *Secular Right*, February 13, 2011; Brooks, "Muslim 'Homegrown' Terrorism in the United States," 43–44; and John Mueller, "Why al Qaeda May Never Die," Skeptics blog, May 1, 2012, nationalinterest.org.
40. See John Mueller and Mark G. Stewart, *Terror, Security, and Money: Balancing the Risks, Benefits, and Costs of Homeland Security* (New York: Oxford University Press, 2011), chap. 2.
41. See also John Mueller and Mark G. Stewart, "The Terrorism Delusion: America's Overwrought Response to September 11," *International Security* 37 (Summer 2012). Poll trends are posted at http://polisci.osu.edu/faculty/jmueller/terrorpolls.pdf.
42. Scott Atran, *Talking to the Enemy* (New York: Ecco, 2010), xiv.
43. Mueller and Stewart, *Terror, Security, and Money*, 1–3.
44. National Research Council of the National Academies, *Review of the Department of Homeland Security's Approach to Risk Analysis* (Washington, D.C.: National Academies Press, 2010). This report received no media attention whatever when it was released.
45. Ian S. Lustick, *Trapped in the War on Terror* (Philadelphia: University of Pennsylvania Press, 2006), 97. See also Mueller, *Overblown.*

46. Bart Kosko, "Terror Threat May Be Mostly a Big Bluff," *Los Angeles Times*, September 13, 2004.
47. Lustick, *Trapped in the War on Terror*, 98.
48. Jeffrey Rosen, *The Naked Crowd* (New York: Random House, 2004).
49. Bernard Brodie, "The Development of Nuclear Strategy," *International Security* 2 (Spring 1978): 68.
50. William Arkin, "Early Warning" blog, *Washington Post*, January 26, 2006.
51. Mueller, *Overblown*, 3.
52. This essay is adapted in part from Walter Laqueur, "The Terrorism to Come," *Policy Review* (August/September 2004): 49–64.

ABOUT THE EDITOR

 **Stuart Gottlieb** teaches at the School of International and Public Affairs at Columbia University, where he is also an affiliate of the Saltzman Institute of War and Peace Studies. His courses and research focus on American foreign policy, counterterrorism, and international security. He formerly served as a senior foreign policy adviser and speechwriter in the United States Senate (1999–2003), and continues to advise and consult on issues related to foreign policy and terrorism.

Gottlieb received his Ph.D. in international relations from Columbia University, and is an adjunct professor at New York University's graduate politics program.

SSAGE research**methods**

The essential online tool for researchers from the world's leading methods publisher

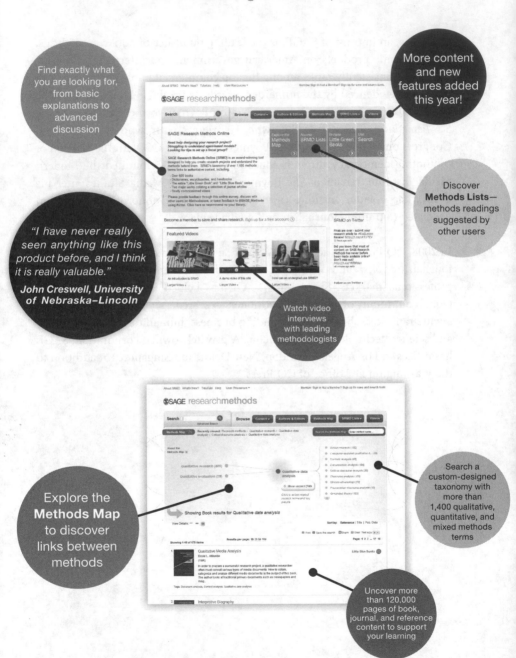

Find exactly what you are looking for, from basic explanations to advanced discussion

More content and new features added this year!

"*I have never really seen anything like this product before, and I think it is really valuable.*"
John Creswell, University of Nebraska–Lincoln

Discover **Methods Lists**—methods readings suggested by other users

Watch video interviews with leading methodologists

Explore the **Methods Map** to discover links between methods

Search a custom-designed taxonomy with more than 1,400 qualitative, quantitative, and mixed methods terms

Uncover more than 120,000 pages of book, journal, and reference content to support your learning

Find out more at
www.sageresearchmethods.com